Fundamentals of Entrepreneurship

Prof. Mata Badal Shukla
M.Com., D.Phil
Professor,
Faculty of Commerce and Management Studies
Mahatma Gandhi Kashi Vidyapith, Varanasi – 221002
and
Formerly,
Dean, Faculty of Commerce & Management Studies
Director, Institute of Management Studies
Head, Department of Commerce
Mahatma Gandhi Kashi Vidyapith, Varanasi
and
Formerly Head and Professor,
Guru Ghasidas Central University, Bilaspur (C.G.)
and
President, Indian Commerce Association (2006)
President, Indian Accounting Association (2006)
Vice President (North), Indian Council for Business Education

KITAB MAHAL

First Edition: 2016
Reprint : 2022
Reprint : 2024

ISBN : 978-81-225-0787-4

Price : ₹540.00

Head Office

Kitab Mahal Publishers
4655/21, Ansari Road (G. F.)
Daryaganj, New Delhi-110002
Phone : 011-23273230/43526875;
(WhatsApp) 9335107914
Email : kitab_mahal@hotmail.com

Published By : Kitab Mahal, 4655/21, Ansari Road, (G. F.) Daryaganj, New Delhi-110002
Phone : +91 9350075776 Email : kitabmahalpublishers@gmail.com
Visit : www.kitabmahalpublishers.com
Printed by : Avatar Offset, 43/2, Site-IV, Sahibabad Industrial Area, Ghaziabad (U.P.)

PREFACE

Business invites opportunities for business and entrepreneurs treat these opportunities to enrich the economic and social wealth of the society. It is rightly observed that a great society is one in which its men think about and practice entrepreneurship. The entrepreneurs assume the risks associated with the business opportunities and convert the available innovations in to products and services that are useful to customers. Entrepreneurship utilises favourable environment for accelerating the pace of economic development, and thus furthering the cause of economic welfare.

With the advent of missions of new government at the centre, Make in India, Skill India and Digital India, entrepreneurship has been assigned a more catalytic role to achieve the goals of faster economic development. Entrepreneurial behaviour ultimately creates opportunities for employment generation. Entrepreneurship inculcates the thoughts of new creations and enterprising vision which again improves the volumes of business. The knowledge of entrepreneurship and its effective implementation have become essential components of the economic growth. Now entrepreneurial abilities, skill and leadership are regarded as a change agent to solve the problems of increasing competition, complexities, uncertainties and emerging conflicts of economic and social values in business.

In the recent past, various universities have prescribed the study of entrepreneurship in their syllabus at the graduate level. Besides, entrepreneurship has also been made as an important part of the curriculum meant for technical education. This transforms the students from employment seekers into employment providers for others.

Efforts have been made to present various aspects of entrepreneurship in the present book in an easy and lucid language. This book is particularly useful for the paper of "Fundamentals of Entrepreneurship" for B. Tech., B.Com., B.B.A., B.A. and vocational studies.

I am highly indebted to my faculty colleagues and faculty members of other universities and colleges for their immense cooperation, help and inputs in finalising the present book. Fascinating presentation of the book is the outcome of special efforts and inspiration of Sri Indresh Kumar Agrawal of Kitab Mahal. I am thankful to him for the timely publication of the book.

I heartily invite views, comments and constructive suggestions from the faculty members of different universities and colleges to make the book more educative and useful.

Prof. M.B. Shukla

CONTENTS

on liberalizing the schemes as well as simplifying the systems and procedures. The initiatives taken in the previous year and accelerated during the year under review resulted into increased retail portfolio of the bank.

EXAMINATION QUESTIONS

Long Answer Questions

1. What is business growth ? Discuss its need for a business firm.
2. Define stability strategy. Also examine its criteria.
3. What do you know by growth strategy ? Discuss its approaches.
4. What is merger ? Examine its types.
5. Define joint venture. Discuss its process.
6. Discuss the nature of integration. Also examine its types.
7. Discuss the nature of backward and forward integration. Examine their rationale.
8. What is diversification ? Discuss its techniques.
9. Why does a firm seek to continue to exist after its main products are either obsolete or out of favour for health or other reasons ?
10. How do joint ventures differ from merger activity ? In what ways are they similar ?
11. What is joint venture ? What are the advantages and disadvantages of joint ventures ?

Short Answer Questions

1. What do you mean by stability strategy ?
2. Explain the features of growth strategy.
3. Discuss the various approached to growth strategies.
4. What to do you mean by joint ventures ?
5. What is mergers and acquisition process ?

Objective Type Questions

1. Conglomeration is a technique to :
   (*a*) expand in the same industry
   (*b*) diversify in other areas
   (*c*) taking over other units
   (*d*) divide the organisation in sub-units
2. Merger means :
   (*a*) Taking over one organisation by another organisation
   (*b*) Combination of two or more businesses
   (*c*) Acquiring controlling interest in other organisation
   (*d*) None of the above
3. Forward integration creates facilities for manufacturing products for which:
   (*a*) Current product is treated as output

(*b*) Current product serves as inputs
(*c*) Outsourcing of raw materials
(*d*) Selling of raw materials to others

4. Integration is meant for :
(*a*) Expanding internally
(*b*) Expanding externally
(*c*) Expanding internally and externally
(*d*) None of the above

5. Backward integration means :
(*a*) Production of raw material
(*b*) Purchase of raw material
(*c*) Production of output
(*d*) None of the above

6. Intensive expansion involves
(*a*) 2 ways (*b*) 3 ways (*c*) 4 ways (*d*) 5 ways

Answers

1. (*b*) 2. (*b*) 3. (*b*) 4. (*b*) 5. (*a*) 6. (*b*)

Reason Based Questions

State with reason whether the following statements are true or false :

1. Under stability strategy, the firm improves its competitive strength.
2. In growth strategy, a firm increases its expected performance in terms of market share.
3. Horizontal merger involves two firms operating in the same kind of business.
4. Conglomerate merger integrates unrelated business activities.
5. Joint venture is a special case of consolidation.

REFERENCES

1. *Glueck, William F., Business Policy Strategy Formation and Management Action,' IInd Edition, p. 117.*
2. *Ghosh P.K., Business Policy. Sultan Chand & Sons, New Delhi, 1996, p. 194.*
3. *Weston J. Fred Chung Kwang S. and Hoag S.E., Mergers, Restructuring and Corporate Control, Prentice Hall of India. New Delhi, 1996, p. 85.*
4. *Acharya B.K. & Govekar P., 'Business Policy and Strategic Management', Himalaya Publishing House, Mumbai, 1998. p. 391.*
5. *'Azhar Kazmi, Business Policy', Tata McGraw Hill Publishing Company Ltd., New Delhi, 1992, p. 165.*
6. *Weston, J. Fred, Chung Kwang S. and Hoag S.E., Mergers. Restructuring and Corporate Control. p. 331.*
7. *Business Standard, New Delhi, June 20, 2006. Special Issue on "The Strategist'*

1

ENTREPRENEUR

Entrepreneur is the most important factor in the process of economic development. He occupies the central place in the growth process because he initiates development in a society and carries it forward. As a change agent, the entrepreneur is the first and foremost a catalyst for change. The function that is specific to entrepreneur is the ability to take the factors of production—land, labour and capital and use them to produce new goods or services. The entrepreneur perceives opportunities. He works as an originator of a new business venture and also tries to improve an organisation unit by initiating productive changes.

Concept of Entrepreneur

The word entrepreneur is derived from the French word 'enterprendre' and its literal meaning is "to undertake." It was applied to leaders of military expeditions in the early 16th century. However, around 1790 A.D., it was used in the context of other types of adventures like architects and contractors of public works.

The Oxford English Dictionary in 1887 states that "entrepreneur simply is the director or manager of a public musical institution; one who puts up entertainments, especially musical performance." A further revision has appeared in it in 1933 and the word entrepreneur had a place in business and would mean "one who undertakes an enterprise especially a contractor acting as intermediary between capital and labour." In this way, undertaking of an enterprise is regarded as entrepreneurship and one who undertakes it—one who coordinates capital and labour for the purpose of production is an entrepreneur. Actually, this emerging class is generally treated as the entrepreneurial class.

Nature of Entrepreneur

The entrepreneur is expected to identify the environmental change as an opportunity and uses the factors of production to produce new goods and services. He is motivated to:

(*i*) the desire to find a private commercial kingdom,

(*ii*) the will to conquer and prove his superiority and,

(*iii*) the joy of creating, getting things done or simply of exercising one's energy and ingenuity.

In this process, entrepreneur is expected to possess certain attitudes and values in order to perform the expected entrepreneurial behaviour. The expectations regarding entrepreneurial values and attributes were termed as entrepreneurial orientation. Entrepreneurial orientation is prerequisite condition for an entrepreneur. Entrepreneurial orientation consists of, (*i*) risk bearing propensity, (*ii*) change process, (*iii*) ambition, (*iv*) long-term profit perspective, (*v*) positive attitudes towards management and workers. The term 'entrepreneur' may be used in connection with those who incubate new ideas, start enterprises based on those ideas and provide added value to society based on their independent initiative.

Thus, there are typical characteristics of a person who takes up entrepreneurial career in preference to other opportunities. He prefers to take a risk and start his enterprise rather than take up a job. In terms of motivation, he has a need for achievement, need for power and need for affiliation. Moreover, it is the profit that induces the prospective entrepreneur to get into the business and start new activities or expand the existing activities. Profit, therefore, is a factor which induces the entrepreneur to organise and utilise the factors of production for development. It does not necessarily mean that entrepreneur is concerned only in the pecuniary profits. He is an innovator to bring change with certain achievement motive and that achievement motive may also mean something more than money. "For such entrepreneurs to function effectively, we need an appropriate social climate." Social climate plays a very important role in the industrialisation of any region. Industrially backward areas in some cases, possess the requisite infrastructure and availability of financial incentives yet they have not succeeded well with their efforts at industrialisation to the desired extent only because they lack entrepreneurs with posititive attitudes, culture and values.

Definitions of Entrepreneur

The term 'Entrepreneur' is defined in different ways. However, no consensus has been arrived at a universally accepted definition of entrepreneur. Important definitions of entrepreneur are given below:

(*i*) Cantillon : *According to him, an entrepreneur is the agent who buys means of production at certain prices in order to combine them into a product that he is going to sell at prices that are uncertain at the moment at which he commits himself to his costs.*

In this definition, *Cantillon* emphasised the function of risk taking and uncertainty bearing. The entrepreneur is designated as a dealer who purchases the means of production for combining them into marketable pıoducts.

(*ii*) J. B. Say : "*The entrepreneur is the economic agent who unites all means of production... the labour force of the one and the capital or the land of the others and who finds in the value of products his results from their employment reconstitution of the entire capital that he utilises and the value of the wages, the interest and the rent which he pays as well as profits belonging to himself.*"[1]

The above definition provides that an entrepreneur is an important agent of production who gets together other factors of production. He further states that the entrepreneur shifts economic resources out of an area of lower productivity into an area of higher productivity and greater yield.

(iii) The New Encyclopaedia Britanica : *It treats an entrepreneur as an individual who bears the risk of operating a business in the face of uncertainty about the future conditions. This definition deals with uncertain future and that causes risk in the operation of a business and entrepreneur is required to bear the risk.*

(iv) Joseph. A. Schumpeter : He defined "*entrepreneur as an individual who carries out new combines of means of production by which there occurs disequilibrium.*"

He further stated that the key individuals in development are the entrepreneurs, who are especially motivated and talented class of people. They foresee the potentially profitable opportunity and try to exploit it. According to him, entrepreneur is basically an innovator and innovator is one who introduces new combinations. Innovations may occur in the following forms :

(a) The introduction of new good—that is one which consumers are not yet familiar or of a new quality of a good.

(b) The introduction of a new method of production that one not yet tested by experience in the branch of manufacture concerned which need by no means be founded upon a discovery scientifically new and can also exist in a new way of handling a commodity commercially.

(c) The opening of a new market that is a market into which the particular branch of manufacture of the country in question has not previously entered whether or not thus market has existed before.

(d) The conquest of a new source of supply of raw materials or half manufactured goods irrespective of whether this source already exists or whether it has first to be created.

(e) The carrying out of the new organisation of any industry, like the creation of a monopoly position (for example through trustification) or the breaking up of a monopoly position.

Schumpeter had postulated that dynamic disequilibrium was brought in by innovation of entrepreneur rather than equilibrium and optimisation. It is the norm of a healthy economy and the central reality for economic theory and economic practice. Basically, entrepreneurs see change as the norm for healthy economy. Usually, they do not bring about the change themselves, i.e., they are usually not inventorys but innovators and this defines entrepreneur and entrepreneurship. It is the entrepreneur who always searches for change, responds to it and exploits it as an opportunity.

(v) Peter F. Drucker : He observed that "*Entrepreneurs innovate. Innovation is the specific instrument of entrepreneurship. It is the act that endows resources with a new capacity to create wealth. Innovation, indeed creates a resource.*"[2]

According to Peter Drucker, successful entrepreneurs, whatever their individual motivation be it money, power, curiosity or the desire for fame and recognition, try to create value and to make a contribution. Still, successful entrepreneurs aim high. They are not content simply to improve an alternative what already exists or to modify it. They try to create new and different values and new and different satisfactions to convert a material into a resource or to combine existing resources in a new and more productive configuration and it is change that always provides opportunity for the new and different products.

In this context, *Drucker* mentioned the concept of systematic innovation. "Systematic innovation consists in the purposeful and organised search for changes and in the systematic analysis of the opportunities such changes might offer for economic or social innovation."[3]

According to him, systematic innovation means monitoring seven sources for innovative opportunity. The first four sources[4] lie within the enterprise whether business or public service institution or within an industry or service sector. They are, therefore, visible primarily to people within that industry or service sector. They are basically symptoms but they are highly reliable indicators of changes that have already happened or can be made to happen with little effort. These four source areas are :

(*i*) The unexpected success, the unexpected failure, the unexpected outside event.

(*ii*) The incongruity between reality as it actually is and reality as it is assumed to be or as it "ought to be."

(*iii*) Innovation based on process need.

(*iv*) Changes in industry structure or market structure that catch everyone unawares.

The second set of sources[5] for innovative opportunity—a set of three involves changes outside the enterprise or industry. (i) Demographic (population changes). (ii) Changes in perception, mood and meaning. (iii) New knowledge both scientific and non-scientific. Thus, on the basis of the above definitions, we can say that "Entrepreneurs are agents of change and growth in a market economy and they can act to accelerate the generation, dissemination and application of innovative ideas. Doing so, they not only ensure that efficient use is made of resources but also expand the boundaries of economic activity. Entrepreneurs not only seek out and identify potentially profitable economic opportunities but are also willing to take risks to see if their hunches are right."[6]

Entrepreneurial Characteristics

An entrepreneur should be one who bears, innovates or imitates and organises the business. Following are the important personality characteristics of an entrepreneur :

1. Change Agent : An entrepreneur is expected to work as a change agent. The entrepreneur is a catalyst for change. He should be alert to the signs that change is needed. "Both external and internal forces can act on the entrepreneurial organisation, just as they do on other organisations. The complex and uncertain environment can create the need to change."[7]

In this context, entrepreneur is the person who recognises the need for change and directs it. Whenever a particular need to change is recognised the entrepreneur becomes the key person to initiate that change.

2. Self Confidence : Entrepreneurs should have confidence in their abilities to make both strategic and day-to-day decisions regarding technical matters, marketing and overall business strategy. They should also feel capable of overcoming any future unanticipated problem. Since entrepreneur is to work as cheerleader and coach while implementing change, he requires capability to overcome any resistance to change. Actually, overcoming any resistance to change requires intense interpersonal efforts and support.

3. Energy Level : To be successful, a new venture requires hard work and dedication. In practice, success of an entrepreneur needs the ability to work for long hours in completing the task before him. Entrepreneurs need an unusually high energy level in order to meet the demands of launching and running a business.

4. Level of Risk : The entrepreneur assumes risk. Entrepreneurs shift resources from areas of low productivity and yield to areas of higher productivity and yield. Of course, there is a risk they may not succeed. But if they are even moderately successful, the returns should be more than adequate to offset whatever risk there might be. Thus, entrepreneurs are typically characterised as risk takers. Successful entrepreneurs actually tend to take moderate risk rather than little risk or excessive risk.

5. Need for Achievement : Entrepreneurs exhibit a high need for achievement which accounts for their seemingly endless drive. Studies show that people with high need achievement like to take risks but only reasonable ones and such risks stimulate them to greater effort. Moreover, *McClelland* found that certain societies tended to produce a larger percentage of people with high need achievement. Thus, high achievers set ambitious short-term and long-term goals that challenge them and that provide great personal satisfaction when achieved.

6. Tolerance for Ambiguity : Imperfection in information is always possible and manager is required to take decisions with incomplete or unclear information. But entrepreneurs even face more ambiguity since they may be doing certain things for the first time and they are risking their livelihood. Thus, entrepreneurs should be comfortable and capable of making decisions based on incomplete or little information. Practically, it is a critical trait for entrepreneurs who face a great deal of uncertainty at the time of starting new enterprise.

7. Locus of Control : General idea that individuals not luck or fate control their own lives. Entrepreneurs work with impression that they are pulling their own strings. Thus, entrepreneurs tend to believe that they have a high degree of control over their lives. Side by side they oppose to believe their lives are governed by luck, fate or other external sources. Since, they feel in control of their lives they should be able to strike out on their own and assess the future prospects by their own calculations.

Functions of An Entrepreneur

1. Innovation : Innovation means doing the new things or the doing of things that are already being done in a new way.[8] This innovation is the process of doing new things. However, there is distinction between creativity and innovation. Creativity is the ability to bring something new into existence. Practically, it is the ability, not the activity of bringing something new into existence. It is possible for a person to conceive of something new and envision how it will be useful but not necessarily take the necessary action to make it a reality. It is also possible that ideas generated in the mind of a man have little value until they are converted into new products, services or processes. But "innovation is the transformation of creative ideas into useful applications but creativity is a prerequisite to innovation."[9]

Schumpeter described entrepreneurs as innovators who use the process of shatter the status quo through new combinations of resources and new method of commerce. It includes new processes of production, introduction of new products, creation of new markets, discovery of a new and better form of industrial organisation. *Peter Drucker* also elaborates that "innovation is the specific tool of entrepreneurs the means by which they exploit change as an opportunity for a different business or a different service. It is capable of being presented as a discipline, capable of being learned, capable of being practised. Entrepreneurs need search purposefully for the sources of innovation, the changes and their symptoms that indicate opportunities for successful innovation. They need to know and to apply the principles of successful innovation.[10] Thus, innovation is the development process. It translates an idea into an application. It requires entrepreneur to work out the detail of product design or service analytically, to develop marketing, obtain finance and plan operations.

2. Risk-Taking : The risk is the condition of not knowing the outcome of an activity or decision. Nevertheless, risk is capable of being evaluated for relative probabilities. Risk bearing means provision for capital in order to enable the entrepreneur to establish and operate the business. Economists like *Cantillon. J.B. Say* and others stressed risk taking as the specific function of an entrepreneur. Entrepreneur is required to reduce uncertainty in his investment strategies by initiating expansion and diversification programmes in the enterprise. In this connection, Drucker observed that entrepreneurial behaviour is risky because so few of the so-called entrepreneurs know what they are doing. They lack the methodology. They violate elementary and well-known rules. So, entrepreneur should try to reduce the level of uncertainty by analysing the problem in proper perspective. Actually, "business game consists of great risks and rewards are also great when risks are successfully covered. The ability to perform services and the risks involved are inseparable. Therefore, for successfully covering the risks, highest order of ability is required. A successful entrepreneur would be one who has trait, patience, sagacity, power of observation and wisdom and ability of discrimination. He should be mentally alert, gifted with discernment, practically acute-minded, shrewd and an exceptionally intelligent person."[11] Thus, entrepreneurs are required to perform this function—risk taking as well as risk bearing at the same time. They are the owner as well as executor of the business enterprise.

3. Organisation and Management : The process of organisation and management includes planning of an enterprise coordination, control and supervision. Prof. *Alfred Marshal* recognised this function as an important function of an entrepreneur. "Entrepreneurs often fall into the trap of thinking that just because their business is small, they do not really need a comprehensive system of organisation and management. They may rationalise that by designing an effective organisational and management control system or they cannot improve their capabilities because of their limited knowledge about possible methods of effective control. But entrepreneur are expected to develop an effective organisation and management system in the organisation. They have to interact directly with employees and exchange information about what is going on in the firm. They tend to be directly involved in their organisation's operational activities to ensure effective control. They are expected to formulate plans, production strategies, financial management and develop marketing channels and management of personnel.

4. Business Decisions : *Arther H. Cole* described an entrepreneur as a decision maker. The decisions with regard to what to produce, how to produce and for whom to produce are to be taken by the entrepreneur himself. In this connection, he has to implement his innovative process. Prof. Cole described the functions of an entrepreneur as :

(*i*) the determination of those objectives of the enterprise and the change of those objectives as conditions required or made advantageous;

(*ii*) the development of an organisation including efficient relations with subordinates and all employees;

(*iii*) the securing of adequate financial resource, the relations with existing and potential investors;

(*iv*) the requisition of efficient technological equipment and the revision of it as new machinery appeared;

(*v*) the development of a market for products and the devising of a new product to meet or anticipate consumers demand;

(*vi*) the maintenance of a good relations with public authorities and with society at large. Thus, the entrepreneur is an institution himself and he performs various functions related with organisation development and management control. He is supposed to bear the risk, manage, innovate, organise and take decisions with regard to his business empire.

Kinds of Entrepreneurs

1. Innovative Entrepreneurs : They are characterised by effective assemblage of information and the analysis of results originated from different set of combinations. According to Schumpeter, innovative entrepreneurs are those who may raise money to launch an enterprise, assemble the various factors, select top executives and set the organisation operational. They also identify the opportunity for introducing a new technique or a new commodity or a new market. These entrepreneurs are quite aggressive in experimentation and putting attractive or viable possibilities into practice. Thus, innovative entrepreneurs are one who believe in introducing new goods, adopt new method of production, develop new market and restructure the organisation under their command.

Mostly, Innovative entrepreneurs are the product of developed nations and they are in position to adopt and implement innovative process in action. But underdeveloped nations are unable to have this type of entrepreneurs as they lack resources and expertise to invest in innovation process.

2. Imitating Entrepreneurs : These entrepreneurs are those entrepreneurs who are unable to innovate the changes themselves but they are capable enough to imitate the techniques and technology innovated by innovating entrepreneurs. Thus, these entrepreneurs are always ready to adopt successful innovation executed by innovating entrepreneurs as there is little involvement of huge capital expenditure in this process. Developing economies or underdeveloped economies need this type of entrepreneurs. Prospective entrepreneur of these nations prefer to imitate the technology, knowledge and skill developed by innovating entrepreneurs. By western standards, an imitative entrepreneur may be a pedestrian figure, an adopter and imitator rather than a true innovator."[12]

3. Fabian Entrepreneurs : These entrepreneurs are shy and lazy in their working. Their dealings are guided by the customs, religion, tradition and past practices. Actually, Fabian entrepreneurs are always conscious in their dealings and believe in skepticism in initiating any change. They do not have any will power to initiate new changes as well as lack desire to adopt new methods innovated by innovating entrepreneurs. Thus, they always believe in tested routes of production and not interested in taking risk. Actually, they are habitual of following the paths directed by earlier entrepreneurs. They avoid in taking challenges in production system and that is why they are unable to maximise the fruits of entrepreneurial actions.

4. Drone Entrepreneurs : These entrepreneurs are those who are not inclined to bring changes in their production system as demanded by the change in consumer preferences, technological innovation, economic and social behaviour of the prospective customers. Market always provides opportunities to the entrepreneurs but this type of entrepreneurs generally fail to use these opportunities in profitable way. Due to this reason, they fail to earn profit or even suffer loss. They are traditional in their approaches and do not make changes in production methods. They generally risk their identity as their product loses marketability and at the end uneconomic or unviable operation pushes them out of the market.

Role of Entrepreneur

Entrepreneur is the most important factor in the economic development of the country. He plays a very important and catalytic role in activating the factors of production leading to the overall economic development. The entrepreneur organises and utilises the various factors and sets productive machinery in action. The availability of entrepreneurs, therefore, is the precondition of economic growth.

According to *Prof. Schumpeter*, the supply of entrepreneur depends on the rate of profit and social climate. It is profit that induces the prospective entrepreneur to get into the business and start new activities or expand the existing activities. Profit, therefore, is a factor which induces the entrepreneur to organise and utilise the factors of production for development. Entrepreneur is an innovator with a certain achievement motive and that achievement motive may also mean something more than money. Social climate also plays its role in attracting prospective entrepreneur to innovate, assume risk and face the music of uncertainty.

According to *Prof. Schumpeter*, there is high degree of risk and uncertainty in economic world and in this context, entrepreneurial behaviour is important as development is a discontinuous process which itself proceeds with spurts.

Entrepreneurial behaviour has a role in ensuring the change required by the development process. Entrepreneur brings innovation or technical know-how to introduce new products and new combinations of production factors. Economic system has a reservoir of unused technical inventions which can be early utilised by the entrepreneurs. According to *Prof. Schumpeter*, "It is no part of his function to find or to create new possibilities. They are always present, abundantly accumulated by all sorts of people."

Entrepreneur also mobilises capital source to have a command over factors of production. *Prof. Schumpeter* rightly observed that entrepreneur needs credit because credit promotes industrial development which in turn deliver new goods. So, resource mobilisation efforts of entrepreneur also ensure the better and effective utilisation of resources available in the country which further accelerates the pace of economic development.

Difference between Entrepreneur and Manager

1. Innovation : An entrepreneur initiates changes in production. These changes are innovative in nature and thereby increase productivity and profit. Manager involves himself in combining the factors of production to produce. He deals with ongoing coordination of the production process which can be visualised as a continual combining of the factors of production.

2. Risk-Taking : An entrepreneur invests heavily in provision of products and services. However, he is expected to take necessary efforts to succeed in his business. He tackles uncertainty and assumes moderate risk. But manager is required to be careful in his decision making process. He is risk-taker and expected to transfer that risk to entrepreneur.

3. Reward : An entrepreneur is risk-bearer and he expects a profit as a reward for his risk-bearing behaviour. However, there is every possibility that there may be loss in his uncertain but risky behaviour. But manager expects a compensation as salary for his managerial efforts.

4. Skills : An entrepreneur knows business intimately. He requires more business acumen than managerial skills. He further needs intuition, creative thinking and innovative abilities. But a manager earns his skill through professional training specially through business schools. He equips himself with analytical tools, people management relations and political skills.

5. Status : An entrepreneur is job provider and not of job seeker. He is vested with powers of ownership, control and management. But a manager is just responsible for the execution of policies formulated by the owner or entrepreneur or his nominated representative or directors on the board. He is totally governed by the policies and programmes of the entrepreneur.

6. Authority : An entrepreneur accepts organisational role models. He believes in transactions and deal making as a basis for basic relationship. He forces his own vision and is decisive and action oriented. He wants freedom, goal oriented, self-relient and self-motivated. But a manager tries to develop a hierarchy as basic relationship. Moreover, Manager wants promotion and believes in corporate rewards. Actually, he is power motivated.

On the basis of the above analysis, we can say that an entrepreneur is generally motivated by need for achievement. It is possible through his innovative and creative behaviour. In practice, it is not sufficient for the entrepreneur to develop entrepreneurial process but it is also important for him to manage that business in an efficient way. Thus, he is responsible for entrepreneurial functions as well as managerial functions. An entrepreneur at the first instance, initiates innovation then it becomes a routine affair to be handled by the manager at a later stage. Actually, entrepreneur perceives and exploits opportunity and the subsequent steps necessary for efficient governance are to be taken by the manager.

EXAMINATION QUESTIONS

Long Answer Questions

1. Define and describe an entrepreneur and discuss the various theories and entrepreneurship.
2. What are the characteristics of an entrepreneur leasdership ? Discuss with reference to Indian conditions.
3. "Entrepreneurial qualities are in-born and cannot be acquired." Analyse this statement and explain the characteristics of entrepreneur leadership.
4. Define entrepreneur. What are the functions of an entrepreneur ?
5. "Development requires resources but resources alone do not produce development." Examine the functions of an entrepreneur in the light of the statement.

6. "An entrepreneur is a person who functions as an innovator, manager and coordinator." Discuss.
7. What are the qualities required in an entrepreneur ? Explain the factors which help in achieving success by an entrepreneur.
8. "Entrepreneurs are dreamers as well as risk bearers." Comment.
9. What are the qualities of a successful entrepreneur ? Suggest a suitable ideal form for selecting entrepreneurs for a developing economy.
10. "Developing economies need imitative rather than innovative entrepreneurs." Comment.
11. Who is an entrepreneur ? How does an entrepreneur differ from a manager.
12. Discuss the different types of entrepreneurs.
13. Discuss the features of Schumpeterian innovative entrepreneurs. Are they found in underdeveloped economies like India ? Explain.
14. Examine the role of an entrepreneur in a developing economy like India.
15. Discuss briefly the following statements :
    (a) "Entrepreneurs are dreamers as well as risk bearers."
    (b) "Entrepreneurial qualities are in-born and cannot be easily acquired."
16. Explain the views expressed by Prof. Peter Drucker in his Theory of Systematic Innovation in regard to entrepreneurial development in a country. How are his views different from the views of Joseph A. Schumpeter in this regard ?
17. "Socio-economic transformation of a society depends on the entrepreneurial capacity of its people." Critically examine this statement.
18. "Development requires resources but resources alone do not produce development." Elucidate and explain the functions of entrepreneur.
19. "Entrepreneur is one who undertakes risk." Explain it and discuss the main qualities of a successful entrepreneur.
20. Bring out the traditional and modern thinking about the role of entrepreneurs in the economic development of a country.
21. "The entrepreneur is the economic agent which lifts the economic resources of an area of lower productivity to the area of higher productivity and greater yield.
22. "The Entrepreneur is a catalyst of development, with him we prosper, without him we are poor." Explain with examples.
23. "A technical entrepreneur may be compared to a craftsman who develops improved quality of goods because of his craftsmanship." How far is this statement correct ?
24. Give a broad classification of Entrepreneurs. How are the "Agricultural Entrepreneurs" different from "Industrial Entrepreneurs" ?
25. "An entrepreneur is a person who functions as an innovator, manager and coordinator of all the tangible and intangible resources." Discuss this statement and highlight the role of an entrepreneur in a developing economy like India.

26. Main function of an entrepreneur is to take risk and bear uncertainty. Discuss the statement citing examples to differentiate entrepreneurship from capital ownership.

Short Answer Questions

1. Describe the functions of an entrepreneur.
2. Explain the entrepreneurial characteristics.
3. Who is an entrepreneur ?
4. Discuss the nature of entrepreneur.
5. Explain the different kinds of entrepreneurs.
6. Distinguish between entrepreneur and manager.
7. Describe the functions of an entrepreneur.
8. Distinguish between professional manager and entrepreneurs
9. Describe the qualities of an entrepreneur.
10. "Entrepreneur is not a gambler, he is risk lover". Do you agree ?
10. "Entrepreneurial and Managerial attributes are common". Comment.
11. "Innovation is the hallmark of entrepreneurship."
12. "Entrepreneurs are exposed to more risks."
13. "Entrepreneurs are basically leaders."
11. Explain the difference between an 'Entrepreneur' and a 'Manager'.
12. What, in your opinion, should be the characteristic features of a successful entrepreneur in India ?

Objective Type Questions

1. According to Schumpeter, Innovation occurs in the following forms :
   (a) 2 (b) 3 (c) 4 (d) 5
2. Innovative entrepreneur ensures :
   (a) Static equilibrium (b) Dynamic equilibrium
   (c) Static disequilibrium (d) Dynamic disequilibrium
3. The Book "Innovation and Entrepreneurship" is written by :
   (a) J. B. Say (b) J. A. Schumpeter
   (c) Peter F. Drucker (d) Cantillon
4. No. of sources for innovative opportunity given by Peter Drucker are :
   (a) 5 (b) 6 (c) 7 (d) 8
5. Fabian Entrepreneurs are characterised by :
   (a) Hardworking (b) Religious and traditional
   (c) Shy and Lazy (d) Ready to take risk
6. Drone Entrepreneurs are those who generally
   (a) Earn super profit (b) Earn normal profit
   (c) Earn profit or even loss (d) Incur losses

7. Systematic Innovation means
   (a) Monitoring different sources of or innovative opportunity
   (b) Developing different types of entrepreneurial behaviour
   (c) Identifying different new business opportunities
   (d) Creating base for systematic creativity
8. Supply of entrepreneur depends on the
   (a) Rate of the profit available (b) Prevailing social climate
   (c) Rate of profit and social climate (d) None of the above

Answers

l-(d) 2-(d) 3-(c) 4-(c) 5-(c) 6-(c) 7-(a) 8-(c)

Reason Based Questions

State with reason whether the following statements are true or false :

1. Fabian entrepreneur are shy and lazy by nature.
2. An entrepreneur works for profit.
3. Entrepreneur should be a dreamer.
4. Entrepreneurial and Managerial qualities are not common.
5. The skills and qualities required for an entrepreneur and a manager are exactly similar in nature.

REFERENCES

1. Say, J. B., *Treatise on Political Economy*, pp. 28-29.
2. Drucker Peter F., *Innovation and Entrepreneurship.* Harper Businsss, New York, 1993, p. 30.
3. *Ibid.*, 31.
4. *Ibid.*, p. 35.
5. *Ibid.*, p. 35.
6. OECD- *Fostering Entrepreneurship*, Paris, 1998, p. 11.
7. Robbins Stephen, P. & Colter Mary, *Management*, Prentice Hall of India, New Delhi, 1998, p. 423.
8. Clemence, R. V. (Ed.), *Essays of Schumpeter*, p. 218.
9. Thomas J. Peters and Robert, H. Waterman, Jr., *In Search of Excellence : Lessons from America's Best Run Companies*, Harper & Row (New York, 1982), p. 206.
10. Drucker Peter P., *Innovation and Entrepreneur ship*, p. 20.
11. Tandon B. C, *Environment and Entrepreneur*, Chugh Publications, Allahabad, 1975, p. 48.
12. Berna, James, J., *Industrial Entrepreneurship in Madras State*, Stanford Research Institute, 1970, p. 7.

2

ENTREPRENEURIAL CLASS

Balanced development of a country, extension of the benefits of economic progress to the backward areas and widespread diffusion of industrial units are the important dimensions of planned development. However, experience of less developed countries shows that their efforts at achieving the balanced regional development would not succeed until such time as they are able to initiate a widely diffused, yet viable industrialisation process which demands for promotion of new entrepreneurship—a vital factor of production for the success of any adventure. Actually, entrepreneur is the most important factor in the economic development of any region or any country. He plays a very important and catalytic role in activising the other factors of production leading to the overall development. The entrepreneur organises and utilises the various factors and sets productive machinery in action. The availability of entrepreneurs therefore is the pre-condition of economic growth.

The dream of owning and operating a business is shared by majority of the population subject to constraints available to them. Motivated by the potential for profit, the freedom available in their own behaviour and the ability to focus their efforts on what they truly enjoy, entrepreneurs continue to strike out on their own. Some potential entrepreneurs prefer their own business in place of their successful careers in other organisations. Some others see entrepreneurship as an attractive option due to their personal problems. Thus, "people who choose to start their own businesses assume many financial risks and work harder and longer than the average employee in an established organisation but they are driven by the potential rewards and the great personal satisfaction that comes in the business ownership."[1] In this context, monetary and achievement motivation have their own role in deciding the level of entrepreneurial behaviour in the country.

In western countries, entrepreneurs had played very important role in accelerating the pace of development and made the people of underdeveloped countries very much conscious of the importance of entrepreneurship in the programme of rapid economic development. Developing nations have begun to realise that for achieving the objectives of development, it is necessary to increase the quantity and quality of entrepreneurship in the country. It is possible for a country to have resources—labour, technology, technical knowledge and capital but its potentiality cannot be fully explored unless there are active and enthusiastic entrepreneurs who have the ability to organise the various factors of production.

Societal Perspective of Entrepreneurial Growth

Historical development of entrepreneurship are governed by different factors. These factors are the important determinants of entrepreneurial growth and thus given a societal perspective to the entrepreneurship. These factors are as follows.[2] :

(*i*) Ethical Value System : Development of entrepreneurial class is a direct function of ethical value system of the society concerned. *Max Weber* opined that the spirit of rapid industrialisation depends upon a nationalised technology, acquisition of money and its rational use for productivity and multiplication of money. These elements are generally governed by specific value orientation of individuals i.e. the tendency of acquisition and rational attitude towards action which are generated by ethical value. *Max Weber* further held the view that there is positive relationship between protestant ethic and the spirit of capitalism.

(*ii*) Minority Group Morale : According to *Hagen* disadvantaged minority group is generally the source of entrepreneurship. It is general perception that technological innovations are caused more by the culturally marginal persons than others. The concept of marginal man is synonymous with the concept of disadvantaged minority. The history of Japan shows that it had regained its lost glory due to this factor. In India too, Parsis had given a lead in entrepreneurship because traditionally they had enjoyed prestige of which they were deprived later. Their strong desire and efforts to receive their lost prestige led them to successful entrepreneurship.

(*iii*) Need for Achievement Motivation : *McClelland* approach suggests that need for achievement motivation is crucial factor in determining the level of industrial and economic activities. Information with regard to principles of rearing boys also maintains a high degree of need for achievement with the underlying motivational structure of puritans. For example, Jains and Parsis progressed economically due to high degree of their need for achievement as a result of their child rearing practices. In practice, motivation directly affects the level of entrepreneurship.

(*iv*) New Ideas and Opportunities—Empirical studies suggest that exposure to new ideas and opportunities also matter for people's entry to manufacturing activities. Indian case studies observed that not religion but exposure to new ideas and values was the common factor between Parsi and Hindu entrepreneurship that encouraged them to opt for manufacturing areas. It is also important to note that social movements *viz.* Brahmo Samaj and Arya Samaj and education had played very important role in exposing the Indian entrepreneurs to western ideas which led them to entrepreneurship. In this context it is rightly observed that "the process of entrepreneurial spread by analysing the differential responses of the social groups to the opportunities provided by the commitment of the political system to industrialisation. Political and cultural systems both have a bearing in explaining the differences in responses.

(*v*) Political Systems : Some scholars held the opinion that political system also plays an important role in entrepreneurial growth. According to Boulding, political structure was the decisive factor in entrepreneurial growth of France and Russia. *Hoselitz* also argued that Japanese entrepreneurship could find active expression and resulted in faster economic progress because her political system properly integrated the industrial and agricultural economy, large, small and handicraft industries, labour intensive and capital intensive technology, traditional and modern social structure and because there was non-existence of colonial disruption. Similarly in India too, the Government policies have contributed significantly towards entrepreneurial growth.

(*vi*) Regional Industrial Climate : Favourable regional industrial climate also motivates people from different parts of the country to develop an entrepreneurial class in that particular region or area. Marwaris, Gujratis, Vaisyas and Jains gave lead in entrepreneurship mostly in Maharashtra and Gujarat but side by side conducive industrial climate also motivated to non-Vaisyas and non-Jains to emerge in entrepreneurship in these areas. Studies also show that first generation entrepreneurs have been motivated to develop their manufacturing facilities in backward area districts and zero industry districts. Actually industrial estates have given further boost to first generation entrepreneurs to set up their industrial units. Unfavourable industrial climate like in West Bengal and Bihar and Eastern Uttar Pradesh has a demoralising effect on the existing entrepreneurs and created an effective barrier for upcoming of first generation entrepreneurs.

Thus, societal perspective to entrepreneurship is quite important in deciding the level of entrepreneurial class in a country like India and different factors are to be assessed in proper perspective.

Socio-Economic Variables of Entrepreneurs

Entrepreneurial behaviour is governed by the combination of socio-economic considerations. In this context, two variables are important : (*i*) Economic Variables (*ii*) Social Variables.

(*i*) Economic Variables : Basically entrepreneurship is the promotion of economic change. Entrepreneurial behaviour is supposed to be directed to materialistic objective of maximisation of economic welfare. "Entrepreneurial activity is a form giving activity—giving form to the wishes of the society to ideas, to the efforts of the factors and to the raw material they process through.[4] These factors promote economic growth and development perspective for the emergence of entrepreneurship. In this context, two kinds of economic factors are important market incentives and stock of capital. Market incentives relate with the new social needs that entrepreneur can attempt to satisfy in new ways. The stock or supply of capital should be adequate to finance new enterprises. Banks and financial institutions must be willing to direct capital to potential entrepreneurs. Thus, according to *J.B. Say* entrepreneurs rationally combine the forces of production into a new producing organisation. *Schumpeter* also states that entrepreneurial behaviour covers the introduction of a new good, a new method of production, new market, a new source of supply of raw materials or half munufactured goods and a new organisation of any industry for creation of a monopoly position or breaking it. In this way, entrepreneur initiates necessary action to reform or revolutionise the pattern of production.

(*ii*) Social variables : Social variables include cultural and social differences in indirect action of entrepreneurial behaviour available from country to country. According to *McClelland*, a social motive to excel that tends to characterise successful entrepreneur especially when reinforced by cultural factors. Certain societies tended to produce a larger percentage of people in the high need achievement. Studies also suggest that entrepreneurial behaviour is also affected by the motives and goals which include wealth, power, prestige, security, self-esteem and service to society.

Thus, social variables consider the entrepreneur as a role performer corresponding to the role expected by the society. Wishes of the society are exhibited through customs and taboo, rewards and restraints, ethnic values and child rearing practices, nationalist attitude and patriotic inculcations and protestant ethic. He is conditioned by the social milieu to which he belongs. Actually sociologists consider social sanctions, cultural values and role expectations as responsible factors for the emergence of entrepreneurial class in a country. Entrepreneurial behaviour is directly controlled by the role expectations of sanctioning groups and the occupational requirements of the job. *Weber* suggests that religious beliefs develop intensive exertion in occupational pursuits, the systematic ordering of means to end and the accumulation of assets. *Hoselitz* opined that culturally marginal groups encourage entrepreneurial behaviour and thus economic development. Due to their ambiguous position, these groups are suited to make creative adjustments and thereby develop practical innovations. In this context *Hagen* rightly remarked that communities and castes are the nursing ground for potential entrepreneurs.

Socio-Economic Origins of Entrepreneurship in India

Emergence of entrepreneurial class is a direct function of varying combination of socio-economic, psychological, cultural and other factors. These are analysed in following ways :

1. Caste Structure/Religion : There are different groups in the society at large. Out of different groups, some social groups produce more effective entrepreneurs. The caste system has played very important role in deciding the level of occupational mobility. Earlier, the main sources of entrepreneurship were the trading castes of Hindu Marwaris and Jain Banias from Gujarat, Rajasthan and Chetiars of Tamil Nadu. But recent development suggests a different picture. Now new springs of entrepreneurship originated among other castes like Brahmins specially in the south. Naidus of the South, Gujarati Patels, Sikhs, Khans and Aroras of Punjab, Mittals of Haryana making entrepreneurial behaviour as popular and socially crazy behaviour. Besides, religion also has an important bearing on motivating the desirable persons to opt for entrepreneurship. According to *Max Weber*, protestant ethic was a commercial factor in fostering the entrepreneurial behaviour among the Christians. However, Hindu and Islam religions are not so effective in fostering such type of behaviour.

2. Family Background : Family background also helps in developing entrepreneurship among the members of the family. General saying is son of a Bania community will remain a bania as family background provides enough awareness about business intricacies. Moreover, size of family, type of family and economic status of the family also determine the entrepreneurial traits. However, modern thinkings suggest that family background has least role in the development process of first generation entrepreneurs. A large chunk of first generation entrepi eneurs are coming from unemployed youth. Similarly, first generation entrepreneurs are quite successful in manufacturing process, belong to those families who were engaged in agriculture or employed in some industrial organisations.

3. Level of Education : It helps the entrepreneurs to develop their entrepreneurial talent more efficiently and effectively. Now days persons having technical background are more keen to develop manufacturing facilities in the area of their expertise. For example, technical personnel in information technology or computer are engaged in IT industry which is now treated as sunrising industry. Thus. entrepreneurship development is directly related with the level of education of potential entrepreneurs.

4. Migratory Character : Potential entrepreneurs are always interested to migrate to those areas where they find a conducive entrepreneurs. In practice there are several factors which influence an entrepreneur to move to a particular area to start his industrial units. It is notable that some communities are more mobile than others. In this connection we can mention the Marwaris, Punjabis and Sindhis who have been found the most mobile moving to each and every point of the country in search of viable prospects.

Numbers of minority groups are often concentrated geographically in neighbourhood enclaves. The reasons for this vary. For example in some countries and regions immigrants may constitute a large share of the minority population. Migrants may have family and other ties to persons who have already migrated towards whom they will naturally gravitate. The perception of hostility towards members of minority groups may also lead to their local concentration. The neighbourhood can thus cushion the immigrant's incorporation into the country by providing both a community and employment. Studies also suggest that such enclaves can strengthen immigrants' capacity to compete in the broaden market as entrepreneurs providing information networks, sources of credit, a loyal consumer base and a steady supply of workers."[5]

5. Clusters of Firms : The regionalisation of entrepreneurial activity can also reflect the phenomenon of clustering. Clustering is the apparent tendency of firms in related lines of business to concentrate geographically.[6] The fame of high-tech clusters such as Silicon Valley of Bangalore and Hyderabad has given an important clue that it is linked with R&D and more and more IT firms are concentrating in these areas. Moreover, clustering of firms at Pune, Gurgaon, Jamshedpur, Naini (Allahabad) enable the entrepreneurs to produce a wide range of goods in these areas. The degree to which economic activities are clustered is often impressive. Clusters in different areas involve varying degrees of interaction between the firms involved, ranging from fairly loose networks of association through to multifaceted entrepreneurship involving a mix of cooperation and competition.

The concept of industrial estates developed by the Government in the country indirectly helps in mobilising potential entrepreneurs to develop their plants in these industrial estates.

EXAMINATION QUESTIONS

Long Answer Questions

1. Write a note on the emergence of entrepreneurial class in India.
2. Explain the socio-economic origins of entrepreneurs in India.
3. Trace the history of emergence and development of entrepreneurial class of India.
4. Explain the societal perspective of entrepreneurial growth in India.
5. "Socio-economic variables are the deciding factors for entrepreneurial growth". Comment.
6. Critically examine the development of entrepreneurship in post Independence era.
7. What are the different stages of economics growth? Outline, briefly, the major achievements of Planning in the industrial growth in India, pointing out the role of entrepreneurs in this development process.
8. Do entrepreneurs emerge only from certain communities and social groups ? Justify your viewpoint.
9. Describe the profile of India entrepreneurs in comparison to the western entrepreneurs.
10. "Emergence of an entrepreneurial class in a country is a direct function of varying combination of the socio-economic, psychological, cultural and other significant factors."
11. Discuss the factors that influence the entrepreneurial growth in a country. Was the entrepreneurial growth in India up to the mark as evidenced by various programmes of socio-economic development initiated by the Government of India from time to time ?

Short Answer Questions

1. What do you mean by entrepreneurial class?
2. Examine the societal prespective of entrepreneurial growth.
3. Explain the socio-economic variables of entrepreneurs.
4. Describe the socio-economic origins, of entrepreneurship in India.
5. Write a note on the emergence of entrepreneurial class in India.

6. Bring out the causes of entrepreneurial crisis and suggest, the remedies for the same.

Objective Type Questions

1. Protestant ethic was advocated by
   (a) Bovee Courtland (b) K. L. Sharma
   (c) Max Weber (d) James Berna
2. Which one is not effective in developing an entrepreneurial class
   (a) Hindu Valayas (b) Jain
   (c) Christians (d) Juda
3. Present Japanese economy is the result of :
   (a) Minority group efforts (b) Samurai group
   (c) Majority group efforts (d) None of the above
4. Clustering means
   (a) Political concentration (b) Geographical concentration
   (c) Social concentration (d) Cultural concentration
5. Achievement Motivation is concerned with
   (a) Peter Drucker (b) Robert H. Waterman
   (c) McClelland (d) J. B. Say

Answers

l-(c) 2-(c) 3-(b) 4-(b) 5-(c)

Reason Based Questions

State with reasons whether the following statements are true or false :

1. Availability of entrepreneurs is the pre-condition of the economic growth.
2. There is a positive relationship between protestant ethic and the spirit of capitalism.
3. Need for achievement motivation is the crucial factor for entrepreneurship.
4. Society is the repository of entrepreneurial resource.
5. Clustering is the apparent tendency of firms in related lines of business to concentrate geographically.

REFERENCES

1. Bovee Courtland Thill Joh. V. Wood Marian Burk and Dovel George P. *Management,* Mcgraw Hill Inl. New York, 1993, p. 368.
2. Sharma Krishna Lal. *Entrepreneurial Performance in Role Perspective,* Abhinav Publications, New Delhi, 1975. p. 11.
3. Bhanushali, S.G., *Entrepreneurship Development,* Himalaya Publishing House, Bombay, 1987, p. 12.
4. Fostering Entrepreneurship, The OECD Jobs strategy, OECD, 1998, p. 97.
5. *Ibid.* p. 92.

3

ECONOMIC SYSTEMS AND ENTREPRENEURIAL BEHAVIOUR

Economic resources are by nature scarce and have different alternative uses. Institutional framework of human and economic endowments is the direct result of production, exchange and distribution related problems. Institutions created with these problems are vested with decision making power available in the particular economic system. Achievement of specific objectives is governed by the constituents of economic system. Environment factors are the by products of economic system and effectiveness of these factors is determined by the variables available in the economy.

Nature of Economic Systems

Economic system consists of those institutions which a given people, a nation or a group of nations have chosen or accepted as the means through which their resources are to be utilised for the satisfaction of the human wants. Actually, society and its institutions are man-made and are moulded and remoulded constantly due to continuous and smooth change available in the society. Moreover, economic systems are also man-made. These systems are governed and determined by the aspiration of the people. "They arise neither from the operation of natural resources nor from the dictation of the super natural power. They arise and are modified time again by the laws which have passed the decrees which authoritative agencies issue, the decision which judicial agencies laid down, the contractual arrangements which people set up among themselves, the customs and habits which people develop and people opinions as to what is right and wrong way, the good or the bad way of doing something."[2] In practice, some individuals are very dominating and effective and posses leadership qualities. They have capacity to bring desired changes on account of their large following. But, the remaining individuals are accept to the existing as well as changing norms of the society.

Thus, economic system consists of those institutions which are accepted by the society at large for the use of available resources. The purpose of utilizing these resources is to maximise the economic and social welfare of the society. It is basically the mechanism which bids people in making their decisions. In other words, an economic system refers to the mode of production, exchange, distribution and the role which the government plays in the economic development of the country.

Determinants of Economic System

Economic systems are formed either by evolution or revolution. However, nature of economy is determined by the following forces."[3]

(*i*) The historic, cultural sources of its people, ideals, desires and attitudes,

(*ii*) Its natural resources including climate.

(*iii*) The philosophies which some or many of its people posses and advocate.

(*iv*) The past and present theorising of its people on how to achieve chosen ideals and goals.

(*v*) The trials and errors of the people in seeking economic end.

Criteria for Economic System

Economic system is different from social, religious and political systems as their objectives and institutions are different. Basically, economic structure of the societies is more or less the same because they are governed by similar production process, same means of transport and communication, same sources of energy and similar resources. With the result, society receives identical goods and services as produced by relevant production process.

In the present day context, there are different economic systems but differ considerably from one another. However, there are not different in terms of economic relationships. The following criteria are used to distinguish one economic system to another:

(*i*) Degree of the ownership of the means of production.

(*ii*) Nature and forms of the functioning of the price mechanism.

(*iii*) Political and administrative setup to qualify the ownership and price mechanism.

Economic system determines the nature of state intervention in the business. Thus, economic system is an integral part of the business environment. Generally, there are three types of economic systems and these are capitalism, socialism and mixed economy.

1. CAPITALISM

Capitalism is purely an economic concept and can be combined with entirely different political, religious, family, educational and other institutions. According to *Prof. Loucks*, "Capitalism is a system of economic organisation featured by the private ownership and the use of the private profit of man-made and nature made capital."[4]

Prof. Pikersgill defined capitalism in the following words: "The capital system is one characterised by the private ownership of the means of production, individual decision making and the use of the market mechanism to carry out the decision of individual participants and the flow of goods and services in markets."[5]

According to *Webbs*, "capitalism, capitalistic system or capitalist civilization means the particular stage in the development of industry and legal institutions in which the bulk of the workers find themselves divorced from the ownership of the instruments of the production in such a way as to pass into the position of the wage earners whose subsistence, security and personal freedom seem dependent on the wall of a relatively small proportion of the nation, namely those who own and through their legal ownership, control the organisation of the land, the machinery and the labour forces of the community and do so with the object of making for themselves individual and private gains.

Thus, in simple words, "Capitalism is an economic system wherein property rights are vested with individuals or their associations, legally recognised as persons, individuals. These persons are not only free to own capital and consumer's goods but also to use and dispose them off as and when they like."

Features of Capitalism

(*i*) Right of Private Property: Private property refers to the right vested in an owner and protected by the society. The owner exercises control over the uses of the properties owned by him. Everybody has a right to acquire private property, to keep it and after his death to pass it on to his heirs as per the system of inheritance. With the result, inequalities of wealth distribution are perpetuated. The rich people become richer and the poor people become poor. Besides, factors of production are owned by private individuals. They are also the owners of the firm and factories.

(*ii*) Freedom of Enterprise: It has three dimensions, *viz.*, freedom of enterprise, freedom of contracts and freedom to use one's property. In the system, everybody is free to opt for any occupation, or start any business or to enter into contracts in a manner most profitable to him. Every citizen has the freedom to form any firm or company or business anywhere he likes provided he has the requisite capital, skill and risk taking capacity.

(*iii*) Consumers Sovereignty: Every consumer enjoys a freedom to have the commodities and the services that he wishes to consume. Consumer is treated as the king. Thus, it means the production decisions are governed by the consumers desires which are reflected in their demand pattern. However, the consumers sovereignty is limited by the consumers income and the availability of goods in the market.

(*iv*) Profit Motive: Profit motive induces the people to undertake any productive activity. Entrepreneurial activity is governed by the profit motive and not by the social service. He is not in the business for social service. He is in the business to earn profit and out of that profit he fulfills his social obligations. It means profit motive of individual governs the formulation of business enterprise. Commodities and services produced by the entrepreneurs are expected to yield maximum profit. Actually, it is the profit motive which induces entrepreneurs to ensure the optimum use of factors of production.

***(v)* Absence of Central Economic Plan:** Freedom of enterprise and property rights rule out the possibility of central direction or central authority. Resource allocation and investment decisions are guided by the market forces. The state has no role to play in the economic planning of the country. Entrepreneurial decision generally decides the nature of product and level of production. It is also influenced by the number of individual consumers who make their decisions without consulting one another. It is the consumer's preferences which finally decide what should be produced and what should not be produced.

***(vi)* Class Conflict:** Capitalistic structure leads to inequal distribution of income and wealth. It further envisages inequality in economic and political power. The society has been divided in two categories: the haves and haves not, which have conflicting interest to each other. Moreover, class conflict is inherent in capitalism.

***(vii)* Role Assigned to Entrepreneurs:** An entrepreneur plays a vital role under this economic order. He directs all productive machinery of the country. It is he who hires the other factors of production and compensates them. He represents the community in the matter of production.

***(viii)* Competition:** The first important function of competition in a capitalist society is pricing of goods and factor services. Prices are determined by free play of market forces. Secondly, competition creates and preserves efficiency in the production process. Capitalism is essentially a free market economy.

***(ix)* Control with Risk:** Golden rule of capitalism is to control and control the business which goes with risk. Investors or entrepreneurs who have invested or taken initiatives with regard to investment of capital and risks have every right to control the business under their command.

***(x)* Rate of Price System:** Price mechanism facilitates the working of capitalism. Price equate the demand and supply of commodities and factors of production. Price guides the producers as to what to produce and what not to produce. Similarly, price also sends signals to the consumers as to what to consume and what not to consume. Thus, capitalism is governed by the price mechanism.

Merits of Capitalism

***(i)* Optimum Utilisation of Resources:** Entrepreneurial activity is guided by the profit motive. Practically, every entrepreneur tries to use the productive resources at his disposal in the most efficient manner with an objective to maximize his profit. There is a keen competition among producers to produce at lowest cost and control wastes to their lowest level. Thus, capitalism ensures the most efficient use of national resources.

***(ii)* Automatic Working:** Price mechanism is the basis of automatic working of capitalism. Price rectifies the distortions available in the economy, if any. Price mechanism also rules out any expenditure to be incurred on the operating system of capitalism.

***(iii)* Higher Level of Productivity:** Under capitalism, control of business rests with the entrepreneur and so he is induced to work hard and work efficiently to earn higher level of profits. Similarly, workers can also earn higher income by improving their efficiency and doing more work. Thus, under this system, entrepreneurs and workers both are enduced to improve their efficiency and put hard work.

***(iv)* Economic Prosperity:** Capitalism encourages potential investors to invest more and more to earn the profit. Larger the investment level larger the level of production and services. Higher investment also ensures higher level of employment opportunities. Society is the most beneficiary of huge availability of goods and services in the market.

***(v)* Improvement in Risk Taking Capacity:** Profit motive also induces entrepreneurs to innovate and assume more risks. Higher the risk, greater is the profit innovations and it leads to improvement in production technique and lowering the costs of production.

Demerits of Capitalism

***(i)* Class Conflict:** Capitalism divides the society into two categories, *viz.*, have and have nots or capital and labour. Thus, they have conflicting interest and look out for an opportunity to fight. The workers want higher wages and less working hours which is against the philosophy of capitalists. Class conflicts ultimately leads to strikes and lock outs which are not in the interest of the society as well as economy.

***(ii)* Exploitations of Consumers:** Economic decisions of entrepreneurs are governed by their self interest and not by social welfare. Entrepreneurs involve themselves in gentlemen's agreements which lead to monopoly in place of competition. Lack of effective competition, manipulative practices of entrepreneurs and the ignorant and the helpless behaviour of individual consumers turn the consumer-king into an abject slave—a victim of exploitation. Thus, consumers are exploited by the unscrupulous entrepreneurs.

***(iii)* Wasteful Competition:** Competition encourages wasteful expenditures like advertisement and selling costs. Actually, consumers are unable to gain from cut throat competition launched by the producers. Competition also leads to the production of too many varieties lead to but these too many varieties lead to wasteful use of economic resources.

***(iv)* Economic Instability:** Excess competition and high saving rates encourage recurrence of trade cycles in the system. Trade cycles are again responsible for over production. Thus, combined effect of these variables leads to economic instability in the economy.

***(v)* Defcctive Allocation of Resources:** Capitalism has its own priorities. It encourages investment in those areas where expected profit is at higher level. In this sense, goods and services required for basic needs of the society is not the goal of the production under capitalism. Capitalism makes available productive resources for the production of luxuries which is meant for rich people. Productive resources are not utilised in producing sufficient quantity of goods for human consumption as poor people has no capacity to compensate with profit to the entrepreneurs.

2. SOCIALISM

Under socialism the instruments of production are owned and controlled by the state. Resources mobilisation and allocation are also governed and regulated by the government. In a theoretical framework, all resources are under the control of public ownership. However, management of these resources are also undertaken as per the wishes of society at large.

Dickenson defined "Socialism as an organisation of society in which the material means of production are owned by the whole community and operated by organisation's representative of and responsible to, the community. According to a general plan, all members of the community being entitled to benefits from the result of such socialised planned production on the basis of equity rights."[6]

According to *Webbs*, "Socialised industry is one in which the national instruments of production are owned by public authority or voluntary association and operated not with a view to profiting by sale to other people, but for the direct service of those whom the authority or association represents."

According to *Loucks*, "Socialism refers to that movement which aims at vesting in society as a whole, rather than in individual's ownership and management of all nature made and man-made producers' goods used in large scale production to the end that an increased national income may be more equally distributed without materially destroying the individual's economic motivation or his freedom of occupational and consumption choices."[7]

Features of Socialism

(*i*) Social ownership and Control: Socialism assumes that ownership and control of means of production are to be vested in the state so that the state may provide work for everybody. Besides, state has a control over means of production and profit of all enterprises go to the state exchequer. The government uses these profits for the benefits of society at a large.

(*ii*) Central Authority: Socialism assumes the existence of a central authority which directs the allocation of productive resources of the community. Similarly, state is responsible for the production and distribution of goods and services. Since means of production are owned and controlled by the state it has authority to direct the production of commodities and the utilisation of resources in the desired channels. Central authority is entrusted with price mechanism which lays down the objective of planning and to settle the targets and priorities of planning.

(*iii*) State Enterprises: Under socialism, state is expected to play its participative role in business. Production is generally initiated and conducted by the state-owned enterprises as there is no role for private enterprises. These state enterprises are responsible for the payment of wages and other costs and keep profit for themselves. These enterprises generally work as an model employer. A state is required to work as a capitalist in terms of landlord and entrepreneurs.

***(iv)* Equality of Opportunity:** Socialism tries to provide equality of opportunity to all. Equitable distribution of income is ensured. Every individual has an equal opportunity to rise in life. Every person has an opportunity to receive educational facility and he can enter a profession of his choice. Every step is taken to provide full opportunity to each and everybody to achieve his goal, mission or objective. Every individual enjoys equality of opportunity regardless of caste, creed, family and religions.

***(v)* Classless Society:** Socialism believes in classless society. There is no distinction between the have and haves not. The main objective of socialist state is to remove the distinction between two classes of labour and capitalists. Severe regulatory measures are generally adopted to check the growth of private wealth. Every individual gets a reward according to his work and ability.

***(vi)* Social Development:** Socialism provides the consideration to social welfare which guides productive resources in the country. Commodities and services of such type and in such quantities are produced which are essential for promoting social welfare. Central authority ensures effective actions for social development of society at large. The state takes necessary steps to ameliorate the lot of the common man by providing adequate medical aid fully and free educational and recreational facilities.

Merits of Socialism

***(i)* Effective Resource Allocation:** Socialism ensures effective allocation of productive resources to different sectors of the economy. Central planning authority just like Indian Planning Commission determines the allocation of resources more economically and optimally among the various productive uses. Central planning authority is also in a better position to assess the basic needs of the people and the intensity of their desires and to entrust the resources to satisfy these desires in the best possible manner.

***(ii)* Improvement in Productive Efficiency:** Under Socialism, production activities are undertaken to increase the social welfare. Central planning authority also ensures availability of improved techniques of production and scientific research to all organisations to improve their productive efficiency. State control reduces the possibility of wasteful expenditure on competitive selling campaigns.

***(iii)* Economic Stability:** Trade cycles are the special feature of capitalism and they create hardships to the producers and consumers. Socialism eliminates trade cycles as means of production are owned and controlled by the state. Central planning authority effectively determines the level of investment and the level of aggregate demand. The state has full authority to prevent the imbalance between aggregate demand and aggregate supply by ensuring effective implementation of regulatory measures.

***(iv)* Accelerating Economic Development:** Under Socialism, state is expected to adopt economic planning as a means of promoting accelerated economic development. Economic planning ensures effective and fruitful utilization of potential productive resources. A planned socialist economy functions effectively according to the development programme and in a systematic manner. Economic planning raises the rates of saving and investment as these are essential to accelerate economic progress.

***(v)* Social Justice:** Socialism develops social justice. The socialist principle provides for a fair and equitable distribution of income for all. There is no provision or role for exploitation of man by man. Inequalities of income are minimized to ensure equal distribution of national income. Socialism also ensures protection against uncertainties relating to income, work and living conditions.

Demerits of Socialism

***(i)* Development of State Capitalism:** Socialism is responsible for state capitalism in place of private capitalism. In the system, state is not merely political authority but it also exercises unlimited authority in the economic area. All powers are generally concentrated in the state and the individuals have no role in the economic decision-making.

***(ii)* Essence of Personal Liberty:** Under Socialism, private individuals have no initiatives as their whole activities are governed by the dictates of the state. With the result, there is no incentive to hard work and stimulus to self improvement; inventive ability, enterprising spirit and the go ahead attitude are some of the causalities of state capitalization.

***(iii)* Essence of Consumer Sovereignty:** Socialism encourages only those consumption and production which increase the level of social welfare. Consumption will have to adjust itself against available production from state agencies. Consumer does not have its own choice. His consumption behaviour is directed and governed by the state philosophy of consumption and production.

***(iv)* Red Tapism and Bureaucratic Management:** Under socialism bureaucracy runs state affairs. But, bureaucrats are not fully trained in running economic machinery. Actually, bureaucracy is considered to be inefficient in running a business. Bureaucracy does not believe in quick decision-making and encourage red tapism and corruption in the system. The Government can and does attract able men but conditions in government services are not conducive to hardworking and effective people.

***(v)* Defective Resource Allocation:** Socialism lacks automatic indicator for the efficient allocation of economic resources. Some commodities are produced in excess and floated while there is shortage of other commodities, resulting in unsatisfied demand. Central economic authority fails to ensure effective production system, viable allocation of resources and efficient working environment. Besides, Government also lacks sufficient resources which are necessary for the efficient running and expanding of industrial units.

3. MIXED ECONOMY

Mixed economy may be defined as a form of economic system, which possesses the elements of both, i.e, market or capitalistic economy and command economy. Thus, it integrates good features of both capitalism and socialism. It relies primarily on the price system for their economic organisation but use a variety of government intervention such as taxes, spending and regulation to handle macro economic stability and market failure.

Under this form of economic system, the means of production are partly owned by the private sector and partly owned by the state. The centralized economy (public sector) and the market economy (private sector) co-exist under this system. Thus, system of mixed economy integrates the good features of capitalism as well as socialism to provide a practical platform for the economic development.

Economic development of mixed economy depends upon the joint co-operation of the government and the private sector. In other words, in a mixed economy, the means of production and productive capital is owned by private entrepreneurs. But, the government also directly regulates, promotes and participates in the working of economy through its statues, policies, programmes and initiatives.

Features of Mixed Economy

(*i*) Co-existence of Public and Private Sector: In a mixed economy, the public sector and the private sector participate jointly for the development of the country. The resources of the country are owned and used both by the government and the private industrialists. There is neither exclusive public ownership of the means of production nor the private ownership. The state is the owner of many sources of economic activities. Besides, private sector also manages and some other economic activities. The two sectors are expected to work on a cooperative basis. But, often they become competitive.

(*ii*) Existence of Economic Planning: Mixed economy implies that both the sectors should function in a properly coordinated manner. Economic planning lays down the broad framework within which the economy as a whole is expected to function to realise specific goals. However, social welfare is the major objective of whole planning process. Government also adopts necessary measures to regulate and influence the private sector so that it may function in the interest of nation. Exclusiveness of private entrepreneurs is regulated by the state or by independent regulatory authorities.

(*iii*) Price Mechanism: Mixed economy is governed by price mechanism and government directives. In other words, market mechanism and administrative pricing structure are the important components of mixed economic system. Products of the private sector are priced by the market forces of demand and supply. On the other hand, prices of goods and services produced by the public sector are determined by the state. Thus, dual pricing is an important work of a mixed economy.

***(iv)* Protection of Consumer Sovereignty:** Under mixed economy, consumers are free to buy commodities and services of their choice. Private entrepreneurs are free to produce commodities according to consumer preferences but under the broad policy framework formulated by the government. The aim of price control is to protect the consumers from the exploitation of private entrepreneurs.

***(v)* Dual Objectives:** Private sector operates with profit maximization motive and public sector is guided by social welfare considerations. Private entrepreneurs are attracted to remain in the business only for profit. Public sector enterprises also earn profit but they transfer this profit to the government for providing social welfare. Public sector judges its success by social profitability. Thus, mixed economy fulfills dual objectives: private profit and social profitability.

***(vi)* Protection of Labour:** Under mixed economic system, the government protects the weaker sections of society including labour. With the help of economic and legislative measures, government tries to protect labour from the exploitation of private entrepreneurs. The government also takes necessary steps to prevent industrial disputes.

***(vii)* Reduction of Economic Inequalities:** In mixed economy, government initiates necessary steps for the reduction of inequalities of income and wealth. The government motivates promotion of backward area development and if need arises participate in the business by establishing enterprises in the backward areas.

Merits of Mixed Economy

***(i)* Benefits of Both Sector:** Mixed economy secures the merits of both capitalism and socialism while avoiding the evils of both.

***(ii)* Protect of Freedom:** Mixed economy protects individual freedom. Under the system, individuals have the freedom of consumption, choice of occupation, freedom of enterprise and freedom of expression.

***(iii)* Supremacy of Price Mechanism:** Price mechanism is allowed to operate under mixed economy.

***(iv)* Reduction in Inequality:** Reducing the inequalities of wealth and class struggle is one of the aims of mixed economy.

(v) Control on Economic Fluctuations: Economic fluctuations can be avoided due to centrally planned economy.

Demerits of Mixed Economy

***(i)* Operational Difficulty:** Mixed economy is difficult to operate. Balancing and adjusting the public and private sector is often difficult.

***(ii)* Possibility of Excessive Control:** Excessive controls and heavy taxes are likely to prevail under mixed economy. These will discourage production in the private sector.

***(iii)* Bureaucratic System:** Problems of red-tapism, nepotism, favouritism, officialdom, etc. are also found in this type of economic system.

***(iv)* Existence of Exploitation:** Mixed economy is described by *Schumpeter* as "Capitalism is the oxygen tent." According to him, it is only a trick of the capitalists to cheat the working class by offering them some temporary advantages like social security and uplift of the depressed classes, etc.

EXAMINATION QUESTIONS

Long Answer Questions

1. Explain the basic philosophy of socialism and elaborate its importance in the present business environment.
2. Differentiate between capitalism and socialism. Also assess their superiority.
3. What is capitalist economy? Explain its merits and demerits.
4. "Business is the product of a number of environmental factors that are always changing." Comment.
5. What do you mean by economic system? Examine its various forms.
6. What is socialism? Evaluate its relevance in the context of economic reforms being implemented in India.

Short Answer Questions

1. What is a socialist economy?
2. What is mixed economy?
3. Explain the basic philosophy of 'socialism'?
4. Explain the features of the 'mixed economy'.
5. What do you mean by central planning authority?
6. What do you mean by Indian economic system?

REFERENCES

1. Louks, William N. Comparative Economic System, Harper & Brothers Publishers, New York, 1957p.5
2. *Ibid.*, p.6
3. *Ibid*, p.4
4. Louks. William N.op.cit.188
5. Pickersgill, garu M.and Pickersgill Soice E., Contemporary Economic System: A Comparative view, New Gersey, Prentice Hall of India, Inc.1974, p.13
6. Dickenson, H.D, Economics of Socialism, 1939, p.11
7. Loucks, William N., op.cit., p.42

4

ENTREPRENEURSHIP

Entrepreneurship is an important facor of industrial development of a country. It is the primary trait of an entrepreneur. The degree and quality of entrepreneurship differ from entrepreneurs to entrepreneurs. However, there are certain cogent determinants which affect the development, progress and growth of entrepreneurship. In practice, entrepreneurship changes the direction of national economies, industries or markets. It initiates new products and develop organisations and means of production to make them marketable. It introduces quantum leaps in technology and forces the reallocation of resources away from existing uses to new and productive uses. It also distrupts the status quo and reshapes the process of economic development and society on a new course.

Concept of Entrepreneurship

Following approaches are used to explain the concept of entrepreneurship :

Economic Approach : Entrepreneurship is the process of initiating a new venture, organising the resources it requires and assuming the risks it entails. Thus, the word 'entrepreneurship' itself derived from 17th century French "enterprendre" which refers to individuals who were undertakers meaning those who undertook the risk of new enterprise.

In his essay 'Sur la Nature Due Commerce In General', *Richard Cantillon* remarked that "entrepreneur is a person who pays a certain price for a product to resell it at an uncertain price, thereby making decisions about obtaining and using resources while consequently assuming the risk of enterprise".

Adam Smith, in his 1776, 'Wealth of Nations' observed that "entrepreneur is an individual who undertook the formation of an organisation for commercial purposes. He is a person with unusual foresight who could recognise potential demand for goods and services. He reacts to economic change, becoming the economic agents who transformed demand into supply".

J.B. Say again a French economist in his 1803 'Traited Economic Palitique' (English version 'A Treatise on Political Economy' published in 1945) reported that an entrepreneur is one who possessed certain arts and skills of creating new economic enterprises, yet a person who had exceptional insight into society's need and was able to fulfil them.

In 'The Principles of Economics', 1871 in which Austrian economist *Carl Menger* remarked that "economic change does not arise from circumstances but from an individual's awareness and understanding of those circumstances. The entrepreneur becomes, therefore, the change agent who transforms resources into useful goods and services often creating the circumstances that lead to industrial growth.

Joseph Schumpeter another Austrian economist remarked in his work "The Theory of Economic Development", 1934 that "Entrepreneurs as a force of creative destruction whereby established ways of doing things are destroyed by the creation of new and better ways to get things done. It is a process and entrepreneurs as innovators who use the process to shatter the status quo through new combinations of resources and new methods of commerce.

Peter F. Drucker in his work Innovation and Entrepreneurship,1985 observed that "entrepreneurship occurs when resources are redirected to progressive opportunities not used to ensure administrative efficiency. This redirection of resources distinguishes the entrepreneurial role from that of the traditional management role.

Sociological Approach : Sociologists consider the entrepreneurship as a process of role performance. Entrepreneurs are expected to be governed by the wishes of the society, customes, ethics values, child rearing practices etc.

Thomas Cocharan concluded in his study 'The Entrepreneur in. Economic Change—Explorations in Entrepreneurial History', 1965 that the entrepreneur represents society's model personality. His performance depends upon his own attitudes towards his occupation, the role expectations of sanctioning groups and the occupational requirements of the job. Society's values are the most important determinant of the attitudes and role expectations.

According to *Peter Marris*, a sociologist, in his study 'The Social Barriers to African Entrepreneurship', 1967, Entrepreneurship requires to assemble or reassemble from what is available very concrete kind of imagination to see what others have missed, sensitivity to business and social environment rest in industrial development and entrepreneurial courage. These are the important factors that make an entrepreneur.

Psychological Approach : In this approach we can mention the concept developed by *McClelland* and *Hagen*. In his work 'The Achieving Society',1961, David C McClelland stated that it is the high need for achievement which drives people towards entrepreneurial activities. Achievement motive is basically measured through child rearing practices which stress standards of excellence, material warmth, self-reliance, training and low father dominance. Individuals with high achievement motive tend to take keen interest in situations of high risk, desire for responsibility and desire for a concrete measure of task performance.

E. E. Hagen also in his study on the theory of social change 'How Economic Growth Begins', 1964 deals about the withdrawal of status respect as the trigger mechanism for changes in personality formation. Status withdrawal is the perception on the part of members of some social group in the society whom they respect and whose esteem they value.

Thus, entrepreneurship is the end result of a complex and varying combination of socio-economic, psychological and other variables.

Definitions of Entrepreneurship

Entrepreneurship is a multifacet activity and defined by different authorities in different ways. Some of the definitions given by them are analysed below :

1. Higgins B. : "Entrepreneurship is meant the function of seeking investment and production opportunity, organising an enterprise to undertake a new production process, raising capital, hiring labour, arranging the supply of raw materials, finding site, introducing a new technique and commodities, discovering new sources of raw materials and selecting top managers of day to day operations of the enterprise."[1]

This definition deals with the functions of an entrepreneur. These functions included handling economic activity, undertaking risk, creating some thing new and organising and coordinating resources.

2. John Kao : "Entrepreneurship is an attempt to create value through recognition of business opportunity, the management of risk taking appropriate to the opportunity and through the communicative and managerial skills, to mobilise human, financial and material resources necessary to bring a project to final end."[2]

In this definition, entrepreneurship is treated as a dynamic and risky process. It incorporates the capital, technology and human talent. Entrepreneurial process itself is the result of art and science.

3. Schumpeter J.A. : "Entrepreneurship as defined essentially consists in doing things that are not generally done in the ordinary course of business routine."[3]

In this definition, Schumpeter emphasised on the innovation process to be undertaken by the entrepreneur. Entrepreneur is required to gather resources, organise talent and provide leadership to make the business a commercial success.

4. Ronstadt Robert C. : "Entrepreneurship is the dynamic process of creating incremental wealth. This wealth is created by individuals who assume the major risks in terms of equity, time and or career commitment of providing value for some product or service. The product or service itself may or may not be new or unique but value must somehow be infused by the entrepreneur by securing and allocating the necessary skills and resources".[4]

This definition identifies the creation of incremental wealth as an end result of entrepreneurship. The process of value creation is a risky process but entrepreneur has to reduce the risks interm of equity and time.

5. Drucker Peter F. : According to him "Entrepreneurship occurs when resources are redirected to progressive opportunities not used to ensure administrative efficiency. He further states that entrepreneurship is not natural;

it is not creative. "It is work. Entrepreneurship requires entrepreneurial management." Specifically, entrepreneurial management requires policies and practices in four major areas.[5]

First, the organisation must be made responsibe to innovation and willing to perceive change as an opportunity rather than a threat. It must be organised to do the hard work of the entrepreneur. Policies and practices are needed to create the entrepreneurial climate.

Second, systematic measurement or atleast appraisal of a company's performance as entrepreneur and innovator is mandatory as well as built in learning to improve performance.

Third, entrepreneurial management requires specific practices pertaining to organisation structure, to staffing and managing and to compensation, incentives and rewards.

Fourth, there are some "do nots" things not, to do in entrepreneurial management.

Thus, in the above definition, *Drucker* tries to give management orientation to entrepreneurship. He further states that the entrepreneurial organisation requires different management from the existing. But like the existing it requires systematic, organised and purposeful management. And while the group rules are the same for every entrepreneurial organisation, the existing business, the public service institutions and the new venture present different challenges. have different problems and have to guard against different degenerative tendencies. There is need also for individual entrepreneurs to face up to decisions regarding their own roles and their own commitments.

On the basis of these definitions, we can say that "Entrepreneurship is a process of innovation that reallocates resources to new opportunities, often creating new opportunities through unusual combinations of resources and the skills of risk taking entrepreneurs.

Characteristics of Entrepreneurship

1. Dynamic Process : Entrepreneurship involves a dynamic process in which new firms emerge from existing firms, grow and unsuccessful ones die. It can be thought of in terms of the Schumpeterian approach of creative destruction. The dynamism of this process is to be evaluated in terms of the rate at which businesses open and close. The complex and uncertain environment can create the need to change and often the entrepreneur is the person who recognises the need for change and directs it. Thus, entrepreneurship is a dynamic process which recognises the need to change and the entrepreneur becomes the key person to initiate any change.

2. Innovation : Entrepreneurship is innovation where new products and services and more efficient production techniques are introduced by the firms that have identified new market opportunities or better ways of meeting existing demands. Innovation means "doing new things or doing the things that are already being done in a new way." It includes new processes of production, introduction of new products, creation of new markets, discovery of a new and better form of industrial organisation. According to *Schumpeter* innovation may occur in the following forms :

(*i*) The introduction of new goods, that is one which consumers are not yet familiar with or of a new quality of goods.

(*ii*) The introduction of new method of production, that is one not yet tested by experience in the branch of manufacture concerned, which by no means be founded upon a discovery scientifically new and can also exist in a new way of handling a commodity commercially.

(*iii*) The opening of a new product market that is a market into which the particular branch of manufacture of the country in question has not previously entered, whether or not this market has existed before.

(*iv*) The conquest of a new source of supply of raw material or half manufactured goods, irrespective of whether this source already exists or whether it has first to be created.

(*v*) The carrying out of the new organisation of any industry, like the creation of a monopoly position (for example, through trustification) or the breakingup of a monopoly position.

3. Risk Taking : Risk bearing means making provisions for capital in order to enable the entrepreneur to reduce uncertainty in his plan of investment and expansion of the enterprise. Entrepreneurs are calculated risk takers. They enjoy the excitement of a challenge, but they do not gamble. Entrepreneurs avoid low risk situations because there is lack of challenge and avoid high risk situations because they want to succeed. They like achievable challenges. Entrepreneurs like to take realistic risks because they want to be successful ; that is they take great satisfaction in accomplishing difficult but realistic tasks by applying their own skills. Hence, low risk situations and high-risk situations are avoided because they are not the source of satisfaction. In short, the entrepreneurs likes a difficult but achievable challenge.

A risk situation occurs when entrepreneurs are required to make a choice between two or more alternatives whose potential outcomes are not known and must be subjectively evaluated. A risk situation involves potential success and potential loss. The greater the possible loss, the greater the risk involved. As a risk taker and bearer, entrepreneur will have to make decisions in conditions of uncertainty, balancing potential success against loss. In practice, selection of risky alternative or a conservative alternative depends on :

(a) the attractiveness of each alternative;

(b) the extent to which entrepreneur is prepared to accept the potential loss;

(c) the relative probabilities of success and failure; and

(d) the degree to which entrepreneur's efforts increase the likelihood of success and decrease the likelihood of failure.

Entrepreneurial traits are inter related with regard to risk taking behaviour. These interrelations are as follows :

(a) Risk taking is related with creativity and innovation and it is an essential part in turning ideas into reality.

(b) Risk taking is related to self confidence. The more confidence entrepreneur has in his own abilities, the greater confidence entrepreneur will have in being able to affect the outcome of his decisions and a greater willingness to take what others see as risks.

(c) Realistic knowledge of entrepreneur's own capabilities is also important. Such realism serves to restrict entrepreneur's activities to situations in which he can affect the outcomes.

Risk taking and creativity are two essential characteristics of entrepreneurs. By trying to be more creative he will also become aware of more productive ideas. When he is able to choose from a number of good ideas, he will be more willing to take the necessary risks to implement his most productive idea.

To some degree, every one is creative under most circumstances, so it is possible to develop a person's creative talents. When he has developed a creative idea, certain risks may be involved in having the idea implemented.

The risk taking ability of entrepreneurs is enhanced by :

(a) their self confidence,

(b) their willing to use their capacities to the fullest extent to move the odds in their favour;

(c) their capacity to assess realistically the risk situation and their ability to alter the odds; and

(d) looking at the risk situation in terms of their established goals.

4. Decision Making : To be entrepreneurial, a person should be creative, specially when it comes to decision-making. He must strongly believe in himself and his ability to make good decisions. It is this decision-making ability that is the distinguishing mark of an entrepreneur.

Managers usually base their decisions on firm data and documentation contained in surveys, reports and committee recommendations. This information has usually been generated in a standardised manner in accordance with techniques used in solving problems. It is possible for a major problem to be split up so that a part of it can be solved immediately—generally to meet an urgent need where the results are fairly certain. A decision is usually reached by an established procedure well understood by management and it may represent a consensus, many individuals being unwilling to accept personal responsibility for the decision in question.

Success of an entrepreneur depends on his ability to make decisions which improve the future profitability of his business. Intuitive decision-making ability, a most valuable entrepreneurial resource comes from years of experience of being exposed to making necessary decisions in increasingly complex situations.

As environment changes, entrepreneur is required to make more judgements and intuitive decisions. Mistake will occur but he must be quick to recognise them and take corrective action. Quantitative data can support his judgement, but will not replace the intuition underlying many of more entrepreneurial decisions.

The entrepreneur may. face various types of problems in his entrepreneurial behaviour. So he should pay due attention to rational aspects of decision-making. The scientific method of problem solving indicates that there are specific procedures to follow in order to solve a problem and make a decision. These usually involve the following steps : (*i*) Become acquainted with the problem in general. (*ii*) Determine the key facts relating to it. (*iii*) Identify major problems. (*iv*) Identify related problems. (*v*) Search for possible causes of the problem. (*vi*) Consider potential solutions to the problem. (*vii*) Select the most feasible solution. (*viii*) Implement the solution; and (*ix*) Verify that the solution is correct. This rational approach is a logical and sensible way to solve most business problems. However, the scientific method will not guarantee that a particular solution will work. It is entrepreneurial leadership and power which are needed to implement a decision/solution successfully.

5. Accepting Challenges : Entrepreneurship deals with challenges which are to be faced by the entrepreneur in his behaviour. In practice, entrepreneurs face a tremendous challenge, a challenge they need to exploit as an opportunity. Biggest challenge before the entrepreneurs is to exploit the available opportunities in instable form. Opportunities are risky and uncertain and thus entrepreneurship deals with risk and uncertain behaviour of the product, price and market. The entrepreneur is required to innovate for which he is innovator. But innovative process is also affected by risk and uncetainty as to what extent prospective customers will support the innovative product in the market. But there is no option before the entrepreneur to avoid this types of challenge. Entrepreneurship considers 'exceptions' and entrepreneurs are supposed to become the examplars.

6. Organisation : Entrepreneurship offers people an alternative to the traditional career path. Starting an innovative new venture takes a great deal of planning, investigation, organisation and perseverance. Entrepreneurship also deals with the approaches used to get into market, the form of ownership the new organisation will adopt, the development of the business plan and sources of funding and managerial support. In an enterprise capital is brought in by the financial institutions and banks, labour by the labourers, land by land owners and all such factors are divorced from one another. They are all separately owned and are scattered all over the country. It is the entrepreneurial process which brings them together and harnesses them to work in production. Thus, entrepreneurship develops talented person who specialises in the work of organising ability. The entrepreneur initiates the work, organises it, supervises it and develops support system to solve the organisational problems in proper perspective.

7. Skilful Management : It refers to effective and viable management of resources of the firm. It has a wide coverage of aspects of setting up objectives, goals, programmes and their management. The entrepreneurcial skills include the ability of the entrepreneurs to deal with new situations, organisations, economic and social forces as available from time to time. The entrepreneur should have skill to get positive support from administrators, policy makers, bankers and financial institutions, infrastructural agencies, customers and workers. He should be able to identify, select and develop executive who can effectively manage and control the human resources. He is also required to stimulate. intiative and enthusiasm in the fulfilment of organisational objectives. He should believe in effective delegation of powers and responsiblities to others.

8. Making the Organisation a Success : Business is a game of skill. Risk and return both are positively correlated. "As the ability' required, service performed and the risk borne are inseparable, ability of the highest order is required to make the entrepreneurship successful."[6] Entrepreneurship motivates the prospective entrepreneurs to undertake the risk of an enterprise by identifying, arranging and combining the productive variables available in the environment. It is the entrepreneurial behaviour which identifies opportunities for introducing and implementing the new ideas with regard to production technique. nature of product, expansion and diversification programme and marketing strategies. So entrepreneurship develops a background where organisation has to get result as expected by the entrepreneur.

Entrepreneur and Entrepreneurship

There is misconception about the entrepreneur and entrepreneurship. General thinking is that there is no difference between the two and both are the same. But conceptually, they are different though in practice they are just like the two sides of a same coin.

Entrepreneur is a person who is a visualiser, creator, innovator, decision maker, risk taker and leader. He is actively engaged in seeking change by exploiting opportunities. Moreover, he accepts risk as part of the process of being entrepreneur. Similarly, he is motivated by independence and the opportunity to create financial surplus or profit.

Entrepreneurship is a process of action to be completed by the entrepreneur. It refers to a process by which entrepreneur is required to complete the innovative process by initiating new or latest technology, idea or perception. Entrepreneurship is a risk taking phenomenon as every thing is uncertain and due to this uncertainty it involves risk and entrepreneur is supposed to bear the risk available in the organisation process if any.

Enterprise is the tool to achieve the objectives of entrepreneurship. The capacity to assume risk independently and individually with an objective to earning profits and encashing the available opportunity to maximise earnings through enterprise are the guiding principles before the entrepreneurs.

Thus, there are three components to understand the conceptual framework of entrepreneur and entrepreneurship. These components are entrepreneur, entrepreneuuship and an enterprise.

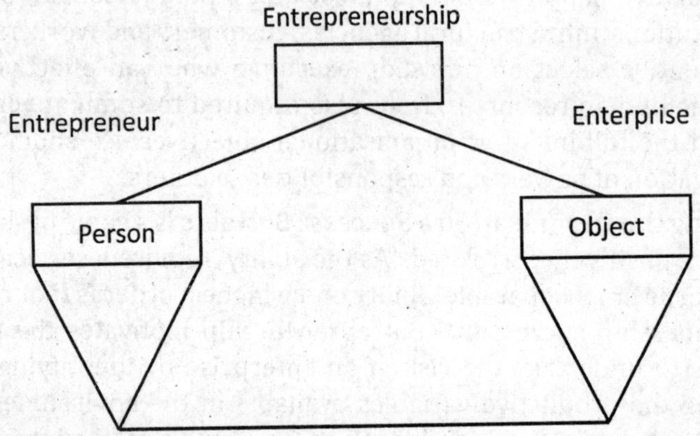

Actually, enterprise is a tool to pursue the business objectives and with the help of an enterprise, entrepreneur ensures production and marketing of goods and services in a viable manner. Entrepreneur is the person who initiates the change by expanding and diversifying the operational behaviour of the enterprise. This is possible only with the help of entrepreneurial process.

Intrapreneurship

Intrapreneurship is concerned with innovation that leads to new corporate divisions or subsidiary venture in established larger firms.[7] Now days, the term intra-preneurship is getting certain degree of propularity in corporate sector.

In practice, corporate entrepreneurship is referred as intrapreneurship. In corporate firm, innovative employees disrupt the company in constructive ways to instigate new products or services. Generally, corporate managers and employees are given freedom to explore new ideas which may be proved as boon in future for the firm. Actually these individuals are expected to create something new within the context of their assignments without having any responsibility or personal stake is their creations. "There is no assumption of personal risk, no assumption of profit and no assumption of loss. In fact, entrepreneurship is not taking place at this point. Entrepreneurship starts when these individuals stop being employees and work as entrepreneurs. They are charged with the responsibility of championing their innovations. These individuals are expected to create an entrepreneurial team that could evolve not a new operating division or a formal subsidiary. The corporate entrepreneurs often still have no direct investment and bear no financial risk. Consequently, they seldom reap rewards beyond bonuses and promotion but they do behave as if they are giving birth to new enterprises."[8]

Thus, intrapreneur is a person who promotes innovation and creativity within a larger enterprise. In certain cases, larger enterprise welcome creative or new ideas and try to motivate their managers and employees to create something new to enlarge the scope of corporate entreprensurship. These motivational efforts involve breaking down formal organisational barriers and control mechanism that have begun to stifle creativity and creating environment that allow people with an entrepreneurial bent to be successful inside the enterprise.

Economic and Social Benefits of Entrepreneurship

The changing environment provides new opportunities for entrepreneurs and as a result entrepreneurship has positively affected the economy and society. Following are the important economic and social benefits of entrepreneurship.

1. Creating Innovation : Development of new enterprises plays an important role in introducing goods and services to the economy. For example as the demand for products and services continues to grow, entrepreneurs continue to innovate to meet the unfulfilled needs of customers.

2. Fuelling Economic Growth : Development of small business is the best way to ensure economic growth, preserve competition, prevent monopolistic control of industries and assure competitive prices for qualty products. Besides, small businesses also create job opportunities for others.

3. Identifying Ownership Opportunities : Entrepreneurship helps people in identifying an option to the traditional job seeking path. Now prospective entrepreneurs try to develop their own business enterprises by identifying viable innovative opportunities. Entrepreneur-ship offers people ownership opportunities where prospective entrepreneurs are supposed to work as job providers in place of job seekers.

4. Enhancing Welfare Amenities : Innovative new enterprises serve society by providing health care facilities, comforts, insurance etc. Entrepreneurs by their own experience try to create products and services that can help others. It is general perception that when individuals experience personal problems or tragedy, they may discover a need for product or service that is not being met. These situations force the inividuals to become innovative in removing their sufferings and at a later stage, this initiates ground for entrepreneurship.

Role of Entrepreneurship in Developing Economy

Entrepreneurship has an important role to play in the economic development of a country like India. The entrepreneur is an economic leader and change agent who have the ability to identify opportunities for ensuring innovation in techniques of produciton, new products, new sources, and new markets. The role of an entrepreneur has now undergone change over the years. Earlier he was expected to bear the risk and uncertainty but now besides these, he is required to coordinate the productive resources in viable way, Moreover, he is expected to take active role in introduction of innovations.

Thus, to ensure accelerated pace of economic growth, developing economies like India require effective entrepreneurial role as they are tied by a chain whose links are in poverty, imbalanced development, under employment, low productivity, traditional culture and stagnatic set of conditions. The resources either remain unutilised or underutilised because people are backward in the sense that they lack skills their knowledge is deficient and they are conservative and immobile. Under these situations only few daring and risk taking entrepreneurs emerge. *Prof. Schumpeter* observed that the entrepreneur is not a man of ordinary managerial ability but he is a man of qualities who introduces something new. Actually, he is reservoir of untapped technical knowledge who can make the proper use of it. He supplies the funds and other resources, plans innovations and takes ultimate decisions.

Development of western economies is the result of entrepreneurship. This has made the people of developing economies very much conscious of the role of entrepreneurship in accelerating the pace of economic development. Now there is growing awareness among the people of developing economies that accelerated pace of development is possible only with the help of entrepreneur ship. It requires to increase the quantity and quality of entreprneurship in the economy. By quality we mean to say that the innovative and imitative entrepreneurs can contribute stimulus for development. It has been rightly observed that "though a country has resources—labour, technology, technical knowlede and capital, its potentialities cannot be fully explored unless there are active and enthusistic entrepreneurs, who have the ability to organise the various factors of productions."[9]

Meier and *Balmin* also stated that "development does not occur spontaneously as a natural consequence when economic conditons are in some sense right : a catalyst or agent is needed and this requires entrepreneurial spirit."[10]

Social conditions also affect the level of development in developing economies. Culture also decides the level of entrepreneurship. People are generally conservative and they are not inclined to bring or accept change. But with favourable environment we can initiate entrepreneurship. A viable business environment is governed by the active, social and cultural behaviour of the people, efficient economic environment and supportive and motivating attitudes of Government.

Since developing economies lack innovative entrepreneurs, so efforts should be made to produce innovating and imitating entrepreneurs. Thus, we can say that entrepreneurship is an indispensable ingredient in economic development of a country like India.

Barriers to Entrepreneurship

Process of entrepreneurship can be affected by regulatory measures and other environmental factors, Barriers to entrepreneurship can stifle innovation if promoted enterprises are protected unnecessarily from the government and competitve forces which generate new ideas. Excessive promotional costs, uncertainty, ineffective political leadership make the potential entrepreneurs to shy away from risk takng behaviour. These barriers are as follows:

(i) Regulatory Barriers : Generally, government regulates entry to markets, defining registration requirement and reporting and disclosure norms and ensuring the tax compliance. In practice, there are different legal forms of business organisations each of which offers different merits and limitations, registration and reporting requirements. These situations force the entrepreneurs to weigh their relative costs and benefits. Normally, the procedure for registering as a sole trader and unlimited liability partnerships are relatively simple and costs are minimal. Formation of private company is also easy and these forms are generally adopted by small entrepreneurs. Besides, for Government support, entrepreneurs are also expected to produce a business plan certified by technical consultancy organisations which attest to the enterprise's viability.

(ii) Mergers and Acquisitions : Flexible merger and acquisition policy generally discourages entrepreneurs and forces them to shy away from entrepreneurial behaviour. They apprehend that whenever they be able to bring success to the enterprise, other entrepreneurs will try to initiate the process of mergers and acqusitions. Effective mergers and acquisitions policy allows entrepreneurs to define their role and ensure smooth sailing for entrepreneurship. It also enables the entrepreneurs to think that they have to run their promoted enterprises for a long long period. Small entrepreneurs are unable to compete with medium and big enterprises and that is the main reason for growing sickness in small enterprises. So, mergers and acquisitions should contain reorganisation process which enable the small entrepreneurs to merge their enterprises making them viable. However, merger and acquisition or reorganisation should be transparent and governed by simple procedures.

(iii) Competition Policy : Gentlemen's agreement among the entrepreneurs to monopolise the market may create problems for potential entrepreneurs, Actually, private barriers to entry can be stifling. Existing entrepreneurs might have interested to suppress competition among them in order to raise prices and exploit consumers. Such agreements invariably require some attempt to keep competitors from offering what the incumbents refuse to in the way of either quantity or quality of product. Collective boycotts could be used for example to deny new competitors supplies of raw materials components and acess to distribution channerls."[11] In this context, it would be necessary to enact competition law so that it will be difficult for dominating firms to unilaterally seek to protect themselves from new competition. The intent to restrict firms to maintain large market shares solely governed by greater efficiency rather than artificial barriers to entry.

(iv) Defective Tax Structure : Higher level of tax doses tend to distort economic activity and reduces profit margin to entrepreneurs. High tax doses lead to a sub-optimal use of resources and a less efficient and dynamic economy. They reduce the returns available to entrepreneurs and discourage them from further creation or expansion. High marginal income and corporate tax rates penalise very successful entrepreneurs. They also reduce firm's liquidity by reducing their capacity to retain more profits for further investment, Similarly, they provide an incentive for tax avoidance and evasion, tending to expand undeclared economic activity. Thus, low tax rates are not the only factor positively affecting the level of enrepreneurship. The relative tax structure on different forms of business organisations can also encourage one form over the other.

(v) Delayed Payments : Delayed payments from big enterprises to small enerprises are the normal feature of small business. They became a problem because of their vulnerability to cash flow constraints and because of their frequently weak bargaining position with respect to purchases. The Government of India has already introduced a separate act "Delayed Payment Act" to protect the interest of small entrepreneurs. Legislation can offer such measures as statutory rights of interest on late payments and the right to sue late paying firms. The Abid Hussain Committee has already recommended the necessary reendments in Indian Companies Act, 1956 to make it mandatory for companies to indicate the amount due to small scale industries in their annual accounts.

(iv) Absence of Protection of Intellectual Property Rights : Innovation is basic root of the entrepreneurship. "Despite the potential benefits offered by research and development of new products and services, firms are reluctant to invest in R & D because the results of such spending on technological discoveries, new products and techniques, can fall easily into the hands of rivals due to the difficulty associated with attaching ownership rights to these results. "So, the Government should try to protect the innovative process developed by the entrepreneurs. It should also try to formulate comprehensive "Intellectual Property Policy" to set an equilibrium between two objectives, first rewarding or compensating creators and inventors for innovation and second promoting the interests of business and the public at large in securing access to science, technology and culture. This, implies granting innovators the rights that are necessary to recoup their investment without stifling competition for an unduly long period of time.

(vii) Defective Administrative and Compliance System Government generally favours small entrepreneurs by granting them tax subsidies and tax incentives to achieve a wide range of economic and social objectives. These measures include tax benefits to promote employee training and R & D, special provisions to SSI's to help them to access financial support extended by financial institutions and special tax provisions to create export promotion zones etc. Tax subsidies and incentives require definitions of the eligible activities, accountability requirements and other administrative procedures and these generate administrative expenses for government and compliance costs for business. Indian bureaucratic system known for its redtapsim also increases the delay in execution of compliance and its costs. So, it would be better to have a trade off between using the administrative system to correct market imbalances and favour particular social goals on the one hand and the objective of cost effectiveness of compliance system on the other.

Thus, entrepreneurship ensures accelerated pace of economic development of the country, It also encourages potential entrepreneurs to innovate for new products and services required by the society at large.

EXAMINATION QUESTIONS

Long Answer Questions

1. Define Entrepreneurship. What are the functions of an entrepreneur ?
2. What do you understand by entrepreneurship ? Discuss the nature and scope of entrepreneurship.
3. Define entrepreneurship and elaborate on its scope and vital role in developing economics.
4. Discuss the methods of identifying entrepreneurship.
5. Entrepreneurship is nothing but a conversion of dreams into viable action." Examine this statement.
6. What do you mean by entrepreneurial barriers ? Discuss these barriers in Indian context.
7. "Economic and social perspectives of entrepreneurship are quite important that is why we should develop entrepreneurship in India." Comment.
8. "Entrepreneurship is nothing but a combined effect of innovation and its effective management." Do you agree with this statement ? Explain.
9. "Entrepreneurship is neither a science nor an art. It is a practice based on knowledge." (*Peter F. Drucker*). Examine this statement, highlighting the characteristics features of entrepreneurship.
10. Critically examine the role of entrepreneurship in economic development of a nation.
11. "Entrepreneurship is the process of initiating a new venture, organising the resources that is required and assuming the risk and uncertainty that it entails." Examine this statement.
12. "Entrepreneurship is an essential tool for economic development." Discuss.
13. In the Indian context, explain the specific role that entrepreneurship has played in the economic development of the country.

Short Answer Questions

1. Discuss the different approaches of entrepreneurship.
2. Explain the characteristics of entrepreneurship.
3. Distinguish between entrepreneur and entrepreneurship.

4. What is entrepreneurship ?
5. Distinguish the benefits of entrepreneurship.
6. Explain the barriers to entrepreneurship.
7. Intrapreneur is the same as entrepreneur.
8. Explain briefly entrepreneurship and explain its main characteristics.
9. What are the factors that hinder the growth of entrepreneurship in our country?
10. Entrepreneur and Intrapreneur are the same.

Objective Type Questions

1. According to economic approach, entrepreneur is
   (a) Risk bearer (b) Profit seeker
   (c) Change agent (d) Manager
2. According to sociological approach entrepreneurship is
   (a) Process of economic change
   (b) Process of role performance
   (c) Process of assembling imagination
   (d) Process of sensitivity
3. Psychological Approach deals with
   (a) Achievement motive (b) Performance motive
   (c) Profit motive (d) Status motive
4. 'The Achieving Society' 1961 is written by
   (a) Hagen (b) McClelland
   (c) Higgins. B. (d) Carl Menger
5. Entrepreneurial traits deal with
   (a) Job providing behaviour (b) Profit seeking behaviour
   (c) Risk taking behaviour (d) Change seeking behaviour
6. Entrepreneurship is ensured by
   (a) Small firm (b) Middle level firm
   (c) Larger firm (d) Subsidiaries
7. Entrepreneurship fails to lead
   (a) New Corporate divisions (b) New subsidiary venture
   (c) Partnership firm (d) None of these
8. Barriers to entrepreneurship stifle
   (a) Risk taking Capacity (b) Innovation
   (c) Profitability (d) Uncertainty

9. Merger and Acquisition
   (a) encourage entrepreneurial behaviour
   (b) discourage entrepreneurial behaviour
   (c) fail to affect entrepreneurial behaviour
   (d) None of these
10. The book "Intrapreneurship" was written by
   (a) Holt David H. (b) Pinchot Gifford III
   (c) Meier and Balmin (d) B.C. Tondon

Answers

1-(c) 2-(b) 3-(a) 4-(b) 5-(c) 6-(c) 7-(c) 8-(b) 9-(b) 10- (b)

Reason Based Questions

State with reason whether the following statements are true or false :

1. Problems faced by small and big entrepreneurs are similar.
2. Entrepreneurship leads to economic development.
3. Entrepreneurship is a practical skill that cannot be taught in classrooms.
4. Entrepreneurs are expected to be governed by the wishes of the society and its practices.
5. Entrepreneurship is the dynamic process of creating incremental wealth.

REFERENCES

1. Higgins. B., *The Economic Development,* p. 219.
2. Kao, John and Steresson. Howard (eds.), *Entrepreneurship — What it is and How to Teach it,* Division of Research, Havard Business School, 1984.
3. Schumpeter J.A., *The Theory of Economic Development* Harvard University Press. 1934, p. 42.
4. Ronstadt. Robert. *C. Entrepreneurship, Text, Cases and notes.* Dover A.I.a Lord 1984, p 28.
5. Drucher Peter. F., *Innovation and Entrepreneurship.* Harper Business. 1993. p 150.
6. Tandon B.C., *Environment and Entrepreneur,* p. 42.
7. Pinchot Gifford. III. *Entrepreneurship,* Harper & Row, New York. 1985, p. 4.
8. Holt. David H., *Entrepreneurship, New venture creation.* Prentice Hall of India. New Delhi. 4, 1998, p. 82.
9. Tandon B. C, *Environment and Entrepreneur,* p. 58.
10. Meier and Balmin. *Economic Development,* p. 300.
11. OESD, *Fostering Entrepreneurship,* p. 57.

5

THEORIES OF ENTREPRENEURSHIP

It is a universal fact that entrepreneurship is an important factor in economic development. An Entrepreneur is the risk bearer and works under uncertainty. But no attempts were made by economists for formulating systematic theory of entrepreneurship. According to William J. Baumol, the economic theory has failed to provide a satisfactory analysis of either the role of the entrepreneurship or its supply.[1] The traditional notion of an entrepreneur is that he brings together the factor inputs and organises productive activity. The traditional models treat the entrepreneurial function like a managerial function. Similarly, in modern growth theory also, any contribution of entrepreneurship is typically contained in a residual factor. This residual, variously termed as 'technical change' or 'coefficient of ignorance'. It includes among other things, technology, education, institutional organisation and entrepreneurship[2].

Different thinkers have evolved different theories of entrepreneurship. Salient features of these theories are as follows :

1. Innovation Theory

This theory was propounded by *J.A. Schumpeter*. According to *Schumpeter*, entrepreneur is basically an innovator and innovator is one who introduces new combinations. In practice, new combination theory covers five cases[3] which are given below :

(i) The introduction of a new good which consumers, are not yet familiar—or of a new quality of a good.

(ii) The introduction of a new method of production, that one not yet tested by experience in the branch of manufacture concerned, which need by no means be founded upon a discovery scientifically new and can also exist in a new way of handling a commodity commercially.

(iii) The opening of a new market i.e. a market into which the particular branch of manufacture of the country in question has not previously entered, whether or not this market has existed before.

(iv) The conquest of a new source of supply of raw materials or half manufactured goods, irrespective of whether this source already exists or whether it has first to be created.

(v) The carrying out of the new organisation of any industry like the creation of a monopoly position (for example, through trustification) or the breaking up of a monopoly position.

Critical Evaluation : In Schumpeterian theory, the main theme is the innovation. He makes a distinction between an innovator and an inventor. According to him, an inventor discovers new methods and new materials. But, an innovator is one who applies inventions and discoveries in order to make new combinations. With the help of these new combinations, he produces newer and better goods which yield satisfaction as well as profits.

In economic development process, entrepreneurs have been assigned a crucial role so that tempo of growth is maintained effectively. Development requires basic changes and entrepreneurs carry out the required changes. Thus, entrepreneurial development brings economic development. Schumpeter's concept of entrepreneurship is quite broad based. Entrepreneurship includes not only the independent business men but also executives and managers who actually undertake innovative functions.

However, Schumpeter's theory suffers from following limitations.

(i) It excludes individuals who merely operate an established business without performing innovative functions.

(ii) Innovating entrepreneur represents the most vigorous type of enterprise. However, this type of entrepreneur is rarely available in developing countries like India.

(iii) It laid too much emphasis on innovative functions. But it ignores the risk taking and organising aspects of entrepreneurship.

(iv) It assumes an entrepreneur as a large scale business man. He is a person who creates something new. But in practice, an entrepreneur cannot have large scale operations from the very beginning.

(v) It fails to provide a suitable answer to question like—Why some countries had more entrepreneurial talent than others?

According to *Schumpeter,* entrepreneurs are not a class in themselves like capitalists and workers. An individual is an entrepreneur only when he actually carries out new combinations and ceases to be an entrepreneur the moment he settles down to running the established business. According to *Schumpeter*, an entrepreneur exists only if the factors of production are combined for the first time. Maintenance of a combination is not an entrepreneurial activity. In this way, combination theory differs from the theory of rent formulated by Ricordo. Ricardo included the term "entrepreneurial ability" as an imdependent factor of production and it is concerned with profit. Thus, this theory fails to provide suitable solutions to the problems.

2. Need for Achievement Theory

This theory was developed by *David. C. McClelland. McClelland* concerned himself with economic growth and the factors that influence it. In this context, he tries to find the internal factors i.e. "human values and motives that lead man to exploit opportunities, to take advantage of favourable trade conditions.[4] That is why he gives importance to the innovative characteristics of entrepreneurial role. The entrepreneur is concerned with need for achievement (n-achievement).

The n-achievement is called as 'a desire to do well, not so much for the sake of social recognition or prestige, but for the sake of an inner feeling of personal accomplishment."[5]

It is this motive of n-achievement that guides the actions of entrepreneur. People with high n-achievement behave in an entrepreneurial way. So it is better to develop n-achievement among individuals to ensure high scale of economic development. In practice, n-achievement motive is inculcated through child rearing practices, which stress standards of excellence, material warmth, self-reliance, training and low father dominance. *McClelland* identified two characteristics of entrepreneurship. First doing things in a new and better way. Secondly, decision making under uncertainty.

This motive is called as the tendency to strive for success in situations involving an evaluation of one's performance in relation to some standard of excellence. People having high need for achievement are more likely to succeed as entrepreneurs.

According to *McClelland*, individuals with high need achievement will not be motivated by monetary incentives but that monetary rewards will constitute a symbol of achievement for them. Similarly, they are also not interested much for social recognition or prestige but their ultimate goal is personal accomplishment. That is why *McClelland* suggests that in order to raise the level of achievement motivation, parents should set high standards for their children.

Critical Evaluation: Research studies on the psychological roots of entrepreneurship reveal that high achievement orientation ensures the success of entrepreneurs. But the empirical tools of concept used by *McClelland* are found to be highly suspect and one wonders how many of the individuals who are judged to have high n-achievement could succeed in utilising it in practice in the present day developing countries unless strengthened by other reinforcing circumstances. At the same time, empirical investigations also need the following:

(*i*) It is necessary to create a climate (especially in educational institutions at various levels) to enable the children to grow to become individuals with high n-achievement.

(*ii*) It is possible to improve the performance of existing entrepreneurs through imparting proper training and education.

3. Status Withdrawal Theory

E. Hagen attempted to formulate a theory of social change. The theory of social change explains that when members of some social groups feel that their values and status are not respected by the society. they turn to innovation to get the respect of the society. According to *Hagen*, entrepreneurship is a function of status withdrawal. This theory provides that a class which lost its previous prestige or a minority group tends to show aggressive entrepreneurial drive.

Hagen postulates four types of events which can produce status withdrawal :

(*i*) Displacement of a traditional elite group from its previous status by another traditional group by physical force.

(*ii*) Denigration of values, symbols through some change in the attitude of superior group.

(iii) Inconsistency of static symbol with a changing distribution of economic power and.

(*iv*) Non-acceptance of expected status on migration to a new society.

Hagen further opined that creative innovation or change is the basic feature of economic growth. He describes an entrepreneur as a creative problem shooter interested in things in the practical and technological realm. Such type of individual feels a sense of increased pleasure when facing a problem and tolerates disorder without discomfort. In traditional societies, positions of authority are granted on the basis of status, rather than individual ability. That is why, Hagen visualised an innovative personality. There are four responses which assess the personality.

(*i*) *Retreatist* : One who combines to work in the society but remains indifferent to his work and position.

(*ii*) *Ritualist* : One who adopts a kind of defensive behaviour and acts in the ways accepted and approved in his society but with no hopes of improving his position.

(*iii*) *Reformist* : One who foments a rebellion and attempts to establish a new society.

(*iv*) *Innovator* : A creative individual who is likely to be an entrepreneur.

Innovation requires creativity and such creative individuals cause economic growth. In practice creative personalities emerge when the members of some social groups experience the withdrawal of status respect. Whenever there is any withdrawal of status respect, it would give rise to innovation—a creative individual who is likely to be an entrepreneur.

Critical Evaluation : The theory acts to distinguish between entrepreneurship and intra-preneurship. There are different factors within the organisation which motivate the executives and professionals to do some innovative behaviour leading to new products and services. Actually, they are not governed by status withdrawal. The theory only suggests that the people, who had enjoyed social standing at some stage in their histories fall into a retreatist phase and with an urge to regain that lost status emerge as entrepreneurial personality. The theory also presupposes a long term perspective for entrepreneurial growth about three to five generations for the emergence of entrepreneurship. But actually it does not happen. In India, first generation entrepreneurs are quite successful in their entrepreneurial behaviour. J.P. Gour of Jai Prakash Industries and Sunil Mittal of Bharti group etc. can be cited in this context.

4. Theory of Social Change

It was *Max Weber* who first of all took the stand that entrepreneurial growth was dependent upon ethical value system of the society concerned. The central figure of the Weber's theory of social change consists in his treatment of the protestant ethic and the spirit of capitalism. Moreover, this theory provides an analysis of religion and its impact on entrepreneurial culture.

Max Weber opined[6] that the spirit of rapid industrial growth depends upon a rationalised technology, acquisition of money and its rational use for productivity and multiplication of money. These elements of industrial growth depend upon a specific value orientation of individuals *i.e.* the tendency of acquisition and rational attitude towards action which are generated by ethical values.

Weber analysed his theoretical formulation by the relationship that he found between protestant ethic and the spirit of capitalism. He found his thesis true about other communities also, e.g. Hindu, Jain and Juda. He held that protestants progressed fast in bringing capitalism because their ethical value system provided them with rational economic attitude, while the Jews and Jains failed to develop industrial capitalism because of their value of 'Pariha' (the restriction on having any contact with other communities)."[7]

According to this theory, driving entrepreneurial energies are generated by the adoption of exogenously supplied religious beliefs. It is these beliefs which produce intensive exertion in occupational persecutes, the systematic ordering of means to ends and the accumulation of assets. For people who believe in this belief (Protestant ethic) hardwork in their walk of life is not only to enable them to have their worldly desires met but also to have their spiritual needs satisfied. Thus, in the Weberian system, the motivating force for entrepreneurial activity is provided by Calvinist ethic irrespective of the cultural background, personality type of the individual and the social environment to which he lives.

Critical Evaluation : The theory of social change propounded by *Max Weber* is based on the invalid assumptions. So expected results are not valid in all cases. These assumptions are as follows :

(*i*) there is a single system of Hindu value.

(*ii*) the Indian community internalised those values and translated them in to day to day behaviour and

(iii) these values remained immune to and' insulated against external pressures and change. The studies further show that Hinduism is not averse to the spirit of capitalism and to adventurous spirit. The Hinduism has contributed a lot in entrepreneurship development in India which is based on capitalism.

5. Theory of Social Behaviour

Kunkel presents a behavioural model of entrepreneurship. Supply of entrepreneurs is a function of social, political and economic structure. Behavioural model concerned with the overtly expressed activities of individuals and their relations to the previous and present surroundings, social structures and physical conditions. According to *Kunkel*, Individuals perform various activities of which some are accepted by the society while others are not. The accepted are rewarded. The rewards act as reinforcing stimulus increasing the probability of repeating that behaviour pattern. This pattern of social behaviour is entrepreneurial behaviour. The supply of entrepreneurship depends upon four structures found in a society.[8] That are as follows :

(i) Limitation Structure : The society limits specific activities and this limitation structure affects all the members (including entrepreneurs) of a society.

(ii) Demand Structure : Material rewards are necessary to lay the foundation for future social gains. Moreover, behaviour of people can be made entrepreneurial by manipulating certain selected components of the demand structure.

(iii) Opportunity Structure : It consists of the availability of capital, management and technological skills, information concerning production methods, labour and markets.

(iv) Labour Structure : It is concerned with the supply of competent and willing labour. The supply of labour is governed by several factors such as available alternative means of livelihood, traditionalism and expectations of life.

Critical Evaluation : The theory assumes the ideal structures for the supply of entrepreneurs. But, generally, there is discrepancy between objectives, structures and the actual incidence of entrepreneurs. It is due to the fact that there are inadequate or incorrect perceptions attached with these perceptions. In practice, entrepreneurship is also governed by the specific combinations of circumstances which are generally not available in the environment.

6. Theory of Leadership

According to *Hoselitz*, entrepreneurship is a function of managerial skills and leadership. Business also requires finance but that is of secondary importance. He further explains that a person who is to become an industrial entrepreneur must have more than the drive to earn profits and amass wealth. In this process, he has to show his ability to lead and manage. In business, there are generally three types of leadership—merchant money lenders, managers and entrepreneurs. In practice, money lenders are market oriented and managers are authority oriented. But entrepreneurs have in addition to these a production orientation-

The merchant money lenders deal in goods/services which is generally acceptable to every one. However, an entrepreneur creates his own commodity and its acceptability is uncertain. Therefore, the entrepreneur assumes more risk as compared to a trader or a money lender. In this context, it is important to note that making profit is not enough to succeed in entrepreneurship. Hoselitz[9] opined that entrepreneurship can develop in a society where its culture permits a variety of choices and where social processes are not rigid. The social conditions should ensure the development of enterprise-oriented personalities.

Hoselitz emphasised the role of culturally marginal groups like Jews and Greeks in Medieval Europe and the Lebanese in West Africa, the Chinese in South Asia, the Indians in West Africa in promoting economic development. Making use of the work of *Stonequist* and *Park*, *Hoselitz* formulated the hypothesis that marginal men, because of their ambiguous position from a cultural or social stand point, are peculiarly suited to make creative adjustments in situations of change and in the course of this adjustment process too, they are able to develop genuine innovations in social behaviour.

Critical Evaluation : It is quite true that marginal men or groups enjoying an ambiguous culture and social position having no bondage of tradition to inhibit them from entrepreneurship development. But there are certain economic and political factors also which encourage the people to initiate entrepreneurial behaviour. For example, Government of India and State Governments are trying to encourage first generation entrepreneurs by offering them various types of incentives and subsidies. Potential entrepreneurs are also opting for enterprise development without cring for social or cultural restrictions.

7. Theory of Model Personality

The theory of *Cocharn* is a sociological theory of entrepreneurial supply.[10] *Cocharn* emphasises cultural values, role expectations and social sanctions as the key elements that determine the supply of entrepreneurs. According to him, an entrepreneur is neither a super normal individual nor a deviant person but represents a society's model personality. His performance is influenced by three factors

- (*i*) his own attitudes towards his occupation.
- (*ii*) the role expectations held by sanctioning groups and
- (*iii*) the operational requirements of the job. In this context, society's values are the most important determinant of the attitudes and role expectations.

Critical Evaluation : The theory deals with only social factors. Profit is the most important factor for encouraging entrepreneur to assume risky behaviour. Even need for achievement starts from profit making process. It is implied in need for achievement process. Besides, entrepreneur is also expected to assume managerial functions. But theory fails to incorporate all these requirements.

8. Theory of Systematic Innovation

Prof. Drucker has developed the theory of systematic innovation. According to him "Systematic innovation consists in the purposeful and organised search for changes and in the systematic analysis of the opportunities such changes might offer for economic or social innovation." Specifically, systematic innovation means seven sources for innovative opportunity.[11]

The first four sources lie within the enterprise, whether business or public service institution, or within an industry or service sector. They are therefore visible primarily to people within that industry or service sector. They are basically symptoms. But they are highly reliable indicators of changes that have already happened or can be made to happen with little effort. These four source areas are :

(*i*) The unexpected—the unexpected success, the unexpected failure, the unexpected outside event ;

(*ii*) The incongruity—between reality as it actually is and reality as it is assumed to be or as it ought to be";

(*iii*) Innovation based on process need ;

(iv) Changes in industry structure or market structure that catch every one unawares.

The second set of sources for innovative opportunity, a set of three involves changes outside the enterprise of industry :

(*i*) Demographics (Population changes) ;

(*ii*) Changes in perception, mood and meaning ;

(*iii*) New knowledge, both scientific and non-scientific.

Prof. Drucker, further remarked that the lines between these seven sources areas of innovative opportunities are blurred, and there is considerable overlap between them. They can be likened to seven windows each on a different side of the same building. Each window shows some features that can also be seen from the window on either side of it. But the view from the center of each is distinct and different.

Critical Evaluation : The theory of sysmatic innovation is quite comprehensive one. The entrepreneur is required to identify different sources of change. Thereafter, he is expected to coordinate these changes with the opportunities available in the environment. But the most important problem attached with this theory is the question of reliability and predictability of seven sources. For example, new scientific knowledge is not the most reliable or most predictable source of successful innovations. However theory tries to provide a comprehensive framework to the entrepreneurship.

Thus, on the basis of above theories, we can say that entrepreneurship is a multidisciplinary area. Actually, entrepreneurship is governed by human factor living in an ever-changing society pursuing simultaneously economic, social and psychological objectives. So unless a theory of entrepreneurship is woven into sociological, cultural. psychological, political and managerial fibre, it cannot give a sense of economic web.

EXAMINATION QUESTIONS

Long Answer Questions

1. Discuss briefly various theories of entrepreneurship. Which one is more suitable for India.
2. Critically examine the innovation theory of entrepreneurship.
3. Discuss in detail various theories of entrepreneurship.
4. Critically examine the Need for Achievement theory of entrepreneurship.
5. Explain the Peter Drucker's theory of entrepreneurship.
6. What do you mean by Need for Achievement ? How does it affect entrepreneurship development ?
7. Critically examine the economic theory of entrepreneurship.
8. Discuss the views of Schumpeter of Drucker in regard to Entrepreneur and Entreneurial Development.
9. Critically examine the Innovation Theory of Entrepreneurship as propounded by J.A. Schumpeter.
10. Explain the views expressed by Prof. Peter Drucker in his theory of Systematic Innovation in regard to entrepreneurial development in a country. How are his views different from the views of Joseph A. Schumpeter in this regard ?
11. Critically examine Walker's view on entrepreneurship and explain in what respect it differs from Drucker's view.
12. Discuss the views of economists, sociologists and psychologists on entrepreneurship.
13. What do you mean by Entrepreneurship ? Bring out the reducing feature of important theories of entrepreneurship.
14. Critically examine the theories of entrepreneurship and their relevance in modern context.
15. Explain the concept of entrepreneurship. Describe briefly the different theories of entrepreneurship. What are the sources of Entrepreneurship ?

Short Answer Questions

1. Explain the features of Innovation theory.
2. Examine the limitations of Schumpeter's theory of innovation.
3. Do you think that Need for Achievement realliy encourages entrepreneurs ?
4. What is status withdrawal ?
5. In what ways, social change is related with entrepreneurship ?
6. Discuss the different structures for the supply of entrepreneurship.
7. How does entrepreneurship is a function of managerial skill and leadership?
8. Critically examine the theory of status withdrawal.
9. What do you mean by social change ? How does it help in developing entrepreneurial traits ?
10. Discuss the salient features of the social behaviour.

11. Critically evaluate the theory of leadership.
12. What do you mean by systematic innovation. Also examine the theory of systematic innovation.
13. Achievement motivation can be instilled in the minds of entrepreneurs.
14. Sociologists' viewpoint is conflicting with the viewpoint on entrepreneurship.
15. Entrepreneurship is all about innovation.

Objective Type Questions

1. "Entrepreneur is basically an innovator" is given in book
   (a) Entrepreneurship in Economic Theory
   (b) Entrepreneurship and Economic Development
   (c) The Theory of Economic Development
   (d) The Achieving Society
2. The Achieving Society is concerned with
   (a) Innovation (b) Probability
   (c) Creativity (d) High Standards
3. Need for Achievement Theory is concerned with
   (a) E. Hagen (b) Schumpeter
   (c) McClelland (d) Peter Kilby
4. Status Withdrawal Theory is given by
   (a) McClelland (b) E. Hagen
   (c) Peter Kilby (d) William Baumol
5. Which one is more useful in entrepreneurship
   (a) Retreatist individual (b) Reformist individual
   (c) Creative individual (d) Ritualist individual
6. Theory of social Change provides analysis of
   (a) Economic value system (b) Ethical value system
   (c) Religious value system (d) Political value system
7. Theory of Social Change was propounded by
   (a) Hoselitz B.P. (b) John Kunkel
   (c) Max Weber (d) K. L. Sharma
8. According to Hoselitz, entrepreneurship is a function of
   (a) Innovation and creativity
   (b) Dream and action
   (c) Managerial skill and leadership
   (d) Capital and Labour
9. Theory of Model Personality is not related with
   (a) Attitudes towards occupation
   (b) Perception towards professionalism
   (c) Role expectation by sanctioning groups
   (d) Operational requirement of the job

10. Systematic innovation considers number of sources for innovative opportunity
    (a) 4 (b) 6 (c) 3 (d) 7

Answers

1-(c) 2-(d) 3-(c) 4-(b) 5-(c) 6-(b) 7-(c) 8-(c) 9-(b) 10-(d)

Reason Based Questions

State with reason whether the following statements are true or false :

1. The viewpoints of psychologists and economists on the making of an entrepreneur are contradictory.
2. "Innovation and Entrepreneurship" is a book written by J.A. Schumpeter.
3. Entrepreneurship is a function of status withdrawal.
4. Innovation requires creativity.
5. First generation entrepreneurs are quite successful in their entrepreneurial behaviour.

REFERENCES

1. Baumol, William, J. "Entrepreneurship in Economic Theory". *American Economic Review, Papers and Proceedings.* Vol. LVII. No. 2 (May, 1968), p. 65.
2. Kilby, Peter, "Hunting the Heffalump" in Peter Kilby (ed) *Entrepreneurship and Economic Development.* The Free Press, New York. 1971. p. 2
3. Schumpeter, Joseph, A. *The Theory of Economic Development* translated by Redver Sopie. Oxford University Press, New York, 1961. p. 66.
4. McClelland, David. *The Achieving Society.* D. Van Nostrand and Co. New York. 1961, p. 210.
5. *Ibid,* p. 110.
6. Max Weber, *The Theory of Economic and Social Organisation.*
7. Sharma, K. L., *Entrepreneurial, Performance in Role Perspective.* Abhinav Publications, New Delhi, 1975, pp. 11-12.
8. Kunkel. John. H., *Society and Economic Growth : A Behavioural Perspective of Social Change,* Oxford University Press, London, 1970. pp. 260-74.
9. Hoselitz. B.F., *Sociological Aspects of Economic Growth,* Vakil Feffer and Simmons, Bombay, 1960, pp. 64-65.
10. Cocharn. Thomas. C, *The Entrepreneur in Economic Change : Explorations in Entrepreneurial History,* Summar, 1965, pp. 26-27.
11. Drucker Peter, F., *Innovations and Entrepreneurship,* Harper Business, New York, 1993, pp. 35-36.

6

ENTREPRENEURIAL ENVIRONMENT

In general, entrepreneurs are required to consider how the environment affect their entrepreneurial decisions so that they will be able to react to potential business opportunities, potential threats and plan for the future. "The term environment refers to institutions or forces that are outside the enterprise and potentially affect' the enterprise's performance." The environment is composed of internal environment and external environment. Internal environment 'consists of forces inside the enterprise that can influence the enterprise and its performance. External environment contains all the forces outside the enterprise.

General environment is that part of the external environment which is composed of forces that have a general influence on the enterprise behaviour. Entrepreneurial environment is directly concerned with general environment and it is the general environment which affects the level of entrepreneurship. These include political, legal, economic, technological, sociological, cultural and international forces.

These factors affect the level of entrepreneurship and entrepreneurs are supposed to undertake environmental analysis for interpreting their potential and real impacts on performance of the firm.

1. Political Environment

Political environment is concerned with general stability of the country in which an enterprise is expected to perform and the political philosophy of party in power towards business. Political forces define the business climate by the constraints they impose and by the activities they permit. They also affect the way business enterprises protect their inventions and patents etc. If political parties believe in well being of the country and society then there will be no problem in maintaining political stability. Political stability ensures effective planning and implementation of economic programmes. Political philosophy of party in power, general political conditions, leadership qualities are the important factors which create political environment. Main factors related with political environment are as follows :

***(i)* Political Philosophy** : Political parties have their own political philosophies. Capitalism, communism, socialism, mixed economy are the economic systems by which political parties are required to explain their stand or opinion. They are also expected to implement their economic agenda in the development of the country. Economic agenda decides the techniques and priorities of economic development. In this way different political philosophy determine the role and forms of entrepreneurial activities.

***(ii)* Political Atmosphere** : Favourable political conditions are necessary for the economic development of the country. Political instability cretes uncertainty while entrepreneurial activities need a clear, certain and comparatively stable government policy. Political instability, public movement etc. are the result of power conflict of political parties of the country. In this situation, entrepreneurs are unable to take a sound business decisions as they need a clear-cut Government policy. Political instability increases the level of risk. So entrepreneurs are required to keep a watch on the possibilities of stability in political activities before involving themselves in entrepreneurial activities.

***(iii)* Quality of Leadership** : In modern scenario, political parties rule the country and thus, leadership of party in power decides the destiny of the country. Matured, decisive, competent and efficient leadership enables the country to have an effective economic growth strategies. Accelerated economic development ensures the well being of the country. So it is for the political leadership to provide sufficient incentive and protection to entrepreneurial activities at the Government level.

2. Legal Environment

In practice, Government regulates all important components of the economy. Government generally try to control the entry, working, selection of resources and their uses in business situations. On these lines, government prepares legal environment of the business. However, it is duty of the government to develop regulatory framework in such a way which creates conducive environment necessary for business activities. Conducive environment encourages entrepreneurial activities in satisfactory way. Factors related with legal environment are as follows :

***(i)* Determining Areas** : Government determines all those areas and conditions under which entrepreneurs undertake their entrepreneurial activities. Under this arrangement, entrepreneurs may be required to take permission or licence from the Government before moving into entrepreneurial activities. Similarly, they are also supposed to take prior permission in availing public facilities and resources. Simple permission/approval arrangement encourages entrepreneurs to opt for more entrepreneurial activities.

***(ii)* Regulation of Entrepreneurial Functions** : Whenever entrepreneurs start their work or their business units or got admitted in the business then Government helps them in accelerating the pace of operations and also regulates the operations as per requirements. In this system, we include all those controls which prohibit the general functions, efforts and performance. So, the Government from time to time directs and regulates the managerial functions of the entrepreneurs.

***(iii)* Regulating Results of Entrepreneurial Activities** : Public regulations are also applicable on all entrepreneurial activities. Regulations with regard to volume of profit, disposal of profit, exhaustion of excess payments etc. are also helpful in creating legal environment. If these regulations are flexible and simple, entrepreneurs may find themselves in more active situation in their entrepreneurial behaviour.

(*iv*) Regulating Relationship Among Various Segments of Economy: Government formulates rules, regulations and enactment of separate Acts for regulating the mutual relationship among the different components of the economy. It helps in avoiding conflicts in entrepreneurial interests or concentrating economic powers in few hands. For example, certain restrictions on appointment of directors on the Board of Directors, abolition of different types of holding companies, regulation of labour laws or takeover codes or corporate governance etc.

3. Economic Environment

Economic environment is of multidimensional nature. It includes all those actions which make the economic activities possible in the country. Economic resources, economic conditions, economic policies, trade policy, labour arrangement, incentives and subsidies are some of the important factors which constitute economic environment. These are discussed below :

(*i*) Availability of Economic Resources : Availability of adequate quantity of natural and physical resources encourages entrepreneurs to undertake more entrepreneurial activities. Effective utilisation of these resources is possible only through entrepreneurship. It will help the entrepreneurs to earn more profit and retain the profit for further expansion programme.

(*ii*) Economic Conditions : Economic conditions govern the enterprise ability to remain viable. Inflation, interest rates, unemployment, per capita income, consumer purchasing power, excahnage rates are some of the important factors which provide sufficient symptoms about the conditions prevailing in the economy as a whole. For example, when inflation rates are high entrepreneurs pay more for supplies and may raise their prices to cover these costs. In case of high inflation rate Government may be forced to initiate regulation of price and wage structure through guidelines etc.

(*iii*) Economic Policies : Economic policies determine the direction and volume of the business. For example in socialist economies decisions with regard to what to produce, how to produce, for whom to produce and how much to produce are to be taken by the Government or central planning system like Indian Planning Commission. Government is responsible for formulating these economic policies to regulate the level of production and consumption. In free economic system, it is for the market forces to decide all these things and Government regulatory role is restricted to a nominal level.

(*iv*) Labour Policies : Labour is an important and active factor for production or service process. Volume of production and costs are governed by the productivity of labour to a large extent. So in practice, the Government should formulate such policy which will ensure timely payment of sufficient wages, strengthen the social security system and improve labour productivity. If entrepreneurs think that labour policy is favourable then they will be motivated to undertake entrepreneurial activity. Current labour environment also enables the entrepreneurs to take necessary decisions. If lockouts and strikes are the game of the day, then it would be very difficult for entrepreneurs to assume risks. Similarly, disciplined labour environment makes the entrepreneurs more active in taking entrepreneurial decisions.

(*v*) Trade Policy : The major objectives of trade policy are to ensure sufficient supply of goods and services in the country and controlling the adverse balance of payments. Entrepreneurs will be motivated to instal new plant or initiate action for expansion if trade policy formulated by the Government is going to increase the supply as per the demand available in the market. Export promotion and import substitution measures also encourage entrepreneurs to opt for more expansion. Establishment of export oriented units (EOU) is a major step in this direction.

(vi) Tariff Policy : Effective tariff policy provides a base for entrepreneurs to undertake more entrepreneurial activities. High tariff rates affect demand level as well as margin available to the entrepreneurs. Determination of tariff structure is to be made to avoid unnecessary reduction in consumer's purchasing power. Neither potential entrepreneurs would like to establish new entrepreneurs nor existing entrepreneurs will believe in expansion process. So, tariff policy should be development oriented enabling the entrepreneurs to undertake more entrepreneurial activities.

(*vii*) Incentives : Incentives are necessary to encourage entrepreneurial activities in the country. It will ensure a high margin at low risk. Interest free loan, exemption from wealth tax, rebate to NRI's. rebate to women entrepreneurs, tax holiday, conversion of sales tax into interest free loan, allotment of land and production sheds at concessional rates, rebate on stamp duty, provision for seed capital, supply of raw materials at concessional rates are some of the important incentives which help in creating conducive environment for entrepreneurship.

(*viii*) Subsidies : Under this scheme, Government creates favourable environment by participating in terms of economic assistance in economic activities already undertaken by the entrepreneurs. There are some activities to which entrepreneurs do not want to undertake or they are not profitable in the short run. Under these conditions, entrepreneurs should be given financial support and assistance to undertake that entrepreneurial activity. Export Import Assistance and subsidy for Research and Development, transport subsidy, subsidy for full efficient plant, subsidy for good testing tools, subsidy for industrial colonies, subsidy for technical consultancy, subsidy for markert survey etc. constitute the subsidy programme of the Government and they encourage entrepreneur to undertake more entrepreneurial activities.

4. Technological Environment

Technological forces constitute the technological environment. These forces include the expertise, procedures, and systems used by enterprises to make profound changes in the transformation process and in goods and services. "Fuelled by scientific research and industrial breakthrough technological forces define new industries and provide enterprises with tools and opportunities to compete more effectively." These factors are as follows :

***(i)* Better Utilisation of Productive Resources** : Latest technology encourages better utilisation of materials and labour. Scientific and technological skills of labour can be improved with the help of technology. Innovation develops technological bases which in turn create more demand for products in the market. Ultimately entrepreneurial possibilities are increased to meet out growing demand for the product.

***(ii)* Increase in Competition Capacity** : Scientific and technological development encourages innovation which ultimately improves product marketability. Cost reduction programme is also possible with science and technology. Use of outdated technology reduces the market potentiality of the product as well as scope for entrepreneurship.

***(iii)* Risk Efficiency** : Technological environment helps in creation of new production techniques. Initially risk is the prime factor of production process but at later stage market absorbs the product risk and stable market is available to the entrepreneurs. Technological development increases the capacity of entrepreneurs to assume more risk in the long run.

***(iv)* Improvement in Productivity** : Wastages of productive resources increase the cost of production. But science and technology help in controlling the wastages of resources and ensure their proper utilisation. New inventions evident the scope of resource utilisation and every resource has its demand in the market.

***(v)* Improvement in Profitability** : Better technological environment ensures better utilisation of resources by controlling the wastages and improving the margins of entrepreneurs. Cost control programme can be implemented successfully with the help of new technology. Thus, technological environment widens the positive gap between price and cost which ultimately increases the profit base. Side by side, it also improves the profitability of the enterprise.

5. Social Environment

Social environment prepares background for entrepreneurial activities. Today business is regarded as a social institution. It forms an integral part of the social organisation having responsibilities to a wider circle of individuals like entrepreneurs, workers and consumers etc. who participate in the business activities. Social structure, social values and conventions, consumerism, labour attitude etc. constitute the social environment. Since an entrepreneur is a part of the society, he is governed by the social values and conventions. An effective but favourable social environment is necessary for entrepreneurship. Factors guiding the social environment are as follows :

***(i)* Social Structure** : Functional division of community in the social structure determines the level of entrepreneurial activities. In India VARNA arrangement is guided by functional distribution of duties like Brahmins, Kshatriyas, Vaisyas and Sudra. In practice, Varna distribution affects the forms of entrepreneurial behaviour. Vaisyas think that their duties lie only in business activities. Marwaries and Gujaratis Vaisyas are proved to be more risk-taking communities. But in recent years there is a dramatic change in the social behaviour. Improvement in level of education, government incentives and subsidies etc. have motivated other varnas of the society to undertake entrepreneurial activities.

***(ii)* Social Values and Conventions** : The values are the belief that shape individual and groups attitudes. Values and attitudes mould peoples behaviour and influence the needs and wants that they seek to fulfil through interaction with business enterprises. Generally, individuals try their level best to protect their social values and conventions. Production of public goods, avoidance of unethical bahaviour, fulfilment of social obligations are being treated as part of the social behaviour and entrepreneurs cannot avoid them in their entrepreneurial behaviour.

***(iii)* Consumer's Opinion** : Consumer's opinion with regard to consumption of goods and services also affects the form of entrepreneurial activities. Economic condition of the consumer, taste, habit, fashion etc. regulate the volume and form of production . A product having more demand due to change in fashion, taste, habit etc. motivates the entrepreneur to undertake production of that product in most of the cases.

***(iv)* Labour Motives** : Labour mentality towards production process also plays an important role in shaping the form of social environment. Generally, there is conflict of interest between the two—employer and employee. There will be more conflict if labour think that employer is their competitor and exploiter, then volume of entrepreneurial activity will be slashed.

6. Cultural Environment

General perception about entrepreneurship development is that it is based on cultural and ethical values. People generally believe that success or failure of an individual or an enterprise is totally governed by the mercy and pleasure of some special God. It is also believed that status is inherited, it is not earned. It is considered that casteism and certain occupations are meant for members of a particular caste, religion or sex. All this results in considerable immobility and inflexibility and thus, labour wasted as the customs are still very powerful in such conditions. In this context, cultural structure and cultural aspirations are important parts of the entrepreneurial environment.

(i) Cultural Structure : Supply of entrepreneurs is determined by the cultural structure. Demographic characteristics also describe the population and its behaviour in regions where an enterprise is located. Family background, level of education, economic conditions of the family etc. also affect the supply of entrepreneurs.

***(ii)* Cultural Aspirations** : Regulation of entrepreneurial trend is also possible through cultural aspirations. If social constraints are being removed it means there is no entry barrier for other castes to enter the business field and supply of entrepreneurs is possible from any source. Change in value system ensures change in the cultural expectations. Now it is possible due to change in the cultural heritage of the country that any person from any caste can enter the field of entrepreneurship.

7. International Environment

International business environment deals with the forces which originate outside the home country in which an enterprise is working or expected to work. These forces like multinational corporations, exchange rates, level of competition from foreign market, position of international capital market etc. influence interactions with people and enterprises. In recent years. globalisation has been identified as an important development affecting the working of business enterprises. As part of the external environment, entrepreneurs are being challenged by an increasing number of global competitors in the consumer's market. These factors include MNC's, globalisation process, GATT/WTO, development of international capital market, etc. constitute an international environment. These are discussed below :

(*i*) Development of Multinational Corporations : International business scenario has created favourable conditions for the development of MNCs in home country. These MNCs have a direct investment abroad and direct interest in the business environment in which they have such investment. Flexibility in direct foreign investment on the part of Government discourages domestic entrepreneurs to establish new enterprises in the home country. MNCs generally have good product image, updated technology, quality control and effective marketing strategies and it is difficult task before the entrepreneurs to compete with them.

(*ii*) Globalisation : In the era of globalisation, Government itself is interested to force the home enterprises to improve their competitive strength in fighting for consumer market in international environment. The globalisation throws both opportunities and challenges to the Indian entrepreneurs. With the opening up of the economy, entrepreneurs are facing tough competition from MNCs. Now they have been forced to reorient their strategies to reduce costs, improve the quality of their products and thereby making survival possible in the competitive market.

(*iii*) GATT/WTO : They have set in motion for expanded multilateral trading system. They place special emphasis on the removal of non-tariff trade barriers and low level of tariffs. The reduction in tariffs and removal of trade restrictions have exposed the Indian entrepreneurs to unexpected challenges. India has ratified the agreement for the establishment of the WTO as a logical step of its endorsement of the Uruguay round of negotiations relating to GATT. Under these situations. Indian entrepreneurs are being forced to change their strategies as there is no option for them except to improve their competitive strength.

(*iv*) International Capital Market : In recent years, globalisation process enables the joint stock companies to approach the international capital market for their funding programme. It is quite true that Indian entrepreneurs are being compelled to adopt international accounting and reporting norms but they are quite successful in launching their GDRs and ADRs in global market. Even now they are trying for listing their instruments in leading international stock exchanges like NASDAQ.

Thus, entrepreneurial environment affects the growth of entrepreneurship in the country. Government should try to create favourable environment for the development of an effective entrepreneurship.

EXAMINATION QUESTIONS

Long Answer Questions

1. Describe the various environmental factors affecting entrepreneurial development. Are these factors available in India? Discuss.
2. "Technological environment makes entrepreneurship efficient and profitable." Discuss this statement.
3. "There is positive correlation between level of entrepreneurship and level of economic development." Comment.
4. How can we develop an entrepreneur? Describe the factors affecting the development of entrepreneurs.
5. What you mean by environmental factors ? Examine their impact on the level of entrepreneurship development.
6. "Cultural revolution has changed the whole structure of entrepreneurial bahaviour in the globalised era". Comment.
7. Explain the factors affecting entrepreneurial development in India, pinpointing the role of government.
8. Discuss various environmental factors which help development of the entrepreneurs in a country, like India. What measures have been taken by the Government of India in this regard?
9. Examine the role of political and legal environment in directing the entrepreneurial activities.
10. Explain the various environmental factors that affect the entrepreneurial development in the context of a developing country like India.
11. "The success of the entrepreneurship depends to a great extent upon its political, social, cultural, legal and economic environment." Discuss above statement in the Indian context.
12. "Socio-Economic and political environment is a major factor influencing entrepreneurial growth in a country." How far is this statement correct in the Indian context ? Give examples to illustrate you answer.
13. What do you mean by entrepreneurial environment? Examine the various components of entrepreneurial environment.
14. Discuss important factors which influence the growth of entrepreneurship. Answer the question with reference to Indian context.
15. Discuss the various factors which affect entrepreneurial development. To what extent, institutional support system helps it?

16. "Entrepreneur is required to adjust his entrepreneurial behavaiour in the changing environment." Comment.
17. "VARNA based entrepreneurial arrangement has been replaced by management oriented entrepreneurial behaviour." Do you agree ? Explain.
18. "Political stability and matured leadership encourage more entrepreneurial activity than other considerations." Comment.
19. Discuss various environmental factors which help development of entrepreneurs in a country like India. What measures have bee taken by the Government of India in this regard ?
20. How do environmental factors effect entrepreneurial development? Do you think government initiations through Entrepreneurial Development Plans (EDPs) are properly designed and implemented to give expected results?

Short Answer Questions

1. What are the various environmental factors ?
2. Explain the various components of political environment.
3. Examine the factors affecting legal environment of business.
4. Describe the constituents of economic environment.
5. What are the technological forces that generally constitute technological environment ?
6. How does social environment affect entrepreneurship ?
7. How far cultural environment is responsible for entrepreneurship development?
8. Do you think that international environment is more responsible for entrepreneurship development of a country ?

Objective Type Questions

1. External environment of business
   (a) Employees behaviour (b) Enterprise behaviour
   (c) Management behaviour (d) Promoter's behaviour
2. Economic policies determine the
   (a) Direction of business
   (b) Volume of business
   (c) Direction and volume of business
   (d) Promoter's behaviour
3. Regulatory framework of business is concerned with
   (a) Enactment of acts (b) Regulations
   (c) Formulations of rules (d) All of the above
4. Inflation is positively related with
   (a) Viability of the firrm (b) Productivity of the firm
   (c) Volume of business (d) None of these

5. Objective of trade policy is not concerned with the following
   (a) Supply of goods and services
   (b) Controlling the adverse balance of payment
   (c) Import substitution measures
   (d) Cost of effectiveness
6. Incentives are not concerned with the following
   (a) Rebates (b) Exemption from tax
   (c) Provision of seed capital (d) Lamp-sum payment
7. Subsidies are
   (a) Concessions (b) Discount
   (c) Repayment (d) None of the above
8. Social structure is composed of
   (a) Functional Division of Society
   (b) Functional Division of Castes
   (c) Functional Division of Community
   (d) None of the above
9. NASDAQ is concerned with
   (a) Indian Capital Market
   (b) Asian Capital Market
   (c) International Capital Market
   (d) None of these
10. Social behaviour is not related to
    (a) Production of public goods
    (b) Avoidance of unethical behaviour
    (c) Fulfilment of social obligations
    (d) Profit earning process

Answers

1-(b) 2-(c) 3-(d) 4-(c) 5-(d) 6-(d) 7-(c) 8-(c) 9-(c) 10-(d)

Reason Based Questions

State with reason whether the following statements are true or false :

1. Religious factors in India support the spirit of entrepreneurship in India.
2. Cultural background influences entrepreneurs.
3. Individual factors are more important than environmental factors while making a person a successful entrepreneur.
4. Functional division of community determines the level of entrepreneurial activities.
5. Incentives are necessary to encourage entrepreneurial activities.

7

ENTREPRENEURSHIP AND ECONOMIC GROWTH

The progress of Indian economic development from 1947 to the present scenario provides further evidence that individuals do respond to incentives in their pursuit of self-survival and accumulation of wealth. Further, the nature of this response depends on the economic climate, particularly the role of the government. India's economy struggled as long as it was based in a system of government regulation with little interaction with economic forces outside the country. The economic reforms have set the stage for substantial improvements in the Indian economy. However, we still need more initiatives, to further advance its economic development. It is quite true that the more recent microeconomic approaches to economic growth is the promotion of entrepreneurial activities. Entrepreneurial efforts have been found to generate a wide range of economic benefits, including new businesses, new jobs, innovative products and services, and increased wealth for future community investment.

Generally, social-cultural-political context within a country foster certain "General National Framework Conditions," which can generate not only the opportunities for entrepreneurship but also the capacity for entrepreneurship — in particular, the skills and motivation necessary to succeed. Together, the entrepreneurship opportunities, on the one hand, and the skills and motivation, on the other, lead to business dynamics that yield creative destruction, a process in which new firms are created and older, less efficient firms are destroyed. The overall result for a country is economic growth.

Now, our country is ready for the implementation of microeconomic policies that will foster entrepreneurial activities. India has taken various measures to lay the foundation for the type of economic growth that can be fostered only by entrepreneurial activities and appropriate economic policies that reflect individual rights and responsibilities. In this context, it is important to mention that, in recent years India has made several important structural changes, including the construction of telecommunications networks and the implementation of a nationwide road construction programme. The entrepreneurial skills include managing risk, building an effective team and raising funds. The functional skills include entrepreneurial abilities in such areas as marketing, finance and product development etc.

Entrepreneurship and Environmental Support System

Efforts are to be made to create a conducive environment for the promotion of entrepreneurship in the country. In this regard, following initiatives should be taken to promote entrepreneurship.

1. Indian government should provide a solid foundation for entrepreneurial efforts. The advocates of an entrepreneurial economy must promote and communicate policies that will provide a clear link between entrepreneurial efforts and overall economic prosperity.
2. Voters and taxpayers must understand the reasons why their government is investing in anything as new as entrepreneurship.
3. Gradual approach is to be taken to convert the political economy into a solid and viable economy. Speedy economic reforms are need of the hour to remove ineffectiveness of various factors of production.
4. The government must mobilise public opinion in favour of new economic policies. Relative success of the economic reforms depends on its effective implementation.
5. Social legitimacy of entrepreneurship can be a critical factor in its success. Respect for individuals starting new firms is an important cultural factor for ensuring high levels of entrepreneurial activities. In short, uncertainty within the culture can lead to resistance.

Thus, it can be easily concluded that India can generate additional economic growth by fostering entrepreneurial activities within its borders, particularly within its burgeoning middle class. Not only has entrepreneurship been found to yield significant economic benefits in a wide variety of nations, but India specifically has reached a point in its development where it can achieve similar results through entrepreneurial efforts. India is poised to generate new business startups in the high technology area that can help it become a major competitor in the world economy. It has a strong educational base suited to entrepreneurial activities, increased inflows of foreign capital aimed at its growing information technology, services sector, and a host of successful new business startups.

Entrepreneurial Approach to Economic Growth: Following suggestions are to be implemented so that entrepreneurial approach can effectively contribute towards economic growth; India must now provide opportunities for

(1) Education directed specifically at developing entrepreneurial skills,

(2) Financing of entrepreneurial efforts,

(3) Networking among potential entrepreneurs and their experienced counterparts.

The government can play a substantial role in helping to provide these types of opportunities. It can also provide appropriate tax and regulatory policies and help the citizens of India to understand the link between entrepreneurial efforts and economic prosperity. However, its overall role must be minimised in business activities to fully realise the benefits of free market and individual self-interest in business innovations.

Entrepreneurial Behaviour and Indian Economic Planning System

India's commitment to planned economic development is a reflection of our society's determination to improve the economic conditions of our people and an affirmation of the role of the government in bringing about the growth performance through a variety of social economic and institutional means. The ultimate objective of Indian planning is to achieve broad based improvement in the living standard of society at large. Rapid growth is essential for expanding incomes and employment. It provides the required resources to finance programmes of social uplift.

Nature of Economic Planning: Economic planning deals with the process of taking decisions with regard to use of available resources for the fulfilment of certain objectives or goals. Actually, planning process decides the nature, mechanism and beneficiaries of production behaviour of the economy.

It is generally defined as a continuous process which involves decisions or choices about alternative ways of using available resources with the aim of achieving particular goals at some time in future. Thus, economic planning develops a mechanism for identification and use of resources for the betterment of society at large.

Features of Economic Planning: Major features of economic planning are as follows:

(i) It is concerned with survey and diagnosis of the present economic scenario.

(ii) It defines policy and objectives to be achieved in future.

(iii) It presents a macro economic projection for the whole economy.

(iv) It formulates strategies through which objectives are to be achieved.

(v) It guides and directs the economy along the path of growth and development.

(vi) It enhances productive capacity in the country.

Types of Planning

1. Comprehensive Planning : It is generally called as imperative planning. It is totalitarian in nature and works on the basis of directions. It comprehends all the inputs and outputs and incorporates innumerable details in respect of resources, factors and commodities and services. Plans formulated under this planning process encompass different units owning resources *viz.* private companies, cooperatives, individuals and public sector. Thus, the blue print for the production of various goods and services, bore upon all the resources owned by the innumerable units of various types available in the economy.

The comprehensive planning is governed by the centralised directions. The directions are based on the use of implementing instruments which give commands to the economy to work in a particular frame work. Implementing instruments consist of positive commands and negative controls. The commands are concerned with orders, fiats and directions with regard to what to do in the economy. However, negative controls are issued in terms of guidelines generally concerned with what not to do.

Naturally, there is a need of centralised agency which formulates these implementing instruments — commands and controls. Since ultimate power of the country rests with the government, so it has the power to authorise Central Agency meant for the purpose. In India, it is the Planning Commission who is responsible for doing all these things. Thus, the government has an active role in comprehensive planning. Market mechanism does not affect the planning process. It is the comprehensive planning which enables the planners to give a concrete shape for vision of the government.

2. Decentralised Planning : It is also called as indicative planning. It is democratic in nature. Under this type of planning, decision making process is dispersed and the implementation of plans is carried through market mechanism. Actually, it involves the dispersal of planning both in respect of formulation of the plans and their implementation. It is argued that the devolution of planning functions is necessary at different levels. Public must have a say in the planning process. It is important to say that public through elections participates in the government and through its representatives shapes the plan process. So in the present scenario in India too, there is need for decentralised planning as Panchayati Raj Institutions are now mandatory and they must have the right to participate in the planning process, as state governments and central government have involved themselves in formulation of their plans.

Decentralised planning also envisages the involvement of the social action groups organised on a voluntary basis. Since these groups are in constant touch with the people, particularly with marginalised and deprived sections of society, they can contribute more in suggestive system of the planning process.

It also assumes that there must be dilution of the planning authority by bringing in non-government agencies like market prices, incentives together with public investment confined only to essential projects rather than the entire economy. Under this planning, planning agencies are involved in forecasting process rather than targeting. They also identify the major factors and sectors that are quite important for the economic growth. They are also required to quantify the contributions of these factors to keep them more effective and viable.

Decentralised planning is also based on an assumption that the market prices decide the nature of choices. It also formulates a framework of prices and other incentives to guide both public and private activity. However, it also earmarks the areas for the development of infrastructural facilities *viz.* roads, education and health. It accommodates government intervention to safeguard the environment from pollution, to eradicate poverty and deprivation, to correct inequalities of income and wealth etc.

Objectives of Indian Planning

At the time of independence, Indian economy was a backward economy. In order to move the economy on the path of development, India adopted a model of planned economic development under the mixed economy structure. The main objectives of planning in India include the following:

(i) **Increase in National Income:** This objective gets translated into an increase in not only the national income, but also in the level of production and real per capita income.

(ii) **Achieving Full Employment:** Unemployment is a curse in any society. It is more so when there is an inadequate social security or its total absence. Employment imparts dignity to human beings and is also an important means of reducing poverty and inequalities. The objective of planning was not to reduce inequalities by lowering the income levels of the richer sections but by raising the income levels of the poorer sections of the society.

(iii) **Reduction in Inequalities of Income and Wealth:** India being an extremely poor country, inequalities of income and wealth translate themselves into absolute poverty and destitution. There can be no difference of opinion regarding the desirability of reducing such inequalities, particularly because they also lead to inequality of economic opportunities.

(iv) **Creation of a Socialist Society:** This was an obvious and generally accepted objective inclusive-of there being equal opportunities of economic advancement for all sections of the society.

(v) **Removal of Bottlenecks:** Removal of Bottlenecks in the way of economic growth such as, low rates of saving and investment, inefficient technology, problems of balance of payments, absence of basic industries and insufficient infrastructure, etc.

(vi) **Industrialisation:** Our plans adopted a strategy of industrialisation of the economy with particular emphasis on heavy and basic industries. Though this strategy also assigned a high priority to agricultural growth, in practice, agricultural and rural development received inadequate attention. Some analysts are of the view that India, with its vast agricultural potential should have first concentrated on the development of agriculture and rural parts of the economy. Such an approach would have generated economic surplus needed for capital formation and investment.

(vii) **Self-reliance:** Our plans also aimed at "self-reliance". Critics claim that this objective was misinterpreted and led to the adoption of wrong priorities. Our plans and policies took it to mean freedom from the need to import and, therefore, a policy of "import substitution" regardless of its cost. The critics hold the view that this objective should have been taken to mean "ability to play for our imports through our export earnings". Viewed this way, we should have added to our export capacity and competitive strength in international markets.

(viii) **Precedence to Public Sector:** In our planned growth, public sector was assigned a place of precedence over the private sector so as to acquire commanding heights of the economy and be in a position to use it for guiding the private sector along chosen lines. This was done while ignoring the fact that public sector undertaking is inherently less efficient than private ones.

Thus, the basic objectives of India's Five Year Plans are rapid economic growth, full employment, self-reliance and social justice. Apart from these basic objectives, each five-year plan takes into account the new constraints and potential/possibilities during the period and attempts to make the necessary directional changes and emphasis.

Approaches of Twelfth Five-Year Plan: Salient Features

(i) The process of restoring fiscal discipline should continue in the Twelfth Plan. This should keep macro-fundamentals broadly in line to ensure faster growth.

(ii) Entrepreneurial capacity in the private sector is matched by an impressive pool of managerial talent and an increasingly skilled workforce. It needs to be strengthened in the years to come.

(iii) The aspiration for change amongst the entire population, especially the young, is an important feature that can help in pushing the economy to a higher growth path. Efforts are needed to ensure that the performance of the economy remains ahead of ever rising expectations in the Plan.

(iv) The Plan will develop support system to offset some important critical constraints arising from the supply side. The most important of these relate to (a) availability of energy, (b) growing evidence of problem with water availability, (c) slower than required improvement in farm output and in the logistics of farm produce, (d) difficulties relating to land acquisition for industry and infrastructure development, and (e) the lack of a credible and fair system for exploitation of mineral resources.

(v) The Planning Commission has explored two alternative targets for economic growth in the Twelfth Plan. The first is a restatement of the Eleventh Plan target of 9.0 per cent growth, which has yet to be achieved. The second is an even higher target of 9.5 per cent average growth for the Twelfth Five Year Plan.

(vi) The sectoral growth rates are broadly consistent with the 9.0 per cent and 9.5 per cent. The 9.0 per cent target requires a significant acceleration in growth in agriculture; in electricity, gas and water supply; and also in manufacturing. However, the main onus for providing additional jobs to the growing labour force will rest on manufacturing and construction and on the services sectors.

(vii) The average investment rate needed during the Plan period is estimated to be 38.5 per cent of GDP for the 9.0 per cent growth with 4.5–5.0 average inflation. The investment rate would have to rise to as much as 41.4 per cent of GDP for the 9.5 per cent growth with 5.0–5.5 rate of inflation.

(viii) To sustain high growth, efforts are needed to expand the productive potential of the economy at a faster rate. In order to achieve an average economic growth rate of 9.0 per cent, the rate of fixed capital formation needs to improve to around 33.5 per cent of GDP over the Plan period.

(ix) Prospects for private corporate investment in the Plan period depend upon many factors, which include India's overall macro economic environment, particularly fiscal deficits and interest rates, the domestic investment climate and India's relative attractiveness as an investment destination compared with other countries. However, optimistic assumptions envisage private corporate fixed capital formation averaging around 12.4 per cent of GDP during the Plan.

(x) The public sector (government and PSUs) will have to contribute its share for raising the rate of fixed capital formation to the desired levels. The fixed capital formation from this sector needs to improve from an average 8.3 per cent of GDP in the Eleventh Plan to an average 9.1 per cent of GDP in the Twelfth Plan. The additional investment of 0.8 percentage points of GDP should be directed largely into infrastructure sectors like energy, roads, transport, irrigation, watershed management, etc.

(xi) The savings needed to finance this level of investment are expected to come from a modest improvement in the savings rate of the household sector, from 23.2 per cent of GDP in the Eleventh Plan to 24.0 per cent in the Twelfth Plan. Private corporate savings are expected to increase from an average of 8.2 per cent of GDP in the Eleventh Plan to 8.5 per cent in the Twelfth Plan.

(xii) For prudent management of the external account, it is desirable that the Current Account Deficit (CAD) should be restricted to an average below 2.5 per cent over the Twelfth Plan period. It is possible to exceed this level for a year or two, but for the five year period as a whole it should work to a limit of 2.5 per cent of GDP, particularly so in the uncertain and volatile global financial conditions that are likely to persist for some time.

(xiii) The projections envisage Gross Budgetary Support (GBS) for the Plan increasing from 4.92 per cent of GDP in 2011-12 to 5.75 per cent of GDP by the end of Twelfth Plan period. The increase in the GBS as a per centage of GDP over a five year period is only 0.83 per cent of GDP. There are several sectors where Plan allocations must increase as a percentage of GDP, notably health, education and infrastructure.

(xiv) Private and PPP investments are estimated to have accounted for a little over 30.0 per cent of total investment in infrastructure in the Eleventh Plan. Their share may have to rise to 50.0 per cent in the Twelfth Plan.

(xv) The pattern of energy demand that may be needed to support 9.0 per cent GDP growth. The total energy requirement (in terms of million tonnes of oil equivalent) is projected to grow at 6.5per cent per year between 2010-11 and 2016-17. This is based on the assumption that the energy elasticity will decline over time.

(xvi) Special attention will be given to competitive pricing and coordination between alternative modes of transport. The resultant integrated policy framework is expected to provide the backdrop for the development of transportation in the Plan.

(xvii) Railways are very important part of any transport network especially for freight movement. They are much more energy efficient than road transport, with a much smaller carbon footprint. Railway safety is also an issue. The entire system is in urgent need of modernisation and this should have top priority in the Plan.

(xviii) The Plan also set seven measurable targets, reflecting the health status to be achieved by the end of the Plan period. These targets related to (i) Infant Mortality Rate (IMR), (ii) Maternal Mortality Ratio (MMR), (iii) Total Fertility Rate (TFR), (iv) Under-nutrition among children, (v) Anaemia among women and girls, (vi) Provision of clean drinking water for all and (vii) Improving child sex ratio for age group 0-6 years.

(xix) The Plan will have priorities convergence among all the existing National Health Programs under the NRHM umbrella, namely those for Mental Health, AIDS control, Deafness control, Care of the Elderly, Information, Education and Communication, Cancer control, Tobacco control, Cardio Vascular diseases, Oral health, Fluorosis, Human

Rabies control, and Leptospirosis. Physical fitness is a prime and basic requirement for insuring good health and there is a growing recognition of the importance of sports for health, physical fitness and nutrition.

(xx) The Plan should aim at locating a Health Sub-centre in every Panchayat and an AWC in every habitation, their formal inter-linkage being a must for integrating the delivery of health, nutrition and pre-school education services.

(xxi) The Plan must try to ensure that all children including differently-able children are able to enjoy equal access to education and educational institutions. A concerted effort is needed to strengthen the system at all levels: elementary education, secondary and higher secondary education and higher education. In parallel, vocational education and skill development efforts need to be strengthened.

(xxii) Strengthening of monitoring and evaluation mechanism including social audit for SSA and MDMS with web-based monitoring for transparency and periodic and sustained third party evaluation. Promoting Adult Literacy with Sakshar Mission as the main vehicle with focus on women, SC/ST and minorities covering all Educationally Backward Blocks (EBBS).

(xxiii) During the Plan period, an additional enrolment of 10 million could be targeted in higher education equivalent to 3 million additional seats for each age cohort entering the higher education system. This would significantly increase the GER bringing it broadly in line with the global average.

Role of Entrepreneurship Economic Growth

The entrepreneur is supposed to create ideas and put them into effect in fostering economic growth and development. Entrepreneurship is one of the most important input in the economic development of a country. The entrepreneur acts as a trigger head to give spark to economic activities by his entrepreneurial decisions. Actually, he is the person who identifies the opportunity, creates and arranges resources and is ultimately responsible for the performance of the business enterprise. He plays a pivotal role in each and every sector of the country. An entrepreneur has been assigned following roles for economic growth of the country:

(1) Creation of Innovative Change : An entrepreneur is a person who always looks for changes. Continuous dreaming helps in idea creation. Idea creation facilitates creativity innovations which are the direct result of creative ideas. Viable innovations lead entrepreneurial behaviour. Entrepreneur is responsible for combining the factors of production in an effective way to enlarge the production base. He also introduces new ideas and new combination of factors. He always tries to introduce newer and newer techniques of production of goods and services. An entrepreneur brings economic development through continuous innovations. According to *Meir* and *Baldwin*, development does not occur spontaneously as a natural consequence when economic conditions in some sense are right. A catalyst is needed which results in entrepreneurial activity to a considerable extent. The diversity of activities that characterises rich countries can be attributed to the supply of entrepreneurs.

(2) Promotion of Capital Formation : Entrepreneurs promote capital formation by mobilising idle savings of public. Compensating investment risk through adequate rate of returns is the basic function of entrepreneur, with this approach entrepreneur motivates the public for more savings. Business ideas creativity and innovation are the important conditions for developing entrepreneurship is the country. Actually, he is responsible for channelising savings for production purposes which in turn gives a multiplier effect to the process of capital formation. They employ their own as well as borrowed resources for setting up their enterprises. Such type of entrepreneurial activities lead to value addition and creation of wealth, which is very essential for the industrial and economic development of the country.

(3) Creation of Employment Opportunities : Most of the economies especially developing countries like India are facing acute problems of growing unemployment. Entrepreneurs provide employment to the unemployed persons. With the setting up of more and more service units by entrepreneurs, indifferent sectors like tiny/small, medium and large sectors of the country, job opportunities are created for others. Thus, through setting up industrial units, he creates job for himself and to the unemployed persons in the society. Besides, these enterprises grow, providing direct and indirect employment opportunities to many more. In this way, entrepreneurs play an effective role in reducing the problem of growing unemployment in persons in the country which in turn clears the path towards economic development of the nation.

(4) Promotion of Balanced Regional Development : The basic function of entrepreneur is to identify opportunities in the prevailing environment, Entrepreneurs help to remove regional disparities through setting up of industries in less developed and backward areas. The Government of India and the state governments both are providing different types of incentives and subsidies for backward area districts and zero industries district. The growth of industries and business in these areas leads to a large number of public benefits like road development transport, health, education, entertainment, and social endowments etc. Setting up of more industries lead to more development of backward regions and thereby promoting balanced regional development.

(5) Increase in Per Capita Income : Each and every country has its own natural and other resources. There is need to optimise the use of these available natural resources. In this context, entrepreneurs convert the latent and idle resources like land, labour and capital into goods and services resulting in increase in the national income and wealth of a nation. With the help of increasing space of entrepreneurial activities owners of factors of production get their price as income as these owners put their resources for productive purposes. Generally, available resources motivate and provide opportunities to the entrepreneurs for the establishment of viable ventures. They explore and exploit opportunities, encourage effective resource mobilisation of capital and skill, bring in new products and services and develop markets for growth of the economy. In this way, they help in increasing gross national product as well as per capita income of the people in a country. The increase in gross national product facilitates further economic growth.

(6) Wealth Creation and Distribution : There is direct relationship in entrepreneurial activity and creation of Job opportunities. People were unable to get job because there was no job and they were poor. Due to entrepreneurial activity unemployed people are getting job as a base for income. Now with the help of job, entrepreneurs can ensure more wealth creation by utilising untapped natural and human resources. Entrepreneurial activity enables factors of production to fetch better price. This process stimulates equitable redistribution of wealth and income in the interest of the country to more people and geographic areas, thus giving benefit to larger sections of the society. Entrepreneurial activities also generate more activities and give a multiplier effect in the economy.

(7) Promotion of Export Trade : Import substitution and export proportion both are important dimensions of favourable balance of trade. Favourable balance of trade is an important ingredient of economic development. Entrepreneurs produce goods and services in large scale for the purpose of earning huge amount of foreign exchange from export. Entrepreneurs through innovation also create new products which are quite helpful for export promotion and import substitution. Thus, import substitution and export promotion ensure economic independence and development of the country.

(8) Encourages Backward and Forward Linkages : Innovation helps in effective entrepreneurship. With the help of latest innovations, entrepreneurs produce huge production, increase product variety, ensure cost effectiveness, improve product demand and sales volumes and also facilitate earnings and profit growth. When an enterprise is established in accordance with the latest technology, it induces backward and forward linkages which ultimately encourages better utilisation of available resources. Thus, it stimulates the process of economic development in the country.

(9) Improvement in Standard of Living : Entrepreneurial activity creates generation employment opportunities. This process leads to increase in income and purchasing power which can be used for consumption expenditure. Increased demand for goods and services boost up industrial activity. Large scale production will result in economies of scale and low cost of production. Marketing process involves creating a demand and then filling it. Entrepreneurs are also responsible for making further innovations. It creates opportunity for production of wide variety of goods and services. It also enables the people to avail better quality goods at lower prices which results in the improvement of their standard of living.

(10) Facilitates Overall Development : Entrepreneurs act as catalytic agent for change which results in chain reactions. Once an enterprise is established, the process of industrialisation is set in motion. This unit will generate demand for various types of resources and there will be so many other units which require the output of this unit. Vertical and horizontal establishment of industrial units optimise the use of resources available in that particular area. This leads to overall development of an area due to increase in demand and setting up of more and more units. In this way, the entrepreneurs multiply their entrepreneurial activities, thus creating an environment of enthusiasm and conveying an impetus for overall development of the area.

(11) Economic Independence : It is a basis for political and social independence. So each and every country is required to make necessary efforts for ensuring economic independence. Development of agriculture sector and industrial sector is quite necessary for economic independence. Both these sectors are complementary to each other and accelerate economic growth. Multidimensional economic growth facilitates economic independence. Thus, it is assumed that entrepreneurship is important for getting economic self-reliance. Export of goods and services on a large scale help in the process of earning of scarce foreign exchange for the country. Efforts for import substitution also facilitate the production of goods and services in the country which ultimately control the imports. Moreover, import substitution efforts serve the foreign exchange for other urgent needs. In this way, import substitution and export promotion help to ensure economic independence of the country.

RURAL ENTREPRENEURSHIP

Indian growth story is directly linked with the rural entrepreneurship development. Farming community is now quite aware about the value of their resources and their usefulness. Similarly, agro based industries are emerging in the rural areas giving a powerful base for rural entrepreneurship.

Diversification into non-agricultural uses of available resources such as catering for tourists, blacksmithing, carpentry, spinning etc. as well as diversification into activities other than those solely related to agricultural usage, for example, the use of resources other than land such as water, woodlands, buildings, available skills and local features, all fit into rural entrepreneurship. The entrepreneurial combinations of these resources are, for example: tourism, sport and recreation facilities, professional and technical training, retailing and wholesaling, industrial applications (engineering, crafts), servicing (consultancy), value added (products from meat, milk, wood, etc.) and the possibility of off-farm work. Equally entrepreneurial, are new uses of land that enable a reduction in the intensity of agricultural production, for example, organic production.

Dynamic rural entrepreneurs can also be found. They are expanding their activities and markets and they find new markets for their products and services in rural areas.

Now, farming community is also interested to convert their land for industrial purposes. In the changed scenario, they are ready to develop agro based units. Industrial units promoted by rural entrepreneurs are in a position to use the available resources at local level by diversification of their land for non-agricultural usage. This type of entrepreneurial venture is an example of a straightforward entrepreneurship and not so much an example of on-farm diversification. It is an example of how seeing and seizing the opportunity are vital ingredients of entrepreneurial success.

These areas are quite popular. They include trade, food processing, handicrafts, production of basic consumer articles, catering, running tourist establishments, and bed and breakfast arrangements.

Although agriculture today still provides income to rural communities, rural development is increasingly linked to enterprise development. Since Indian economy is more and more globalised and competition is intensifying at an unprecedented pace, affecting not only industry but any economic activity including agriculture, it is not surprising that rural entrepreneurship is gaining in its importance as a force of economic change that must take place if many rural communities are to survive. However, rural entrepreneurship demands an enabling environment in order to flourish.

Examination Questions

Long Answer Questions:

1. What is entrepreneurship? How does environmental support system encourage entrepreneurship?
2. Discuss the features of Indian Planning system. How does it promote entrepreneurship?
3. Critically examine the salient point of Twelfth Plan Approach for Indian economy.
4. Critically examine the role of entrepreneurship in economic growth of the country.
5. What is rural entrepreneurship? How does it ensure rural development?

Short Answer Questions:

1. What is economic growth?
2. What do you mean by General National Framework Conditions?
3. What do you mean by entrepreneurial support system?
4. What are the objectives of Indian planning?
5. What is rural entrepreneurship?

Objective Type questions:

1. Entrepreneurial skill includes except the following:
   (a) Managing risk
   (b) Building an effective team
   (c) Paying dividends at higher scale
   (d) Raising funds
2. Functional skills do not include entrepreneurial abilities in areas
   (a) Marketing
   (b) Finance
   (c) Product development
   (d) Farming
3. Innovative change does not concern with the following change:
   (a) Style
   (b) Design
   (c) Efficiency
   (d) Structure

Answers

1-(c) 2-(d) 3-(c)

8

ENTREPRENEURSHIP AND EMPLOYMENT GENERATION

Each and every body needs bread, clothing and housing facilities at least to survive in the society. For this one is ready to work for gainful employment. Each member of society is a part of human resource network and he is ready to contribute in the economic development process of the country. Unemployment deals with a situation. However, productive and services systems have their own limitation in generating employment opportunities to these people. Functional behaviour of these productive and services systems is affected by various barriers which generally affect the working of business organisation. So, there is growing mismatch between the supply and demand of human resources and excess supply of work force becomes the basis of unemployment.

The generation of productive and gainful employment, with decent working conditions, on a sufficient scale to absorb our growing labour force must form a critical element in the strategy for achieving inclusive growth. Past record in this respect is definitely inadequate and the problem is heightened by the fact that the relatively higher rate of growth achieved during the last decade or so is not seen to generate a sufficient volume of good quality employment. Efforts are required to focus on diagnosing the reasons for past failings observed in the employment situation and to reverse at least some of the adverse employment outcomes associated with the pattern of economic growth in the recent past.

The basic weakness in our employment performance is the failure of the Indian economy to create a sufficient volume of additional high quality employment to absorb the new entrants into the labour force while also facilitating the absorption of surplus labour that currently exists in the agricultural sector, into higher wage. Non-agricultural work requires migration of such surplus workers to other areas for productive and gainful employment in the organised or unorganised sector. Women agricultural workers in families where the male head has migrated, also require special attention given the need for credit and other inputs if they are self-employed in agriculture or for wage employment if they do not have land.

Unemployment generally constitutes two aspects. These are seasonal unemployment and disguised unemployment. In the words of the Ninth International Conference of Labour Statisticians, "where persons in employment who are not working full time would be able and willing to do more work than they are actually performing or when the income or productivity of persons in employment would be raised if they worked under improved conditions of production or transferred to another occupation, account being taken of their occupational skills." These are the persons with very low income levels. The International Labour Organisation (ILO) focused on the poverty approach to the employment problem. It says that unemployment is concerned with those persons who have abnormally low earnings as unemployed.

Conceptual Framework for Employment Creation

Entrepreneurs are required to invest their valuable funds in creation of financial and physical assets for the successful operation of the business enterprise. The main objective of an enterprise is to generate income for the entrepreneurs and their families. The physical assets involved in business operations are need to be acquired, serviced and repaired. All these activities require human labour fully or in part, depending on the level of business sophistication and technology employed. Human labour has a price, whether it is family labour (referred to as self-employment) or non-family labour (wage employment). The remuneration received by family members is critical to a household's ability to access basic needs, improve livelihoods and create assets.

Employment is generally categorised in two broad categories: agricultural and non-agricultural. Agricultural employment is mainly rural/land based crop and livestock farming, including fish culture, and rural employment generated therefrom in marketing and processing. Second type of employment is non-agricultural employment, which is defined as urban based largely encompassing service subsector employment, formal and informal manufacturing and large-scale enterprises. Agriculture sector and Industrial sector are both complementary to each other. Employment generated by agricultural marketing and processing incorporates those labour-using activities that procure, process and market farm produce. With regard to dairy marketing and processing, the agents involved comprise raw milk traders, dairy processors and traders in processed dairy products. However, these agents also hire services from others to repair their equipment, provide transport etc., which in turn provides indirect employment from the dairy enterprise.

In present economic system, entrepreneurship is argued to be far more important than it ever was. There is a general agreement that all jobs in the last couple of decades have been created by startups spearheaded by energetic entrepreneurs. The large companies, if anything, have been steadily losing jobs.

Entrepreneurial ventures vary widely in their characteristics, from self-employment or necessity based entrepreneurship at one end of the spectrum to opportunity based entrepreneurship at the other, that seeks to revolutionise the world by leveraging new technology and creating new markets. Opportunity based entrepreneurship is usually based on significant innovation in the realm of technology, business process or the like and is set up to grow, right from inception.

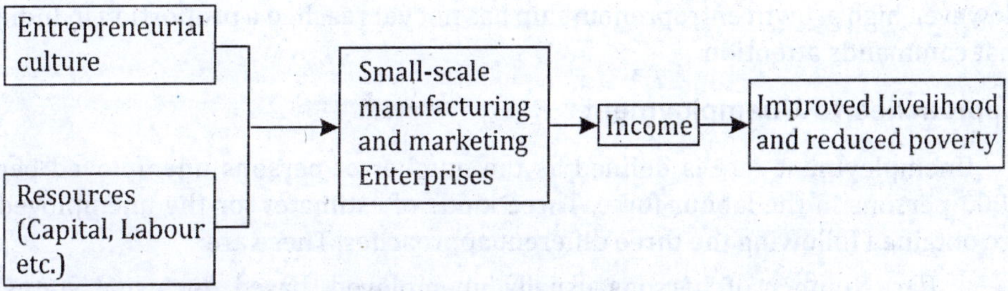

Source: Barrett, and Reardon (2000).

(Figure 1)

India has a long history of entrepreneurship, as evidenced by centuries of business and commercial activity and the existence of generations old business groups and families. The Global Entrepreneurship Monitor studies suggest that the entrepreneurship in India has predominantly been necessity based rather than opportunity based. However, entrepreneurs are not able to create desired impact on the economy through job creation. Thus, the challenge of entrepreneurship in India is, how to increase the incidence of potentially high growth entrepreneurial ventures? In real life scenario, Indian entrepreneurs are in dilemma. They are facing the problem of clarity and uncertainty in government policies and programmes.

Indirect tax regimes favouring the small enterprise have suppressed scale and encouraged firms to remain small. Labour laws that limited the mobility of labour forced entrepreneurs to fear growth in employee strength. Poor infrastructure has led entrepreneurs to create their own and in the process, lock up precious capital which should have been deployed to grow the business. Inadequate availability of land with clear titles, and owner-occupant friendly policies have led to the diversion of scarce capital towards unproductive investments in land and buildings. Poor judicial enforcement of property rights and private contracts has led to sub-optimal business practices, such as make instead of buy and own instead of rent. Perhaps the most damaging impact of our deeply entrenched policy regime of the past has been the effect it had on the entrepreneurs' own beliefs concerning economy of scale, diversification and efficiency wages that limit their propensity to grow.

The era of liberalisation, privatisation and globalisation in the last two decades has brought about some mitigating effects in many of the above areas. The present era of economic reforms has facilitated the high growth ventures that have established themselves during this period points to a positive role played by the new economic policies in opening up areas with huge pent up demand for private investment and providing unrestricted access to the state of the art technology available in the world. There are some sectors which are being seen as fast emerging areas. These areas are telecommunication, power, transportation, logistics, media etc. These sectors have seen significant entrepreneurial activity both from traditional business houses and first generation entrepreneurs.

However, high growth entrepreneurship has not yet reached a proportion in India that commands attention.

Approaches to Unemployment

Unemployment rate is defined as the number of persons unemployed per 1000 persons in the labour force. Three kinds of estimates for the unemployed are obtained following the three different approaches. These are:

(i) Number of persons usually unemployed, based on 'usual status' approach,

(ii) Number of persons unemployed on an average in a week, based on the 'weekly status' and

(iii) Number of person-days unemployed on an average during the reference periods of seven days preceding the survey.

The **first** estimate indicates the magnitude of persons unemployed for a relatively longer period during a reference period of 365 days and approximates to an estimate of chronically unemployed. Some of the unemployed on the basis of this criterion might be working in a subsidiary capacity during the reference period. The former is called as the usually unemployed according to the principal status and the latter, the usually unemployed excluding the subsidiary status workers (us adjusted) which admittedly will be lower than the former.

The **second** estimate based on the weekly status gives the average weekly picture during the survey year and includes both chronic unemployment and also the intermittent unemployment, of those categorised as usually unemployed, caused by seasonal fluctuations in the labour market.

The **third** estimate based on the daily status concept gives average level of unemployment on a day during the survey year. It is the most inclusive rate of 'unemployment' capturing the unemployed days of the chronically unemployed, the unemployed days of the usually employed who become intermittently unemployed during the reference week, and the unemployed days of those classified as employed according to the priority criterion of current weekly status.

Types of Unemployment

1. **Open Unemployment :** It is also called as structural unemployment. It deals with a situation where a large labour force does not get employment opportunities that may yield them regular income. It is notable that under this situation workers are willing to work and able to work but they do not get employment due to non availability of complementary resources especially capital. The rate of capital accumulation lags behind the rate of population growth.

2. **Disguised Unemployment :** Under disguised unemployment opportunities are not open for every one and remain concealed. This type of employment is a work sharing device *i.e.,* existing work

is shared by a large number of workers. In such a situation, even if many workers are withdrawn, the same work can be continued by few workers. The contribution of such labourers to production is quite negligible. Disguised unemployment is a common feature in agriculture based economics.

3. **Underemployment :** It is concerned with those situations where labourers are unable to get employment opportunities in terms of their ability and workable time. Thus, it has two approaches: (a) A situation i.e., in which a labourer does not get the type of work he is capable of opportunity due to lack of suitable jobs (b) A labourer does not get sufficient work to absorb him for the total length of the working hours a day. Second form of unemployment is also known as seasonal unemployment.

Causes of Unemployment

1. **Poor Economics Growth:** Each and every economy has its own agenda to ensure its proper economic growth. Unemployment is the direct result of poor rate of economic growth. The size of employment generally depends on the level of development and its implementation process. Due to poor implementation of planning process employment is inadequate and due to inherent problem employment opportunities have not been created for the unemployed people.

2. **Backward Agriculture:** Due to poor mechanisation and modernisation programme agricultural productivity is quite low. Land holding is uneconomic. Agriculture is a seasonal occupation. There is an absence of supplementary employment opportunities. Consequently, people in rural areas are chronically and partially unemployed. The institutional reforms like land reforms, consolidation, ceiling of land holding and tenancy reforms have not been effectively implemented due to political and administrative ineffectiveness. Non-co-operative attitude of the farmers is also responsible for backwardness of Indian agriculture.

3. **Higher Population Growth:** Higher level of population adversely affects the per capita availability of employment opportunities. Growing size of population improves supply side of work force but at the same time there is no way to increase the demand for labourers in agriculture and industry. Agriculture sector is supplying different types of raw materials to the industry but entrepreneurs are unable to create job opportunities in terms of growth in population.

4. **Ineffective Employment Strategies:** Indian planning system fails to formulate effective employment strategies. The Government of India has formulated different employment generation schemes but due to poor implementation process they are unable to generate adequate opportunities in the economy.

5. **Poverty:** It is quite true that growing use of intensive technologies affect employment generation even though efforts are required to develop more

industries in rural areas using locally available resources. Underdeveloped countries are in the grip of vicious circle of poverty, which in turn, greatly influences the pattern of employment opportunities in the country. Poor people are unable to make any gainful use of existing resources.

6. Use of Capital Intensive Technologies: In India, capital is scarce and surplus labour is available in the system. Problem of unemployment is directly linked with the continuous decay of cottage and small scale industries. Under these circumstances, the country should adopt labour intensive techniques of production.

7. Ineffective Education System: Our education system is ineffective as it provides purely academic knowledge which is not job oriented. Since independence efforts are being made to popularise technical and professional education but these facilities are not adequate. There is an urgent need to go for vocational education to solve the problem of unemployment. At present, we are also facing the problem of employability. Skill development is required among the educated youths to improve their employability.

8. Declining Rate of Cottage and Small Industries: Cottage and small industries are able to create more jobs and also they use available local resources. But, now a days they do not have bright future as they have to compete with medium and big size industries.

9. Lack of Entrepreneurial Behaviour: Supply of entrepreneurs is restricted to metro cities, so the job opportunities are restricted to these cities. However, they are also facing other infrastructural problems. No efforts have been made to develop entrepreneurial behaviour especially among rural people who can generate more employment opportunities in these areas. Due to lack of entrepreneurship, they are unable to get themselves to be involved in productive activities.

10. Regional Disparities: Regional imbalance also encourages unemployment. Some regions have sufficient resources but they are unable to use available resources to accelerate their economic development process. But some are crying for resources to ensure their economic development. This disparity is largely responsible for slow growth of employment opportunities in backward regions. Under these situations two types of problems are affecting the growth. On the one hand we are unable to use existing resources for the development of that particular area and secondly, we are unable to generate employment opportunities as these areas have no industrial units due to required resources.

11. Defective Social System. The defective social system of the country is responsible for the growing unemployment. People are still superstitious and illiterate and not able to control their family size. They are contributing in population explosion. Effective awareness programme is to be initiated to make the small family as an important agenda for socio economic development.

Role of Entrepreneur in Generation of Employment Opportunities

In the era of globalisation, liberalisation and privatisation dimensional perspective of business is also changing. Business is changing as per need of the society and economy. Therefore, generation of employment opportunities is the primary task of entrepreneurs. It is quite true that entrepreneurs not only perceive ideas, but also make sincere efforts to convert them into realty. In the process they provide various employment opportunities to the people of the society. Scope of business is quite broad based. It includes industries, trade and services. Manufacturing process is the main activity of the business. In this process entrepreneur creates various types of employment opportunities in the areas of technical and non-technical sides. Trading and service are supporting mechanism for manufacturing activities. In trading activity which is directly related with the manufacturing and final consumption activity entrepreneurs are supposed to create large number of employment opportunities in areas of purchasing and selling, supply chain management etc.

Trade itself is not a complete activity, because during course of trade—purchase or sale of commodities, various constraints like time, exchange and finances are experienced. Some activities are helpful in solving these constraints and make the trading process easy. Such activities are known as service activities meant for trade. In recent years service sector is at emerging pace and provides good services to the society. It creates new avenues of employment in different sub-sectors. Important areas are as follows:

1. **Finance and Banking Services :** Finance is the 'base of trade' and 'lifeblood of the business', because finance is required right from the start of business activities to its operation. The financial requirements are fulfilled by banks and finance companies. So, these companies provide employment to their owners and provide employment to staff — Agents, Cashiers, Accountants, Branch Managers, Collection Agent and Security Staff, etc.

2. **Insurance Services :** There are two types of risks involved in business activities—systematic and unsystematic risks. Every entrepreneur wants security from these risks. He wants an insurance umbrella for damage to the commodities stored in the godowns and during the course of their transportation. The insurance sector has attracted the entrepreneurs and businessmen towards it. Insurance agents and development officers are doing commendable job through Life Insurance, General Insurance and Marine Insurance. The insurance sector has provided self-employment to large number of insurance agents and salary employment to the staff working in these insurance companies.

3. **Stock and Commodity Exchange :** Stock and Commodity Exchanges are engaged in providing auxiliary services to the business. These exchanges provide trading platform or facilities for purchase or sale of shares, debentures and securities and commodities. These exchanges need a large number of persons. But, stock activities can be performed only by members, who are supposed to work as bulls and bears. In such conditions, some entrepreneurs have established

their enterprises to do the stock marketing, whereby others have got self-employment. They appoint also staff in their offices and, therefore, they are getting their livelihood from these exchanges. Produce Marketing is an organised market, where purchase and sale of agricultural commodities are taking place. Commodity exchanges facilitate trading in industrial commodities and other finished and semi-finished commodities. Thus, these activities also result into creation of employment.

4. Consultancy Services : In India, consultancy sector is an emerging sector for employment generation. Hence, various types of consultancy centres, like Health Centres, Management Centres, Academic Institutions, Professional or Business Advisory Centres, General Insurance Advisory Centres, Legal Consultancy Centres and Marriage Advisory Bureaus, etc. have been established, creating self-employment opportunities to the people. Now online solutions have also been made available. The entrepreneurs are earning their livelihood, as self-employed persons. Besides, they are also providing employment to large number of persons working in these centres.

5. Placement Services : At present, various Educational, Technical and Professional Institutions are engaged in imparting knowledge to their students. But, imparting knowledge is not sufficient. These institutions are also trying to facilitate their students to get employment. In these situations entrepreneurs are providing placement services to needy students. Thus, through placement services, they can get self-employment for themselves and are also able to provide employment to large number of people in this mechanism.

6. Agency Services : The business has now become very complex, so it is not possible for an individual entrepreneur alone to carry out all business activities. For effective performance of several business activities, he requires the agency services provided by the Agents, Brokers, Goods Senders, Auctioners, Refinancer and Import-Export Agents, etc. Thus, these agents have been able to get self-employment. They are also providing employment to helping hands required in these services.

7. Packaging Services : Packaging is the container or wrapper of the products. It also provides safety to the products. Packaging requires good packing material, efficient packing staff and transport facility. For packaging services, large number of persons are either self-employed or get employment in packaging process.

8. Transport Services : An entrepreneur during the course of establishment of an industry or a business, needs services of various transport means. He generates employment opportunities in the following ways:

(i) ***Direct employment :*** The entrepreneurs use various means of transportation, *viz.* Roads, Railways, Airways and Seaways for carrying of raw material and sending the finished goods to the market, which enhances the source of employment and many people get employment.

(ii) ***Indirect employment:*** In course of hiring transport services, an entrepreneur is indirectly helpful in providing employment to the operators, drivers, mechanics etc.

Thus, the entrepreneur provides direct contribution through transport of goods and passengers from one place to another. It also increases the income of the country.

9. Warehousing Services: Manufacturers produce goods at large scale and consumers purchase these goods in small quantities as per their requirements. As a result, the produced goods are required to be stored in cold storages, warehouses etc., and thus it provides self-employment to staff, labour, transporters etc.

10. Communication Services: Communication services facilitate business activities. It reduces the distance between the entrepreneurs and the consumers. The Postal, Telegraph and Telephone Services provided by the public sector companies alone are not adequate to meet the growing requirements of the business world and society at large. So, various services, like – S.T.D., I.S.D., P.C.O., Courier, Mobile, Internet, etc. have been developed in the private sector also where entrepreneurs get self-employment and also provide employment to large number of young people.

11. Advertising Services: Advertisements provide information with regard to quality, prices, sources of availability etc. of products to the potential consumers. For this purpose, many individuals and organisational advertisement agencies have started their working and they require artists, designers, scanners, drawing experts etc. for preparing copies of advertisements, for pasting of advertisements and so on. They also need various experts of print media as well as electronic media to give advertisements on television, etc. So, the advertising services provide self-employment and salary employment to substantial number of persons.

12. Accounting and Reporting Services: Accounting compliance is a statutory requirement for every business organisation so that profit and loss of the business may be assessed properly. Accounting professionals provide their expertise for the purpose. Thus, they get self-employment and also provide employment to supporting staff. Besides, they also provide help in preparation of various types of reports, like project reports and viability reports, etc. Actually, preparation of these reports also requires services of experts as per mandatory requirement. The persons with the abilities and qualities have adequate opportunities of self-employment in this sector. Financial audit, social audit, environmental audit, energy audit etc. require the services of chartered accountants, cost accountants environmental engineers etc.

13. Safety and Security Services: In the process of business operations, every industrialist, and business organisations require security, safety and protection. The Government also provides security through various agencies, but these efforts are not adequate. In such conditions, private entrepreneurs have started providing security services. The entrepreneurs have established security service agencies by deploying the services of ex-army personnel, guards, peons, clerks, watchmen and managers, etc. In this way, entrepreneurs are providing employment opportunities for various segment of society.

14. Marketing Services: Every manufacturer, businessman, industrialist and consumer desires to have commodities and services at his own place. Now some entrepreneurs have developed organisations to provide all these services as per requirement of the consumers. Besides, employment is also available to persons who are ready to work with these services.

15. Event Management: It relates with social and cultural dimensions of the society. Every person arranges some events in his life from time to time, on the occasions of marriage, birth of a child or marriage anniversary etc. Nowadays, organising these events, is directly linked with event management. It is a fast emerging area where entrepreneurs perform all these events by charging huge fees. Thus, they create self-employment for themselves and also provide employment to other persons who are engaged in the event management services which is getting popularity in government sector also.

Various government departments and organisations also organise various events, such as Independence Day, Republic Day, Gandhi Jayanti, Women's Day, Debate Competitions, Speech Competitions, Cricket Matches, Blood Donation Camps etc. So, persons who are expert in making these arrangements for such events may get good opportunities for employment.

16. Entertainment Entrepreneurs: At present, entertainment is a growing industry. In practice, there are various sources of entertainment, *viz.*, dance, music, singing, mono-acting, cartoon framing, story writing, dialogue writing, poetry recitation, videography, videogames and photography etc. Some entrepreneurs have selected these areas of entertainments as source of their livelihood. Besides, they are also providing employment to several persons, by utilising their services in the process of these entertainments.

Suggestions to Improve Employment Opportunities

Entrepreneurs are required to implement the following suggestions to improve employment opportunities in the country:

1. Development of Effective and Viable Infrastructural Facilities : At the macro level, the government has to focus on upgrading and making available quality physical infrastructure like power, roads and transportation etc. Effective coordination is also required among all stakeholders to ensure speedy implementation of projects. It will enable entrepreneurs to conserve capital and direct it to their core competence—innovation.

2. Development of Knowledge Infrastructure : Effective and viable efforts are required to create and upgrade the knowledge infrastructure. Two thirds of the R&D expenditure in India is involved in the government and public sector, which is exactly the opposite of the trends in U.S. So, entrepreneurs should try to give more thrust on R & D programme to reap the benefits of innovation. Untapped available natural resources can also be utilised with the help of innovations.

3. Proper Channelisation of Risk Capital : Policies have to be geared up to channelise the early stage risk capital towards sustaining vibrant innovative activity. There has been a significant increase in the number of government innovation funding programs to support new ideas falling into various domains. This directional shift in focus from controlling economic activity to promoting innovation is an important development. Actually, private venture capital in India has tended to be growth capital rather than risk capital. But, at the operating level, the rules, regulations and processes have not been evolved with this change in focus.

Remedial Measures

Following steps are to be implemented to solve the problem of unemployment:

1. **Enlargement of Employment Opportunities :** In this case two strategies need attention. First are dealt with the expansion of the industrial sector and second one is broad basing the service sector. In recent years efforts have been made to enlarge the scope of service sector in the country. So, this should be continued to absorb more and more persons in the service sector.

2. **Increase in Capital Formation :** Sufficient and effective measures are required to increase the level of capital formation in the country. It will help in maintaining the existing activities ensuring the establishment of production and services units in the country. Increasing level of capital formation improve the volume of the work in the country. Besides, more investment in capital goods also ensures faster growth of employment opportunities.

3. **Balanced Approach in Use of Technology :** Efforts are required to use combination of capital intensive and labour intensive technologies of production with the moderate use of capital intensive technology. We can easily ensure the viability of cottage & small scale activities and agricultural activities. Capital intensive technologies also help in creation of bigger plants like steel, fertiliser, petrochemicals etc. These industries also help in the development of ancillary industries. With these efforts we can create more employment opportunities.

4. **Man Power Planning :** It helps in managing human resources in scientific manner. Educated youth are not getting jobs due to their poor employability. To overcome this problem, we need skill development of educated youths as per the requirements of industries. Besides, efforts are also required to ensure adequate provision of nutritive foods, health facilities elementary education training for some jobs etc. for better supply of labour work force.

5. **Special Employment Programmes :** These are different types of people who need special support system so far problem of unemployment is concerned. These are landless agricultural labourers, marginal farmers, village artisans, tribal people and people living in the hilly areas. The programme should be initiated for them in the form of direct employment as on rural capital works. Mahatma Gandhi National Rural Employment Guarantee Act (MNREGA) has made a positive impact in creation of employment opportunities in rural areas.

Guaranteed Wage Employment—Mahatma Gandhi National Rural Employment Guarantee Act (MNREGA)

Workfare programmes have been important programme interventions in India and elsewhere in developing countries since long. These programmes typically provide unskilled workers with short-term employment on public works. They provide income transfers to poor households during periods when they suffer on account of absence of opportunities of employment. In areas with high unemployment rates and under employment, transfer benefits from workfare programmes can prevent poverty from worsening especially during lean periods. Durable assets that these programmes create have the potential to generate second-round employment benefits as requisite infrastructure gets developed.

We have a long history and experience in implementing wage employment programmes. However, beginning with Jawahar Rojagar Yojana in 1989, the outreach of these programmes increased significantly as in the period 1989 to 2006, ultimately culminating in NREGA. These wage employment programmes implemented by State Governments with Central assistance were self-targeting, and the objective was to provide enhanced livelihood security, especially to those dependent on casual manual labour.

Based on the experience of these programmes the NREGA was enacted to reinforce the commitment towards livelihood security in rural areas. The Act was notified on 7 September, 2005. The significance of NREGA lies in the fact that it creates a right based framework for wage employment programmes and makes the government legally bound to provide employment to those who seek it. In this way the legislation goes beyond providing a social safety net, and towards guaranteeing the right to employment.

The objective of the NREGA is to enhance the livelihood security of the people in rural areas by guaranteeing 100 days of wage employment in a financial year to a rural household whose members volunteer to do unskilled manual work. The Act further aims at creating durable assets and strengthening the livelihood resource base of the rural poor. The choice of works suggested in the Act address causes of chronic poverty like drought, deforestation, soil erosion etc., so that the process of employment generation is on a sustainable basis. However, NREGA is not supply driven but demand driven. Resource transfer under NREGA is based on the demand for employment and this provides another critical incentive to states to leverage the Act to meet the employment needs of the poor. The delivery system has been made accountable as it envisages an Annual Report on the outcomes of NREGA to be presented by the Central Government to the Parliament and to the state legislature by the State Government.

Funding

The Central Government bears the costs on the following items:

(i) The entire cost of wages of unskilled manual workers.

(ii) 75% of the cost of material, wages of skilled and semi skilled workers.

(iii) Administrative expenses as may be determined by the Central Government, which will include, inter-alia, the salary and the allowances of the Programme Officer and his supporting staff and work site facilities.

(iv) Expenses of the National Employment Guarantee Council.

The State Government bears the cost on the following items:

(i) 25% of the cost of material, wages of skilled and semi skilled workers (as a ratio of 60:40 is to be maintained for wages of the unskilled manual workers and the material, skilled/semi-skilled workers' wages, the State Government has to bear only 25% of the 40% component, which means a contribution of 10% of the expenditure).

(ii) Unemployment allowance payable in case the State Government cannot provide wage employment on time.

(iii) Administrative expenses of the State Employment Guarantee Council.

EXAMINATION QUESTIONS

Long Answer Questions:

1. What do you mean by employment generation? How do entrepreneurs create employment opportunities in the society?
2. "Entrepreneur is a part of society and he should try to develop it." Comment.
3. Critically examine evaluation of job opportunities in different sectors of Indian economy.
4. How does entrepreneurship help in employment generation? Give suggestions to improve it.
5. Discuss the causes of unemployment? Suggest remedial measures to solve the problem of unemployment.

Short Answer Questions:

1. What is unemployment?
2. What is disguised unemployment?
3. What are the approaches to the unemployment?
4. What are the objectives of MNREGA?
5. What do you mean by seasonal unemployment?

Objective Type Questions:

1. MNREGA is concerned with
   (a) Education
   (b) Employment
   (c) Environment
   (d) Economic Planning

2. Services are included in
   (a) Primary sector
   (b) Core sector
   (c) Ancillary sector
   (d) Auxiliary sector
3. Unemployment is not concerned with the following:
   (a) Open unemployment
   (b) Under employment
   (c) Voluntary unemployment
   (d) Disguised unemployment

Answers

1-(b) 2-(d) 3-(c)

9

ENTREPRENEURSHIP AND SOCIAL STABILITY

Business is created by individuals. Technically, these individuals are promoters or entrepreneurs. At the first instance, it is the social trait which encourages the individuals to take a lead for business behaviour. Entrepreneurial behaviour of these individuals need recognition from their own group, community and society. Acceptability of entrepreneurial behaviour by social institutions is a basic requisite condition for the survival of entrepreneurs. It is the society which expect that the entrepreneurs are part of its own system and they have to serve the purpose of societal interest. These individuals are the part of society. Group of individuals constitutes community and it is the basis for the society itself. All individuals or groups of the society are unable to assume risk as business itself is a risky phenomenon. However, some of these individuals are ready to take risk and come forward for the promotion of business. Actually it is the social environment which provides base for the entrepreneurial behaviour. There are certain social factors which guide the operational behaviour of entrepreneurs. These factors include attitude of people to work, attitude to wealth, family, marriage, religion, education, ethics and social responsibility of business.

Definitions of Society

According to *Ginsberg* "A society is a collection of individuals united by certain relations or modes of behaviour which mark them off from others who do not enter into these relations or who differ from them in behaviour."

Parsons also defined the society in following way "Society may be defined as the total complex of human relationships in so far as they grow out of action in terms of mean-end relationships, intrinsic or symbolic."

According to *Prof. Wright* "Society is not a group of people. It is the system of relationships that exist between the individuals of the group."

Features of Society

(i) It is the whole system of social relationships and not a mere agency for the comfort of the beings.

(ii) It is a permanent institution and is a kind of natural organisation which has emerged out of natural instincts of man.

(iii) Nature of society consists not in the external factors of interdependence or likeness or authority but in the state of mind of the beings who compose society. Three main types of societies—tribal, agrarian and industrial have been marked out on this globe. The African society is tribal, the Indian society is agrarian (peasant) while the American society is industrial.

(iv) It exists only when the members know each other and possess common interest or objects.

(v) The members who constitute society are required to show their likeness and their interdependence. They must have a community of feeling.

Nature/Definition of Social Structure

S.F. Nadel defined the social structure as follows "We arrive at the structure of a society through abstracting from concrete population and its behaviour, the pattern on network of relationships obtaining between actors in their capacity of playing roles relative to one another."

According to *Ginsberg* "Social structure is concerned with the principal forms of social organisation *i,e.* types of groups, associations and institutions and complex of these which constitute societies,"

According to *Talcott Parsons* "Social structure is used to the particular arrangement of interrelated institutions, agencies and social patterns, as well as the status and roles which each person assumes in the groups,"

Features of Social Structure

1. It is an abstract and intangible phenomenon.
2. Individuals form are the units of associations and institutions. In this way, these associations and institutions are the units of social structure.
3. Pattern of social structure is created by the institutions and associations which are interrelated in a particular arrangement.
4. It refers to the external aspect of society which is relatively stable as compared to the functional or internal aspect of society.
5. It is a 'living' structure which is created and maintained for a time and changes.

Social Structure of India

(i) ***Birth*** – This is a happy occasion in the family. Ceremonies and rituals are held to celebrate the occasion. The birth of male child is good symptom for the survival of the family. In some areas, the birth of a girl is looked down upon.

(ii) ***Men*** – In the Indian society, a man is considered to be the bread-earner and shoulders the responsibility of the family. He is very dominating by nature and prefers to rule over his women. They are active members of the family and they ensure sense of protection to the family members.

(iii) ***Women*** – Historically, women have played a significant role in the social and political structure of the country. In the ancient times, women enjoyed much freedom, but with advent of the Muslims and the purdah system they were marginalised to some extent. Generally, women are very submissive in nature. However, due to improved education levels, women have become more assertive. Now, women are joining jobs to make themselves self-reliant.

(iv) ***Marriage*** – This is an important social obligation which most Indians adhere to. It is given much importance by society. Marriages are generally arranged, but now many are choosing their own partners in urban areas. Children born outside a marriage are looked down upon. Marriages are conducted with elaborate rituals and much money is spent on this occasion.

(v) ***Family*** – The family as a unit is given much importance. Couple members of the family are supposed to adjust themselves. Having children is an emotional issue, divorces are generally shunned. The family system nurtures the well-being of the children. Nowadays, due to modernisation cases of divorces are increasing in number. At present, divorce is being used as a solution to settle an unhappy marriage. But in general, people like to retain the family unit.

(vi) ***Patriarchal Set-up*** – India is mostly a patriarchal set-up, with the father having control over the family unit. The man controls the reins of the family unit. He is the head of the family. The eldest male member has much say in the matters of the family.

(vii) ***Matriarchal Set-up*** – It is linked with the improvement in education level. This type of set-up is available specially in Kerala where women are the dominant force. They decide the issues of the family. Literacy in Kerala is 100 percent and majority of the women are in employment.

(viii) ***Caste System*** – The social structure is based upon the caste system. The society is divided into four major castes — Brahmans, Kashtriyas, Vaisyas and the Sudras. The Brahmans are the priests and are considered to be the uppermost caste. The Kshatriyas are the warriors, the Vaisyas are the business class and the merchants and the Sudras are the working class. Intercaste marriages are not permitted as a rule, although now it has become quite common in the urban areas. Now with growing urbanisation, the caste system is becoming obsolete.

(ix) ***Death*** – This is truth of worldly life. This is also important occasion in the family system. Death is considered to be inevitable. Ceremonies are held on this occasion and even after the death of a person, yearly rituals are performed by the family members to remember departed soul.

Thus, Indian society is very complex, yet remains intact as people follow certain guidelines laid down by the society. They prefer not to deviate from it.

Social System

Social system is a derivative of social structure. Social structure is the 'means' through which the social system functions. Thus, the social system refers to functional aspect of social structure"

According to *Talcott Parsons* "A social system consists in a plurality of individual actors interacting with each other in situation which has at least a physical or environmental aspect."

Social system is constituted by the actions of individuals. It involves participation of an actor in a process of interactive relationship in accordance with social norms. On the basis of their interaction and interrelationship they create a pattern which is called social system.

Features of Social System

1. Pluralistic Society : It consists of individuals having different ethnic, linguistic, religions and caste backgrounds—for example, our society is a pluralistic society with a complex social order characterised by a multiple of ethnic, linguistic, religions and caste divisions. Hindus constitute the majority community. Muslims are concentrated in J & K, Assam, Bihar, U.P., Kerala and West Bengal. Christians are concentrated in the small states of North East—Nagaland, Meghalaya, Arunachal Pradesh, Mizoram and also in Kerala and the Sikhs are concentrated in Punjab.

2. Predominantly Rural Society : Base of Indian society is rural society as majority of people live in villages are now developing. Earlier, these villages were suffering due to lack of civic amenities, employment opportunities, roads, transport facilities, electricity, hospitals and schools. But now in rural areas situation is improving. The gap between rural-urban development scenario is being reduced as government is providing more and more funds under different schemes for the development of rural areas. They have also started enjoying some fruits of industrialisation and development. The government has launched various schemes for ameliorating the conditions of rural people.

3. Poverty : Poverty of masses especially in rural areas is an important feature of Indian social system. The government has initiated different schemes and programmes for the welfare of weaker section of the society. Even today, a large number of people continue to live below the poverty line. The economic development of the society through organised plans and all round industrial and technological development is need of the hour. The government has enhanced the volume of investment in rural sector but their impact is negligible.

4. Illiteracy and Ignorance : Illiterates constitute a big part of Indian social system. A large number of Indians are still illiterate. The population explosion and poverty combined with inadequate resources and efforts have all combined to perpetuate the problem. The political process continues to be predominated by illiterate masses but still leadership is being controlled by urban elites. The government has already enacted the Right to Education Act, 2010 making provision of compulsory and universal education to all. Sarva Shiksha Abhiyan is the most effective tool now to eradicate illiteracy and ignorance prevailing in the Indian society. Level of education has quite improved. But these efforts are required to continue to improve the literacy rate on continuous basis.

5. Linguistic Diversity : There is growing instances of communalisation of society on language basis. Languages should be free from societal divisions and they should also be used as enriching knowledge. Inspite of this communalisation of language is an important factor which is polluting the social fabric of Indian environment. On the basis of language, Indian society stands divided into linguistic groups. The Constitution of India recognises as many as 15 languages as the major languages which are spoken by 87% of population. Linguistic diversity and emotional and parochial love of people for their regional languages have forced the government to accept and follow the principle of reorganisation of Indian States on the basis of languages i.e. the creation of linguistic states.

6. Racial Diversity : India is inhabited by people having racial connections. People of the North are of Aryan races, whereas the people of South represent the Dravidian race. In the Eastern States people have affinity with Mongolian race. The racial inter-mixing is improving and mobility of labour has eroded this gap. The principle of unity in diversity is accepted and yet diversities are many a time allowed to dominate the objective of unity. The constitution does not permit racial discrimination and provides for secularism as the best way. But in actual operation, socio-political processes and racial factors still play an important role in creating racial diversity.

7. Caste and Casteism : Caste and casteism are important features of Indian social system. The constitution provisions abolishing untouchability and discrimination on caste and creed basis has taken a great step towards their dilution, if not elimination of caste and casteism. But in the actual process of Indian society, caste and casteism continue to be major factors. However, improved literacy and growing pace of urbanisation will improve the situation. Moreover, constitution provisions for reservation of seats and jobs for the people belonging to scheduled casts and tribes have failed to produce the desired integrative effect. Caste system has deep historical roots and it will take time to reduce the impact of caste system. Caste system is playing an integrative role but only at the group level. It has helped in the formation of social groupings.

8. Communalism : The presence of communal tension and the periodic outbreak of communal riots have been the bone of Indian social system. Regional and communal political parties are always trying to take the benefits of these events. Exploitation in the name of religion, election campaigns based on communal lines and use of religion as a pressure group are practical by political parties. Communalism is still a big strain on India's efforts towards nationalism. The menace of communalism continues to be a big danger to the unity and integrity of the nation.

9. Regionalism : Religious, linguistic, cultural and caste diversities prevailing in the Indian society are responsible for grouping regionalism. The adoption of federal structure presupposes the existence of some regionalism due to which the division of power is done between the federal government and the federating units. India is not an exception to generalisation. But, regionalism should not create barriers in the overall development of the country.

10. Tradition and Modernity : Tradition and modernity both are in existence in the Indian society. The attempts of modernisation of traditions as well as traditionalisation of modernity are simultaneously ensuring balancing act in the society. Modern trends and pressures like politicisation of caste, lessening of caste consciousness among the urban elites, operationalism of modern western tools of administration and government etc., are also affecting and diluting the impact of tradition. Some times modernity also gets coloured with traditionalism when the social and political elites talk in terms of age old glorious traditions of India. The Indian approach is quite realistic one and development programmes are trying to maintain a balancing act between traditional modernity.

11. Problem of Social Communication : Indian social system faces the problem of social communication. Social structure of Indian society is based on the different types of myth prevailing in the Indian society. This has created unnecessary gap between the elites and the masses. This problem is clearly reflected between high and low castes, illiterates and literates, urbanites and ruralites etc. Indian social structure consists of religious, regional, linguistic and caste diversities. These variables are responsible for social conflicts among the various institutions of Indian society. Social institutions are close to each other. However, these institutions are supposed to adjust themselves in a changing Indian society.

Dualism in Indian Society

Dualism refers to uneven development in various segments of economy. It is an important characteristic of an underdeveloped country. In each affected segment, some components are well developed and are experiencing high growth rate. They are able to provide means for high standard of living for the persons engaged in them. In contrast, it also contains some highly backward components. The persons who are engaged in those subset of activities are, on an average, very poor. Moreover, the developed and backward component of the segment of activities is not segregated by geographical boundaries.

Thus, Economic dualism arises due to uneven economic development within a country. The division of a single economy into two sectors that appear to be at different levels of development is referred to as a dual economy. A dual economy is usually a sign of markets working poorly. In India's case, the labour and credit markets do not function properly due to a great degree of skewness of endowments such as education, land, and social ability (caste, religion and gender influence this).

Dualism may also be viewed from other aspects. It enforces simultaneous existence of advanced and backward technologies in some economic activities.

Some economic activities are highly capital intensive and are characterised by—

(i) speed and availability of information, and processing techniques;

(ii) the speed of decision-making and implementation;

(iii) high labour productivity;

(iv) long gestation periods of the projects; and so on.

In contrast, some economic activities are based upon primitive and old techniques. They are highly labour intensive, but are characterised by low labour productivity. Beside this, activities based upon backward techniques have poor or no organisation. It is because of this that they are often termed as "informal sector". Frequently, even a given type of economic activity is simultaneously undertaken with diverse technologies and production processes ranging from highly labour-intensive to highly capital-intensive ones. Economic dualism results in the creation of two separate sectors — the modern and traditional. In India, that would be modern industry and services versus a traditional rural sector. Both need each other to coexist (for example, the former needs food from the latter, and the latter needs fertilizers and connectivity from the former), and yet run differently from one another.

The best example of dualistic structure can be seen in transport facilities. In this sector there is co-existence of different means of transport ranging from human and animal driven carts to vehicles using advanced technology and mechanical system.

In Indian economy, the presence of dualism can be seen in various sectors such as in food items, water availability, and use of computer. In food items, it may exist from road-side eating places to five star kitchens. Processed and packed food, including junk items, may be available in the midst of undernourished and starving people. Expensive water may be available in abundance with widespread scarcity of ordinary safe drinking water. Use of computers and sophisticated electronics can be there together with non-availability of basic reading and writing material to the general public.

Dualism also reflects itself in large-scale income disparities. In that sense, a backward economy is a dualistic one both in rural and urban areas. In rural areas, the advance components of dualism are found in the form of developed mining, fisheries, plantations, use of agricultural machinery, use of chemical manure and so on. In contrast, backward segments are represented by small and fragmented farms, abundance of unskilled as landless agricultural workers, disguised, unemployment and subsistence farming.

Urban dualism shows itself in the form of posh offices, hotels, and restaurants, shopping complexes, entertainment centers and residential buildings. There is variety of financial institutions providing financial services. Information services and technology are easily available, economical and of high standard. In contrast, there are urban slums populated with the very poor lacking even basic civil amenities. Employment-wise, we have very highly paid executives and in contrast those who provide lowly paid menial services.

ROLE OF ENTREPRENEURS IN BRINGING SOCIAL STABILITY

1. **Objective of Self-Sufficient Society :** Society needs goods and services as a source to improve their well being. The entrepreneurs try to increase the production through their business enterprises, producing goods and services as per the needs of the local community, providing employment to people to earn their income and improve their savings and capital formation, contribute towards export promotion and import substitution etc. Thus, the entrepreneurs through their behaviour fulfil the dream of establishment of a self-sufficient and stable society.

2. **Enrichment of Ethical Values :** The entrepreneur develops the ethical values for the society to ensure social stability. He stresses upon maintaining moral values, ideals and standards in the managerial process of various business activities. Entrepreneur is a part of whole value system of the society.

3. **Social Development :** Entrepreneurs are part of the society and society is developed by the entrepreneurs. Entrepreneurs are required to create business organisation and through this organisation they have to fulfil their dream to earn profit and producing goods and services for the benefits of the society at large. They make best possible efforts for utilisation of available physical and human resources, providing employment to local people and also fulfilling his social responsibilities towards various groups of the society. Each segment of society has a right to get job opportunities in business enterprise if they have necessary qualification and experience etc.

4. **Changes in the Social Framework :** Entrepreneurs make changes in the social framework with the help of latest innovations. These innovations facilitate society's progress by introduction of new products, new markets, new techniques, new sources and establishment of new industries. Innovations are responsible for change in design and style of consumption behaviour which ultimately increase the level of society.

5. **Control on Social Evils :** Entrepreneurs are also making efforts for the development of social endowments. These endowments include development of education, health, social welfare services and transport facilities. These endowments improve the level of thinking of the society. These entrepreneurs are responsible for establishment of new industries and expansion of the existing industries. Entrepreneurs also provide employment to needy persons and encourage them towards creativity or entrepreneurship. It raises the standards of living of such people, which will be helpful in removing of several social evils. Employment is a path of creation of moral values in society.

6. **Removal of Economic Problems :** There are certain problems like, class conflicts, polluted environment, slum areas and social crimes, etc. which affect the Indian Society most. Entrepreneurs through their tiny, small, medium and large enterprises are trying to give purchasing power to the unemployed persons of the society. It eliminates class conflict in the society. Development of rural entrepreneurship also got success in controlling social crimes.

7. **Provision of Employment Opportunities :** The entrepreneurs increase the opportunities for employment. They establish new enterprises and expand

the existing establishments in different areas of the country. Growing level of entrepreneurial profit and retained earnings further improve the business operation and consequently further employment improve the opportunities.

8. Removal of Poverty : The entrepreneurs are responsible for creating direct and indirect employment opportunities to the unemployed persons. Increase in scale of production, development of new products and expansion of new enterprises and markets have to increase the level of employment opportunities in the country. Thereafter, people get earnings for their survival and enjoyment of life. Due to increase in income people further create more demand for products and services. Consequently, poverty gets reduced in the country. In this regard, *Nurkse* has stated that, "The entrepreneurs enlarge the path of economic progress, through which the country gets rid of the vicious circle of poverty."

9. Improvement in Standards of Living : The entrepreneurs are known for their new techniques, new products and new markets. These efforts enable the society to consume variety of products and services. Increase in availability of adequate and innovative products and services improve the standard of living of the society. Growing level of consumerism further creates the scope of innovations.

10. Social Changes : New ideas are responsible for creativity. Creativity in turn is the basis for innovations. Viable innovations fuel the entrepreneurial actions. Thus, entrepreneur is a creative agent of social change. Each and every segment of the society become the partner in the progress of the country. Actually, these measures ensure a dynamic and stable society in the country.

Social Entrepreneurship

The terms social entrepreneur and social entrepreneurship were used first in the literature on social change in the 1960s. The terms came into widespread use in the 1980s and 1990s, promoted by *Bill Drayton* the founder of Ashoka : Innovators for the Public, and others such as Charles Lead beater. From the 1950s to the 1990s Michael Young was a leading promoter of social enterprise and in the 1980s was described by Professor Daniel Bell at Harvard as 'The world's most successful entrepreneur of social enterprises because of his role in creating favourable environment for them.' During the nineteenth and twentieth centuries some of the most successful social entrepreneurs successfully straddled the civic, governmental and business worlds – promoting ideas that were taken up by mainstream public services in welfare, schools, and health care.

One well-known contemporary social entrepreneur is Muhammad Yunus, founder and manager of Bangladesh Grameen Bank and its growing family of social venture businesses, who was awarded a Nobel Peace Prize in 2006. The work of Yunus and Grameen echoes a theme among modern day social entrepreneurs that emphasised the enormous synergies and benefits when business principles are unified with social ventures. In some countries, including Bangladesh, social entrepreneurs have filled the space left by a relatively small state. In other countries, particularly in Europe and South America, they have tended to work more closely with public organisations at both the national and local level.

Today, non-profit and non-governmental organisations, foundations, governments and individuals also play the role to promote, fund and advise social entrepreneurs around the planet. A growing number of colleges and universities are establishing programs focused on educating and training social entrepreneurs.

Social Entrepreneurs as a Change Agent— Social entrepreneurs can play an important role in social sector in the following ways:

(i) Adopting a mission to create and sustain social value (not just private value);

(ii) Recognising and relentlessly pursuing new opportunities to serve that mission;

(iii) Engaging in a process of continuous innovation, adaption, and learning;

(iv) Acting boldly without being limited by resources currently in hand; and

(v) Exhibiting heightened accountability to the constituencies served and for the outcomes created.

Conceptual Framework of Social Entrepreneurship

A social enterprise is an organisation that achieves large scale, systematic and sustainable social change through a new invention, a different approach, a more rigorous application of known technologies or strategies, or a combination of these. Actually, Social entrepreneurship describes an entrepreneurial venture that aims to achieve a particular social goal through positive externalities, in addition to profit.

Business entrepreneurship typically measures performance in profit and return, but social entrepreneurs also take into account a positive return to society. Social entrepreneurship typically furthers broad social, cultural, and environmental goals and is commonly associated with the voluntary and not for profit sectors. Profit can at times also be a consideration for certain companies or other enterprises.

Entrepreneur whose work is aimed at progressive social transformation is expected to improve the social endowments in the country. A business to drive the transformational change. While profits are generated, the main aim is not to maximise financial returns for shareholders but to grow the social venture and reach more people in need effectively. Wealth accumulation is not a priority, revenues beyond costs are re-invested in the enterprise in order to fund expansion programme.

Thus, the social enterprise is a collective term for a range of organisations that trade for a social purpose. They adopt one of a variety of different legal formats but have in common the principles of pursuing business-led solutions to achieve social aims, and the reinvestment of surplus for community benefit. The objectives focus on socially desired, nonfinancial goals and their outcomes are the nonfinancial measures of the implied demand for and supply of services.

Components of Social Entrepreneurship

(i) Identifying a stable but inherently unjust equilibrium that causes the exclusion, marginalisation, or suffering of a segment of humanity that lacks the financial means or political clout to achieve any transformative benefit on its own;

(ii) Identifying an opportunity in an unjust equilibrium, developing a social value proposition, and bringing to bear inspiration, creativity, direct action, courage and fortitude, thereby challenging the stable state's hegemony; and

(iii) Forging a new, stable equilibrium that releases trapped potential or alleviates the suffering of the targeted group, and through imitation and the creation of a stable ecosystem around the new equilibrium ensuring a better future for the targeted group and even society at large.

According to *Perrini & Vurro* (2006) social entrepreneurship is a dynamic process created and managed by an individual or team (the innovative social entrepreneur), which strives to exploit social innovation with an entrepreneurial mindset and a strong need for achievement, in order to create new social value in the market and community at large.

Skoll Foundation has also stated that the social entrepreneur aims for value in the form of transformational change that will benefit disadvantaged communities and ultimately society at large. Social entrepreneurs pioneer innovative and systematic approaches for meeting the needs of the marginalised, the disadvantaged and the disenfranchised populations that lack the financial means or political clout to achieve lasting benefit on their own.

FEATURES OF SOCIAL ENTREPRENEURSHIP

(i) It indicates the group or person's efforts

(ii) It aims at creating social value, either exclusively or at least in some prominent way;

(iii) It shows a capacity to recognise and take advantage of opportunities to create that value ("envision");

(iv) It employs innovation, ranging from outright invention to adpting someone else's novelty, in creating and/or distributing social value;

(v) It is willing to accept an above-average degree of risk in creating and disseminating social value; and

(vi) It is unusually resourceful in being relatively undaunted by scarce assets in pursuing their social venture.

EXAMINATION QUESTIONS

Long Answer Questions:

1. What is society? Explain its features?
2. What do you mean by social stability? How does entrepreneurship ensure it?

3. What is social system? Examine the role of entrepreneurship in bringing changes in social system?
4. What are the reasons for social instability? Evaluate the role of entrepreneurship in removing social instability.
5. What do you mean by dualism in Indian society? Critically examine the government steps to reduce the dualism in Indian society.

Short Answer Questions:

1. What is Society?
2. What is social system?
3. What do you mean by social stability?
4. Why we need social stability?
5. What do you understand by dualism?
6. Who is a social entrepreneur?

Objective Type Questions:

1. Society is a
   (a) group of people
   (b) system of relationship between
   (c) individuals having different behaviour
   (d) community structure.
2. Muhammad Yunus is a
   (a) Innovator
   (b) Entrepreneur
   (c) Intrapreneur
   (d) Social entrepreneur.
3. Duality refers to
   (a) Haves and have nots
   (b) Class conflict
   (c) Classless society.
   (d) Uneven development.

Answers

1-(b) 2-(d) 3-(d)

REFERENCES

1. Musselnian V.A., and Hugnes, E+1, Introduction to Business Issues and Environment, p.533
2. Schncider.E.V, Industrial Psychology., p.514

10

Entrepreneurship and Balanced Regional Development

Each and every developed and developing nations have their own problems of regional development. Some parts of the country are highly developed and some parts are severely affected by lack of resources and facilities. Some regions are quite rich in natural resources but they are poor because they are unable to utilise their existing resources. Similarly, some regions are lacking in natural resources even then they are ensuring their development through technological development. So, there is a need for stability in the development process of the country by adopting the process of balanced regional development of the country.

Balanced development of different parts of the country, extension of the benefits of economic progress to the less developed regions and widespread diffusion of industry are among the major aims of planned development. Expansion of the economy and more rapid growth increase progressively the capacity to achieve a better balance between national and regional development. In striving for such a balance, certain inherent difficulties have to be met, especially in the early phases of economic development. In the interest of development itself, the maximum increase in national income should be achieved and resources obtained for further investment. The process is a cumulative one, each stage determining the shape of the next. In some fields, as in industry, intensive and localised development may be inevitable. In other areas, also efforts are required to provide for more dispersed advance in sectors like agriculture, small industries, power, communications and social services. Sufficient investment is also needed in economic and social overheads to create numerous promising centres for growth. Once a minimum, in terms of national income and growth in different sectors is reached, it becomes possible to provide in many directions for a larger scale of development in the less developed regions. A large country with extensive natural resources, viewing each phase of its development in the perspective of a long-term plan. It is obvious to realise a high and sustained rate of growth but also to enable its less developed regions to come up to the level of the rest.

Nature of Balanced Regional Development

Balanced regional development does not mean equal development of regions in the State. It simply implies the fullest realisation of a region's potential so that the benefits of overall economic growth are shared by the inhabitants of the region.

Balanced regional development may be defined as the creation of equal opportunities for all people to participate in, contribute to and benefit from development. It also requires a balanced development which is based on human development. It is the process of enlarging people's choices as to what they do and can do in their lives. Poverty limits the opportunity of many people to develop their capabilities and thereby limits their choices as to what they can do in their lives and how they can participate in development.

The present wave of globalisation is expected to free the Indian consumer from the exploitation of the incompetent domestic producers. The challenge posed by globalisation must be converted into an opportunity under the multilateral trade system. The New Economy producers in the software sector are already doing it. Those in the Old Economy sector must be facilitated to accept this challenge and to adapt to the new trade environment. "Globalisation has to deliver what working people and their families everywhere aspire to—a decent job, security and a voice in the decision making process." Globalisation is the only process through which we can remove regional imbalances. It ensures free flow of investment opportunities to exploit the natural resources and unemployed population of poor regions of the country. The objective should, therefore, be to make globalisation work and not to shoot it down, which will render living conditions in the developing world even more unacceptable

Objectives of Regional Development

The main objectives of regional development are increase in national income and more balanced development of different parts of the country. They are thus related to one another and, step by step, it becomes possible to create conditions in which resources in terms of natural endowment, skill and capital in each region are fully utilised. In each region the nature of the problem and the impediments to rapid development in particular fields should be carefully studied, and appropriate measures devised for accelerated development. The essential object should be to secure the fullest possible utilisation of the resources of each region, so that it can contribute its best to the national pool and take its due share from the benefits accruing from national development.

Need for Balanced Regional Development

1. **To Accelerate the Development of Economy :** Balanced regional development is required to ensure accelerated pace of development. It also facilitates the development of every region based on the availability of natural resources in that particular area. Maximum utilisation of manpower available in that area can also be ensured for the development.

2. **To Develop the Economy Smoothly :** It facilitates hasslefree development of the economy. If all areas are equally developed then there is possibility of

mutual cooperation in these areas. In case of regional imbalances, lower level of income of backward areas will succeed in diluting the growth achieved by the developed areas. It will affect the goods and service being produced in the developed areas. Secondly with the help of balanced regional development barriers affecting transport and supply of goods etc. can be also removed. It will also help in minimising the inflationary pressure on the economy.

3. To Develop and Conserve Resources : The major objective of regional development is to ensure maximum utilisation of available local resources. Process of regional development also put control on the destructive use of resources. Establishment of different industrial units makes possible for the better utilisation and conservation of natural and human resources available at local level.

4. To Promote Large Employment Opportunities : Availability of regional disparities in underdeveloped economy encourages income, employment and production at low level. Establishment of industries in different areas and development of infrastructure facilities in backward areas create more employment opportunities. It also improves per capital production and income.

5. To Maintain Political Stability : Balanced Regional Development is also required to maintain political stability. If regional disparities exist in some areas and increase in income in other areas then it may become a danger point for the nation as a whole. Backward areas demand separation from the main stream to fulfil their dream of development.

6. To Defend the Country: Regional development is quite important from the point to save the country from foreign aggression. If all areas are equally developed and industries are quite dispersed then air attack can be faced without any hurdles. If some regions have been developed and industries are concentrated in some areas the external aggression can put the economy in problem. Thus, balanced regional development is necessary from the view point of National Defence and its safety.

7. To Control Social Evils: With the help of balanced regional development, concentration of industries in big towns and cities can be easily controlled and it also helps in removing social evils in these areas. Industrial concentration encourages different types of pollution and thus, adversely affect the health and efficiency of people living in that particular area. Cost of living also increases which ultimately improves poverty and public unrest. Balanced regional development is necessary to control all these social evils.

Strategies for Balanced Regional Development

(i) The growth potential of each region should be fully developed, but in the precise manner in which this goal is achieved and the stages of growth will not be identical.

(ii) Some regional factors, such as those connected with physical features and geographical location, cannot be easily altered, but there are others which can be influenced by raising levels of education and skill, developing power and, generally, by applying science and technology on a larger scale.

(iii) Large scale industries, specially basic and heavy industries, frequently serve as a spearhead of intensive and broad-based development. However, not all regions can offer equally favourable conditions for the development of industry.

(iv) It is also possible to over-estimate the significance of the location of large industrial units in relation to the living standards of the bulk of the population.

(v) To initiate infrastructure development and diversified programmes, the basic and capital goods industries and other large industries.

(vi) Keeping in mind the availability of related raw materials, possibility to develop other industries need to be fully explored, such as labour intensive industries of the traditional type, small scale industries of the modern type, agricultural processing industries, forest industries, assembly operations and recreational industries.

(vii) Each region should endeavour to identify, plan for and promote industries which are specially suited to its conditions and for which it can provide relatively greater facilities.

Policies For Regional Development

(i) The priority was given to programmes related to agriculture, community development, irrigation, especially minor irrigation, local development works etc. which spread over the entire area within the shortest possible time;

(ii) Ensuring provision of facilities such as power, water supply, transport and communications, training institutions etc. in areas which were lagging behind industrially or where there was greater need for providing opportunities for employment;

(iii) Launching programmes for the expansion of village and small industries.

(iv) In the location of new enterprises, whether public or private, consideration is to be given to the need for developing a balanced economy in different parts of the country. In particular this aspect was to be kept in view, where the location of an industry was not determined almost entirely by the availability of raw materials or other natural resources.

(v) The regional aspects of development were dealt with in three different ways: (a), through the plans of states, emphasis was given to programmes which had a direct bearing on the welfare of the people in different parts of the country, (b) special programmes were undertaken in particular areas where development had either received a temporary setback, or was being held back by certain basic deficiencies; (c) steps were taken to secure more dispersed development of industry which, in turn, created conditions for development in several related fields.

(vi) Programmes of agriculture, community development, village and small industries, irrigation and power, communications and social services have the widest coverage, and aim at providing basic facilities and services to people in all regions.

(vii) Special schemes were formulated for particular areas which had difficult problems to face. The programme included medium as well as minor irrigation schemes, construction of embankments for flood protection and land reclamation and contour bunding schemes.

(viii) In the location of public sector projects, the claims of relatively backward areas have been kept in view wherever this could be done without giving up essential technical and economic criteria. The location of several important projects like the steel plants has been determined on the basis of expert study and on economic considerations.

(ix) While in the selection of sites for basic capital and producer goods, industries' proximity to raw materials and other economic considerations have naturally been important, it was felt that in a wide range of consumer goods and processing industries it was possible to foster regional patterns of development. These include cotton textiles, sugar, light engineering industries such as bicycles, sewing machines, electric motors, radio receivers, re- rolling of steel and non-ferrous metals.

(x) To some extent the development of new processes and new uses of raw materials has assisted in the spread of industry. Thus, a beginning was made with the use of bagasse as raw material for paper, and a number of paper factories based on the use of bagasse have been approved for being set up in sugarcane growing areas. In encouraging better use of local resources care had been taken to ensure that a balance is maintained between regional distribution and considerations of economy in production.

(xi) Village and small industries are spread all over the country and various forms of assistance provided by the Central and State Governments are made available in the areas according to the programmes which are undertaken. Industrial estates have been set up in all states, and increasingly they are to be located in the smaller towns and rural areas.

(xii) It provides extensive opportunity for the development of different parts of the country. In drawing up these plans, the broad objectives have been to enable each state to contribute its best towards increasing agricultural production, to secure the largest measure of increase in income and employment feasible, to develop social services, in particular, elementary education, water supply and sanitation and health services in the rural areas, and to raise the levels of living for the less developed areas.

(xiii) Efforts were made to enlarge the possibilities of development in areas which have, in the past, been relatively backward. Thus, for instance, the intensive development of agriculture, extension of irrigation, village and small industries, large-scale expansion of power, development of roads and road transport, provision for universal education for the age-group 6-11 years and larger opportunities for secondary, technical and vocational education, improvements in conditions of living and water supply, and programmes for the welfare of scheduled tribes and castes and other backward classes will go a long way to provide throughout the country the foundations for rapid economic development.

(xiv) Poverty and under-employment are specially acute in areas with heavy pressure of population and in those with scanty development of natural resources. The large programme of rural works will help expand opportunities for work in these as well as other areas. In some parts of the country there will be considerable development in plantation industries, specially tea, coffee and rubber. Large industrial projects, river valley projects and others described later will also serve as vital centres for future growth.

(xv) Location for basic industries has generally to be based on technical and economic considerations. Moreover, in the case of industries which may be able to export a significant proportion of their output, in the national interest the location of new or additional capacity has to be guided by the need to secure economies of scale and to enhance the ability to compete in foreign markets.

Problem of Regional Disparities

Even today India suffers from several problems like those of regional disparities and income inequalities. It is because, India presents a picture of extreme regional disparities in terms of such indicators of economic development/growth as per capita income, the proportion of population living below poverty line, working population in agriculture for living, the percentage of urban population of total population, percentage of workers in manufacturing industry and services sectors.

Indian economy is richly endowed with productive resources and potential of achieving a stage of self sustained growth. In India, inter-regional disparities are so wide and persisting that they cannot be ignored. Economic activities which spell prosperity are not evenly spread throughout the country. In some states industries, financial institutions are concentrated whereas in some states or regions even infrastructure like roads, banks, electricity and water are not available. In some regions infrastructure facilities are in huge quantities, but there is no proper use. Per capita State Domestic Products (SDP) are in variation. Some states such as Punjab, Haryana, Maharashtra are having higher per capita SDP whereas, M.P., Bihar, Jharkhand have less per capita SDP. Bihar, J&K, M.P. and Orissa recorded a lower growth rate and this contributed to the slow growth in their per capita income. An important reason contributing to widespread regional economic disparities in India is the effect of Green Revolution and uneven development of infrastructural facilities.

The Planning Commission has tried to overcome the problem of regional disparities in the following three ways:

(i) The recognition of backwardness factor to be taken into account in the transfer of financial resources from the centre to states;

(ii) Special area development programmes directed at development of backward areas;

(iii) Measures to promote private investment.

Income Inequalities in India is another important problem. This problem arises because of two things:

(a) In a market economy such inequalities lead to inequalities of economic opportunity.

(b) Distribution of income and wealth is closely linked to distributive justice.

In India, incidence of inequality and poverty go hand in hand. Both are widespread and feed each other. The major trends in this regard are given below:

(a) The number of poor below poverty line has increased in absolute terms,

(b) The structure of economic system generates inequalities.

(c) Trends of public budgets and evasion of taxes strengthen inequalities in India.

Role of Government in Infrastructure Development

Infrastructure (also termed as social overheads) has always been recognised as one of the crucial determinants of developmental level of an economy. It comprises those facilities for conducting various productive economic activities, which are not industry-specific. That is to say, these facilities are not designed to serve individual industries. They are there to aid and promote all kinds of economic activities. By their very nature, they tend to be commercially non-viable, but the economy cannot progress and sustain its developmental level without them.

Infrastructure is commercially non-viable because of –

(i) long gestation period; (ii) high capital investment;
(iii) low rate of profitability; (iv) pilferage of facilities.

The very nature of "socialist-democratic welfare state' enshrined in the Constitution of India implies that Government has a spectacular role to play in developing the infrastructure for laying the foundation for economic and industrial development. Facilities like transportation, communication, information technology, roads, education, supply of power, fuel, water etc., as well as development of human resources, facilities for education, training and development and overall socio-economic development of the people are the responsibility of Government. Even since the independence, Government of India has made substantial investment on all these aspects; particularly plan outlay was very significant in these areas. An all-round progress in different segments of infrastructure has been recorded. This is true both of physical and social infrastructure. Expansion of different modes of transportation and communication has been phenomenal. The generation of electricity has multiplied by number of time. Increased in irrigation facilities has been very large. Banking facilities has also been increased substantially. Rapid spread of education, health and other services again bear the testimony to this.

But state has its own limitations. The supply of infrastructure has fallen short of requirements due to lack of financial resources. The available infrastructure suffers from low productivity, underutilisation or misutilisation of available infrastructure.

In view of the above limitations of the public infrastructure the Government took initiative to change the policy in the year 1991. In the post-reform period beginning with 1991 there has been a paradigm shift in the government's attitude *vis-a-vis* infrastructure. The Government of India has opened infrastructure sector particularly banking, power, communication, insurance etc. for private sector participation. In post reform era, in addition to taking steps to improve the performance of infrastructure provision under their direct control, government is responsible for creating policy and regulatory framework that safeguards the interests of the poor, improves environmental conditions and coordinates cross-sectoral interactions, whether services are produced by public or private providers. Government is responsible for developing legal and regulatory framework to support private involvement in the provision of infrastructure services.

Problem of Income Inequalities in India

The income inequalities and poverty are the important problems before the policy makers in under developed and developing economies like India. This problem of income inequalities in India arises because of two things:

(i) In a market economy such inequalities lead to inequalities of economic opportunity.

(ii) Distribution of income (and wealth) is closely linked to distributive justice.

In India, incidence of inequality and poverty go hand in hand. Both are widespread and feed each other. The major trends, in this regard, are given below:

(a) The number of poor below poverty line has increased in absolute terms.

(b) The structure of economic system generates inequalities.

(c) Trends of public budgets and evasion of taxes strengthen inequalities in India.

Post Reform Period Effects: The major factors which attribute to income inequalities are as under:

(a) shift in earnings from labour to capital income;

(b) rapid growth of service sector particularly banking, financial institutions, insurance and real estate with a consequent explosion in demand for skilled workers; and

(c) a drop in the rate of labour absorption during the reform period associated with an increase in regional inequality, especially in the incidence of rural poverty.

Thus, the government is making all efforts through their poverty eradication programmes and others measures under plans to reduce the income inequalities.

Entrepreneurship is the active process of recognising an economic demand in an economy and supplying the factors of production (land, labour and capital) to satisfy that demand. The goal of the entrepreneurship is to generate profit. Entrepreneur has a role to play in insuring an equality in property in the society by introducing small scale enterprises in the undeveloped or rural area. He introduces new ideas and creates new market by utilising the local resources and generating employment for the local people. Large scale industries lead to disparities between rural and urban areas, so as far as social stability and balanced regional development are concerned. Small scale enterprise is the ultimate option which can only be done by an entrepreneur.

There is a wide range of significant contributions that entrepreneurs can make to the development process. Entrepreneurship raises productivity through technical and other forms of innovation. It is a powerful tool of job creation. Entrepreneurs play a strategic role in commercialising new inventions and products.

Entrepreneurs play a critical role in the restructuring and transformation of economy in rural area. They also help in reducing the ossification of established social institutions and the concentration of economic power. They make markets more competitive and thereby reduce both static and dynamic market inefficiency. Entrepreneurs stimulate a redistribution of wealth, income and political power within societies in ways that are economically positive without being politically disruptive. Entrepreneurs improve the social welfare of a country by harnessing dormant, previously overlooked talent. The unique feature of entrepreneurship is that it is a low cost strategy of economic development, job creation and technical innovations. Other agents of change may accomplish the same ends, but not as cost effective as entrepreneurs. This can be accomplished by setting up enterprises, initially as a small scale. Entrepreneurship can bring a great change in socio-economic condition of undeveloped areas and thereby accelerate the growth and development of a nation in a sustainable way.

Role of Entrepreneurs in Balanced Regional Development of Industries

1. Knowledge of Market Conditions : Market conditions motivate the entrepreneurs to think in terms of establishing industrial units. An entrepreneur has full knowledge of the markets. He seeks answers for different questions *viz.*, where is the good market for a particular product? Where particular product and service are to be produced? What will be the cost of production of a product at that place? To what extent the labour and capital will be available in the area? What is the prospective demand for the commodity? what should be the price of the commodity, extent and type of competition and the measures to face the competition etc. Entrepreneurs establish industries in those areas, where most of the factors are favourable to him.

2. Government Support System : Entrepreneurial behaviour is quite sensitive. It needs effective government support system for ensuring balance regional development. Governments are required to provide various types of facilities—allotment of land at concessional rates, provision of basic infrastructure facilities at the allotted place, easy availability of various resources, finance facilities at reasonable rates of interest, exemptions from taxes, supply of modern techniques and machineries on easy instalments, good facilities for marketing, etc. The entrepreneurs may come forward to avail these facilities for establishment of new industrial units and expansion of the existing units.

3. Optimum Use of Resources : The nature is kind enough to all countries and areas with one or the other resources, free of cost, of course, in varying degrees. These resources include natural and human resources etc. The entrepreneurs use various resources in production of various commodities and services, as they possess entrepreneurial qualities.

4. Reformative Social Structure : Basic theme of the entrepreneurship is the continuous innovation. Entrepreneurs are required to bring necessary changes in the social structure. They bring modernity to traditionalism in Indian society. They also ensure changes in the life style of the society by giving opportunity to earn their income through gainful employment. The society has become industry oriented, misbeliefs have reduced, several obsolete traditions have come to an end. With the result, the entrepreneurs do not hesitate to bear risks and establishing industries in far flung areas.

5. Improvement In Productivity : Innovations lead to improvement in productivity of man, machines and materials. The efforts of the entrepreneurs lead to improvement in productivity. They provide opportunities to people for leading active life, so that they can gainfully utilise these resources.

6. Multi Dimentional Development : Nature has several diversities, having certain uniformity also. The entrepreneurs are required to assess these diversities and use them for prosperity of human beings. The entrepreneurs are expected to have various capabilities, like—intelligence, sharp memory, far-sightedness, dedication, courage, knowledge of various new techniques, awareness towards the opportunities, knowledge of market conditions etc.

7. Self-Sufficient Society : The entrepreneurs have important role in establishment of self-sufficient society, by producing goods and services as per their requirement. They also produce products as per demand in foreign market.

8. Removal of Regional Disparities : In a developing economy like India, central government as well as state governments both are trying to involve entrepreneurs for the development of different regions. Entrepreneur gets various facilities to establish industries in such areas like—zero industry districts and backward areas district. For this purpose, government provides land and capital at concessional rates. Exemption in taxes and various types of subsidies are also provided for the establishment of industries in the backward areas.

Globalisation and Regional Imbalances

In the present era of economic development, no economy can stand alone and immune from the developments in the foreign countries. Each and every country is, therefore, legitimately affected by what happens in the rest of the world. The international transmission effect is more speedy, more substantial and more sustained than ever before. Now each country especially developing economy like India is trying to survive in the context of global scenario. Globalisation has given a new orientation to the world economies. Globalisation deals with opening up of the economy for world market by attaining international competitiveness. It simply indicates interaction of the country relating to production, trading and financial transactions with the developed industrialised countries of the world. It offers both challenges and opportunities to the developing countries. To maintain their economic and political identity, developing countries are trying to reorganise their economic, legal, social and political structure for facing the challenges of international competitiveness. India is also reorienting itself to globalise its systems for improving its international competitive strength.

Indian economy had experienced major policy changes in early 1990s. The new economic reform, popularly known as, *Liberalisation, Privatisation and Globalisation* (LPG model) aimed at making the Indian economy the fastest growing economy and globally competitive. The series of reforms undertaken with respect to industrial sector, trade as well as financial sector aimed at making the economy more efficient. With the onset of reforms to liberalise the Indian economy in July of 1991, a new chapter has dawned for India and her billion plus population. This period of economic transition has had a tremendous impact on the overall economic development of almost all major sectors of the economy, and its effects over the last decade can hardly be overlooked. Besides, it also marks the advent of the real integration of the Indian economy into the global economy.

All the countries of the world developed equally. Some countries are highly developed economically and some other countries are still developing and some more are under developed. Several factors are responsible for such variations among the nations besides political factors as mentioned below:

(i) The availability of sufficient natural resources,

(ii) The quality of human resources and also its quantity,

(iii) Abundance of financial resources, and

(iv) Technological skills, efficient management skills among the people.

Regional imbalances are the by-products of the above factors. The problem of regional imbalances is highly critical for almost all the countries of the world. There have always existed a variety of inter-regional and inter-state variations in terms of all macro indices linked with economic and social issues. There is what is known as 'declining areas' or 'special areas' within the frontiers of each country. These typical areas qualify for special government assistance to uplift them from a state of stagnation or near stagnation, resulting from local unemployment, industrial imbalance, declining industries, over-population, and a variety of other economic and social 'pulling' factors. The problem is highly alarming in developing countries most of which suffer from acute and lasting differences in prosperity between geographical regions. This phenomenon of regional income differentials is termed as 'regional dualism'. India is no exception to this.

In India, regional imbalance has been one of the major concerns before policy makers and planners. There had been a huge gap between active and vibrant regions and hinterlands during pre-independence period in terms of availability of facilities and this has resulted in the form of unequal levels of development both in terms of economic and human. The foremost problems of regional development are concerned with (a) classifying regions, (b) measuring the inter-regional differences in prosperity/poverty, and (c) pulling through economic and other measures, the declining areas so that they are bestowed with equitable and balanced distribution of national prosperity and well being.

One of the main consequences of regional imbalances is the migration of people to the developed areas. For instance many skilled people from India migrated to the developed nations. Similarly within India, people from rural areas or under developed regions have been migrating to highly developed cities or regions. Hence, Mumbai city has been facing the menace of population pressure on its resources. Violence, law and order problems are the other consequences of such migrations to the developed regions from under developed or developing regions. Almost all the major cities in India do face very high intensity of population. Some of such cities are New Delhi, Kolkata, Chennai, Mumbai, Bangaluru, Hyderabad, Pune, Ahmedabad etc.

Demand for Separate State

There have been demands for separate states in India since independence. In the recent past, a separate Telangana State was created from Andhra Prasesh, a separate Chhattisgarh state was created from Madhya Pradesh, Jharkhand from Bihar and Uttaranchal from Uttar Pradesh. These demands for separate states are mainly due to lack of economic development in such regions. The economic development of a particular region is measured based on per capita income, gross state domestic product, poverty, unemployment etc. In India, Bihar, Orissa, Rajasthan, Madhya Pradesh, Uttar Pradesh and North-eastern states are comparatively economically backward when compared to the remaining states. Maharashtra, Gujarat, Tamilnadu, and Punjab like which are comparatively highly developed. In Andhra Pradesh state, there are three regions namely the coastal region, the Rayalaseema region and the Telengana region. Among these three regions, the Telangana was the most backward due to lack of resources, negligence by successive governments, poor quality of infrastructural facilities etc.

Need for Restructuring of Economy

This era of reforms has also ushered in a remarkable change in the Indian mindset, as it deviates from the traditional values held since Independence in 1947, such as self-reliance and socialistic policies of economic development, which mainly due to the inward looking restrictive form of governance, resulted in the isolation, overall backwardness and inefficiency of the economy, amongst a host of other problems. This is despite the fact that India has always had the potential to be on the fast track to prosperity. Now that India is in the process of restructuring her economy, with aspirations of elevating herself from her present desolate position in the world, the need to speed up her economic development is even more imperative. And having witnessed the positive role that Foreign Direct Investment (FDI) has played in the rapid economic growth of most of the Southeast Asian countries and most notably China, India has embarked on an ambitious plan to emulate the successes of her neighbours to the east and is trying to sail herself as a safe and profitable destination for FDI. The process of globalisation not only includes opening up of world trade, development of advanced means of communication, internationalisation of financial markets, growing importance of MNCs, population migrations and more generally increased mobility of persons, goods, capital, data and ideas but also infections, diseases and pollution. It is the integration of economies of the world through uninhibited trade and financial flows, as also through mutual exchange of technology and knowledge. Ideally, it also contains free inter-country movement of labour. In context to India, this implies opening up the economy to foreign direct investment by providing facilities to foreign companies to invest in different fields of economic activity in India, removing constraints and obstacles to the entry of MNCs in India, allowing Indian companies to enter into foreign collaborations and also encouraging them to set up joint ventures abroad; carrying out massive import liberalisation programmes by switching over from quantitative restrictions to tariffs and import duties.

Suggestions for Removing Regional Disparities

1. **Review of the Problem :** Neutral evaluation is necessary for the problem of regional disparities. The central government or the state government both are required to use any equal measurement to identify the level of regional disparities.

2. **Arrangement of Adequate Capital :** The central government should sanction adequate fund to the state government for the development of backward areas. The central government should take its own initiative for the development of big projects in the identified area. However, funding and other facilities are to be supplemented by the central government to the state government. Moreover state government should be made accountable for the development of backward areas.

3. **Special Development Programme :** Separate development programmes for each area should be prepared on the basis of Techno economic survey of the area. These development programmes should integrate the projects like use of technology in agriculture, water conservation, food control, transport and telecommunication etc. Social and institution reforms should also be included in these programmes.

4. **Establishment of Industrial Estates :** Industrial estates should be developed to remove regional disparities. New industrial infrastructure policy should be formulated to enable the small towns to have big industrial estates. It will facilitate the removal of regional disparities. At the initial stage, government should provide all support for the development of industrial estates.

5. **Arrangement of Integrated Programme :** Integrated development programme should be prepared for the development of village and small industries in backward areas. All infrastructural facilities like power, water supply, transport, communication, training institutions and finance etc. are to be arranged by the state government.

6. **Development of Growing Point :** Establishment of growing points is the best incentive for industrial development in backward areas. This type of policy assuring the establishment of urban dwellings will encourage migration of labour from neighbouring villages to the cities for livelihood. It will reduce manufacturing or construction costs and increase the inflow of income earned from cities for the funding of rural development. It will also ensure new thoughts and new product techniques for the development of rural areas.

EXAMINATION QUESTIONS

Long Answer Questions

1. Discuss the nature of balanced regional development? Discuss its rationale.
2. Critically examine the various strategies for regional development.
3. Discuss the government policy for regional development.
4. Discuss the problem of regional disparities. Also examine the role of entrepreneurs in removing regional disparities.

5. Discuss the different issues involved in regional development. Evaluate the role assigned to entrepreneurs to solve these issues.

Short Answer Questions

1. What do you mean by balanced regional development?
2. What are the objectives of balanced regional development?
3. What are the factors responsible for regional disparities?
4. How does infrastructural facilities help in regional development?
5. How does entrepreneurs are motivated for balanced regional development?

Objective Type Questions:

1. Regional imbalances are the byproduct of the following except
   (a) Insufficient Population
   (b) Insufficient Resources
   (c) Lack of financial resources
   (d) Lack of Higher education
2. Parameters for regional disparities do not include the following:
   (a) Per capita income
   (b) Proportion of Population living below Poverty line
   (c) Gross capital formation
   (d) Percentage of working population in agriculture
3. Per capita State Domestic Product is the highest in the following state.
   (a) Haryana
   (b) Bihar
   (c) U.P.
   (d) M.P.

Answers

1-(d) 2-(c) 3-(a)

11

ENTREPRENEURSHIP AND FOREIGN TRADE

Each and every country has its own strengths and limitations with regard to supply of goods and services. Export and import of goods and services in a country is largely governed by the supply of these goods and services and government policy for the purpose. However, in the era of globalisation whole world is a global village. There is increasing space for global linkages with different economies. Level of foreign trade also affects the level of balance of payments. Stability of currency also depends upon the position of balance of payment to a large extent. Every country is interested to improve its export performance and try to maintain a favourable foreign trade. Now in current scenario, more and more parts of the domestic economy are exposed to international markets. It is but natural that developing economy like India should expand the base of its foreign trade. Level of mutual dependency among the various countries is improving and it has made more and more countries vulnerable to changing scenario of international markets.

Entrepreneurship and Foreign Trade

Each and every country has its own strengths and limitations with regard to supply of goods and services. Export and import of goods and services in a country is largely governed by the supply of these goods and services and government policy for the purpose. However, in the era of globalisation whole world is a global village. There is increasing space for global linkages with different economies. Level of foreign trade also affects the level of balance of payments. Stability of currency also depends upon the position of balance of payment to a large extent. Every country is interested to improve its export performance and try to maintain a favourable foreign trade. Now in current scenario, more and more parts of the domestic economy are exposed to international markets. It is but natural that developing economy like India should expand the base of its foreign trade. Level of mutual dependency among the various countries is improving and it has made the more and more countries vulnerable to changing scenario of international markets.

Emerging Dimensions of India's Foreign Trade

A. Merchandise Trade — Salient features of India's merchandise trade are as follows:

(i) Over the last ten years, India's merchandise trade (on customs basis) increased manifold from US$ 195.1 billion in 2004-05 to US$ 764.6 billion in 2013-14. As per the World Trade Organization (WTO), India's share in global exports and imports increased from 0.8 per cent and 1.0 per cent respectively in 2004 to 1.7 per cent and 2.5 per cent in 2013. Its ranking in terms of leading exporters and importers improved from 30 and 23 in 2004. to 19 and 12 respectively in 2013. While India's total merchandise trade as a proportion of gross domestic product (GDP) increased from 29.0 per cent in 2004-05 to 41.8 per cent in 2013-14. India's merchandise exports as a proportion of GDP increased from 12.1 per cent to 17.0 per cent during the same two time periods. There were considerable differences in the growth rates within the two time periods which owed largely to the global uncertainty, prolonged weakness in some areas and volatility in global commodity prices since 2008. In particular, global crude oil prices were a major factor in the process of elevated levels of merchandise trade deficit.

(ii) There was a very high growth of 40.5 per cent in 2010-11 and growth of merchandise exports moderated to 21.8 per cent in 2011-12. The high growth in two years led to overall exports crossing the US$ 300 billion mark. In 2012-13, though exports were still above the US$ 300 billion mark, growth in exports could not be sustained and marginally declined by 1.8 per cent. During 2013-14, however, exports recovered to post a growth of 4.7 per cent (US$ 314.4 billion). In 2014-15 (April-January), growth of exports moderated to 2.4 per cent (US$ 265.0 billion *vis-a-vis* US$ 258.7 billion in the corresponding period of the 2013-14).

(iii) India's merchandise imports grew by 28.2 per cent in 2010-11 and the high growth continued through 2011-12 driven by broad-based expansion in imports of gold and silver, POL group and non-POL, and non-gold and silver group. In 2012-13, there was only modest decline in the growth rates of gold and silver as well as non-POL imports, leading to continuance of elevated level of total imports of around US$ 490 billion. In 2013-14, in view of the sharp depreciation of the rupee owing to domestic and external factors, the government placed restrictions on gold imports which led to a sharp decline therein of 46.4 per cent. With domestic activity remaining weak, non-POL and non-gold and silver imports also declined by around 7 per cent, which along with the fall in gold imports led to overall decline in imports lo US$ 450 billion. In 2014-15 (April-January), imports grew by 2.2 per cent to US$ 383.4 billion as compared to US$ 375.3 billion in 2013-14 (April-January). While the value of POL imports declined by 7.9 per cent in 2014-15 (April-January), gold and silver imports grew by 8.0 per cent in 2014-15 (April-January). Non-POL and non-gold and silver imports which largely reflect the imports needed for industrial activity grew by 7.8 per cent in 2014, 15 (April-January), after registering a decline of 0.7 per cent and 6.9 per cent respectively in 2012-13 and 2013-14.

(iv) These developments in nominal terms broadly reflect the trends. It is useful to decompose the growth rates in terms of changes in quantity and price, which are best indicated by the quantum and unit value indices that reflect terms of trade. The change in quantum index for exports broadly corresponds directionaly with nominal growth in US dollar and rupee terms, albeit at much lower rates. 2012-13 being an exception when in US dollar terms there was negative growth as against a high positive growth rate in the quantum index. In the case of the quantum index of imports, there was greater directional divergence with the nominal growth rates expressed in US dollar and rupee terms. The changes in unit value indices of exports and imports were broadly in positive territory with the exception of 2009-10. The outcome in terms of trade was reflected in the deterioration evidenced in 2011-12. This deterioration owes to the oil price shock which could be reversing in the second half of 2014-15.

(v) The oil price shock was amplified given the large import dependence that had kept imports at elevated levels since 2011-12 and the relative sluggish global demand constraining overall export growth. India's subsequent resilience owed to the diversification processes that encompass both commodity composition and direction of trade.

B. Composition of Trade - Main constituents of foreign trade are as follows :

(i) The commodity composition of India's trade has undergone many changes since liberalization and has been driven by trade policy, movements in international prices, and the changing pattern of domestic demand. Manufactured goods constitute the bulk of exports — over 63 per cent in recent years, followed by crude and petroleum products (including coal) with a 20 per cent share, and agriculture and allied products with a share of 13.7 per cent share. The top seven product groups accounting for nearly 80.9 per cent of India's total exports in 2014-15 (April-December) were: petroleum products (19.4 per cent share): gems and jewellery (13.0 per cent share): agriculture and allied products (12.0 per cent share): textiles and allied products (11.6 per cent share): chemicals and related products (10.1 per cent share): transport equipment (8.5 per cent share) and machinery (6.3 per cent share).

(ii) Growth in exports of petroleum and agriculture and allied products which had been in positive territory for the last four years, turned negative in 2014-15 (April-January). Gems and jewellery exports which exhibited a declining trend in 2012-13 and 2013-14 continued to register a declining trend in 2014-15 (April- January). In the case of electronic goods, there has been continuous decline in exports since 2012-13. During 2014-15 (April-January). some sectors like transport equipment; machinery, chemicals and related products, textile and allied products and base metals registered positive growth in exports.

(iii) Marine products and leather and leather manufactures recorded relatively high growth in 2012-13. 2013-14, and 2014-15 (April-January). While the shares in terms of nominal value of exports (conversely imports) may be high in some sectors, the import (export) component may also be high and therefore it would be instructive to look at value added.

(iv) One of the major items in India's import basket is the POL group, which accounted for 36.6 per cent of India's total imports in 2013-14. POL imports surged with a growth of 46.2 per cent in 2011-12, mainly on account of significant increase in global crude oil prices *vis-a-vis* 2010-11. The growth in imports of POL, moderated to 5.9 per cent and 0.4 per cent respectively in 2012-13 and 2013-14.

(v) Capital goods imports are another major group which declined continuously from 2011-12 onwards. Within capital goods, imports of machinery registered positive growth in 2014-15 (April-January). Gold and silver imports accounted for I 1.4 per cent of India's total imports in 2012-13 and 7.4 per cent in 2013-14. These imports declined by 9.0 per cent and 40.4 per cent respectively in 2012-13 and 2013-14 but registered a positive growth of 8.0 per cent in 2014-15 (April-January). Imports of pearls and precious and semi-precious stones grew bv 5.4 per cent in 2013-14 and declined by 3.9 per cent in 2014-15 (April-January).

C. **Direction of Trade:** Major directions of foreign trade are as follows :

(i) There has been significant market diversification in India's trade in recent years—a process that has helped in coping with the sluggish global demand, which owes to a great extent to the weakness in the euro zone. Region-wise India's export shares to Europe and America have declined over the years—from 23.6 per cent and 20.1 per cent respectively in 2004-05 to 18.6 per cent and 17.2 per cent respectively in 2013-14. Conversely, the shares of India's exports to Asia and Africa have increased from 47.9 per cent and 6.7 per cent respectively in 2004-05 to 49.4 per cent and 9.9 per cent respectively in 2013-14. The change in direction immediately prior to the global financial crisis and since 2010-11 indicates the process of diversification underway.

A comparison of India's trade in the pre-crisis (2004-05 to 2007-08) and post-crisis period (2010-11 to 2013-14) shows that India's exports and imports from Europe, the USA and Singapore have declined, while its trade with Asia and Africa has increased.

(ii) In 2014-15 (April-December), India's exports to the European region grew by only 0.2 per cent. India's exports to Africa and America grew by 12.9 and 14.5 per cent respectively and to Asia, a major destination accounting for nearly 50 per cent of India's exports, by 2.2 per cent in 2014-15 (April-December). Within Asia. India's exports to South Asia grew by 23.8 per cent (mainly due to high export growth to Sri Lanka, Nepal, and Bangladesh) and 8.8 per cent in the case of West Asia-Gulf Cooperation Council (GCC) (UAE, Saudi Arabia and others). India's exports to other regions of Asia witnessed a contraction—declining by 4.4 per cent to North East Asia (consisting of China, Hong Kong, Japan). 7.2 per cent to the Association of South East Asian Nations (ASEAN), (consisting of Singapore, Indonesia, Thailand, Malaysia) and 8.5 per cent to Other West Asia (Iran, Israel and others)—in 2014-15 (April-December). Countrywise India's exports to the USA and UAE— major destinations with a share in India's total exports of 12.5 per cent and 9.7 per cent respectively in 2013-14—grew by 11.2 per cent and 11.9 per cent in 2014-15 (April-December). However, India's exports to China (4.7 per cent share) and Belgium (2.0 per cent share) declined by 14.7 per cent and 10.7 per cent during the same period. Since 2012-13, there has been a contraction in India's exports to Singapore and Indonesia.

(iii) The share of Europe in India's imports also declined from 23.0 per cent in 2004-05 to 15.8 per cent in 2013-14, while the shares of Asia and Africa increased substantially from 35.6 per cent and 3.6 per cent in 2004-05 to 60.7 per cent and 8.1 per cent respectively in 2013-14. The share of America in India's imports has also increased from 8.8 per cent to 12.8 per cent during the same period. China is the major source of India's imports, accounting for 11.3 per cent of India's total imports, followed by Saudi Arabia (8.1 per cent share), the UAE (6.5 per cent share) and the USA (5.0 percent share) in 2013-14. In 2014-15 (April December). India's imports from China grew by 18.7 per cent. However, there was contraction in India's imports from Saudi Arabia, the UAE, and USA by 14.2 per cent, 7.9 per cent and 7.9 per cent, respectively during the same period. Imports from Switzerland and Singapore also declined in 2012-13 and 2013-14 but picked up with a positive growth in 2014-15 (April-December).

D. Trade Deficit : Major trends of trade deficit are as follows :

(i) In 2013-14, India's trade deficit (on customs basis) declined to US$ 135.8 billion from a high level of US$ 190.3 billion in 2012-13, mainly on account of a decline in the growth of imports (8.3 per cent), even though growth in exports was sluggish at 4.7 per cent. The decline in imports owed to lower growth in oil imports (0.4 per cent) and negative growth in gold and silver imports.

(ii) However, in 2014-15 (April-January) trade deficit increased marginally by 1.6 per cent to US$ 118.4 billion as against US$ 116.5 billion in 2013-14 (April-January). Low export growth (2.4 per cent) and import growth (2.2 per cent), resulted in a modest increase in trade deficit by US$ 1.8 billion. Nevertheless in terms of levels, trade deficit being close to last year reflects on external-sector polices including trade policies.

Internal Trade and Inter-Regional Trade

Internal trade is one where goods and services are transacted or exchanged between two individuals or firms or institutions with in the country. This is also known as domestic trade. Whereas inter-regional trade or international trade is trade where goods and services are exchanged among different countries or regions across political frontiers. It is also known as foreign trade, overseas trade or external trade. Main distinction between the two include the following:

(i) Internal trade takes place within political boundaries of a country whereas inter-regional or international trade is the trade between two or more regions or nations with different political boundaries.

(ii) The principal difference between internal and inter-regional or international trade is that the latter involves the use of different type of currencies and each region (country) follows different foreign exchange policies, trade policies etc.

Balance of Payments

Balance of payments of a country is a "systematic record of all economic and commercial transactions between the residents of the reporting country and residents of foreign countries." This account is for a period of time, normally one year. These transactions are as between residents of one country with those of other countries.

Mechanisms of Balance of Payments

Balance of payments is maintained on a double entry system with credits and debits of equal size. For every transaction, there is corresponding entry on both the credit and debit sides. If exports are indicated as a credit for outflow of goods on current account, a corresponding entry of debit is shown for claim on a foreign company or country or increase in foreign assets or claims on foreigners. Imports are indicated debit item for the inflow of goods and the credit item for being paid out is shown by increase in foreign liabilities, reduction of foreign assets or outflow of funds or claims on us. In this way, for every credit/debit entry on current account, there is a corresponding entry on capital account to match the former. Unilateral transfers include gifts, donations etc., There is no corresponding payment or change in assets or liabilities due to unilateral transfers. The contra entry is donations or gifts on the debit side and for the credit; it is the flow of goods from out of the country. Generally all debits are not matched with credits due to differences in sources and timing of events. If there is discrepancy then a balancing entry is made as errors and omissions.

Components of Balance of Payments

A- Current Account

Current account, deals with only those transactions of current nature which are resulting in incomes or expenditure and not leading to asset formation are recorded. Current account includes the following sub-heads (a) Transactions of merchandise of visible items of goods, namely, exports including re-exports and imports, (b) Transaction on invisible account, namely, foreign travel, transportation, banking, insurance and other services, interest, dividends, royalties, Government embassy expenditures etc., (c) Unilateral transfers like gifts, donations, charities etc., (d) Non-monetary gold movements. All the above items can take place on private account or government account and may be subject to government restrictions or controls, if any.

B. Capital Account

Capital account deals with those transactions which are short-term capital inflows and outflows for private purposes, official purposes or banking purposes. Private flows of capital include private company remittances for working capital purposes to subsidiaries or branches of foreign companies or short-term loans, grants etc., from foreign banks, international financial institutions, foreign government etc. These short-term flows may be for investment purposes or speculation on private account or for compensatory purposes on government account. These can also be banking funds are also included for short-term purposes.

Long-term capital movements also include private or governmental transactions. The private flows include loans and advances granted to private parties (buyers' credit), investment in shares, bonds, debentures etc., by Indians abroad or by foreigners in India, investment in joint ventures, consultancy, turn-key projects, deferred payment credits etc. Such flows on official account also take place through governments or governmental agencies or financial institutions in India are also involved in these flows on official account These flows or transactions include lines of credit, foreign government loans, credits, grants etc., for private long-term purposes.

The capital account provides a framework of changes in foreign assets and liabilities of the country. It also affects its creditor/debtor position. An excess of foreign assets over foreign liabilities shows a net creditor position and *vice versa*. Net changes in current account are reflected by a corresponding and opposite change in the capital account, changing the foreign assets and liabilities position of the country. Current account is like an income and expenditure statement with surplus of deficit in it transferred to capital account which is like a balance sheet. If all these accounts do not tally, errors and omissions are added to balance the corresponding column of balance of payments. In an economic sense, a country has a surplus or deficit in its balance of payment, when its transactions other than those merely financing the real transactions are not in balance.

Balance of Trade and Balance of Payments

Balance of trade is the difference of payments made for import of goods and those received for exports of goods i.e. it includes only visible imports and exports. If receipts are more than the payments, then it is said to be favourable. If payments made for imports exceed export earnings, then it is said to be unfavourable.

Balance of payment, on the other hand, shows payments and receipts on account of all external transactions of a country *vis-a-vis* other countries. This includes mercantile export and imports of visible and invisibles as well as the capital transactions. In other words, balance of payments is systematic record of all economic transactions during the period, generally a year, between the reporting country and the rest of the world. It is a summary of transactions made in foreign exchange and transfer of goods and evidence of debts and ownership suitably classified and segregated between the business and government and other institutions of one country and rest of the world for a period of time, generally a year.

Balance of trade, thus, is only a part of balance of payments. The most important difference between the two is that whereas there may be a surplus of deficit in balance of trade during a period, the balance of payment will always be in balance in the accounting sense.

Disequilibrium in balance of payments means long period deficits or surplus in the current account of balance of payments of a country.

Disequilibrium in Balance of Payments

Balance of payments is a statistical record of all economic transactions visible and invisible between the residents of the economy and rest of the world during a specific period of time usually one year.

Disequilibrium in balance of payments refers to the difference between receipts and payments as revealed by sectional accounts of varieties of items in various groups and not in total debits and credits in the balance of payments as a whole, because it will always be in balance as per the rule of double entry system of book keeping. Disequilibrium in balance of payments may be in the form of surplus or deficit. It is surplus in balance of payments when total receipts from the rest of the world exceeds the total payments and in deficit if a country's receipts from foreigners fall short of payments to foreigners.

Any disequilibrium (a deficit or a surplus) in the balance of payments when it persists continuously is certainly undesirable because of its disastrous effects on the country's economy and orderly world trade. Some of the important measures to correct surplus in balance of payments include revaluation, exchange, appreciation, boosting imports by reducing import controls. However, disequilibrium in the form of deficit in balance of payments is more harmful to a country's economic growth and is, therefore, to be corrected sooner than later.

Balance of Payments Developments

Salient features of development in India's Balance of Payments are as follows:

(i) Post the 2008 global financial crisis. Emerging Market Developing Economies (EMDEs) had to face periodic shocks or stresses emanating from policies in advanced economies as well as through financial channels notwithstanding the efforts of the G-20 at coordination of policy responses to the crisis. The Indian economy had to weather the shocks which got amplified on account of confluence of weak external demand and relatively strong domestic demand with large dependence on crude oil imports whose price levels remained elevated until the second half of the current fiscal. These shocks led to widening of the CAD in 2011-12 which continued through the first quarter of 2013-14. With external financing sources remaining volatile, the less than adequate quantity and deteriorating quality of financing resulted in a sharp depreciation of the rupee. The policy responses that were put in place in 2013-14 helped overcome the stress through reduction in the levels of CAD and this, along with ample financing, led to reserve accretion that helped build resilience—a process that continues through the current fiscal.

(ii) In the first half of 2014-15. India's external-sector position was benign and comfortable. Two important developments were that: (a) lower trade deficit along with moderate growth in invisibles resulted in lower CAD and (b) there was a surge in capital inflows, enabled by higher portfolio investment, foreign direct investment (FDI) and external commercial borrowings (ECB). Higher capital inflows were in excess of the financing requirement or CAD and resulted in accretion in foreign exchange reserves.

(iii) Data on merchandise trade available beyond the first half discussed in an earlier section indicates that trade deficit continues to remain broadly at comparably moderate levels and the monthly data on financial inflows and foreign exchange reserves available unmistakably points to reserve accretion and the copious nature of external financing.

(iv) A part of the moderate trade outcome owe to the recent fall in international prices of crude petroleum. Given the above developments and considering the current conjuncture opportune, the Government decontrolled the prices of high speed diesel on 19th October 2014 and lifted the restrictions placed on gold imports on 29th November 2014.

Balance of Payments: Overall position of Balance of Payments in summary form is given in Table 11.1.

Table 11.1 : Balance of Payments : Summary (US$ million)

	2009-10	2010-11	2011-12	2012-13 (PR)	2013-14 (P)	2013-14 H1 (Apr.-Sept. 2013)	2014-15 H1 (Apr.-Sept. 2014)
1. Current Account							
i. Exports	182442	256159	309774	306581	318607	155152	166974
ii. Imports	300644	383481	499533	502237	466216	238941	240188
iii. Trade balance	–118202	–127322	–189759	–195656	–147609	–83789	–73214
iv. Invisibles (Net)	80022	79269	111604	107493	115212	56830	55272
A. Services	36016	44081	64098	64915	72965	35239	36069
B. Transfer	52045	53140	63494	64034	65276	32744	32757
C. Income	–8038	–17952	–15988	–21455	–23028	–11153	–13554
Current account balance	–38181	–48053	–78155	–88163	–32397	–26959	–17942
2. Capital Account							
i. External assistance	2890	4941	2296	982	1032	130	606
ii. ECBs	2000	12160	10344	8485	1 1777	2455	3429
iii. Short-term debt	7558	12034	6668	21657	–5044	589	69
iv. Banking capital	2083	4962	16226	16570	25449	11487	–542
of which Non-resident deposits	2922	3238	11918	14842	38892	13700	6473
v. Foreign investment	50362	42127	39231	46710	26386	7762	38385
A. FDI	17966	11834	22061	19819	21564	14589	16183
B. Portfolio investment	32396	30293	17170	26891	4822	–6827	22202
vi. Other flows	–13259	–12484	–7008	–5105	–10813	–6619	–3407
Capital account balance	51634	63740	67755	89300	48787	15806	38539
3. Errors & Omissions	–12	–2636	–2432	2689	–882	453	–2522
Capital account balance (including errors & omissions)	51622	61 104	65323	91989	47905	16259	36017
4. Overall Balance	13441	13050	12831	3826	15508	–10701	18076
5. Reserve Change	–13441	–13050	12831	–3826	–15508	10701	–18076

Source : RB I

Notes: PR: Partialy Revised; P: Provisional; (-)indicates increase; + indicates decrease

Current Account Developments in 2014-15 (April-September)

(v) Data on balance of payments (BoP), which is available with a lag of approximately one quarter, indicates that in the first half of 2014-15, there was a year-on-year improvement in trade account (on BoP basis) as a result of low growth in imports overcoming the moderation in merchandise export growth. Merchandise exports grew by 7.6 per cent in 2014-15 (April-September) to US$ 167.0 billion. However, in the second quarter there was some deceleration in export growth owing to moderation in oil prices from an average of US$ 105.1 per barrel in 2013-14 (second quarter) to US$ 98.9 per barrel in 2014-15 (second quarter).

(vi) The outcome in terms of imports was again somewhat mixed in the two quarters of the first half of the current fiscal relative to last year. This was largely due to the base effect of high gold imports in the first quarter of 2013-14 and a sharp correction in such imports in the second quarter of 2013-14 as against a steady pick-up in the first quarter of 2014-15 followed by a surge in imports in the second quarter reflecting seasonal demand spike and the easing of restrictions on gold imports.

(vii) The mixed outcome also owed to the pick-up in non-gold non-POL imports in 2014-15 relative to the compression in 2013-14. Invisible account covers (a) services, (b) transfers and (c) income. The surplus therein has been a major factor that moderated the large trade deficits from spilling over to the CAD. Services (net) continued to be dominated by software exports and witnessed a growth of 2.4 per cent to US$ 36.1 billion in 2014-15 (April-September) as against US$ 35.2 billion in the corresponding period of the previous year. Transfers (net) mostly remittances—were around US$ 32.7 billion in the first half of both 2013-14 and 2014-15. While software services and remittances provide surpluses, net income is an outgo that reflects interest/dividends payable and has a large bearing on the level of net international investment position. Income (net) is dominated by investment income and was US$ 13.8 billion in 2014-15 (April-September) as against US$ 13.4 billion in 2013-14 (April-September). As a result of the above developments. CAD was placed at US$ 17.9 billion in 2014-15 (April-September) as against USS 26.9 billion in the same period of 2013-14. As a proportion of GDP, the CAD declined from 3.1 per cent in the first half of 2013-14 to 1.9 per cent in the first half of 2014-15.

Capital/Finance Account Developments in 2014-15 (April-September)

(i) There was marked improvement in the net capital/financial flows both in terms of quantum and quality in the first half of 2014-15. Net financial flows were at US$ 36.0 billion in the first half of 2014-15 compared to US$ 16.3 billion in the first half of 2013-14. Net foreign investment, an important financial flow, surged from US$ 7.8 billion in 2013-14 (April-Seplember) to US$ 38.4 billion in 2014-15 (April-September). Net ECB was the other important item of the capital/finance account of the BoP which also improved from US$ 2.5 billion in 2013-14 (April-Seplember) to US$ 3.4 billion in 2014-15 (April-September). Net banking capital witnessed a decline from US$ 11.5 billion to (-) US$ 0.5 billion during the same period.

(ii) The financial account was dominated by direct and portfolio investments which are non-debt creating in nature. The net flows in the form of FDI and portfolio investment were more than sufficient to finance the CAD during this period. While higher net FDI flows reflect a positive outlook about the growth potential of the domestic economy, robust portfolio inflows in 2014-15 were underpinned by reduced external-sector vulnerabilities of the domestic economy and benign global financial conditions aided by the prospect of additional European Central Bank easing. Given the net capital flows and the CAD levels, accretion in foreign exchange reserves was US$ 18.1 billion (BoP basis) in the first half of 2014-15 as against drawdown of US$ 10.7 billion in 2013-14 (April-September). In 2014-15 (up to December, 2014) there has been a net inflow of US$ 28.5 billion in foreign institutional investors (FII) investment as compared to an outflow of US$ 4.5 billion in the corresponding period of 2013-14.

(iii) The latest data on FD1 inflows (net) available is for the period April-December 2014 and places these inflows at US$ 24.2 billion as against a level of US$ 20.7 billion in the same period in 2013-14. In so far as non-resident Indian (NRI) deposits are concerned, the lower levels of US$ 10.0 billion in April-December 2014 relative to April-December 2013 (US$ 35.1 billion) become broadly similar when adjusted for the one-off swap scheme. The above developments in the current and capital accounts indicate further accretion to reserves on BoP basis beyond the first half of the current fiscal.

Measures to Control Deficit: Some of the important methods to overcome deficit in balance of payments include the following:

(i) Devaluation : Devaluation means lowering of the value of the domestic currency in terms of foreign currencies. When the value of domestic currency decreases in terms of foreign currencies, the local commodities become cheaper in the international markets, i.e. the exports increase. It is, however, necessary that the other countries should not devalue their currencies and that the devaluation must be rellected in increase in exports and decrease in imports. Devaluation policy is successful subject to satisfaction of certain conditions.

(ii) Deflation : Deficits in balance of payments are caused by increase in imports. The aim of deflation is to curtail the demand for foreign goods. Deflation means fall in prices and incomes. Reduction in money income will bring about a fall in the demand for imported goods. Deflation should, however, be used very cautiously because it leaves a trail of unemployment and fall in wages in the economy.

(iii) Exchange Control : Exchange control refers to the regulation of exchange rates by the Government and also the restriction on the conversion of the local currencies against foreign currencies. Exchange controls may be direct or indirect depending upon the international trade conditions. The major forms of exchange controls are intervention and restrictions.

(iv) Import Duties and Quotas : The most common method of foreign trade is to impose duties or tariffs on the imports. Import duties reduce the demand for foreign goods considerably and thus, release pressure on the foreign exchange. It should, however, be remembered that the imports of essential consumer goods and crucial raw material cannot be stopped altogether, unless the country develops sufficient power to produce them domestically. Domestic industries may also be protected through tariffs.

Measures to Control Deficit: Some of the important methods to overcome deficit in balance of payments include the following:

(i) Devaluation : Devaluation means lowering of the value of the domestic currency in terms of foreign currencies. When the value of domestic currency decreases in terms of foreign currencies, the local commodities become cheaper in the international markets, *i.e.*, the exports increase. It is, however, necessary that the other countries should not devalue their currencies and that the devaluation must be reflected in increase in exports and decrease in imports. Devaluation policy is successful subject to satisfaction of certain conditions.

(ii) Deflation : Deficits in balance of payments are caused by increase in imports. The aim of deflation is to curtail the demand for foreign goods. Deflation means fall in prices and incomes. Reduction in money income will bring about a fall in the demand for imported goods. Deflation should, however, be used very cautiously because it leaves a trail of unemployment and fall in wages in the economy.

(iii) Exchange Control : Exchange Control refers to the regulation of exchange rates by the Government and also the restriction on the conversion of the local currencies against foreign currencies. Exchange controls may be direct or indirect depending upon the international trade conditions. The major forms of exchange controls are intervention and restrictions.

(iv) Import Duties and Quotas : The most common method of foreign trade is to impose duties or tariffs on the imports. Import duties reduce the demand for foreign goods considerably and thus, release pressure on the foreign exchange. It should, however, be remembered that the imports of essential consumer goods and crucial raw material cannot be stopped altogether, unless the country develops sufficient power to produce them domestically. Domestic industries may also be protected through tariffs.

Thus, unfavourable balance of payments (especially deficit) can be corrected by promoting exports and curtailing imports, foreign collaborations, encôuraging FDI and remittances in the country, foreign loans, counter trade etc.

Challenges before Indian Foreign Trade

1. Challenge of becoming a major player in world trade: The challenge for India is to achieve a share in world trade commensurate with its size. Despite making great strides in its export growth with 20 per cent plus growth continuously from 2002-03 to 2007-08, India has not made much progress in terms of the share in world trade. While India's exports were higher than those of China till 1954, they started lagging thereafter. If India can attain at least half of China's share in world exports, the impact on its employment and manufacturing activity will be enormous. While trade policy measures, shift in focus to some markets and some products, trade facilitation, tariff reforms etc. have helped in some measure. If India has to achieve a substantial share in world exports, a big push will be needed.

2. Challenge of real diversification of India's exports : While India has diversified its export basket as well as export markets over the years, substantial diversification in tune with world demand has not taken place. This can be seen by matching India's exports with the top 100 imports of the world at the six-digit HS level. The exercise based on PCTAS data 2010(data for 2008) shows that India's presence in these top items of world demand is negligible except for a few items such as diamonds and jewellery, oil cakes, t-shirts, men's/boy's trousers, flat rolled iron products, and maize (corn). There are many electronic, electrical, and engineering items (the three Es) in the top 100 imports of the world where India's presence is negligible.

3. Challenge of increasing export competitiveness : India's export competitiveness is being challenged not only from China and the South East Asian countries but also from the newly emerging Asian countries, less developed countries like Bangladesh, and small countries like Vietnam in items like textiles. At macro level, the two major determinants of export competitiveness are the exchange rate and inflation reflected in the real effective exchange rate (REER). As per the RBI, there has been a distinct divergence between the movements of six-currency and 36-currency REER indices so far during 2010-11. While the six-currency REER remained above base level by 16 to 20 per cent, signifying higher inflation differentials with these economies, the 36-currency REER largely remained below or around base level, implying that inflation in India has been comparable to or below the levels prevailing in its trading partners in the developing world.

4. Challenges related to tariff reforms : India has been progressively lowering peak customs duty. The fall in peak duty has not led to the feared collapse in revenue collections. The duty cuts have neither wiped out the domestic manufacturing sector nor resulted in large-scale unemployment as forecasted by many. The data show that progressive peak duty cuts have been accompanied by rise in customs duty collections. However, further bold tariff reforms with minimum revenue loss are needed to reach levels comparable to those in ASEAN both for peak rate as well as total duty.

5. Challenges related to FTAs/Comprehensive Economic Cooperation Agreements (CECAs) in the absence of successful WTO negotiations : The proliferation of FTAs in the world is characterised as the 'spaghetti bowl' in which trade criss-crosses in a complex fashion between countries based on tariff differentials and complicated rules of origin. In recent years, India too is a part of many regional and bilateral groupings. While there are benefits from these FTAs for Indian exports, in some cases the benefits to the partner countries are much more, with net gains of incremental exports from India being small or negative. FTAs also lead to a new type of inverted duty structure with duties for final products being lower from FTA partners compared to duties for the previous-stage raw materials imported from non-FTA countries. This acts as a disincentive to local manufacturing which is not competitive against FTA imports because of the inverted duty structure phenomenon.

6. Challenges related to services trade : Services trade is uncharted territory with plenty of opportunities and challenges. A more conducive environment for trade in services can be created by liberalising FDI in services as FDI inflows and trade in services have a close relationship given the nature of intra-firm trade of multinational parent firms with affiliates; rationalising taxes in services like shipping and telecom; going forward with totalisation agreements; streamlining domestic regulations like licencing requirements and procedures, technical standards, and regulatory transparency which can help in the growth and export of services; and continuing with the focus on services in multilateral and bilateral negotiations. These, along with systematic marketing of services, collection and dissemination of market information by setting up a portal for services, streamlining the services data system, and a more focused, coordinated, and synchronised policy by the different agencies involved, could help the services sector make further strides.

The structure of a country's exports affects its prospects for economic growth. It would be better for a country to have a technology-intensive structure for its export efforts. It is quite true that India is trying to develop a sound industrial base, its export structure is still dominated by low-technology products. A low-technology export structure has simply facilitated the export of products as textiles, garments, simple metal and plastics products, and furniture. However, these types of products are produced by low-skilled labour and are undifferentiated, so they do not yield the competitive advantages necessary for broad economic growth. A high technology export structure includes products *viz.* complex electronic machinery, precision instruments and fine chemicals. This type of structure, based in complex skills and fast-changing technologies, generally does yield competitive advantages and export based economic development.

Both export promotion and import substitutions are the two sides of the same coin to maximise the earnings of foreign exchange. The main object of both is to earn foreign exchange or save foreign exchange. However, the significant difference is that in export promotion, efforts are made to earn foreign exchange by directly exporting services and goods to the foreign countries. But in import substitution, efforts are made to increase the level of foreign exchange by restricting the spending and use of foreign exchange.

Export Promotion

Sufficient foreign exchange is required for the economic development of the country. It is required for the imports of necessary plants and technologies. Similarly, there is need of foreign exchange to fulfill other import obligations. Therefore, there is urgent need to earn more and more foreign exchange through export promotion to minimise the adverse gap on balance of payments.

Export promotion means export encouragement. Under this process encouragements and incentives are given to existing exporters and new exporters for export promotion. Generally, specific efforts, inducements and assistance for increasing the sale of commodities and services in the foreign countries is known as export promotion. In other words, export promotion implies all those governmental and non-governmental efforts which are made for increasing the exports of the country. In modern age, export promotion has become the essential requirement for all countries. Today, not a single country is fully self-sufficient and every country aspires to promote exports. India is a developing country, for whom export promotion is quite necessary. In practice following form of study are generally taken for export promotion.

(i) To give cash subsidy to exporters.

(ii) To direct the commercial banks to give adequate credit to exporters.

(iii) To give permission for import of some capital goods, other permissable machineries and other necessary raw materials in exchange of export obligations.

(iv) To give subsidy in railway freight and shipping freight for sending the goods for export.

(v) To allow deductions in terms of custom duty, income tax and other taxes to exporters.

Need for Export Promotion in India

1. To Correct Unfavourable Balance of Trade : India's external trade is generally affected by advance and thus there is decline in foreign exchange reserve. It creates problem in implementation of economic planning. So export promotion is a tool to correct the adverse balance of external trade and earn larger foreign exchange barely for giving dynamism to Indian economy.

2. To Reduce Foreign Loans : Increasing discharge of forward exchange planned economic development and adverse foreign trade have forced the government of India to resort to foreign loans. Effective export promotion policy helps in earning of foreign exchange to meet out the repayment of loans and their interest obligations etc.

3. To Get Development Project Successful : To meet out the growing need of foreign exchange for import of marchionesses and other equipments etc., they have to provide sound base for export promotion. With this way we can earn foreign exchange to get the projects completed in time and ensure the accelerated economic development of the country.

4. To Get International Market for New Products : Planning economic development programmes have enabled the innovators and entrepreneurs to produce new products. So they need interactional market for these products. Export promotion incentive encourage them to go for international market and earn foreign exchange for their country.

5. To Make Economy Self-Reliant : Self-reliance in every field is necessary for sustainable economic development. If we are able to produce every thing in the country there may be continuous decline in import burden and foreign loans. Thus, earning maximum foreign exchange is necessary for attaining self-reliance.

Role of Government in Export Promotion

1. Board of Trade : The government of India has established Board of Trade to study the problem of external trade and monitor the policies from time to time. The Board of trade is also responsible to give its suggestions to the government on the following affairs.

(a) Development of goods

(b) Expansion of production capacity

(c) Reform in export marketing structure and channels

(d) Arrangement of trade services of trading community with regard to export programmes.

2. Export Promotion Councils : Various Export Promotion Councils have been established by the Government of India to such cooperation to consumers, producers and exporters in export trade and ensure mutual coordination among these parties. These councils are also responsible for providing consent only services and suggestions to producers. At present these export promotion councils provide counselling in the areas of cashew nuts, cotton textiles, Silk, leather and leather products, jewellary, diamonds, plastics, spices etc.

3. Commodity Boards : Different Commodity Boards have also been established by the Government of India to promote production and development of different commodities. These are mainly related to tea, coffee, cigarettes, rubber and tobacco etc.

4. Export Inspection Council : The Government of India has established various Export Inspection Councils under Export Quality Control Improvement Programme upto, 1963 for ensuring quality control in exportable goods. The main function of the councils is to inspect the goods before their loading so that only quality goods are exported. It will ensure the protection of brand, good will and prestige of the exporters and country both in the field of export trade.

5. Establishment of Indian Institute of Foreign Trade : The Government of India has established Indian Institute of Foreign Trade in 1964. It is responsible for providing training to manpower for foreign trade. It is also engaged in conducting market survey and research.

6. Establishment of Export Credit and Governmental Corporation : It was established in 1964. The main function of the corporation is to undertake insurance for export related risks. It also provided export credit facilities to exporters.

7. Establishment of Trade Development Authority : It was established in 1976. The main function of this authority is to motivate entrepreneurs of small and medium size institutions for larger exports. It is also responsible for facilitating other activities with regard to export business.

8. Export Processing Zone : The Government of India is providing all facilities for the establishment of export processing zones. It is an important export promotion plan. Production units working under Export Processing Zones are responsible to ensure hundred percent of their production.

9. Indian Council for Trade Fairs and Exhibition and Directorate of Commercial Publicity : It is responsible for organising industrial and trade fairs and exhibition in the country as well as in foreign countries. It also helps in providing necessary information about Indian goods to agencies involved in import of Indian goods in foreign countries. The Directorate of Commercial Publicity, Government of India also provides cooperation and coordination as a supplement agency in foreign trade.

10. Establishment of Various Corporations: The Government of India has established various corporations to work as channelising agency in import and export business. These are State Trading Corporation (STC), Minerals and Metals Trading Corporation(MMTC), Project And Equipment Corporation, Handicrafts Export Corporation Cathedral Corporation etc.

11. Trade Agreements : Trade agreements are playing very important role in improving the volume of export business. Association of South East Asian Nations (ASEAN), European Economic Community (EEC), South Asian Association For Regional Cooperation (SAARC) have been promoted to ensure smooth functioning of the trade agreements.

12. Establishment of Marketing Development Fund : It was established in 1963 to provide financial assistance and support to manufacturers engaged in production of exportable items and goods. Assistance is also given to those who are producing Indian goods in foreign countries.

13. Establishment of Export-Import Bank : The Government of India has established EXIM Bank in 1982 with a capital outlay of ₹200 crores. It provides credit facilities to exporters and importers.

14. Other Measures : The Government of India is also providing following facilities for export promotion :

(i) Cash Compensatory Support Scheme.
(ii) Customs Duty Concession.
(iii) Duty Drawback Scheme
(iv) 100% Export Oriented Unit Scheme.
(v) Direct Tax Concession.

Benefits of Export Promotion

1. Increase in Foreign Exchange : Entrepreneurs produce innovative variety of products and services which are also useful for foreign markets. With the help of export, they can earn more foreign exchange to ensure favourable balance of payments. Entrepreneurs are also supposed to follow the slogans *viz.* 'Export or Perish' and 'Less use, more export' etc. as a guiding philosophy for export promotion. In this way, they can earn more foreign exchange by exporting goods and services.

2. Production and Distribution of Products : The main function of the entrepreneur is to produce and distribute products and services for domestic sale and export. To ensure more exports, the government generally announces several facilities, incentives and policies for export promotion. It also changes and revises the policies, guidelines, rules and regulations from time to time. The entrepreneurs can take advantages of these facilities, required in various ways and comply with the policies and take decisions for production and distribution of various commodities for export purposes.

3. Development of Markets: Export promotion measures facilitate the Indian entrepreneur to increase export trade. Export efforts also enable the entrepreneurs to come in contact with the foreign markets. They can easily gather detailed information about foreign markets and also undertake market research for drawing useful conclusions with regard to market expansion and development.

4. Development of Brand Image: Since entrepreneurs are expected to produce exportable items, they are required to ensure quality products. Quality products actually ensure growing customership and thereafter develop good brand image of the entrepreneurs in foreign markets. In future, it is the brand image which creates further demand for Indian products and services in foreign countries.

5. Economic Prosperity: The entrepreneurs can play important role in earning foreign exchange through export promotion. Earning of foreign exchange is quite important for a developing country like India. Entrepreneurs can also utilise these foreign exchanges for the import of required raw materials, semi-finished materials, machineries, techniques and technology. These steps ultimately improve economic prosperity.

Obstacles In Export Promotion

(i) **Foreign Competition :** Indian goods in foreign countries are facing tough competition. Exporters are facing difficulties in selling their commodities. Bangladesh is the toughest competitor in jute products. The cotton textiles are facing competition from China and Japan. Sri Lanka and Indonesia are also providing severe competition in tea.

(ii) **Defective Policies of Indian Exporters :** Policies being pursued by the Indian exporters also create problem in export promotion. The biggest problem is that Indian exporters are not sending goods as approved in sample. Importers return the goods and by this way prestige of the country is affected adversely.

(iii) **High Price :** Cost of production of Indian goods in most of the cases is quite high. Actually higher cost of production makes the Indian exporters out of the market. China is quite successful in supplying goods at competitive costs. Sometimes, Government of India is forced to compensate the loss of Indian exporters due to higher cost of production as they exported their goods under export promotion scheme.

(iv) **Substitute Products :** Traditional items are dominating the list of goods being exported by the country to foreign countries. Now, these items and goods have substitutes in international market and adversely affecting the export performance of these goods. Jute bags are being replaced by plastic bags. Artificial silk is replacing the demand of cotton textiles.

(v) **Tariff Policies:** Many countries have imposed higher import duties and fixed the import quota on Indian goods, thus, there are declining demand for Indian goods in these countries. About two third of total exportable goods are being affected by this mechanism.

(vi) **WTO Effects :** In the era of globalisation countries are required to adjust with the competitive conditions prevailing over the globe. Developing countries especially India are facing problems with regard to export promotion as they can not subsidise their exportable items. Providing incentives for export is also against the WTO agreements. India is signatory of all these agreements so it cannot subside export except to motivate exporters for becoming more and more cost effective and competitive.

Suggestions For Export Promotion: Main suggestions for export promotion are given below :

(i) **Export Marketing Research :** Indian Trade Association and Indian Institute of Foreign Trade are involved in the market research to identify the countries where export of Indian goods is feasible. Production schedule and export plans are to be formulated by keeping the results of above market research.

(ii) **Improvement in Quality and Designs** : To compete with foreign producers Indian manufacturers are required to improve quality and designs of their products. They have to give more emphasis on quality control process. These exercises enable the importers to get quality products and also help in the export promotion programme.

(iii) **Cost Competitiveness** : Indian manufacturers are required to control their cost of production. Effective Production behaviour and control on wasteful expenditure will reduce the cost of production. It will improve the cost effectiveness as well as strengthen the competitive position of the exporters.

(iv) **Wide Publicity** : Efforts should be undertaken to give wide publicity about the new products and existing products by the exporters. Reliable and effective advertisements may improve the image of the exporters as well as demands of the products. Government corporations like STC and MMTC should also be involved in the process of publicity of Indian goods in foreign market.

(v) **Incentive to Export Promotion** : Government should try to give more infrastructural incentives for the production of exportable items to avoid the provisions of the WTO agreements. Establishment of Special Economic Zones is a viable decision to improve the export performance. Easy availability of raw materials and power etc., will improve the production base as well as competitive strength of the exporters.

(vi) **Trade Agreements:** Bilateral and multilateral agreements are necessary with those countries who are imposing ban or restrictions on export of Indian goods. With the help of these agreements we can easily enter the desired market and improve the volume of export.

Import Substitution

Import substitution means production of those goods in the country itself which are being imported from foreign countries. Thus, Import substitution means to have own production of commodities and services in place of importing them. In other words, Import substitution implies such concept, under which a country carries out the production or manufacturing of such commodities and services, which are to be imported from the foreign countries. Efforts for import substitution include the following :

(i) If domestic supply of goods is not available in the country then efforts are made to create production capacity or create or develop new sources of production of importable goods within the country.

(ii) If domestic supply of a product or goods is not adequate then efforts are required to expand the supply or production of goods in the country.

(iii) To protect the domestic industries from foreign competition, if domestic industries are making loss due to competition or there is increase in foreign supply in the country.

Import substitution becomes the main basis for the formulation of economic and trade policies. Shortage of foreign exchange due to widening of gap in the import and export can be reduced by producing more goods or their substitutes in the country itself.

Benefits of Import Substitution : Major benefits of import substitution are as follows :

(i) It reduces import.

(ii) It eases the problem of foreign exchange.

(iii) It reduces foreign dependence.

(iv) It corrects balance of payments.

(v) It ensures forward move towards self reliance

(vi) It improves employment position by establishing more production capacity or production units.

Role of Entrepreneurs in Import Substitution : The role of entrepreneurs in import substitution can be assessed in the following ways:

1. Saving of Foreign Exchange : Entrepreneurs are also producing goods and services which can be used for those products which are being imported from foreign country. By producing substitute products and services, entrepreneurs try to save valuable foreign exchange. At a later stage, consumer becomes habitual of substitute products.

2. Creation of Employment Opportunities : When entrepreneurs produce the goods and services in the country which can be used as a substitute of the imports, employment opportunities are generated in the country and utilisation of capital also becomes possible.

3. Increase in National Income : Import substitution efforts also help to save foreign exchange which ultimately leads to increase in national income. Any increase in national income improves the well-being of the society. It also enables the country to optimise the use of available resources in the country.

4. Self-Reliance: Import substitution reduces the dependence on imports from foreign country. Various entrepreneurial activities for increasing production and services not only reduces the dependence on imports from foreign countries, but also reduce the foreign exchange crisis. It also motivates other potential entrepreneurs to get involved in these activities.

5. Accelerating the Pace of Industrialisation : Import substitution efforts accelerate the pace of industrialisation in the country. Entrepreneurs are generally encouraged by the incentives and subsidies to work for import substitution efforts. They invest more capital to enlarge the scale of production. In this way, they try to supply quality goods and services to the society and thereby restricting the imports and thus, saving the foreign exchange.

Suggestions to Improve Import Substitution : Following suggestions are to be implemented to make the import substitution more effective :

1. Priority should be given to production of those goods which are not being produced in the country. For this purpose foreign collaboration should be encouraged in each and every desired segments.
2. Incentive for import substitution should be allowed on the lines of cash incentive scheme.
3. Concessional funding arrangement should be given to those production units which are engaged in production of goods under import substitution.
4. Import duty should be reduced with reference to goods under import substitution.
5. Exemption in custom and excise duties should be given in case of raw materials used for production of goods under import substitution.
6. Concessional tariff policy should be formulated for import of coal etc.
7. Necessary exemptions should be allowed in income tax, sales tax and additional depreciation for production of goods under import substitution.

Role of Entrepreneurs in Earning Foreign Exchange

Increasing space of global village ensures free movement of man, material and money from one country to another country. Saving of foreign exchange is also necessary to check the vicious circle in import-export. Improving entrepreneurial behaviour leads to higher level of production and increases the earning of foreign exchange. In this context, role of entrepreneurs can be assessed in following ways:

1. Production of Products and Services : Entrepreneurs produce the goods and services. They are using their surplus production for exports. Export efforts enable them to identify the further scope of exports of other products. Thus, exports create temptation among the entrepreneurs to produce a variety of products and services for earning more foreign exchange.

2. Minimise Foreign Dependence : Imports are always costly in terms of foreign exchange as well as in terms of trade. Entrepreneurs have to play their role in this context. Entrepreneurs through their innovative behaviour can easily produce goods and services which can be treated as a substitute for imported items. By this process, they can minimise foreign dependence for the supply of goods and services in the country.

3. Production of Import Substitution Items: The Government of India has completely banned the import of some commodities, whereas import of some other goods and services has been declared as restricted items. In such conditions, entrepreneurs may fulfil the need of earning foreign exchange by producing commodities included in list of import substitution.

4. Innovative Approach: The entrepreneur is always ready to take the advantages of all favourable opportunities. He carries out production by suitably identifying the opportunities and also starts providing new range of services in the foreign market.

5. Increase in Exports: Entrepreneurs search viable opportunities in diversified export items. In some cases, Government also provides incentives for the production of exportable items. The combined effect of these measures increases the level of export.

6. Industrial Progress: Concept of global village has created an environment of competition and cost effectiveness. Entrepreneurs ensure a speedy industrialisation and target the large scale production. In this way they can easily compete with foreign producers and get the foreign market under their control.

Role of Entrepreneurs in the Development of Special Economic Zones (SEZs)

India recognised early the effectiveness of the export processing zone (EPZ) model in promoting exports, with Asia's first EPZ set up in Kandla in 1965. With a view to overcome the multiplicity of controls and clearances; absence of world-class infrastructure; and an unstable fiscal regime to attract larger foreign investments in India, the Special Economic Zones (SEZs) Policy was announced in April 2000. SEZs in India functioned from 1 November 2000 to 9 February 2006 under the provisions of the Foreign Trade Policy and fiscal incentives were made effective through the provisions of relevant statutes. The SEZ Act 2005, supported by SEZ Rules, came into effect on 10 February 2006, providing for drastic simplification of procedures and for single window clearance on matters relating to central as well as state governments. The SEZ Rules provide for different minimum land requirements for different classes of SEZs. In addition to seven Central Government SEZs and 12 state/private-sector SEZs set up prior to the enactment of the SEZ Act 2005, formal approval has been accorded to 580 proposals out of which 374 SEZs have been notified. The performance of SEZs has been reasonably good despite some criticism.

Performance of SEZs in India— SEZs are becoming increasingly important in India's exports. The performance of SEZs is mainly examined in three areas, exports, employment and investment.

(i) Exports: A total of 130 SEZs are already exporting. Out of this 75 are information technology (IT)/ IT enabled services (ITES), 16 multi-product and 39 other sector specific SEZs. The total number of units in these SEZs is 3046. The physical exports from the SEZs have increased by 128 per cent to 494.08 crore in 2013-14. When the whole world including India was reeling under the effects of the global recession, growth in exports from SEZs was 128 per cent in 2009-10 compared to a paltry 0.7 per cent growth in total exports from India.

Exhibit : Exports from the Operational SEZs

Year	Exports		Growth over Previous Year
	Value in ₹Crores	Billion USD	
2005-2006	22,840	5.08	-
2006-2007	34,615	7.69	52%
2007-2008	66,638	14.81	93%
2008-2009	99,689	22.15	50%
2009-2010	2,20,711	49.05	121%
2010-2011	3,15,868	70.19	43.11%
2011-2012	3,64,478	81.00	15.39%
2012-2013	4,76,159	88.18	31%
2013-2014	4,94,077	82.35	4%

One of the criticisms SEZs face is that exports are mainly from the old SEZs which were formerly free trade zones (FTZs) and not from greenfield SEZs. It is interesting to know that not only have many greenfield SEZs started exporting but also the exports of new SEZs, i.e. SEZs notified under the SEZ Act 2005, have grown rapidly over the years resulting in the highest share of 54 per cent for this category in 2013-14 compared to Central Government SEZs and State Government/private SEZs established prior to the SEZ Act 2005.

(ii) Employment: Out of the total employment of 6,44,073 persons in SEZs, an incremental employment of 5,09,369 persons was generated after February 2006 when the SEZ Act came into force. At least double this number obtains indirect employment outside the SEZs as a result of the operations of SEZ units. This is in addition to the employment created by the developer for infrastructure activities.

(iii) Investment : The total investment in SEZs till 31 December 2014 is approximately $2,14,871 crore including $1,96,972 crore in the newly notified zones. In SEZs 100 per cent FDI is allowed through automatic route. The Government's role has been more as a facilitator by fast tracking the approvals rather than providing any direct monetary support. SEZs being set up under the SEZ Act 2005 are primarily private investment driven.

Problems before SEZ Programme : Industrial units working under SEZ development programmes are facing following problems-

1. Land acquisition programme in 2008 created problems for the developers who started setting up SEZs. Demand was good and abundant capital available. So, there was a rush to set up SEZs as most developers hoped to attract sufficient clients. That turned out to be an over-estimation. Singur and Nandigram erupted and reframed the debate on land acquisition. Till then, the government had been buying land for industry, often on the pretext of 'public purpose' and at sub-market prices, lending credence to the charge of SEZs being a 'land play'. Amid mounting

public backlash, the government stopped. Industry had to now negotiate with landowners and also pay market prices.

2. Due to global recession in 2008 and till today cash evaporated from the world economy, including India. Real estate prices tumbled and developers fell into a debt trap. They had no money to build, and with the apparent land arbitrage in SEZs gone, they had less reason to build one.

3. The draft of the Direct Tax Code (DTC), which was released in late 2009 has also created tax implications for the entrepreneurs working under SEZ Programme.

4. The budget 2014-15, shows that the commerce and finance ministries pulling in different directions. No income tax for SEZs became history. Finance minister Mr. Jaitley, citing equal sharing of the corporate tax liability and foregone revenues of ₹5,473 crore, slapped a 18.5% minimum alternative tax (MAT) on SEZs, he also levied a 15% tax on dividends declared. This has affected out cash flows of SEZ's.

EXAMINATION QUESTIONS

Long Answer Questions

1. What do you mean by export promotion and import substitution? Explain the steps taken by the state for export promotion.
2. Explain the composition and direction of India's foreign trade.
3. Describe the measures taken by the government for export promotion.
4. Discuss the role of entrepreneurs in export promotion and import substitution.
5. Critically examine the role of government in export promotion and import substitution?

Short Answer Questions

1. What is import substitution?
2. What is export promotion?
3. What are the obstacles in export promotion?
4. Distinguish between export promotion and import substitution?
5. How do entrepreneurs contribute in the earning of foreign exchange.

Objective Type Questions

1. Export promotion affects Balance of Payments
   (a) Adversely
   (b) Favourably
   (c) Neutral
   (d) None of the above

2. Export promotion assistance does not include the following:
   (a) Cash Subsidy
   (b) Export credit
   (c) Liberal import licence.
   (d) Tax incentive.
3. Special Economic zones Policy was announced in
   (a) April 2000
   (b) September 2000
   (c) March 2000
   (d) December 2000

Answers

1-(b) 2-(c) 3-(a)

12

Entrepreneurship and Consumerism

Entrepreneurs and consumers are the two sides of the same coin. They are supposed to mutually fulfill their individual expectations. However, in practice, entrepreneurs are guided by the profit considerations. Even if situation permits they are always ready to exploit the consumers at large. Consumers are part of the society. They expect that entrepreneurs will provide goods and services of standard quality at reasonable price in reasonable time. So there is always a possibility of conflicting interest between the two. Thus, in these situations, consumers have no option except to go for their movement to protect their interests. Consumerism is nothing but a well designed movement to protect the interests of consumers. Actually Consumer movement is a socioeconomic movement to protect the rights of consumers in relation to the goods purchased and services availed.

It is a collective consciousness on the part of consumers, business, government and civil society to enhance consumers' satisfaction and social welfare which will in turn benefit all of them and finally make the society a better place to live in. Consumerism is still in its infancy in our country, thanks to the sellers market and the government monopoly in most services.

Nature and Definitions of Consumerism

Consumerism refers to wide range of activities of government business and independent organisations designed to protect rights of the consumers. Consumerism is a process through which the consumers seek redress, restitution and remedy for their dissatisfaction and frustration with the help of their all organised or unorganised efforts and activities. It is, infact a social movement seeking to protect the rights of consumers in relation to the producers of goods and providers of services. Infact consumerism today is an all-pervasive term meaning nothing more than people's search for getting better value for their money.

According to McMillan Dictionary (1985), "Consumerism is concerned with protecting consumers from all organisations with which there is exchanged relationship. It encompasses the set of activities of government, business, independent organisations and concerned consumers that are designed to protect the rights of consumers". The Chamber's Dictionary (1993) defines consumerism as the protection of the interests of the buyers of goods and services against defective or dangerous goods etc. "Consumerism is a movement or policies aimed at regulating the products or services, methods or standards of manufacturers, sellers and advertisers in the interest of buyers, such regulation may be institutional, statutory or embodied in a voluntary code occupied by a particular industry or it may result more indirectly from the influence of consumer organisations."

Rights of Consumers

(i) Rights against exploitation by unfair trade practices.

(ii) Right to protection of health and safety from the goods and services the consumers buy or are offered free.

(iii) Right to be informed of the quality and performance standards, ingredients of the product, operational requirements, freshness of the product, possible adverse side effects and other relevant facts concerning the product or service.

(iv) Right to be heard if there is any grievance or suggestions.

(v) Right to get the genuine grievances redressed.

(vi) Right to choose the best from a variety of offers.

(vii) Right to a physical environment that will protect and enhance the quality of life.

Reasons for Emergence of Consumerism

1. Growing Exploitation through Restrictive and Unfair Trade Practices: Consumers are exploited by a large number of restrictive and unfair restrictive and unfair trade practices. The monopolistic and restrictive trade practices are available for restricting competition and increasing the market imperfections to the common detriment, consumer exploitation through unfair trade practices that mislead or dupe the customers has become widespread.

2. Deceptive Advertising : Advertising is an important means used by producers to deceive consumers. The actual purpose of advertising is informing the consumer about the use and quality of different products. To this extent, it is useful. However, it has two most important ill effects for which consumers face problems. These ill effects are as follows: (i) The cost of advertising is added to the selling cost and this increases the prices; and (ii) It can be deceptive and can misguide the consumers. Companies can claim qualities with no scientific basis and they can keep the consumers in dark by not disclosing the risks associated with the use of their products.

3. Fictitious Bargains : Suppliers of goods and services generally bargain with consumers to improve their sales volumes. Fictitious bargains are the common form of deception. Many devices are used to lure buyers into believing that they are getting something for nothing or at a nominal value for their money. Prices may be advertised as generally reduced and cut when in reality the goods may be sold at sellers' regular prices. Now-a-days suppliers are giving a slogan to improve the volume of their business like buy two and get one free.

4. Low Level of Consumer Awareness : In India, consumer awareness is low due to the apathy and lack of education among the masses. Consumers are not aware about their rights—to be informed about product quality, price, protection against unsafe products, access to variety of goods at competitive prices, consumer education etc. Consumerism is affected by the lack of education and information resources, testing facilities, competent leadership, price control mechanism, and adequate quasi-judicial machinery.

5. Globalisation Effect : In the era of globalisation it is impossible for the buyer to examine the goods before hand and most of the transactions are concluded by correspondence.

Growing level of information technology and emergence of e-commerce related innovations, the consumers are unable to get confirmatory test benefits etc about the product. As a result buyer is being misled, duped and deceived day in and day out. Mahatma Gandhi rightly remarked that "A Consumer is the most important visitor on our premises. He is not dependent on us, we are on him. He is not an interruption to our work; he is the purpose of it. We are not doing a favour to a consumer by giving him an opportunity. He is doing us a favour by giving an opportunity to serve him."

6. Problem of Adulteration : Due to lack of effective certification mechanism we are witnessing the widespread practice of adulteration. Supervisory staff involved in the checking process are also not doing justice to consumers. With the result adulteration is practised by suppliers at several points in the supply chain-right from the producer to the ultimate consumer. In agricultural commodities adulteration is widespread as these products have more chances for adulteration.

Components of Consumerism

1. Self-protection by consumers themselves is quite necessary. Consumer must be aware of his rights, raise voice against exploitation and seek redressal of his grievances.
2. Consumers' consciousness determines the effectiveness of consumerism. It is the duty of the consumer to identify his rights and protect them.
3. Voluntary Consumer Organisations are engaged in organising consumers and encouraging them to safeguard their interests.
4. The success of consumerism lies in the realisation of the business that there is no substitute for voluntary self-regulations. Little attention towards the business will not only serve consumers interest but will also benefit them.
5. The government should formulate necessary code of conduct for the suppliers of goods and services. Some businesses in India have come together to adopt a code of conduct for regulating their own activities.
6. Effective regulatory mechanism for the business should be developed by the government to protect the interest of consumers.
7. Consumerism has over the time developed into a sound force designed to aid and protect the consumer by exerting, legal, moral and economic pressure on producers and service providers.

Consumer Awareness Scheme[1]

Consumer movement is slowly gaining ground in our country, but it is still in its infancy stage. The success of consumer movement mainly depends upon the level of consumer awareness generated in the country by educating the consumers about their rights and responsibilities. Within India the level of consumer awareness varies from state to state depending upon the level of literacy and the social awareness of the people. Educating more than 110 crore people of various categories of population particularly those in rural areas where consumers are more susceptible to exploitation, on various subject matters on consumers interests which are being dealt by different Ministries/Departments, is a gigantic task that can be undertaken only through a sustained national programme with adequate funds made available for the purpose.

Consumer Welfare Fund[2]

Consumer Welfare Fund was created in 1992 with the objective of providing financial assistance to promote and protect the welfare of the consumer, create consumer awareness and strengthen consumer movement in the country, particularly in rural areas. The Department of Consumer Affairs operates the Fund, setup by the Department of Revenue under the Central Excise Act, 1944.

Consumer Protection

Consumer movement is a socio-economic movement which seeks to protect the rights of consumers in relation to the goods purchased and services availed. Government has been according high priority to better protect the consumer interests. The Department of Consumer Affairs, has initiated a number of steps to promote a responsible and responsive consumer movement in the country. Such measures include the use of multimedia publicity campaign for promoting consumer awareness and encouraging consumers' involvement through efforts of Government and Non-Governmental Organisations and others.

Consumers, all around the world, are victims of poor quality, unsafety, under measurement, adulteration and false promises. Indian consumers suffer and lose thousands of crores of rupees every year due to adulteration and quality deceptions. Consumer protection means the protection of the consumers from their exploitation by the unfair trade practices of the producers. Consumer protection is that instrument in the hands of consumers which protect their hard earned money and creates the 'value for money' in this new era of New Public Management.

Some of the important factors of consumer protection are: international endeavours, consumer cooperatives, public sector consumer movements, consumer advocates, legal measures and individual enlightened consumers but the most important legal measure to protect the rights of the consumers is the Consumer Protection Act, 1986.

Objectives of Consumer Protection

(i) To create suitable administrative and legal mechanisms which would be within the easy reach of consumers and to interact with both, Government and Non-Governmental Organisations to promote and protect the welfare of the consumers.

(ii) To involve and motivate various sections of society including consumer organisations, women and youth to participate in the programme.

(iii) To generate awareness among consumers about their rights and responsibilities, motivate them to assert their rights so as not to compromise on the quality and standards of goods and services and to seek redressal of their disputes in consumer forum, if required.

Role of Entrepreneurs in Augmenting and Meeting of Local Demand

Local demand means the demand for any particular commodity or service at a specified place at the given prices. India is a vast country having different types of cultural and sociological ethos. In real situation, demand for goods and services are directly linked with the socio-cultural framework of the society. The entrepreneurs are also playing their role in the following way:

1. Creating Local Demand:

(i) Tiny and small entrepreneurs are mostly first generation entrepreneurs. They know the locally available resources. Utilising local resources they produce goods and services and try to fulfil the local demand of the people. These producers produce goods services as per the requirements of community on occasions of different festivals like Dushehra, Diwali, Ram Navmi, Id-ul-zuha, Navaratri etc.

(ii) Actually, local demand of a particular product or service induces the entrepreneurs to go for production at local level. Wooden baskets and furniture, netting and weaving, papad making, preparation of jute products are increasingly providing space for rural entrepreneurship. Due to change in cultural behaviour of Indian society entrepreneurs are now engaged in business of tent houses, keeping various types of tents, furniture and halls ready for marriages and other events. Lighting and floral decorations are also being arranged by them. They create more value addition through catering services as per the requirements of the customers. Thus, by supplying locally suited goods and services, the entrepreneurs create desires among the local people and convert this desire into demand. This demand further increases the level of purchase of commodities and services at local level.

2. Increasing and Maintaining the Local Demand: Keeping the prevailing external and internal environment in mind, entrepreneurs create local demand by supplying goods and services as per innovative style to the society at large. They are also playing their role on regular basis in maintaining demand for existing products and creating further demand of innovative products and services. For it, they give advertisements and also adopt various sale promotion techniques, like free sample, operational demonstrations, rebates, reduction sale etc.

3. Improving Consumer Satisfactions: The entrepreneurs make several efforts to meet the local demand, like after sale service, complain redressal, establishing coordination between demand and supply of various commodities etc.

EXAMINATION QUESTIONS

Long Answer Questions:

1. What do you mean by consumer protection? Discuss its objectives.
2. Explain the features of consumerism. Also explain the problems of Consumerism in India.
3. What is consumerism? Discuss the reasons for growing consumerism in India.
4. What is local demand? Examine the role of entrepreneurs in meeting local demand.

Short Answer Questions:

1. What do you mean by local demand?
2. What do you mean by consumer awareness?
3. What do you mean by consumer welfare fund?
4. What is consumer protection?
5. What do you mean by consumers?
6. What do you mean by unfair trade practices?
7. What are the purposes of consumer movements?

Objective Type Questions:

1. Consumerism is the process under which consumers seek the following for their dissatisfaction and frustration
   (a) Redress
   (b) Restitution
   (c) Remedy
   (d) All of the above
2. Jago Grahak Jago is a
   (a) Consumer welfare scheme
   (b) Consumer awareness scheme
   (c) Consumer Protection scheme
   (d) None of these
3. Local demand is a demand for commodity or service
   (a) At a specified Place
   (b) At a given price
   (c) Linked with local socio-cultural environment
   (d) All of the above

Answers

1-(d) 2-(b) 3-(d)

REFERENCES

1. Annual Report, 20010-11, Ministry of Consumer Affairs Food and Public Distribution, Government of India, p.35
2. *Ibid*, p.36

13

WOMEN ENTREPRENEURSHIP

Entrepreneurship does not differentiate the sex and women entrepreneurs can improve their gender lot by initiating into entrepreneurial activities. "Women have always been the major contributor of human capital since inception and creation of this universe. Earlier, they were confined to household activities but time is changing very fast. In the changed scenario, awareness has motivated women to start their own enterprises and contribute to the family income".[1] Now there is growing awareness among women that entrepreneurship opens up a new field for them and they can achieve their cherished profession which has independence and self support.

Nature of Women Entrepreneurs

The term "women entrepreneur" deals with that section of the female population who venture out into industrial activities i.e. manufacturing, assembling, job works, repairs/servicing and other businesses.

Women entrepreneurs may be defined as the women or a group of women who initiate, organise and operate a business enterprise. Women are expected to innovate, imitate or adopt an economic activity to be called women entrepreneurs.

The Government of India has treated women entrepreneurs of a different criteria-level of women participation in equity and employment position of the enterprise. As such "women entrepreneurs is defined as an enterprise owned and controlled by a woman having a minimum financial interest of 51 per cent of the capital and giving at least 51 per cent of the employment generated in the enterprise to women."

Thus, on the basis of above definitions we can say that women enptrepreneurs are those entrepreneurs who have taken initiative in promoting and running an enterprise by having a controlling interest in that particular enterprise.

Women Entrepreneurs' Enterprise, as defined for the first time in 1988, laid down that an enterprise owned and administered by a woman entrepreneur with a minimum financial interest of 51 per cent in the share capital and giving at least 50 per cent employment to women would be treated as Women's Enterprise. The investment ceilings were kept at par with the limits specified in 1985 for other units, *i.e.* upto ₹35 lakh for SSI units and upto ₹45 lakh for ancillaries. This definition was revised in August 1991, by dispensing with the employment criterion for women workers.

Currently, the women's Enterprise is defined as a small scale industrial unit/ industry related service or business enterprise managed by one or more women entrepreneurs in proprietary concerns in which she/they individually or jointly have a share of capital of not less than 51 per cent as partners/shareholders/ directors of private limited companies/members of cooperative societies.

Features of Women Entrepreneurs

Following are main entrepreneurial traits of women entrepreneurs[2] :

(*i*) Imagination : It refers to the imaginative approach or original ideas with competitive market. Well planned approach is needed to examine the existing situation and to identify the entrepreneurial opportunities. It further implies that women entrepreneurs have association with knowledgeable people and contracting the right organisations offering support and services.

(*ii*) Attribute to work hard : Enterprising women have further ability to work hard. The imaginative ideas have to come to a fair play. Hard work is needed to build up an enterprise.

(*iii*) Persistence : Women entrepreneurs must have an intention to fulfil their dreams. They have to make a dream translated into an enterprise. Studies show that successful women have worked hard. They persisted in getting loan from financial institutions and other inputs. They have persisted in adverse circumstances and in adversity.

(iv) Ability and desire to take risk : The desire refers to the willingness to take risk and ability to the proficiency in planning, making forecast, estimates and calculations. Profits are the reward of risk. Enterprising women take risk but the risk is well calculated. It offers challenges where chances of survival and failure are on equal footing.

Women bntrepreneurship in India

Basically, Indian women have been one career that is marriage. But in present scenario, they are being shifted to teaching, professional career, office work, nursing and medicine. Moreover, they now started to engineering and business affairs. Actually participation of women in entrepreneurial behaviour is comparatively a recent phenomenon.

The Fourth All India Census of MSME reveals that Total number of registered enterprises was 15.53 lakhs out of which 2.15 lakhs units were registered as women enterprises. An enterprise (Manufacturing or a Service) managed by one or more women entrepreneurs in proprietary concern, or in which she/ they individually or jointly have a share capital of not less than 51% as Partners/ Shareholders/Directors of Private Limited Company/Members of Co-operative Society is called a 'Woman Enterprise'.

Women Entrepreneurs in the urban areas have a better concentration in capital intensive industries viz. paper and paper products, leather products, rubber products, chemical products, machinery and transport equipment.

Government Policy Support

The Industrial Policy, 1991 has laid emphasis on the development of entrepreneurship among women. It provides that "merely making longer resource allocation for women within the prevailing pattern and structure of development would not yield the desired results. The policy has a strategy for the holistic development of women. This would help develop their personality and at the same time improve their economic and social conditions. This policy with this end in view has redefined women's units as units in which they had the majority shareholding and management control.[4]

The policy has further envisaged special training programmes to support women entrepreneurs. Accordingly, women entrepreneurs are receiving training through Entrepreneurship Development Programmes (EDPs) conducted by various institutions and organisations both at the central and state levels. Study suggests that EDP is getting popularity among women entrepreneurs specially in the items like readymade garments, dress designing, food products, export oriented handicrafts, plastic products, soft tiles and herbal preparations.

The Small Industries Development Organisation (SIDO) is also providing technical schemes for the establishment of SSI units. Keeping in mind the promotional requirements of women entrepreneurship, the SSI Board in 1991 revised the definition of women units by deleting the condition of employing 50 per cent of women workers. It has given a further boost to women entrepreneurs to undertake more entrepreneurial activities and avail of other facilities available to SSI units.

SIDBI Efforts

The SIDBI has also been trying to promote women entrepreneurship. The SIDBI on its part has also undertaken various development initiatives towards this goal. The Bank has designed programmes with a focus on women *viz.* Mahila Vikas Nidhi, Mahila Udyam Nidhi, Micro Credit Scheme, Women Entrepreneurship Development Programmes etc. Mahila Vikas Nidhi (MVN) is SIDBI's specially designed fund for the economic development of women. MVN aims to bring about the economic improvement of women especially the rural poor by providing them avenues for training and employment opportunities by facilitating the creation of infrastructural and training facilities. The basic activity involves the setting up of Training-cum-Production-Centres (TPCS) and for the purpose, a judicious mix of loan and grant is extended to accredited NGOs. In addition, activities like vocational training, strengthening of the marketing setup for the products of the beneficiary group, arrangement for the supply of improved inputs, production and technology improvement are also covered under the MVN scheme. Under MVN, the cumulative assistance of ₹60 million has been provided to 133 NGOs benefiting about 17,500 women. Training-cum-production centres set up by NGOs under MVN mostly attend to activities like sericulture, spinning, weaving, knitting, embroidery, coir-products blockprinting, handloom, bamboo products, handicrafts, bakery-products, shoe-making etc. These programmes are formulated with the twin objectives of—

(*i*) providing training and extension services support to women entrepreneurs through a comprehensive package suited to their skills and socio-economic status, and

(ii) extending financial assistance on liberal terms to enable them to set-up industrial units in the small scale sector.

PROMOTIONAL SCHEMES FOR WOMEN ENTREPRENEURS

Central Government has formulated the following important schemes that are made specifically at women entrepreneurs.

1. Trade Related Entrepreneurship Assistance and Development Scheme For Women (TREAD)

With a view to encourage women in setting up their own ventures, the government launched a Scheme, namely, "Trade Related Entrepreneurship Assistanc and Development (TREAD) during the 11th Plan. The scheme envisaged economic empowerment of women through the development of their entrepreneurial skills in non-farm activities. There are three major components of the scheme :

(*i*) Government of India grant upto 30% of the Local project cost to the Non-Government Organisations (NGOs) for promoting entrepreneurship among women. The remaining 70% of the project cost is financed by the lending agency as loan for undertaking activities as envisaged in the project.

(*ii*) Government of India grant upto ₹1 lakh per programme to training institutions/NGOs for imparting training to the women entrepreneurs.

(*iii*) Need-based Government of India grants upto ₹5 lakhs to National Entrepreneurship Development Institutions and any other institutions of repute for undertaking field surveys, research studies, evaluation studies, designing of training modules etc.

Operationalisation of the Scheme

The scheme envisages that Women Associations/NGOs/SHGs should prepare composite bankable proposals for a group of women entrepreneurs, and submit it to the bank, which are signatories to participate in the scheme, namely, Syndicate Bank, State Bank of India, Canara Bank and Allahabad Bank. The Bank examines the proposal and issues approval.

2. Micro and Small Enterprises Cluster Development Programme (MSE-CDP)

(a) Existing Clusters: A cluster is defined as a group of enterprises, normally, 20 or more producing same/similar products/services. The Cluster Development Programme (CDP) being implemented envisages diagnostic study of identified clusters of traditional skill-based MSEs to identify appropriate technologies and their providers and to facilitate adoption of available technology meeting the specific needs of the end users. The Cluster Development aims at enhanced competitiveness, technology improvement, adoption of best manufacturing practices, marketing of products, employment generation etc. The scheme provides assistance for capacity building, common facilities, marketing etc. the delivery, assimilation and diffusion of the identified technology from its producers to the recipient user/cluster of small enterprises.

Types of Interventions

(*i*) *Soft Interventions* : Capacity building activities in the cluster where no fixed asset is acquired or formed. Soft interventions, *inter alia*, include :

(*i*) Diagnostic study
(*ii*) Forming association : Trust building and developing identity
(*iii*) Capacity building,
(*iv*) Organising workshops, seminars,
(*v*) Training and exposure visits,
(*vi*) Market development,
(*vii*) Launch of website,
(*viii*) Common piocurement,
(*ix*) Common/complementary sales and branding.

In the past, depending upon the type of cluster, assistance available for soft interventions has varied in the range of ₹25-35 lakhs per cluster. Currently an internal ceiling of ₹10 lakhs for soft intervention under this Scheme is available. The Government is trying to bring upwards. Clusters of women's enterprises are entitled upto 90% assistance for soft interventions.

(ii) *Hard Interventions* *:* These are tangible "assets" like :

(i) Setting up of Common Facility Centre (CFCs),
(ii) Mini tool rooms,
(iii) Design centres,
(iv) Testing facilities,
(v) Training centres,
(vi) R and D centres,
(vii) Common raw material bank/sales depot, etc.

There can be other tangible assets that could be set up by the Women's Clusters, as long as they are put to common use. For hard interventions, it is necessary to form a Special Purpose Vehicle (SPV) which could be a registered society, or a cooperative society, or company, or a trust or any other legal entity—in which at least 20 to 30 members of the Cluster contribute and participate. Other Cluster members who do not join this SPV could also sign up as users. The Common Facility Centre that is set up by the SPV as a hard intervention is entitled to the highest level of assistance from the MSME Ministry, i.e., upto 90% of the project cost. This covers the cost of machinery, plant, equipment, laboratory and other tangible assets. The balance 10% of the project cost would have to be contributed by the SPV or by the State government or the Local government. But, land and building are not covered under this "Project Cost" and will have to be provided by the SPVs of the Women's Enterprise Clusters or by the State government or by some other agency.

(iii) Infrastructure Assistance : Infrastructure assistance includes the construction of basic amenities like power, approach roads, drainage, water supply and storage and the like. MSME Ministry's assistance for this component is presently limited to 40% of the total cost—though the government is trying to increase this level. Only one element of Infrastructure Assistance, i.e., Display or Exhibition Centres (which could consist of show-rooms with attached stores) are entitled to a higher level of assistance in so far as Women's Clusters are concerned, i.e., 90%. This Display/ Exhibition Centre could be built by the Women's Clusters, SPV within the Cluster, or near the Cluster or even in adjoining markets of towns—as long as they exhibit and market the products manufactured by the Women's Clusters.

(b) Creation of Physical Infrastructure : This Ministry implemented the IID Scheme to provide developed sites with infrastructural facilities like power distribution network, water, telecommunications, drainage and pollution control facilities, roads, exhibition/display centres, raw materials, storage and marketing outlets, common service facilities and technological backup services etc. This scheme has been subsumed in the MSME-Cluster Development Programme. All the features of IID Scheme have been retained. To create physical infrastructure exclusively for women enterprises central grant of 40% of the project cost subject to a maximum of ₹2 crore is available. The Ministry of MSME is making efforts to enhance the quantum of grant to 80% in a project of ₹10 crore.

Operationalisation of the Scheme

(i) A Cluster Development Executive (CDE) is required for executing and monitoring all soft interventions in a cluster. Normally, a CDE can be a DIC Officer/MSME-DI officer/retired expert or even hired person from Non- Government Sector.

(ii) The hard interventions in a cluster and creation of physical infrastructure require to set up a users body/special purpose vehicle which could be society/trust/company to be formed by the cluster beneficiaries.

3. Credit Guarantee Fund Scheme

The Government introduced the Credit Guarantee Fund Scheme for Small Industries in May, 2000 with the objective of making available credit to SSI units, particularly tiny units, for loans upto ₹25 lakhs without collateral/ third party guarantees. The Scheme is being operated by the Credit Guarantee Fund Trust for Small Industries (CGTSI) set up jointly by the Government of India and SIDBI. The Scheme provides for collateral free credit facility (term loan and/or working capital) extended by eligible lending institutions to new and existing SSI units/Small Scale Service and Business (industry related) Enterprises (SSSBEs) including Information Technology and Software Industry upto ₹25 lakhs per borrowing unit. In the case of women enterprises, the guarantee cover is upto 80% of the credit subject to a maximum guarantee limit of ₹20 lakhs. The Member Lending Institutions (MLI) availing of guarantee from the Trust have to pay a one-time guarantee fee of 1.5% of the credit facility (comprising term loan and/ or working capital) sanctioned by the lending institution to the borrower and annual service fee of 0.75% per annum on the amount of credit facility extended by the MLI, which is covered under the scheme.

Operationalisation of the Scheme

The entrepreneurs whose bank finance is approved by the lending bank may ask the bank to obtain guarantee from the Credit Guarantee Trust Fund. This facility is available online to the lending banks and clearance from the Trust is conveyed in a day or two.

4. Support For Entrepreneurial And Managerial Development

MSME DIs regularly conduct EDPs/MDPs for existing and prospective entrepreneurs and charge fee for such courses. To encourage more entrepreneurs from among the SC/ST, women and physically challenged groups, it is proposed that such beneficiaries will not be charged any fees but, instead, paid a stipend of ₹500 per capita per month. 50,000 entrepreneurs will be trained in IT, Fashion Technology, Catering, Agro and Food Processing, Pharmaceutical, Biotechnology etc. through specialised courses run by MSME DIs. 20% of courses conducted by these institutions shall exclusively be for women.

5. Exhibitions For Women Under Promotional Package For Micro and Small Enterprises Approved By CCEA Under Marketing Support

DC (MSME) has formulated a scheme for women entrepreneurs to encourage Small and Micro manufacturing units owned by women in their efforts at tapping and developing overseas markets, to increase participation of representatives of small/micro manufacturing enterprises under SIDO stall at International Trade Fairs/Exhibitions, to enhance export from such units.

The government has decided to encourage women entrepreneurs to participate in the International Exhibitions. For this purpose, the following steps have been taken by the government :

(i) provide rent free space in the exhibitions

(ii) reimburse 100% economy class air fare for one representative

(iii) reimburse shipping cost upto ₹15,000, The overall ceiling shall, however, be ₹1.25 lakhs.

Problems of Women Entrepreneurs

Women entrepreneurs are facing the following problems :

(i) Banks and financial institutions do not have faith in women entrepreneurial abilities so they consider women applicants a higher risky than men loanees. They look for men behind the women applicants.

(ii) They lack ability to bear economic risk, social risk, technical and environment risk.

(iii) They have peculiar problem in domestic affairs like husband and child care etc.

(iv) They have low level of favourable family background in the field of family cooperation, education, occupation and entrepreneurial base.

(v) Women have led a protected life. So, they are handicapped by their inability to travel from one place to another place for business reasons.

(vi) They lack high achievement motivation. They have preconceived notions about their role in life and this inhibits achievement and independence.

Suggestions to Promote Women Entrepreneurship

(*i*) Women entrepreneurs should be treated a separate target group for all entrepreneurial development programmes.

(ii) Vocational training facilities are to be developed by the Government for women. It is a first stage in developing women entrepreneurship.

(iii) Institutional support system should be designed to suit the requirements of women entrepreneurs.

(iv) Encouragement should be given to appropriate technologies, equipment and practice for reducing their druggery and increasing their efficiency and productivity.

(v) Government should try to involve women entrepreneurs in decision making process meant for entrepreneurship development.

Thus, more and more potential women candidates should be motivated to join entrepreneurial activities. For this purpose, effective entrepreneurship development programme is necessary to suit their requirements.

EXAMINATION QUESTIONS

Long Answer Questions

1. What do you know by women entrepreneurs ? Critically examine their present position in India.
2. Discuss the nature of women entrepreneurship. Also examine their role in Indian context.
3. Discuss the rationale of women entrepreneurship in India. Do you think that Government should be the only agency to be involved in development of women entrepreneurship.

4. Explain the objectives of women entrepreneurship. Also discuss the problems and prospects of women entrepreneurship in the country.
5. "Institutional support System is also necessary for. women entrepreneurship and SIDBI is moving in all right direction" Do you think so ? Explain.
6. "Family background and social taboos are main factors behind slow growth of women entrepreneurship in our country," Comment on this statement.
7. "Effective leadership qualities and will power are the prerequisite conditions for developing women entrepreneurship in the country." Give your opinion on this statement.
8. Discuss the problem of women entrepreneurs in India.
9. "In our country, women entrepreneurs have been able to establish themselves properly like their male counterparts." Discuss.

Short Answer Questions

1. Who is women entrepreneur ?
2. Explain the features of women entrepreneurs.
3. Discuss the Government policy support for women entrepreneurs.
4. Examine the SIDBI efforts in developing women entrepreneurs.
5. Describe the problems of women entrepreneurs.
6. What is the present position of women entrepreneurship in India.
7. Give suggestions to promote women entrepreneurship in India.

Objective Type Questions

1. A woman entrepreneur is supposed to have a minimum financial interest in share capital of entrepreneur's enterprise

   (a) 35 per cent (b) 51 per cent
   (c) 25 per cent (d) None of these

2. Employment condition for women's enterprise to female workforce

   (a) At least 50 per cent (b) 26 per cent
   (c) 51 percent (d) 75 per cent

3. Mahila Vikas Nidhi is being managed by

   (a) IDBI (b) SBI
   (c) NABARD (d) SIDBI

4. The most important constraint before the woman entrepreneur is

   (a) Risk bearing capacity
   (b) Peculiar problem in domestic affairs
   (c) Family background
   (d) Lack of achievement motivation

5. Women entrepreneurship may be developed with the help of
   (a) Treating women entrepreneurhip as a separate target group
   (b) Providing vocational training
   (c) Literacy drive
   (d) Ensuring high achievement motivation

Answers

1-(c) 2-(d) 3-(d) 4-(b) 5-(b)

Reason Based Questions

State with reasons whether the following statements are true or false :

1. In our country, women entrepreneurs have been able to establish themselves properly like their male counterparts.
2. Contribution of women NGOs have dismal role in empowerment of rural women.
3. Nowadays, the problems faced by women entrepreneurs are not very different from those faced by their male counterparts.
4. Indian women have one career that is marriage.
5. Women entrepreneurs are those who have a minimum financial interest of 51% of the capital.
6. Women are not able to establish themselves properly as entrepreneurs in India.
7. Women are yet to establish themselves as entrepreneurs in India.

REFERENCES

1. Paul Jose, Ajith Kumar N., Maulilly Paul, T. *Entrepreneurship Development,* Himalaya Publishing House, Mumbai 1996 p. 65.
2. Srivastava, S.B. *A Practical Guide to Industrial Entrepreneurs,* Sultan Chand and Sons, Delhi, 1992, 385.
3. Paul Jose, Ajith Kumar N. Maupilly, Paul, T., *Entrepreneurship Development,* p. 49.

14

ENTREPRENEURIAL BEHAVIOUR

Creativity and innovation are special breeds of planned change that organisations actively seek to promote in the system. Creativity is the process of developing a novel idea or a new way of approaching an old idea, is the spark of innovation, the transformation of creative ideas into products or process that fulfil customer needs. In practice, a wide variety of forces can affect organisational change but therefore forces which are responsible for exerting powerful influence in today's economy. These are the intensified pressure of competition, the internationalisation of the marketplace, the accelerated pace of technological advancement, and the rapid change in consumer values and life-styles. Combined impact of these forces and other environmental forces, motivate and compel managers to take a closer look at how creativity and innovation can help their organisations adapt to the environment, influence the environment, or shift domains, both today and tomorrow. In addition to helping organisations respond to the environment, the opportunity to pursue creative and innovative changes can provide individual and group challenges that motivate employees and managers alike to higher performance. Creativity and innovation often being spontaneously sparked by a particular organisational problem or an insight into an organisational opportunity. Such changes may be planned and implemented through informal, episodic activities. However, to consistently contribute to organisational performance, creativity and innovation must be systematised and incorporated into the organisation's daily activities. A variety of factors are involved, but three key elements are particularly crucial for institutionalising creativity and innovation : planning, organisational culture and organisation structure.

If we are to thrive in business, we must be creative. Success in business today demands constant innovation. Generating fresh solutions to problems, and the ability to invent new products or services for a changing market, are part of the intellectual capital. They also give a company or business organisation its competitive edge. In a world of change, success comes from looking for the next opportunity and having the ability to find hidden connections and insights into new products or services, desired by the customer. Developing the radar to spot an opportunity, takes creativity. While brainpower is our most valuable resource, great ideas are in short supply. Successful business organisations or companies now place a premium on attracting and keeping talent because wealth flows directly from innovation. Creativity is the root of innovation. It is a process and a skill which can be developed and managed throughout the entire organisation. "Creativity is marked by the ability or power to create-to-bring into existence, to invest with a new form, to produce through imaginative skill, to make or bring into existence something new." "Creativity is the process of bringing something new into being... creativity requires passion and commitment. Out of the creative act is born symbols and myths. It brings to our awareness what was previously hidden and points to new life. The experience is one of heightened consciousness—ecstasy". "A product is creative when it is (a) novel and (b) appropriate. A novel product is original not predictable. The bigger the concept, and the more the product stimulates further work and ideas, the more the product is creative."

Nature of Creativity

There are many definitions each emphasising a different facet of creativity.

1. **Approach of Outputs of Creative Efforts** : It describes creativity as "the discovery of something that is novel but also useful or relevant or economical or elegant or valuable."[1]

2. **Approach of Novel Hypothesis** : It explains the gravity of a creative act. "The product or outcome of a creative effort must be both significant and strikingly different from the beaten track."[2]

However, *Don Mackinnon* has stated that mere novelty of a product does not justify its being called creative. There are certain conditions for a product to be treated as creative :[3]

(i) The product must be adaptive to reality.

(ii) It must serve to solve a problem, fit the need of a given situation, accomplish some recognisable goal.

(iii) The creative product must be produced, developed, evaluated, communicated etc.

(iv) Product is aesthetically pleasing.

(v) It significantly changes our view of the world.

3. Approach of Creative Process : According to this approach, "creativity is divergent thinking, the seeking of relationship between previously unrelated concepts or frames of reference of exploring the underknown".[4] However, it may be possible that the result of this effort may or may not be creative but the effort indicates the important features of the creative process, for example wide search or exploration, leaps of imagination, incubation, developing fresh insight, etc. Generally, routinised nature of the work adversely affect the imaginative capacity of the individual and consequently limits the scope of creativity. Due to this reason, science and arts are generally more creative pursuits than the factor work or vocational training programmes.

4. Approach of States of the Being : Under this approach, "creativity is identified with openness in expressing feelings, receptivity to ideas, concern for others, desire to grow as a person and actualise one's potential etc."[5] In this context, it is feasible to compare creative and non-creative persons from the same profession. There are certain additional personality traits and abilities that distinguish creative person from non-creative persons like the greater love of complexity of the creative?, their more bizarre fantasy life but simultaneously a high degree of contact with reality their greater dependence of judgement. The ability to come up with many varied and uncommon ideas or solutions also seems to distinguish creative from non-creative persons, as also their ability to notice anomalies, issues, paradoxes etc."[6]

Thus, the above different approaches relating with creativity indicates that they are affected by different limitations. If we evaluate creativity only in terms of novelty and usefulness or elegance of a product, we will find that this creative product may have been discovered or produced either accidentally or by a non-creative process. Nowadays, innovation are highly institutionalised. Most of the researchers are based on individual/particular problem area and scientific methods are applied or tested to that particular problem area. Similarly, dreamer would be the champion creative if we judge the creative by the creative process instead of the creative product. The dreamer is more concerned with the extent of imagination and divergent thinking, combinational play, the relating of remote ideas and these factors enable the dreamer of the creative process at their floodtide during dreaming. If creativity is to be evaluated in terms of the characteristics of the creative person such as lack of inhibition, receptivity, curiosity, idea flows etc., the child who will be in a better position, leading scientists, artists, thinkers and poets. So, we can say that creativity is concerned with the employment of a playfully exploratory rather than a mechanical process of problem-solving, by a person who is open and curious and imaginative rather than by a person who is inhibited and conventional to find solution or design that are novel (and yet useful) rather than merely run of the will." Convergent thinking helps in this divergent thinking process where the thinker is supposed to make some critical choices like establishing an original line of enquiry or thinking.

Constituents of Creative Abilities

(i) Fluency : It measures a person's ability to come up with a number of solutions to a given problem. Those that come up with a large number of uses would be called ideationally fluent person. Ideationally fluent person tends to come up with a greater variety of solutions as well as with a larger number of unusual solutions that persons who are ideationally not fluent.

(ii) Flexibility : It is the ability to provide a large variety of solutions to respond to a problem from a variety of viewpoints. Another ability that is also required is the ability to use a variety of approaches in problem , solving.

(iii) Originality : It is the ability to come up with unusual but appropriateness. A related ability is the ability to come up with relationship between ideas or two frames or references.

(iv) Problem Sensitivity : It is the ability to notice the unexplained, the unsatisfactory or the incongruent or the ability to sense the problems.

(v) Unravelling causes and effects : It is the ability to go to the roots of a phenomenon by unravelling its causes and equally to visualise its consequences. It is a vital ingredient to scientific creativity as well as in artistic creativity.

(vi) Elaborateness : It is the ability to elaborate on a theme. Actually, it is the difference between the idea that man has considerable creative potential and a full-fledged training programme for increasing creativity. The ability to elaborate is indispensable in putting a creative idea to work.

(vii) Problem Restructuring : It is the ability to go behind the surface features of a problem and see what the real problem is.

Constituents of creative abilities are not available in equal measures in the same individual. The individual who can deal fluently may not be very original and *vice versa*. It is, therefore, inappropriate to categorise a person as creative or uncreative without, specifying the dimensions on which he has high ability and the ones on which he has more limited ability.

Types of Creativity

Generally, quality of creation determines the types of creativity. Various authors have suggested different types of creativity. These are as follows :

1. **Abraham Maslow :**According to him nature of creativity deals with the following aspects :
   - (*i*) *Primary Creativity* : It deals with spontaneous creations. Spontaneous creations, as in a child belong to primary creativity,
   - (*ii*) *Secondary Creativity* : It is more deliberate and skilled as in the application of ideas and insight to inventions.
2. **Ainsworth Land :** According to him there are the following levels of creativity :
   - (*i*) Elaborative
   - (ii) Improvement oriented
   - (iii) Combination or syntheses of superior quality
   - (iv) Transformation (such as the emergence of a new approach or paradigm through the destruction of the old)
3. **Iring Taylor :** *Iring Taylor* has suggested the following quality hierarchy :
   - (*i*) *Spontaneous Creativity* : It is similar to Maslow's primary creativity. It deals with spontaneous creations.
   - (*ii*) *Technical Creativity :* It involves striking improvement in a process that increases the level of proficiency or efficiency.
   - (*iii*) *Inventive Creativity* : It involves ingenuous new combination of materials or ingredients. In this context, we can mention the Edison's light bulb or Bell's telephone.
   - (*iv*) *Innovative Creativity* : It involves far-reaching application of more basic ideas such as management applications of principles of

psychology to develop a much more effective system for motivating staff.

(*v*) *Emergentive Creativity* : It consists of new revolutionary principles for an art or a science such as the psycho-analytical concepts of *Freud* or the relativity concept of Einstein or Picasso's cubist ideas.

Generally, emergentive creativity is intrinsically not so much superior to expressive, technical, inventive or innovative creativity. According to *Khandwala*, these are simply different forms of creativity and each can vary enormously in quality. The quality or level of creativity is related to the level of novelty and appropriateness of the creative effort. The lowest level is where novelty is minimal and appropriateness (to a situation or a context) is marginal, the highest when both are exceptionally high. Moderate levels of either or both indicate intermediate levels of creativity. The implication in that we need not move from expressive to emergentive creativity. Rather, to improve the quality of any type of creativity we need to move in two directions simultaneously, towards greater relevance or appropriateness of whatever we are trying to create. This means we should get better at both divergent thinking and also at acquiring a deep understanding of reality."[7]

Creative Process

The creative process in organisations involves three steps : idea generation, problem solving or idea development and implementation.

1. Generation of Ideas : The generation of ideas in an organisation depends first and foremost on the flow of people and information between the firm and its environment. It is greatly stimulated by external contacts. For example, the vast majority of technological innovations, have been made in response to the conditions in the marketplace. If organisational managers are unaware that there is potential demand for a new product or that there is dissatisfaction with already existing products, they are not likely to seek innovations. Outside consultants and experts are important sources of information for managers, because they are frequently aware of new products, processes, or service developments in their fields. The generation of ideas is more likely to promote innovations when those ideas issue from the grass-roots level of the organisation. She argues that empowering people on the lower levels of organisations to initiate new ideas within the context of a supportive environment is a valuable means of implementing successful innovations.

2. Idea Development : Idea development is dependent on the organisational culture and processes within the organisation. Organisational characteristics, values and processes can support or inhibit the development and use of creative ideas. Commitment to the rational problem-solving approaches are discussed. The organisational structure also plays an important role. Rigidity structured organisations that inhibit communication between departments will often keep potentially helpful people from knowing that a problem exists. By creating barriers to communication, such organisations may also prevent problem solutions from reaching managers who need them.

New ideas are propelled through the organisational system by a variety of means, one of which is the policy of making external commitments to consumers even before a new computer product has actually been built.

3. Implementation : The implementation stage of the creative process in organisations consists of those steps that bring a solution or invention to the marketplace. For manufactured goods, these steps include engineering, tooling, manufacturing, test marketing and promotion. While a high rate of innovation often reduces short-term profitability, it is crucial for long-term growth.

Forms of Creativity

(i) Creative Representation : It needs intimate knowledge of whatever is sought to be represented and also a freshness of perspective. The child creativity is largely representational. It directly paints with its available skills what it feels and thinks."[8]

(ii) Abstractive and Inferential Creativity : It needs a capacity to penetrate the fog, the noise and other directions and to see what it all adds up to." The capacity to transform a mess into a logical structure or design is needed the most for this sort of creativity. The capacity to build models out of the mess (that is simplify reality) spot anomalies intuit underlying principles perform "what if sorts of mental experiments generalise etc. are important for this sort of creativity."[9] The Scientist's creativity is abstractive and inferential where they are expected to discover the hidden patterns and code of things.

(iii) Elaborative Creativity : It deals with the process of flushing out imaginatively an insight or an abstraction or an inspired idea. It requires strength in associative thinking, *i.e.*, in the capacity to think of interesting association of one's core idea, the ability to develop an idea, see its consequences and interesting application etc. There is a sort of chain reaction in which the core idea gets linked to other ideas which in turn get linked to still other ideas and so on." It is an attractive process similar to formation of a crystal or a coral reef.

CREATIVE THINKING

Basically, there are two types of thinking or problem-solving activities. These are convergent and divergent thinking.

1. Convergent Thinking

It consists of those abilities, which helped a person get to the right solution in problem that had one right solution. For example, good memory, logical ability etc. It also consists of mechanisms of thought that help the person get a good definition of the problem when the problem is complex or vague, to analyse the problem in depth, to select a solution (or the method of getting a solution) out of many that may be available to put together a solution (i.e., to synthesise a solution) and to refine a solution and make of an efficient one.[10] It is rational thinking. In this thinking, the information provides one right answer or recognised best or conventional answer. It is also required to grasp an unclear problem. Categorisation, logical thinking, analysis, comparing, evaluation are critical factors in this phase of problem-solving. In the problem-solving process, "Problems are such that there is only one right answer or at best a few right answers and these answers can easily be discriminated from the many wrong ones. Also, given the problem, anyone knowing the basic logical, mathematical or memory operations can reach the right answer.""

Mechanism of Convergent Thinking

(i) Clarificatory Mechanism : A problem is an unmet goal or an unwanted effect often accompanied by insufficient information as to what is wrong, why is it wrong, how to set it right and/or what would constitute setting the problem right.[12] It incorporates phases like:

(a) verbalising a problem,

(b) listing the components of the problem,

(c) analogies and comparisons.

(ii) Analytical Mechanism : It involves several related processes of clarification :

(a) breaking a problem down into its components (factoring of the problem),

(b) seeking relationships among components,

(c) identifying components of a problem into more abstract forms,

(d) defining issues, constraints variables,

(e) imposing constraints on a problem like making assumptions, establishing criteria of evaluation,,

(f) costing or selecting by comparing and evaluating alternatives,

(g) working backwards from a solution to the present situation,

(h) building a model of the problem situation and manipulating its components to see alternative outcomes.

(iii) Synthesis Aiding Mechanism : It deals with various stands of thought or the various parts of a complex situation in the form of brief notes, which generally trigger the act of synthesis. Synthesis is the act of seeing the pattern among components the whole in the parts, the unity in the diversity. A mechanism that aids synthesis once the analysis is completely made is that of aggregation. Some of the factors also help in the act of the synthesis :

(a) incubation,

(b) inconsistent or extreme elements, and

(c) broad model.

(iv) Optimising Mechanism : Optimising is the process of refining a solution until the solution is of acceptable quality. It involves a number of mechanisms such as :

(a) substitution of parts,

(b) addition of components,

(c) deletion of unnecessary ingredients,

(d) modification of elements,

(e) alteration of the relations between the components,

(f) formalising the criteria for evaluating potential solutions.

2. Divergent Thinking

It is an imaginative phase of creative thinking. According to *Guilford*, "The unique feature of divergent production is that a variety of responses is produced. The product is not completely determined by the given information ... Divergent thinking ... comes into play whenever there is trial and error thinking ... "Further, in divergent thinking operations, we think in different directions, sometimes, searching, sometimes, seeking variety."[13] Actually, divergent thinking is the main characteristic of creative thinking. "Divergent thinking is undertaking search for solutions that may involve substantial departures from beaten track. It involves using approaches or perspectives that may be uncommon or unusual, often resulting in a variety of solutions. Some of which may be quite novel."[14]

Mechanisms of Divergent Thinking[15]

(i) Development of a working definition of the problem.

(ii) Formulation of objectives and procedures, etc.

(iii) Use of associative thinking for developing for more and more alternatives.

(iv) Reinterpretation of constraints to help in restructuring process of original problems.

(v) Evaluation of possible solution to make the further searching possible.

(vi) Setting the mind to synthesise imaginary solutions.

(vii) Launching brain storming to generate unconventional alternatives or solutions.

(viii) Searching solutions to counter the use of conventionally advanced alternatives.

(ix) Re-assessment of basic assumptions required for current approaches.

(x) Encouragement or facilitation to conceiving process of far out possibility by creating distortion or avoidance of problem constraints.

(xi) Assessment of negative consequences of non-availability of solutions and doing efforts for generating solutions to the problem.

(xii) Seeking interesting far-out analogies to the problem situations and an exploration of their mechanics.

(xiii) Diverting attention from a mindset or obsessions, side tracking.

Techniques of Creative Thinking

1. Brain Storming

It is a group technique, but it can also be used by individuals. The brainstormer takes up a fairly clearly stated problem which has many possible solutions such as how to increase plant productivity or how to develop interest among children in science. Thereafter, the individual or panel of brainstormer is encouraged to 'brainstorm", *i.e.,* generate in a rapid-fire fashion novel solution to the problem. All criticism or evaluation of any idea during this brainstorming phase is generally discouraged. Brainstorming is based on the principle that quantity of ideas begets quality and to get many ideas, it is necessary to suspend evaluation of ideas during the idea generation phase.

Features of Brainstorming

(i) It is not useful as a technique where the problem has a unique solution that can be reached by analysis.

(ii) Specific topic is required for brainstorming process. In the absence of specific topic, brainstorming will not be very fruitful.

(iii) It leads to many ideas. Once the ideas are generated, then it is necessary to identify a few ideas for more intensive investigation.

(iv) It has a wide acceptability. It creates more ideas. Participants in brainstorming session are free, give more ideas or large number of options.

(v) It is a powerful technique in which participants are motivated to give suggestions for solving the specific problem meant for brainstorming session.

(vi) It provides a democratic and collaborative culture specially in case of divergent thinking.

Principles of Brainstorming

1. During the generating phase of ideas, evaluation process is to be deferred. It is more relevant specially in case of evaluation of negative and critical kind of ideas.
2. Encouragement should be given to generating more and more ideas. It will provide more opportunity for generating more brilliant ideas. Principle of "Quantity begets quality" should be implemented.
3. It would be better to encourage more fantastic ideas. A fantastic idea is the one, which does not seen at all to be a practical idea. It will discourage conventional patterns of thinking. It is true that fantastic ideas are not

practicable but they trigger other ideas that might not only be novel but also useful.

4. It is better to welcome other's ideas or one's own previous ideas. It would also be better to open to the suggestive power of other's or one's own earlier ideas.

2. Attribute Analysis

It attempts to generate alternative ways of satisfying the major characteristics of a product or activity. It is useful for designing or redesigning a specific product or service or an activity.

It also combines the convergent thinking principle of forming categories with the brain storming principle of generating many alternative solutions. Crawford has suggested the following steps[18] in attribute analysis :

(a) Identification of major attributes of an object or an activity.

(b) Generation of many alternative ways of securing the possible attribute.

(c) Evaluation of alternative designs in terms of criteria like cost, marketability, etc.

According to *Crawford,* magic inspiration is not the only or even major source of creativity. Much creativity arises from changing the attributes of an object or an activity, or from grafting on to the object or activity an attribute or attributes of some other object or activity.

Principles of Attributes Listing

Crawford has given the following principles of attribute listing :[19]

(i) Creativity deals with inspiration. It also includes adaptation and experimentation.

(ii) Creation includes combination of different products or ideas as well as allows the modification of an attribute or assimilation of different attributes of other things.

(iii) Concrete alternatives are to be searched and in case of need also modify the current attributes of an object.

(iv) Creativity deals with looking for closely related substitutes of an existing or current attribute. Thereafter, it can be upgraded to more and more far-out alternatives.

(v) Creation is a continuing stream of modifications repaired by ideas in use or in practice in current scenario. It also ensures necessary changes in products or objects.

Thus, we can say that the more specific the object or activity one wished to change, the better would be the results given by attribute listing. It also helps in separating the modifiable from the unmodifiable attributes of the objects. It also encourages to concentrate attention on the modifiable attributes. In this context, the following procedures are required :

(a) listing of all the obvious attributes of an object or activity, e.g., current sise, colour, shape, functions, weight, major function, steps, subprograms etc. for an activity,

(b) identifying some of these attributes that can possibly be altered without destroying the main function of the object or activity,

(c) stating the alternative attributes as more abstract.

Steps Involved in Attribute Listing

(i) Listing of basic but modifiable attributes or properties or specifications of a particular object or activity.

(ii) Generating alternatives to the current attribute or specification.

(iii) Listing abstract or generic attributes of a concrete object or activity. It helps in generating more ideas in place of listing the concrete attributes.

3. Synectics

It is a group technique specialised in using a variety of analogies in problem-solving. The word synectics has been adopted from the Greek word synecticos in corporating diverse elements. Technique of Synectics is quite popular in practice for finding innovative approaches to a number of intractable technical problems. "Synectics is a difficult technique but its principles of constructive psychological strain is most practical. It consists of mechanisms—analogies and metaphors—that bend and stretch the mind in every direction through the stuff of poetry. It also help in charming the mind for creating novel visions and insights."

Major **analogies** under this technique are as follows :

(i) Direct Analogy : It involves discussing an analogy of the problem situation from a very different field. It also undertakes a direct comparison of phenomenon under discussion with some other similar phenomenon. In this context, it is better to say that the more far fetched the analogy, the greater the probability that the angle suggested by the analogy. Actually, it has not previously been thought of by anybody.

(ii) Personal Analogy : It requires the problem-solver to project himself into a situation and report back his experiences of that particular situation like what he feels, sees, hears, thinks etc. This type of enquiry, sometimes helps in yielding dramatic discoveries.

(iii) Fantasy Analogy : Under this analogy, the person concerned is asked to release his imagination from real life constraints and, in effect, day-dream. Group members are required to imagine a constraint free solution as in case of enjoying wish fulfilling daydreams. They are also urged to fantasise some perfect solution even if it flies in the face of known scientific principles."

(iv) Symbolic Analogy : It requires group members to furnish pithy but poetic or paradoxical phrases for a situation. However, the leader is expected to take a key word or even undertake some discussion and ask the group members to come up with a short, provocative phrase that captures the essence of the word under discussion. Moreover, it should be aesthetically satisfying or paradoxical." Examples of symbolic analogy (book titles) are progressive ingestion for forest fire, discrete infinity for multitude, involuntary willingness for receptivity, impure aggressor for acid etc.

4. Checklist of Questions

It provides tentative solution to a barrage of questions. Some of these questions are quite straightforward questions : For example, how can we modify the solution to make it more economical, or can we find other uses of-the solution ? Questions are the creative acts of intelligence for they could be so designed as to force a dramatic shift of perspective. In this context, *Edward de Bono* has suggested the use of PO (Provocative Operation). "PO consists of mechanism of breakdown habitual approaches such as an irrelevance, a joke, an inversion, etc. According to him, "people often fall into a problem-solving rut. That is, they tend to solve problems using "old think" consisting of habitual, logical, orderly evaluative or ideological ways of dealing with problems."[21] An irrelevance such as a random number or a random image or a joke may break the mental set, derail the habitual approach to generate lateral thinking and possibly help the mind to discover a fresher, more creative approach.

Process of Creative Problem-Solving

The following stages are involved in the process of creative problem-solving :

(i) Preparation : The preparation phase is one in which the problem solver familiarises himself with the problem. It involves the investigation of the problem in all directions, including a full understanding of what the problem is and the constraints within which it has to be solved. It requires detailed analysis through known procedures etc.

(ii) Incubation : It is the letting go of the problem by the conscious mind and allowing it to ferment below the level of consciousness. Incubation is often necessary for insights to occur in solving difficult problems. According to *William Kirkwood*, "incubation helps in abandoning the prevailing lines of thought and provides a fresh start. It also helps the mind to forget some self-imposed constraints on thinking. It enables subconscious transformation of data because during the lull in conscious problem-solving, other data stored in memory as well as fresh data from outside get a chance of interacting with the problem data."[22]

(iii) Illumination : It is being struck by a solution in a eureka like experience. According to *Rosamond Harding*, "illumination is the state of inspiration and oftenly accompanied by two distinct and vivid impressions; the sense of possession and the sense of compulsion."[23]

(iv) Verification : It is an evolution or verification of perspective solution. It also deals with required and refinement of inherent implications.

Creative Performance

Motivation exists at various levels and it affects creative performance. It also motivates persons for creative thinking. The following factors motivate people to go for creative performance.

1. Release of Inner Tensions : According to *Freud*, a person creates to release or act out his or her inner tensions. Thus, creation is a relief from tension, a sort of indirect catharsis, culminating in the fulfilment of unconscious wishes.[24] *Van Gogh* also suggests that conflict ridden people generally sublimate their inner tensions, *i.e.*, express them in works that are socially acceptable such as painting or poems.[25] Similarly, it also suggested that creaters are really narcissists (narcissists are those persons who wish to enjoy self, admire and be admired.) i.e., they create in order to be admired.

2. Intrinsic Satisfaction : "It is argued that people create because of the intrinsic satisfaction they get from the very process of creation."[26] This process is marked as it is by facing challenges and overcoming obstacles, solving technical and/or aesthetic problems, giving birth to something that is one's own, acquisition of new skills and knowledge and the exhilaration of the moments of inspiration, is intrinsically so exciting that once someone tastes its sweet and spicy nectar he or she is looked. Money and auction, though welcome, become secondary."[27]

3. Human Necessity : Necessity is the mother of inventions. All kinds of human needs have led to acts of creation. Actually any human need when it is felt powerfully enough can if the circumstances are favourable, precipitate an act of creation or invention. The drive for money and power has led to vast enterprises and power structures. Similarly, the need to create and to make a distinctive contribution are the springboards of much scientific and artistic creativity. *Abraham Maslow* has stated the need for self-actualisation, which also encourages people to go for creative performance. One need is for personal growth, for the development of one's potential, the need to become everything that one is capable of becoming". On the other hand, it is also suggested that altruism or the need to contribute to other's growth, which is called an extension motivation and is another act of the need for self-actualisation."[28] Instead of being concerned only with personal growth, the altruism is concerned with the growth and development of other people as well. This, too, is an unending guest and, therefore, an endless potential motivator of innovative behaviour."[29]

4. Urge for Creating Original : It is the most important factor affecting people to go for creative performance. This is the need to create, to discover, to pioneer to do something original and distinctive."[30] This is a need that not only makes one develop his or her potential, it is a need that implies, one to seek a distinctive expression of one's potential. It is the difference between seeking to develop one's potential as an artist and seeking to be a highly original artist. When awakened, this turns into a supremely powerful motive of creative behaviour, for added to the satisfaction of personal growth or the growth of others, depending upon one's focus in the thrill of invention and novelty."[31]

CREATIVITY AND INNOVATION

The term 'creation' relates with founding and an origin. Creativity is concerned with the generation of new idea and innovation, translates new idea into a new product or an organisation. Innovation means doing the new things or the doing of things that are already being done in a new way." This innovation is the process of doing new things. However, there is distinction between creativity and innovation. Creativity is the ability to bring something new into existence. It is possible for a person to conceive of something new and envision how it will be useful but not necessarily take the necessary action to make it a reality. It is also possible that ideas generated in the mind of a man have little value until they are converted into new products, services or processes. But "innovation is the transformation of creative idea into useful applications but creativity is a prerequisite to innovation.

Schumpeter described entrepreneurs as innovators who are the process to shatter the statues quo through new combinations of resources and new method of commerce. It includes new process of production, introduction of new products, creation of new markets, discovery of a new and better form of industrial organisation. *Peter Drucker* also elaborates that "innovation is the specific tool of entrepreneurs to exploit change as an opportunity for a different business or a different service. It is capable of being presented as a discipline, capable of being learned, capable of being practised! Entrepreneurs need search purposefully for the source of innovations, the changes and their symptoms that indicate opportunities for successful innovation."[32] Thus, innovation is the development process. It translates an idea into an application. It requires entrepreneurs to work out the details of product design or service analytically, to develop marketing, obtain finance and plan operations.

Types of Innovations

(i) Technical Innovation : It is concerned with innovations in the processes by which production takes place and also with innovation in the products themselves. It is also called pure innovation. It is creation of something radically different from existing technologies or products. An innovation may have no competitors as its birth, thereby giving a monopoly to the individuals who hold the legal rights to the invention. New inventions can create new products, thereby new industries. Generally, it is also treated as product oriented innovation which involves developing goods and services that incorporate entirely new and novel breakthrough advances. Over the product life cycle, large organisational units develop to exploit these products and markets as they mature.

(ii) Non-Technical Innovation : It is concerned with innovation missions, styles of management, growth strategies, management systems and organisational structures to office decor and flexitime." It is also treated as process innovation.

It is incremental and evolutionary. Its purpose is to make existing industries more efficient. It refers to small changes in design, product formulation and manufacturing, materials and service delivery that firms make to keep their product upto date and their costs down. It also involves making improvements to existing pioducts and production or other organisational process.

Phases of Innovation

Innovation has two phases— (i) Design Phase and (ii) Implementation Phase:

(i) Design Phase : The design phase is marked by much divergent thinking and creativity, brainstorming, search for alternatives etc. Research studies suggest that the management of the design phase needs to be marked by great administrative flexibility and authority exercised by the expert in a given situation, open communications, sharing information, much discussion etc."[33]

(ii) Implementation Phase : It requires a very different mode of management. It is not that important for divergent creative thinking, as for putting the chosen innovation to work. Much planning needs to be done, careful coordination and control and evaluation of progress.

Risk, Uncertainty and Innovations

'Risk' is the condition of not knowing the outcome of an activity or decision. Nevertheless, risk is capable of being evaluated for relative probabilities. It is variability of outcomes (or returns). If there is no risk, return is certain. "A business organisation working under risk free environment would continue to expand forever, because a negative outcome could not occur. Therefore, risk is a limit to ever expanding entrepreneurship."[34] That is why entrepreneur needs risk bearing capabilities. Risk bearing means provision for capital in order to enable the entrepreneur to establish and operate the business.

'Uncertainty' is a situation in which the entrepreneur understands the problem but does not have complete information on the possible alternatives and the likely consequences of each alternative. It also refers to thc "confidence entrepreneurs have in their estimates of how the world works; their understanding of the causes and effects in the environment. If there is no uncertainty, then the environment can be perfectly known. If this is true, then everyone can know it (at least for a price) and it could be a source of lasting profit for anyone."[35] So entrepreneurs working under a condition of risk have enough information to estimate the probable outcomes of each alternative, they have insufficient information to estimate probable outcomes when they operate under a condition of uncertainty." Most of the decision entrepreneurs make occur under a condition of uncertainty, primarily because environmental uncertainty make the future unpredictable."[36]

Types of Uncertainty

1. **Structural Uncertainty** : It relates with certain structural conditions and constraints generally imposed due to the entry of a new venture into

emerging industries. There are only the unknown future and the entrepreneur's will to succeed. "Traditional ways of doing things" "rule of thumb", "standard operating procedures" or "usual and customary practices are not going to help the entrepreneur. Technological uncertainty is the best example of structural uncertainty. It focuses on the final configuration of resources, especially technological resources which is still unsettled. Firms are as laboratories trying new combinations of technology, human resources and organisational system to discover what works. Successful combinations are adopted by other firms as fundamental and further experiments are conducted to refine the concepts and practices.

2. **Strategic Uncertainty** : It deals with the situation where complete information is not available regarding level of competition, number and name of competitors, types of products and process on which competitors are working and government policy about new industry. New ventures in emerging industries are often unaware of these important variables and this type of uncertainty creates problem before them. Government regulatory authorities who have been assigned to regulate emerging industries are also unable to formulate effective guidelines for their regulatory framework and existing rules are generally confusing and useless.

3. **Resources Uncertainty** : It is concerned with availability of resources in the firm's input markets. New ventures generally fall problem in their fund raising programme from the financial markets because financial sources are unfamiliar with the new industries risk and return profile. Professional managers also face a career risk and economic uncertainty when joining firm in emerging industries. "The procurement of raw material supplies and parts may also be difficult during the industry's emergence. If the inputs are also employed by other industries, there may be shortages until the vendors can adjust their capacity. If the inputs are newly created, developed or engineered, they may be of uneven quality and in short supply. In either event, input costs are likely to be at their highest during the emergence stage."[37]

4. **Customer Uncertainty** : It relates with output or customer market. Generally, incomplete information is available with regard to buyer needs and wants, income levels, demographic characteristics, psychographics profile, and buyers perception etc. and new ventures in emerging industries fail together these informations on sound footings. They also, face uncertainty about customers resistance over the prices and the points of products. They are also under pressure to face the wrath of customers regarding product differentiation and sustainability, branding, standardisation, market behaviour etc. Generally, customers are confused by the variety of product offerings, the lack of standardisation, the perception of rapid obsolescence and the erratic quality of some competitors.

Innovation usually means embarking on an uncertain voyage. Uncertainty can be of many origins. There may be uncertainty as to the approach needed to get to the innovative product creativity.

This type of uncertainty is technological in character. There may also be uncertainty about the preferences of the intended users of the Innovative product or service. There may be uncertainty associated with the costs and benefits of the innovation.

Developing Organisational Creativity and Innovation

Creativity is best nurtured in a permissive climate, one that encourages the exploration of new ideas and new ways of doing things. Many managers find it difficult to accept such a climate. They may be uncomfortable with a continuing process to change, which is the essential accompaniment of creativity. They may also be concerned that a permissive atmosphere encourages the breakdown of discipline or cost control. The following conditions are necessary for developing organisational creativity.

1. ***Develop an acceptance of change*** : Organisation members must believe that change will benefit them and the organisation. This belief is more likely to arise if members participate with their managers in making decisions and if issues like job security are carefully handled when changes are planned and implemented.
2. ***Encourage new ideas*** : Organisation managers, from the top to the lowest-level supervisors, must make it clear in word and deed that they welcome new approaches. To encourage creativity, managers must be willing to listen to subordinates' suggestions and to implement promising ones or convey them to higher level managers.
3. ***Permit more interaction :*** A permissive, creative climate is fostered by giving individuals the opportunity to interact with members of their own and other work groups. Such interaction encourages the exchange of useful information, the free flow of ideas, and fresh perspectives on problems.
4. ***Tolerate failure :*** Many new ideas prove impractical. Effective managers accept and allow for the fact that time and resources will be invested in experimenting with new ideas that do not work out.
5. ***Provide clear objectives and freedom to achieve them :*** Organisation members must have a purpose and direction for their creativity. Supplying guidelines and reasonable constraints will also give managers some control over the amount of time and money invested in creative behaviour.
6. ***Offer recognition :*** Creative individuals are motivated to work hard on tasks that interest them. But, like all individuals, they enjoy being rewarded for a task well done. By offering recognition in such tangible forms as bonuses and salary increase, managers demonstrate that creative behaviour is valued in their organisations.

On the basis of the above framework, efforts are needed to develop conducive environment in the organisation, then we can hope for viable creativity and innovation.

EXAMINATION QUESTIONS

Long Answer Questions

1. What do you mean by creativity ? Also examine its types and forms.
2. What is creativity thinking ? Examine its techniques.
3. What is brainstorming ? Explain its various principles.
4. What do you mean by attribute analysis ? Examine its principles.
5. What is synectics ? Evaluate its major analogies.
6. What is creative Process ? Examine the various steps involved in it.
7. What is creative performance ? Examine the factors affecting creative performance.
8. What is convergent thinking ? Explain its mechanism.
9. What do you mean by divergent thinking ? Evaluate its mechanisms.
10. What do you mean by uncertainty ? Examine its different types.
11. "Heuristic is the process of developing new ideas through a progression of thoughts and insights". Comment.

Short Answer Questions

1. Explain the steps involved in attribute listing.
2. Explain the process of creative problem-solving.
3. How is creativity related with innovation ?
4. Distinguish between risk and uncertainty.
5. Explain the types of innovation.
6. Examine the phases of innovation.
7. Explain the conditions required for developing organisational creativity.

Objective Type Questions

1. Creativity is the result of
   (a) planned change (b) systematic change
   (c) unsystematic change (d) Frequent change
2. Business is
   (a) Profitable activity (b) New Profitable activity
   (c) Creativity activity (d) uncertain activity
3. Edison's light bulb is the result of
   (a) Spontaneous creativity (b) Technical creativity
   (c) Inventive creativity (d) Innovative creativity

4. In case of brainstorming
   (a) Criticism is encouraged
   (b) Criticism is banned
   (c) Criticism is discouraged
   (d) Criticism is not possible
5. Synectics is concerned with
   (a) Single technique
   (b) Individual technique
   (c) Group technique
   (d) None of these

Answers

1-(a) 2-(c) 3-(c) 4-(c) 5-(c)

Reason Based Questions

State with reasons whether the following statements are true or false :

1. Creativity is the root of innovation.
2. Creativity requires passion and commitment.
3. A product is creative when it is novel and appropriate.
4. Innovation is the specific tool of entrepreneur.
5. Innovation is essential for entrepreneurial success.
6. Heuristics is the process of developing new ideas through a progression of thoughts and insights.
7. There are four phases of entrepreneurial development programme

REFERENCES

1. Frank Barron, *Creative Person and Creative Process,* Holt Rine Hart and Winston, 1969, New York, p. 20
2. Khandwalla Pradcep, *Fourth Eye.*
3. Donald W. Machinnon, *Creativity,* London, 1970, pp. 17-32.
4. *Ibid.,* p. 8
5. Abrahim Maslow, *Motivation and Personality,* Harper, New York, 1954, p. 8
6. Torrance E. Paul, *Rewarding Creative Behaviour,* Prentice Hall.
7. *Ibid.,* p. 12
8. *Ibid.,* p. 10
9. *Ibid.,* p. 11
10. *Ibid.,* p. 62
11. *Ibid.,* p. 2
12. *Ibid.,* p. 102
13. Guilfor D.J.P. *Intelligence, Creativity and Their Educational Implications, C.* San 'Diego : Robert R. Knappl, 968), p. 21.
14. *Ibid.,* p. 66
15. *Ibid.,* 7D-71.
16. Meadow Arnold, Parnes, Sidney J. and Reese Hayne, Influence of brain storming Instructions and Problem Sequence on a Creative Problem Solving Text. *Journal of Applied Psychology,* Vol., 43, 6.1969.

17. Os born Alex. F., *Applied Imagination* (New York, Scribner's 1963; Indian Edition Allahabad, St. Paul's Society, 1961) Chs. 19 and 20.
18. Crawford R.P., *The Techniques of Creative Thinking : How to use your ideas to Achieve Success,* Hawthorne Books, New York, 1954, p. 46.
19. Cranford, R.P., *Ibid.,* p. 46.
20. Gordon W.J.J., *Synectics : The Development of Creative Capacity.* Harper and Row, Newyork, 1961. p. 72.
21. Khandwalla, P., *Fourth Eye,* p. 29.
22. Kirkwood, William G., Effects of incubation sequences on Communication and Problem Solving in Small Groups, *Journal of Creative Behaviour,* Vol. 18, 1, 1984, p. 46-61.
23. Harding, Rosamond E.M., *An Anatomy of Inspiration,* Frank Cass, London, 1967, p. 13.
24. Freud Sigmund, *Introductory Lectures in Psycho-analysis and Hogarth and the Institute of Psycho-analysis, London.* Vol. IX-1959.
25. P. Khandwalla, p. 102.
26. Teresa M Ambile, *The Social Psychology of Creativity,* Springer Verlag, New York, 1983, p. 4.
27. P. Khandwalla, p. 102.
28. Abraham Maslow, *Journal of Creative Behaviour,* Vol. 19, 1, 1985, pp. 30-37.
29. Udai Pareek : A Motivational Paradigm of Development, *Journal of Social Issues,* Vol. 24. 2. 1968, pp. 115-122.
30. J.W. Getzels and M. Csiksenmihalyi, The Creative Artist as an explorer in J. Mc. V Hunt (ed.). *Human Intelligence* (Newyork Transaction, 1972) and Johan P. Houston and Sarnoff A. Medmick, Creativity and the need for novelty, J. *of Abnormal and social Psychology,* Vol. 66, 1963, pp. 137-141.
31. Pradip Khandwalla, p. 104.
32. James Ulterback, The process of technological innovation within the firm, Academy of Management, Journal, Vol. 12, 1971, pp. 75-88.
33. Tom Burns and G.M. Sacker, *The Management of Innovation,* Tavi Stock London, 1961, p. 14.
34. Penrose, E. The Theory of the Growth of the Firm. Johan Wiley, 1959, Newyork, pp. 56-57.
35. Dollinger, Marc, J., *Entrepreneurship,* Pearson Education Ltd., New Delhi, 2003, p. 33.
36. James W. Frederick Son, *"The Comprehensiveness of Strategic Decision Process,* Extension, observation, future Directions." Academy of Management Journal 27. No. 3, 1984, pp. 445-466.
37. Dollinger Marc, J., *Op.cit,* p. 134.

15

ENTREPRENEURSHIP DEVELOPMENT PROGRAMMES

Entrepreneurship is one of the inputs in the economic development of a country. The supply of entrepreneurial spirit/talent is a function of entrepreneurial competencies as also the business and industrial climate prevailing in the country. "It is a common experience any where that entrepreneur is a scarce but most important agent of economic development of any country. The supply of entrepreneurs always lags behind the need generated by the requirements of development efforts".[1] So, the need for an effective entrepreneurial class arises from the need to speed up the process of economic development.

Entrepreneurs are not just born they can be developed and trained in entrepreneurial activities. However, they must be motivated to develop their own innovative entrepreneurial enterprises for the production of goods and services. Generally, every body does not have the capacity to become a potential entrepreneur. Development of an entrepreneur means inculcating entrepreneurial traits into a person; imparting the required innovaiton, developing the management and building the entrepreneurial attitude. The process of entrepreneurial development incorporates equipping a prospective entrepreneur with institutional support system and backup used for enterprise development and sharpening his entrepreneurial competencies.

Nature of Entrepreneurship Development Programme

Entrepreneurship Development Programme (EDP) means "a programme designed to help a person in strengthening and fulfilling his entrepreneurial motive and in acquiring skills and capabilities necessary for playing his entrepreneurial role effectively. Towards this end, it is necessary to promote his understanding of motives, motivation pattern, their impact on behaviour and entrepreneurial value.

Thus, EDP is desigend to identify persons with entrepreneurial abilities and to train them to set up new enterprise. In a simple way, it deals with careful identification and potential entrepreneurs, need based entrepreneurial training and pre and post-project implementation, follow-up support.

Rationale of EDP

(i) EDP is meant for developing those first generation entrepreneurs who on their own cannot become successful owners of enterprises.

(ii) The effective entrepreneurial class is necessary to speed up the porcess of activating the factors of production to ensure higher rate of economic growth.

(*iii*) EDP ensures potential entrepreneurs of backward and tribal areas to set up their enterprises with the help of government and institutional support system.

(*iv*) EDP helps in dispersal of economic activities in different regions by providing training and other support to local people.

(*v*) EDP develops the persons who are interested to work as job providers by establishing enterprises not to those who are job seekers. Thus, it helps in creation of employment opportunities.

(*vi*) EDP improves the standard of living of the weaker sections of society and involvement of all sections in the process of economic growth.

(vii) EDP develops motivaiton and competence necessary for successful launching, management and growth of the enterprise.

Thus, EDP is necessary to motivate the potential enrepreneurs to convert their dreams into action. However, it is not expected to create any magical result. It is a continuous process of training and motivating them to set up enterprises in a big way.

General belief about the EDP is that individual can be developed and their perception can be changed. They may be motivated to convert their dreams/ideas into action through an effective EDP. However, it is notable that EDP is not merely a training programme. It also develops social and organisational framework which enable the potential entrepreneurs to perceive opportunities and learn to respond to them. in this way, EDP is a process of [2]

(i) enhancing the motivation, knowledge and skills of the potential entrepreneurs,

(ii) arousing and reforming the entrepreneurial behaviour in their day to day activities,

(iii) assisting them in developing their own ventures or enterprise as a sequel to entrepreneurial action.

Objectives of EDP

(i) To accelerate the process of entering into business for those who come from business families;

(ii) To encourage first generation entrepreneurs who do not have any business background;

(iii) To develop and strengthen the entrepreneurial competencies of prospective entrepreneurs;

(*iv*) To provide help in identification and formulation of viable projects;

(*v*) To arrange support system about the process and procedures of setting up of an enterprise;

(*vi*) To import training in managerial understanding and skills;

(*vii*) To provide post-training assistance and monitoring facilities.

Thus. EDP which basically covers the areas of non-financial incentives is an important promotional activity that has assumed special importance in the context of broadbasing the entrepreneurial cadre and encouraging particularly small, medium and tiny sector entrepreneurs. Moreover, EDPs are expected to achieve major objectives like identifying the entrepreneurial base and creation of self employment opportunities.

Evolution of EDP

Earlier, Government and other agencies were responsible for supporting potential entrepreneurs to set up their units specially in backward and tribal areas. In this context, Small Industries Service Institute and SIET Institute in the sixties tried to fill the information gap which existed and were relevant for small entrepreneurs. 'The entrepreneurs required a lot of information for setting up a business and in that context the contribution of these programmes was essentially in the area of disseminating knowledge on financial, technical and managerial aspects. To that extent, these programmes were not basically programmes towards entrepreneurship development, but were in the nature of supportive programmes for the existing and the new entrepreneurs."[3]

However, it was visualised that creation of industrial development corporations and other external facilities has failed to develop an effective and sufficient condition for entrepreneurship development. There must be an effective framework to develop the qualities of the individual who respond to the external opportunities i.e. availability of funds, financial incentives etc. Similarly, efforts should also be made so that social and organisational factors help potential entrepreneurs to perceive the opportunities and learn to respond to them.

At present, existing entrepreneurs basically emerged out of the natural growth of entrepreneurial talent of certain communities like Marwaris, Gujaratis, Parsi's and South Indian Brahmins. This type of entrepreneurs is a highly motivated group but problem is that they be often interested in quick profits or high profits, opportunities which are normally concentrated in the already well-developed areas.

So, it would be more important to have a broad-based entrepreneurial source to command the tempo of economic growth. In this context, entrepreneurial training can make a lot of difference in performance of the entrepreneurs. By motivating non-entrepreneurial participants to start a viable enterprise, we can easily develop a valid substitute for natural institutions like business families or existing entrepreneurs.

Features of EDP

To ensure success of EDP, it would be better to incorporate the following features:

(i) Identification and careful selection of entrepreneurs for training ;
(ii) developing the entrepreneurial capabilities of the trainee ;
(iii) ensuring a viable industrial project for each potential entrepreneur ;
(iv) equipping the trainee with basic managerial understanding ;
(v) helping him to secure necessary financial, infrastructural and related assistance, and
(vi) subsidised training cost to ensure commitment of participants.

Government Initiatives for EDP and Training

In the era of liberalisation, privatisation and globalisation along with ongoing IT revolution, capable entrepreneurs are making use of the opportunities emerging from the evolving scenario. However, a large segment of the population, particularly in the industrially backward regions/rural areas generally lags behind in taking advantage of these opportunities. Therefore, there is a need to provide skill development and entrepreneurship development training to such people in order to bring them to mainstream of economic growth.

Entrepreneurship development and training is, thus, one of the key elements for development of micro and small enterprises (MSEs), particularly, the first generation entrepreneurs. To undertake this task on regular basis, the Ministry of Micro, Medium and Small Enterprises has set up three national-level Entrepreneurship Development Institutes (EDIs). These are the National Institute for Micro, Small and Medium Enterprises (NI-MSME), Hyderabad; the Indian Institute of Entrepreneurship (HE), Guwahati and the National Institute for Entrepreneurship and Small Business Development (NIESBUD), NOIDA, (UP). Further, the Ministry has been implementing [in addition to the schemes operating by the Office of the Development Commissioner (MSME)], an important scheme, namely, Scheme for Assistance to Training Institutions. The main objectives of the scheme are development of indigenous entrepreneurship from all walks of life for developing new micro and small enterprises, enlarging the entrepreneurial base and encouraging self employment in rural as well as urban areas, by providing training to first generation entrepreneurs and assisting them in setting up of enterprises.

EDP and Training Programmes for first Generation Entrepreneurs

MSME-DIs are imparting varieties of training programmes for first generation potential entrepreneurs, existing industrial workers and managers. The ultimate aim is to promote the MSME sector of the country by inculcating entrepreneurial culture in the respective area as well as to enhance productivity of the existing industries of that State/Area. It also provides various common facilities to existing industries of the area and helps them in improving the techno managerial skill.

(i) Industrial Motivation Campaigns (IMCs) : Industrial Motivation Campaigns (duration of 1-2 days) are organised to identify and motivate traditional/nontraditional entrepreneurs having potential for setting up MSEs so as to lead them towards self-employment. Emphasis is being given to organise the maximum number of programmes in rural/remote areas particularly for weaker sections of the society.

(ii) Entrepreneurship Development Programmes (EDPs) : Entrepreneurship Development Programmes are being organised as a regular training activity to cultivate the latent qualities of youth by enlightening them on various aspects that are necessary to be considered while setting up Micro, Small & Medium Enterprises. These programmes are conducted generally for technicians/artisans for motivating them towards self-employment. The course contents of such Entrepreneurship Development Programmes are so designed as to provide useful information on product/process design, manufacturing practices involved, testing and quality control, selection and usage of appropriate machinery and equipments, project profile preparation, marketing avenues/techniques, product/ service pricing, export opportunities, infrastructure facilities available, financial and financial institutions, cash flow etc. No fees is charged from SC/ST, women and physically handicapped participants in the stipendiary programmes, rather a stipend of ₹500 per month is provided to a person belonging to candidates under the promotional package. Emphasis is being made to organise special programmes in rural areas particularly for weaker sections of the society.

(iii) Entrepreneurship-cum-Skill Development Programme (ESDPs): Comprehensive training programmes are organised to upgrade existing skills and to create new skills in workers and technicians of existing units by organising various technical training courses for them. The basic objective has been to provide training to unskilled/semi-skilled workers engaged in MSE sector and to equip them with better and improved techno-managerial skills of production. Emphasis is being made to organise the maximum programmes in rural areas particularly for weaker sections of the society. Specific tailor-made programmes are organised for the skill development of socially disadvantaged groups (OBC, SC, ST, Minorities and women) in remote regions/pockets of the States. The target groups for these programmes are SC/ST/OBC/women/ minorities and other weaker sections. These programmes are also called 'Out-Reach Programmes as these are conducted in rural/less developed areas.

Programmes so far organised, *inter alia,* included Herbal Cosmetics, High Fashion Garments, Hosiery, Food and Fruit Processing Industries, Information Technology, Hardware Maintenance, Soap and Detergents, Leather Products/ Novelties, Servicing of Household Electrical Appliances and Electronic Gadgets, Gem Cutting and Polishing, Engineering Plastics, Tour operators, Mobile repairing, Beautician, CAD/CAM, etc. No fee is charged from SC, ST, women and physically handicapped in the stipendiary programmes, rather, stipend of ₹500 per month is provided to SC, ST, women and physically handicapped candidates under promotional package.

(iv) Management Development Programmes (MDPs) : The basic objective of imparting training in management subjects is to improve the MSMEs in the decision making and in enhancing productivity/profitability. Potential entrepreneurs are trained so that they can set up and run their own enterprises.

(v) Business Skill Development Programme (Tailor-made Course): Tailor-made courses, namely, Business Skill Development Programme (BSDP) has been introduced for new Entrepreneurs through Select Business Schools/ Technical Institutions etc. The programme has been devised to encourage educated unemployed youth/students basically from Business Schools/Technical Institutes to start self-employment ventures of MSEs.

(vi) Entrepreneur-cum-Skill Development Programme (ESDP) on Biotechnology : Biotechnology is playing an important role in diverse sectors such as human and animal health care, plant and agriculture sciences, food and nutrition, environment etc. The areas of tissue cultures, bio-fertilizers, biopesticides, mushroom cultivation, solid waste management etc. are given priority for ESDPs.

Course Contents and Curriculum of EDPs

The course contents of an EDP should be formulated as per the objectives of the EDP's. It should consist of the following :

1. General Approach to Entrepreneurship : The participants should be given exposure about the conceptual framework of entrepreneurship role, expectation, Entrepreneurial environment etc. Innovative behaviour related issues should be focused to enlighten the entrepreneurs about their future challenges and prospects. Besides, development agencies should try to design appropriate strategies enabling the potential entrepreneur to tackle different risk inherent in an innovation activity. These risks are as follows :

(i) *Technical risks :* the risk of not knowing enough about the technical processes, materials etc.

(ii) *Economic Risks :* the risk of market fluctuations and changes in relation to raw materials etc.

(iii) *Social Risks :* the risk inherent in the development of new relationship.

(iv) *Environmental Risks :* risk which result from environmental changes in the manager's work as an outcome of the new activity.

Moreover, prospective entrepreneurs should be given a detailed information with regard to facilities generally provided by the government and other agencies involved in promotion of entrepreneurship.

2. Motivational Training : Motivational training inputs are meant for developing the motivation of potential entrepreneurs and their enterprise building skills. Besides, motivational inputs also include psychological games, tests, goal setting exercises, role play etc. The motivational inputs will be aimed at increasing the participants, understanding of the entrepreneurial personality and entrepreneurial behaviour and bring about through self-study, changes in self-concept, value, skills thereby leading to positive entrepreneurial behaviour. The major motivational inputs may be given in the beginning of the training programme on full time basis though the learning effected through them will be reinforced and used" throughout the training programme. The understanding of the entrepreneurial personality and behaviour will be supplemented through interface with one or two successful as well as not so successful entrepreneurs.

3. Developing Management Skills : Prospective entrepreneurs should be given exposure in different types of management problems. It would sharpen their management skills. The management problems take different forms and the management patterns are peculiar to the situation. So, training for exposing managerial skills will be arranged in keeping the situational requirements. However, managerial aspects should include production planning, labour laws, cost analysis, financial accounting, selling arrangements, taxation laws etc.

4. Training for Project Management : Project inputs are required to help the potential entrepreneurs to develop their project ideas into bankable projects. They should be given acquaintance with the industrial opportunities in the area and also necessary guidance on product selection. Necessary knowledge about project feasibility, viability and implementation should also be given to the potential entrepreneurs. Under project preparation, technical feasibility includes selection of technology, availability of raw materials, selection of location and site, availability of plant and machinery, infrastructure facilities, roads, transport, power, manpower/personnel requirement. Similarly, market analysis, level of competition, capital cost, working capital requirement, estimated cost of production, projected sales volume, profitability estimates, expected rate of return, projected cash flows and break even analysis are different aspects that have to be incorporated in assessing the commercial viability of the project. Sufficient exposure is necessary with regard to financing of the project. Financing arrangement generally includes sources of financing, promoters contribution, level of institutional financing, seed capital, investment subsidy etc. Prospective entrepreneurs should be instructed about the importance of timely implementation of project. They should be given proper training about scheduling of various activities, provision for effective supervision and need for avoiding delay and consequent cost escalation.

5. Structural Arrangement : Training inputs also aim at familiarising the participants about the proposed structural arrangement for the business or industrial unit. They should be given adequate familiarisation about government policy regarding development of industries, especially with regard to small scale industries, registration and licensing procedures, forms of organisation like proprietary, partnership, private company and joint stock company, institutional setup etc.

6. Support System : In most of the cases, participants are generally first generation entrepreneurs and they do not know about the government and institutional support system. Support system may also be used as motivational inputs to encourage the participants about their future prospects. They should be familiarised with the incentives/concessions available, tax-incentives, tax holiday, backward/zero industries districts concessions, soft loan scheme, special schemes for technicians etc. This should be followed by acquainting them with procedure for approaching government departments and agencies, applying for and obtaining these concessions from them.

7. Factory Visits/In-plant Training : Practical exposure is also necessary. Depending upon their products the potential entrepreneurs may feel the need to gain more knowledge about the production process etc. by visiting some of the similar units in production. For this purpose, factory visits may have to be arranged. Similarly, entrepreneurs who select relatively sophisticated products will be expected to have a good idea of the product and the process facilities should be arranged for in-plant training or prototype development on exceptional basis.

Government Support System for EDP and Training to Entrepreneurship Development Institutes

Under the scheme, assistance is provided to existing and new training Institutions for establishment of Entrepreneurship Development Institute (EDI) and strengthening of their training infrastructure on a matching basis. Ministry provides assistance on a matching basis, not exceeding 50 per cent of the project cost or ₹150 lakhs whichever is less (90 per cent or ₹270 lakhs of the project cost whichever is less, for North-Eastern States and Union Territories of Andaman & Nicobar and Lakshadweep Islands) excluding cost of land and working capital. The balance 50 per cent of the matching contribution (10 per cent for State level EDIs in North Eastern States including Sikkim or Union Territories of Andaman & Nicobar and Lakshadweep Islands) should come from the concerned Institute, State/UT Government, public funded institution(s), NGOs/Trusts/ Banks/ Companies/Societies/Voluntary organisations etc.

The assistance would be for creation of infrastructure. The land will have to be provided by the State Government or any other institution or by the applicant. Financial assistance would be for construction of building, purchase of training aids/equipments, office equipments, computers and for providing other support services e.g., libraries/data bases etc. The costs of land, construction of staff quarters etc. would not qualify for calculation of matching grant from the Central Government. All the proposals under this scheme are required to be recommended by and routed through the concerned State/UT Government.

Now, new component of training has been added under this scheme. Assistance would be provided under the scheme to the following Training Institutions, for conducting Entrepreneurship Development Programmes (EDPs) and Entrepreneurship cum Skill Development Programmes (ESDPs) and Training of Trainers (ToTs) programmes in the areas of Entrepreneurship and/or Skill Development.

(a) National level EDIs (including branches),

(b) Training Institutions established by Partner Institutions (PIs) of national level EDIs,

(c) Training/Incubation centres of NSIC,

(d) Training cum Incubation Centres (TICs) set up by NSIC

(e) Other Training institutions with proven professional competency, capacity and experience, approved under the scheme.

Skill Development (SDP) training would normally be of 100 to 300 hours (1 to 3 months). Entrepreneurship Development (EDP) training would be of 72 hours (2 weeks) and Trainer's Training for 300 hours.

Phases of EDP

1. Pre-training Preparation : It comprises policy issues related to the objectives of the Programme : laying down criteria of success; recruitment, selection and training of trainers; development of training materials for different levels of applicant population of entrepreneurs and publicity strategy.

2. Entrepreneurial Training : It centres on the entrepreneurs themselves. Allied issues to be tackled-location, methodology, use of training material, trainer—trainee relations and coordination among faculty from different development institutions.

3. Post-training Care : This consists of making available necessary information, counselling and support to the entrepreneur in his enterprise-building efforts.

It is notable that every EDP has to pass through these phases and each phase involves a considerable amount of work some times within the organisation, but most of the time in cooperation with other development institutions. Any deficiency in any of these phases can affect the outcome of the programme.

Organisations for EDPs

At present various national and state agencies are engaged in organising EDP's for first generation entrepreneurs. These agencies are as follows :

1. National Institute For Entrepreneurship and Small Business Development (NIESBUD), Noida, UP.

The National Institute for Entrepreneurship and Small Business Development (NIESBUD) was set up on 6th July, 1983. The basic objectives of the Institute are promotion and development of micro, small and medium enterprises including enhancement of their competitiveness through different activities. The Institute is envisaged to serve as apex national resource institute for holistic development of entrepreneurial activities throughout the country. The major activities of the Institute include :

i. Evolving model syllabi for training various target groups;

ii. Providing effective training strategies, methodology, manuals and tools;

iii. Facilitating and supporting Central/State Governments and other agencies in executing programmes of entrepreneurship and small business development; and

iv. Conducting programmes for motivators, trainers and entrepreneurs who are commonly not undertaken by other agencies and organising activities which help in developing an entrepreneurial culture in the society.

Government, aimed at increasing the supply of skilled manpower for meeting the growing demands in different sectors, the Institute conducted a total of 126 Entrepreneurship-cum-Skill Development Programmes for 3173 participants, which largely represented Women, SCs/STs/OBCs and other Weaker Sections of the Society. The Entrepreneurship-cum-Skill Development Programmes were in the trades of Computer Hardware and Networking, Mobile Repairing, Cutting and Tailoring, Retail Management, Costume Designing and Tailoring, Computer and Tally Account, Animation, Desk Top Publishing (DTP), Hospitality and Biotechnology.

The Institute has been organising different kinds of training activities in active association with the Ministry under the Scheme 'Rajiv Gandhi Udyami Mitra Yojana (RGUMY)' in its capacity of Udyami Mitra, undertakes activities like selection of entrepreneurs, identification of the capabilities, selection of suitable projects and assistance in preparation of the project reports. So far 434 prospective entrepreneurs have been assisted. Besides, the Institute has been instrumental in creation of the Units/Self-Help groups etc. (294). While the Institute has been instrumental in getting the Loan sanctioned in 260 cases, the same has been disbursed in 110 cases. 108 beneficiaries have filed the Memorandum with the concerned District Industry Centres (DICs).

The Institute has been appointed as a Gateway Agency by the Ministry of Panchayati Raj, Government of India under its Rural Business Hub Scheme (RBHS) for the Five districts : Chamoli and Champaran (Uttarakhand); Sirmor (Himachal Pradesh); Patna (Bihar) and Banswara (Rajasthan). The concept of Rural Business Hub aims at halting the migration of the rural population to urban areas, to develop the concerned areas into a Hub of income generating activities and is being implemented at the Panchayat/Block level in a Public/Private Panchayat Partnership (PPPP) mode. The institute has been assigned 24 clusters by the Office of the DC (MSME), KVIC, Coir Board and U.P. Government. The Diagnostic Study of all the Clusters has been completed and the respective reports approved by the concerned agencies. The major intervention being taken up in all the Industrial Clusters is technological upgradation aimed at cost reduction in production, reduction of pollution and improvement in working environment through HR Development. The implementation of Soft Intervention in 6 Industrial Clusters (O/o DC {MSME} and UP Government) has also been taken up. The organisational set-up in terms of SPV/Consortium formation has been completed in all the Clusters. Besides, basic Programmes of Lean Manufacturing such as 5S, 3M are being implemented in all the 6 Clusters to improve the method of processing and production resulting into enhanced productivity, better quality and reduction in wastage of time and man-hours. Being the final year of the implementation of the SFURTI Scheme, the Institute as Technical Agency is engaged in the process of Evaluation and Monitoring for assessing the impact of the implementation of different interventions. The Institute completed the process of identification of the machines, their supplier(s) etc. at all the four Coir Clusters assigned to the Institute in the State *of* Karnataka. All the CFCs are expected to be functional soon. The work of implementation on various parameters including formation of SHGs and Consortium is in progress in different KVIC Clusters.

During 2009-10, the institute organised other activities such as Training-cum-Incubation Centre for Garment Manufacturing. It conducted a total of 123 training activities for 3134 beneficiaries most of them being women and belonging to weaker sections of the society. The programmes, which were predominantly organised in the rural areas, were in the trades of Sewing Machine Operators; Garment Drafting and Construction; and Machine Embroidery and Tracing and Artificial Gems and Jewellery. A total of 514 participants were assisted to get direct wage employment in the different units of the Industry, viz; M/s. Textile Exports; M/s. New Delhi Export House; M/s. Rag Trade India etc. Besides, the Centre initiated its participants into the micro enterprise building process through execution of small orders for stitching of the clothes in their respective neighborhood and also facilitated the trainees in forming Self-Help Groups for undertaking income generation activities.

2. Entrepreneurship Development Institute of India (EDII)

It was established in 1983 by financial institutions like IDBI, IFCI, ICICI, State Bank of India and Government. EDII has been spearheading an entrepreneurship movement throughout the country with a belief that entrepreneurs need not necessarily be born, they can be developed through well-conceived and well-directed activities :

Objectives of EDII

(i) augment the supply of trained entrepreneurs through training;
(ii) generate a multiplier effect on opportunities for self-employment;
(iii) improve managerial capabilities of small scale industries;
(iv) contribute to the dispersal of business ownership and thus, expand the social base of Indian entrepreneurial class;
(v) contribute to the creation and dissemination of new knowledge and insight into entrepreneurial theory and practice through research;
(vi) augment the supply of trainer-motivators for entrepreneurship development;
(vii) participate in institution-building efforts;.
(viii) sensitise the support environment to facilitate potential as well as existing entrepreneurs to establish and manage their enterprises;
(ix) promote micro enterprises at rural level;
(x) inculcate the spirit of entrepreneurship amongst youth;
(xi) collaborate with similar organisations in India and other developing countries to accomplish the above objectives.

EDP Initiative

EDII has been trying to provide EDP facilities in different dimensions. These dimensions are :

(i) Entrepreneurship in education
(ii) Microfinance and micro enterprise development
(iii) Performance and growth of existing entrepreneurs
(iv) Performance improvement of ED institutions and ED Programmes.

It has also designed and implemented several national and international training programmes and workshops for the academic community and for entrepreneurs.

3. Indian Institute of Entrepreneurship (IIE), Guwahati

The Indian Institute of Entrepreneurship (IIE) was set up at Guwahati in 1993. It took over NI-MSME's NER Centre w.e.f. 1st April, 1994. Over the period, the Institute has expanded its activities to a great extent covering all facets of MSME activities. Since its establishment and upto December, 2009, the Institute has organised more than 1800 training programmes/workshops/seminars/ meets. The Institute has obtained ISO-9001-2000 certification. The promotion of new entrepreneurs has been the major focus of training activities organised by the Institute. In order to promote new entrepreneurs, the institute organises rural, general and women EDPs, crash course on self-employment and sector specific EDPs.

The institute under the sponsorship of the M/o MSME, initiated a unique programme of Comprehensive Entrepreneurship Development (CEDP) on gem stones processing and hosiery and woolen garment manufacturing. The Institute imparts skill development training to prospective entrepreneurs and artisans through a six-month and three-month certificate courses in Gem stone processing and Hosiery processing, respectively, at its training centres at Guwahati, Aizwal, Sikkim and Arunachal Pradesh. It also provides incubation facilities and technical support and guidance and market linkages to prospective entrepreneurs in these sectors. The state-of the-art Jewellery Designing and Manufacturing Training Centre, established with support from the Ministry, provides forward linkages to the existing Gemstone Cutting and Polishing Centres. The Institute has been organising seminars, workshops, meets and conferences for providing forum for interaction and exchange of views by various agencies and entrepreneurs.

In keeping with the trend of the recent worldwide phenomenon of entrepreneurship development through area approach, IIE initiated' cluster development efforts to develop the languishing small and traditional industrial sector in the North Eastern Region. The Handloom cluster at Imphal, sponsored by DC, Handloom formed a good number of SHGs' of weavers with financial linkage. The institute also started Handloom Clusters in Uttarakhand. The institute is mandated as the Technical Agency for 11 Scheme of Fund for Regeneration of

Traditional Industries (SFURTI) clusters for Eastern and North Eastern Region. It provided guidance and handholding support to the CDAs and Implementing Agencies (IAs) for carrying out diagnostic studies and preparation of action plans along with validation of action plans through CDCG meetings. Further, for smooth functioning of the programme, IIE was involved in monthly and quarterly monitoring of the clusters for assessing progress of the clusters in qualitative and quantitative term *vis-a-vis* developing templates and tools for monitoring and evaluation. It also provided linkages with various business development service providers and support/technical institutions. Besides, IIE as the Technical Agency had been extending handholding services to CDAs and IAs at different stages of implementation of these eleven clusters.

The institute organised eight sensitisation workshops on cluster development under the Regional Resource Centre (RRC) for all the States of North Eastern Region during the year 2009-10. The prime focus of these workshops was to orient the prospective stakeholders of cluster development—the officials from the Industries Departments and from Banks and Financial Institutions in these states for a collective effort in cluster development initiative in. a more participatory manner in the light of the RRC. Eighteen awareness programmes were organised on cluster development approach. The RRC also arranged two exposure visits to Saharanpur in UP and Dimapur in Nagaland.

The Institute provided guidance and handholding support to the CDAs and Implementing Agencies (IAs) for carrying out diagnostic studies and preparation of action plans along with validation of action plans through CDCG meetings. Further, for smooth functioning of the programme, IIE was involved in monthly and quarterly monitoring of the clusters for assessing progress of the clusters in qualitative and quantitative term *vis-a-vis* developing templates and tools for monitoring and evaluation. It also provided linkages with various business development service providers and support/technical institutions. Besides, the institute as the Technical Agency had been extending handholding services to CDAs and IAs at different stages of implementation of these eleven clusters.

4. Small Industries Development Organisations (SIDO)

Recognising the need for training in improving and upgrading the skill of workers and management personnel, the SIDO has formulated programmes for various types of training. It offers following courses :

(i) Appreciation course in Industrial Management;

(ii) Specialised courses in such areas as production management, marketing management, financial management, export management and materials management etc.

(iii) Adhoc incentive courses on subjects like inspection and quality control, work study, salesmanship etc.

At present SIDO has 16 specialised institutes responsible for training, research and development of product design and processes. Besides, it has designed EDPs to identify persons with entrepreneurial abilities and to train them to set up new small /tiny industries. These EDPs are meant for separate target groups. These groups include[6]

(i) educated unemployed,

(ii) women,

(iii) weaker sections,

(iv) rural artisans,

(v) physically handicapped,

(vi) students,

(vii) defence personnel,

(viii) technocrats,

(ix) entrepreneurs under self-employment scheme.

5. National Institute for Micro, Small and Medium Enterprises (NIMSME), Hyderabad

NI-MSME, formerly known as National Institute of Small Industry Extension Training (NISIET), was set up in 1960 and is presently located at Hyderabad. The Institute has benefited not only the Indian micro, small and medium enterprises (MSMEs) but also those in other developing countries through a plethora of activities and, thus, helped in promoting self employment and enterprise development. The Institute is constantly evolving in accordance with the changing times, modifying its focus with the emerging needs of MSMEs and providing solutions in the form of consultancy, training, research and education. NI-MSME's programmes are designed to have universal relevance for successfully training the entrepreneurs to face challenges and emerging competition in the era of globalisation. Over the years, the Institute has gained immense experience and expertise in the areas of entrepreneurship development, technology, management and information services. NI-MSME's inherent capacity to innovate, together with its modern infrastructure, has enabled the Institute to excel in its endeavour of MSME promotion.

NI-MSME has always been conceiving specialised need-based programmes, workshops and seminars in tune with the changing policy and economic scenario. The primary aim of these activities has been to enable the enterprises and the supporting systems to deal effectively with aspects that directly or indirectly affect the success of enterprises. NI-MSME has developed profitable interface with several international agencies like CFTC (Commonwealth Fund for Technical Co-operation), UNESCO (United Nations Educational, Scientific and Cultural Organisation), UNDP (United Nations Development Programme), Ford Foundation, GTZ of Germany, USAID (United States Agency for International Development), and ILO(International Labour Organisation), to name a few.

6. Small Industries Development Bank of India (SIDBI)

It was established in April 1990 and earlier it was a wholly owned subsidiary of IDBI. Now, it is an independent company and was separated from IDBI in 1997. The aim of SIDBI's EDPs is to build and nurture a reservoir of entrepreneurs through training motivation and guidance. The Bank's strategy for entrepreneurship development involves support to NGOs and specialised agencies for conducting specially designed programmes covering various target groups ultimately aimed at the promotion of rural enterprises.

The EDPs are normally of a 6 weeks duration coupled with proper practical training inputs. Agencies specialised in conducting EDPs like Entrepreneurship Development Institute of India, Institutes of Entrepreneurship Development (IEDs), Centre for Entrepreneurship Development (CEDs), Technical Consultancy Organisations (TCOs) and NGOs have been supported for conducting the EDPs for specific target groups.

The SIDBI is constantly endeavouring to address the problems related with management deficiency and a low level of skill and technology by specially designed two programmes like Small Industries Management Assistance Programme (SIMAP) and Skill-cum-Technology Upgradation Programme (STUP). The objective of SIMAP is to develop a cadre of industrial managers specifically trained to assist the SSI entrepreneurs in their multiple responsibilities. The STUP is structured to improve the performance of the existing SSI units by developing/strengthening managerial skills and the technical competence of the entrepreneur and senior executive of the small enterprises.

A few specialised technical institutes like Central Institute of Plastic Engineering and Technology (CIPET), Rural Technology-Institute (RTI) and UP Electronics Corporation have also been extended assistance for conduct of product specific EDPs.

Critical Evaluation of EDPs in India

The present stage of development of EDP as a factor contributing to the industrialisation of backward and other areas is far from satisfactory. In spite of the spurt in EDP activity, it is observed that by and large efforts have remained limited to certain areas and the approach in general has been somewhat haphazard. The programmes conducted by the various agencies vary in duration, selection procedures, course contents etc. The contribution of EDPs is very uneven among regions.

EDPs are presently operating only in a few states/centres effectively. Their dispersal to rural/backward areas is not upto the mark. Even within each industrially developed state, there are many areas which have remained backward. This has happened not because of lack of supportive activities but for lack of entrepreneurs or intrinsic factors such as adverse terrain, soil, climate etc.

Lessons learnt from these EDPs suggest that enough attention is not being given to streamline and coordinate all activities related with programmes to get the maximum results. Experience also shows that existence, calibre and willingness of the support system greatly influence the success of the programme but it is an other important area where our EDPs are at loss. They are more attuned to maintenance function than to the development function. Moreover, EDPs are costly affair now a days. These programmes have fancy budgets. Estimates suggest that they ranked from ₹2 lakh to ₹5 lakhs. EDPs with such fancy budgets cannot become popular in developing economy like India.

It is also remarkable to note that our EDPs are modelled on the classical theory of entrepreneurship and they are geared to meet out the need of elitist small group, while the larger groups are being helped through the extension and assistance programmes without any systematic EDP effort to meet their needs.

Inspite of above situations, agencies are doing their sincere efforts to popularise the EDPs to first generation entrepreneurs. EDPs are governed by dynamic process and we have to consolidate and * improve our performance whatever has been learnt from these EDPs.

Suggestions to Make EDPs More Effective

Following suggestions are necessary to be implemented in improving the viability of EDPs :

1. The structure and composition of EDPs taking into account the regional variations need to be streamlined.
2. The programme should have a practical content and needs a lot of inter-institutional organisational arrangement to make it a success.
3. Effective support services should be linked with EDPs for better results. Financial institutions specially SIDBI's representatives and lead bank's nominees should be associated with the programme.
4. Potential entrepreneurs who have business experience, education and skills should be tapped first for EDPs. Then efforts will be made to cover entrepreneurs from the non-traditional class i.e. without business and industrial experience but having the potential of becoming successful entrepreneurs.
5. Inter-disciplinary approach/thrust should be given to the EDP. Intensive follow-up work will have to be done and systematised in the process to make it accessible to entrepreneurs in formal and informal forms.
6. A token fee may be charged from the participants to ensure their commitment towards EDPs. Payments of stipend to participants may be avoided as far as possible.
7. EDPs should have conceptual clarity and right conception and analysis. It should be designed to meet out the objectives already set and imagination to tackle unusual problems.

Thus, EDP is necessary for promoting entrepreneurship but its course contents and conceptual framework must be able to motivate first generation entrepreneurs in setting up their viable enterprises at the first instance.

EXAMINATION QUESTIONS

Long Answer Questions

1. Describe and evaluate the various entrepreneurial development programmes in India. Offer your valuable suggestions in this regard.
2. Do you agree with the view that entrepreneurs can be developed through appropriately designed entrepreneurial development programmes? Describe the basic pre-requisites of a successful entrepreneurial development programme.
3. "Entrepreneurs are born and not made." Do you agree with this statement? Evaluate the relevance of entrepreneurial development programme in this context.
4. What do most of the entrepreneurship development programmes in India provide to a prospective entrepreneur ?
5. What do you mean by entrepreneurial development programme ? Is it necessary to have it in ensuring the accelerated pace of industrialisation ?
6. How can we develop an entrepreneur ? Describe the factors affecting the development of entrepreneurs.
7. "Etrepreneurs are born and not made." Discuss.
8. What do you mean by entrepreneurial development programme ? Examine its relevance and stages.
9. Critically evaluate the various entrepreneurial development programmes initiated by the Government of India.
10. Make out a case for entrepreneurial development programmes. Also enumerate the operational problems involved in entrepreneurial development programme conducted in India.
11. What are the objectives of the entrepreneurial development programmes ? Critically evaluate the various entrepreneurial development initiated in our country by the Central and State Governments.
12. Review and evaluate entrepreneurial development programmes in India.

Short Answer Questions

1. Discuss the entrepreneurship development programmes in India.
2. Describe the contents of a Entrepreneurship Development Programme.
3. "Entrepreneurship development programmes are not successful in India." Comment.
4. What is entrepreneurship development programme ?
5. Discuss the objectives of entrepreneurship development programme.
6. Describe the evaluation process of EDP.
7. Discuss the main features of EDP.

8. Discuss the organisations involved in EDP in India.
9. Critically examine the EDPs in India.
10. Give suggestions to make the EDPs more effective.

True/False Questions

Tick True or False position of the following statements :

1. Entrepreneurs are made not born.
2. Entrepreneurship Development Programme are not successful in India.
3. Entrepreneurial guidance bureau is controlled by the Indian Investment Centre.
4. Small Industries Development Organisation is engaged in consultancy work.
5. EDII is established by the Government of Gujarat.
6. NIESBUD provides EDP facilities.
7. Generally EDP consists of three phases.
8. Everybody does not have the capacity to become a potential entrepreneur.
9. EDP is necessary to motivate the potential entrepreneurs to convert their dream into action.
10. EDP is not merely a training programme.

Objective Type Questions

1. EDP meant for developing
   (a) Professional skill
   (b) Entrepreneurial motive
   (c) Personal qualities
   (d) Entrepreneurial monitoring
2. EDP is required to help
   (a) Existing entrepreneurs
   (b) First generation entrepreneurs
   (c) Future entrepreneurs
   (d) None of the above
3. Following is not involved in EDP
   (a) Identification of entrepreneurs for training
   (b) Selection of entrepreneurs for training
   (c) Developing entrepreneurial capabilities
   (d) Arranging infrastructural facilities
4. EDII was developed by the
   (a) Government of India
   (b) State Government of Gujarat
   (c) All India Financial Institutions
   (d) Public Sector Banks.
5. NIESBUD was established in
   (a) 1980
   (b) 1983
   (c) 1986
   (d) 1989

6. SIDO is not responsible for organising functional management
   (a) Appreciation courses (b) Regular courses
   (c) Specialised courses (d) Ad hoc Incentive course
7. Skill-cum-Technology upgradation programme (STUP) is designed by
   (a) NISIET (b) SIDBI
   (c) NIESBUD (d) ED11
8. EDP should incorporate
   (a) Regional variations (b) Practical contents
   (c) Inter-disciplinary approach (d) All of the above
9. Entrepreneurial Behaviour is governed only by
   (a) Hereditary character (b) Training support system
   (c) EDP (d) None of the above
10. EDPs should be organised normally by
   (a) 4 weeks duration (b) 6 weeks duration
   (c) 8 weeks duration (d) None of the above

Answers

1-(b) 2-(b) 3-(d) 4-(c) 5-(b) 6-(b) 7-(b) 8-(b) 9-(d) 10-(b)

Reason Based Questions

State with reasons whether the following statements are true or false :

1. Entrepreneurial development programmes (EDPs) have, in true sense, helped in producing a large number of entrepreneurs across the country.
2. Entrepreneurship is a practical skill that cannot be taught in classrooms.
3. There is no need to have formal education upto some level to become an entrepreneur.
4. There are four phases of entrepreneurial development programme.
5. Objectives of entrepreneurial development programmes (EDP) is to create growth of entrepreneurship.

REFERENCES

1. Bhanushali, S.G., *Entrepreneurship Development,* Himalaya Publishing House, Mumbai, 1987, p. 213.
2. Singh, N.P., *Emerging Trends in Entrepreneurship Development: Theories and Practice,* IFDM, New Delhi, 1985, p. 96.
3. IDBI, *Entrepreneurship Development Programmes,* 1980, p. 18.
4. IDBI, *Entrepreneurship Development Programmes,* p. 36.
5. IDBI, *Entrepreneurial Development Programmes,* 1980. p. 44.
6. SIDBI, *Report on SSI Sector,* p. 77.

16

IDENTIFICATION OF BUSINESS OPPORTUNITIES

A potential entrepreneur is interested to involve himself in only those business processes which are viable and have a demand in the market. At the same time, he is required to select a particular option out of different options available to him. For example, he has to select a particular business or industry then he is required to evaluate what will be the form of that particular product or service and possibilities of that particular industry or business in the prevailing scenario. Identification of a business opportunity as per the market demand, approach of support system towards a particular product are some of the important problems generally encountered by the potential entrepreneurs. In other words, finding out the possibilities of a business or industry is generally regarded as identification of Business opportunity.

Business Opportunity

In practice, an entrepreneur is termed as an opportunity seeker. He is supposed to identify, explore and then select a viable business opportunity. Business opportunity is an attractive project in terms of adequate rate of return which motivates the entrepreneur to accept that particular project for making investment decision. Entrepreneurs generally assess different possibilities and select only highest reward paying possibility for execution. Thus, a business possibility may take the shape of business opportunity only when that possibility is being capable of as commercially feasible. In this context, two major criteria are important for making a possibility as a business opportunity, *(i)* favourable market demand or excess of demand over existing supply available in the market and (ii) adequate rate of return on investment that is generally equal to normal rate of return and risk premium attached to that particular business opportunity. However, these two criteria must be feasible in terms of technical, production, commercial and managerial viability otherwise there is no utility in having such type of rate of return.

Objectives of Identification of Business Opportunities

1. To evaluate the possibilities of developing and utilising physical resources of a particular region from the technical and economic

point of view.

2. To study and examine the small, medium and large scale industrial possibilities keeping in mind the requirement of the region and country as a whole. These possibilities must be technically feasible and economically viable.
3. To identify those industries which are not based on local resources but they can be established on the basis of economic consideration keeping in mind the future requirement of the region or country as such.
4. To recommend by certifying the usefulness of other possible industries for the region.
5. To assess and estimate the capital, labour, transport, power, fuel, raw material for feasible industries.
6. To study the short and long run development possibilities of the region with regard to agriculture, irrigation, forestry, fisheries, minerals and labour etc. and recommend an effective programme for balanced economic situations of region concerned.
7. To evaluate the impact of achievement in financial resources, production, employment and initial requirement of capital in industrial development process.

Thus, from the practical point of view it is necessary to conduct survey of related conditions for the assessment of different dimensions of industrial feasibility. Actually, survey identifies those areas and directions which are necessary for the balanced development of region, state or industry concerned and prepares background for the proposed development. Site of plant location is governed by the local and all India conditions and side by side requirements of capital, power, fuel, raw materials and labour also affect the identification process of business opportunities. In this way, identification of business opportunities includes the collection and analysis of related data on region, area and feasible product concerned and taking necessary decision about their potentiality for development. An entrepreneur should try to give due importance in his decision making process as it governs the future of his business.

Factors Affecting Identification of Business Opportunities

1. Volume of Internal Demand : An entrepreneur should try to assess the pattern of internal demand of proposed product or industry in which he is planning to involve himself. Demand of product or industry is generally governed by the level of national income, per capita income and population etc. Normally, higher the level of income higher will be the demand of product in the market.

2. Availability of industrial Raw Materials : Availability of raw material also determines the business opportunities as it decides the level of future production. Easy availability of raw material generally encourages the entrepreneur to adopt positive steps for establishment of industrial units. If there is shortage of raw material or existing units are facing the crisis of raw materials it means there is no use to develop more units in that particular industry. An entrepreneur is expected to assess his position to what extent he will be able to ensure proper supply of raw materials for smooth production.

3. **Availability of Internal Resources** : Generally, there are three phases of a business opportunity—promotion, expansion and diversification. Availability of viable opportunity and adequate rate of return motivate entrepreneur to undertake entrepreneurial activity but again with the condition that he has to have some seed capital of his own, personal connections etc. Existing entrepreneur is required to test his existing capability to mobilise internal resources for expansion. If he does not have any additional internal resources it may not be viable to increase the capacity of production. Similarly, he has to examine the rationale to what extent internal resources can be utilised for future expansion programme, and if he is ready to utilise that resource he will again think that this diversion is not going to affect the level of present operation. So, it is necessary to give due consideration on internal resources before initiating a particular decision.

4. **Form of External Assistance** : Identification of business opportunities also involves the marking of sources from which financial and other facilities are expected to come. Volume of support and facility, their sources and conditions also affect the identification process. Easy accessability to these facilities and assistance will also accelerate the process of identification. Government generally provides subsidy and incentives for promotion of industrial units. Availability of favourable environment for subsidy and incentives helps the entrepreneurs to take prompt decisions.

5. **Possibility of Export** : Export potentiality is an important criterion for measuring efficiency of a particular industry. If an entrepreneur is planning to establish a particular unit which has export potential, certainly it will increase the level of expected earning. Moreover, he can easily avail the subsidy, incentives and concessions given by the Government for export promotion efforts. Besides, he can also meet out research and development requirement through export income. These steps will enable the entrepreneurs to improve the quality of particular product as well as its competitiveness in the market.

6. **Analysis of Performance of Existing Units** : Objective analysis of performance of existing units is to be undertaken to ensure success in identification of business opportunities. Detailed analysis is required for employment position and its potentiality in unit concerned, quantitative and qualitative dimensions of capital (fixed and working capital), fixed assets, product range, value addition through manufacturing or processing, requirement of financial support and foreign exchange, marketing problems, sales performance, export potentiality, forms of assistance, infra-structural facilities, forms of organisation and structure of industry etc. This type of analysis will help the entrepreneur to have an idea about the prevailing situation in existing units.

7. **Gathering Information Regarding Proposed Industry Development** : An entrepreneur is expected to take a decision about the establishment of a particular

industrial unit after completing the process of identifying business opportunities. In other words, he has to finalise a proposal with regard to development of a particular product in a particular industry after undertaking a detailed study of prevailing position. But before giving a final shape to a particular proposal he is again supposed to critically examine the nature of product, proposed additional capacity, expansion of existing industry, form of expansion of new units, capital investment for establishing a new unit, additional requirement of power, employment and production etc. Critical analysis of these aspects will provide a sound base to entrepreneur in taking a particular decision.

8. Level of Risk in the Business : There are different types of risk generally involved in a particular business. These risks are technical risks, economic risks, social risks and environmental risks. Technical risks deal with the risk of not knowing enough about the technical processes, materials etc. However, economic risks are the risk of market fluctuations and changes in relation to raw materials etc. Risk inherent in the development of new relationships is treated as social risk. Environmental risks are the risks which result from environmental changes in the entrepreneurial work as an outcome of the new activity. Thus, entrepreneur has to assess the implications of these risks at the time of identification of business opportunities.

Business Opportunities in Major Group of Industries

Entrepreneurial opportunities are available in the following major group of industries :

1. Manufacturing : It deals with conversion cycles. Entrepreneurs convert raw materials into semi-finished products and finished products. Manufacturing organisations use raw materials to produce goods in terms of physical items. Goods are tangible, so they can be touched, seen, measured and otherwise physically evaluated by customers. Manufacturing business requires more investment in equipment, energy and raw materials and that is why risks are generally much greater in comparison to other types of business, like wholesaling, retailing and service industries.

2. Wholesaling : It deals with transferring of goods from manufacturers to retailers at certain remuneration or commission. Actually, wholesalers are middlemen between manufacturers and retailers. They provide servies to the retailers such as fast delivery or credit services that enhance the value of the product. Small entrepreneurs play dominant role in wholesaling business. "Wholesalers buy product in bulk from manufacturers, store it in a place convenient to retailers and then sell it as retailers call for it. Besides having a few employees, a wholesaler usually has relatively few customers most of whom tend to buy large volume, repeating customers"[1]. Under wholesaling business, entrepreneurs calm the feathers of retailers whose promised goods have failed to arrive or chasing after suppliers who have failed to deliver.

3. Retailing : It deals with customers directly in supplying goods. Retailers purchase products from either wholesalers or manufacturers and supply or sell the same to the customers or end users. They provide different types of services to consumers, such as personal attention, wide selection or credit terms. In this way, they also add value to the product specially stores, Departmental stores, super market, convenience stores, discount stores and retail outlets are the different types of retail business.

4. Services : It deals with activities that provide some value to the recipient such as financial, legal, medical, or recreational benefits. Service organisations do not deal in a product but they produce services. "Services such as education and health care are intangible, so they cannot be physically examined before they are produced. Moreover, services are generally produced at the same time the customer uses them, so they cannot be stores."[2] Entrepreneurial skill competency and efficiency govern the efficacy of services business. Due to this reason, services hold a magnetic attraction for the entrepreneurs. "Services are open to innovation, and no other industry group offers entrepreneurs a higher return on their investment of time. Often, an entrepreneur can run a service business alone."[3] Doctors, advocates, accountants, consultants, advisors, computer experts work independently and easily develop their image among their clients or customers.

New Venture

A new venture is any organisation still in its formative stages. Basically, new ventures are founded by individuals intending to change the environment of a given industry by the introduction of either a new product or a new production process. Although money new ventures grow into large organisations, during their formative stages they face unique risks and present special challenges to their owners. Changes are the law of nature. External environment generally cause problems for established businesses and create opportunities for potential entrepreneurs. Technological changes, economic changes, change in social values, and deregulation, etc., affect the thinking and creativity of dreamers and innovation and are the direct result of change available in environment.

Role of New Ventures

1. Sparking Innovation : New ventures generally play crucial role in introducing new goods and services to the economy. Often, new ventures employ major entry wedges like new product or services, parallel competition and franchising. A New product or services are relatively rare and if they are composed of new technology, they may be hard to imitate. According to *Peter Drucker*, it is called "being first with the most" strategy. Parallel competition is a "me too" Strategy that introduces competitive duplications into the market. These duplications are parallel, not identical to existing products or services. It is possible with a small innovation or variation in an already well accepted and well recognised product line or service systems. From chasing develops a proven marketing formula for success and expands it. Franchise avails the benefits of visibility and recognition, logical cost savings, volume buying power, lower employment and training costs and the ability to use the mass media for advertising efficiently.

2. Improvement in Social Endowments : Innovative new ventures assist the society by providing improvement in social endowments like health, education and social welfare programmes. Improved social endowments ensure better health care facilities, comforts and further improvement in standard of living. Personal experiences and market surveys enable the entrepreneur to create products and services which can easily help the different segments of society.

3. Accelerating Economic Growth : Small and tiny industries are nursery beds for first generation entrepreneurs. "Economists view a healthy small business community as the best way to full economic growth, preserve competition, prevent monopolistic control of industries and assure competitive prices for quality products."[4] These industries also play crucial role in creating job opportunities.

4. Developing Entrepreneurs : New ventures provide people an alternative to the traditional career path, e.g., service opportunities. They motivate people to act as job providers in place of job seekers. With the result, new goods and services are available for the society at large. Government subsidies and incentives, institutional support system etc. enable the minorities and women to opt for entrepreneurship as a choice of career.

Approaches to New Ventures

1. Starting a New Business : A start-up organisation is one, which is created by the entrepreneur himself. "A start-up gives the entrepreneur greater freedom in selecting goods or services location, facilities, equipment, suppliers and professional services. Similarly, a start-up is not bound by the established procedures or legal commitments that an existing business often carries and a start-up avoids the possibility of inheriting problem customers, problem suppliers or problem employees."[4] However, there are certain limitations which affect start up organisations. There are problems involved in bank loan, identification of prospective employees and their training and development: constraints of designing an organisation, shortage of good locations and difficulties in getting customers, etc.

2. Purchasing an Established Business : Sometimes, potential entrepreneurs purchase established business to avoid problems involved in a start-up organisation. Potential entrepreneurs also interested to purchase existing firm because there are certain benefits inherent in existing businesses. "The existing firm has already invested the time and effort required to choose a good or service to produce, select a location, establish a customer base, hire employees, select suppliers, design the organisation structure and create operating procedures. The track record of the business can be evaluated and compared with competitors in the industry."[5] Inspite of these favourables factors, potential entrepreneurs may face problems like poor location, poor reputation, outmoded facilities, obsolete inventory and technology and unfavourable contractual agreements.

3. Purchase of Franchise : Franchising is a marketing system by which the owner of a service, trade marked product or business format grants exclusive rights to an individual for the local distribution and or sale of the service or product and in turn receives payment of a franchise fee, royalties and the promise of conformance to quality standards".[8] Some of the entrepreneurs who avoid technicalities of start-up business or purchasing an existing firm opt for the benefits of franchising which include an established brand name and company identity, well defined policies and procedures and assistance in both starting up and managing the enterprise. However, potential entrepreneur faces certain limitations of franchise business. These limitations limit the freedom of entrepreneurs, the franchise fee, start-up costs and royalty fee normally paid whether the franchise makes a profit or not, can be a hardship for a small business especially if revenue is lower than expected. And even if a concept is franchised, it can still fail.

Starting of a New Venture

Identification of business opportunities provide a framework for entrepreneurial activities. A framework is generally governed by different stages. These stages are : pre-startup stage, startup stage, early growth stage and later growth stage.

1. Pre-Startup Stage : It is defined as a period that precedes any attempt to generate sales. It starts with the idea that is available from creative process and ends at the point of being consciously perceived as commercial venture. During this stage focus is generally given on product, service and market planning. Entrepreneurs are supposed to believe that their ideas are feasible and commercially viable through the development of an enterprise. There are generally four activities to new venture.

(i) Identification of Business Concept : It incorporates conceptualisation of business and it is possible only with the extension and shaping of creativity process into visions of useful products and services. Potential entrepreneur is required to fill up the gap already existing in demand pattern of goods and services.

(ii) Product Market Study : If entrepreneur is satisfied that a particular product is feasible, then he has to initiate product research. Either, he has to arrange patents etc., or he is supposed to manage actual R & D to design the item necessary for production. On the other hand, market research is the process of identifying the potential customers for that particular product. Entrepreneurs generally manage these things by seeking necessary help from professionals.

(iii) Financial Planning : It deals with financial resources or funds. New ventures are generally financed by personal savings of the entrepreneurs. But at a later stage entrepreneurs have to attract capital through loans etc. At this stage financial planning is generally based on verifiable information. Most ventures need seed capital at this stage and startup stage. "Seed capital may be defined as the cash needed for product development, market research and initial operating expenses before sales revenue can begin to offset business expenses."[7] However entrepreneurs are required to assess their stake in the proposed business, investment by family members and their personal financial capabilities outside business interest.

(iv) Pre-startup Implementation : It comprises a set of well-timed activities that have to be accomplished. It is a stage when entrepreneur is expected to prepare himself for necessary action and do certain things before launching a particular project. At this stage, entrepreneur is required to establish relations with outside parties for necessary supplies. He has to maintain contacts with those who are ready to join the administrative system of the proposed organisation.

Here, entrepreneur has to arrange resources, purchase beginning inventary, hiring of resources needed and seeking necessary permission, approval licences, leases, facilities and equipment etc.

2. Startup Stage : It is concerned with the initial period of business. In this stage, entrepreneurs require to focus on implementation and early positioning. It is the first step into income generating activity of the firm. He has to formulate strategies to meet his business objectives and positioning the venture for a long period in the market and industry. These points are relevant.

(i) Fulfilling Business Objectives : New venture will generate adequate projected revenue. For this purpose projected sales has to be used as measuring criteria. Analysis of break even point, variable costs, cash flow is to be undertaken in proper way to establish a relationship between the projected sales and estimated costs. In this situation it would be easier to have a clear-cut idea about fulfilling the business objectives.

(ii) Enterprise Positioning : Positioning is the process of organising the enterprise to provide product and services to a particular customer group. Effective business idea ensures the successful operation of a business. So, there is a need to ensure a clear-cut concept of the product and its growth potential in future. However, efforts would be made to ensure the survival of the business in short-run as well in the long-run However, enterprise is to be positioned to achieve long-term objectives. If product or service is viable in the short-run then it is that enterprise is to be positioned to take benefits of growth potential of that particular product or service. Thus, positioning or reposiuoning of enterprise is a continuous process and efforts are necessary to plan it during the pre-startup stage.

3. Early Growth Stage *:* It considers three symptoms : Very sow percewed comfort zone and very rapid. Very slow is an indication hat sales increase slowly as product has a limited market at its early stage or nature of product itself effect slow sales. In case of perceived comfort zone incremental growth in sales is possible as resources can be ensured by increasing the volume of sales. This process will easily ensure profit as an entrepreneurial objective. Very rapid situation indicates a rapid increase in sales as new products gain wide accep ance in new markets. It indicates a positive reaction from the consumer demand side. It ranges from slow growth through incremental higher sales to explosive growth through quantum changes In consumer demand Thus, entrepreneurs are concerned with rapid changes in sales and resources. Thus, it is very sensitive development in the life of the venture and it needs intense monitoring. Reversals are possible in these situations. It is possible for the entrepreneurs to have low growth potential in future and he needs to re-position his enterprise for the

4. Later Growth Stage : It may be regarded as a stage when the enterprise experiences slower growth rate and industry concerned has attracted competitors. The general symptom of this stage is mat required to make a successful transition from family business to professionally managed companies. Most of the family businesses or private companies have to be converted into joint stock companies and entrepreneurs are generally ready to convert their holdings into tradeable securities in stock exchanges. Initial public offerings (IPOs) are generally planned by them. Entrepreneurial cadre is generally replaced by professional managers.

Thus new venture development represents a different sets of environment. But only few ventures are able to have all these four stages to their life Some ventures do not survive for a long period due to their inherent weaknesses. Other ventures are started by those entrepreneurs who have no intention to expand their enterprise beyond a certain, limit for example comfort zone of operations. Similarly, there are certain entrepreneurs who would like to believe in rapid growth but may not be interested in converting their business into professionally managed companies. Actually, they the the entrepreneurs who would not like to dilute their personal identity with the firm or enterprise.

EXAMINATION QUESTIONS

Long Answer Questions

1. What are the objectives of identifying business opportunities ? Discuss the factors affecting the identification of business opportunities.
2. What is business opportunity ? How are business opportunities identified ?
3. Discuss the different stages of starting a new venture.
4. Define business opportunity. Discuss the objectives of identifying business objectives.
5. Examine the nature of business opportunity. Also explain the factors affecting business opportunities.
6. Discuss the process of starting a new business.
7. What is business opportunity ? Examine the process of identifying the business opportunities.
8. "Identification of business opportunities is the first essential condition for the entrepreneurship." Explain and discuss the factors affecting the identification of business opportunities.
9. What do you mean by business opportunities ? How can you identify them.

10. If you were a prospective entrepreneur with a flair for fabric designing, how would you carry out the opportunity scanning and identification process for your abilities ?
11. Describe the factors that you will take into consideration for conducting market demand analysis for a small scale garment manufacturing unit.
12. You are an entrepreneur, planning to set up a software development unit in your city. Explain the variables you would use and the steps you would follow to conduct your market demand analysis.

Short Answer Questions

1. What is business opportunities ?
2. What are the objectives of identification of business opportunities ?
3. Explain the factors affecting identification of business opportunities.
4. Describe the process of starting a new business.

Objective Type Questions

1. Business opportunity relates with
   (a) Business possibilities
   (b) Commercially feasible projects
   (c) Risk projects
   (d) Favourable market demand
2. Early growth stage falls to consider following symptoms
   (a) Very slow (b) Perceived comfort zone
   (c) Very rapid (d) Rapid
3. Very rapid situation indicates
   (a) Increase in production (b) Rapid Increase in production
   (c) Rapid increase in sales (d) Increase in sales
4. Enterprise positioning is meant for
   (a) Short-term arrangement (b) Continuous process
   (c) Long-term process (d) None of the above

Answers

1-(b) 2-(d) 3-(d) 4-(c)

Reason Based Questions

State with reasons whether the following statements are true or false :

1. Adequate rate of return on investment is generally equal to normal rate of return.
2. Demand of product is generally governed by the level of national income, per capita income and population.

3. Services are generally produced at the same time the customer uses them, so they cannot be stored.
4. A new product or services are relatively rare and if they are composed of new technology, they may be hard to imitate.
5. Parallel competition is the strategy that introduces competitive duplications into the market.

REFERENCES

1. Siropolis, Nicholas, C, *Small Business Management,* Houghton Miffin Company, Boston, 1990, p. 70.
2. Courtland, L. Bovee and John, V. Thill, *Marketing,* McGraw-Hill, New York, 1992, p. 5-6.
3. Siropolis, Michalas, C, *Small Business Management, p.* 72
4. Courtland, Bovee, John, V. Thill, Marian Burk Wood and George P. Dovel, *Management,* McGraw-Hill Int. New York, 1993, p. 376.
5. *Ibid,* p. 376.
6. Fry, P., Entrepreneurship : *A Planning Approach* (Minneapoilis/St. Pual: West, 1993), p. 118.
7. John W. Wilson, *The New Ventures :* Adisson Wesley, 1985, p. 109.

17

PROJECT MANAGEMENT

Projects are the means for development and economic upliftment leading to an improvement in the quality of life of the people. The need to achieve these objectives assumes additional relevance in situations prevailing in developing countreis which can afford neither frittering away of capital resources nor loss of time in achieving the objectives set for these projects. Since projects provide the building blocks for generating additional capital, it is imperative that delays in project implementation and attendant cost overruns are kept to a minimum. Actually, projects are crucial for the process of development and economic growth. Any delay in the implementation of projects would in addition to cost overruns lead to substantial loss of production.

Nature of Project

The dictionary meaning of project is speculative imagination. It deals with three dimensions : innovation, vision and risk. So it is a scheme of something to be done in a viable framework.

According to *Gittinger*, "project is a whole complex of activities involved in using resources to gain benefits."[1]

"A Project is a single use plan and aimed at achieving a specific one time goal. Projects integrate fewer activities and resources and are often developed as sub-units of programme."[2]

Encyclopaedia of Management also defines a project as an organised unit dedicated to the attainment of a goal—the successful completion of a development project on time, within budget in conformance with predetermined programme specifications."

A project is defined as "a non-routine-repetitive one-off undertaking, normally with discrete time, financial and technical performance goals". The definition is descriptive and because of the endless variety of projects, most of the definitions are of this nature. As another: "A project can be considered to be any series of activities and tasks that:

(i) have a specific objective to be completed within certain specifications;

(ii) have defined start and end dates;

(iii) have funding limits (if applicable); and

(iv) consume resources (i.e., money, time, equipment)

Thus, on the above definitions we can say that project is a cluster of activities where resources are invested from its inception to its completion to generate a given result within a framework of approved time and cost schedules.

Characteristics of a Project

1. **Investment Pattern** : Project requires funding support for its successful identification and execution. In a particular time framework, entrepreneur has to invest necessary funds in terms of seed capital and installation and development of fixed assets. Funds are to be blocked during gestation period without creating any money. Thus, project involves capital investment for the purpose of developing production or service facilities.

2. **Expected Return** : Capital investment is required in project but returns are expected only after the project completion. However, an entrepreneur invests funds in project only when he foresees a viable operation in future. It means there must a series of expected return in future. If project is not profitable or unable to generate adequate return in future then it will not motivate entrepreneur to block his resources in that particular project.

3. **Time Limit** : Project requires a timely completion so efforts are needed to realise the objectives or completion of project within a framework of approved time and cost schedules. With the delay in completion of projects huge investments will remain in the pipeline resulting delay in income inflows and employment generation. In this context, a progress measurement system for evaluating the physical progress of the project and its coordination activities based on separate weightages assigned for input effort sequential requirement in equipment assembly and sequential requirement in process has to be developed to avoid time over-run and cost over-run.

4. **Location** : Entrepreneur generally decides the site or location of his project. Actually, site selection is a tough decision and he is required to evaluate the suitability of options. Availability of consumer market in that particular area or easy accessability to labour and raw materials affect the decision of entrepreneur in site selection so location affects the viability of the project. Cluster approach is getting popularity now days when units having similar production behaviour are generally located in particular area or region.

PROJECT MANAGEMENT

Project Management in the modern context is a highly sophisticated and fast developing concept and practice." Project management has been defined as "the process of planning and directing a project from its inception to its completion in a given time at a given cost to generate a given result." So in modern era, project management is the need of the hour. Entrepreneur is supposed to follow effective project management to get a better result from his proposed investment. Actually, efficiency of investment depends on the effective management of both time and cost behaviour. Viability of an enterprise depends on the success in accelerating the flow of benefits from particular investment project.'

Components of Project Management

An important facet of any project management activity is the selection of the organisational model for the project. An appropriately designed organisation provides the essential framework for efficient project management. However, it is desirable to develop a functional approach with centralised policy farmulation and decentralised implementation. In this regard, following components are integral parts of the project management.

1. **Project Planning, Monitoring and Control** : It is an important component for the effective and timely implementation of the project. In order to make the implementation effort more effective, it is necessary that the approach to project implementation should be based on a culture of detailed planning which ensures that each activity is planned at a suitable level to the minutest detail. A structured and integrated system of planning and review should be adopted.

2. **Pre-investment Activities Planning** : Generally, there is delay in project implementation owing to inadequate attention being paid by the entrepreneur to the timely completion of a host of preparatory activities necessary for ensuring the smooth execution of the project. It is therefore, essential that at the inception of a project a pre-investment activity network is prepared identifying all activities on which action must be initiated in advance and indicating the scope, responsibilities, time schedule and inter-relationship of these activities.

3. **Procurement and Contract Management** : Delay in project execution is also due to delay in procurement and award of construction contracts. So, it is necessary to divide the total project into a number of well defined and manageable work packages or systems. Each package consisting of inter-related equipments and services that can be advantageously engineered and procured should have clearly identifiable terminal points and tie-ups with the other packages. Care has to be taken to ensure that the packages for each project are mutually exclusive and collectively exhaustive.

4. **Quality Assurance** : This is a vital area in which entrepreneur is expected to take concerted efforts in ensuring quality in project execution. Quality standards are relative phenomenon and they have to be maintained from designing stages. Quality defects during manufacture, erection and commissioning result not only in enormous delays but also in lower operational reliability. In order to ensure that the implementation effort will result in a reliable operating plant that has been efficiently built in accordance with applicable codes and standards, it is essential that a comprehensive quality assurance programme be developed commencing from the design and carried through the stages of receipt of materials, manufacture storage, erection and commissioning.

5. **Cost Engineering and Budgeting** : It covers a detailed cost estimates for the project. It also includes updated estimates at regular intervals based on actual expenditure incurred and the preparation of cash flows in consultation with the planning group. The budgeting process is a vital management tool not only for providing a basis for control over expenditure and for cash forecasting, but also a system to ensure coordinantion of inputs and results by all sub-systems.

The process of budgeting should be from bottom upwards with each work area defining its budget in physical units linked with progress and targets and a centralised group integrating these into a comprehensive organisation budget both in physical and financial parameters.

6. Site Management : It is concerned with selecting a suitable site for the project execution. Site planning should integrate the work plan with the phased quantification of input resources including materials and work fronts and check points for inspection and quality control. To ensure effective implementation of site systems there is need for regular interaction between the entrepreneur and his team members responsible for project execution. Site management also incorporates the construction, management systems and procedures, responsibilities and inter-relationships required for timely execution of the project.

Project Life Cycle

Each stage of the project cycle plays an important role in the systematic project planning process. A project has to complete three stages :

1. **Pre-Investment Stage** : It is concerned with laying down the objectives of the project. On the basis of practical study, theoretical framework is required to be developed under this stage. Demand forecasting, strategies to achieve objectives, evaluation of resources characteristics, financial profile and project financing, cost-benefit analysis and pre-investment appraisal are some of the important variables to be taken into under this phase. Besides, it also covers organisational design, selection of consultancy organisation, design criteria, construction planning and planning for contract management. This is the stage where project idea is to be converted into an investment proposal.

2. **Construction Stage** : Once an investment decision is taken its execution is necessary. Thus, it is related with developing infrastructure for the project. Entrepreneur is required to invest necessary resources in fixed assets like land and buildings, plant and machinery, township development and other endowment facilities like transport, communication and other services. Development of organisational framework like control systems, production organisation, personnel organisation and marketing organisation are required to be developed under this phase. Procurement of materials, erection of facilities, organisation of progress review meetings are also initiated under this stage. It also covers trial-run process.

3. **Normalisation Stage** : It starts with processing of input and generating outputs. It initiates routine procedures to produce goods and services for which project has been developed. It requires working capital financing for raw materials and other consumable items. It also operationalises the fixed assets like plant and machinery etc. already developed in construction stage.

Objectives of Project

1. **Promotional Objectives** : It is concerned with the development of new production facility by the entrepreneur in a particular industry segment.

Innovative behaviour leads to new product development and entrepreneur is expected to produce new product. So, creation of production facility for new product through project execution is the only option before the entrepreneur.

2. Balancing Objectives : If entrepreneur thinks that capacities of different production units are not properly balanced then he may opt for carrying out economic and efficient repairs to maintain continuous production. He may also go in for additions to existing plants. However, in this process, it is necessary for entrepreneur to have sufficient value addition to meet out the investment already made in addition of balancing plants. Actually, balancing projects should not only yield higher revenue but also be in a position to remove or minimise inefficiency due to under-utilisation of capacity in other units.

3. Modernisation Objective : It is initiated due to either the plant outliving its utility resulting in higher maintenance cost or due to technological changes in production/process technology. Thus, it is but natural for the entrepreneur to undertake modernisation programme to remain competitive in the market. Modernisation improves products, production and processes. It also increases the capacity of enterprise to remain in the business and competitiveness with available competitors.

4. Replacement/Maintenance Objectives : It is concerned with relatively small in nature and cover only parts of the plant capacity. For example replacing a turbine by electricity power generating plant. To avoid obsolescence, it is necessary to resort for replacement with the help of replacement/maintenance, products are to be maintained at the same level or there may be improvement in operational efficiency of the plant. By initiating this process we can easily minimise the maintenance cost and avoid production loss.

5. Expansion Objective : Expansion projects are embarked upon to produce a larger volume of current product ranges or to meet out anticipated growth in demand for its products or increase in market share for the products. Under this process, additional facilities are to be developed to supplement the existing resources or for assuring supply of critical inputs. However, basic objective behind expansion project is to encash the additional opportunities available in the market.

6. Diversification Objectives : Existing entrepreneurs also would like to enjoy profitable investment opportunities in new area or in sun-rising industries. Besides, spreading over the risk and investible resources may also be the objective of expansion project. Diversification projects also enable the enterprise to generate income from different areas where investment was not made earlier.

Factars to be Considered in Preparation of a Project

(*i*) Compatibility with Entrepreneur : Project is to be prepared as per the interest, personality and resources of the entrepreneur. Proposed project should fit into the entrepreneurial abilities and training of the entrepreneur. Project must be in a position to offer prospects of rapid growth and high return on capital to be invested by the entrepreneur.

(*ii*) Consistence with Government Priorities : Government from time to time declares its intention about the industrialisation approach of the country. That is generally reflected in Industrial Policy Resolution of the Government. So, project should be inconsistent with national goals and priorities, consistent with governmental regulations on environmental effects, foreign investment policies and licensing procedures etc,

(*iii*) Availability of Inputs : Project needs certain supplies, resources and inputs. Entrepreneur should try to assess the requirement of resources and inputs required and he must assure himself to what extent these supplies are available within manageable limit. Availability of technical knowhow, availability of power supply etc. have to be assessed in evolving a project.

(*iv*) Adequacy of Market : It relates with extent of present market and market share, competitors and their market share, export market, quality, price profile of the product, sale and distribution system, projected increase in consumption, social and demographic trends and patent protection.

(*v*) Reasonableness of Cost : It is necessary to assess the cost structure of the proposed product and what extent it will enable the entrepreneur to realise an acceptable profit with a competitive price. Entrepreneur should try to examine the cost of individual inputs and rate of normal return/expected return available in the industry as such. Entrepreneur should consider the cost of material inputs, labour cost, overheads, administration expenses, selling and distribution cost, services and economies of scale.

(vi) Acceptability of Risk Level : Projects are vulnerable to business cycles, technological changes, competition from substitutes and imports and governmental controls over price distribution and environmental pollution etc. Thus, entrepreneur should examine his position to what extent he is ready to accept technical risk, economic risk, social risk and environmental risk etc.

Thus, project management provides a long term base to the enterprise to operate in the market. Continuity in income, accelerated income flows and diversified risks are the motivating force to embark upon new ventures/new projects.

Nature and Functions of Project Manager

A Project Manager (PM) is generally found entangled in the continuous circle of doing, learning and changing. Only managers with the requisite skills and sufficient amount of enthusiasm and dynamism can withstand the pressures in these incessant operations. An ideal PM should have the following skills and personal attributes :

Skills

- Planning ability
- Organising capacity
- Team building skill
- Technical skill

- Conflict resolution ability
- Administrative skill
- Interpersonal skill
- Diplomatic skill

Personal Attributes

- Drive, Initiative and sound leadership traits
- Confidence, persuasion, aggressiveness and never-say-die attitude.
- Ambitious and forceful
- Effective communicator
- Flexible and adaptable
- Ability to identify problems and suggest solutions
- Good coordinator
- Quick Decision-maker
- Creative and enthusiastic.

EXAMINATION QUESTIONS

Long Answer Questions

1. What is a project ? what are its objectives ?
2. What factors should be taken into account while preparing a project ? Evaluate need of project formulation to make project effective.
3. How will you judge the feasibility of a new product ? Explain with the help of an illustration.
4. Define project, also evaluate its characteristics.
5. What is project management ? Explain is components.
6. Discuss the nature and life cycle of a project.
7. "Entrepreneur is required to consider a large number of factors in preparation of project and they are imperative to be evaluated." Discuss.
8. What is project ? How is it formulated ?
9. Discuss the nature of a project. Also examine the steps necessary in identification and formulation of a project.
10. What do you understand by project design and network analysis ? Prepare a project design.
11. Give a classification of project. Discuss various phases of project life cycle ?
12. Why is the stabilisation phase considered one of the most critical phases in the life of an enterprise ? Outline the main challenges at this stage and suggest suitable strategies to overcome them.

Short Answer Questions

1. What is a project ?
2. Explain the feature of a project.
3. Describe the components of project-management.
4. What is project life cycle ?

5. Discuss the objectives of a project.
6. Explain the factors to be considered in preparation of a project.

True/False Questions

Tick the True/False of the following statements :

1. A project is a single plan.
2. Site management incorporates construction management system.
3. Pre-investment activities involve identification of factors responsible for delay in project execution.
4. Quality standards are relative phenomenon.
5. Project life cycle is irrelevant with project management.
6. Diversification projects help in generating more income from existing projects.
7. Projects are vulnerable to business cycles only.
8. Increase in market share is not concerned with project management.
9. Balancing projects minimise inefficiency.
10. Normalisation stage with processing of input and generating output.

Objective Type Questions

1. Project is not concerned with the following
   (a) Innovation (b) Vision
   (c) Risk (d) Creativity
2. A project is a
   (a) Cluster of activities (b) Single activity
   (c) Group of activities (d) None of these
3. Gestation period is concerned with
   (a) Time over run (b) Cost over run
   (c) Labour turnover (d) Viability of the firm
4. Progress measurement system deals with evaluating
   (a) Financial progress (b) Physical progress
   (c) Output performance (d) Labour relations
5. Cluster approach indicates
   (a) Different production behaviour
   (b) Similar production behaviour
   (c) Unified production behaviour
   (d) None of the above
6. Efficiency of investment is governed by
   (a) Time behaviour of project (b) Cost behaviour of project
   (c) Both (d) None of the above

7. Project management is not concerned with the following
   (a) Functional approach
   (b) Centralised Policy formulation
   (c) Decentralised implementation
   (d) Decentralised policy formulation
8. Project life cycle is not concerned with the following
   (a) Pre-investment stage (b) Construction stage
   (c) Normalisation stage (d) Stabilisation stage
9. Modernisation improves
   (a) Products (b) Production
   (c) Processes (d) Capacity
10. Expansion Project helps in
    (a) Supplementing the existing resources
    (b) Arturing supply of critical inputs
    (c) Encashing additional opportunities
    (d) None of the above

Answers

1-(d) 2-(a) 3-(d) 4-(b) 5-(b) 6-(a) 7-(d) 8-(d) 9-(d) 10-(c)

Reason Based Questions

State with reasons whether the following statements are true or false :

1. All the elements of general management are always present in project management.
2. Project does not involve forecasting.
3. Entrepreneurial projects fail due to insufficient management.
4. Project cost have direct relation with economic benefits derived from it.
5. Expansion project helps to encash the additional opportunities available in the market.
6. Managing project is different from managing regular business.
7. A project is a single plan.
8. Project life cycle is irrelevant with project management.
9. Projects are vulnerable to business cycles only.
10. Increase in market share is not concerned with project management

REFERENCES

1. Desai Vasant, *Dynamics of Entrepreneurial Development and Management*, p. 196.
2. Bovee Courtland, Thill John. V. Wood Marian Burk and Dovel George P. *Management*, p. 213.

18

PROJECT IDENTIFICATION AND CLASSIFICATION

It is the first and most crucial stage of the project cycle. Entrepreneur has several investment opportunities but he is supposed to select only a few potential projects for preliminary evaluation. Opportunities encourage the entrepreneur to do something if situation is viable. Every new business opportunity is unique. Each will have something that sets it apart from others even if it is no more than the personality of an entrepreneur.

In a free enterprise system markets arise for new products and services from wants and needs of consumers. It is for the entrepreneur to identify opportunity based on both wants and needs. Thus, project identification is concerned with the collection, compilation and analysis of economic data for the eventual purpose of locating possible opportunities for investment and with the development of the characteristics of such opportunities.'

Identification Process: Identification process is concerned with conscious identification of a viable product idea that logically addresses an opportunity. An opportunity is defined as the identification of a gap in need and the likelihood that if a product was developed to fill the need it would also be wanted, *i.e.*, there would be effective demand." Thus, identification of business opportunity is the result of interaction between the entrepreneur and his environment.

In this context, *Peter Drucker* has identified three kinds of opportunities : additive, complementary and breakthrough. Additive opportunities are those opportunities which enable the entrepreneur to utilise the existing resources in better way without in any way involving a change in the character of business. Complimentary opportunity results in introduction of new ideas and involve change. Breakthrough opportunities incorporate fundamental changes in both the structure and character of a business. A certain level of risk is always involved in these opportunities. However, additive opportunities are least risky but greater risk is available in complementary opportunities. Breakthrough opportunities carry highest degree of risk. But level of risk is directly attached with the level of return involved in these opportunities. That is breakthrough opportunities hold highest rate of return and guiding spirit behind entrepreneurial behaviour which is innovative behaviour. Higher the level of innovation higher the level of return attached with that innovative process.

Product Idea: Product idea is the result of idea generation, incubation, illumination and implementation. Idea generation is the way one conceives of a product but a formal product means drafting the first design and questioning its feasibility. However, it requires a transition activity which enables the enrepreneur to take a decision to pursue that idea or not. If answer is yes an incubation period occurs in which an inventor or R&D team is expected to explore product ideas, experiment and try different types of confirmatory tests. In the meantime, inventor or R&D team puts forward proposal for product development requiring a commitment of time and money. "When this is achieved, the illumination stage-or implementation stage occurs in which the company gears up for test production, completes patent work, develops an engineered protoype and at the end, actually produces a limited run of new products. These are tested, markets are studied and various certificates of opproval are secured before the company enters the final stage of diffusion. Diffusion is the process of expanding into full production and into the consumer target markets while continuing to improve the product to meet consumer's expectations."[2] Thus, identification of product idea provides help in identification of a relevant project, .

In this process, three dimensions are generally included : inputs, outputs and social cost and benefits. Input dimension ensures that project will utilise raw materials, fuel & power, manpower, and finance etc. to produce output. Output indicates the capacity of the project to produce goods and services, income and employment generation etc. In practice, quantity and quality of product/output decide the level of market capacity to absorb the particular output. Generally, projects have social dimensions where assessment process is initiated to evaluate the sacrifices which the society will be expected to make and the expected benefits will accrue to the society from a particular project.

Steps in Project Identification

The identification of a project provides only the green signal for the preparation of feasibility report (FR) for appraisal and investment decision. The inputs for identifying a project can be resourced from different sources : government agencies, banking and financial institutions, trade and industry associations, and other international organisations and collaborative agencies. However, entrepreneur is required to ensure identification of optimal projects which will contribute maximum to the growth and other objectives of the enterprise. The essential steps for project identification relates to studying the following:

(i) Available raw materials,

(ii) Available technology and skills.

(iii) Position of substitutes available in the market.

(iv) Information with regard to import of commodities which can be indigenously manufactured.

(v) Inter-industry relationships,

(vi) Performance of existing industry in which specific product related project is being planned.

(vii) Availability of development plans.

(viii) Position of old project if any. However, in actual practice, these steps are hardly scientifically studied and followed by the entrepreneur at the time of project identification. The projects many a time come spontaneously on the basis of ideas and possibilities of demand or availability of some raw materials and not an outcome of scientific investigation and systematic search for feasible projects.

Testing Criteria for Project Identification

At the time of investment decision, entrepreneur is required to take concerted efforts to assess the social and economic costs and profitability of the project with the help of Social Cost Benefit Analysis (SCBA) technique. Projects are accepted or rejected many a time on the basis of economic viability assessed on the basis of application of accounting prices, premium on foreign exchnage, shadow wage rate etc. But at the identification stage, projects are identified mainly on the basis of felt need and/or technical feasibility and/or financial viability. Moreover, it would be better to examine the following issues in detail with regard to project identification:

(i) the organisational structure and nature of project planning capability to be developed by the entrepreneur;

(ii) what analysis/studies need to be undertaken at the identification stage;

(iii) how and to what extent the use of social cost benefits analysis (SCBA) should be used at the identification stage;

(iv) whether some guidelines should be provided for undertaking necessary studies; and

(v) how to ensure the availability of shelf of the project for the concerned objective.

Constraints in Project Identification and Execution

There are two types of constraints. These constraints are Internal and External constraints.

Internal Constraints

Internal constraints are those constraints which arise due to limitations of entrepreneurial management responsible for project execution etc. These are as follows:

(i) Non-availability of required project planning capability with entreperneur from where the project idea originates is the first major constraint. Unless such capability is created and project identification is done on more scientific basis and well in advance after taking expected benefits into consideration the adoption of sophisticated approaches/method for selecting or rejecting projects at the time of taking final investment decision will serve very little purpose in ensuring implementation of optimal project.

(ii) Entrepreneur, while preparing feasibility report, focuses on the problem of non-availability of realistic cost estimates and time schedule. This becomes a major constraint in scrutinising evaluation and investment decisions thereby delaying the total project realisation. A sound information system on cost and time schedule would help in reducing the pre-investment decision-making time and effort of an entrepreneur.

(iii) Another constraint is the non-procurement of equipments/materials in time. It is largely due to the fact that entrepreneur's inefficiency in placing the order in time as well as non-cooperation of suppliers in making necessary supplies in time. Most of the time for lack of proper monitoring & followup, timely ordering of equipment and materials are delayed. These lapses are mainly attributable to entrepreneurial inefficiency.

(iv) Non-involvement of project management in formulation of project objectives and goals is another constraint. Since, it is not involved in formulation of project objectives, there is no binding force in terms of accountability for project execution in time. Project management team may face the problem in achieving the unrealisitc goals of the project

External Constraints

(i) Rapid changing technology and its consequent need of specialised manpower. Entrepreneurs are facing to adjust themselves with the fast changing scenario in these sectors.

(ii) Delay in deliveries from Indian equipment suppliers due to shortage of basic materials, the need to import certain items, power-cuts, lack of sufficient experiene, outdated business methodologies etc.

(iii) Implementation of projects faces hurdles due to government policies and regulations. Delay in government approval, licensing, foreign collaboration agreements, foreign exchange approval, environment clearance etc. creates problems before the entrepreneur.

(iv) Lack of standardisation of the equipments which creates a problem in finding a ready alternative to overcome a contract delivery failure. Inflationary market trends which use artificial shortages and consequent overrum of time and cost estimates.

Dimensions of Project Environment

Entrepreneur is required to identify suitable opportunities. There are different options with various dimensions like product/service, technology, equipment. scale of production, market, time phasing, location etc. It is a thorough job for the entrepreneur to select with such wide dimensions. The crucial factor in identifying opportunities for project investments is the understanding of the environment in which one operates; sensitivity to emerging opportunities and possibilities thereof, analysis of tangible/intangible factors and lastly the destiny of the entrepreneur. The various dimensions of the environment are:

(i) Business environment
(ii) Industrial policy
(iii) Regulation of industrial development
(iv) Regulatory framework for foreign investment
(v) Promotional measures for industrial development
(vi) Liberalisation and new economic policy etc. Thus, an understanding of the business environment which shows the opportunities available, applicable regulations and controls, incentives and facilities provided, would benefit potential entrepreneurs in identifying promising and beneficial investment opportunities.

Present Position of Innovation Management in India

In the dynamic and ever-changing environment, change is the key to success. As the invention emanates from need, the change in demand needs to innovate. The fierce competition in the customers' market has enforced the entrepreneurs to innovate so as to lead and survive for a long period. Innovation is a process where new products and services and more efficient production techniques are introduced by the entrepreneurs that have identified new market opportunities or better ways of meeting existing demands. "Innovation means doing the new things or the doing of things that are already being done in a new way."[3] Thus, innovation is an art of doing new things. However, there is distinction between creativity and innovation. Creativity is the ability to bring something new into existence. Practically, it is the ability not the activity of bringing some thing new into existence. It is possible for a person to conceive of something new and envision how it will be useful but not necessarily take the necessary action to make it a reality. The ideas generated in the mind of a man have little value until they are converted into new products, services or processes. "Innovation is the transformation of creative ideas into useful applications but creativity is a prerequisite to innovation."[4]

Schumpeter has described entrepreneurs as innovators who use the process to shatter the status quo through the new method of commerce. It includes new processes of production, introduction of new products, creation of new markets, discovery of a new and better form of industrial organisation. *Peter Drucker* also elaborates that "innovation is the specific tool of entrepreneurs as the means by which they exploit change as an opportunity for a different business or a different service. It is capable of being presented as a discipline, capable of being learned, capable of being practised." Entrepreneurs need search purposefully as the sources of innovation and they need to know and to apply the principles of successful innovation.[5] Thus, innovation is the development process. It translates an idea into an application which adds value to the existing products and enhances its utility in the light of attributes intended in changed environment. It requires entrepreneurs to workout the details of product design or service analytically to develop marketing, obtain finance and plan operations.

Need for Innovators

In India, J.C. Bose and Dr. C.V. Raman's keen sense of observation and perseverance lead them to discover new phenomena in the last half century. However, the country has not been able to produce such curious men having outstanding ability to make fundamental discoveries in science and technologies. The Indian scientists have contributed more to incremental knowledge or minor innovation. In this context, it is important to mention that continuous efforts are needed to make the research and development activities. For this purpose, grass-roots innovators and communities with traditional knowledge and documents should be encouraged to popularise their innovations in the society through prototype designs or products. Besides protecting their intellectual property rights, planning process should be strengthened to link innovation, investment and enterprise to make the innovative efforts/creative work a strong movement. It is quite correct to say that individuals are creative. But the question arises that, is society capable enough to recognise and reward these innovators? General practice in India is that the innovative people have been ignored or harassed until they were recognised by other nations. It is notable that central as well as state governments are also not serious in supporting indigenous science and innovations. There were announcements of intent to provide six per cent of the GDP to education. However, no steps have been taken to popularise research and development activities in concrete terms. Government is incurring huge expenditure on information technology, but formal sector has been affected by severe resource crunch for innovations. There are fewer students in the area of science and technology researches and the inadequate funding from the Government also severely affects the innovative projects.

Thus, in present scenario, it would be better to ensure innovations for business survival and success. Actually, managing innovations effectively has become the key to the growth of India in the context of increasing competition owing to the globalisation and emergence of disruptive technologies across the world. Both business managers and corporates need to constantly innovate, so as to stay ahead in the competition. Increasing competition leads to the emergence of disruptive technologies, thereby making the existing technologies obsolete. The future would not be about eliminating disadvantage but about creating new advantages. Moreover, "poverty has compelled Indians to have the cerebral edge as the country clearly had an edge when it came to innovations."[5] Similarly, efforts are also needed for innovations in customer relationship management and on the human touch in strengthening customer relations. New technologies would enable corporate to better their products and services. Human touch is quite imperative for successful business models.

National Innovation Foundation—India

The Department of Science and Technology (DST) India helped the establishment of the National Innovation Foundation (NIF)—India, on Feb 28th 2000, with the main goal of providing institutional support in scouting, spawning, sustaining and scaling up grassroots green innovations and helping their transition to self supporting activities.

The foundation has a Governing Council chaired by Dr. R. A. Mashelkar, Former Director General CSIR and President Global Research Alliance. Professor Anil K. Gupta, President SRISTI and Professor Indian Institute of Management Ahmedabad, is the Executive Vice-Chairperson of NIF.

For the last many years the Honeybee Network and Society for Research and Initiatives for Sustainable Technologies and Institutions (SRISTI) have been scouting innovations by farmers, artisans, women etc. at the grassroots level.

Grassroots Innovations Augmentation Network (GIAN) scales up innovations, from the HoneyBee database of innovations, through value additions in innovations to sustain creativity and ethics of experimentation. GIAN was conceived at the International Conference on Creativity and Innovation at Grassroots (ICCIG), jointly organised by IIM Ahmedabad and SRISTI.

Objectives of NIF

(i) To help India become an innovative and creative society and a global leader in sustainable technologies by scouting, spawning and sustaining grassroots innovations ;

(ii) To ensure evolution and diffusion of green grassroots innovation in a selective, time-bound and mission oriented basis so as to meet the socio-economic and environmental needs of our society ;

(iii) To provide institutional support in scouting, spawning, sustaining and scaling up grassroots green innovations as well as outstanding traditional knowledge and helping their transition to self supporting activities ;

(iv) To seek self reliance through competitive advantage of innovation based enterprises and/or application of "people generated sustainable technologies" at grassroots level ;

(v) To build linkages between excellence in formal scientific systems and informal knowledge systems and create a knowledge network to link various stakeholders through application of information technology and other means ;

(vi) To promote wider social awareness, and possible applications, of the know-how generated as a result of these initiatives in commercial or social spheres and encourage its incorporation in educational curriculum, developmental policies and programs.

Mission of NIF

To help India become an inventive and creative society and a global leader in sustainable technologies without social and economic handicaps affecting evolution and diffusion of green grassroots innovations. To meet its objectives in scouting, awarding and incubation of grassroot innovations, NIF has set up five dedicated departments to execute innovation to enterprise development models :

(i) Scouting and Documentation

(ii) Value Addition and Research and Development

(iii) Business Development and Micro Venture

(iv) Intellectual Property Management

(v) Dissemination and Information Technology Management

Technology Business Incubators (TBI)

The need for instruments such as TBI has been recognised the world over for initiating technology led and knowledge driven enterprises. Studies also show that such mechanisms help not only in the growth of technology based new enterprises but also in improving their survival rate substantially (from 30 per cent to over 70 per cent). TBIs also facilitate speedy commercialisation of research outputs. The TBIs usually provide the following types of services :

(i) Market survey/marketing assistance,

(ii) Business planning and training,

(iii) Organising management/technical assistance,

(iv) Assistance in obtaining statutory approvals,

(v) Information dissemination on product ideas/technologies,

(vi) Syndicating finances,

(vii) Arranging legal and IPR services,

(viii) Using facilities of the Host Institute (HI) at nominal charges,

(ix) Work space for a limited period

(x) Common facilities of TBI such as communication, conference, computers.

Objectives of TBI

(i) Creation of technology based new enterprises,

(ii) Creating value added jobs and services,

(iii) Facilitating transfer of technology,

(iv) Fostering the entrepreneurial spirit,

(v) Speedy commercialisation of R&D output,

(vi) Specialised services to existing SMEs.

Criteria for Selection of Location : Ideally, a TBI should be located near a source of technology and knowledge, i.e., around R&D Institutions/Academic Institutions or it should have strong links with such institutions to ensure optimal use of the already existing expertise and facilities, thus, keeping the cost of the TBI on lower side. Locating TBIs in such location could also reduce time lag between technology development and its commercialisation. Further, as the success of a TBI largely depends on its location and management besides quality of tenant enterprises, the following aspects relating to the HI need to be kept in view while selecting location of the TBI :

(i) R&D track record and subsequent commercialisation of R&D output,

(ii) Dedicated team of R&D persons,

(iii) Industrial milieu in the region,

(iv) Proximity to other R&D/academic institutions,

(v) Infrastructure, facilities and expertise available,

(vi) Strong commitment and willingness of the HI.

Thrust Areas : Each TBI would focus on not more than 2-3 thrust areas. The thrust areas for a TBI would be identified, based on the following :

(i) Expertise and facilities available in the HI,

(ii) Track record of the HI in the chosen areas,

(iii) Industrial climate in the region,

(iv) Market potential/demand in the region.

To begin with, TBIs are proposed to be promoted in the following selected thrust areas which have potential for faster growth :

(i) Information and Communication Technology (ICT)

(ii) Application of biotechnology

(iii) New materials including nano materials

(iv) Instrumentation and maintenance

(v) Agriculture and allied fields

(vi) Garments and fashion technology

(vii) Services

Facilities Required : The TBIs should mainly draw upon the existing facilities available in the HI including land and building. However, certain essential facilities, which need to be created in a TBI are given below :

(i) Modern work space,

(ii) Communication facilities,

(iii) Computing facilities,

(iv) Vital equipment needed in identified area

(v) Library and information centre

(vi) Training and conference facilities

Sponsorship : The TBI may be promoted by the selected HI and DST jointly. The HI has to provide the requisite land and building for the TBI. Other related and interested agencies could also be involved as sponsors.

Activities of TBI

Each TBI would be required to plan and undertake specified activities based on the identified thrust areas. However, the following set of activities is suggested as general guidelines :

(i) Provide specialised services to existing SMEs in the region,
(ii) Facilitate technology commercialisation,
(iii) Consultancy,
(iv) Training including short courses,
(v) Technology related IPR issues, legal and quality assurance services,
(vi) Marketing,
(vii) Assistance in obtaining and other clearances,
(viii) Common facilities,
(ix) Assistance in preparation of business plans,
(x) Technology shows/technology clinics/trade fairs.

Organisation Status of TBI

The TBI should itself represent a dynamic model of sustainable business operation and generate revenue as well as profits. As per the guidelines of the Department regarding legal status of new Technology Business Incubators it has become mandatory to register the new TBIs as an autonomous body functioning as a society registered under Societies Act of 1860/or as a non-profit making section 25 company. The affairs of the TBI should be managed by an Advisory Board. The Board of the TBI should help not only in development of a strategic plan containing quantifiable objectives to achieve the desired results but also in managing the TBI efficiently and effectively. The Board should have representation from the promoters and reputed professionals. This may include representatives of DST, SIDBI, HI, industry, VC companies, Entrepreneurs, student bodies and tenants of the TBI. A committee should also be set up for selection of tenant firms.

Performance Parameters and Expected Output

The performance of TBIs would be judged, based on the following parameters:

(i) Number of tenant enterprises promoted and their growth pattern,
(ii) Number of businesses graduating successfully and their growth,
(iii) Number of new jobs generated,
(iv) New technologies commercialised,
(v) Quality of services offered,
(vi) Number of consultancy jobs undertaken,
(vii) Net revenue earned,

(viii) Return on Investment,

(ix) Upgradation/modernisation facilitated in existing units.

Special Features of TBI : Special features of TBI are as follows :

- Dedicated management team
- Well defined tenant selection and graduation system
- A set of value added services
- TBI to be run as a business entity
- Periodic performance evaluation

Thus, the TBIs besides providing a host of services to new enterprises (and also to existing SMEs in the region) also facilitate an atmosphere congenial for their survival and growth. The essential feature of a TBI is that the tenant companies leave the incubator space within 2-3 years.

National Science and Technology Entrepreneurship Development Board (NSTEDB)

The National Science and Technology Entrepreneurship Development Board (NSTEDB), established in 1982 by the Government of India under the aegis of Department of Science and Technology, is an institutional mechanism to help promote knowledge driven and technology intensive enterprises. The Board, having representations from socio-economic and scientific ministries/ departments, aims to convert "job-seekers" into "job-generators" through Science and Technology (S&T) interventions.

Objectives of NSTEDB

(i) To promote and develop high-end entrepreneurship for S&'T manpower as well as self-employment by utilising S&T infrastructure and by using S&T methods.

(ii) To facilitate and conduct various informational services relating to promotion of entrepreneurship.

(iii) To network agencies of the support system, academic institutions and Research and Development (R&D) organisations to foster entrepreneurship and self-employing using S&T with special focus on backward areas as well.

(iv) To act as a policy advisory body with regard to entrepreneurship.

Support for Entrepreneurial and Managerial Development of MSMEs (INCUBATOR)

The concept of Business Incubation is a relatively new concept for MSMEs. The "Support for Entrepreneurial and Managerial Development of Small and Medium Enterprises (INCUBATOR)" Scheme of the NMCP makes available a new window for supporting and nourishing businesses based on new ideas. Under the scheme, knowledge institutions like Engineering Colleges, Research Labs etc. are provided financial assistance for incubating each of the new ideas. The Incubator provides technology guidance, workshop and lab support and linkages with other agencies for successful launching of the business and guides the entrepreneurs in running the business for the next 2-3 years.

Problems and Prospects for TBIs

TBIs model had great scope for creation of a new generation of entrepreneurs who in turn would provide jobs and generate national wealth as well. "The scope is there but the difficulty lies in the lack of understanding of the concept by the beneficiaries. However, necessary actions are being taken to address the problem, which include awareness creation through workshops and seminars and talks by successful entrepreneurs. The thrust areas in which DST proposes to promote TBIs include information and communication technology, bio-technology, new materials, instrumentation and maintenance, agriculture and food processing, technology, biotechnology, new materials, instrumentation and maintenance, agriculture and food processing, garments and fashion technology and services."

Thus, on the basis of above analysis, we can say that Indians have always been entrepreneurial. India has already produced great stalwarts like JRD Tata, Walchand Hirachand, GD Birla, S.L. Kirloskar and Dhirubhai Ambani. There are a few significant economies across the world where Indian entrepreneurs have not struck deep roots, a few countries where they are not amongst the most successful of the immigrant communities. The Indian spirit of enterprise straddles the entire spectrum from silicon valley to wall street, from the Kiranawala to high tech start up, from shipping and steel to software, from manufacturing to service and from Dunkin Donuts to hotmail.com. However, the key question is to introspect with a sense of urgency to have a depth analysis of how can India be a much more powerful incubator for entrepreneurship in the years to come, given the sise of our country, our brain power and business acumen ?

Suggestive Framework

Following suggestions are to be implemented for ensuring incubating process at an accelerated pace :

1. There is a need to ensure systematic changes in our method of education. Currently, the system pigeonholes individuals into a narrow range of discipline and straight jackets them into rigid career tracks. Given the overwhelming emphasis on grades, creativity and independent thinking and uptaking a backseat. The need of the hour is an education system that fosters exploration, questioning and debates. A system that can help each student to pursue a path that best stimulates their creativity and challenges him or her. The objective should be to create citisens who have the ability to think laterally. Students who are equipped to step out into the real world and become thought-leaders rather than products of machinery that churns out yet another commodity.

2. There is also need of a shift in societal and individual attitude at different levels. More often than not, our social environment tends to suppress precisely those attributes that are prised highly in an entrepreneurial culture. For instance, our system still remains largely driven by a credential-oriented mentality that discourages individuals from deviating from traditional educational and professional paths. Striking out in an unknown direction is frowned upon and failure entails a very heavy price. Regrettably, our environment also accords considerable premium to conformity. The nail that sticks out get hammered. In this context, we need to develop a much greater tolerance for the thinkers, the socalled eccentrice and the mavericks. Because, very often, they are the ones who turn out to be the visionaries.

3. There is also a compelling need to get the institutional framework right. To start an entrepreneurial activty, get the financing in place, to obtain the approvals and get the process kick-started is a back-breaking and concerted exercise. Generally in case of a business failure, the aftermath degenerates into a legal quagmire. However, recent guidelines on venture capital funding will give a fillip and provide a meaningful avenue for entrepreneurs to realise their vision more speedily and easily.

4. There is a need to innovate for giving Indian entrepreneurs a head start. For instance, government can easily design suitable micro equity arrangements for entrepreneurs. The government should develop micro stock exchanges to address the need of the entrepreneurs. The Internet certainly makes this possible. Given Indian genius in financial innovation—for example, the badla system and hundi—this is certainly within our grasp. Such arrangement would considerably lower the threshold at which businesses could reduce debt and replace it with equity capital, thereby helping spawn many more entrepreneurs.

5. Entrepreneurship is a quality that large business enterprises require as much as small start-ups and much more today than ever before. The challenge for large corporates is to turbo charge the entreprenurial islands within. Going forward, such a structure would be more conducive to pursue experiments to innovate, to develop cutting edge products, to dream new and better ways of running the business and creating value in an unfettered manner. In essence, to create thought-leaders—people who are perpetually willing to step out of the box, think laterally and go that extra mile to make huge positive impact on the organisation. The idea is to have entrepreneurs and partners in business rather than just employees.

6. The Government should try to push the entrepreneurship beyond the boundaries of business. Entrepreneurship should be much broader in its scope. There is a need to have entrepreneurs in all walks of life in government, in the public sector, in educational institution, in non-governmental organisations and in social endeavours too.

7. There is a need to look upon entrepreneurs as role models in the society because it is only they who contribute in a great measure to the process of wealth creation and nation building. They are the persons who create the order out of disorders. Actually, they are not job seekers, they are job providers to others. Thus, they also contribute in job creation activities. That is why, government has already taken many proactive initiatives. Among these are, rewriting some of the more restrictive regulations, building a world class science park for technopreneurs and a total overhaul of educational system etc.

8. A proper network with effective feedback system should be developed to provide training and development facilities to the budding entrepreneurs.

Thus, efforts are needed to developed well-rounded individuals who would be the entrepreneurs of the future. It is, in this context, society, potential entrepreneurs and government should play their respective roles in developing a conducive environment for multidimensional development of the economy as a whole.

Project Classification

Taxonomy refers to classification. The location, type, technology, sise, scope, and speed of a project are normally the factors which determine the effort needed in executing a project. Broadly, projects can be categorised as :

(i) Defensive, *i.e.*, aimed at strengthening the present position or status, and

(ii) Aggressive, *i.e.*, those concerned with giving new ways of service or entering new commercial line etc.

Project could be classified as major, medium or mini depending on the size of financial outlay required for implementation.

Depending on the speed for execution, the categories could be :

(i) normal, where required time is allowed;

(ii) crash, where additional cost are considered to gain time; and

(iii) disaster, where anything needed to gain time is allowed.

Projects could be further classified :

(i) as national/international;

(ii) as industrial/non-industrial;

(iii) depending on level of Technology, like hi tech/low tech

(iv) according to size : mini, medium, large, mega etc.

(v) according to type of ownership—public/private/joint sector/ cooperative etc.

(vi) based on the nature such as balancing, modernisation, replacement

Projects are generally classified in the following ways :

1. Quantifiable and Non-Quantifiable Project : Quantifiable projects are concerned with quantification of targets and development of particular project is made to produce particular product/service in terms of units, quantity etc.

Project engaged in physical production, power generation, mineral production etc, are treated as quantifiable projects. Non-quantifiable projects are those projects where quantitative assessment is not possible. These projects are related with social endowment projects like health, education, social welfare, rural development etc. Family welfare, empowerment of women and development of children, labour welfare etc., are important areas of non-quantifiable projects.

2. Sector Projects : Economy is generally divided among different sectors to ensure effective project development. For example, Planning Commission identifies defferent sectors and allocates resources for project development accordingly. These sectors are :

(i) Agriculture, Irrigation, Food security and Nutrition,

(ii) Industry and minerals,

(iii) Energy,

(iv) Transport and communication,

(v) Environment and forest,

(vi) Special area programmes and

(vii) Science and Technology.

3. Techno-Analysis Projects : These projects include factor intensity oriented projects, causation oriented projects, and magnitude oriented projects. Factor intensity oriented projects deal with capital intensive projects or labour intensive projects. Investment in plant and machinery and R&D programmes and human resource is the basis for deciding that what type of project is capital intensive projects or lobour intensive projects. Availability of demand for goods and services, availability of raw materials, avaibility of skills or other inputs are the important criteria for treating a project as causation oriented projects. If a particular product or service is not available to meet out growing demand then projects development is meant for such purpose is treated as causation oriented projects. Similarly, if certain types of raw materials are not available then efforts to develop a particular project to ensure supply of that raw material is also regarded as causation oriented projects. In case of magnitude oriented projects, level of investments generally used as a deciding criteria. For example, classification of project in different scales—large scale, medium scale or small scale projects is totally governed by the level of investment required in these projects.

4. Objective-wise Projects : All India financial institutions generally extend financial support to meet out the objectives for which funds are required. These projects are classified as New projects, Expansion projects, Modernisation projections, Diversification projects.

Criteria for Selecting a Particular Project

(i) Size of Investment : Entrepreneur is responsible for the promotion of a project. He is required to make his own promoters contribution. There are two types of financial institutions—state level and national level. State level financial institutions like State Financial corporations and State Industrial Development corporations contribute a lesser amount to the total investment required for the project. Thus, under this category only small scale industry and medium size industry can be considered for financial support. But in case of All India financial institutions, medium size and large size industry can be considered for financial arrangement along with promoter's contribution for the purpose.

(ii) Location : A new entrepreneur is expected to locate his project in backward area districts or zero industry districts to avail subsidy, concessions and tax incentives. Similarly, small entrepreneurs are supposed to development to develop their projects in industrial estates developed by state industrial development corporations. It will also facilitate them to avail all infrastructural facilities at one place.

(iii) Technology : First generation entrepreneurs basically opt for proven technology which is indigenously available. It enables the entrepreneurs to work smoothly. However, large-scale sector projects require high technology which is generally governed by latest technology. Projects having foreign collaborations are generally based on foreign technology.

(iv) Equipment : the entrepreneur is expected to select best equipments, plants, machineries etc, for ensuring an effective operational framework for production function. In certain cases, state small industries corporations also ensure supply of equipments etc, to small entrepreneurs. But in case of collaborative projects, foreign collaborators also ensure supply of equipment etc. to agreed projects.

(v) Marketing : Innovative entrepreneurs are quite successful in launching their products in the market but this type of behaviour is quite risky one at the first instance. However, entrepreneurs are required to assess the position of market through market survey etc. Availability of product range, substitutes, price structure, level of competition etc. affect the market potentiality of the product to be launched by the entrepreneurs.

Thus, it would be better for the entrepreneur to assess the implications of above factors before opting for launching a project.

EXAMINATION QUESTIONS

Long Answer Questions

1. What do you understand by project identification ? Explain the internal and external constraints in project identification.
2. Discuss the nature of a project. Also examine the steps necessary in identification and formulation of a project.
3. What is Project ? Describe the factors generally considered in the process of project identification and formulation.
4. Describe various steps involved in project identification. Briefly discuss difficulties experienced by entrepreneurs in the process of project identification.

5. What is project identification ? Briefly describe the steps involved in the identification of a project.
6. What are the major sources of project ideas ? What precautions should be taken by an entrepreneur at the time of selection.
7. "Project identification cannot be complete without identifying the characteristics of the project." Discuss. Also state internal and external constraints in a project identification exercise.
8. How, as a small entrepreneur, would you decide whether the product or service you want to offer to the market has sufficient demand or not ? Identify the key variables that you would need to measure for a product like Readymade office shirts in order to be able to find out whether sufficient demand exists for it.

Short Answer Questions

1. What do you mean by identification of a project ?
2. What is product idea ?
3. Discuss the steps involved in project identification.
4. Explain the testing criteria in project identification process.
5. Discuss the constraints in project identification and execution.
6. Discuss the different dimensions of project environment.
7. What are the different types of a project ?
8. Examine the criteria for selecting a particular project.
9. Distinguish between project identification and formulation.

Tick the True/False of the Following Statements

1. Every new business opportunity is unique. (T)
2. An opportunity is defined as the identification of a gap in need and the likelihood. (F)
3. Number of kinds of opportunities identified by Peter Drucker is five. (T)
4. Breakthrough opportunities carry highest degree of risk. (F)
5. Higher the level of innovation, higher the level of return attached with that innovative idea. (T)
6. Identification Stage also examines social cost benefit approach. (F)
7. Limitations of entrepreneurial management are generally called internal constraints. (T)

Objective Type Questions

1. Project identification deals with

(a) Viable product idea (b) Logical opportunity

(c) Effective demand (d) None of the above.

2. Additive opportunities are necessary to :
   (a) Have a dream for future (b) Utilise existing resources
   (c) Create new resources (d) All of the above.
3. Complementary opportunities result:
   (a) Introduction of new idea
   (b) Introduction of new product
   (c) Introduction of new culture
   (d) All of the above.
4. Breakthrough opportunities in corporate fundamental changes in—
   (a) Structure of the business
   (b) Character of the business
   (c) In both the structure and character of the business
   (d) None of the above.
5. Product idea is the result of—
   (a) Idea generation (b) Incubation
   (c) Illumination (d) All of the above.
6. Non-availability of required project planning capability is due to—
   (a) Poor professional management
   (b) Poor entrepreneurial management
   (c) Poor general management
   (d) None of the above.
7. Lack of standardisation of the equipment is due to—
   (a) Internal constraints (b) External constraints
   (c) Government barriers (d) Regulatory barriers.
8. Following is not concerned with quantifiable project—
   (a) Power generation (b) Mineral production
   (c) Family welfare (d) Water supply.
9. Factor intensity oriented projects are—
   (a) Capital intensive projects
   (b) Labour intensive project
   (c) Technology oriented project
   (d) a and b boh.
10. Non-quantifiable project is not concerned with the following :
   (a) Food security and nutrition
   (b) Empowerment of women
   (c) Labour welfare
   (d) Education for all.

Answers

1. (a) 2. (b) 3. (a) 4. (c) 5. (d) 6. (b) 7. (b) 8. (c) 9. (d) 10. (a)

REFERENCES

1. Desai, Vasant, *Dynamics of Entrepreneurial Development and Management* p. 155-
2. Holt David. H. *Entrepreneurship,* p. 166
3. Schumpeter J.A. The Theory of Economic Development. Harvard University Press, 1934 p. 42.
4. Thomas J. Peters and Robert H. Waterman Jr. In Search of Excellence : Lessons from America's Best-Run companies. Haprer & Row New York, 1982 p. 206.
5. Drucker Peter F. Innovation and Entrepreneurship.
6. Business Line. Dec. 6, 2001.

19

PROJECT FORMULATION

Project formulation relates with second stage of project cycle. It is a pre-investment exercise to determine whether to invest, where to invest, when to invest and how much to invest. The project feasibility reports are meant to provide required information for assessing technical, financial, commercial, organisational and economic viability of the project. Project formulation deals with comparative appraisal of project idea developed in a particular form. In practice, a project idea is to be evaluated in terms of technical feasibility, financial feasibility and social cost benefits analysis.

Nature of Project Formulation

Project formulation is a process in which an entrepreneur is required to undertake an objective assessment of different dimensions of an investment proposition of project idea. The basic purpose of this process is to determine the total impact of the proposed project. Project formulation is an important strategy of pre-investment phase where product idea is to be converted into a project idea. It helps in achieving the objectives of the project—maximum benefits at minimum cost in a particular period of time.

"Project formulation is the systematic development of a project idea by evaluating its various components to take an investment decision"

It involves a screening process through which a project idea is to be developed. With the help of a project idea entrepreneur can easily formulate the objective of the project. Generally, these objectives comprise two types of objectives—general objectives and operations objectives. Entrepreneur has to clearly define their objectives as it will enable him to quantify the targets of physical, financial, human and other resources. A general objective indicates the expected objective of the project. But operational objectives mention the results expected from the implementation of the project.

Stages of Project Formulation

1. **Feasibility Analysis:** It involves the evaluation of a project idea to what extent a detailed investment proposal is required. Generally, three alternatives are available in the context of project idea evaluation. If project idea is feasible, it means entrepreneur can move to next step. If project idea is not feasible, it is an indication that it would be better to abandon the idea. However, if it is not

possible to arrive at a conclusion, then entrepeneur should try to collect more relevant data and analyse the same for arriving at a conclusion.

Feasibility study should focus on the issues like (i) general information of the industry as a whole ; (ii) objectives of the proposal; (iii) alternative ways. if any, of attaining the objectives and better suitability of the proposed project, (iv) project description, gestation period, costs, technology proposed, anticipated life of the project etc., (v) demand analysis, total demand/requirements of the country including anticipated imports and exports and share of the proposed project, (vi) capital costs and norms assumed activity-wise and yearwise, (vii) operating costs and norms; (viii) revenue and benefits estimation etc.

2. **Techno-Economic Analysis:** It is concerned with the identification of the project demand potential. It also helps in choice of optimal technology. Information originating from this analysis is generally used as a basis for project design. Market analysis is also inbuilt process of this analysis by which entrepreneurs can easily evaluate the capacity of the economy to abosrb the output of the project. Demand potentiality of the product also decides the nature of technology to be used. Thus, techno-economic analysis includes two components: determination of project demand potential and selection of optimal project strategy. In this way, techno-economic analysis ensures a unique individuality to the project.

3. **Project Design and Network Analysis:** It defines micro activities of the project and their interrelationships. The project activities are to be developed in sequential order along with time allocation for each and every activity. Network drawing is generally developed with the work plan having estimated time framework. Thus, a working plan defining individual activities with an estimated time allocation constituting the project design

4. **Input Analysis:** It helps in determining the resource requirements of the project. It is basically concerned with the identification, qualification and evaluation of inputs required for the project. Inputs consist of materials, human resources etc. It evaluates the nature of resources in terms of recurring and non-recurring requirements and the sources from which these rsources will be arranged. Thus, input analysis is composed of three components: *(i)* nature of resources that a project will consume; (ii) magnitude of the resorces needed ; and (iii) pattern of supply of inputs.

5. **Financial Analysis:** It measures the project costs, operating costs and fund requirements. With the help of financial analysis, entrepreneur compares the various projects on the basis of generally accepted scale of measurement. Ratio analysis, profit analysis and projected fund flow analysis etc. are generally used as analytical tools to decide the estimated financial performane of the project. Financial analysis also seeks to find out whether the project will generate revenue to realise the ultimate objective for which it has been initiated.

6. **Cost Benefit Analysis:** It evaluates the project from the viability point of view. In this context, basis of assessment is the project design. It takes into account the apparent direct costs and direct benefits of the project. There are certain

entities generally attached with the project and with the project development, they have to sacrifice and gain in years to come. Thus, cost-benefit analysis provides a micro as well as macro dimensions of costs and benefits attached with the project.

7. **Social Cost Benefit Analysis:** It is an assessment of expected total costs to be incurred and benefits derived out of project that is under consideration from the community point of view. Social benefits expected include possibility of financial and out of pockets reduction in service costs, availability of increased resources improvement in domestic resource capacity, increase in foreign exchange, possibility of import substituion, employment generation, spin off effects, improvement in industrial development, improvement in standard of living and improvement in environment. On the other hand, society is expected to incur sacrifices in favour of expected benefits. These social costs include financial and out of pocket costs, contingencies, environmental costs. technology transfer, maintenance costs, reduction in foreign exchange. disguised unemployment, pollution costs, congestion in mobility and other spontaneous and instant costs.

8. **Pre-Investment Analysis:** It indicates that project proposal is now ready for formal approval and in final shape. With the help of different analysis undertaken by the entrepreneur various conclusions already drawn to present a clear picture. Now these conclusions also help different agencies—project sponsoring agency, project implementation agency and external consultancy agency—to take a particulr decision whether to accept the project proposal or not. This analysis enables the agencies/entrepreneurs to have a clear idea about the acceptability of a project proposal.

Project Feasibility

An entrepreneur is expected to involve himself in only those projects which are technically sound, financially feasible, economicially beneficial, commercially dependable and organisationally effective and adequate. To achieve these objectives, he undertakes feasibility studies.

Feasibility study is defined as a formal investigaion of profitable opportunity which leads to rational decisions about making an investment decision.

Feasibility studies consist of market analysis, technical analysis, financial analysis and social profitability analysis.

1. **Technical Feasibility Study :** It is "an attempt to determine how well the technical requirements of the industry can be met, which location would be most advantageous and what the size of the plant should be." In technical analysis, efforts are generally made to review the infra-structural facilities like land, builiding, transportation, availability of raw materials, position of power, production shed, township development, project location in terms of advantages/ disadvantages, proposed size in terms of economic size, evaluation of technical know-how and project schedule.

2. **Market Feasibility Study** : It is also generality called an economic feasibility study. It evalutes the market factors like market growth potential and

location of competitors. Market survey is most popular method for assessing the market feasibility study. In this study, efforts are necessary to analyse whether the prodction of the proposed unit would be absorbed in the market or not. These projections are generally governed by market forecasts of the project. Overall demand forecasts of various categories is quite helpful in achieving the above objectives. These forecasts are regularly prepared by the professional agencies involved in marketing network. Besides, level of competition is also assessed under this study enabling the entrepreneur to assess his strength and weaknesses in the market.

3. **Financial Feasibility Study:** It deals with evaluation of the estimates of cost of the project to ensure that it contains all provisions for contingencies and are realistic. Assessment of sources of finance and position of fund tie-up is undertaken in this study. Entrepreneur is expected to maintain an effective debt-equity ratio. Similarly, he is also required to contribute his contribution as per laid down norms. A critical examination of financial projections is necessary to ensure the paying capacity of the project in respect of future dividends, repayment of debt obligations and servicing of interest etc.

4. **Commercial Feasibility Study:** It evaluates the commercial aspects of the arrangement of the project. It also examines the arrangement process for procurement of machinery and equipments. The whole evaluation process includes the progress regarding placement of orders of equipment, procedure for selection and tendering etc. Arrangement process for sale of goods and services is also included in this study.

5. **Social Profitability Study:** It is defined as a process of evaluating a project in terms of total impact which the project will have on the economy of the nation. Actually, it is a resource investment proposition where the national interest is involved. It helps in evaluating individual projects within the planning framework which indicates sectoral policy objectives and resource allocation. In this context, national planning process and objectives are used as basis for social profitability study.

Feasibility Report

It is a master report prepared from information collected through feasibility studies and consists of various tables, reports and statements. It incororates introductory information on background of the industry to which the project belongs and the organisation prepraring the report. It provides adequate information for project appraisal etc. Besides, financial institutions also use this report for evaluation before extending financial assistance to the enterprise concerned. Following are the contents[1] of a feasibility report.

I. Executive Summary

II. Project Background and History.

III. Market and Plant Capacity

(i) Demand and market supply
(ii) Sales and marketing
(iii) Production programme
(iv) Plant capacity

IV. Material Inputs
(i) Materials and inputs
(ii) Supply programme

V. Location and Site
(i) Location
(ii) Plant site and local conditions
(iii) Environment impact

VI. Project Engineering
(i) Layout and physical coverage of the project
(ii) Technology and equipment
(iii) Civil engineering

VII. Plant Organisaion and Overhead Costs
(i) Plant organisation
(ii) Overhead costs

VIII. Manpower
(i) Labour (skilled)
(ii) Staff (administrative and sales)

IX. Project Implementation

X. Financial and Economic Evaluaiton
(i) Total investment outlay
(ii) Project financing
(iii) Production cost
(iv) Profitability
(v) National economic evaluation.

Difference Between Feasibility Report and Project Report

1. Feasibility Report (FR) presents relevant facts before the top management or entrepreneurs enabling them to accept or reject the project. On the other hand, Detailed Project Report (DPR) involves the preparation of detailed specifications and designs, enginering drawings, site investigation, foundation designs etc. as well as time schedule for project implementation.

2. FR is concerned with pre-investment decision but preparation of DPR is a post-investment decision. FR provides basis on which the investment decision is taken whereas DPR is used as a work plan for the implementation of a project.

3. FR deals with an exploratory research and hence needs a span of 6 to 15 months. However, DPR is an official document prepared with a lot of care and diligence. It needs one year to two years after the investment decision is taken by the entrepreneur or the top management.

4. FR is reliable for a short period of time till the investment decision is made about a project. But DPR guides the entire project and even if any variation is available in the project data then it can be compared and observed. Besides, DPR serves all practical purposes in the project development and for future reference.

Thus, feasibility report is expected to serve as a preliminary assessment of the overall worthwhileness of a project idea. Actually, feasibility report describes the nature and complexity of the project as well as a general view on investment range. However, it always gives an opportunity to revise the actions and rectify mistakes before they are taken for approval etc. Moreover, it pre-supposes the economic and social benefits to be derived from the project.

Essentials of Conducting Feasibility Studies

The guidelines formulated by the UNIDO regarding conducting feasibility studies are as follows :

1. **Scope of the Project** : The scope and magnitude of the project should be clearly defined. This should include all activities scheduled to happen which play important role in commissioning the project successfully and auxiliary operations related to the production extraction, off-site transport, storage of inputs and the off-site construction of major equipments to be used on the site and other off-site and on-site ancillary activities. The computation of project costs can also be facilitated by treating the components as sub-projects, the sum of which yield the investment and production costs of the entire project.

2. **Procurement of Data for Studies** : Efforts are required to estimate the investment and production costs accurately as well as costs and time involved in collecting these data. Investment cost estimates should be based on the following points :

   (i) Inviting tenders based on specifications and bills of quantities.

   (ii) Exercising on prices of similar projects to estimate costs governing specification and bills of quantities.

   (iii) Applying the unit cost constituents derived from homologous operational projects such as measuring in cost per cubic metre of hemmed space or cost per square metre of constructed area.

   (iv) Estimating the total for groups of equipment in iunctional project parts based on the costs of comparable existing projects.

   (v) Annual inflation rates, change in foreign exchange rates, differences in local conditions, different regulations and laws governing industry and accessibility of the construction sites should also be taken into account at the time of undertaking feasibilities studies.

3. Verification of Alternatives and Assumptions : It deals with evaluation of available alternatives regarding choice of technology, equipment, capacity, location, financing etc., factors and assumptions governing these to arrive at a particular decision.

4. Proposed Cost Structure : It deals with spending of costs for the project deliverables. These costs include material costs, research costs, labour costs, overhead costs, distribution or octroi costs etc. There are certain costs which do not always result in outflow of funds like depreciation and loss on sale of fixed assets etc. They may be inputed for opportunity costs or sunk costs that are incurred of which some may be explicit costs and some may be implicit to the production or operation process. Thus, it would be ideal to lable all the necessary expenditure incurred during the project implementation which deserves to be treated as cost.

5. Scheduling the Operation : There are certain techniques like PERT, GERT, CPM, Q-GERT, ZBB etc. which are generally applied for efficient time management. However, these activities are segregated and accordingly miniscule schedule are prepared and their linkage are formed to make the project scheduling process more understable and executable.

6. Currency Management : Generally, there are two types of currencies, local currency and foreign currency, required for the project financing. Local currency should be available for convenient spending and foreign currency (Convertibility) is required for importing the requisite goods and services. Efforts are required to arrange these currencies to avoid delay in project execution.

7. Contingencies : There are two types of contingencies affecting the timely execution of projects. There are inflationary pressures on money market and physical shortages of the materials in the market due to short supply and storage. Project manager is supposed to estimate these contingencies as precisely as possible and necessary arrangement for them is to be made by him for successful implementation of the project.

8. Project Team : It would be better to conduct the feasibility study under the guidance of project team. The composition of the team should be as follows :

(i) an industrial economist

(ii) a market analyst

(iii) an engineer or a technologist who is well versed with appropriate project

(iv) an mechanical and industrial engineer

(v) a civil engineer

(vi) a management expert who is also able to deal with accounting aspects of industry.

Besides certain other technical persons like soil expert, land surveyors and other laboratory technicians should be made available to help the team in feasibility study.

9. Expansion Projects : It is concerned with those existing projects where expansion of scale of operation and scope of coverage is proposed. In order to formulate a comprehensive project proposal, it is necessary to integrate the data of expansion of project with those of the existing enterprise. In this context, it would be better to evaluate the effectiveness and adequacy of existing internal organisation structure and supporting facilities in consonance with the size of the expansion project. There is need for some modifications or adjustments then that have to be taken in account in case of expansion proposal. However, financial evaluation of an expansion project should also the break-even and sensitivity analysis as well as scanning the funds flow and cash flow statements of the ongoing project.

10. Cost Studies : Generally, there are some well-established norms for calculating the pre-investment costs, which varies from project to project. It relates with the cost of studies to the estimated number of man-months required. Cost per man-month is calculated in each Individual case in respect of core salaries, travelling, dearness, mapping, writing and printing allowances and other office overheads. Investment costs of pre investment studies are approximately :

(a) an opportunity study ranges from 1 to 0.2 per cent of the total cost;
(b) Pre feasibility study ranges from 1.5 to 0.25 per cent;
(c) feasibility study ranges from 2 to 0.3 per cent depending on the size of the project.

11. Accuracy of Cost Estimates : Normally estimates of investment and costs of production vary as per the different studies in progress. The ideal variation on these estimates can in all the three cases be as follows :

(a) opportunity studies may vary + (-} 30%
(b) Pre feasibility studies may vary + (-) 20%
(c) Feasibility studies may vary + (-) 10%

12. Agencies Involved in Conducting Such Studies : Now-a-days public and private sector agencies are involved in conducting feasibility studies. The public sector agencies who render the support services to new project investigators include NCAER, New Delhi, CESS, Hyderabad, ICSSR, New Delhi, PUSA-ICAR, New Delhi, TIFR, Mumbai etc. Similarly, private sector agencies which are also engaged in these studies are ORG, Mumbai, IMRB, New Delhi, TCS Mumbai etc.

Project Selection

Product idea is used as a basis for project idea. But project idea is generally screened with the help of technical, economic and financial feasibilities. Thus, project selection is the end result of translated product idea into project idea through effective feasibility studies.

Selection Criteria

Selection criteria are valuable tools for the systematic and objective analysis of projects. There are different selection criteria generally used with regard to project selection which are grouped as (1) Specific Criteria. (2) General Criteria.

1. *Specific Criteria* : These are concerned with economic development of the country. These criteria are as follows :

(*i*) ***Factor Intensity Criterion :*** According to this criterion, entrepreneur should accept and excecute those projects which are expected to help in utilising the abundant resources. Besides, some factors are scarce in availability but efforts should be made to use scarce resources as complimentary with the abundant resources. Optimum product mix with the help of abundant resources and scarce resources are advisable in this context.

(*ii*) ***Size and Complexity Criterion*** : This criterion encourages those projects which are small at their primary stage but there is growth potential for higher size. So stepping stone theory is the basis for this criteria. Size of project should be growth oriented and small scale unit is to be developed as medium scale and medium scale as large scale at a later stage of development process. Thus, large scale enterprises using more complicated techniques and yielding distant returns must wait for a later stage when simple entrepreneurial skills and attitudes have been learned.

(iii) ***Foreign Exchange Benefits Criterion*** : This criterion deals with earning possibility of foreign exchange. It means a project that can earn foreign exchange must be given preference in selection to other projects which are not expected to earn foreign exchange.

(*iv*) ***Commercial Profitability Criterion*** : It considers the profitability aspect of the project. It uses net profit after taxes deducting all costs as basis for evaluating commercial profitability of the project. In practice, measurement of profitability is governed by important factors like (a) estimated capital cost of the project, (b) estimated costs of production and (c) estimated receipts from the sale or realisation from the projects's output.

(*v*) ***National Economic Profitability Criterion*** : It evaluates the approximate rate of return to the national economy on an investment in a project taking into account all major measurable economic costs and benefits. It is notable that an efficient allocation of investment resources is achieved by equating the social marginal productivity of capital in its various uses. Thus, national economic profitability is defined as the total net measurable rate of return to the economy on an investment.

2. ***General Criteria*** : These criteria are concerned with entrepreneur's own interests. These criteria are as follows :

(*i*) Entrepreneur has a technical capability in a particular field.

(*ii*) Entrepreneur is interested to seek financial support from fianancial institutions and that finance is meant for specific project.

(*iii*) Regional bias of the entrepreneur to develop a particular project in a particular region keeping in mind the availability of local resources,

(*iv*) Entrepreneur has an intention to develop a project in particular field seeking a dominating status in that particular field.

Considerations Required for Project Selection

There are two types of considerations to be kept in mind at the time of project selection : (1) Macro Considerations and (2.) Micro Considerations

Macro Considerations

They need a detailed and more comprehensive planning, policy formulation and hard work to improve the total mechanism of an economy. Basically, these are concerned with national level projects. These include the following points :

(i) Overall growth available in different sectors of an economy at a particular period of time.

(ii) Availability of resources to allocate for priority sectors and correcting the imbalances, if any, among the sectors of an economy.

(iii) Identification and allocation of scarce resources required for developing high or key priority areas meant for public needs.

(iv) Regulating and controlling fiscal and monetary framework of the country as required in changing scenario.

(v) Adjustment required in maintenance of wage policy, exchange rate policy and credit regulatory mechanism available in the country.

(vi) Ensuring motivation in rational resource allocation, capital mobilisation and maintaining a balance of payments equilibrium in the country.

Sectoral Considerations

(i) Making the investment plan more realistic and matching it with available resources.

(ii) Ensuring at least the costs and benefits of the projects at par.

(iii) Ensuring effective implementation of multiple projects by managing resource crunch, time over-runs and cost over-runs, etc.

(iv) Priority should. be given to completion of ongoing projects in place of under-taking new projects. However, if launching of new project is urgently required, then it should not affect the implementation process of currently ongoing projects in terms of costs or time spent.

(v) Rational decision-making process is to be put in place on the basis of lessons drawn from the experiences available in the execution of past projects.

(vi) Cost-benefit analysis of project is to be undertaken on scientific appraisal system.

(vii) Investment plans are to be bifurcated in terms of core and non-core projects. This would help in making the investment plans more effective and flexible.

EXAMINATION QUESTIONS

Long Answer Questions

1. Explain in brief the elements of project formulation.
2. What is project formulation ? Explain the need and significance of project formulation.
3. How will you judge the feasibility of a new project ? Explain with the help of an illustration.
4. What factors would be taken into account while preparing a project? Evaluate the need of project formulation to make the project more effective.
5. What is Feasibility ? Discuss the different types of feasibility studies.
6. What do you mean by Feasibility Report ? What are its contents ? How does it differ from Project Report ?
7. What are the criteria for project selection ? What are the basic points to be kept in mind while selecting the project ?
8. What do you understand by project design and network analysis ? Prepare a project design.
9. As a manager, how would you formulate a project ? Give specimen of a project report.
10. How will you examine the financial and technical feasibility of a project ? Discuss.
11. Explain in brief the stages of project formulation.
12. What are the basic inputs required for analysis of competitive situation and market assessment by an entrepreneur planning to set up a small unit for making low cost detergent ? Discuss.

Short Answer Questions

1. What is project formulation ?
2. What are the stages involved in project formulation ?
3. What is feasibility analysis ?
4. What is techno-economic analysis ?
5. What is social cost benefit analysis ?
6. What is project feasibility study ?
7. Discuss the contents of feasibility report.
8. What are the main differences between feasibility report and project report?

9. What are the criteria for selecting a project ?
10. What is pre-investment analysis ?

Objective Type Questions

1. Project formulation relates to
   (a) Fourth stage of project cycle
   (b) Second stage of project cycle
   (c) Third stage of project cycle
   (d) First stage of project cycle
2. The purpose of project formulation to determine the
   (a) Total impact of the proposed project
   (b) Major impact of the proposed project
   (c) Minor impact of the proposed project
3. Techno-Economic analysis deals with identification of the
   (a) Supply potential (b) Demand potential
   (c) Export potential (d) Import potential
4. Input analysis relates with
   (a) Funding requirement (b) Material requirement
   (c) Labour requirement (d) Resource requirement
5. Project design defines
   (a) Micro activities of the project
   (b) Macro activities of the project
   (c) Allied activities of the project
   (d) Individual activities of the project
6. Feasibility study is defined as a
   (a) Formal investigation of profitable opportunity
   (b) Informal investigation of profitable opportunities
   (c) Intensive investigation of profitable opportunities
   (d) None of the above
7. Project selection is
   (a) Product idea is used as a basis for project idea
   (b) Project idea is used as a basis for product idea
   (c) Both are the same
   (d) None of the above
8. General criteria is concerned with
   (a) Entrepreneur's own interests
   (b) Economic development of the country
   (c) Business Environment of the country
   (d) None of the above

9. Specific criteria is related with
   (a) Economic development of the country
   (b) Business Environment of the country
   (c) Entrepreneur's own interests
   (d) None of the above
10. Network drawing is generally developed with
    (a) Action plan (b) Feasibility report
    (c) Work plan (d) None of the above

Answers

l-(b) 2-(a) 3-(b) 4-(d) 5-(a) 6-(a) 7-(a) 8-(a) 9-(a) 10-(c)

Reason Based Questions

State with reasons whether the following statements are true or false:

1. Teriam costs and benefits are quantifiable.
2. Social cost benefit analysis CSCBAT of a project only considers the viewpoints of the society, does not incorporate the viewpoints of the promoter of the project.
3. Project cost has direct relation with economic benefits derived from it.
4. Social cost benefit analysis is must for project justification.
5. Project does not involve forecasting.
6. SCBA lays stress on redistribution of project pay offs.
7. Feasibility Report is same as appraisal report.
8. Social cost benefit analysis (SCBA) of a project includes financial analysis of the same.
9. While carrying out financial feasibility of a project, promoters have a tendency to inflate the figures of projected profitability statement.
10. Project feasibility consists of 3 feasibility study.
11. Marketing feasibility is the most important among other feasibility studies.
12. Technical feasibility is more important than financial feasibility.
13. It is easier to achieve Break Even Point in the capital intensive units as compared to labour intensive units.

REFERENCE

1. Rao, P.C-K., *Project Management and Control,* Sultan Chand and Sons. New Delhi, 1998, p. 52.

20

PRODUCT SELECTION

Earlier it was an easy job of an entrepreneur to select a product. He was free to select any product which he thinks, that product is profitable and viable from the market point of view. There were different criteria like technological knowhow, financial resources, a rough estimate of demand on which entrepreneur was expected to apply his mind before launching that product in the market. But today conditions have changed and became complex. Purchasers are replacing the role of sellers and they are now more competitive. Process of selection of a product has now been considered as an important decisional area. Today, if entrepreneur selects and develops a particular product, it means that he has considered the dimensions like customer's satisfaction, position of competitors, interest of dealers, infrastructural facilities, need for efficiency and socio-economic conditions prevailing in the society etc. and collected necessary information about them.

Concept of Product

Manufacturing organisations use raw materials to produce goods, physical items like car, T.V., utensils, icecreams etc. Goods are tangible and they can be touched, seen, measured and otherwise physically evaluated by customers. Further, "the customer does not generally have to be present during production, goods can be manufactured in a central location and then stored until needed or shipped to a location where customers can obtain them. In contrast, service organisations produce services, activities that provide some value to the recipient such as financial, legal, medical or recreational benefits. Services such as education and healthcare are intangible, so they cannot be physically examined before they are produced. Moreover, services are generally produced at the same time the customer uses them, so they cannot be stored."[1] Various organisations offer products that are a combination of goods and services. Manufacturing organisations provide various services along with the tangible items they produce, just as service organisations frequently include goods in their services offerings Bajaj Finance Ltd.; Escorts Finance Ltd., provide financial services for scooter and tractor buyers. Similarly, Indian Hotels Ltd., (Taj group) a service enterprise takes orders for airlines and prepare meals, etc. but their menu items are tangible goods. The combination of goods and services produced by manufacturing and service organisations determines the unique challenges being faced by the managers.

Product Development Process

It is an extension of the innovation in products and production system. It deals with the following stages :

1. **Idea Generation Stage** : It is concerned with visualisation process of a model product. Product ideas may be contributed by entrepreneurial insight, creative mind mapping or accidentally stumbling upon an idea through a corridor of related activity. Entrepreneurs require to evaluate all ideas and inventions. However, only commercially viable product ideas are picked up through the process of screening and eliminating the non-viable ideas.

2. **Incubation Stage** : It is concerned with formal development of a product or development of prototype for product concerned. It completes three phases like development of product design, prototype development and commercialisation process. Besides, consumer testing of the prototype or proposed product provides a ground for the final selection of the most promising model for mass production.

3. **Implementation Stage** : It involves limited manufacturing facility for the proposed product. This is a preliminary effort to put actual product into the field and together with market feedback. It also helps the entrepreneur to learn through trial and error and to get additional valuable clues for product improvement and other necessary modifications. Thus, it is consist of making a transition from prototype development to development of limited manufacturing facilities.

4. **Commercialisation Stage** : If entrepreneur thinks that product acceptability in the market is good and satisfactory, it means that implementation stage has given a green signal to produce that product with or without expected modifications. Now production department can initiate mass production of the product and marketing department is free to lunch a full-fledged advertising and promotion compaign for mass distribution. However, new product is much like a child that needs guidance and support during the formative years.

Sources of Product Concept

An entrepreneur generates product idea through his own environment. Industrial journals, technical publications, research and development institutions, regional research laboratories, modern scientific research institutions, market surveys are the major sources through which entrepreneur gathers information about product idea. There are certain marketing agencies and R&D institutions which are engaged in arranging patents etc. to potential enpreprepreneurs. Thus, entrepreneur selects a particular product out of different product ideas available to him for further development and production.

Product Design

It is "systematic process for the development of new goods and services or for the improvement of existing goods or services."[2] This process is important for both manufacturing and service organisations. R&D departments are engaged in creating and improving products. They generally enjoy autonomy in persuing their designs, often with little regard for the problems that those designs might present during production.

Business organisations in competitive markets are being forced to think that competitive advantage results from the overall ability to bring new products to market and satisfy customers and not necessarily from the ability to design the most elegant or most sophisticated products. However, it requires communication and cooperation between designers and the managers and workers in manufacturing finance, marketing, human resources departments etc.

Necessary Precautions Regarding Product Selection

An entrepreneur is expected to take the following precautions in selecting a particular product for launching purposes :

(*i*) Production process should not be long and time consuming.

(*ii*) Product process should be smooth and easy going.

(*iii*) Demand of the product should be adequate and continuous.

(*iv*) Industry of the product should have growth potentialities.

(*v*) Product should be acceptible in the market and some degree of competition is always better.

(*vi*) Plant, machinery and equipment meant for the product, industry should be easily available in the market.

(*vii*) Raw materials should be locally available. If they are not locally available, they should be easily available from other places in shortest possible time.

(*viii*) Technologists, artisans and workers meant for industry concerned should be available in the market at reasonable price tag.

(*ix*) Product should have a minimum support base in terms of export potential.

Product Life-Cycle

It describes the passes of goods and services through a sequence of marketing stages. Every product, whether It is a tangible item or a service, passes through a series of marketing stages that make-up the product life cycle. At each stage, managers must consider how to allocate resources to maximise sales and profits. Generally, the following stages are involved in product life-cycle :

1. **Product Development Stages** : In order to survive in a competitive environment; a manufacturing organisation must innovate and complete the new product development as fast as they can. When the product is under development, the company makes an investment but gets no sales in return.

2. Introduction Stage : Under this stage, companies put the product into the market. It requires long period. Sales for the new product build slowly, providing low or no profits because of. the expenses relating with development and introduction.

3. Growth Stage : In this stage, companies are offensive in their product awareness programme and consumers are getting attracted to the product. With the result, sales and profits improve substantially. Under this stage, competitors also enter the market and they start competitive advertising and consumers are persuaded to buy the product.

4. Maturity Stage : In this stage sales continue to rise in its early part but they rise at decreasing rate. At the end of this stage, sales start falling. Though sales increase, profits do not keep pace and tend to fall. Thus, in this stage, sales and profits peak and slowly decline.

5. Decline Stage : In this stage, sales start declining at a faster rate. Thus, sales drop off and profits erode.

Factors Affecting Product Selection

Entrepreneur is guided by different factors in selecting a particular product for project execution.

1. Technical Knowledge : Availability of technical capability to entrepreneur helps him in selecting a product in that particular technical field. Similarly, if entrepreneur himself have gained substantial amount of experience in manufacturing and marketing of particular product then the selection of such a product would be helpful to him.

2. Availability of Market : It also plays a crucial role in the selection of the product. A wide market creates more demand for the product and market risk will also be reduced in that way. The entrepreneur should have a clear cut answer about the product market—How to sell and where to sell ? Local market may be useful for small scale units but they have to expand their market at a later stage.

3. Financial Strength : Manufacturing process of a product needs huge fund in capacity creation, prototype development, R&D. working capital expenses required at preliminary stage and payment of royalty etc. Entrepreneur should ensure his position to what extent he is ready to invest in the product as wellas to maintain liquidity of the business.

4. Position of Competition : Product performance in market is also governed by the level of competition available in that particular market. Market share of existing competitors and their products range. possibility for new competitors, availability of substitutes etc. affect the market viability of the product.

5. Priority of Products : In certain cases products belong to the priority sector indutries and certain products are reserved for exclusive production in small scale sector. In those cases level of competition is comparatively less in comparison to general products. Similarly, certain products are listed by the

Government for exclusive purchase from the small scale sector. Thus, if particular product belongs to these categories these considerations generally receive more weightage in Selection of the product.

6. Seasonal Stability : Continuity in demand of a product during the whole year has a stable market than to a seasonal product. Seasonal inelasticity of a product affects favourably in the selection of a product. Side by side, sales of product should not be affected by abnormal fluctuations. An entrepreneur should prefer only those products which have continuous demand in the market.

7. Restriction on Imports : It encourages entrepreneur favourably in selection of a particular product. In case of ban or restriction on import of a product, domestic market provides considerable scope for such a product as there will be no or restricted supply of imported goods. Naturally. entrepreneur would favour the production of those items which fall under ban list or restricted list of import.

8. Supply of Raw Materials : Adequate supply of raw material is necessary to maintain a continuous production process of a product. Entrepreneur should also try to ensure a continuous supply of raw materials in desired quantity for whole of the year. Local supply or external supply also affect the selection of a product. In case of external supply, entrepreneur will be required to maintain compratively a high level of inventory or raw materials. It will require more blocking of funds for a long period.

9. Availability of Incentive and Subsidy : Government generally provides different types of incentives, concessions, tax exemptions, tax rebate etc. on production of certain items which are treated as import substitutes or as an essential item. Obviously, entrepreneur will select those items which enjoy these advantages.

10. Ancillary Products : In case of product to be produced by ancillary units, it means, it will serve as a major component for the parent industry. In this situation, there will be a ready demand for the product and entrepreneur can easily select this product for proposed project.

11. Locational Advantage : There are certain products which are meant for production only in free trade zones, export promotion zones, special export promotion zones. Government also provides export incentives and tax concessions etc. to these units, so it would be better for the entrepreneur to select these items for production purposes. Availability of big consumer market in nearby areas also affects favourably in selection of a product.

12. Licencing System : As per industrial policy, government formulates licencing policy from time to time. In certain products, it is must for the entrepreneur to seek necessary licences from the government authorities. Capacity addition is also regulated by the licence under certain conditions. Generally, in case of a licenced product licence seeking process is also quite cumbersome. Thus, problem in seeking for these licences also affects the selection of a product.

13. Government Policy : Product selection process should also be analysed in terms of Government policy and its impact. If Government policy is favourable to a particular product then selection of that particular product will prove helpful to the entrepreneur. If entrepreneur is planning to produce a particular product which is not in the interest of the society in that case Government policy will not support the entrepreneur. Thus, in the long run production of a product which is not in favour of society at large will not serve the entrepreneurial purpose.

On the basis of above analysis, we can say that entrepreneur should give due weightage to these factors at the time of selection of a product. Defective selection of a product will create more problems for the entrepreneurs and these problems will affect entrepreneur adversely in the long run. So, he should be cautious enough towards selection of a product as it is the first and most important step in entrepreneurial behaviour.

EXAMINATION QUESTIONS

Long Answer Questions

1. What is product selection ? Discuss its importance for entrepreneurial success.
2. What is product selection ? Illustrate how is a product selected.
3. Discuss the concept of new product. Discuss the factors affecting the product selection.
4. What do you mean by product selection? Discuss the sources of product concept.
5. Examine the need of product selection. What are the necessary conditions which should be kept in mind in product selection?
6. Give a classification of project. Discuss various phases of project life cycle?

Short Answer Questions

1. Discuss the different stages of product development process.
2. What are the factors which generally affect product selection?

Objective Type Questions

1. Product development process involves :
   (a) One stage (b) Two stage
   (c) Three stage (d) Four stage
2. Incubation stage deals with:
   (a) Sample development (b) Idea development
   (c) Prototype development (d) None of the above.

Answers

1. (d) 2. (c)

Tick the True/False Answers

1. Idea generation stage is a visualisation process.
2. Implementation stage is concerned with providing facility for mass production.
3. Product acceptance is necessary for commercialisation stage.
4. Favourable government policy creates more product demand.
5. Seasonal in elasticity of a product affects favourably in the selection of a product.
6. Ancillary Products need more effective advertising.

Answers

1. (T) 2 (F) 3 (T) 4 (T) 5 (T) 6 (F) 7 (T) 8 (F)

REFERENCES

1. Courtland, L-Bovee and Johan V. Thill, *Marketing,* McGraw Hill, New York, 1992, p. 5-6.
2. Pearson, Bracker and White, *Operation Management Activities of Small, High Growth Electronics Firms,* p. 23.

21

PROJECT APPRAISAL

Project appraisal is an exercise whereby an entrepreneur or sponsoring financial institution undertakes an objective assessment of various dimensions of an investment proposal meant for financing decision. It is an ex-ante analysis of a designed investment proposal. The objective of an appraisal process is not only to decide whether to accept or reject the investment proposal but also to recommend the ways in which the project can be redesigned or reformulated so as to ensure better technical, financial, commercial and economic viabilities. The project appraisal which is an essential tool for judicious investment decisions and project selection is a multidisciplinary task and professionals drawn from different fields are quite helpful in undertaking independent project appraisal.

Concept of project appraisal may be defined as a method of presenting a choice amongst competitive usage of resources in a convenient and comprehensive fashion to achieve the laid-down objectives of the economic development plan.

Thus, project appraisal is an analysis of cost and benefits of a project proposal. Its basic objective is to ensure a rational allocation of limited resources to various investment opportunities.

Objectives of Project Appraisal

(i) to assess future expected contributions of project alternatives.

(ii) to undertake analysis of various cost and benefit components of proposed alternatives .

(iii) to develop a conceptual framework for monitoring and evaluating the proposed actions.

Project Appraisal Process

Generally project appraisal process entails two steps :

1. **Classification of effects of a project** : Under this process probable effects of a project are categorised to evaluate the value of an action proposed. Generally, certain actions are easily predictable and other actions are less amenable to predictions. For example, quantitative effects of an action are easily predictable rather than the qualitative action.

2. **Assessment of effects of a project** : This process identifies the effect of a project in terms of desirability. A project may have benefits and cost effects both

at the same time but from different angles : entrepreneur, society or Government. For example, construction of a dam may contribute in the national income by generating power and irrigational facility but it may not be in the interest of local community who may be displaced from that particular area.

Project Appraisal and Project Evaluation

Project appraisal is an ex-ante analysis of a designed project proposal. It assesses and determines the expected costs and benefits of a proposed project. Project appraisal is a pre-investment decision-making process. But project evaluation is an ex-post analysis of an executed project. Thus, project evaluation is a post-investment evaluation process. It evaluates and compares the actual benefits derived and effective costs incurred on the project. Besides, it also compares the expected project results (ex-ante) with the realised results (ex-post) to get an idea to what extent project is successful in its objective.

Importance of Project Appraisal

(*i*) It provides specific and predicted results.

(*ii*) It tests the desirability of a project.

(*iii*) It generates information to determine the success or failure of a project.

(*iv*) It develops or uses existing norms to forecast the rate of success or failure of a project.

(*v*) It verifies the hypothesis developed for the project.

Aspects of Project Appraisal

(*i*) Gestation period.

(*ii*) Location.

(*iii*) Life of the project.

(*iv*) Choice of technology and technical feasibility.

(*v*) Capital costs and norms as well as phasing of capital cost.

(*vi*) Operating cost and norms as well as likely availability of assumed infra-structure facilities in time and required quantity and volume.

(*vii*) Quantification of economic costs and social benefits etc.

Tools of Project Appraisal

Following tools are generally used with regard to project appraisal :

(*i*) Financial Appraisal

(*ii*) Economic Appraisal

(*iii*) Technological Appraisal

(*vi*) Socio-economic Appraisal

(*v*) Managerial Appraisal

I. FINANCIAL APPRAISAL

It deals with financial analysis to ensure initiation of financial conditions and system for the sound execution and efficient operation of the project. Financial analyst is required to monitor and keep track records of various operations like costing, procurement, engineering, marketing, tax management etc. Financial analysis covers the following ***aspects*** :

(*i*) Cost Analysis : It estimates and evaluates the expected cost of production. It covers analysis of future costs, opportunity cost, imputed costs, incremental cost, interest cost, depreciation and income tax etc. In project analysis, these costs are analysed to provide a relevant base to cost structure.

(*ii*) Pricing : It relates with price determination strategy. Expected price framework decides the level of expected demand in the market. So, it should be determined judiciously and be competitive. Nature of market also affects the capacity of price determination. If demand for a products is inelastic then entrepreneur will be in position to charge a high price.

(*iii*) Financing : It deals with resource mobilisation programme in future. It also relates to expected strategy for effective utilisation of resources. Expected rate of return and cost of capital is to be compared for making debt-equity mix.

(*iv*) Income and Expenditure : It is concerned with estimates, expected income and expenditure with regard to the project under consideration. With the help of expected income and expenditure, entrepreneur will be able to have an idea about cost of production and expected profit.

(*v*) Capital Budgeting : Capital budgeting is concerned with the allocation of the financial resources among the available investment opportunities. The consideration of investment opportunities involves the comparison of the expected future streams of earnings from a project with the immediate and subsequent streams of expenditure for it.

Evaluation of Investment Proposals

An entrepreneur is expected to consider a number of investment proposals regarding various projects. But funds available with him are always limited and it is not possible for him to invest available funds in all the proposals at a time. Thus, it would be better to select from amongst the various competing proposals, those which give the highest benefits. There are various methods of evaluating profitability of capital investment proposals. These are as follows :

A. Traditional Methods.

(*i*) Pay Back Period

(*ii*) Accounting Rate of Return

B. Discounted Criteria.

(*i*) Net Present Value Method

(*ii*) Internal Rate of Return

(*iii*) Profitability Index

1. Pay Back Period : It provides an answer to the question—How will it take to pay back its cost? An enterprise may accept or reject an investment proposal depending on its target pay back and/or depending on the risk involved in the project. Thus, the period which it takes the cash inflow from a capital investment project to equal the cash outflow. Actually, it indicates the length of time required for the stream of cash proceeds by an investment to equal the initial expenditure incurred. Formula used for the calculation of pay back period is as follows :

$$ARR = \frac{\text{Average Profit after taxes}}{\text{Average investment}}$$

Project will be accepted if the actual pay back period is less than the expected or predetermined pay-back. However, project will be rejected if the actual pay-back period is more than the expected or predetermined pay-back.

Merits : Following are the main merits of pay-back period.

(*i*) It is simple to understand and easy to calculate.

(*ii*) It weighs all returns equally ignoring even distant returns. It has an inherent hedge against economic depression.

(*iii*) It saves in cost and requires lesser time and labour as compared to other methods of capital budgeting.

(*iv*) It reduces the possibility of loss due to obsolescence as it prefers investment in relatively shorter period projects.

(*v*) It enables entrepreneur to select an investment which yields quick return of funds.

Limitations : Main limitations of this method are as follows :

(*i*) It does not take into account the cash inflows earned after the pay-back period and hence the actual profitability of the project cannot be correctly assessed.

(*ii*) It ignores the time value of money and does not consider the magnitude and timing of cash inflows. It assesses all cash flows as equal though they accur in different periods.

(*iii*) It avoids the cost of capital which is a very important factor in making sound investment decision.

(*iv*) It fails to determine the minimum acceptable pay-back period. Usually, it is a subjective decision.

(*v*) It suits only small projects requiring less investment and time.

2. Accounting Rate of Return : It is also called Average Rate of Return. It estimates the rate of return on proposed capital investment that the project should yield. It is based on accounting profits rather than cash flow. It is defined as the percentage of average profit after tax to average investment calculated over the life of the project. For this purpose, capital employed or average investment and profit earned are determined according to commonly accepted principle of accounting. Following formula is used to calculate ARR.

$$ARR = \frac{\text{Average Profit after taxes}}{\text{Average investment}}$$

If ARR is more than the predetermined rate of return then project can be accepted. If ARR is less than the predetermind rate of return then it will be rejected. However, ranking of mutually exclusive projects depends on the higher ARR.

Merits : ARR has the following advantages :

(*i*) It is simple to calculate and easily understandable.

(*ii*) It is based on readily available accounting information.

(*iii*) It considers total benefits associated with entire life of the project.

Limitations : Following are the main limitations of ARR :

(*i*) It ignores time value of money.

(*ii*) It places more emphasis on profit and not on cash flows which are more relevant for investment proposal.

(*iii*) It does not consider the reinvestment of profits achieved over a period of time.

(*iv*) It is incompatible with the objectives of the firm.

(*v*) It fails to differentiate between the size of the investment required for each project. Competing investment proposals may have the same ARR but may require different average investment.

3. Net Present Value : It is the value obtained by discounting all estimated cash outflows and inflows of an investment proposal by chosen hypothetical target rate or return of cost of capital. Thus, it requires the computation of the present values of all future cash inflow using some predetermined minimum desired rate of return, also called cut-off rate. It is generally based on the cost of capital.

It takes into consideration the time value of money and attempts to calculate the return on investments by introducing the factor of time element. It recognises the fact that a rupee earned today is worth more than the same rupee earned tomorrow. So, it is based on the fact that the cash flow arising at different periods of time differ in value and are not comparable unless their equivalent present values are found. The present value of Re. 1 due in any number of years can be found with the use of the following formula.

$$PV = \frac{1}{(1+r)^n}$$

PV = Present value

r = rate of interest/discount rate

n = number of years

If the NPV is positive or is exactly zero, it means that the investment proposal should be accepted. On the other hand, if the NPV is negative it should be rejected.

Merits : Following are the main advantages of NPV:

(*i*) It introduces the time value of money and is suitable to those situations where uniform cash outflows and uneven cash inflows or cash flows at different periods of time are available.

(*ii*) It indicates all future flows in today's values. Thus, direct comparison between two mutually exclusive projects are possible.

(*iii*) It considers the earnings over the entire life of the project and the true profitability of the investment proposal can be evaluated.

(*iv*) It is relatively simple and reliable method of project appraisal.

(*v*) It takes into account the objective of maximum profitability.

Limitations : Following are the main limitations NPV :

(*i*) It is comparatively more difficult to understand and operate.

(*ii*) It is biased towards short run projects.

(*iii*) Its accuracy is governed by the accuracy of the predicted future cash flows and interest rates.

(*iv*) It does not consider non-financial data like the marketability of the product.

(*v*) It is not easy to determine an appropriate discount rate.

4. Internal Rate of Return : According to this method, all cash flows in respect of the project including the initial investment are discounted to their present value by using the appropriate rate of discount. This method also helps in calculating the exact rate of return or appropriate rate of return which the investment proposal is expected to achieve. When the cost of capital is used by the company as the discounting rate and the net present value is positive the project yields a surplus and therefore it can be taken-up for implementing. In this context, discounting cash flow technique has three steps :

(*i*) Estimating the initial investment and the yearly cash inflows and outflows currently for the entire life of the project.

(*ii*) An appropriate rate of discount is used to discount all cash flows.

(*iii*) Striking the net present value by setting off the present value of inflows against the present value of outflows.

When the rate of discount is changed the net present value of the cash flows will also change and at one stage the net present value will become zero. In other words, at this rate the present value of inflows will be equal to the present value of outflows. The rate of discount at which the net present value is zero is called the Internal Rate of Return (IRR) of the project. It is calculated by finding out the consecutive rates of discount between which the net present value changes sign and using the method of interpolation to find out the exact rate. If the IRR exceeds the enterprise's target DCF return, the project should be accepted. On the contrary, if the target DCF return exceeds IRR the project should be rejected.

Merits : Main merits are of IRR as follows :

(*i*) It makes possible the financial appraisal of the project and gives the exact discounting ratio at which the NPV is zero.

(*ii*) It indicates the symptom—higher the IRR the better is the profitability of the project. The IRR is to be more effective in justifying the financial viability of the project.

(*iii*) It takes into account the time value of money and can be usefully applied in situations with even as well as uneven cash flows at different periods of time.

(*iv*) It considers the profitability of the project for its entire economic life and hence enables evaluation of true profitability.

(*v*) Under this method calculation or assumption of cost of capital is not necessary. IRR suggests maximum rate that a project can earn—whether the firm's cost of capital is given or not.

(*vi*) It provides for uniform ranking of various proposals due to the percentage rate of return.

(*vii*) It is also compatible with the objective of maximum profitability and is considered to be a more reliable technique of capital budgeting.

Limitations : Following are the main limitations of IRR :

(*i*) It is difficult to understand and is the most difficult method of evaluation of investment proposals.

(*ii*) It assumes that the earnings are reinvested at the internal rate of return for the remaining life of the project which is not a justified assumption particularly when the average rate of return earned by the firm is not close to the internal rate of return.

(*iii*) It is not appropriate for mutually exclusive proposals.

(*iv*) Its dependability for decision making depends on the extent of accuracy of future financial projections.

(*v*) The results of NPV method and IRR method may differ when the projects under evaluation differ in their size, life and timings of cash flows.

5. Profitability Index : It is also called Benefit Cost Ratio. It is the ratio of present value of expected future earnings discounted at a required rate of return to an initial cash outflows. It is expressed as profitability index. Thus, it indicates the relationship between present value of cash inflows and the present value of cash outflows. Following formula is used for the calculation of Profitability Index. Present value of cash inflows

$$\text{Profitability Index } \frac{\text{Present value of cash inflows}}{\text{Present value of cash outflows}}$$

If the profitability index is more than one, the project will be accepted. It will be rejected if the index is less than one. Projects are ranked in terms of index and preference is given to projects which have comparatively higher ranks.

Merits : Merits of Profitability Index are as follows :

(*i*) It is conceptually sound.

(*ii*) It takes into account the time value of money.

(*iii*) It provides ranking of projects which helps in selection of projects.

Limitations : Limitations of this method are as follows :

(*i*) It is vulnerable to different interpretations.

(*ii*) Its computation process is complex and tedious.

II. ECONOMIC APPRAISAL

It is used to measure the suitability of the project in terms of economy or society as a whole. Thus, it gives a macro dimension to project appraisal process. Following measures are used to the economic appraisal.

(i) Economic Rate of Return (ERR) : It is the rate of discount which equates the real economic cost of project outlay to its economic benefits during the life of the project. It also measures the rate of return to the economy or society and not the individual entrepreneur. Financial viability considers the current market prices and costs but fails to represent the true value from the national or economic point of view. However, it uses shadow prices which reflect the real cost of inputs to the society and real benefits of the output rather than market prices. Basically, cost of the project, working capital requirements, operating cost and labour components are revalued on the basis of international prices, conversion factors and shadow wage rates etc. On the basis of these revalued costs, a stream of cash outflows, inflows and net flows are calculated and then discounted to achieve an economic internal rate of return.

(ii) Break-Even Analysis : It is used in two terms—narrow sense and broad sense. In broad terms, break-even analysis refers to the study of relationship between costs, volume and profit at different levels of production or sales. But in narrow terms, it refers to a technique of determining that level of operation where total revenues equal total costs i.e. the point of no profit, no loss. The most important aspects of this analysis are, cost must be divided into fixed and variable costs. Fixed capital remains constant over the entire range of output, variable cost varies in a constant ratio with volume; selling price do not change during the period; one product is included in the sales curve or if more than one, the sales mix remains constant throughout the period under consideration; the relationship between fixed and variable costs does not vary during the period; and productivity remains constant. If any of these factors change, the existing relationship between cost and revenue will change, requiring that a new analysis is made. Thus, the minimum level of production and sales at which a unit will continue to run is not 'no profit no loss'. Technically it is called break-even point and it is the first goal of any project to reach at this level. It can be expressed in terms of volume of production or as a percentage of plant capacity utilisation. The formula used in calculation of BEP is as follows :

$$\text{BEP (units)} = \frac{\text{Total fixed cost}}{\text{Contribution per unit}}$$

$$\text{BEP (Rs.)} = \frac{\text{Fixed cost}}{\text{Contribution}} \times \text{Sales}$$

Or

$$\text{BEP} = \frac{\text{Fixed cost}}{\text{P/V ratio}}$$

P/V Ratio = Contribution *over* Sales.

Thus, BEP analysis gives more emphasis on contribution margin. Contribution margin is the difference between the per unit sale price and the variable cost per unit. The contribution is the minimum requirement to cover the total fixed costs.

The BEP analysis is quite helpful in deciding the fate of two mutually exclusive projects having a different cost structure. It also serves as an important tool to indicate which project is the cheapest and cost effective during a particular period.

(iii) Domestic Resource Cost (DRC) : It measures the resource cost of manufacturing a product as against the cost of importing/exporting it. It also shows the long term comparative advantage a country generally enjoys in the production of a particular product. Thus, it indicates a relationship between the total rupees spent in terms of domestic resources for manufacturing a product against the foreign exchange requirement of import etc. Moreover, it is the measure of total Indian currency spent to save a unit of foreign currency by developing import substitutes or earning a unit of foreign currency by exporting a particular product.

In this way, we can say that output from any project adds to domestic availability of the product and side by side reducing the imports to the extent of output of the project or increasing the level of exports if the product is being exported. With the help of this process, we can easily save the foreign exchange to the extent of imports reduced or earn the foreign exchange to the extent of exports already increased. Thus, Domestic Resource Cost (DRC) is therefore calculated as the quantum of domestic resources or costs deployed in production to the net foreign exchange saved or earned.

(iv) Effective Rate of Protection (ERP) : It measures the net protection available to a particular stage of manufacturing. Generally government regulates the level of production of particular product by imposing various tariffs and quantitative controls and extending subsidies to the manufacturers. Domestic costs of material inputs are also affected to this initiative. In the international market, competitive strength of the product is governed by the adjusted costs and prices. Thus, ERP is based on the value addition. Value addition is the difference between selling prices of a product and the cost of the material inputs. ERP is calculated on the basis of the following formula :

ERP = Value added at domestic prices—Value added at international prices.

or

$$\text{ERP} = \frac{\text{Value added at market prices}}{\text{Value added at world prices}} - 1$$

In the above formula, it has been assumed that there should not be difference in value of production computed at domestic prices (DVPI) and value added at international prices fWVA) as there is no role for tariffs, quantitative controls and subsidy etc. But in practice, Governments specially in developing economies impose tariffs or quantitative controls and subsidise the exports as an effective measure of protection for domestic product. That is there is ERP or difference in these factors.

III. SOCIAL COST BENEFIT ANALYSIS

It is an assessment of expected total costs to be incurred and benefits derived out of a project that is under consideration from the society or community point of view. It means a project is considered to be socially viable if the benefits which accrue from the project serve the larger social purpose. The main feature of these benefits is serving the interest of those who have no stake in that project. The benefits resulting from a project enjoyed by some others who do not directly contribute or pay for such benefits. Such benefits are like creation of additional employment opportunities, development of backward areas or districts, growth in village and rural Industries or development of ancillary projects of substantial advantage to rural areas and community in general. Social costs like harmful effects of industrialisation, environmental pollution or scarcity of resources etc. are taken into account under social cost benefit analysis.

Thus, in social cost benefit analysis, all costs and benefits irrespective to whom they accrue and regardless of whether they are paid for or not are relevant. The society's concern for savings and investments is reflected in social costs benefit analysis where savings are valued higher than consumption. So, the acceptance or rejection of project is viewed in term of total social or national impact like its effect on national planning, employment, consumption, savings and foreign exchange flows.

IV. TECHNOLOGICAL APPRAISAL

It is concerned with adequacy and suitability of the plant, plant layout and design; supplies of plant and machinery and reputation of the machinery and equipment suppliers. It also evaluates the technology required, technological alternatives and possibility to select appropriate technology etc.

Objectives : Objectives of technological appraisal are as follows :

(*i*) to examine the rationale of proposed technology and provide an insight into future technological developments.

(*ii*) to assess the possibility of goal achievement with the preferred technology.

(*iii*) to avail better available technology in terms of cost effectiveness and efficiency.

(*iv*) to search a technology which can be adjusted with present level of technical skills by initiating orientation and training programmes.

(*v*) to select a better technology which is environmentally viable.

Components of Technological Appraisal : Following are the important ingredients of technological appraisal[1] :

(*i*) the state of existing and available technology (domestic and foreign);

(*ii*) training needs of personnel for the present technology and for the new technology;

(*iii*) availability of technical knowhow;

(*iv*) input base for the technology or its compatibility with the input substitutes;

(*v*) future progressive integration of the technology for modifications or refinements;

(*vi*) wide product mix and its byproducts;

(*vii*) minimisation of waste loss or scrap in the process or its development;

(*viii*) factor intensity (labour intensive or capital intensive);

(*ix*) stability to changes and its relative obsolescence;

(*x*) other techno-economic considerations (side effects of technology transfer on the labour lay-off etc.).

Factors affecting Technical Appraisal

1. Feasibility of selected technical process : In modern era, technology is affected by frequent changes and also by obsolescence. So, it is important that adopted technology should be assessed in terms of technical information available on its technique, plant and equipment to be used in the production processes.

2. Scale of operations : A minimum scale of operation is required to ensure economic viability of the unit. Productivity can also be ensured by allowing economic operation at minimum scale. For example, in India minimum cane crushing capacity is required for the development of a sugar project.

3. Location : It has an important bearing with regard to the sources of raw materials, availability of power, fuel, transport, skilled and unskilled labour and in relation to the markets to be served by the project.

4. Plant & equipment and layout : Entrepreneur is required to consider the suitability of the plant and machinery, reputation and experience of the suppliers etc. Plant layout at the location site should be assessed in term of the possible need of future expansion. It should also be examined with reference to the site plan.

5. Supply of water, power and fuel etc. : Plant operation needs adequate supply of water, power and fuel etc. Full assurance of these supplies be obtained from different government agencies and other suppliers. Alternative arrangements like diesel generating sets should be examined with reference to availability of finance etc.

6. Waste, effluents and by-products disposal : Certain industries like sugar, chemical etc. are responsible for release of effluents, waste etc. and they are harmful to human and marine life. In such cases effluent may require proper treatment before it can be discharged in a river. So, waste and effluents management is required from the regulatory point of view.

7. Construction schedule : It requires scrutiny of physical elements of the project from the engineering design work to the installation and testing of equipment and commercial production. Estimated project cost is largely affected by the realistic assessment of the construction schedule. Pre-operating expenses as an element, of project cost should be estimated in proper way as it helps in calculation of lotal project cost.

8. Technical know-how : Generally, entrepreneurs lack technical experience. So it may be necessary to arrange facilities for technic know-how. It there is provision lor technical agreements then be necessary to examine the responsibilities and function of technical collaborators.

9. Cost estimates : Cost estimates need careful examination of the assumption on which they have been based. It has to be done with regard to plant and machinery, buildings and other fixed assets. Similarly, provision for escalation in the prices of imported and indigenous machinery made in the project report be examined with regard to current economic situations and the market conditions. Arrangement of equipment and spare parts should also be examined in the context of operational requirements.

If till the appraisal stage the estimates are preliminary or somewhat detailed but containing lots of assumptions and other conditions likely to change, then the immediate task of the entrepreneur is to prepare a definite cost estimates. It also ensures that the project is completed as originally envisaged in financial terms. It is important to note that detailed estimates should be based on prevailing market conditions with adequate safety margins built in. This safety margins are required due to (i) general inflationary trends, (ii) to provide for small and sundry items which might have been overlooked while preparing the estimate and (iii) unforeseen market conditions where due to certain pressures developed, project supplies have to be ensured by offering bonus or incentive to suppliers for maintaining schedules.

V. COMMERCIAL APPRAISAL

It involves investigation of arrangements for buying plant and machinary, arrangement for obtaining raw materials and for marketing of products. The examination would include the progress regarding placement of orders for equipments, procedure for selection and tendering etc. The arrangement for sale of finished goods also to be looked into.

The examination process also involves to evaluate whether the proposed arrangement will ensure the best value for the money spent. Appointment of sole selling agents, regional distributors, dealers and the justifications for their appointment and the terms on which these agents and dealers will be appointed are examined in detail. The entrepreneur's own marketing forecasts are also examined.

Following are some of the factors that may be responsible for wrong results during a market survey conducted with the help of a questionnaire :

- Not using relevant and right questions for the product/service under study;
- Sample of respondents chosen not being representative;
- Investigator not being experienced in such a survey;
- Respondents not being able to understand the questions;
- Respondents deliberately giving wrong answers;
- Investigators filling up the questionnaire with their own answers, without actually conducting the survey, in order to avoid painstaking work;
- Investigators improper handling of the interviews.
- Investigators not taking care to validate the data with a view to checking inconsistencies and avoiding biases;
- Investigators not being competent to apply statistics and correlation methods;
- Investigators making wrong interpretation of answers received;
- Respondent not having faith in this kind of survey and taking it casually.

VI. MANAGERIAL APPRAISAL

It deals with evaluation of competencies, skill and reliability of management. This would also involve review of their past track record and competence. Actually, quality of management affects the success of an industrial project to a large extent. Generally, it is not expected that an entrepreneur should have experience in a particular industry but he is supposed to appoint adequate experienced personnel in the areas of production, finance, personnel and marketing. Professionals should also be drawn from technical, administrative and accounting sides. If entrepreneur is interested to have technical and financial collaboration with a foreign firm of repute, the entire process should be thoroughly examined and necessary remedial measures should be adopted by him.

EXAMINATION QUESTIONS

Long Answer Questions

1. Discuss the methods of project evaluation, specially for project for small business.
2. How do you go ahead with your work of project appraisal ? Explain the different methods employed for this purpose.
3. What do you understand by project appraisal ? Discuss the merits and limitations of average rate of return method or project appraisal.
4. Discuss the process of project appraisal. What are the different aspects of project appraisal ?
5. Discuss the methods of socio-economic evaluation of product.
6. What is project appraisal ? How is it done ?
7. Most of the Projects in India are unable to complete due to cost over-run and time over-run." Discuss with causes and way out.
8. What is Break-Even analysis ? Discuss its role in project appraisal process.
9. What do you mean by technological appraisal ? Discuss the different factors governing project appraisal.
10. Define project appraisal. Also distinguish between project appraisal and project evaluation.
11. Discuss the different tools of project appraisal.
12. What do you mean by evaluation of investment proposals ? Examine various evaluation techniques of investment proposal.
13. What is Social Cost Benefit analysis ? Discuss its importance in project appraisal.

Short Answer Questions

1. What are the major components of project appraisal process ?
2. Explain the objectives of project appraisal.
3. Examine the importance of project appraisal.
4. Distinguish between project appraisal and project evaluation.
5. Examine the main aspects of project appraisal.
6. Discuss the major tools of project appraisal.
7. What is pay back period ?
8. What is economic appraisal ?
9. What is profitability index ?
10. What is break-even analysis ?

Objective Type Questions

1. Project appraisal is an
   (a) Export analysis
   (b) Expert analysis
   (c) Profitability analysis
   (d) None of the above
2. Gestation period is concerned with
   (a) Idea creation period
   (b) Incubation period
   (c) Implementation period
   (d) Commercialisation period
3. Pay back period deals with
   (a) Period required for profit earning process
   (b) Period required for cost of investment recovery
   (c) Period required for fixed cost recovery
   (d) None of the above
4. NPV method relates to
   (a) Time value of money
   (b) Inflated value of money
   (c) Present values of all future earnings
   (d) None of the above
5. NPV formula is
   (a) $\frac{1+P}{n^2}$
   (b) $\frac{1+P}{n^2}$
   (c) $\frac{1}{(1+r)^n}$
   (d) $\frac{1}{(1+r)^n}$
6. Internal rate of return ensures
   (a) NPV is positive
   (b) NPV is zero
   (c) NPV is negative
   (d) None of the above
7. Profitability index enables the project to be accepted if it is
   (a) Positive
   (b) Negative
   (c) Zero
   (d) None of the above
8. Economic rate of return considers
   (a) Economy as a whole
   (b) Society as a whole
   (c) Both of the above
   (d) Individual entrepreneur
9. Formula for DEP is Fixed cost
   (a) $\frac{\text{Fixed cost}}{\text{PV Ratio}}$
   (b) $\frac{\text{Fixed cost}}{\text{Contribution}} \times \text{Sales}$
   (c) A + B are the same
   (d) $\frac{\text{Contribution}}{\text{Sales}}$

10. ERP is governed by
    (a) Value creation (b) Value addition
    (c) All of the above (d) None of the above

Answers

1-(c) 2-(c) 3-(b) 4-(c) 5-(c) 6-(b) 7-(a) 8-(c) 9-(c) 10-(b)

Reason Based Questions

State with reasons whether the following statements are true or false :

1. Neither pay back period nor modified pay back period takes into consideration time value of money for appraising a project.
2. NPV, IRR are project appraisal techniques.
3. If the IRR exceeds the enterprise's target DCF return, the project should be accepted.
4. RR method is not appropriate for mutually exclusive projects.
5. Profitability Index and benefit cost ratio are the same.

REFERENCE

1. Rao, P.C., *Project Management and Control,* Sultan Chand and Sons. New Delhi, 1998, p. 84.

22

Project Report

Generally, an entrepreneur is required to prepare a project report before a project is undertaken. It assesses the demand potential of the proposed product, works out the cost of capital invested and operational costs and side by side expected profitability of the proposed project. Practically, it is a pre-investment study of investment proposal but encompasses a thorough investigating process covering economic, technical, social, managerial and commercial aspects. It is important to note that after finalising the feasibility studies a detailed project report (DRP) is required to be drawn up based on the data and results obtained from the studies. The preparation of the DPR is the final and most important stage of pre-investment phase of the project.

The formulation of DPR is undertaken only after the investment decision is taken on the basis of the technical, economic and financial feasibility studies so that the expensive efforts involved in the preparation of DPR are not wasted. At the time of formulation of DPR there are certain designs and data are necessary. These include process designs, layout drawings, construction data etc.

Nature of Project Report

DPR is a working plan for implementation of project proposal after investment decision has been taken by the entrepreneur. Thus, feasibility studies provide ground for taking a particular investment decision but DPR is prepared only when a particular investment decision has been taken by the entrepreneur and it provides ground for project implementation. In this way, a project report may be defined as a report which provides all necessary information of the unit proposed to be set up for the manufacture of a product or rendering a service. A project report enables the entrepreneur to know how much money, manpower and material would be required to set up the project, type of machine and technology required and the economic gains from the project. Information regarding economic, technical, financial, managerial and production aspects of the project/service are covered by the project report.'

Now projects require sophisticated technology and in turn huge funds are required through financial institutions and banks. Thus, high technology involve higher cost in the project implementation and as such entrepreneur cannot afford to tolerate the failure of the project. So, it would be better to have a project report formulated by the experts in the field.

Objectives of Project Report

(*i*) To plan in advance about the fulfilment of expected performance in the area of marketing, technology, finance, personnel, production, customer satisfaction and social endowments.

(*ii*) To evaluate the organisational objectives to what extent they are achievable. For this purpose entrepreneur is expected to consider the input data, analyse the data, predict outcome, choose best alternatives, take action, measure results with predictions.

(*iii*) To make efforts to quantify the objectives as well as enabling them to be measurable, tangible, verifiable and attainable.

(*iv*) To assess the implications of constraints on resources. These resources include manpower, equipment, financial and technological.

(*v*) To avail financial support from the financial institutions as they require a systematic project report to evaluate the desirability of financing the project.

(*vi*) To examine the course of action as suggested in the project report. Generally, successful implementation of a project is governed by the course of action as given in project report.

On the basis of the above objectives, we can say that it is possible for the entrepreneur to formulate the project idea but formulation of a project report is to be done by a team of professionals as it requires a multidisciplinary approach. Thus, project report is basically a guide which outlines the course an entrepreneur proposes to embark upon. But before the report is presented, the entrepreneur must be made to understand that the report is for him and not for the financial institutions from which funds are likely to be sought. If it is conceived as a document only for financial institutions, its objectivity is lost. When an entrepreneur approaches a professional for preparing a project report he normally does have a nebulous/preliminary idea of what he proposes to pursue. A lot of discussions need to be held with the entrepreneur to find out whether he is merely acting on various suggestions. The entrepreneur's interest in the project is vital for making the task of report preparation easy; the consultant would then only have to organise the ideas in a report format, working out the financial implications of each action or event in the proposed project. Depending on the nature of the business proposed, an organisational set up needs to be formed. After this, advice from the professional is needed.

Process Involved in Preparation of DPR

Techno-economic feasibility study provides inputs for the preparation of DPR. In this context, following processes are involved.

(*i*) Break down all project components, time phase and schedule them minutely and prepare accurate cost estimates, furnishing with necessary and relevant assumptions and calculations;

(*ii*) Develop baselines for controlling time and costs that help in implementation of the project;

(*iii*) resources to implement the project.

Issues Involved in DPR : It includes the following issues :[2]

1. Critical and Routine Issues : Depending on its nature, every project has a critical issue—it may be, among other things, technology, trained manpower, raw materials and management. A project consultant must be able to identify the critical issue, and convince the entrepreneur that it has been duly taken care of in the report. More than this, there are routine issues. These need to be effectively monitored and taken the appropriate provision for alternative sources. Therefore, in preparation of the project, the critical factors should be outlined so that the entrepreneur can pay attention to effective implementation of the project.

2. Infrastructural Aspects : After ensuring that the critical issues are taken care of, aspects like technical feasibility and various production processes, pricing and so on, need to be looked into and the consequent financial implications are thoroughly examined to arrive at the proposal. Technical analysis also include, discussions on the nature and size of the land identified, fencing, infrastructure, power, communication facilities, machinery, the technology (whether indigenous or foreign) and the other facilities required for the production of goods/services of the desired quality. While planning for the basic infrastructure, the overall cost of the equipment and other facilities must be evaluated. When this is done, a clear picture of the project cost emerges.

3. Market Potential and Feasibility : Generally, the market rather than technology is the major cause for the failure of the project. In most of the cases, all project reports vouch for the market potential of the product under consideration, which is assessed through macro surveys. However, efforts should be made to get an idea of the marketing cost incurred in assessing the market potential. Moreover, financial institutions do place must trust on demand projections based on population studies and analysis. Invariably, a detailed market survey by a professional institution is required to identify the market potential, the methodology of selling and the marketing feasibility. Therefore, even if the entrepreneur wants to rush through the whole exercise, the consultant must convince him that a little more time spent on gauging the marketing feasibility is beneficial as any wrong decision on this front would jeopardise the project in the long run.

4. Capacity to Fall Back : While preparing a project report, the capacity to fall back must be deliberated at least from the following three angles :

(*i*) ***Entrepreneurs:*** In the event of the entrepreneurs failing to deliver, whether there is an in-built mechanism by which any of the others in the organisation or any group to which they belong, can take care of the project must be looked into. The financial soundness of the entrepreneurs must therefore be carefully examined (*ii*) ***Raw Materials :*** Continuous dependence on one raw material supplier is risky. Therefore, alternative sources of raw materials need to be identified and incorporated in the project report and

(*iii*) ***Market :*** There is a tendency to totally bank on buy-back agreements. Some project reports glorify these points. Relying on just one buyer is again risky. Even if their terms may not be as attractive as the original buy-back arrangement the project should include alternative buyers. These are applicable especially in the case of foreign technical collaborators.

5. Core Competencies and Competitive Edge : In a competitive world, no project, however exclusive it may be, can be free from competition. In this regard, core competency would definitely help. And if the project has the same competency it must be highlighted. Core competence is an intrinsic value addition obtaining in a project and which cannot be easily replicated by the deployment of other resources such as time, money, training, human resources and other inputs.

Analysis Generally Covered in Project Report

A project report generally requires a multi-disciplinary approach and following set of analysis is incorporated in it :

(*i*) Technical analysis comprising system analysis using technique of operation research to sort out complex problems like allocation problems, replacement problems, inventory problems, scheduling and queuing of operations with use of PERT/CPM, linear programming, integral programming, goal programmings and simulation etc.

(*ii*) Marketing research to forecast demand for goods/services which may be produced on implementation of the project, capture market and elicit cooperation of the consumers etc.

(*iii*) Financial analysis to project future cash flows, profitability, evaluate not to do cost benefit analysis, profit planning, budgeting and resource allocation etc.

(*iv*) Techno-economic analysis suggesting to adopt optimal technology for project size/objectives, to explore economic conditions to absorb project's products etc.

(*v*) Project Design and network analysis i.e. detailed work plan to the project and its time profile.

(*vi*) Input output analysis etc.

Contents of Detailed Project Report : Contents of the DPR are as follows :

(i) Deviations from the feasibility study.

(*ii*) Drawings.

(*iii*) Physical topographical information.

(*iv*) Rates and basis for various cost estimates.

(*v*) Water and power supply guarantee from Power Boards/Local authority.

(*vi*) Estimates relating to land, site development, mainpart structures, auxiliary plant structures, administrative and other buildings, roads and saved areas, railway sidings, water supply, effluent disposal, storm water drainage, power supply, construction, plant and equipment, compound wall/fencing, plant layout and equipment, machinery, spares, foundation, erection, electrification, material handling equipments.etc.

(*vii*) General import duty rates, freight and handling, insurance and contingencies.

(*viii*) Assessment of working capital requirements with due consideration of inventory and credit policies consistent with marketing network proposed.

Development of ancillary industries is an additional criterian meriting the clearance of DPR for new projects and expansion of existing facilities. The requirements in this regard are :

(*i*) All DPRs must indicate the parts, components etc. with approximate annual quantities proposed to be procured from ancillary industries around the project, for use in construction, operation and maintenance.

(*ii*) When applying for industrial licence or letter of intent, where applicable, the items proposed to be procured from ancillary industries around the project must be stated.

(iii) Before finalising foreign collaboration agreements, consideration should be given to items obtainable from ancillary industries.

Format of Project Report

There is no prescribed format for the preparation of a project report but a project report should contain mainly the following set of information in general.

1. General Information : It may include information about industry and its status in the economy, present production and demand, indicating licensed, installed capacity, Government policies and export potential. Thus, bio-data of entrepreneurs, industry profile, constitution and organisation and product details etc, should be included as general information.

2. Project Description : It analyses the different aspects of physical infrastructure and other facilities, location of plant and its advantages, raw materials survey giving specifications and quality of raw materials required and their availability, availability of technical know-how, water, power and fuel supply and arrangement for effluents treatment, environmental clearances, list of plant, machinery and equipment, capacity of the plant, research and development facility. Communication system and transport facilities are the other important aspects generally discussed in project description. Besides, implementation and construction programme in the form of CPM/PERT are also included in it.

3. **Market Potential** : Demand and supply position of the product proposed, broad market trend of the product within and outside the states for 5 years, price expected to be realised from the proposed product, marketing strategy, after-sales service, impact of seasonality factor, provision of transport facility are the important points generally considered to get an idea about market potential of the proposed product.

4. **Capital, Cost and Sources of Finance** : An estimate of the various components of capital items required by the unit should be given in the report. Costs of the project that have to be incurred on fixed items are to be analysed in proper perspective. Land cost inclusive of development expenditue incurred on the land, buildings to be erected for housing the plant and machinery, the administrative office, stores, services etc. requirements, estimates to be included in the project cost. Plant and machinery including other equipments and their estimated cost, off-site facilities, utilities and auxiliary facilities, preliminary expenses, contingencies, cost of spares, repairs and maintenance during trial run and commissioning period, pre-commissioning and commissioning expenses are also included in project report. Project report should also incorporate present and probable sources of finance. The sources of funds should equal the cost of the project as otherwise the project cannot be set up in full. The resources to be generated in term of owner's equity, long term loans and deposits and funds from financial institutions should be given separately. Margin of financing—broad pattern to be indicated in detail.

5. **Assessment of Working Capital**: Working capital margin details of estimation be given in the project report. At the initial stage of the project, the estimate of working capital requirements should be made and shown along with the total cost of the project. Different components of working capital requirement should be analysed keeping in mind the production cycle and expected cash flows from the product.

6. **Other Financial Aspects** : These aspects include cost of production, profitability and cash flow statement. Cost of production should show the project broad pattern at least for five years—design capacity, break-even point of production cost, effect of variation of cost of raw materials, utilities, selling price etc. be indicated and elaborated. Price trend of raw materials and finished goods be discussed. Profitability for five years after commissioning the project should be worked out in the prescribed format. Cash flow statement and pay back period should be worked out for the project. Decision-making analysis like IRR, DSCR, BEP, Pay-Back Period, Debt-Equity Ratio, Sensitivity analysis and Economic cost benefit analysis are also given in the report.

Thus, project report is most important document which outlines the course an entrepreneur proposes to execute in near future.

EXAMINATION QUESTIONS

Long Answer Questions

1. What is meant by project report ? What are its salient contents ?
2. Describe the need and significance of preparing a project report.
3. You are required to set up a small business enterprise and in this connection, prepare a project report.
4. What is project report ? How is it formulated ? Explain.
5. Discuss the contents of a project report.
6. What is project report ? Explain its significance.
7. Discuss the nature and objectives of a project report.
8. Examine the different steps involved is preparation of a detailed project report.
9. What is project report ? Explain its scope.
10. Discuss the nature and format of a project report.
11. Define project report. Also explain its scope and objectives.

Short Answer Questions

1. What is detailed project report ?
2. Explain the objective of project report ?
3. Discuss the contents of detailed project report.
4. Explain the components of a project report.

Objective Type Questions

1. DPR is a :
   (a) Working plan (b) Action plan
   (c) Implementation plan (d) None of the above
2. Following is not a critical issue :
   (a) Technology (b) Workers
   (c) Product (d) None of the above.
3. Capacity to fall back :
   (a) Capacity to have main strategy
   (b) Capacity to have alternative strategy
   (c) Capacity to have subsidiary strategy
   (d) None of the above.
4. Core competency is related with :
   (a) External value addition (b) Intrinsic value addition
   (c) Internal value addition (d) None of the above.

Answers

1.(b) 2.(a)3.(b) 4.(b)

Reason Based Questions

State with reasons whether the following statements are true or false:

1. Feasibility Report is same as Appraisal Report.
2. Project report deals with all aspects of proposals.
3. Project report is formulated by entrepreneurs.
4. Entrepreneur is guided by project reports.
5. Project description is a part of detailed project reports.

REFERENCES

1. Paul Jose, Ajith Kumar N. and Mampfilly Paul. T., *Bntrepreneurship Development* Himalaya Publishing House, Mumbai 1996, p. 90
2. Bhat V. Prasanna, Preparing a Project Report, *The Business line,* Nov. 29, 1999.

23

PROJECT DESIGN AND NETWORK ANALYSIS

An entrepreneur is required to develop a product idea and that idea is to be converted into project—a shape to the product idea. But architects and engineers get that project idea through designing process. Designing process is necessary as designs represent the entrepreneurial dream. So, designs through models and prototypes are necessarily to be accurate to match the entrepreneurial objectives otherwise the entire efforts in designing may prove to be a futile exercise. Designing is always aimed at optimising the resources in accordance with the entrepreneurial interest and priorities, the layouts and dimensions may then be established which define the performance standards. Project design may be defined as the individual activities which go into the corpus of the project and their interrelationship with each other. It enables the entrepreneur to identify the streams of events which must take place for the successful execution of the project.

Project management deals with project formulation and its implementation. Project formulation basically concerned with scientific selection of a project. But effective implementation of project ensures an optimum allocation and utilisation of time and resources meant for various components of the project. In this context project design and network analysis are the important tools and have their own role in project management specially at implementation stage.

Need of Project Design

For the successful implementation of aproject, a dynamic and realistic project design is necessary so as to monitor the progress of the project and highlight the variations if any in time for corrective action. Work design is necessary due to the following :

(*i*) Formulation of realistic drawings and other designs as per the requirement of the project.

(*ii*) Scrutiny and approval of construction drawings.

(*iii*) Scrutiny and approval of work estimated.

(*iv*) Scrutiny and approval of specifications and other conditions of work tenders,

(*v*) Tackle and give solution pertaining to process scheme/design which may crop up during the construction stage.

Techniques of Project Design

***(i)* Data Management Techniques** : An efficient data collection, storage and retrieval system is the key to proper planning, quick and judicious decision making. To obtain optimum benefits, the system must have the necessary capability to reflect data in a manner that it matches fully with the requirements and satisfies the different levels of need on a complex user environment. In project work, the data relating to previous projects, similar project handled by other entrepreneurs and the latest development in the field of procurement, construction and erection is essential for effective designing system. Therefore, a scientific design data storage and retrieval system is an important requirement for the work design.

***(ii)* Planning and Scheduling Techniques** : Modern scientific project management techniques for planning, scheduling and monitoring are essential for successful project completion. The physical verification of progress, forecasting of bottlenecks, resource planning, annual budgeting and cost control form an integral part of the composite system. Master networks for the top management are prepared to coordinate the various functional plans, to identify the interface events and to provide the top management with a means to authorise and control work and expenditure. The two schedule approach of keeping cushion time for having the internal execution and control network on optimistic time estimates is adopted. All the schedules and milestones are drawn on the optimistic network. Area-wise networks are prepared to coordinate the various functional plans. Detailed schedules and charts are prepared to depict phasing of time *vis-a-vis* resource utilisation and also to provide a basis for visually tracking the performance.

***(iii)* Contract Management Techniques** : A time schedule for inviting various tenders and bids is made in advance so as to fit in the master network and is advertised in the initial stages of project planning. This builds up pressure on various agencies responsible for preparation of tender documents, specifications, layout etc. to work those specific programmes. Tenders are invited in two parts, the first part covers only technical specifications and experience of the firm on the basis of which shortlisting is done. The competitive prices of only shordisted tenderers are considered.

***(iv)* Equipment Categorisation Techniques** : A continuous process project involves a large number of equipments and components. Non-availability of even a small item can hold up erection and commissioning of the project. Unless a detailed and properly codified equipment list is prepared well in advance the last minute delays due to missing/short supply items are inevitable. This detailed equipment list further classifies each equipment as vital/essential/desirable. The VED analysis is useful for cost control. The list also identifies scarce/difficult/easily available items along with manufacturing cycle. SDE analysis is used for phasing and sequencing of order placement.

***(v)* Project Engineering Techniques** : A detailed list of drawings specifying the scope covered and its supply schedule must be prepared In advance and distributed to the engineering wing and project site. The phased issue of drawings is interlocked with the construction schedule. This induces a strong supplier and consumer interaction for maintaining the supply line. Efficient project engineering techniques call for integration of the basic load data received from the main machinery supplier with available information on auxiliary equipment and past data for items yet to be ordered to enable early preparation of design drawings. Construction drawings could however incorporate the actual data relating to auxiliaries.

(*vi*) Construction Management Techniques : It would be for the entrepreneurs to engage more than one construction contractors to avoid monopolistic pressures, greater deployment of resources, decrease in the probability of total work freeze due to labour trouble and to increase competition and flexibility. In order to save time and cost of the construction, optimum level of mechanisation needs to be determined. This would include development of cranes, material handling equipment, hoist, concrete batching plant, earth moving equipment etc. The entrepreneur must keep his eyes and ears open to developments in construction techniques. These may not only reduce the time and cost of construction but may also improve the quality. Examples are manufacture of controlled concrete and use of slip form shuttering for silos, overhead tanks etc.

Factors Affecting Project Design

(*i*) Design Specification : It lays down the basic parameters of performance and cost. It deals with two processes. (a) an entrepreneur identifies a need for project that he wishes to promote and requests an engineer/architect to design and make a platform for its construction ; (b) through R&D activities the entrepreneur identifies a market opportunity and set about designing a product that fulfils the objective. There are two ways to complete this process: First step assumes that potential customers/existing customers provide design specification and in that case market is assured. However, in the second case entrepreneur or consultant/ expert is required to create a product that will meet the requirement.

(*ii*) Availability of Technology : Generally, there are two options before the firm : either it has to develop technology internally by incurring huge funds for the purpose or there may be pressure to design for an in-house manufacture by using existing facilities. There may be another option to avail the chance of using foreign product design. Whatever may be the case, product specification and detailed design should be tested against the best practice of existing projects. Research and design consultancy firms also provide help and advice to the entrepreneurs.

(*iii*) Experience of Project Design Team : Firm can also ensure the use of skills and experience of the project design team. But in most of cases design team is concerned with existing designed items. Design team may find it difficult to consider designing a new range of products as per the expectations of the potential consumers as it does not have the detailed designed expertise or factory facilities.

(*iv*) Prevailing Designs Culture : A design specification may have customer orientation and acceptance but there is need to have an effective control on the design process. Customers are not ready to accept a quick change in product design etc., but they can be motivated or persuaded to accept a particular design in the long term by adopting a slow change process. Entrepreneurial culture is governed by this fact to a large extent. Designers are different, their culture stresses innovation, so creativity and problem-solving ability etc. can be initiated with the help of R&D activities. Cultural variations can be tackled or promoted by arranging professional training to project design team.

Need of Network Analysis

Network analysis is concerned with evaluation of time and resources profile of project activities. It also deals with identification process of optimising the particular course of action in terms of available time and resource constraints. It develops a clear picture of the work elements of the project and also their sequential relationship.

Thus, network analysis is a system which develops for projects by analysing different project activities. Projects are broken down into different components and activities and then they are arranged in a logical sequence. It also decides the priority of different activities as to which activity will be completed simultaneously and which others sequentially.

Nowadays projects are characterised by high level technology. Several specialised disciplines' are involved in them which call for participation of multiple agencies at various points of time. Their functions are interdependent. For new and complex projects, the simple technique of barchart for planning, scheduling and monitoring does not suffice. It falls short of the requirements. The technique of network analysis such as PERT/CPM provides a new system approach to the management of such project. The techniques have proved to be extremely beneficial and effective in closing the gap between promise and performance. It is increasingly being realised that the answer to the problem of slippages in projects does not lie merely in providing extra resources but lies more in their effective scheduling and monitoring by PERT/CPM.

In this way, Network Analysis is useful in the process of planning, scheduling and monitoring in the context of time management of a project.

"Planning refers to what is to be done, how it is to be done and who is to do it. Scheduling refers to when it is to be done and how much is to be done. Monitoring refers to checking how much has been done and what needs to be done. However, effective project management calls for management of all the sub-systems in an integrated way. Planning, scheduling and monitoring therefore must involve all the sub-systems simultaneously." A Network actually constitutes the heart of such a planning, scheduling and monitoring system.

Types of Network

1. CPM Network : It is a deterministic network. It has two time-cost estimates for each individual activity. One time-cost estimate is concerned with normal situation and the other estimate is meant for the crash situation. However in practice, it does not incorporate any statistical analysis in determining such time estimates. The activities to be taken up and the time each may consume are not likely to vary from what was reckoned at the time of development of the network.

2. PERT Network : The Programme Evaluation and Review Technique (PERT) deals with the liklihood that the single value given as the estimated time for completion of activities is going to have a degree of error associated with it. Instead of taking a single time, three time estimates for each activity is required.[2]

(*i*) optimistic time—how long the activity would take if the conditions were ideal;

(*ii*) most probable time—time if conditions were normal;

(*iii*) pessimistic time—how long the activity would take if a significant proportion of the things that could go wrong, did go wrong.

3. Decision Network : It assumes that the activity may vary and thus some degree of probability is associated with each possible alternative activity. However, the total of all these probabilities for the various alternatives is 1. But the time duration required for each alternative is deterministic.

4. GERT Network : The Graphical Evaluation and Review Technique is the most complex network, treats both activity and time as probabilistic factors. It presents a project as a set of processes of operations called activities which are generally available in certain sequencial order. All activities are necessarily to be completed to make the project accomplished.

Thus, for progressing the project in a coordinated manner the entrepreneur or his project team must work out the list of tasks against detailed time scales and decide upon which tasks are to be taken up parallelly and which ones sequentially. The tasks so determined can then be expressed in terms of critical path network. Often enough, activities come to light at this stage itself which might otherwise have been overlooked. This alone repays the effort in drawing up of the network, even without regard to the degree of control which the network will afford later on in the execution of the project.

This critical path network provides an opportunity, for time analysis—slippages had advance fulfilment of the different activities against planned time schedules. But this by itself is not enough. For one has to be content with the fact that the resources available will always be rather limited in the context of an overall plan. Activities therefore must be re-arranged wherever feasible, for a more practical and effective utilisation of the available resources. To do this it is necessary to keep in focus on the following alternatives :

(a) Plan for fixed resources and accept the fact that this will extend the time schedule or

(b) plan for a fixed schedule and resort to crash programmes without regard to the costs involved, or

(c) plan for a judicious mixture of the two above.

However, in making the choice overenthusiasm should be avoided. Entrepreneur or project team should avoid in placing more emphasis on drawing up impressive looking networks covering forecasts of many months ahead without the slightest justification for what they have planned. If basic estimates and concepts are unrealistic no prediction in regard to resource schedules set down in smallest details, can serve any useful purpose. Realities and practicabilities are many times more important than the preparation for minute details.

EXAMINATION QUESTIONS

Long Answer Questions

1. What is project design ? Discuss its rationale.
2. Discuss the different techniques of project design.
3. What do you know by project design ? Explain the factors affecting a project design.
4. What do you mean by network analysis ? Discuss the various types of network analysis.
5. Critically examine the importance of project design and network analysis in project management.
6. What is network analysis ? Explain the nature of network techniques and network planning.
7. Examine the need of project design. Also discuss the various techniques of project design.
8. What do you mean by project design ? Discuss the factors affecting project design.
9. Examine the rationale of network analysis. Explain its different types.
10. What do you understand by project design and network analysis ? Prepare a project design.

Short Answer Questions

1. Examine the rationale of project design.
2. Discuss the main techniques of project design
3. Explain the factors generally affect the project design.
4. Why do you need network analysis ?
5. Explain the various types of networks.
6. What is CPM ?
7. What is PERT ?
8. What is decision net work ?
9. What is GERT?
10. What is VED analysis ?

Objective Type Questions

1. Designing process deals with
   (a) Entrepreneurial behaviour
   (b) Entrepreneurial training
   (c) Entrepreneurial compensation
   (d) Optimising the resources

2. Work design helps in
   (a) Formulating project reports
   (b) Developing DPR
   (c) Giving solution regarding process scheme
   (d) Creating construction drawings
3. Planning and scheduling techniques are necessary for
   (a) Project Identification (b) Project Selection
   (c) Project Completion (d) Project Appraisal
4. Project design is affected by
   (a) Project Engineering (b) Design Specifications
   (c) Technology Transfers (d) Constructions Techniques
5. CPM Network indicates the following
   (a) Financial estimates (b) Time cost estimates
   (c) Cost estimates (d) Production estimates

Answers

l-(d) 2-(c) 3-(c) 4-(b) 5-(b)

Mark as True/False Answer

1. Project management deals with project formulation and its implementation.
2. Project designs represent the entrepreneurial dream.
3. VED analysis is meant for project maximisation.
4. Network analysis is independent of planning process.
5. Network analysis is governed by sequential relationship.

Answers

1 (T) 2 (T) 3 (F) 4 (F) 5 (T)

REFERENCES

1. Choudhary, S., *Project Management.* Tata McGraw Hill Publishing Company Ltd. New Delhi, 1995, p. 144.
2. Maylor Harvey. *Project Management,* Mac Millan India Ltd. Delhi, 1996, p. 66.

24

LOCATION OF AN ENTERPRISE

Location of an enterprise is an important entrepreneurial decision as it affects the operational as well as financial performance. So, entrepreneur is required to identify that location at which the enterprise will have easy access to physical, economic and social endowments. The general objective in selecting a location is to minimise total cost of production and distribution. The selected location should be in a position to help in generating maximum revenue and provide an opportunity for further growth and expansion. An entrepreneur is expected to evaluate his targets in terms of time and cost variable and try to select a proper location and seek possession of the site before the zero date. Generally, financial institutions are also interested to inspect the location or site of the plant before sanctioning any loan to the enterprise concerned. Efforts should also be made by the entrepreneur to remove all uncertainties associated with the site before the zero date. Entrepreneur should also know that any change in location or site at a later date not only targets will be missed but even the viability of the project may also be lost. Thus, ideal location site helps in smooth and efficient functioning of an enterprise. It ensures a reduction in costs as well as improves productivity and financial viability of the enterprise.

Need for Enterprise Location

(*i*) To promote the establishment of a new enterprise.

(*ii*) To undertake expansion, decentralisation and diversification necessary for meeting increasing demand of products.

(*iii*) To manage the situations arising due to non-renewal of existing lease of an established enterprise.

(*iv*) To develop new location if existing location has been declared as undesirable or unsuitable.

(*v*) To arrange a new location by shifting from existing location due to change in market pattern, depletion of raw materials, change in production processes and transport facilities, etc.

(*vi*) To open new branch or production facility at new places for increasing the volume of production and distribution activities.

Importance of Enterprise Location

Selection of plant location or site is quite important due to the following reasons :

(i) It enables the enterprise to operate smoothly, efficiently and with the minimum cost.

(ii) It controls wastages in efforts and talents of the entrepreneurs.

(iii) It reduces uncertainty in results.

(iv) It encourages effective mobilisation of raw materials, labour and potential customers.

(v) It develops the area by attracting other potential entrepreneurs and endowments like physical, economic and social variables.

Steps in Enterprise Location

Following steps are important in selecting a particular location or site for the plant :

(i) Selection of the region.

(ii) Selection of the locality or community.

(iii) Selection of the exact site and

(iv) Selection of an optimum site.

Generally, entrepreneur is free to select any location or site for his plant development. However, regulatory provisions of the government also affect the choice of plant location or site.

Location, Localisation and Planned Location of Industries : Location is concerned with a particular site where entrepreneur is interested to establish his enterprise or plant having lowest cost objective. If a particular industry is concentrated mainly in one area is called as localisation of industries. For example, Kolkata and Mumbai are known for jute and textiles industry respectively. Planned location of industries is a systematic approach by which location of industries is planned to give each region or area or place a variety of industries to promote dispersal of industries. For example, in Ludhiana, different types of industries have been developed and no particular industry is concentrated in that particular area.

Factors Influencing the Selection of Location of an Enterprise or a Plant or a Project

1. Availability of Land : Land should be large enough to meet out present requirement with provision for further expansion. Land should be for industrial use (land usage pattern to be adhered to) and proper layout of plant and equipment must be possible as per the technical feasibility study. Drainage level of land, soil testing report (should be suitable for the construction of the factory) should be favourable to the project requirements.

2. Availability of Raw Materials : Availability of required quantity and quality of raw materials at a reasonable cost is an important factor for determining the location of an enterprise. Cost of materials generally constitutes a major chunk of total cost of production and thus, the impact of raw materials on location depends upon their nature and the source of their deposits.

3. Supply of Manpower : Every enterprise requires an adequate supply of manpower with appropriate skills. Availability of skilled manpower, cost of labour, labour expectations, local culture affect the supply of manpower to the enterprise. Sometimes, it becomes difficult to obtain high skilled people to work at very remote places with big town facilities. Alfred Weber rightly remarked that "an industrial site will deviate from the point of minimum transportation cost to the cheaper labour centre if the additional cost of transportation at the new centre is more than compensated by the savings in labour cost." However, this situation has been changed. Labour is mobile and there is a level of minimum wages fixed by the Government from time to time. Moreover, certain industries are capital intensive and they require less labour.

4. Transport and Communication Facilities : Transport services are required for assembling of materials and distribution of products. At the time of selection of a particular location efforts should be made to ensure that transportation facilities are easily available at reasonable rates. Site should be well connected by road and rail or nearer to national highways, major railway yard etc. Transportation of equipment, material, product and personnel is an important requirement and it should be ensured in time and in efficient manner.

5. Proximity to the Market : Availability of consumer market also affects the viability of the enterprise. An entrepreneur tan improve his customer relations if they are available in nearby areas and easily render rapid services to them. Enterprises engaged in the production of perishable commodities and those producing for a local market are also interested to develop their plants in potential consumer's area as it would ensure a reduction in transportation cost involved in distributing the finished products. Actually, an enterprise tends to disperse only if they find a new consumer market.

6. Water, Power and Fuel : Uninterrupted operations of an enterprise is the result of sufficient supply of water, power and fuel etc. In this context, efforts are required to assess local sources of water. Besides, required water supply to be assessed in terms of water conditions or sub-soil water etc. Availability of power in the region is to be evaluated in terms of actual requirements. Some industries consume lot of power (Aluminium) or water (Paper industry) and these variables are a very important factor for them. Nowadays, industries are facing the problem of power shortages" and they are shifting to the fuel option—coal. For example, coal is the major source of fuel for the iron and steel industry and these industries are located near the coal mines.

7. Regional Development : In our country, government is pursuing the policy of balanced regional development to solve the problems like slum, disparity of income and wealth and optimum use of resources. In order to ensure balanced regional development, government has declared certain areas as backward areas and zero industry areas. Government gives certain benefits like tax benefits but it is necessary to evaluate the process to what extent they would outweigh the disadvantages.

8. External Economies : In some cases, an enterprise prefers to be located in those centres where other industrial units are already located. There are certain facilities like transportation, warehousing, banking, insurance, communication and factoring services etc. which are easily available and industrial units tend to be concentrated in these areas. Besides, raw materials are also available at cheaper prices and in large quantity. For example, by-products of one enterprise may be used as raw material by another enterprise. Enterprises working as distilleries are generally located in nearby areas of Sugar mills because they supply molasses as raw materials to distilleries.

9. Personal Factors: Personal preferences and prejudices of an entrepreneur also affect the selection of location. Entrepreneurial preferences are also affected by law and order, political stability and safety etc. Thus, entrepreneurs prefer to locate their enterprises in those areas which are safe and free from law and order problems.

10. Local Laws and Regulations : In certain cases local laws and regulations impose restrictions on the development of industrial units in special areas. For example, consent of various agencies like local Panchayat, municipality, government, state planning bodies is mandatory for the entrepreneurs otherwise they cannot run their enterprises in municipal or local areas. Similarly, high rate of income-tax, sale-tax, octroi, etc. discourage entrepreneur to develop their plant in a particular area or state. But facility of tax holidays encourages them otherwise to develop their units in a particular area or state.

11. Ecological and Environmental Factors : Certain industrial units are required to be governed by the ecological and environmental provisions of Pollution Control Act. Industrial units are required to follow the norms of Pollution Control Board. They have to make efforts for the disposal of effluents as directed by the pollution control authorities. They have to arrange the nearest source where effluent (after treatment) could be discharged.

Government Locational Policy

Industrial location has received closer attention of the government and policy planners in recent times. Actually, location policy is an extension of the policy of development of backward areas and industrial disposal. It deals with negative aspect and positive thrust. The negative aspect is concerned with preventive measures for developing new units in the already advanced areas and urban, metropolitan centres with the dictates of the government from time to time. But positive thrust deals with instruments like concessional finance, investment tax incentives subsidies etc. which are being used by the government to develop new units in backward and zero industries districts of different states. With the help of positive strategy, government is trying to ensure effective dispersal of industrial units to backward areas. The government has already formulated a policy that "The new unit should not be located within the standard urban area limit of a large metropolitan city having a population of more than ten lakhs and in the urban area of a city with a population of more than 5 lakhs.

Industrial undertakings are free to select the location of a project. In the case of cities with population of more than a million (as per the 1991 census) however, the proposed location should be at least 25 km. away from the standard urban area limits of that city unless it is to be located in an area disignated as an "industrial area" before the 25th July 1991.

Electronics, computer software and printing (and other industry which may be notified in future as "non-polluting industry") are exempt from such locational restriction. Relaxation in the aforesaid locational restriction is possible if an industrial licence is obtained as per the notified procedure.

The location of industrial units is further regulated by the local zoning and land-use regulations as also the environmental regulations. Hence, even if the requirement of the locational policy as stated above is fulfilled, but the local zoning and land-use regulations of a State government, or the regulations of the Ministry of Environment do not permit setting up of an industry at a location, then the entrepreneur would be required to abide by that decision.

Thus, selection of location of an enterprise is an important decision and entrepreneur should try to assess the implication of the above factors. These factors affect the survival and viability of the enterprise in the long-run.

EXAMINATION QUESTIONS

Long Answer Questions

1. You want to set up a small scale unit, which industry would you like to set up and where should it be located ? Explain with the help of a suitable example.
2. What do you mean by location of an enterprise ? Discuss the factors governing the selection of location of an enterprise.
3. Critically examine the Government policy with regard to location of industries in India.
4. What do you mean by location of an enterprise, localisation of industries and planned location ? How do they affect the entrepreneurial behaviour ?
5. Examine the need for an enterprise location. Also evaluate different steps involved in enterprise location.
6. "Government policy of planned has failed to ensure proper development of industries." Comment.
7. Assume that you are an entrepreneur, planning to start up a full service auto repair and maintenance centre. What are the factors that you would need to consider before taking the location decision for your enterprise ?

Short Answer Questions

1. Examine the need for enterprise location.
2. What do you mean by enterprise location ?
3. Discuss the importance of enterprise location.
4. What are the major steps generally involved in enterprise location.

5. Distinguish between location and localisation of industries.
6. Discuss the basic features of present government locational policy.
7. Explain the determinants of location of an enterprise.

Objective Type Questions

1. Under the present government policy new unit should not be located within the area of standard urban areas

   (a) 16 Kms (b) 20 Kms
   (c) 25 Kms (d) 30 Kms

2. General objective of selecting a location is not the following

   (a) Minimise the cost of production
   (b) Minimise the distribution cost
   (c) Minimise the cost of capital
   (d) None of the above

3. External economies affect location

   (a) Generally (b) Exceptionally
   (c) All of the above (d) None of the above

4. Location of enterprise is concerned with

   (a) Entrepreneurial Decisions (b) Managerial Decisions
   (c) Government Decisions (d) Resource Decisions

5. Steps required in an enterprise location

   (a) 3 (b) 4
   (c) 5 (d) 6

Answers

1-(c) 2-(c) 3-(b) 4-(a) 5-(b)

Reason Based Questions

State with reasons whether the following statements are true or false :

1. Location of an enterprise is governed by industrial policy.
2. Location and localisation both are the same.
3. New units should not be located within the metro pollutant city having 10 lakhs population.
4. Pollution control is in concurrent list.
5. Environmental clearance for chemical units is not mandatory.

25

PROJECT MONITORING AND CONTROL

Monitoring and control process is an important dimension of the project management. Project management is an integrated multidisciplinary function aimed at completing the project successfully through systematic planning, organising, execution and control. Since it is multidisciplinary in nature, an aggressive team or task force, consisting of persons drawn from the various functional specialist departments of planning design and engineering operation and maintenance, finance, constructions, procurement and stores and personnel and entrusted with the project management.

Project monitoring deals with the process of keeping a careful check of project activities over a period of time. To work to its full potential, any kind of project needs to set out proposals and objectives. Then a monitoring system should be worked out to keep a check on all the various activities, including finances. This will help project staff to know how things are going, as well as giving early warning of possible problems and difficulties.

The purpose of Project Monitoring and Control (PMC) is to provide an understanding of the project's progress so that appropriate corrective actions can be taken when the project's performance deviates significantly from the plan.

A project's documented plan is the basis for monitoring activities, communicating status and taking corrective action. Progress is primarily determined by comparing actual work product and task attributes, effort, cost and schedule to the plan at prescribed milestones or control levels within the project schedule or work breakdown structure (WBS). Appropriate visibility of progress enables timely corrective action to be taken when performance deviates significantly from the plan. A deviation is significant if, when left unresolved, it precludes the project from meeting its objectives. The term "project plan" is used throughout these practices to refer to the overall plan for controlling the project. When actual status deviates significantly from the expected values, corrective actions are taken as appropriate. These actions may require replanning, which may include revising the original plan, establishing new agreements, or including additional mitigation activities within the current plan.

Monitoring typically involves measuring the actual values of project planning parameters, comparing actual values to the estimates in the plan, and identifying significant deviations. Recording actual values of the project planning parameters includes recording associated contextual information to help understand the measures. An analysis of the impact that significant deviations have on determining what the corrective actions to take is handled in best possible way.

Role of Management Team

Top management generally constitutes a project management to ensure proper monitoring and control of the project. The management team is required to monitor the following :

(a) the quantity and quality of the project's end result or product,

(b) the time schedule of the project,

(a) the mobilisation and allocation of resources to complete the project within budget estimates.

In practice, monitoring of these variables reflect the level of competency and efficiency of project management and the degree of successful project completion.

An efficient project management uses modern sophisticated techniques and is continuously enriched by its learning curve. It is forceful and capable of foreseeing problems and staying clear of them, bull dosing away the problems and achieving project completion ahead of time and within the limits of cost estimates. To be efficient, the management team must be committed, and responsible. It must take initiative, inspiring all those involved in the project work to support and supplement its efforts. The team has to be conscious of the time value of money and useful cost of procrastination and indecision. Efficient project management budget and controls include the use of resources made available to it, to the fullest advantage.

Project Monitoring

Monitoring of project is done at the implementation stage as well as at the operational stage. During the implementation stage, the project is monitored through :

(i) Regular reports, furnished by the promoters, which provide information about placement of orders, construction of buildings, procurement of plant, installation of plant and machinery, trial production, etc.,

(ii) Periodic site visits,

(iii) Discussion with promoters, bankers, suppliers, creditors and others connected with the project,

(iv) Progress reports submitted by the nominee directors,

(v) Audited accounts of the company,

(vi) Reconciliation of the progress with implementation schedule as envisaged,

(vii) Check on deployment of funds.

Functions of Monitoring Team

The project manager monitors the overall project. A project manager is responsible to monitor and control his relevant division of his project. The divisional project manager reports to the overall project manager of any risks.

Jointly, divisional project managers and overall project manager should :

(i) identify risks, potential project problems, as early as possible,

(ii) identify when goals may not be met,

(iii) identify when constraints may be violated,

(iv) ensure that contingency plans occur before unrecoverable problems occur,

(v) provide and receive project status for the phases and total project.

When there is a significant chance that the goals of the project will not be met, this risk should be reported to upper management. Also, when the constraints of the project may be violated, specifically, costs being overrun and schedules significantly slipped, these risks will be reported. When there are disagreements between the phase project manager and overall project manager, then resolution will be escalated to the change control board. Lack of resolution there could escalate to upper management.

Monitoring Process

It is concerned with evaluating the project performance. It also identifies the significant deviations to take remedial actions. Following steps are involved in monitoring process :

1. ***Monitor progress against the schedule***— Progress monitoring typically includes the following :

(i) Periodically measuring the actual completion of activities and milestones,

(ii) Comparing actual completion of activities and milestones against the schedule documented in the project plan schedule,

(iii) Identifying significant deviations from the project plan budget and schedule estimates in the project plan.

2. ***Monitor the project's cost and expended effort***— Effort and cost monitoring typically includes the following :

(i) Periodically measuring the actual effort and costs expended and staff assigned,

(ii) Comparing actual effort, costs, staffing and training to the estimates and budget documented in the project plan budget and estimates,

(iii) Identifying significant deviations from the budget in the project plan budget and schedule.

3. ***Monitor the attributes of the work products and tasks***— Refer to the Measurement and Analysis process area for more information about developing and sustaining a measurement capability used to support management information needs. Refer to the Project Planning process area for more information about the establishing estimates of work product and task attributes of work products and tasks. Monitoring the attributes of the work products and tasks typically includes the following :

(i) Periodically measuring the actual attributes of the work products and tasks, such as size or , complexity, or service levels (and the changes to thethese attributes),

(ii) Comparing the actual attributes of the work products and tasks (and the changes to thethese attributes) to the estimates documented in the project plan estimates,

(iii) Identifying significant deviations from the estimates in the project plan estimates.

4. ***Monitor resources provided and used***— Refer to the Capacity and Availability Management process area for more information about monitoring and analysing capacity. Refer to the Project Planning process area for more information about planning the project's resources. Examples of resources include the following :

(i) Physical facilities,

(ii) Computers, peripherals, and software used in design, manufacturing, testing and operation,

(iii) Networks,

(iv) Security environment,

(v) Project staff,

(vi) Processes.

5. ***Monitor the knowledge and skills of project personnel***— Refer to the Project Planning process area for more information about planning for needed knowledge and skills needed to perform the project. Monitoring the knowledge and skills of the project personnel typically includes the following :

(i) Periodically measuring the acquisition of knowledge and skills by project personnel,

(ii) Comparing actual training obtained to that documented in the project plan,

(iii) Identifying significant deviations from estimates in the project plan.

6. ***Document the significant deviations in the project planning parameters.***

Post Project Evaluation Process

The concerned evaluation is more or less than the same as performance evaluation with predetermined estimates. The projections in the feasibility reports form the basis for comparison of actual performance with the projections. Post-project evaluation seeks to answer questions like, to what extent the forecasts and projections made have actually materialised, how movement decisions proved in reality, what lessons were learnt etc. On completion of a project, the actual growth in demand is ascertained and compared with market projections of anticipated growth in demand of products, expected market share and selling prices are determined. Besides an initial assessment of market projections, market share and selling price require to be assessed over a period of time. The technical evaluation comprises of evaluation of actual rated capacity, availability of materials and their sources, difficulties in imports as against projections. These evaluations throw up meaningful lessons for the future. The financial performance/projections reflected in the feasibility report and DPR are analysed under various heads based on actual of each. A more difficult post-project evaluation is the economic evaluation due to the time-lag involved in the manifestation of social costs and benefits.

Reviews of financial/cost performances are comparatively easy as compared to evaluation of operational performances. The latter calls for a reasonable period for assessing the performance. In this period, the local and external events affecting the performance which are beyond the control of the organisation are identified. In evaluation of public sector projects there are deficiencies in evaluating processes and procedures. Low allowances for contingencies, insufficient scrutiny of project proposals, underestimation of feasibility reports to avoid approval of higher authorities, absence of norms, inappropriate project selection criteria, inconsistent financial policies, unscientific and subjective evaluation of social cost and and benefits, delay in granting approval and a host of other hurdles and problems plague an effective post-project evaluation.

Expert reviews have been carried out in the past, analysing the causes of cost and time overruns in various spheres of activity and at various levels (internal and external) in a project environment. Studies indicate that cost overruns and time overruns could, to a considerable extent, by minimised (if not totally eliminated) by resorting to sound project estimating. The various techniques that are adopted in this regard are more in the form of lessons from past failures. There are controllable, uncontrollable and non-controllable factors for cost-and time overruns. Uncontrollable factors are not totally non-controllable. It is a question of a managerial competence and environmental factors.

Deviations in Project Execution

Initial time schedule and budgetary price may be unrealistic when project is of non-repetitive nature. So, there is problem of deviations. Absence of expediting and follow up with supplier and contractor. Absence of periodic co-ordination meeting for project speed up and remedial measures are some of the important factors responsible for this type of deviations. Selection of contractor on the bas of lowest quotation, ignoring financial standing of the contractor selected and, as a result, the job get stranded at the meet of the project for financial problem of the contractor. Frequent change over at the mid-stream of the project also create deviation in the project execution. Shortage of fund before the project authority, lack of dynamism, poor leadership and lack of dedication are also responsible for project deviations.

During the course of project execution, there are possibility of time and cost overruns. Cost overrun is associated with time overrun for simple reason of time inflation. Due to cost overrun, projects gets stuck up for want of additional fund, viability of project gets disturbed and fresh look is necessary.

Cost overrun is injurious to the project execution. Fund is costly today and may not be available easily. If viability is affected due to cost overrun and this fact with viability is suppressed by management, the company becomes sick since its birth.

Time over-run : It is the delay in time during actual execution from the schedule date of completion of project. Time overrun causes loss of profit, increase in interest burden, etc.

Cost over-run : The amount by which the actual cost incurred in completing the project exceeds the budgetary cost.

Stages of Cost Over-runs

The cost overruns can occur at various stages in the execution of projects. The various stages are as follows :

(i) Pre-feasibility stage : Costs tend to rise due to delays and passage of time. Acquiring land and obtaining environment and other clearances are usually beset with procedural bureaucratic delays. Securing necessary approvals, from regulatory agencies and financial bodies is yet another reason for delays and consequent increase in costs. Inadequate communication facilities, poor quality of roads, absence of sufficient water sources and such other infrastructure inadequacies add to time slippages and cost overruns. The failure to plan important resources, facilities, tie-ins and inputs needed for timely construction and putting into operation is another major reasons for cost overruns.

(ii) Evaluation stage : The better the evaluation, greater the chances of eventual project success in terms of meeting time schedule and budget. In practice, the evaluation is hurried through by an inadequate study, resulting in lack of clarity on the project scope and underestimate of cost and resources. These, in turn, necessitates subsequent changes in project scope, non-freesing of specifications and revision of resource and cost estimates.

In addition to the above, wrong selection of location influenced by factors other than technical, and the incompetence of consultants who are again selected by extraneous considerations. These led to wrong economic studies and misleading fund flow statements and projections causing financial impediments.

(iii) Choice of technology : There is a tendency of selecting technology on considerations of credit offered by the supplier rather than of technical necessities. Very often, the technology chosen happens to be outdated. Also even before finalising process flowsheets and diagrams, detail engineering and preparation of shopping lists is started. Cost overruns and schedule slippages are also attributed to delay in competing detail engineering, non-availability or insufficient availability of design data, delay in the freesing of design and specifications, absence of an engineering schedule causing delay in the release of drawing for procurement. Improper scrutiny and approval of drawing and specifications also lead to revisions and rework at a later stage escalating project costs.

(iv) *Contracting and procurement* : In this stage, the major causes for cost overruns and project delays are the casual approach to the preparation of tender documents and late release of those documents; wrong selection of vendors fabricators/contractors and delays in evaluating bids.

(v) *Commissioning stage* : Sometimes, project work is completed but due to certain reasons, they are unable to reach commissioning and startup stage. External factors are not under the control of project manager. For example, linking the railway siding with the main line of railways, availability of raw materials and labour in final clearances from the local authorities also create the problems in commissioning and start up the projects.

Mechanism to Control and Time Over-runs

The key to avoid cost overruns and time slippages is to follow sound project management practice. These practices must lead to project success with reference to time, cost and performance. Mechanism to control cost and time overruns are as follows :

(a) The selection or choice of the project is made after an in-depth feasibility study from all angles technical, operational and economic,

(b) The project is undertaken after satisfying all statutory regulations and completing all arrangements for raising funds,

(c) The various phases of the project are thoroughly analysed and planned with utmost cohesion and integration and execute it with highest possible efficiency.

Issues in Project Monitoring and Control

(i) *Line of Balance Technique (LOB)* : It is a device for planning and monitoring the progress of an order, project or programme to be completed by a target-date. Critical dates are established for various major activities like positioning of materials, specific contributory tasks to be accomplished, sub-assemblies and sub-projects are to be completed etc. For these purposes, LOB contains elements of PERT. In LOB, tasks are represented by vertical bars of a length, proportional to their production (or end point) requirements and are plotted sequentially in the vertical bar chart. The desired progress is indicated by a stair-step profile line derived by connecting the tops of the schedule bars. This profile line is the LOB. As the project is pursued, progress of each task is plotted on LOB chart as a vertical bar. At a point of time, the gap between the top of a bar and LOB would show where a delay, exception or deficiency has taken place. Different LOBs are constructed for each check date, for a number of closely related tasks. LOB is a useful control technique. It is a more detailed management oriented charting technique for monitoring progress. LOB chart shows in a comparative picture of committed and actuals of different phases of activities in a project, thereby highlighting areas beyond schedule. Key milestone events, cumulative time schedules and percentage progress are inputs to the LOB Hnns are identified. unner and lower control limits are imposed where variations are anticipated. LOB concept is used with advantage for performance control.

(ii) *Zero Date of a Project* : The final step in establishing a project is the fixation of Zero Date. The Zero Date of a Project signals the effective start of the Project. The clock starts ticking from that date. The Project completion period will be counted from this date and, therefore, anything that affects the performance of the project will have to be defined or established or started by this date. This applies not only to time, cost and technical parameters of the project, but also to infrastructural facilities, formation of a new company or division, governmental clearances and many other activities needed for putting up the project. All those activities which must be completed before the Zero Date are known as pre-project activities. Since it is difficult to initially fix a definite date for the start of a project, all planning is done in terms of the number of weeks/months from the Zero Date. After the pre-project activities take a definite shape, the zero Date is exactly defined.

(iii) *Key Man Insurance* : People are the most important resource of an organisation, especially those whose expert knowledge and skills cannot be replaced. Key person is one whose loss would materially affect the business or credit of an organisation resulting in reduced sales, profits and even survival, at times. Key men includes key woman. Every successful organisation would normally have one or more such key man whose loss would be a hindrance for the continued success of the organisation. The key man is a person who possesses excellent skill and knowledge, is a valuable source of business and a chief source and strength of the organisation's credit. The organisation would have to incur additional expenses to find and recruit a suitable replacement or find an alternative person from the existing employees and train him to be fully functional in the role of the person who has been lost, more so, if the person happens to be a key person.

Key man Insurance is a new and innovative concept to protect the interests of the business organisation in case of premature death of the key man. The insurance policy is owned by the business organisation to whom the 'proceeds are payable in the event of the death of the key man. The insurance indemnifies the organisation from adverse effects due to the lo ss of the key man

Some *salient features* of the key man insurance policy are :

(i) The key man should be an important officer of the company;

(ii) He should have high educational qualifications;

(iii) His services should be of paramount importance and vital to the organisation;

(iv) Neither he nor any of his family members should have major shareholding in the company;

(v) Key man should not derive any benefit from the insurance;

(vi) He should have at least three years' standing in the company;

(vii) Key man insurance cannot be taken if the profits are declining;

(viii) The sum assured on the Life of the key man is normally equal to 10 times his gross yearly emoluments. The premium paid for key man insurance is allowed as a business expenses by the Income Tax authorities.

(iv) Project Rating Index (PRI) : When a firm evaluates a large number of project ideas regularly, it may be helpful to streamline the process of preliminary screening. For this purpose, a preliminary evaluation may be translated into a 'Project Rating Index' (PRI). The steps involved in this exercise are detailed below:

(a) Identify the factors relevant for project rating.

(b) Assign weights to these factors, depending on their relative importance.

(c) Rate the project proposal on various factors, using a suitable rating scale (typically a 5-point or 7-point scale).

(d) For each factor, multiply the factor rating with its weight to get the factor score.

(e) Add all the factor scores to get the overall 'Project Rating Index (PRI)'.

Once the Project Rating Index (PRI) is determined, it is compared with a predetermined hurdle value to judge whether the project is *prima facie* worthwhile or not. When a selection has to be made between competing project with the highest PRI gets the choice of selection.

EXAMINATION QUESTIONS

Long Answer Questions

1. What do you mean by project implementation ? What are the prerequisites for successful implementation of projects ?
2. How are projects evaluated ? Also explain its importance.
3. What do you mean by project monitoring and control ? Briefly discuss one project control technique for control of a project.
4. What are the prerequisites for successful implementation of a project ? Do you agree that projects fail due to lack of proper implementation of the projects ?

5. "Project control is a must for the success of any project." Comment upon the statement in the light of proper control techniques.

Short Answer Questions

1. What is project monitoring ?
2. What is time overrun ?
3. What is cost overrun ?
4. What do you mean by zero date of a project ?
5. What is project rating index ?

Objective Type Questions

1. Management team for monitoring is constituted by the
   (a) Chairman (b) Board of director
   (c) Top management (d) None of the above
2. Cost over run affects the following
   (a) Cost of the project (b) Viability of the project
   (c) Profit margin (d) All of the above
3. Stages of cost overruns include the following
   (a) 2 (b) 3
   (c) 5 (d) 6

Answers

l-(c) 2-(a) 3-(c)

Reason Based Questions

State with reasons whether the following statements are true or false :

1. Project monitoring process is a pre project scenario.
2. Zero date of a project deals with effective start of the project.
3. Keyman insurance is concerned with the insurance policy of workers.
4. Line of balance technique contains elements of PERT.
5. Time overrun is caused due to inflation.

REFERENCES

1. Jerry Adam, *Project Monitoring,* John Wiley & Sons Inc. 2002, p. 86
2. Neal Whitten, *Managing Software Development Projects,* John Wiley & Sons, Inc., 1995,p. 162
3. The Institute of Costs and Works Accountants of India, *Financial Management and International Finance,* Kolkata, 2008, p. 8.

26

PROJECT FINANCING

Project financing is the technique of sourcing and evaluating various means to fund a project at optimum cost. The fund can be mobilised both from internal as well as external sources. There are no common sources of project finance applicable to all projects whether in the public, joint or private sectors. Some sources are exclusive for public sector projects while some others are exclusively for private sector projects. Similarly, some sources are common to all projects. The listing of public sector companies on stock exchange is another source of finance (Public participation in equity capital of public sector units) to these companies. Private sector projects are mostly taken up with capital raised in the capital market. Sources depend on the undertakings, size and the nature of the industry, for example, raising funds through commercial paper is dependent on the tangible networth, working capital limit, listing in stock exchange, etc.

Project Financing discipline includes understanding the rationale for project financing, how to prepare the financial plan, assess the risks, design the financing mix, and raise the funds. In addition, cogent analyses is generally used to know of why some project financing plans have succeeded while others have failed. A knowledge-base is required regarding the design of contractual arrangements to support project financing; issues for the host government legislative provisions, public/private infrastructure partnerships, public/private financing structures; credit requirements of lenders, and how to determine the project's borrowing capacity; how to prepare cash flow projections and use them to measure expected rates of return; tax and accounting considerations; and analytical techniques to validate the project's feasibility.

Project finance is the finance for a particular project, such as a mine, toll road, railway, pipeline, power station, ship, hospital or prison, which is repaid from the cash-flow of that project. Project finance is different from traditional forms of finance because the financier principally looks to the assets and revenue of the project in order to secure and service the loan. In contrast to an ordinary borrowing situation, in a project financing, the financier usually has little or no recourse to the non-project assets of the borrower or the sponsors of the project. In this situation, the credit risk associated with the borrower is not as important as in an ordinary loan transaction. Most important aspect of project financing is the identification, analysis, allocation and management of every risk associated with the project.

Sources of Project Finance

The major sources of obtaining project finance are : 1. Long term rupee funds, 2. Short term rupee funds 3. Foreign currency funds.

1. Long Term Funds

Main sources of long term funds are as follows :

(i) Equity Share Capital : The equity shareholders are the owners of the company, who enjoy the rewards and bear the risks of the business. However, unlike other forms of ownership, the liability in this case is limited to the extent of the nominal value of the shares taken up. The equity capital again can be subdivided into the promoters' contribution and the public subscription. The capital investment of promoters who set up the project and implement it is termed the promoters' contribution. The main sources of equity capital are :

(a) *The core promoters' contribution :* The real promoters or the core promoters who actually conceive the idea to incorporate the company and perform the basic legwork of the project.

(b) *Public equity :* The equity capital subscribed to by the general public in a public issue or private issue come under this category.

(c) *Bodies corporate :* Under the Companies Act, 1956 even bodies corporate are allowed to hold shares, thus, bodies corporate, companies, trusts, HUF, etc. (except partnerships) may hold equity shares.

(d) *Institutions :* The financial institutions also may subscribe to the equity in the form of underwriting developments, firm allotments in public issue, seed or venture capital.

(ii) Preference share capital : Preference share capital has some characteristics of equity capital and some characteristics of debt capital. It is similar to equity capital because here also dividend is to be paid. It resembles debt capital because the rate of dividend is fixed and the preference shareholders do not have a voting right. Further, in case of profits they have a preference over the equity shareholders in case of dividend and also at the time of repayment.

(iii) Internal generation of funds : Sometimes, the schedule of implementation provides for a time gap between completing of one stage of project leading to production being commenced and then the second phase of expansion. This expansion may be envisaging funds from operations arising out of the first phase of commercial production itself. Thus, where internal cash accruals is proposed to be taken as a source of finance, the profitability statement should, all the more, be thoroughly scrutinised as then one uncertain element (profit from operations) becomes the basis of another uncertain element (internal accruals as means of finance).

(iv) Debentures : Debentures are instruments for raising long term debt capital. Secured debentures are protected by a charge on the properties of the issuing company. Debentures may be fully convertible, partially convertible or non convertible. A company planning to issue debentures has to issue a prospectus and take the permission of the Securities and Exchange Board of India. It is also listed on the stock exchanges and traded.

(v) Long term loans : These loans are mostly provided by financial institutions. Development banks and development financial institutions, both national and international, play a vital role in the financing of the projects. They provide long-term institutional finance, called "Term Loans". They provide financial assistance to industrial projects which are employment-oriented and export-oriented. The other types of projects that enjoy this assistance are those which promote import-substitution, those established in backward areas, those promoted by new entrepreneurs, those who use local technology, conserve energy and control pollution. Besides providing term loans, the financial institutions/banks offer financial guarantee. These institutions also provide foreign currency funds.

(vi) Lease financing : In lease financing, the leasing company pays the full price of all required equipment and then lease them out to the lessee under a lease agreement providing for there payment of the principal and the interest amount in quarterly or monthly instalments. At the end of the lease period, the ownership of the equipment is transferred to the lessee at a nominal residual value. The lessee need not invest the capital in full as one time single investment. When the lessee pays the lease instalments, the amount paid is allowed as deduction for tax purposes. The demerits of lease financing are the high rate of interest payment. Further, the depreciation allowance cannot be claimed. Moreover, the leased assets cannot be transferred by lessee and also do not contribute to net worth.

2. Short Term Fund

It is also called working capital funding. This is very common form of bank assistance being availed by the companies. Although most of the capital is employed in purchase of plant and machinery, construction of factory premises/ building etc., however, there is a time element between production and sales. To purchase the initial lot of inputs like raw material, consumables and to meet the various initial expenses like wages etc., some amount of liquidity is needed. The financial assistance is called the working capital assistance. This is a rotating credit and normally the security offered and accepted is the stock and other movable securities.

These are required to operate the project as working capital. The main sources for this type of fund are commercial banks, public deposits, commercial papers, supplier's credit.

(i) Commercial Banks : Commercial banks are a major source of short term finance for business enterprises. Commercial banks, lending norms for working capital are based on the recommendations of the Tandon Committee. The working capital requirement is very large in the case of very large projects. In such cases, several commercial banks may form a consortium and provide working capital finance to the large enterprises. The large amount of working capital, approximately ₹640 crores to Reliance Industries is provided by a consortium of nationalised banks with Syndicate bank as the lead bank.

(ii) Public Deposits : Public deposit is deposits accepted by the public by :

(a) public and private non-banking non-financial companies,
(b) public and private limited non-banking financial companies,
(c) Government companies since 1980,
(d) branches of foreign companies,
(e) partnership firms, and
(f) Proprietary concerns.

(iii) Commercial Papers : Commercial papers, as a source of short-term financing of working capital needs, is a recent phenomenon. The commercial paper was introduced by RBI in early 1990 with a view to enable highly rated corporate borrowers to diversify their sources of short term borrowing. Commercial paper is a short term unsecured promissory note issued by finance companies and certain industrial concerns. The main features of the commercial papers are :

(a) Commercial paper is an unsecured promissory note tied to any transaction. It is privately placed with investors through the agency of banks and other financial institutions.
(b) The issuing company should have the tangible net worth of ₹5 crores; enjoy a working capital limit of not less than ₹10 crores; be listed on stock exchange; obtain a minimum credit rating from an approved credit rating agency, such as CRISIL; and have a minimum current ratio of 1.33.

(iv) Suppliers Credit : Suppliers credit available for one to three months for supply of raw materials and other inputs is a source of short term financing. With the introduction of just-in-production and inventory control techniques in a right political and economic climate, situation may arise when the working capital requirements will be very little, making it possible to pay the suppliers of raw materials and other inputs from the sale proceeds of finished good.

3. Foreign Currency Funds

Many large projects involve expenditure in foreign currency. All foreign exchange requirements require either RBI or Government approval which also specifies the source of funds. Foreign currency fund requirements are mostly obtained through loans from development bonds, external commercial borrowings, tie-up loans, assistance from International Companies like IFC, ADB, CDC, and Euro Issues etc.

(i) External Commercial Borrowings : External commercial borrowing is the amount borrowed by the government through designated agents from All India Financial Institutions. The government generally borrow these amounts in the international money market to meet the massive exchange deficits. The lenders include Asian Development Bank and International Monetary Fund. Any existing undertaking is permitted to make direct commercial borrowing if the Department of Economic Affairs is satisfied with the proposal submitted to it. Direct external commercial borrowing of the total foreign exchange requirements may be permitted while the other part should be financed through rupee payments quadrilateral aid or free foreign exchange releases. But, if a project is 100 per cent Export Oriented Unit (EOU), the entire foreign exchange component is allowed to meet through direct external commercial borrowings.

(ii) External Aids : External aid, available only through the government, is of two types : bilateral and multilateral aid. Bilateral aid as the name implies, is an aid from one government to another government. Generally, the donor is an industrially affluent one, and the recipient or beneficiary belongs to developing or underdeveloped country. Multilateral aid is available from international financial institutions like the world bank group, consisting of internal bank for development, Internal Development Association, IFC, Multilateral Investment Guarantee Agency and the ADB.

(iii) Assistance from International Financial Corporations : The IFC provides financial assistance to the private sector in the developing member countries. The assistance takes the form of equity participation loan, usually in collaboration with other investors. The DEAs clearance is necessary for any undertaking in the private sector to approach IFC for financial assistance. It can grant loans in the currency of the member country or Switzerland for meeting foreign currency expenditure. The equity participation is only in the currency of the member country. Normally, the amount of assistance is between 5 and 50 million US dollars subject to a maximum of 25% of the project cost. Loans are repayable in 7 to 12 years with normal interest and usual commitment charges on undisguised amounts of sanctioned loans. The IFC does not require any guarantee from the government.

(iv) Investment from Oil Exporting Developing Countries : An important source of foreign assistance is the investments from institutions and individuals from oil exporting countries in Africa and Persian Gulf which are not industrially advanced. Such investments can be in equity, loans, debentures, bonds etc. subject to certain limits and restricted to new enterprises, hotels and hospitals. Clearance from RBI is needed for such investments.

Issues in Project Financing

(i) Resource optimisation in Projects : Projects use a number of resources, be it men, machines or materials in order to achieve the project completion. Many of these resources are scarce and need to be controlled so that there is optimum utilisation of the scarce resources. This can be achieved by scheduling of activities to obtain resource levelling, i.e., reduce or minimise the variation in resource requirements over the duration of the project, keeping in view the constraints on the project duration.

The other aspect is to reschedule the activities where there is a restriction on the availability of the resources. Program Evaluation and Review Technique (PERT) can be used with advantage for resource optimisation. Initially, the activities with slack are rescheduled. If the resulting resource requirements are still excessive, then the activities on the critical path must be carefully examined to determine where the greatest resource reduction can be made per-unit time increase in project duration. As the activities on the critical path are rescheduled resulting in an extension of the project duration, the effects optimally scheduling the activities with slack should be constantly re-evaluated. This process of extending the schedule of the critical path activities and then the activities on the slack path must be continued till the overall project schedule meets the maximum resource requirements available. The procedure, therefore, is essentially one of considering alternate schedules to find solutions to problems of resource limitation.

(ii) Inter-corporation Loans : Private sector companies often resort to temporary transfer of funds From one unit/company to another with a view to helping the unit/company which is in need of financial resources. This is done against a reasonable rate of interest. Such loans between corporate bodies are known as 'inter-corporate loans'. In case of Public Sector units also, such transfer of funds is possible with the approval of the government. Government/Centre for Good Governance have laid down guidelines for effective utilisation of this facility for financing projects/organisations.

(iii) Capital Rationing : Capital Rationing is resorted to when funds available are inadequate to undertake all projects, which are otherwise acceptable. Capital Rationing may arise because of internal limitations or external constraints. Internal Capital Rationing is caused by setting a limit by management to its capital expenditure outlays. External Capital Rationing arises out of the inability of the firm to raise sufficient funds from the market at a given cost of capital. When Capital has to be rationed among competing projects, the projects need to be selected based on appropriate criteria like Return on Investment (ROI). Several techniques—discounting as well as non-discounting—are available for evaluation of projects. A sensitivity analysis also needs to be conducted to gauge the effects of certain parameters on the overall profitability of the projects to be chosen, since capital is scarce. Risk Analysis and Risk Mitigation/Allocation also play a vital role in the choice of the projects. Otherwise, the safety of the scarce Capital Investment in the projects might be in jeopardy.

(iv) Risk Minimisation Process : Financiers are concerned with minimising the dangers of any events which could have a negative impact on the financial performance of the project, in particular, events which could result in :

(a) the project not being completed on time, on budget, or at all;

(b) the project not operating at its full capacity;

(c) the project failing to generate sufficient revenue to service the debt;

(d) the project prematurely coming to an end.

The minimisation of such risks involves a three step process. The first step requires the identification and analysis of all the risks that may bear upon the project. The second step is the allocation of those risks among the parties. The last step involves the creation of mechanisms to manage the risks. If a risk to the financiers cannot be minimised, the financiers will need to build it into the interest rate margin for the loan.

EXAMINATION QUESTIONS

Long Answer Questions

1. What is project financing ? Examine its different sources.
2. Discuss the role played by development banks and developmer financial institutions in project financing.
3. What is Lease Financing ? What are its merits and demerits with reference to Project Financing ?
4. What do you mean by resource optimisation in projects Evaluate its importance.
5. Describe the role of State Financial Corporations and commercial banks in project financing.
6. Critically comment on the coordination of the state financial corporations and commercial banks for the success of the industry in the current context.

Short Answer Questions

1. What is equity financing ?
2. What is capital rationing ?
3. What do you mean by corporate loans ?
4. What is working capital finance ?
5. What is lease financing ?

Objective Type Questions

1. Owners funds are
   (a) Short term funds (b) Mid term funds
   (c) Long term funds (d) None of the above
2. Equity Capital is concerned with
   (a) Dividend (b) Interest
   (c) Bonus (d) None of the above
3. Working capital loan is concerned with
   (a) Purchase of buildings (b) Purchase of plant.
   (c) Purchase of raw materials (d) Purchase of brands.
4. Purpose of project financing
   (a) Minimising the cost (b) Optimising the cost
   (c) Reducing the cost (d) None of the above

5. IFC provides funds for
   (a) Public sector projects
   (b) Private sector projects
   (c) Both public sector and private sector projects
   (d) Joint sector projects

Answers

l-(c) 2-(a) 3-(c) 4-(b) 5-(b).

Reason Based Questions

State with reasons whether the following statements are true or false :

1. Development Financial Institutions (DFIs) are meant to provide working capital of SMEs.
2. It is easier to achieve Break Down Point in the capital intensive units as compared to labour intensive units.
3. Debentures are losing its shine in project financing.
4. Public-Private Partnership is getting popularity in project financing.
5. Project financing is always financed by the external sources.

27

PROMOTING A BUSINESS ENTERPRISE

An entrepreneur is one who converts his dream into action and that action is related with promotion of a business enterprise. An entrepreneur identifies the business opportunities, analyse its prospects, concieves the idea of business enterprise and mobilises resources like men, machines and materials, managerial skill and promote the new enterprise. So entrepreneur is also expected to work as promoter of a business enterprise. He is required to take all entrepreneurial decisions with regard to setting up of a new enterprise. An enterprise cannot come into existence without the pioneering work of a person who is called entrepreneur or promotor. According to *G.W. Gerstenberg* "Promotion may be defined as the discovery of business opportunities and the subsequent organisation of funds, property and managerial ability into a business concern for the purpose of making profits therefrom." Thus, promotion includes generation of business or product idea, identification of business opportunities, investigation, assembling, financial arrangement and launching of an enterprise as a going concern.

Need for Business Plan[1]

Every entrepreneur wants to know what to do before he chalks out his business plan. There are crucial areas which the founder should research on before taking the next step. "First, there should fundamentally be no flaws in the business idea, the fashion, conviction and tenacity of the entrepreneur are highly important for any business to succeed." "The most important thing which the best entrepreneurs possess is passion to make it happen. However, they also ask themselves, why will this business work when most others will fail. Thus, understanding the odds." Most business plans never raise money. Many fail for opportunity related reasons, lack of scope, or industry-related reasons. For instance, it is too easy to enter the market—thus, increasing the chances of competition, or the entrepreneurial team might lack what it takes to cope with different market forces. First, entrepreneur must try and avoid disaster, by identifying any flaw in a new business idea. This saves time and money, which could have otherwise been wasted on fundamental flaws. The next step, once these flaws are identified, is to modify or abandon them all together before it is too late. Just as new buyers do a test drive before buying car, this is a road test for entrepreneurs.

Fatal flaws are uncovered, leaving the entrepreneur glad that he didn't put too much into that business plan. In case, there are flaws identified that are not fatal in nature — they can be fixed by targeting a different market, or changing the product or even entering at a different value chain, say, as a distributor not manufacturer and by improving skills in the team.

Most flaws were already identified—this is the best case scenario for start-ups, and also the rarest. This acid test provides the start-up with solid evidence based research to make an effective business plan. Every entrepreneur should be prepared to make a decision on whether it is worth fixing a particular business plan or abandoning it altogether. Second is to address each hurdle as you start building business plan so you are more prepared while facing investors or launching your business. There are crucial elements to keep an eye on : markets, industries and the entrepreneur team.

Markets and industries aren't the same thing. Many a time, the difference between markets and industries are fuzzy. A market consists of a group of current customers with ability to buy products—buyers, whereas an industry is one which offers products that are similar but not the same.

Macro and micro-level research is important. While assessing the scenario in a macro perspective is relatively simple, due to the overload of data available over the internet. Micro level is difficult to invest time in, say mentors.

At the micro level, entering market is a critical barrier to overcome, since customers are already satisfying their needs in some way. In such cases, the entrepreneur must understand customer needs better and fulfil them better than that was being done before.

Review your team with more depth than just their character or ability to perform. See how well they fit into the role for your particular business idea. Most industries are unattractive. Therefore, identify which industry your business will be in, on a broader spectrum, because if your eye is too narrow, you will end up neglecting close substitutes, thus, not noticing competitors ! Make sure you work out what threat your company would face with others coming into your market. In markets where the buyer and supplier power are both strong, you will be stuck in the middle, which will be challenging to overcome. In case of entering a very competitive market, make sure there is enough business for everyone to get a slice of the pie! Lastly, check if the team you are assembling is capable, do they have the knowledge, can they deliver on critical success factors. It is always better to tick all these boxes before writing a business plan. Have a question or a business issue that you would like our mentors to give their insights on ? Tap into a rich pool of experienced business leaders who can mend your business to success.

Factors to be Considered in Promotion of Business Enterprise

1. Selection of Line of Business : The process of starting a new enterprise begins when an entrepreneur has some viable idea. He is expected to analyse the profitability and level of risk involved and the probable amount of capital required. He is supposed to prepare a feasibility report containing survey of various feasible opportunities which indicates the various lines of business he can easily set-up. There are different criteria to evaluate the feasibility of a line of business and in this context most popular criterion is expected rate of return on capital invested. However, entrepreneur prefers a particular line of business which is expected to give a higher rate of return.

2. Choice of Form of Organisation : There are different options available before the entrepreneur about the choice of form of organisation. Actually, choice of organisation decides the authority of the entrepreneur. Size of business also determines the form of organisation. An entrepreneur prefers company form of organisation if production is to be undertaken on large scale basis. Sole proprietorship and partnership are suitable for small and medium scale operations. But nowadays small scale and medium scale entrepreneurs also prefer company form of organisation due to flexibility and universal acceptability.

3. Financing Proposition : The entrepreneur is required to arrange necessary fund for the initiation and continuation of business enterprise. In case of small enterprises, the entrepreneur generally arranges funds from their own savings. But large scale enterprises, need huge funds and entrepreneur is required to mobilise financial resources from financial institutions and capital market. The entrepreneur is also required to take decisions like size of long term fund, size of short term fund, cost of capital, optimum capital structure, expected rate of return on investment and suitability of time for raising resources.

4. Plant Location : The location of a business enterprise is an important factor that affects its viability. The entrepreneur has to search out to a particular location where his enterprise will have easy access to raw materials, labour, power, market and other support services. Efforts should be made to select a location which is optimum in nature and it can ensure a lowest cost of production and distribution.

5. Size of the Unit : Generally, technical, managerial, financial and marketing forces affect the size of the firm. Some forces prefer larger size of operation and some other forces tend to restrict the size of the unit. If entrepreneur thinks that he will be able to market his products and mobilise sufficient financial resources then the best option is the large scale production. However, it would be better for the entrepreneur to initiate operation at small scale or minimum scale and after getting favourable response from the business environment, he can switch over to medium and large scale operations. Business risks and uncertainty also affect the size of the unit. An entrepreneur if interested to be successful, he should consider and analyse the impact of various forces in proper perspective. He should identify an optimum size to achieve his entrepreneurial objectives.

6. Machine and Equipment : These requirements are governed by different factors like nature of product and production process, availability of funds, size of production, managerial skill etc. In practice, mechanisation is necessary to improve productivity of factors of production as well as to reduce the cost of production per unit. However, before installation of machines and equipments care should be taken to assess the availability of spare parts, repair and maintenance services etc. in the market.

7. Plant Layout : The basic purpose of plant layout is to ensure efficiency and economies in production process. An efficient plant layout is one that allows materials to move through various operational phases in shortest possible time. Efforts should be made by the entrepreneur to hire the services of experts/ technocrats to design a suitable layout of physical facilities. The layout should ensure optimum utilisation of men, machines, equipment and space. It should be designed to reduce the delays in production process. Availability of space and nature of production process decide the type or pattern of layout to be developed in the factory campus.

8. Availability of Labour Force : Basic theme of the entrepreneurial activity is that an entrepreneur is a job-provider and not a job-seeker. Thus, he is required to appoint skilled and unskilled work-force and management personnel. Availability of right type of work-force is necessary for the successful operation of the enterprise. Besides, entrepreneur should try to arrange training and development facilities to his work-force. Moreover, work-force should also be motivated to achieve their desired goals.

9. Completion of Procedural Formalities : Sole proprietorship or partnership firm does not require registration formalities. Only certain nominal formalities are required to be completed by the entrepreneur with regard to permission of municipal authorities or sales-tax authorities etc. So, small scale operation attracts nominal government regulations. But in case of company form of organisation entrepreneur is required to complete formalities with regard to registration, commencement of business, listing of shares, registration of products and brands etc.

10. Launching the Enterprise : An entrepreneur is expected to arrange necessary resources like men, machine, materials, money and managerial skill. Then he is supposed to develop an organisation structure and ensure an effective division of work among the managers and other employees. Functional organisation structure is quite helpful in achieving entrepreneurial objectives. It also ensures smooth production system and supply of goods and services in the market.

Requisites of Successful Enterprise

1. Well Defined Organisational Goals : An entrepreneur should try to define the objectives for which a business enterprise has been developed. These objectives should incorporate main objectives, subsidiary objectives and other objectives. Besides, functional areas should also be defined keeping in mind the nature of product, size of the unit etc.

2. Effective Planning : Planning involves decision making i.e. making choices out of certain alternative courses whether they are alternative sets of objectives or alternative paths of reaching them. So, entrepreneur is required to plan his decisions with regard to various activities of the enterprise. This process is governed by business forecasting. Plans also include objectives, policies, programmes, schedules, budgets etc.

3. Effective Organisation System : It rests with the nesting process. It creates the shell or anatomy of an organisation within which workers and managers perform their basic functions. It ensures co-ordination in their operations and facilitates the achievement of business objectives. The entrepreneur should try to develop an effective organisation structure to indicate authority and responsibility relationship in a proper way.

4. Financial Resources : The entrepreneur should develop an efficient management of finance function. Investment decisions, financing decisions and dividend decisions should be performed in an objective way to achieve entrepreneurial goals. An optimum capital structure is highly desirable.

5. Plant Size, Layout and Location : Optimum size ensures lowest average cost per unit. Proper layout improves efficiency and avoids wastage of resources. Similarly, proper location reduces cost of operation. These decisions are crucial decisions and entrepreneur should take these decisions very carefully as they affect viability of the firm.

6. Professional Management : It helps in achieving the objectives of the enterprise. Professional managers ensure desired results from the people working in the enterprise and they effectively co-ordinate the various functional areas of the enterprise.

7. Marketing : Good enterprise-customer relation pays the firm in the long run. So, marketing strategy should be customer oriented. The entrepreneur should try to develop an effective distribution channel supported by viable brands and product ranges. Besides, efforts are needed to develop customer loyalty by developing popular brands, mono or trade marks.

8. Human Relations : An effective two-way communication system should be developed between workers and managers. Effective machinery should be installed to handle worker's reactions, suggestions and grievances in minimum possible time. Management should treat the workers as human beings and effective steps are necessary to provide welfare amenities to them.

9. Innovation : An entrepreneur is an agent of change. With the help of continuous research and development activities, innovations should be encouraged in the organisation. Innovation creates imperfection in the markert which ultimately increases the volume of sales and profits.

Establishing A Small Enterprise

The main steps involved in the establishment of small enterprise are as follows :

1. Selection of the product.
2. Selection of site.
3. Preparation of the project report.
4. Selection of form of business organisation.
5. Clearance from Environmental Regulatory Authorities.
6. Registration with state authorities.
7. Provision/arrangement of long term fund.
8. Working capital finance from banks.
9. Statutory licences and clearances.

10. Purchase of land and building.
11. Selection of personnel/workers.
12. Installation of plant and machinery.
13. Procurement of raw materials.
14. Power connection and water supply.
15. Trial productions.
16. Launching final production process.
17. Marketing of the product.

Thus, efforts are required by the promoter to formalise these steps at the time of launching of a new enterprise.

EXAMINATION QUESTIONS

Long Answer Questions

1. What type of entrepreneurial decisions have to be taken while launching a new enterprise ?
2. What is promotion of a business enterprise ? What factors are generally taken into account in promotion of a business enterprise ?
3. What are the requisites of a successful business enterprise ?
4. What do you know by promotion of a business enterprise. Also discuss various factors affecting the promotion process of a business enterprise ?
5. Define promotion. Also explain the requisites of a successful business enterprise ?

Short Answer Questions

1. What are the factors generally considered in promotion of business enterprise ?
2. Explain the requisites of successful enterprise.
3. Explain the steps involved in starting a new venture.

(M.G.K.V.P. MBA 2003)

Objective Type Questions

Tick the True/False nature of the following statements

1. Optimum size ensures reasonable average cost.
2. Managerial capability decides the size of the unit.
3. Functional organisation is helpful in achieving entrepreneurial objectives.
4. Promotion is defined as discovery of business opportunities.

Answers

1. (F) 2. (F) 3. (T) 4. (F)

REFERENCES

1. Business Line, April 25, 2011, p. 11

28

Small Scale Sector in India

The small scale industries (SSIs) have a crucial role in a developing economy like India. They play a strategic role in the progress of the country. These industries by and large represent a stage in economic transition from traditional segments to modern segments. The traditional nature of this process is reflected in the diversity of these industries. Some SSIs employ simple skills and mechanism while many other units use modern and sophisticated technology. Now, our economy is facing a challenge of economic growth. It has to accelerate the productivity of many important areas like agriculture and industry by improving their techniques of production. SSIs have been assigned to fulfil these expectations in more economic and diversified way.

SSIs constitute an important part of the Indian economic structure. They integrate a continuing element in the scheme of national planning. They are a strategic part of the Indian economy as well as a progressive and effective decentralised sector which is closely related with agriculture and medium and large scale industries. The whole scheme of a socialistic pattern of society with employment for all rests on the decentralisation and wide distribution of economic activity, entrepreneurship and economic advantages. The basic social philosophy underlying Indian planning is that to develop medium and large scale sector only to take advantage of modern technology. Over the rest of the field, SSIs will be encouraged to play their active role. If there is change in scale, that has to be developed with the help of mutual cooperation—both horizontal and vertical.

Rationale of SSIs

Following are the main rationale to support SSIs in India.

1. The Factor Price Argument : It is commonly argued that for various institutional reasons, labour used in large enterprise is priced well above the levels at which it is used in small scale industries. The SSI sector which uses more labour and less capital per unit of output will have relatively lower costs as their training and development costs are quite low. Besides, large enterprises are ready to pay more as they have to attract more stable migrants from rural areas. Cost of developing commitments among them to firm specific is also quite high. But small units make greater use of the unstable labour with high turnover because in their case the stability-efficiency relationship for the work-force is much weaker. Their labour cost is much less expensive as they generally use less expensive often second hand machines which need less training to use and whose cost of damage from misuse is less. The high labour productivity in large firms enables the firm specific labour to claim a share of profit or rent created. The motivation of an exclusive labour force can only be sustained if management is sympathetic to profit sharing ideas. Unionisation of labour force in large enterprises is another important variable. But these types of problems are not available in small scale enterprises.

The administrative, selection and insurance costs of loans from the banking system are quite low in SSIs as compared to large enterprises. The information cost for assessing an SSI project is often a substantial lump-sum amount which works out much cheaper per unit of credit as the sise of the loan increases. Besides, the sise of acceptable collateral which reduces lenders risk obviously increases with firm sise. For small firms, particularly new established ones, the only security available for a potential lender is its personal credit evaluation of the entrepreneur himself. Thus, process of receiving capital and loan in SSIs is quite simple and cheap.

2. The Distribution of Income Argument : There are three ways in which an economy with a larger presence of SSIs would have a more equal distribution of income :

(i) Small units with a lower capital labour ratio would generally have a larger share of value added acruing to the workers;

(ii) Entrepreneurial income could be expected to be more widely distributed; and

(iii) The typically large wage differential between the small and large firms implies that when the former have a larger share in total output more of the income accruing to labour goes to lower wage groups i.e. there is a more equitable distribution of labour earnings. Equity considerations require that SSIs should be promoted. But mere horizontal growth of SSIs without rise in productivity or upward mobility will not improve distribution of labour earnings.

3. Other Arguments : Following are the other reasons for promoting SSIs :

(i) Product Differentiation : Small firms generally cater to the low income groups and will therefore used to concentrate on brands which emphasise basic product attributes such as cleaning powder over some cosmetic properties such as fragrance. When firms of different sises produce ostensibly the same product (for example a bar of soap) the qualities contained in different brands of soap will differ markedly. Simple technologies could be more appropriate in the production of the basic attributes meeting with demand from low income consumers. Small or micro enterprises may be able to use such technologies successfully with low capital labour ratios, while larger capital intensive firms catering to the high income segment may use more mechanised technologies to produce the attributes demanded by wealthier consumers.

(*ii*) ***Consumers Satisfaction*** : SSIs some times produce luxury products, making intensive use of skilled labour, which essentially cater to the luxury segment of the market and which the large firms cannot supply. Elements in the market structure, such as monopoly pricing, advertising and barriers to entry accentuate product market segmentation which increases the economic distance between large and small firms. It is possible that in many lines of production, this type of product market segmentation helps to perpetuate industrial dualism. It is also argued that the welfare of low income groups is best served by promoting low quality products without the additional attributes. This would not only meet the basic needs of poor consumers but the less mechanised techniques used in the manufacture of these products would produce more income for the very same consumers because of the higher labour intensity of such techniques. If products made with less mechanised techniques are priced cheaper, then they would obviously be bought by poor.

(*iii*) ***Flexibility*** : Generally, SSIs are better able to adopt to changing conditions of business environment. Studies suggest that traditional mass production units have been less successful in this regard than small establishments based on a modern version of the craft principle that flexible tasks and machines augment the craftsmen's skills and ability to produce even more varied products. In India, the development of a vast network of very small enterprises is impressive, spreading through the villages and small cities and towns. These units range across the entire spectrum of modern industry from shoes, agarbatti, ceramics, textiles, garments, agricultural equipments and machine parts. It is important to note that the quick response to changing economic conditions which is often the special advantage of SSIs is much more feasible in an economy undergoing liberalisation.

(*iv*) ***Contribution to Export-Potential*** : Studies also suggest that a strong and viable small scale sector is necessary for successful export oriented growth. In the early stages of manufactured export growth. SSI comply a significant role since products are labour intensive, demand changes rapidly, due in part to world economic fluctuations and output growth is demand driven. Small firms have the advantages of low overheads and the capacity to respond quickly to changing conditions. There is a growing international preference for high-quality personalised items, often skill intensive inplace of mass-produced ones. Such products require flexibility which often gives the smaller firm the advantage.

(*v*) ***Fostering Entrepreneurship*** : SSI is also expected to perform better than larger firms in contribution to decentralisation and the fostering entrepreneurship. Support of SSI has often been based in part on the hope of reducing the excessive infrastructure and social costs associated with large assembly plants and large urban agglomerations. It is also important to note that very small specially household units are much more widely dispersed including a fairly high density in rural areas than the small and medium firms. SSIs also help in the promotion of a widely based class of small entrepreneurship.

Objectives of SSIs

1. To create immediate and permanent employment opportunities to public at large at a relatively small costs;
2. To meet a major part of the increased demand for consumer goods and simple producer's goods;
3. To facilitate the mobilisation and exploitation of resources which might otherwise remain inadequately utilised;
4. To bring about an integration of the development of these industries with rural economy and large scale industries;
5. To ensure a more equitable and justifiable distribution of national income to society at large.

Importance of SSIs

1. SSIs are much more labour intensive than large scale industry. They provide more scope for the employment of workers.
2. Elasticity in technical and economic organisations in SSI sector is higher as compared to large scale concerns. Flexibility ensure better innovation.
3. Small units have got better adoptability to variable production and market conditions. They have capacity to adjust themselves with the changing environment.
4. SSIs are expected to earn more quick returns on the capital invested in such industries where; gestation period is quite short in comparison to medium and large industries.
5. The social cost of developing small units specially handicrafts and village industries is lower.
6. SSIs are also sustainable as they are essential for combating poverty and unemployment.
7. SSIs ensure balanced regional development. These industries can be developed in almost all areas including backward, tribal, hilly and inaccessible areas. Thus, they are helpful in achieving a wider spatial dispersal of industrial activities and reducing regional economic imbalances.

Thus, the SSIs have a unique place in a strategy of labour intensive industrial growth. Due to several policy initiatives taken by the government this sector has helped to achieve a reasonable growth in industrial employment, specially at a time when employment in the organised sector has stagnated.

Nature of SSIs

Industrial units constitute small scale units, medium scale and large scale units. This type of categorisation is generally based on the sise, capital resources and the number of workers engaged upon.

Similarly, Village and Cottage Industries are an integral part of the SSI sector. The Planning Commission considers the Village and Small Industries Sector in its entirety and its definition includes traditional sectors such as Khadi, village industries, Handlooms, Sericulture, Handicrafts, Coir and the modern sector including powerlooms and SSIs.

Generally, distinction is made between small scale industries and cottage industries on two different issues : (a) small scale industries are mostly located in urban centres as separate units but the cottage industries are normally associated with agriculture and provide subsidiary employment in rural areas; and (b) small scale industries produce goods with mechanised equipments partially or fully but the cottage industries involve activities mostly by hand and are performed primarily with the help of household workers.

The Fiscal Commission also laid down the basis in 1950 for the distinction between the small scale and cottage industries. "A cottage industries thus one which is carried on wholly or primarily with the help of member of the family either as a whole or a part time occupation. A small scale industry, on the other hand, is one which is operated mainly with the hired labour usually 10 to 50 hands. Accordingly, the Industries (Development and Regulation) Act, 1951 exempted small scale units employing less than 50 workers with power and less than 100 workers without power from the system of registration. This exempted industries were termed as small scale industries.

Fixed capital investment in a unit has also been adopted as the other criterion to make distinction between small scale and village Industries and the large scale industries. This limit is being continuously raised upward by the Government.

Conceptually, Small Industry can be of three different types : *First,* there are traditional village industries and this includes handicrafts. *Second,* there are unregistered household and non-household units which are not covered by the Factories Act of 1948. *Third,* there are registered factories. The official definition laid emphasis on registration aspect. In this way small industry means the third category alone. This is the sector that is concentrated in and around urban centres. Traditional village industries are not included SSI sector. Small industry also does not include activities like handloom, powerloom, sericulture and coir making. These are under the perview of special boards and are not included in the small industry categorisation.

Historical Perspective of the Official Definition of SSIs

The first official definition of SSI was coined in 1950, in terms of the sise of gross investment in fixed assets (plant and machinery, land, building), as well as on the strength of the workforce in the unit concerned. This criterion underwent a number of modifications over the years. In the latter part of the fifties, the change effected in defining an SSI unit was mainly a shift from a workforce-criterion to an investment-criterion.

The SSI sector[1] in India covers a wide spectrum of industi categorised under small, tiny and cottage segments ranging from small artisans/handicraft units to modern production units with signifcation investments. This sector has acquired a prominent place in the socio-economic development of the country as it not only acts as a 'nursery' for the development of entrepreneurial talent, but also produces a wide range of 7500 products.

The term Small Scale Industry evokes different meanings for different agencies. The Planning Commission, Government of India, views the entire Village and small Industries (VSI) Sector as a part of the SSI sector. The National Sample Survey Organisation under the Central Statistical Organisation (CSO), Government of India, defines the entire industry sector in terms of organised and unorganised segments, as well as in terms of Industrial enterprises run by households and non-households. The Central Excise Department, on the other hand, distinguishes SSIs on the basis of the annual turnover of the units (up to a maximum limit of ₹10 million). The Reserve Bank of India (RBI) adopts an expanded definition of SSIs which includes traditional industries as well. The Industrial policy planners in the Small Scale Industries Board define SSI on the basis of investment in plant and machinery (an upper limit of ₹10 million) and cover residual units which do not fall under the assistance programmes of any of the Statutory Boards.

The SSI is currently defined in terms of investment ceilings on the original value of the installed plant and machinery.

Major **components** of SSI have been defined as under.

Small Scale Industrial Undertaking: An industrial undertaking is defined as a small scale unit if the investment in fixed assets in plant and machinery does not exceed ₹10 million. The Small Scale units can get registered with the Directorate of Industries/District Industries centre in the state government concerned.[2]

The RBI uses an expanded definition of SSI which includes[3]:

(*a*) Small scale industrial undertakings which are engaged in the manufacture, processing or preservation of goods in which the investment in plant and machinery does not exceed ₹1 crore. These would, inter alia, include units engaged in mining or quarrying, servicing and repairing of machinery;

(*b*) Tiny enterprises whose investment in plant and machinery does not exceed ₹25 lakhs;

(*c*) Powerlooms;

(*d*) Traditional industries which require high workmanship and technique as also village and household industries producing common goods of consumption, predominantly by using simple tools.

(*e*) The decentralised and informal sectors like handlooms, handicrafts, coir etc. and

(*f*) The industry related service/business enterprises which are notified as such.

The Government has raised the ceiling of investment in plant and machinery for SSI Sector. Small scale industrial units are those with investments in plant and machinery upto ₹1 crore other than a few specified industries such as pharmaceuticals, textiles and sports goods where the cutoff investment limit stands at ₹5 crores.

Ancillary Industrial Undertaking : An industrial undertaking which is engaged or is proposed to be engaged in the manufacture or production of parts, components, sub-assemblies, tooling or intermediates, or the rendering of services is termed as ancillary undertaking. The ancillary undertaking has to supply or render or propose to supply or render not less than 50 per cent of its production or services, as the case may be, to one or more other industrial undertakings. The investment in plant and machinery, whether held on ownership terms or on lease or on hire purchase, should not exceed ₹10 million.

Tiny Enterprises : A unit is treated as tiny enterprise where investment in plant and machinery does not exceed ₹2.5 million, irrespective of the location of the unit.

Medium Enterprises : Medium enterprises (ME) as those units with investment in plant and machinery above the small scale industry limit and upto ₹10 crores.

The definition of SSI is linked to the question of ownership. SSI units cannot be controlled or owned or be a subsidiary of any other industrial undertaking. This implies that in Proprietary/Partnership firms, the combined investment of all the units set up by the same proprietor/partners should not exceed the total investment limit fixed for an SSI. As regards the formation of an SSI as a limited company the equity investment by other companies in SSIs should not exceed 24 per cent.

The objectives of such classificatory changes are aimed at :

(i) facilitating and boosting the growth to SSI in the private sector.

(ii) promoting SSIs within the framework of the social and economic policy of the country.

(iii) encouraging technology modernisation among existing units.

(iv) aiding technically qualified entrepreneurs to set up new units with advance technology.

(*v*) improving product standards creating opportunities for in-house R&D.

(*vi*) providing greater thrust to export.

Small industry has been subjected to various controls and regulations in terms of the IDR Act, 1951 and other relevant statutes. The restriction on ownership is unique in the Indian context and has been introduced primarily to prevent large companies from obtaining fiscal and other concessions by setting up of SSI units as "fronts". This also discourages the misuse of incentives by establishing more than one SSI unit, in the same line of production, by the same set of entrepreneurs.

Micro, small and medium enterprises as per MSMED Act, 2006 are defined based on their investment in plant and machinery (for manufacturing enterprise) and on equipement for enterprises providing or rendering services. The present ceilings on investment for enterprises to be classified as micro, small and medium enteprises are as follows:

Exhibit 29.1

Classification	Manufacturing Enterprises*	Service Enterprises**
Micro	₹25 million/₹25 lakh (US$ 50,000)	₹1 million/₹10 lakh (US$ 20000)
Small	₹50 million/₹5 crore (US$ 1 million)	₹20 million/₹2 crore (US$ 0.4 million)
Medium	₹100 million/₹10 crore (US$ 2 million)	₹50 million/₹5 crore (US$ 1 million)

* Investment limit in Plant & Machinery
** Investment limit in Equipment
*** ₹50 = 1 US$

The term "Village Industries" has been redefined in amended KVIC, Act, 1956 as "any industry located in a rural area which produces any goods or renders any service with or without the use of power and in which the fixed capital investment per head of artisan or worker does not exceed ₹1 lakh (₹1 lakh and 50 thousand in case of village industry located in hilly area) or such other sum as may by notification in the Official Gazette, be specified from time to time by the Central Government".

Nature of Manufacturing Sector

In the Indian set up, the industry universe can be divided into various segments[4]. Factory sector (large scale units—non SSIs); Factory sector (Small scale units); and the village and small industries sector (VSI). SSI units are defined on the basis of investment in plant and machinery with upper ceilings and no minimum investment is prescribed at the lower-end. The VSI sector covers a wide range of industries that differ from one another in terms of the nature of products manufactured, techniques used, scale of production, location and marketing, etc.

The VSI sector has further been divided into two broad sub-sectors, *viz.*

(i) Modern Small Scale industries.

(ii) Traditional Industries.

SSIs (both in the Factory/Non-Factory sectors) and power-loom units are covered under modern small scale industries; while traditional industries include segments like handlooms, khadi and village industries, handicrafts, sericulture, silk and coir. Traditional industries are generally artisan based, located mostly in rural semi-urban areas and have a nominal investment in plant and machinery. Modern SSIs are mostly those units that use power driven machinery and possess better production techniques as compared to traditional sector units. Thes, units are generally located in close proximity to large industrial centres of urban areas.

Further, Factory sectors are termed as Organised Sector Units. These units are registered under the Factories Act, 1948. The remaining units of the SSI segment and other traditional industries fall under the VSI sector and are termed as Unorganised Sector Units. Such units are not registered under the Factories Act as they employ either less than 20 workers (if power is not used) or less than 10 workers (if the unit is using power in the industrial unit. In other words, Central Statistical Organisation's (CSO) categorisation of Organised and Unorganised Sector units is based on the criteria of employment in combination with the use/ non-use of electric power.

Growth and Performance of SSI Sector In India

SSI's constitute an important part of the informal sector in India. The informal sector presents a vast potential for using factors of production such as labour at their true opportunity cost. SSIs have, therefore, been the focus of the industrialisation strategy geared to generate employment and have received a special emphasis in successive five years plans, when a policy thrust is given to SSIs, the question that arises is how will that influence overall industrial growth.

It is believed that SSIs should be at least as efficient as their counterparts in the other sectors in an efficient utilisation of resources. This is specially important in developing courties like India where a resource crunch is a major hurdle to economic growth. The relative emphasis on SSIs has been mainly due to two reasons :

(i) they are more labour intensive; and

(ii) they have higher capital productivity.

Until recently, SSIs have benefited from the promotional and supportive policies of the government. However, in the present scenario of deregulation, SSIs may have to face competition from large scale industries and survive much from government support. One necessary condition for the existence of these units under the condition of deregulation is efficiency and they have to maintain their tempo for growth.

Definition of MSMEs

The Central Government, in exercise of the powers conferred by Sub-Section (1) of Section 7 of Micro, Small and Medium Enterprises Development Act, 2006, after having obtained the recommendations of the Advisory Committee under Sub-Section (4) of Section 7 of the Act in this regard, hereby notifies the following enterprises, whether proprietorship, Hindu Undivided Family, association of persons, cooperative society, partnership or undertaking or any other legal entity, by whatever name called :

1. In case of enterprises engaged in the manufacturing or production of goods pertaining to any industry specified in the First Schedule to the Industries (Development and Regulation) Act, 1951, as :

(a) a micro enterprise, where the investment in plant and machinery does not exceed twenty-five lakh rupees;

(b) a small enterprise, where the investment in plant and machinery is more than twenty-five lakh rupees but does not exceed five crore rupees; or

(c) a medium enterprise, where the investment in plant and machinery is more than five crore rupees but does not exceed ten crore rupees;

2. In case of the enterprises engaged in providing or rendering of services, as :

(a) a micro enterprise, where the investment in equipment does not exceed ten lakh rupees;

(b) a small enterprise, where the investment in equipment is more than ten lakh rupees but does not exceed two crore rupees; or

(c) a medium enterprise, where the investment in equipment is more than two crore rupees but does not exceed five crore rupees.

Micro, Small and Medium Enterprises

Micro, Small and Medium Enterprises (MSMEs), including khadi and village/ rural enterprises credited with generating the highest rates of employment growth, account for a major share of industrial production and exports. They also play a key role in the development of economies with their effective, efficient, flexible and innovative entrepreneurial spirit. The socio-economic policies adopted by India since the Industries (Development and Regulation) Act, 1951 have laid stress on MSMEs as a means to improve the country's economic conditions.

Micro, Small and Medium Enterprises Development Act, 2006

The MSMED Act was notified in 2006 to address policy issues affecting MSMEs as well as the coverage and investment ceiling of the sector. The salient features of the Act include :

(i) Setting up of a National Board for MSMEs

(ii) Classification of enterprises

(iii) Advisory Committees to support MSMEs

(iv) Measures for promotion, development and enhancement of 'MSMEs

(v) Schemes to control delayed payments to MSMEs

New Grouping of Micro, Small and Medium Enterprises

On 9 May, 2007, the Ministry of Small Scale Industries and the Ministry of Agro and Rural Industries were merged to form the Ministry of Micro, Small and Medium Enterprises (MSME). This Ministry now designs policies, programmes, projects and schemes and monitors their implementation with a view to assist MSMEs and helps them scale up.

The primary responsibility of promotion and development of MSMEs is of the State Governments. However, the Government of India, supplements the efforts of the State Governments through different initiatives. The role of the Ministry of Micro, Small and Medium Enterprises (M/o MSME) and its organisations is to assist the States in their efforts to encourage entrepreneurship, employment and livelihood opportunities and enhance the competitiveness of MSMEs in the changed economic scenario.

The schemes/programmes undertaken by the Ministry and its organisations seek to facilitate /provide :

(i) adequate flow of credit from financial institutions/banks;
(ii) support for technology upgradation and modernisation;
(iii) integrated infrastructural facilities;
(iv) modern testing facilities and quality certification;
(v) access to modern management practices;
(vi) entrepreneurship development and skill upgradation through appropriate training facilities;
(vii) support for product development, design intervention and packaging;
(viii) welfare of artisans and workers;
(ix) assistance for better access to domestic and export markets, and
(x) clusterwise measures to promote capacity-building and empowerment of the units and their collectives.

The majority of people living in rural areas are drawing their livelihood from agriculture and allied sectors. However, the growth and balanced development of other sectors such as industry and services are also necessary to sustain the growth of Indian economy in an inclusive manner. The Government of India is striving to improve the economic and social conditions of rural population and non-farm sector through a host of measures including creation of productive employment opportunities based on optimal use of local raw materials and skills as well as undertaking interventions aimed at improving supply chain; enhancing skills; upgrading technology; expanding markets and capacity building of the entrepreneurs/ artisans and their groups/collectives.

Organisational Set-up of Ministry

The Ministry of MSME is having two divisions called Small Scale Industry (SSI) Division and Agro and Rural Industry (ARI) Division. The SSI Division is allocated the work, *inter-alia,* of administration, vigilance and administrative supervision of the National Small Industries Corporation (NSIC) Ltd., a public sector enterprise and the three autonomous national level entrepreneurship development/training organisations. The Division is also responsible for implementation of the schemes relating to marketing and export promotion. SSI Division is also responsible for preparation and monitoring of Results-Framework Document (RFD) as has been introduced by the Cabinet Secretariat under Performance Monitoring and Evaluation System (PMES). The ARI Division looks after the administration of two statutory bodies called the Khadi and Village Industries Commission (KVIC), Coir Board and a newly created organisation called Mahatma Gandhi Institute of Rural Industrialisation (MGIRI). They are also supervising the implementation of the Prime Minister's Employment Generation Programme (PMEGP).

The Ministry is duly assisted in its efforts by Office of the Development Commissioner (MSME) {O/o DC (MSME)}; the Khadi and Village Industries Commission (KVIC); the Coir Board; the Mahatma Gandhi Institute for Rural Industrialisation (MGIRI); the National Small Industries Corporation (NSIC) Ltd.

and the three autonomous national level entrepreneurship development/training institutes, *viz.* National Institute for Micro, Small and Medium Enterprises (NI-MSME), Hyderabad; National Institute for Entrepreneurship and Small Business Development (NIESBUD), Noida and Indian Institute of Entrepreneurship (HE), Guwahati.

Census Initiative for MSMEs

The Micro, Small and Medium Enterprise (MSME) sector is one of the most vital sectors of the Indian Economy in terms of employment generation, the strong entrepreneurial base it helps to create and its share in production. Effective policy formulation and implementation for the promotion and development of this sector, requires a sound database. Prior to the enactment of micro, small and medium enterprise development (MSMED) Act, 2006, which has come into effect from 2nd October, 2006, this sector was known as Small Scale Industries sector.

Performance of MSMEs

The micro, small and medium enterprises (MSME) sector contributes significantly to the manufacturing output, employment and exports of the country. It is estimated that in terms of value, the sector accounts for about 45 per cent of the manufacturing output and 40 per cent of the total exports of the country. The sector is estimated to employ about 59 million persons in over 26 million units throughout the country. Further, this sector has consistently registered a higher growth rate than the rest of the industrial sector. There are over 6000 products ranging from traditional to high-tech items, which are being manufactured by the MSMEs in India. It is well-known that the MSME sector provides the maximum opportunities for both self-employment and jobs after agriculture sector.

Exhibit 29.2
MSMEs Performance: Units, Investment Production and Employment

Sl. No.	Year	Total Working Enterprises (in Lakh)	Employment (in Lakh)	Market Value of Fixed Assets (₹ in Crore)
I	II	III	IV	V
1.	2006-07	361.76	805.23	868,543.79
2.	2007-08	377.36	842.00	920,459.84
3.	2008-09	393.70	880.00	977,114.72
4.	2009-10	410.80	921.79	1,038,546.08
5.	2010-11	428.73	965.15	1,105,934,09
6.	2011-12	447.64	1,011.69	1,182,757.64
7.	2012-13	447.54	1,061.40	1,268,763.67
8.	2013-14	488.46	1,114.29	1,363,700.54

Problems of Small Scale Industries

Small Scale Industries have vest potentialities but they could not progress satisfactorily. Their performance is not good as they they face the following problems :

(i) Inefficient Labour : Labour is major but active player in small scale industries. But they lack training and developmental opportunities in small scale sector. So they are unable to contribute as expected from them. Since size of small units is not always optimal so they are also unable to understand the importance of training and development. Level of education of workers working in small scale sector is also low and they fail to cope up with the challenges of modern production system. Professionals and technocrats are also not interested to join small scale as this sector is not ready to compensate them properly. So small entrepreneurs are facing.the constraint of inefficient labour force and unable to improve their productivity.

(ii) Defective System of Supply of Raw Materials : Small scale industries are facing the problem of short supply of raw materials. Small size and weak financial position also force them to unutilise the services of middlemen to get raw materials on credit from suppliers. Canalising agencies like state level small industries corporations. STC, MMTC and Handloom Development corporations are not providing much help in arranging adequate supply of raw materials at right price in right time. So, they fail to utilise their full production capacity and it also increases their cost of production which adversely affect their competitive strength in the market.

(iii) Absence of Credit Facility : Historically, SSIs have had privileged access to bank finance through cheap priority sector lending. Since interest rates were fixed lower for them than the market rates, they did not reflect the higher risks and costs of investing in small borrowers. SSIs also benefited from the subsidies implicit in the tax standards for provisioning for bad and doubtful debts. The deregulation of interest rates in present scenario forces them to pay more. The benchmark rate of interest for banks is the price lending rates—a higher rate reflects the risks of lending to individual borrowers. Consequently, interest rates have risen sharply for small scale units. The priority sector lending scheme hardly softens the burden since not more than ₹2 lakh can be borrowed under this scheme. Besides, SSIs are also unable to generate resources as they lack systematic way to communicate their work to the capital markets and muster support from the intermediaries. Due to poor financial image, they generally fail to get their credit facility at reasonable costs.

(iv) Lack of Machinery and Equipment : SSIs are also facing the problem of inferior supply of machinery and equipments etc. Most of companies which are engaged in production of plants and machineries, are meant for medium and large scale companies. Only selected companies or few producers are engaged in the production of plant, machineries and equipments for small scale sector. So they generally charge high price for their capital goods supplies from small scale units. Besides, bargaining power of SSIs is not so much and they have to work with available machinery and equipments in the market. They have also been forced to use second-hand machines. It also affects the production performance of SSIs.

(v) Huge Number of Bogus Small firms : Government policy favours SSIs in terms of concessions, subsidy and incentives. This has prompted the so called entrepreneurs to develop bogus firms on paper to avail government subsidies and incentives. It makes impossible for the genuine firms to get due concessions, subsidies etc. from the government. They indirectly help the medium and large scale enterprises in availing raw materials etc. at reduced rates. Availability of cheap finance also encourages the bogus firms to operate in the small scale sector.

(vi) Unsuitable Location : Selection of location for the development of plants etc. also creates problem before the SSIs. The choice of location is generally governed by different consideration like availability of infrastructural facility, the cost and tenure of acquisitions, availability of labour and the proximity of markets. Small entrepreneurs are not properly trained in deciding about suitable location. Actually, they select their location due to other considerations like availability of cheap land, family busines, sentimental attachment to their traditional ancestral property etc.

(vii) Competition from Large Scale Units : SSIs are facing the problem of competition from their other counterparts—medium and large scale industries. Since 1991, a large number of items reseved for small industries are now freely importable. The Government has also announced that it is considering a phased removal of quantity restrictions on consumer goods imports over a period of five years. Medium and large scale industries are also producing goods which are competing with the goods being produced by the SSIs. So in practice, SSIs are unable to compete with large scale units as their size is small and products are not cost effective.

(viii) Obsolete Technology : SSIs lack latest technology as they do not have any techological support from the Government and other technological institutes and laboratories. But in practice, technology alone can ensure quality and high level of productivity. R&D efforts are costly venture and SSIs do not have resources to finance these programmes individually and internally. Small enterprises have a very limited choice with regard to foreign collaboration and technological support too. Their potential partners overseas have a better reputation for innovation but the investment climate in India is not yet hospitable enough to attend them in small scale sector. Special steps have not yet been taken to address the issues of collaboration between Indian and overseas small industries.

(ix) Absence of Organised Marketing Facility : Small Scale industries are unable to spend huge amount on the development of marketing facilities as they lack resources. Lack of standardisation, poor design and quality, lack of precision and proper finish, absence of after-sales service, ignorance about potential market, financial weaknesses are some of the problems which constitute the marketing problems as such and SSIs are facing these problems in their selling process.

(x) Poor Recoveries : It is general practice for buyers to avail credit facility from sellers. SSIs lack bargaining power in dictating their terms to the potential buyers for their products. Provision for credit facility with regard to sales is forced upon the SSIs by potential purchasers. Initially, credit period ranges between one month to three months. But purchasers generally avoid timely payments. A situation has now developed in which buyers do not pay their dues to SSIs for more than 12 months. It created working capital problems before the SSIs.

Remedial Measures

SSI's are holding a very important place in the industrial system of the country. Thus, suitable measures are necessary to remove these bottlenecks in the optimum operation of SSIs. These remedial measures are as follows :

(i) Effective Planning : SSIs are required to conduct detailed survey of the existing situations prevailing in small scale sector and draw productive programmes for them. Study suggests that very few small entrepreneurs launch their operations on the basis of a careful plan. A detailed feasibility study or detailed project report is highly essential for small entrepreneurs to start their units. Without proper planning, they may be affected by improper location, inexperienced consultancy services, improper technology, under-estimation of costs etc. So, SSI's are required to initiate effective action plan for their survival.

(ii) Improvement in Techniques of Production and Proper Technology: SSIs should try to improve their techniques of product and adopt modern technology. Government consultancy organisations and laboratories have an important role to play in this context. They have to arrange viable and modern techniques of production to them as they are unable to expend money on this count. Besides, SSIs should keep themselves abreast of development in technology. They should also try to give a lead if possible financially, in research and development efforts. They should also believe in continuous innovation and then they can remain in their business.

(iii) Training and Development : SSIs should make concerted efforts in imparting proper education and training to workers engaged in this sector as they are valuable asset of industry. Expenditure on training and development activities should be treated as an investment. Small Industries Associations should also involve themselves in providing knowledge and skills required for them in the changing environment. Workers should be encouraged to innovate themselves in the production process as it would enable the SSI's to compete with their medium and large scale counterparts. For this purpose effective motivation and reward system is highly desirable.

(iv) Provision of Infrastructure Facilities : Development-finance, power arrangement, water supply etc. are necessary for the smooth functioning of SSIs. State development corporation, small industries corporation, state technical consultancy organisations are engaged in provision of these facilities. But their support system needs further improvement. Development of industrial estates has solved this problem to a certain extent but efforts are needed to develop more industrial estates to accommodate more small units.

(v) Regular Supply of Raw Materials : Small Industries Development Corporations and other canalising agencies responsible for the supply of raw materials to small scale sector should take necessary action to maintain a continuous but proper supply of raw materials to SSIs They should also ensure that bogus firms are to be excluded from this type of support. Government should also intervene from time to time in arranging cheaper imports of raw materials for them.

(vi) Adequate Credit Arrangement : For SSIs, traditional sources of financing offer little scope for expansion and alternative means like venture capital are yet to be developed for them. SEBI has formulated guidelines for venture capital and there is hope for better finance facility for this sector. Besides, priority sector lending scheme should be made more broad-based and credit limit is to be enhanced. The SSIs depend more on their own funds and loaned fund from non-banking sector as they are unable to get proper support from banks and other funding agencies. The SIDBI is trying to provide these facilities but intermediaries involved in the system are creating problems for them. So, SIDBI should try to bring transparency and effectiveness in its functioning.

(vii) Effective Marketing Arrangements : SSIs should focus on brand product and market development. They should try to remain in the market and special thrust should be given on quality improvement programme. Products at low costs and passing on the benefits to consumers would go in long way to improve their marketing performance. The large companies earn handsome profits from marketing The products of small units by charging a much higher price from the customers. The reason is they have brands. So, SSIs should try to popularise their products in the market which will provide them separate product and brand identity. This strategy will benefit them in the long run However, efforts should be made to maintain standards and quality of the output then they will get positive support from their potential customers.

(viii) Development of Suitable Machinery : SSIs should try to develop separate suitable machineries for taking initiative with regard to problems faced by them. SSI's have different typical problems and that have to overcome by taking offensive strategies. SSIs Association should be offensive and objectively clear in their goals in pleading their cases with the Government. Associations like FICCI, Assocham and CII are more powerful in maintaing their relations with the Government. They should also involve themselves in focusing attention on the problems being faced by their members through seminar, conferences etc So, similar strategies should be adopted by the small industries associations to protect their members' interest with the Government.

Abid Hussain Committee Recommendations with Regard to SSIs Problems and their Solutions

The committee has identified the following problems with regard to SSIs and offered suggestions to remove bottlenecks in their operations :

1. Credit Related Problems

Credit available to SSIs is high in cost, not timely and inadequate in volume, SSI's financing also provides that there is little interactions between term loans and working capital. Term loans are available directly from SFCs and SIDCs whereas working capital is available from commercial banks. Thus, problem of SSIs is that when they are able to access term loans they failed to obtain adequate working capital, so there is need to develop a single window approach.

As regards interest rates, the SS sector had the benefit of lower interest rates during the administered interest rate regime. After rate deregulation, only loans of upto ₹2 lakhs are getting these low interest rates. Since SSI's are usually seen by commercial banks as being more risky, they naturally levy interest rates much higher than the Prime Lending Rate (PLR) on them. Consequently SSI sectors have gone from subsidised interest rates before economic reforms to rates higher than what large companies receive. Main credit related problems are given below :

(i) Absence of a credit rating agency exclusively for SSI Units.

(ii) Financing for technology upgradation and modernisation.

(iii) Delay in realisation of sales proceeds.

(iv) Non-availability of start-up equity assistance to small SGEs and venture funds to innovative projects,

(v) Inadequate marketing infrastructure and credit for intangible marketing expenditure.

(v) Need for functional autonomy for existing support service agencies such as TCOs, SISIs and the need for encouraging the setting up of private sector business service enterprises in the clusters.

(vii) Inadequate credit to micro enterprises.

(viii) Need for resource support for shifting polluting units.

Suggestions

(i) Restructuring of Funding Agency : Under the multi-agency approach for financing SSEs term finance is provided by SFCs and working capital by banks. Lack of coordination between the two has been the major cause for the difficulties faced by SSE entrepreneurs. So, it is necessary that the distinction between term lending and working capital institutions be done away with and banks and SFCs increasingly get into making composite loans. It is essential for a single agency to provide all the credit requirements of an SSE under one roof though there could be some impediments in implementing the idea in the initial years.

(ii) Credit Ratings For SSEs : The term lending institutions and banks have legitimate concerns about the low recovery of loans and these have to be faced squarely. Under these situations, recovery rates have to rise to increase the stock of financial resources that can be allocated to small enterprises. Recovery rates can be increased only if banks and financial institutions have access to reliable information and monitoring is more important. In this context, options include: credit rating, community guarantee, data bank on credit information and the measures required to make them more effective. Credit ratings can be extended to small enterprises. SIDB in cooperation with the national credit rating agencies should promote the establishment of local credit rating agencies for this purpose. Community guarantee is appropriate where the clients do not possess adequate collateral. In this context, cluster associations be allowed to stand as guarantors and their cooperation should be enlisted for this purpose. So efforts will be made to build databases of credit information. Information about the credit record of individuals will be the most effective means to check defaults. The information that banks and financial institutions share with data banks does not have to be divulged to the general public but can be utilised by a closed group of members bound by suitable rules. The cost of lending can also be decreased if SDBI is allowed to borrow low cost funds in international capital markets. A supporting guarantee from the government including sharing the exchange rate risk can enable SIDBI to borrow at very low rates of interest.

(iii) Equity Participation : Encouragement of SSE start-ups also requires improved access for entrepreneurs to additional equity funds. SSE's are not able to access equity funds from capital markets until they grow to a certain level. To sort out this problem, government has already established the National Equity Fund. SIDBI has been operating the fund from Government of India and from its own contributions.

However, the National Equity Fund would operate much better if disbursement of its resources is decentralised to the cluster level. In order to mitigate the shortage of risk capital required by SSEs, there is need to encourage the setting up of Equity Funds by a majority of the specialised branches of commercial banks and local area banks (LABs). SIDBI could contribute upto 50 per cent of these equity funds out of the National Equity Fund. It would be much more likely for these clusters to have new creditable entrepreneurs who could be assistance to technocrat entrepreneurs with inadequate resources. Resources from these funds should also be available to assist existing SSE's in further expansion.

(iv) Development of Bills Culture : The Government has already enacted the Delayed Payments Act. But it has not so far has the desired result and SSEs continue to be plagued by non-payment of their dues, particularly by large enterprises. In this way, SSEs are indirectly providing working capital credit to large enterprises rather than vice-versa. The Act could be made more effective by inclusion of stringent provisions for non-payment of dues to SSIs. Besides commercial banks. SIDBI and SFCs have also attempted to solve the problems relating to timely realisation of sale proceeds by discounting the bills arising out of sale of components/intermediaries by SSEs. The Bill culture should be encouraged in greater measure to mitigate the problems of delayed payment of receivables of SSEs.

The RBI should consider measures which would promote the covering of purchases from SSEs suppliers through the bills route. In annual accounts of large companies information be provided on a statutory basis on the extent of accounts payable to small enterprises. Factoring services should be developed by SIDBI to provide discounting facility to SSEs.

(v) Venture Capital Arrangement : Two important developments have undermined the foundations on which the venture capital industry was able to grow so far. One, the era of low-cost capital has come to an end as the Indian development finance organisations have had to raise capital from the stock markets. Secondly, the venture capital companies now face competition from private equity funds and non-banking finance companies which have entered into later stage financing in the form of "bought-out" deals.

So far the venture capital funds set up by private enterprises do not seem to have made any significant impact in supporting start-up ventures due to paucity of funds and their inability to tap the capital market. Pursuant to the announcement made in the 1996-97 budget. SIDBI has a scheme to contribute 50 per cent of the corpus of venture funds of private and public sector companies provided they are fully dedicated to SSEs. Effective steps need to be taken for setting up of regional and sector-specific venture funds. This, coupled with the liberalised tax incentives to venture capital companies will go a long way in easing the flow of credit to innovative SSE ventures.

Against this background, venture capital companies have to find alternative means to survive in a competitive market. They will have to access capital from other large funds who can share the extraordinary risks of investing in start-up ventures. The returns from investments can also be raised by better management with experience in this specialised business. Finally, the transaction costs are so high that venture capital companies are unable to afford investments of a value less than ₹40 lakh while most small-scale investments are below this threshold level.

Several changes are required in the Indian regulatory system before venture capital companies can make a perceptible difference to small companies. The entry of private pension funds would have to be permitted and free entry of private insurance companies would have to be possible. Moreover, the rules under the Insurance Act 27-A and 27-B stipulating investment of more than 70 per cent of the investment in public sector bonds will have to be abolished.

The 1991 SSI policy had proposed an enactment of a Limited Partnership Act so that it would be easier for SSE entrepreneurs to secure additional funding from the other partners who could invest as sleeping partners. This is another source of SSE funding. Besides, Limited Partnership Act be enacted as soon as possible.

The proposed Act should also incorporate the law governing limited management partnerships. These rules should lay down the rights and obligations of the managers and the investors. Since expertise would have to be sought from management companies overseas, the rules for the repatriation of their profits should also be spelt out.

(vi) ***Credit Requirement of Tiny Enterprises :*** The credit problems of tiny enterprises are even more acute and therefore require special attention. They particularly reauire exceptional assistance at the time of entry when the budding entrepreneur may not have any credit history or collateral. The financial intermediaries in the formal sector (SIDBI, commercial banks, SFCs, regional rural banks, co-operative banks) attempt to cater to SSE needs in an undifferentiated manner. In the process, smaller units have lost out to the relatively larger ones over the years, their problems typified by inadequate and delayed credit, procedural bottlenecks and institutional limitations as manifested in the insistence on collateral and a general lack of sympathy with the needs and constraints of tiny enterprise owners.

The result—high mortality rate, high incidence of default, shortage of funds and stunted growth—are just symptoms of a systemic problem: the inability, both structural and attitudinal. of the formal system to reach out to the smaller clients on a sustained basis.

For ensuring that the tiny sector is not bypassed by the commercial banking system, it should earmark a minimum of 70 per cent of its priority lending allocated to the small-scale sector to the tiny sector.

An alternative system of financial intermediation should be evolved to deal exclusively with the tiny sector's needs. This may be done primarily through augmenting the existing system with active involvement of district co-operative banks, private sector. LABs and NGOs including business/industry associations. These institutions will be working at the district level confining their activities to not more than three districts. This would ensure better appreciation of local requirements and minimisation of transactions (and costs) both for the intermediary as well as the borrower. These institutions need to be seif-sustaining in the long run. They should also have access to the existing avenues of refinancing by NABARD and SIDBI.

To help those entrepreneurs without sufficient collateral towards procuring bank loans, it is suggested that a revolving collateral reserve be created at the intermediary level. In order to compensate the financial intermediary for the loss arising out of default for the first five years of their operation, the state governments should subsidise default upto 20 per cent of the total which would be brought to nought in the sixth year in a phased manner. The subsidy should be available on a matching basis to the intermediaries against their contribution for creating the collateral reserve by setting aside a share in profits. Income tax exemption to the extent of this provision may be made available as an additional incentive. This would be applicable only to district level intermediaries. The National Equity Fund may also be made generally accessible to the intermediaries to build this collateral reserve.

Composite loans (term loan plus working capital) would be made available to tiny units from a single source with an enhanced limit of ₹10 lakh from the present limit of ₹50,000. However, while scheduling the repayment, only the term loan component would be considered. The working capital component would be governed by the level of activity. Under this scheme, banks and financial institutions should not take any collateral from entrepreneurs.

2. Problems with Regard to Support Services

In this context two problems are easily identifiable, firstly access to a diverse range of support service sources—whether government, private companies, consultancies, educational institutions or business associations—is necessary for individual small companies to identify the one most suitable for them. Therefore, the government's role gets restricted to part financing of services without any bias for any particular source. Secondly, support services such as technical assistance, training, market development and information should be available as a single package for them to be effective. In India, however, government is the primary source of support services and a coordinated programme for joint delivery does not exist.

Suggestions : Following suggestions are given to tackle the problems related to support services :

***(i) Technology Development*:** The survival of enterprises in the large majority of natural clusters has been threatened by endemic technological obsolescence. The first alarm bells rang when the exports of low-quality products fell. In some product segments,such as electronic components. Indian companies have braced themselves for competition from MNCs and have pressed their vendors to upgrade quality. In other cases such as diesel engines in Ludhiana, new opportunities for diversification into related products like electric generators and automotive components have been foregone due to technological limitations.

The slow pace of technological progress is not necessarily inherent to small-scale enterprises in India. These companies catered to a price-sensitive home market disinterested in quality. Correspondingly, most household enterprises have been promoted by poorly educated entrepreneurs unable to absorb new information. Many of them also manufacture products like furniture or crude tobacco-based products where technology is stagnant.

The critical barriers to technological development, however, are decidedly policies and regulatory practices governing factor markets in India. For one, labour laws have driven proprietors to contract work to numerous household enterprises equipped with primitive techniques. In some cases, biased allocation of government subsidy has favoured obsolete products such as diesel engines and has driven modern lightweight and fuel-efficient engines using aluminium alloys out of the market. In an industry like food processing, the Prevention of Food Adulteration Act has vested the monopoly of food testing with the government. Now only these antiquated government-owned laboratories are unable to conduct tests required by a modern food processing industry, they also deny access to information about the required standards, particularly to small-scale enterprises, so there is need to take urgent action to amend or repeal laws that are a barrier to technological progress. The Bureau of Industrial Standards played a catalytic role in stimulating technological improvements in the past but is not reportedly doing so now. In the electronics industry, an acute need for common infrastructure for development of instrumentation, calibration and precision tools has been left but help has not been forthcoming. The crafts and textile enterprises have expressed an urgent need for design facilities that is not being met. Similarly, training and quality control facilities need to be refurbished in consonance with emerging demands. So government should share the costs of providing these services in collaboration with the private sector and voluntary organisations.

The technology support required by small-scale industries includes research and development support, testing and calibration, assistance in environmental technology, assistance in pollution control mechanisms, and assistance in improving quality, particularly through the achievement of designated industrial standards. In each of these areas of assistance, new technology support institutions are necessary, which could provide these services effectively. These services could be provided most effectively through institutions based around clusters of similar industries so that they are able to specialise as well as reap economies of scale.

In order to provide a focus and to promote the various schemes suggested above for assisting in technology upgradation and R&D for SSEs, National Research Institute for Small Scale Enterprises be established. This Institute would be expected to operate as a networking institution and a clearing house for policy studies and technology issues that get raised by small-scale industries. It would promote the establishment of R&D networks on a clusterwise or sectorwise basis, depending on where demand for technology appears to be most urgent; it would find funding mechanisms for promoting R&D relevant for SSEs; it would promote the establishment of institutional mechanisms to achieve these purposes. It is proposed that this institute be promoted jointly by the central government and apex industry associations.

(ii) Training Facility : Human capability is a prerequisite for absorption of technological developments. With rapid changes in the business, economic and technological environment, it is becoming increasingly necessary to improve training of new worker and organise continuous retraining of workers already in service. Whereas many large firms have their own in-house training mechanisms, small firms do not have such facilities.

The central government should initiate a special exercise to start a training programme for technicians in both the industry and service sectors. A mechanism should be evolved to obtain participation in this activity by companies, industry associations, state governments and the central government. The Ministries of Industry, Labour and Education should set up a special Task Force with adequate representation from state governments and industry associations to work out the modalities for such a scheme. The state governments should make provision for matching funds to be provided for establishing such skill development centres.

India needs to emulate such programmes as this would be the quickest way to acquire expertise, especially in manufacturing processes, quality control and standardisation. Suitable tax incentives should also be devised to make this possible.

In the area of entrepreneurship development, in spite of having a number of national and state-level entrepreneurship training institutions, only around 10 per cent of the potential target could be accessed through new training facilities. So efforts to create and develop entrepreneurship training institutions are highly imperative in every state. Simultaneously, the performance of the existing state-level institutions must be reviewed and strengthened. The NEDB can shoulder this responsibility with the help of national resource institutions in the field of entrepreneurship.

(*iii*) *Marketing Assistance* : SSEs, due to their sise, do not have the resilience or wherewithal to spend on marketing. SIDBI has initiated action in providing assistance for tangible marketing activities like setting up of showrooms and warehouses, organising trade fairs/exhibitions both in India and abroad and permanent exhibition centres. It also finances intangible expenses like cataloguing, advertising, branding and participation in trade fairs and exhibitions. Commercial banks too can offer similar facilities against guarantees from local community/industry associations. A separate fund needs to be set up for patenting and branding. On the lines of Marketing Development Assistance Fund set up earlier in Exim Bank with World Bank assistance, a fund be created and operated through SIDBI for assisting targeted SSE exporting units. The central government's India Brand Equity Fund (IBEF) may also be suitably enlarged to enable SSEs to have a share in the assistance from the IBEF.

(*iv*) *Market Development for the Tiny Sector* : Strengthening the links of the tiny sector with the rest of industry is one aspect of ensuring markets for the former, especially in the capital and intermediate goods sector. A suitable mechanism be evolved to promote marketing outlets specialising in marketing products manufactured by the tiny sector. Efforts may also be made to develop common brand names for such products.

(*v*) *Franchising* : The marketing of SSI products and services can also be promoted by a more widespread adoption of franchising. So government should consider the removal of the 24 per cent limit on equity holding in SSEs by large companies and foreign investors. This removal would make it easier for franchising companies to take equity positions in SSEs which become their franchisees. This would be applicable for both manufacturing and service SSEs. The restoration of the excise duty exemption for branded goods would also help in the promotion of franchising as a concept.

(*vi*) *Government Procurement and Market Promotion* : Government currently procures 409 products from the small-scale sector on a preferential basis and pays a premium of 15 percent on them. Studies show that the goods were bought mainly from the large units. The reason seems to be the relatively lower transaction costs of dealing with the larger companies.

The old system of preferential procurement by the government obviously needs to change. Involuntary purchase by the government is against the basic principles of free markets. Such a system also perpetuates technological obsolescence in small companies since it does not demand improvements in quality. In any case, government procurement will not be a significant factor unless means are found to lower the transaction costs of purchases from the small-scale sector.

The effectiveness of government procurement can be enhanced through cooperation with cluster associations. Transaction costs can be lowered if orders are placed with these associations and they distribute the work to individual companies. They can also mediate with the government for prompt payment of bills. And if technical assistance is developed with procurement, collaboration with cluster associations can also enable the government to procure goods of superior quality without a proportionate increase in price.

Research shows that in India, small companies do not have a good reputation for quality and delivery. In turn, they are harried by problems of delayed payment and uncertainty about their outlets. The most important channel is the wholesaler who offers relatively low prices but. a stable outlet. On the other hand, prices are higher close to the final consumer where the prospect of a brand presence improves. Clearly, linkages with markets have to be strengthened if small enterprises are to grow. The emergence of department store opens a new and promising opportunity for small firms. Department stores are keen on direct links with manufactures but large companies have established relationships with traditional distribution channels. Small firms do not have such loyalties. However, consistency in quality and prompt delivery would be absolutely important here.

An effort be made in collaboration with cluster associations to build links with department stores. A programme should be undertaken for greater exposure to high-quality products available with small companies. Technical assistance should be made available through SIS1 for small companies to meet the desired standards of quality. The cluster associations should stand guarantee to the quality of the product.

(*vii*) *Information Services :* Generally, paucity of information available to entrepreneurs and that is not disseminated in an organised form by reputed database companies. It is also important to note that NSIET in Hyderabad has tried to develop a specialised database 'SENBDOC for small companies but failed to implement it due to budgetaiy cuts.

Considerable effort is required to create a database industry in India. This would mean that database vendors should have access to sources of information in the various government departments. Conversely, the government should have a policy to price information. The government has already enacted legislation on freedom of access to information. It will provide necessary help in preservation and sharing of information to SSIs in the country.

Government should try to develop cluster based organisations for providing technical support to SSEs. One of their specific functions should be to provide internet based information services to their constituents. SSEs can also build up on-line relationships with customers as well as suppliers. They will then be able to source from the best suppliers and sell to the best customers, thereby making them more competitive.

3. Problems of Infrastructure Development

Historically, the SIDCs were conferred the authority to acquire land, develop it as industrial estates and sell sheds and plots to entrepreneurs. Their mandate did not include the development of related infrastructure such as effluent treatment, power, etc. The Central Government's Integrated Infrastructure Development scheme and the SIDBI Development of Industrial Areas programme have not really taken off so far. In future industrial parks should develop all the distinct components of infrastructure and not just land.

The spontaneously formed clusters have expanded to a level where their further growth will not be possible without a rapid development of their infrastructure. The private sector will find it attractive to invest in such regions because their residents have a high willingness to pay for public services. So both central and state governments should redirect their existing growth centres and other infrastructure development schemes to existing SSE clusters.

Low government participation impedes large infrastructure projects. The state needs to share some of the risks and subsidise some project components, especially where social benefits are higher than the private gain. Furthermore, the government can play an important role as guaranter. It may also have to share some commercial risks, in the initial stages to attract greater interest from the private sector.

India, moreover, needs expertise to cater to the emerging demand for science and incubation parks as seedbeds of technological innovation. These parks have burgeoned in developed and newly industrialising countries to commercialise technology transferred from universities. Indian educational institutions have evinced interest in science parks.

The private sector investment be encouraged for the development of industrial parks. State governments have invested significantly in existing industrial estates and growth centres. Some have functioned very well and others have not. These existing estates provide a good opportunity to invite private sector participation in their upgradation and management. This could raise resources for state governments to invest elsewhere, while improving the functioning of existing estates. But a clear framework for these activities would be required, and rules of the game regarding rights, responsibilities and duties of industrial park companies would have to be made transparent.

Suggestions

(i) Shifting of Polluting SSE Units to Conforming Areas : Some SSE clusters have happened to come up in urban and metropolitan areas and are now causing unacceptable level of pollution. Courts are acting on citisen, NGO and government complaints, directed to such SSEs to relocate their units. Besides providing infrastructure in the conforming areas, a strategy has to be devised by the concerned state governments in coordination with institutions and banks for providing need-based facilities/finance to these polluting units for shifting their enterprises. Installation of in-house effluent treatment plants and common effluent treatment plants in the clusters may also have to be supported by these agencies.

State governments should also have the latitude to decide on the terms for entering into partnership with the private sector. A variety of mechanisms such as leasing of the estate, contracting of services, management contracts or special purpose vehicles can be designed in accordance with the objectives to be achieved and the peculiar characteristics of the region. Moreover, feedback from cluster associations should be sought to avoid errors made in the past.

(ii) Role of Business Associations : Participation of business associations in a whole host of activities is highly desirable. Subsequent to the economic reforms, the national-level associations are undertaking many more promotional activities for their constituents than before. However, at the local level, they still function largely as lobbying groups.

The government, particularly at the state level, must initiate action to activate the city/cluster-level business associations so that they can participate actively in the many activities of small scale business. The government should actively take part in designing all the support mechanisms indicated, particularly by way of providing matching funds. The central government should open a purposive dialogue with the national-level business associations to help in this endeavour at the local level.

Private participation in infrastructure development raises several contentious issues of risk sharing and pricing of goods previously available free to consumers. Business associations can be instrumental in dissemination of information and resolution of disputes.

4. Problems of Institutional and Legal Innovation

Progress in the reform of the Byzantine social legislation governing small and meduim-scale industry has been tardy. Alternatives to the antediluvian systems for insurance and social security, currently in practice, have not been found much effective. Earlier attempts at reform have been mired in the conflicting perceptions of individual ministries supervising the diverse laws. The nuisance of corrupt inspectors goes unchecked due to low liability for negligent and arbitrary implementation of the law. Finally, the implementation of environmental laws could be simpler and more effective if recourse is taken to deterrence mechanisms instead of administrative methods.

Presently, the idea and definition of small enterprise stems from the Industries (Development and Regulation) Act, 1951. It is quite clear that this legislation does not adequately reflect the concerns of the small enterprise sector. The I(D&R) Act is basically structured to regulate large industries through mechanisms such as licensing. The administration of small industries is, rightly, a state subject.

Typically, the state governments could have their own laws to support small enterprise development. However, a uniform promotional framework is desirable to service the overall interests of promoting small enterprises. It will also enable compatible structures vis-a-vis banking institutions. corporate bodies and issues of national concern such as employment. rural development and social welfare.

Suggestions

(i) Separate Law for Small Enterprises : The Government of India should enact a separate law for small scale units. The law could provide for :

(i) Definition of small enterprises.

(ii) Constituting the All India Small Enterprises Board under the law.

(iii) Aspects of small-scale enterprise promotion.

(iv) Involvement of the industry associations in regulation and promotion activities. Constitution of appropriate "industry facilitation councils" to resolve disputes and various concerns using techniques of mediation and arbitration.

(v) Voluntary registration of small-scale enterprises.

(vi) Provision for labour welfare measures for all small enterprises, provisioning also for all clearances and approvals through a single agency. Such a single business law called the "Basic Law for Small Enterprises" will be a superior instrument for governing small enterprises. This will obviate the need for a host of ministries administering diverse laws such as the Minimum Wages Act. the Shops and Establishments Act, Workmen's Compensation Act as applicable to SSEs. Such a law can be implemented by the normal judicial process.

(ii) Review and Modernisation of Laws : There is now adequate identification of all the laws affecting the functioning of SSEs (e.g. the Mahapatra Committee Report. The Report of the Committee to Suggest Simplification of Procedures of Various Approvals of Industrial Projects at the State Level (1994) constituted by the Mintsry of Industry, and many reports compiled by business associations). Governments at both the state and central levels should review these reports and act on them. It will ensure modenisation of outdated laws, repeal of obsolete ones and greater transparency. These steps will do much to mitigate the tyranny of the arbitrary inspector raj.

(iii) Consolidated Inspection System : While the government acts to simplify and modernise laws, it is necessary to act immediately to reduce or eliminate the harassment of SSEs. Governments at both central and state levels must "cluster" inspectors to stop repeated inspections from different departments. Departments must be made to cooperate so that inspection is done on a consolidated basis. Further, cluster associations should participate in this activity to do away with harassment and corruption.

(iv) Initiation of Self Certification Process : A move must be made towards self-certification. SSEs could be asked to specifically certify that they are complying with regulations. Beyond that. Inspection could be done periodically on a random basis. This can be made transparent by an open drawing of lots on a monthly basis through a random number generator in defined special jurisdictions. Once again, business associations can assist in this activity to promote transparency.

(v) *Development of Autonomous Business Service Funds :* Efforts should be made to create autonomous Enterprises Business Services Funds at the state level to finance a variety of projects in collaboration with the private sector. They would be able to garner funds from multilateral funding bodies as well as international and national donor organisations if they are governed by an independent board outside the government. A guiding principle would be that disbursements will be made only against specific projects suggested by state governments or by business associations. The funds should be staffed by experienced professionals.

The central government should provide the seed money for creating such funds in a few states. States should be made to compete for the seed money and those contributing the highest matching funds, including contributions from the private sector, should be selected. This will ensure that adequate commitment is forthcoming for such projects.

EXAMINATION QUESTIONS

Long Answer Questions

1. Discuss the nature and role of small business in a country like India.
2. What are the main problems of small scale industries in India ? How can they be rectified ? Examine government's policy in this regard.
3. What is the role of small business in Indian economy ? Evaluate the measures taken by the government for promoting small business units.
4. Discuss the importance of small units in India and examine the policy of the government in relation to them.
5. "Studies reveal that only a very small percent of small enterprises prove successful". Analyse the reasons for such a state of affairs.
6. "Small scale units need entrepreneurial, skill and professional management." Examine this statement.
7. Enumerate the managerial problems of small scale units in India. As a manager, how could you solve them ?
8. Define an ancillary. Briefly discuss steps to handle day-to-day problems of an ancillary industry ?
9. What are the main problems of small scale industries in India ? How can they be rectified ?
10. Critically evaluate the recommendations given by Abid Hussain Committee in the context of small scale Industries.
11. Examine the significant role of the small scale industries in the economic development of India. Do you think that these industries could not show that dynamism which we expected because they lacked largely the entrepreneurial skill and professional mangement ?

12. What do you understand by small scale industries ? Critically examine the government policy with regard to small scale industries.
13. What do you mean by Small Scale Industries ? Evaluate the government policy with regard to Small Scale industries.
14. What role is played by the small scale industries in the economic development of a country ? Discuss the policy followed by the Government of India for their promotion and growth outlining its strengths and weaknesses.
15. Discuss the role of small business units in increasing employment and exports in India. Offer your suggestions in this regard.
16. Elucidate the managerial problems of small enterprises and suggest the remedies to solve the same.

Short Answer Questions

1. Enumerate the problems of Small Scale Industries.
2. Discuss the rationale of SSIs.
3. Explain the nature of SSIs.
4. Examine the importance of SSIs.
5. Evaluate in brief the performance of SSIs.

Objective Type Questions

Tick the True/False of the following statement :

1. SSIs are better able to adopt to changing canditions of business environment.
2. Small units with lower capital labour ratio have a larger share of added value.
3. Village and cottage industries are an integral part of the SSI sector.
4. A cottage industry is one which is carried on with outside work force.
5. Ancillary industrial undertaking is supposed to supply its 40% production to other industrial undertakings.

Answers

1. (T) 2. (T) 3. (T) 4. (F) 5. (F).

Reason Based Questions

State with reason whether the following statements are true or false :

1. SME Act was passed in 2006.
2. 4th All India Census was started in 2005.
3. SIDBI provides direct finance to MSMEs.
4. Total investment in small scale undertakings should not exceed ₹1 crore
5. Total investment ceilings should not exceed for tiny units ₹25 lakhs.

REFERENCES

1. SIDBI Report on SSI Sector, 1999. pp. 23-25.
2. SIDBI Report on SSI Sector, 1999, pp. 25-26.
3. Report of The High Level Committee on Credit to SSI, 1998, p. 2.
4. SIDBI Report on SSI Sector, 1999, p. 27.

29

GOVERNMENT POLICY FOR SME SECTOR

Development of Small Scale Industries in India is desirable on account of allocative efficiency as well as equity considerations. But for the development of any sector in the economy as such is governed by the policy instruments of the Government. So, in the context of small scale sector too, evaluation of policy initiative is necessary to the extent government policies and programmes have favoured the development of this sector in the countiy as a whole. However, policy instruments need to be developed which do not just protect the SSI's indiscriminately but help them in a dynamic and changing environment. This would result in more efficient firms which are able to exploit the opportunities for growth. Further, these instruments must ensure that firms with different efficiencies and potentials for growth derive differential benefits from the assistance.

Since independence, the Government of India has formulated different policies and programmes for the development of Small Scale industries in the country. These policies can be analysed in the following way :

The Industrial Policy Resolution, 1948

An Industries conference was convened in December, 1947 which had recommeded that the Government should establish a Cottage Industries Board to foster the growth of SSI's. The Government proposed to create suitable machinery to implement the recommendations that included the setting up of a Cottage and Small Scale Industries Directorate.

The Industrial Policy Statement of 1948 had recognised the specific role of SSIs and stated that cottage and small scale industries are particularly suited for better utilisation of local resources and achievement of local self sufficiency in certain essential goods.

The Industrial Policy Statement, 1956

The Industrial Policy, 1956 stated that the objective of the state policy will be "to ensure that the decentralised sector acquires sufficient vitality to be self supporting and its development is integrated with that of the large scale industry. The state will, therefore, concentrate on measures designed to improve the competitive strength of the small scale producers."

The policy further states that the equity is the guiding principle for SSI development. It said : "Small Scale industries provide immediate large scale employment, offer a method of ensuring a more equitable distribution of national income and facilitate an effective mobilisation of resources of capital and skill which might otherwise remain unutilised.

Thus, the policy recognised the role of SSI's in providing employment opportunities, mobilising local skills and capital resources and integration with the large sector. For this purpose, an emphasis was placed on the creation of facilities such as industrial estates and rural community workshops to provide the required production technologies, other amenities and incentives.

The Industrial Policy Statement, 1977

The Industrial Policy, 1977 categorically criticised the earlier industrial policies and it mentioned that "the emphasis on industrial policy so far has been mainly on large industries, neglecting cottage industries completely, relegating small industries to a minor role."

This watershed policy provided for a heightened role for this sector, by considerably expanding the list of products reserved for manufacture by small industry a facility launched in 1967. Its important planks were :

(*i*) Whatever can be produced by small, cottage industries must be produced only by them.

(*ii*) The small scale industries were divided into three categories :

  (a) Cottage and household industries which provide self-employment on a large scale;

  (b) A tiny sector was brought in, for enterprises with investment in plant and machinery of upto ₹1 lakh and situated in towns and villages with population less than 50,000.

  (c) Small-Scale industries comprising industrial units with an investment of upto ₹10 lakhs and in the case of industries with an investment of fixed capital upto ₹15 lakhs.

(*iii*) Legislation to be introduced to recognise and protect the self-employed in cottage and household industries.

(*iv*) The focal point of development to be shifted away from big cities and state capitals to district head quarters where the District Industries Centre would be the nodal agency for the sector.

(*v*) Special arrangements for marketing to be made by providing services such as product standardisation, quality control, marketing surveys etc.

(*vi*) The reserved items list was increased from 180 to 504 and further to 807 items.

Thus, if we compare the provisions of 1977 policy with the industrial policy of 1956 we will find that there are no major structural changes but only a shift in emphasis. The Industrial Policy Statements of 1977 laid down more explicit emphasis on small scale and cottage industries, khadi handloom and development of rural industries.

The Industrial Policy Statement, 1980

The Industrial Policy, 1980, indicates the need for intensifying the development of small industries through integrated industrial process and fostering complementarity between large and small sectors. The policy also recognised the importance of ancillary industry and accelerated the development of rural and backward areas. Its main planks were :

(*i*) Investment limit raised to ₹20 lakh for SSI as a whole.

(*ii*) Investment limit for tiny sector raised from ₹1 lakh to ₹2 lakh.

(*iii*) Higher limit for capital investment in ancillary units at ₹35 lakh. The upward revision of limit of investment for small units, the government opined that

 (a) this would eliminate the tendency of circumventing the present unit by under-estimating the value of machinery and equipment, falsification of accounts or resort to benami units.

 (b) to help genuine small scale units particularly those being set up by young and technically qualified entrepreneurs to come up and

 (c) to facilitate long overdue modernisatin of the existing small scale units.

Besides, with the policy, Government had also proposed the following initiatives :

(*i*) Approval of project proposals for 100 per cent export oriented units and the expansion of existing units exclusively for exports.

(*ii*) A 'modernisation package' envisaged for small and village industries to suit the requirements of each industry and included aspects such as appropriate location, the optimum use of energy and the adoption of the right type of technology.

(*iii*) Maximum time for approval of technology projects was reduced to 30 days.

(*iv*) For the import of technology, entrepreneurs were allowed to collaborate directly, provided the royalty payment was below 5 per cent on domestic sales and 8 per cent on exports.

Critical Evaluation

The Policy shows that there is no major conflict of interest between the small scale and large scale sector. However, it fails to encourage the cottage and small scale industries having lower capital output ratio for initiating higher growth and expansion of employment opportunities. Studies suggest that there are 50 per cent bogus small scale units. Moreover, the SSIs are labour intensive units and they are unable to compete with capital intensive units and they will lose all benefits. Upward revision in investment limits and re-definition of small scale units is a recognition of cost realities but it will in no way contribute to curbing benami ownership.

The Industrial Policy Statement, 1985

Due to inflationary pressure on the economy the Government had raised the investment ceiling for SSI to ₹35 lakhs and for ancillaries to ₹45 lakhs.

The Industrial Policy Statement, 1990

The Government had taken the following measures to re-orient industrial growth to serve the purpose of employment generation, dispersal of industry in the rural areas, and to enhance the contribution of SSIs in exports.

(*i*) The investment ceiling in plant and machinery was further revised to 60 lakhs (from ₹35 lakh), for ancillaries to ₹75 lakh (from 45 lakh) and tiny units to ₹5 lakh (from ₹2 lakhs) however, locational condition of population limit of 50,000 as per 1981 census would continue to apply.

(*ii*) The small units which undertook to export 30 per cent of their annual production by the third year were to be permitted a hike in investment to ₹75 lakh.

(*iii*) A new scheme of central investment subsidy exclusively for SSI sector in rural and backward areas capable of generating higher level of employment at lower capital cost to be implemented.

(*iv*) To ensure timely flow of need-based credit to the small sector, the Government has set up the Small Industries Development Bank of India (SIDBI) under the control and management of IDBI.

(*v*) Special emphasis was to be laid on training of women and youth, expansion of activities of Khadi and Village Industries Commission (KVIC) as well as KVIB. A special cell to be established in SIDO and state Directorate of Industries to assist women entrepreneurs, import training and conduct Entrepreneurship Development Programme (EDPs) with a view to widen entrepreneurial base.

(*vi*) To reduce bureaucratic controls and simplify procedures particularly in the field of labour legislation as a step to eliminate interference of inspectors in SSI units.

The Industrial Policy Statement, 1991

On August 6, 1991 the Government of India announced its new small sector industrial policy entitled policy measures for promoting and strengthening small, tiny and village enterprises." The main objective of this new policy is to inject higher degree of vitality and growth impetus to this sector in order to attain a higher growth rate in respect of its output, employment and exports. The main highlights of this policy are summarised below :

(*i*) De-regulation, de-bureaucratisation and simplification of rules, regulations and procedures in connection with the establishment and maintenance of these small scale units.

(ii) Recognising industry related services and business enterprises within small scale industries, irrespective of their location with an investment upto ₹5 lakhs.

(iii) Arranging adequate and regular flow of credit on a normative basis and to improve the quality of its delivery for smooth and viable operation of the small scale sector.

(iv) To shift emphasis from subsidised/cheap creadit except for specified target groups to ensure adequate flow of creadit on normative basis.

(v) To provide access to capital markets by allowing 24 per cent equity participation by other industrial undertakings.

(vi) To arrange suitable legislation to ensure prompt payment of small industries bills.

(vii) Introduction of a new scheme of integrated infrastructure development to promote industrialisation in rural and backward areas.

(viii) Setting-up of a Technology Development Cell (TDC) in the Small Industries Development Organisation (SIDO) for providing technology inputs for improving productivity and competitiveness of the products produced by the small sector.

(ix) Ensuring market promotion of the products produced by small sector through cooperatives, public institutions and other specialised professional or marketing agencies and consortia approach.

(x) Establishing export development centre in Small Industries Development Organisations (SIDO).

(xi) Introduction of a limited Partnership Act to limit the financial liability of new and non-active partners/entrepreneurs to allow foreign companies upto 24 per cent.

Critical Evaluation

The new small industries policy has tried to create a new era in the sphere of small scale sector. It paves the way for liberalisation by introducing the concept of equity participation by Indian companies and foreign outfits. It also represents the intentions and actions of the government but they are not sufficient for effective implementation of the policy. There are a number of things which are needed to be done at the state level and district level for the promotion of SSI units. The policy is totally silent on the growing problems of bogus units and sickness in small scale sector. It has also failed to provide a cheap credit facility to SSI units.

Economic Reforms and Small Scale Sector

An industrial undertaking is defined as a small scale unit if the invesunent in fixed assets in plant and machinery does not exceed ₹10 million. The Small Scale units can get registered with the Directorate of Industries/District Industries

Centre in the State Government concerned. Such units can manufacture any item including those notified as exclusively reserved for manufacture in the small scale sector. Small scale units are also free from locational restrictions. However, a small scale unit is not permitted more than 24 percent equity in its paid-up-capital from any industrial undertaking either foreign or domestic.

Manufacture of items reserved for the small scale sector can also be taken up by non-small scale units, if they apply for and obtain an industrial licence. In such cases, it is mandatory for the non-small scale unit to undertake an export obligation of 50 per cent. In addition, if the equity holding from another company (including foreign equity) exceeds 24 per cent, even if the investment in plant and machinery in the unit does not exceed ₹10 million, the unit loses its small scale status. An IEM is required to be filed in such a case for delicensed industries and an industrial licence is to be obtained in the case of items of manufacture covered under compulsory licensing.

A small scale unit manufacturing small scale reserved items, on exceeding the small scale investment ceiling in plant and machinery by virtue of natural growth, needs to apply for and obtain a Carry-on-Business (COB) Licence. No export obligation is fixed on the capacity for which the COB licence is granted. However, if the unit expands its capacity for the small scale reserved items further, it needs to apply for and obtain a separate industrial licence.

It is possible that a chemical or a by product recoverable through pollution control measures is reserved for the small scale sector. With a view to adopting pollution control measures, government have decided that an application needs to be made for grant of an industrial licence for such reserved items which would be considered for approval without necessarily imposing the mandatory export obligation.

SMALL SCALE INDUSTRIES DURING PLAN PERIOD

Planning Commission treats small scale industries as an integral part of the village and small industries (VSI) sector. This sector comprises modern and traditional segments of industry. The modern segment includes small-scale industries (SSI) and powerlooms which use modern technology in the manufacturing process. The traditional segment consists of handlooms, sericulture, khadi & village industries (KVI), coir , industries, handicrafts and wool' development (unorganised sector). Provision with regard to small scale industries during different plans has been given below :

1. First Five-Year Plan (1951-1956)

During this period, All India Small Industries Board was established to formulate plans for the development of small scale sector industries. Besides, provision for reservation of certain items for exclusive production in this sector was also made during this plan period.

2. Second Five-Year Plan (1956-1961)

The second plan was aimed at dispersal of industries throughout the country. About 60 industrial estates were set up and certain large industries were prohibited from undertaking expansion in the areas meant for Small Scale Sector.

3. Third Five-Year Plan (1961-1965)

The third plan stressed on improvement in the techniques of production without affecting employment. Out of ₹264 crore ear-marked for the development of small scale and cottage industries only ₹240.76 crore could be utilised, 346 industrial estates were developed during this plan period.

4. Fourth Five-Year Plan (1969-1974)

It has focussed on the following issues :

(*i*) Administration of credit facilities under the State Aid to Industries Act,

(*ii*) Training and common service facilities and quality marketing services to small industries and

(*iii*) Consolidation of Industrial Estates programme.

5. Fifth Five-Year Plan (1974-78)

It was aimed at the following :

(*i*) Development of different small industries so as to facilitate the attainment of the goal of removal of poverty.

(*ii*) Removal of inequality in consumption standards through the creation of large scale opportunities for fuller and addtional productive employment and improvement of skills.

6. Sixth Five-Year Plan (1980-85)

The goals of sixth five-year plan related with small scale sector comprise the creation of additional employment opportunities, fuller utilisation of existing capacities, development of entrepreneurial skills and expanded efforts on export promotion. Thus, the programme for village and small industries was designed so as to achieve the following objectives :

(*i*) Improvement in the levels of production and earnings, particularly of the artisans, through measures like upgrading of skills and technologies and production oriented marketing etc.

(*ii*) creation of additional employment opportunities on a dispersal and decentralised basis.

(*iii*) Significant contribution to growth in the manufacturing sector through inter alia, fuller utilisation of existing installed capacities.

(*iv*) Establishment of a wider entrepreneurial base through appropriate training and package of incentives.

(*v*) Creation of a viable structure of village and small industries sector so as to progressively reduce the role of subsidies and

(*vi*) Concerted efforts in export promotion.

7. Seventh Five-Year Plan (1985-90)

The seventh plan contributed towards improvement of economical and occupational profile or rural, semi-urban and weaker sections of rural communities as well as regional dispersal and structural diversification. Special emphasis was laid on upgrariadon of technology to improve competitiveness, ancillarisation, provisions of design development and testing facilities and comprehensive marketing support. The guiding principles of the Seventh Plan for the small scale sector were as follows :

(*i*) to ensure adequate supply of wage goods and consumer articles of mass consumption at reasonable prices and acceptable quality;

(*ii*) to maximise the utilisation of the existing facilities through restructuring, improved productivity and upgradation of technology;

(*iii*) to concentrate on development of industries with large domestic market and export potential;

(*iv*) to user in sunrise industries with high growth potential and relevance to the needs;

(*v*) to evolve integrated policy towards self reliance in strategic fields and opening up avenues of employment for skilled and trained manpower.

8. Eighth Five-Year Plan (1990-1995)

The Eighth Plan has envisaged the following plan of action for the growth of small and village industries :

(*i*) Provision of incentives for the development of village/household enterprises including khadi and village establishments, handlooms. handicrafts, sericulture.

(*ii*) Exploring avenues for securing proper integration of small industries with larger ones.

(*iii*) Integrated application of industrial policy with technology policy and fiscal policy.

(*iv*) Induction of a measure of technological dynamism so that production efficiency of small sector is improved and its products can find a place in the market on a competitive basis.

In this way, overall endeavour of the plan is to ensure that small sector should not only act as a source of productive employment and livelihood to millions of people but that is must also in generation of an entrepreneurial revolution in the country as a whole.

9. Ninth Five-Year Plan (1997-2002)

The small scale sector has shown considerable resilience and inbuilt strength. After the opening of the economy, its growth rate has been about two to three percentage points higher than that of large and medium industries. The sector has matured and is in a position to make a much greater contribution to the national economy as well as to meet the competition from large industry including multi-nationals. The highlights of the provisions already made in Ninth Plan for small sector are given below :

(*i*) The SSI sector will be provided with necessary incentives and support including making available credit to facilitate its growth and development leading to increased contribution to output, exports and employment generation.

(*ii*) The definition of small scale sector will be broadened from small scale industries to small scale enterprises (SSE) which will include not only industrial enterprises but also business enterprises.

(*iii*) Incentive credit and promotional facilities would be made available to all SSEs. This would promote entrepreneurship, rapid growth of industrial and business ventures in small scale sector and thus additional employment.

(*iv*) The list of products reserved for small scale sector will have to be continually reviewed upwards periodically to take account of inflation and to enable the small scale sector to reap the economies of scale and effect upgradation of technology to withstand the emerging competition, particularly in the export market.

(*v*) The financial institutions will be motivated to offer factoring services on a large scale to the small scale sector in addition to the present system of discounting bills. The non-banking financial companies (NBFCs) would need to be encouraged through suitable financial incentives to provide/earmark enhanced loans/lending to the SSI units.

(*vi*) Friends and relatives of SSI entrepreneurs could be given fiscal incentives at par with those investing in large units/public limited companies to lend to SSI units.

(*vii*) The financial and management base of SFCs and SIDCs may be suitably strengthened to enable them to provide better services to the SSI sector. Banks/financial institutions may concentrate upon cluster approach and set up specialised branches in such clusters of SSI concentrations. Setting up Local Area Banks (LAB) by financially strong and better managed SSI associations would also help in making available adequate credit to the SSI units.

(*viii*) Technology upgradation, transfer and acquisition of appropriate technology would be encouraged through enhanced flow of credit from financial institutions (FIs) and encouragement would also be given for adoption of higher quality parameters and quality consciousness amongst the SSI units.

Small Scale Sector (MSMEs) and Twelfth Plan : 2012-2017

The Micro, Small and Medium Enterprises (MSME) Sector has emerged as a highly vibrant and dynamic sector of the Indian economy over the last few decades. It is estimated that this sector contributes about 45 per cent of manufacturing output and 40 per cent of total exports of the country and employs about 69 million persons in over 29 million units throughout the country. Within the MSME

Sector there is a significant concentration of Micro Enterprises, both in terms of working enterprises and employment. There are over 6,000 products ranging from traditional to high-tech items manufactured by the MSMEs. The sector also covers the enterprises established in khadi and village industries and coir sector.

New Definitional Framework: Recognising the contribution and potential of the sector, the definitions and coverage of MSE Sector have been broadened significantly under Micro Small and Medium Enterprises Development (MSMED) Act, 2006. Service sector, an important emerging sector, has also been included under this Act, depending on its category into Micro, Small and Medium Enterprises. The criteria of investment limit in plant and machinery is the only parameter, used to categorise the enterprises in the sector in the country.

Nomenclature and Classification of MSME (Manufacturing)	**Ceiling on Investment in Plant and Machinery (in INR)**
Micro	25 lacs
Small	5 crore
Medium	10 crore

Status and Key Challenges

MSME Sector has been consistently registering a higher growth rate than the overall growth of the industrial sector. During the first four years of the Eleventh Plan, MSME Sector exhibited a growth rate of 13 per cent on an average. There are some inherent challenges faced by the sector which have a strong impact on its growth. These relate to (i) availability of credit and institutional finance (ii) outdated technology and innovation (iii) need for skill development and training (iv) inadequate industrial infrastructure (v) marketing and procurement.

The Twelfth Plan explores various aspects of MSME Sector, relating to the growth of the sector. These may be classified under six important verticals to provide theme-based focus, while devising any strategy for the sector. These are (i) finance and credit (ii) technology (iii) infrastructure (iv) marketing and procurement (v) skill development and training (vi) institutional structure, however, keeping in view of the unique status of the khadi and village industries and coir sector in the Indian economy, it was decided that there will be separate recommendations for these sectors. Similarly, concerns of unorganised sector and special areas and groups would be given due consideration while formulating any programmes/schemes under the aforementioned six major verticals.

Strategies of the Plan For SMEs

(A) Credit and Finance

(i) Credit is a crucial input for promoting growth of MSME Sector, particularly the MSE Sector, in view of its limited access to alternative sources of finance. Access to information, simplification of loan procedures and interest subvention for micro enterprises are enabling features for timely and affordable credit to MSMEs. The Plan should provision resources for promoting e-platforms for information flow and simplification of procedures. To address the risk perception of banks, particularly for lending to MSEs, the Credit Guarantee Scheme needs to be strengthened, with enhanced budgetary support. There should be substantial increase in the number of MSEs covered under the Performance and Credit Rating Scheme which is a facilitating factor for easy access to credit with liberal terms.

(ii) The reach of the MSEs to the banking network has to be substantially enhanced through setting up of branches near clusters. While there has been an effort to facilitate credit to clusters by financial institutions such as SIDBI, reach and thereby coverage needs to be increased. In fact, a cluster-centric approach is the best bet for addressing the credit needs of the MSME Sector because of reasons of operational convenience and trust building.

(iii) Access to finance needs to be enlarged through alternative sources of capital such as private equity, venture capital and angel funds. This is crucial for facilitating the growth of knowledge-based enterprises which have high potential in the Indian context. Further, prospective enterprises in emerging areas such as nanotechnology, biotechnology, aero-space and defence applications would also require such alternative sources of finance since traditional channels are unable to meet their needs.

(iv) There has to be aggressive market intervention, such as promoting companies for market making and ensuring scaling up of operations of SME exchange. The Plan has to provide resources for such market interventions.

(B) Technology Upgradation and Support for Emerging Sectors

(i) Technology will be the foremost factor for enhancing the global competitiveness of Indian MSME Sector. The Prime Minister's Task Force on MSMEs has identified low technology, generally used by the MSME Sector, as a major cause for poor competitiveness of the sector.

(ii) The main focus needs to be on developing appropriate technologies for various manufacturing processes to bring down cost, develop collaborations between private and public sector on boosting R&D, and facilitate absorption of globally competitive technologies. Also, separate schemes of the ministry for installation of plants and equipments with advanced technologies *viz.*, CLCSS and NMCP components may be merged into one scheme, skill development and capacity building.

(iii) Lack of skilled manpower and information as well as lack of reach to modern technology are affecting the growth of the MSME Sector. Among its major recommendations, the Prime Minister's Task Force has identified lack of skilled manpower as a road block for the growth of the MSME Sector. The Ministry of MSME has been mandated to provide skill to 42 lakh persons during the Twelfth Plan period. Strategies for this, including enhancing training capacities for skilling and industry-led skilling and training programmes have been covered previously in the Human Resources Development Section.

(C) Infrastructure Development

(i) Cluster-based intervention has been acknowledged as one of the key strategies for comprehensive development of Indian industries, particularly the Micro and Small Enterprises (MSEs). The Ministry of MSME has adopted the cluster approach as a key strategy for enhancing the technical and physical infrastructure as well as capacity-building of micro and small enterprises and their collectives in the country. Since 1994, Ministry had also been supporting creation and upgradation of industrial infrastructure in the States under Integrated Infrastructural Development (IID) Scheme, which was subsumed under MSE-CDP in October, 2007.

(ii) Land and infrastructure constraints are a major problem, particularly in metros and bigger cities. As production processes of majority of MSEs can be accomplished in flatted factories, flatted factory complexes may be encouraged by providing financial support likewise. Accommodation problem of industrial workers may be addressed to a great extent by supporting dormitories (in or around industrial estates/areas). SPVs may run the dormitories on sustainable basis.

(iii) Maintenance of industrial estates (mainly maintenance of roads, drainage, sewage, power distribution and captive power generation, water supply, dormitories for workers, common effluent treatment plants, common facilities, security and so on) is a critical component for successful functioning of the industrial enterprises in any industrial estate/industrial area. It would be appropriate to handover maintenance of industrial estates to the industry associations, local bodies, State Government agencies and SPVs on self-sustaining basis. World over high-tech and innovative enterprises start in modular industrial estates. To encourage such ventures, modular industrial estates are proposed to be set up near centres of excellence like IITs.

(iv) The Cluster Development Programme of the Ministry of MSME (MSE-CDP) may be continued in the Twelfth Plan period with streamlining of interventions and also ensuring the sustainability of clusters developed. The Programme should also address the requirements of the large unorganised manufacturing sector.

(D) Marketing and Procurement

(i) Marketing and procurement are the other areas where MSMEs face more challenges than opportunities. The challenges range from procurement of raw materials to lack of market information. MSMEs face several constraints in the marketing and procurement front due to their limited manoeuvrability in such wide ranging activities either on account of lack of finance or on account of lack of awareness. While marketing of products of MSMEs mostly depends upon the market forces and individual efforts of the enterprises, Government and its organisations can play the role of a facilitator to help MSME Sector in these endeavours.

(ii) There are multiplicity of market development assistance programmes to support MSMEs, like participation in domestic and international trade fairs, bar coding, packaging and standardisation within the Ministry. There is a need for rationalisation and consolidation of such programmes under different broad heads.

(iii) However, schemes especially in areas of use of ICT for creating cluster-level, state-level and national-level B2B portals with connectivity to international markets and marketing infrastructure may be required in the Twelfth Plan such as setting up of testing facilities and establishment of information dissemination centres and display-cum-exhibition centres.

(iv) The plan allocation for such schemes can be made under the infrastructure vertical and technology vertical (ICT Scheme), respectively. The vacant land available in the premises of MSME DIs and DICs can be put to use for construction of display-cum-exhibition centres and establishment of information dissemination centres.

(v) Setting up of marketing organisations in clusters in PPP mode through formation of SPVs, which would form the focal point at the cluster level for all marketing-related activities, such as e-marketing, branding, advertising, barcoding and so on could be considered in the Twelfth Plan.

(vi) National Small Industries Corporation (NSIC), the autonomous outfit of Ministry of MSME may be the apex organisation to coordinate market development activities under different schemes.

(vii) The Government has recently introduced a Public Procurement Policy for the MSME Sector. Further, there is also need for inclusion of private sector in the procurement policy for the MSME Sector. An offset under defence purchases has vast potential for MSME Sector. There is need for setting up a mechanism in the Ministry of Defence to ensure that the offsets under defence purchases are suitably focused to support SMEs in upgrading their capacities.

(viii) All new and existing schemes should be merged into one scheme, namely Marketing Development Assistance Scheme.

(E) Institutional Structure

(i) The Institutional and legal framework for promotion and development of Micro, Small and Medium Enterprise (MSME) Sector of India is spread both at the National and State level. The primary responsibility for the development of MSMEs lies with the State Governments and Government of India supplements their efforts through a range of initiatives. The Prime Minister's Task Force in its report have made significant recommendations on liberalising the policy regime for the MSME Sector, *viz.*, introduction of Insolvency Act, liberalisation of labour laws, liberalisation of Apprenticeship Act, strengthening of district industry centre and so on.

(ii) The following issues need to be immediately addressed to unshackle the growth of the MSME Sector (i) environmental issues (ii) labour issues (iii) exit policy (iv) amendment of MSMED Act (v) restructuring of the DICs and MSME-DIs.

(iii) On the environmental issues, it is recommended that policies be made uniform pan-India with appropriate relaxation of the controls for the MSMEs. Regarding the labour issues, the immediate need is to consolidate the plethora of labour laws and acts into one user-friendly law. The enactment of Micro, Small and Medium Enterprises Development (MSMED) Act, 2006 is a harbinger for the growth of the MSME Sector. However, there is an urgent need to strengthen the various provisions of the Act along with enactment of the rules under the various sections.

(iv) However, the implementation of the process of filing of Entrepreneurs' Memorandum is still very tardy. Application of e-governance for streamlining of the procedures and for that purpose setting up of an information and database network among the DICs, MSME-DIs and the Ministry may be considered.

(v) The provision regarding the delayed payment under the MSMED Act was another facilitator for ensuring regular cash flow to the micro and small enterprises against the supplies made. The Micro and Small Enterprises Facilitation Councils (MSEFC) stipulated under the Act to be set up at the State level where foreseen as facilitators to the MSEs.

(vi) However, most of these MSEFCs are not operating efficiently. In fact, in some States they are yet to be constituted. The group recommends immediate action for upscaling the activities of these MSEFCs and introduction of an information and communication network for operation and monitoring of these MSEFCs. A budget of ₹100 crore may be allotted for ICT enabled upscaling of the EM filing and MSEFC operations.

(F) The Unorganised Sector

(i) The Prime Minister's Task Force on MSMEs have stated that no discussion on MSME can be completed without a full treatment of the unorganised sector. More than 94 per cent of MSMEs are unregistered with most of them being in the informal/unorganised sector. The Task Force has commented that in addition to the growth potential of the sector and its critical role in the manufacturing and value chains, the heterogeneity and the unorganised nature of the Indian MSMEs are important aspects that need to be factored into policy making and programme implementation.

(ii) Policies/programmes for the larger sized MSMEs need to address issues relating to growth, marketing, access to raw material, credit, development and technology upgradation. Programmes for the micro and small enterprises in the unorganised sector need to address similar issues for improving their productivity and competitiveness. In addition, they must address requirements of social safety nets for workers in these, more vulnerable enterprises. The future strategy should focus on providing social security to the unorganised workers in the MSME Sector in terms of the mandate under Unorganised Workers Social Security Act (UWSSA).

(iii) The policies for the MSME Sector would have to be devised especially in the areas of skill formation and credit and technology upgradation, and should meet the special needs of the informal sector. Instead of consigning these responsibilities to other departments, the Ministry of MSME will have to actively provide an enabling environment for the unorganised sector to flourish and integrate with the organised sector. Towards this, it is suggested that separate approaches/ schemes for the unorganised sector be built into the broad verticals—credit, technology, skill formation and so on. For example, some of the important suggestions can be incorporated into the flagship MSE-CDP Scheme as these can be done on a cluster basis. Apart from this, the Ministry may work out the modalities of how enterprises in the sector can be registered.

Plan Outlays for Village and Small Scale Industries

According to the industrial policies and programmes, the public sector outlay on small industries has been Increased during successive plans. The outlays for the public sector for village and small scale industries is given in Exhibit 29.1.

Exhibit 29.1
Total Public Sector Outlay on Small Industries

Plan & Period	Small Industries	Village and Small Industries (VSI)	VSI Percentage share in Total Plan outlay
First Plan (1951-56)	5.20	33.70	2.14
Second Plan (1956-61)	56.00	180.00	4.00
Third Plan (1961-66)	113.10	240.80	2.81
Annual Plan (1966-69)	53.50	126.10	1.90
Fourth Plan (1969-73)	96.20	242.60	1.54
Fifth Plan (1974-78)	221.70	592.50	1.50
Annual Plan (1979-80)	104.80	255.70	2.10
Sixth Plan (1980-85)	616.10	1951.90	1.78
Seventh Plan (1985-90)	1120.50	2752.70	1.49
Annual Plans (1990-92)	N.A.	1819.00	1.50
Eighth Plan (1992-97)	1629.55	2932.55	1.44
Ninth Plan (1997-2002)	4303.85	5808.89	1.24
Tenth Plan (2002-2007)	5534.00	7873.00	1.42
Eleventh Plan (2007-2012)	10330.00	12238.00	1.18
Twelffh Plan (2012-2017)	24124.00	29182.00	1.21

Source : Various Plan documents

From Exhibit 31.1, it is observed that Planning Commission has made a very nominal percentage of total plan outlay for village and small industries. It is also important to note that the share of outlay on VISs out of the total Plant outlays has shown a non-linear trend. The proportion of fund allocation to the sector was highest in the Second Five-Year Plan and thereafter it has gradually declined.

Policy Environment for MSMEs

Various policy initiatives were taken during the year to support the MSME Sector. As a follow up of the comprehensive policy package announced by the Hon'ble Prime Minister in August, 2000 for the SSI and tiny sectors. The policy measures included full excise duty exemption upto a turnover of ₹1 crore, provision of 12 per cent capital subsidy for technology upgradation in select industries, one time capital grant of 50 per cent of SSI Associations for developing and operating testing laboratories and an increase in the coverage of the ongoing integrated infrastructural development scheme.

Policy Environment

Considering the importance of holistic development of the MSME sector to the overall economic development of the country, Hon'ble Finance Minister announced a number of measures in the Union Budgets of 2009-10 and 2010-11 having positive impact on the sector, in addition to fiscal stimulus packages by Government of India and a number of monetary easing and liquidity enhancing measures by Reserve Bank of India to counter the negative fallout of the global slowdown on the Indian economy.

Prime Minister's Task Force on MSMEs

The Hon'ble Prime Minister had constituted a Task Force on Micro, Small and Medium Enterprises under the Chairmanship of Shri T. K. A. Nair, Principal Secretary, Prime Minister's Office to review the problems of the MSME Sector. SIDBI was also represented in the Task Force. The Task Force had set up seven subgroups in the areas of Credit, Marketing, Infrastructure/Technology/Skill Development, Exit Policy, Labour, Taxation, Matters relating to Special Package for North East and Jammu & Kashmir. The Task Force submitted its report to Government of India on January 30, 2010 with a number of recommendations on the above issues concerning MSMEs.

RBI Monetary Policy Measures

RBI has taken a number of accommodative monetary easing and liquidity enhancing measures in the wake of the global economic crisis, which have helped to instil the confidence in the market participants and mitigated the adverse impact of the crisis on Indian economy. Some of these measures have since been reversed by Reserve Bank of India in a calibrated manner in line with new macro economic development. The salient measures by RBI were :

(i) Decided to mandate banks to switch over to the system of Base Rate from July 01, 2010 as suggested by the Working Group on Benchmark Prime Lending Rate (PLR) system.

(ii) Proposed to mandate banks not to insist on collateral security in case of loans upto ₹10 lakhs as against the present limit of ₹5 lakhs extended to all units of the micro and small enterprises (MSEs) sector as recommended by the RBI Working Group on Credit Guarantee Scheme of the Credit Guarantee Fund Trust for Micro and Small Enterprises (CGTMSE).

(iii) Banks have been urged to keep in view the recommendations made by the Prime Minister's Task Force and take effective steps to increase the flow of credit to the MSE sector, particularly to micro enterprises. The Reserve Bank will monitor the performance of banks in this regard. The Task Force recommended several measures having a bearing on the functioning of MSMEs, credit, marketing, labour, exit policy, infrastructure/technology/skill development and taxation

(iv) With a view to increasing banking penetration and promoting financial inclusion, domestic commercial banks, both in the public and private sectors, were advised to put in place a Board-approved Financial Inclusion Plan (FIP) in order to roll them out over the next three years and submit the same to the Reserve Bank by March, 2010.

(v) To put in place an appropriate monitoring mechanism of the working of the SLBC/District Consultative Committees (DCC).

(vi) To expand the terms of reference of the Working Group on introduction of Priority Sector Lending Certificates (PSLC) to also include review of the pros and cons of inclusion of bank lending to micro finance institutions (MFIs) under priority sector lending.

Budget-2015-16 And MSMEs

Amidst India's evolving economic environment, MSMEs have been advocating revision of the basic structure of definition of MSMEs to provide for a higher capital ceiling. MSME which contribute to about eight percent of India's GDP play a vital role in the country's growth. In India MSMEs contribute 40 percent of the country's total export. MSMEs provide employment to more than 60 million people and are producing more than 8000 quality products for the international and Indian market. Permanent Establishment (PE) norm will be modified to encourage fund managers to relocate to India. General Anti Avoidance Rule (GAAR) will be deferred by two years. It will apply to investments made on or after 01-04-2017, when implemented. In order to facilitate young entrepreneurs rate of income tax on royalty and fees for technical services will be reduced from 25 per cent to 10 per cent. To generate greater employment opportunities the benefit of deduction for employment of new regular workman to all business entities will be extended. The eligibility threshold of minimum 100 regular workmen will be reduced to 50.

Basic custom duty on certain inputs, raw materials, intermediates and components in 22 items is proposed to be reduced to minimize the impact of duty evasion. All goods except populated printed circuit boards for use in manufacture of ITA bound items are proposed to be exempted from SAD. The Finance Minister proposed to create a Micro Units Development Refinance Agency (MUDRA) Bank, with a corpus of ₹20,000 crore, and credit guarantee corpus of 3,000 crore, which will refinance Micro-Finance Institutions through a Pradhan Mantri Mudra Yojana. He added that priority will be given to SC/ST/OBC enterprises in lending.

Finance minister has stated that the government would allocate Rs 20,000 crore through Micro Units Development Refinance Agency (MUDRA) Bank for the SME sector and will enhance credit facility to boost the growth of small businesses and manufacturing units. He also allocated Rs 1000 cr for support of Start-ups. Finance Minister again reiterated on his promise to set up expert committee for legislation on single-window clearance.

The Government's 'Make in India' initiative and its thrust on expanding the share of manufacturing to India's goss domestic product (GDP) has the potential to transform the fortunes of the micro, small and medium enterprises (MSMEs) in the country. Also with focus on Digital India and Swachh Bharat Abhiyan, the sector will get the needed impetus.

Salient Features (2015-16) of Budget Proposals

(i) The SMEs sector faces the core challenge of lack of low cost credit facilities. To address this problem the government has announced to set up a Mudra Bank with a corpus of ₹20,000 crore. This micro financing will play a vital role for SMEs by enabling them to gain access to basic things like raw materials and other necessary resources which are important to run their business.

(ii) Finance Minister has state that, "We also have to encourage and grow the spirit of entrepreneurship in India and support new start-ups. Thus, can our youth turn from being job-seekers to job creators." With this focus on empowering youth, skill development and special focus on self-employment will have huge positive impact on our socio-economic scenario, though the accurate implementation is very crucial for its long term impact.

(iii) In addition, the government is establishing a mechanism to be known as SETU (Self-Employment and Talent Utilisation) which will support all aspects of start-up businesses and other self-employment activities. FM has allocated ₹1000 crore under this scheme for technology start-ups and has claimed to create world class incubators. It will be interesting to know how government will be facilitating the formation of such entities by people who know the business, as after all it's a specialized job.

(iv) The Finance Minister has also announced Atal Innovation Mission and earmarked ₹150 crore for the innovation promotion platform involving academics, entrepreneurs, and researchers.

(v) In order to facilitate young entrepreneurs, income tax rate on royalty and fees for technical services will be reduced from 25 per cent to 10 per cent. Moreover, the benefit of deduction for employment of new regular workman to all business entities will be extended to generate greater employment opportunities. The eligibility threshold of minimum 100 regular workmen will be reduced to 50.

(vi) Basic custom duty on certain inputs, raw materials, intermediates and components in 22 items is proposed to be reduced to minimise the impact of duty evasion.

(vii) The clarification of tax pass-through for investors who register as AIF1/AIF2 category investors is a huge relief as this means the fund managers are not subject to tax terrorism. This clarity will ensure that overseas investors will find greater comfort in investing in private equity funds and venture in India. In addition, a credit guarantee fund of ₹3,000 crore will help small business units to fight their funding needs to some extent.

(viii) Another positive measure in the Budget is unveiling a comprehensive bankruptcy code by 2015-16. The new code will hopefully contribute to the business environment improvement.

Various measures like GST, public procurement policy, allocation of capital spending in infrastructure, introduction of internationally competitive direct taxes, sharp slash on few indirect taxes and simplification of tax regime such as subsuming of education cess and the secondary and higher education cess in central excise duty and permission to issue digitally signed invoices and electronic records will certainly result in ease of doing business.

(ix) The presence of entities that invest in venture and private equity funds is an important aspect while creating a successful early-stage ecosystem for start-ups. Currently, majority of such entities invest in Indian VC/PE funds are overseas meaning that the Indian fund managers have to deal with sector risk and country risk as well while marketing to overseas entities. The FM could have either converted his 1000 crore for start-ups or announced a different provision which would facilitate flow of domestic capital to Indian VC funds.

(x) Also, there are no big bang reforms and not enough tax sops. Increase in service tax, cut in MSME ministry budget for some key schemes, lack of specific guidelines on skill development are some prominent drawbacks as well.

Largely, the budget has some good policies for SME sector but if the government falls short in implementation of these ideas and do not take strong initiatives in the course of the year then the overall impact will be a disappointing one.

Critical Evaluation

Some announcements made in the Union Budget with regard to the MSMEs would greatly benefit the sector, but it is important that the Government puts in place a proper delivery mechanism. However, that said the Government should also specify the norms concerning the funding of the MSME sector and should make the rules easier for MSME entrepreneurs opting to exit from any failed business. It is notable that the move to form a committee to study the 'financial architecture' of the MSMEs was welcome as much of the service sector initiatives were also MSMEs. Rapid urbanisation has also fuelled its growth. He said the entrepreneurs from the service sector running services like small food joints and working as mechanics or electricians, finance was a major constraint as they had to borrow at a hefty interest of 10-20 per cent a day.

Lauding the initiative of the Union Finance Minister to recognise the role of this sector in the local economy as most of them ran their enterprises close to where they lived, he said the service sector entrepreneurs were also vulnerable to vagaries of nature and even if they could not ply their wares, they had to pay daily interest on the money they had borrowed. He felt that the move to understand the financial architecture of this sector would lead to removing the glitches it faced in sourcing finance. He suggested a comprehensive study be made before the report is presented to Government.

The proposal to create a ₹10,000 crore fund to act as a catalyst for attracting private capital to aid the MSMEs was welcome. Generally, investment was from the promoter and his close relatives/friends and by asset mortgage. Already, SIDBI provides venture capital in a small way and there were efforts by private individuals also to extend financial help for start ups. But the norms for lending to be spelt out clearly because of the risk involved in funding though the returns also would be great if the ideas proved to be successful. The large size of the venture capital also would make the available pool substantial when others join in. However to the proposal to revisit the question of definition of what constituted MSME, he said the MSME Development Act, formulated in 2006, specified the ceiling on capital equipment for manufacturing units in the MSME sector as ₹25 lakh for micro units, ₹5 crore for small units and ₹10 crore for medium enterprises. For the service enterprises, the limit on investment in plant and machinery ranged from ₹10 lakh to ₹5 crore. Given the rise in investment requirement needed, it is felt that this ceiling should be revised upwards.

The Budget proposals would greatly benefit the MSME sector but all depended on implementation and the 'delivery should be effective'. Even on the issue of evolving a simple exit route for MSMEs, the SARFAESI Act contained 'draconian' provisions and even for default of a small portion of a loan availed, lenders opted for auctioning of pledged property worth several times the value of loan taken. There is need for the creation of a 'systematic exit route' so that the promoters were able to salvage whatever they could do from a failed effort. The intention of the Government was welcomed but the real impact of it would depend on the details of the policy once finalised, he said.

Annexure 1

New Support System for Medium and Small Size Enterprises

Rejuvenating small businesses both in the formal and informal sectors is crucial for generating employment opportunities for the teeming millions in the coming years.

Improving Business Environment : Short, Medium, and Long-term Steps

Over the next few years, the government, both at the centre and in states, has to consider ways of improving the business environment for small businesses.

While the longer-term solution is a wholesale revamping of the laws and regulations governing business, a number of steps can be taken in the short-term, and a number of policy experiments could be initiated.

Steps in the Short Run

1. Create a website with all the rules and regulations applicable to business across states and the centre. This would be an extremely important portal for the centre, states and entrepreneurs, given that regulation is scattered. Ebiz set up by the Department of Industrial Policy and Promotion (DIPP) has already done some work which can be built on. Over time, the website can also carry best practices from across the states.
2. Review the existing regulatory landscape for outdated regulations which can safely be done away with. A more ambitious task would be to create a model regulatory structure from first principles that initially could apply just to SMEs.
3. Strengthen grievance redressal mechanisms against inspections. For example, in Karnataka firms can successfully appeal and obtain redressal within three to five days. To help make the redressal process effective, ensure that copies of all documents generated in the inspection and redressal process are provided to forms.
4. Minimise human interaction and shift reporting/data submission to an online-only mode whenever possible, e.g. for routine registration, repeated filing of information and reporting of information. The committee could work with Ebiz on this.
5. Shift important decision making from the inspector to higher-level officers, who are generally more trusted by firms. The inspector's remit would be to observe and document violations, while significant penalties could be the remit of senior officials.
6. Create a system for self-certification and third-party certification. Allow this to stand in for a wide variety of inspections of regulations deemed lower priority or less critical for public good. Follow a risk-management approach where only high-risk decisions/larger companies/companies that do not have a record of compliance are subject to frequent inspection.
7. Allow firms a time period to remedy faults/lack of compliance rather than penalise them immediately. The focus of inspections should shift from penalising defaulters to helping them gradually comply with regulations.
8. The existing separation of land into commercial and residential plots is detrimental to setting up MSMEs. One solution would be to designate land for mixed use and make it available to micro-enterprises when they start out. Another would be to create pre-approved blocks in new industrial zones, where permissions for a wide variety of activities has been obtained.
9. A lot of land is held by developmental authorities, PSUs, and large firms. These land banks stay unutilised. The government could institute a 'use it or

lose it' policy to free up locked land, which can be used for industrial estates, common facilities, incubators etc.

10. Flexible choices should be offered to employees and employers that reflect the evolution and wider availability of social security and health benefits from providers like the New Pension Scheme (NPS) and Rashtriya Swathya Bima Yojana (RSBY).
11. A coupon system could be introduced for purchase by employers who recruit and pay casual workers (daily, weekly, and other short duration or seasonal employment), with the price of a coupon including a premium for social benefits, to replace the cumbersome system of contributions and reporting that currently exists. It should be easy to attach a coupon to the Aadhaar number of the worker, thus obviating the need to file many forms.
12. Apprenticeships are currently stifled under an outdated and burdensome 1961 Act. The Apprenticeship Act should be rewritten/amended.
13. Amend the MSME Act of 2006 to provide a mechanism for the orderly handling of financial distress by introducing a temporary stay, followed by orderly and speedy liquidation, revival, or sale options.

Medium-term Steps

1. Get states to share best practices on business regulations and see what can form the basis for tried and tested regulatory change.
2. Based on these inputs, create a state-approved model regulatory structure that is available for businesses opening up in NIMZs. The model should include details on entry regulation, land/site allotment and development, regulations including labour, taxes and safety/environment compliance norms including self-certification, third-party certification, deemed certification, and risk-based inspections, as well as conditions for exit.
3. States would of course have the freedom to depart from the model structure. Departures can be monitored to see what works.
4. A more permanent entity (along the lines of the Australian Productivity Commission) can be set up as the knowledge base for work on the business environment and the champion for change.

Long-term Steps

Indian legislation governing business needs to be thoroughly revamped. A committee could be constituted, with the mandate to propose a more streamlined and modern set of laws, especially in the areas of taxation, labour, environment, and safety. Preliminary work can be started here, but in controversial areas, the focus has to be on building consensus for the time being.

Facilitating Growth of Small Businesses

The informal/unregistered segments of manufacturing have been performing below potential due to lack of adequate and low cost financing, rising input costs, competition from imports, and an unfavourable business environment in general. As discussed in para 9.2, the share of unregistered manufacturing value added in overall GDP is on the decline. The informal sector lacks easy access to credit and technology. The productivity gap between the informal and formal industry sectors remains large. The role of small businesses and the informal sector is of utmost importance in meeting employment-generation targets. Industrial policy need to focus on labour-intensive and resource-based manufacturing in the informal sector. Growth of the informal sector and small businesses is constrained by a large number of laws, rules and inspections. Operational compliances are required individually for almost all activities carried out by small businesses. Because of the regulatory and fiscal burden, small businesses trend to avoid becoming medium and formal.

The role of small businesses and the informal sector is of utmost importance in meeting employment generation targets. Industrial policy need to focus on labour-intensive and resource-based manufacturing in the informal sector.

State governments are formulating and implementing heterogeneous sets of regulations. Apart from inspections and compliances, insolvency provisions make it difficult to restructure and rehabilitate sick and dying businesses in the small and medium enterprises sector. Procedures to buy and acquire land are costly. Registration of land sale and purchase deeds, transfer of title and acquiring of construction permits are complicated and time-consuming procedures. While some states have taken steps to promote ease of doing business in recent years. The majority of states are still far from having a friendly eco system for small businesses. India's 'Ease of Doing Business' ranking by the World Bank has gone down from 131 to 134 out of the 189 countries in 2014. There is need to build a consensus on best practices to be applicable to all states and to promote self-certification, e-filing, and e-returns.

There is need to build a consensus on best practices to be applicable to all states and to promote self-certification, e-filling, and e-returns.

Skill Development

Skill development is vital not only for reaping the benefits of demographic dividend, but also for greater inclusive growth. To bride the demand-supply mismatch of skilled persons, the National Skill Development Corporation (NSDC) has approved 158 proposals till March 2014. The overall commitment to 129 training proposals and 29 sector skill councils stands at ₹ 2215.89 crore. A total of 19,54,300 persons have received job-oriented skills training through NSDC skilling partners since 2010, of which 60 per cent have been placed in different sectors. During 2013-14. NSDC partners trained 10,05,074 people across a wide array of sectors ranging from healthcare, manufacturing electronics and hardware, tourism, hospitality and travel to banking, financial services, retail, information technology, and textiles in 366 districts. The National Skill Certification and Monetary Rewards Scheme, popularly known as STAR with a budget of ₹ 1000 crore provides monetary reward to those who wish to acquire a new skill or upgrade existing skills. The scheme became operational on 16 September, 2013 and has enrolled more than 4 lakh trainees in 206 courses. As on 31 March, 2014, 3,44,545 trainees have completed their training with 559 partners in 6402 centres across the country. Under the special skills training initiatives called 'Udaan', a private sector-led skills training programme for diploma holders, graduates, and postgraduates of Jammu & Kashmir, 61,893 people from 47 corporates across the country have been trained. By 31 March 2014, 4318 people had joined training from 36 corporates, of whom 1451 have completed their training. The target for the next year is to enrol 8000 people from Jammu & Kashmir. Skills development is vital not only for taking advantage of the demographic dividend, but also for more inclusive growth.

NEW GOVERNMENT INITIATIVES FOR 2014-15

Referring to Medium, Small and Micro Enterprises (MSME) as the 'backbone' of the economy, Finance Minister Arun Jaitley said his Government proposes to set up a ₹10,000-crore venture capital fund intended to be a catalyst to attract private capital. The fund will "provide equity, quasi-equity, soft loans and other risk capital for start-up companies," he said.

Heeding the long-standing demand of the sector, Jaitely also announced that the definition of MSME would be reviewed to provide for a higher capital ceiling. At present, the ceiling for manufacturing is ₹25 lakh for micro enterprises, ₹5 crore for small units and ₹10 crore for medium enterprises. He said a committee which would include members of the Finance Ministry, the MSME Ministry and the Reserve Bank would be set up to examine the sector's financial difficulties and will submit its report in three months.

"The revision of the MSME definition for high capital ceiling will enable them to get greater credit from the market, in turn helping them grow and expand," said R. Narayan, Founder and CEO, Power2SME, a B2B buying platform for such enterprises.

The Budget also proposed to offer easier exit norms. "An entrepreneur-friendly legal bankruptcy framework will also be developed for SMEs to enable easy exit". A ₹200-crore fund was also announced to promote innovation, entrepreneurship and the agro industry, and also a country-wide district-level Incubation Accelerator Programme to support new entrepreneurial ideas. The budget also proposed to allocate ₹200 Cr for setting of six more mega textiles clusters in Bareilly, Lucknow(Uttar Pradesh), Surat, Kutch(Gujarat), Bhagalpur(Bihar), Mysore(Karnataka), and one in Tamil Naidu.

Further ₹50 Cr has been provided for trade felicitation centre and a craft museum in Varanasi(UP), to promote handlooms products.

The city is known for hand woven Banarsi Silk Sarees mostly made by muslim weavers who are now struggling to survive after the entry of cheap Chinese imitations.

Critical Evaluation

The new policy package aimed at stepping upcredit flows to the small and medium sector. The package is a clear recognition that industrial and manufacturing activity is extremely important and government places great emphasis on industrial resurgence.

EXAMINATION QUESTIONS

Long Answer Questions

1. Discuss the importance of small units in India and examine the policy of the government in relation to them.
2. Critically examine state policy in respect of growth of small enterprises with particular reference to liberalisation policy.
3. "The post-independence policies' and strategies followed by the Government of India represent entrepreneurial orientation.' Discuss.
4. Describe and evaluate the Government policies and their effects on entrepreneurial development in India. Offer your valuable suggestion also.
5. Critically examine the present government policy with regard to small scale enterprises in India.
6. Write a critical note on the role of Government of India policy and the small scale enterprises. Offer your suggestions in this regard.
7. To what extent present Government policy is responsible for bringing solution in entrepreneurship development ? Offer your suggestions to bring necessary improvement in the process.
8. "Step-motherly treatment of Government to small scale industries is the main cause of deteriorating situation of small scale industries in India." Do you agree ? Support your answer with reasons.
9. "Parental role of Government in the development of small scale units should be discountinued and they should be given a level playing field ? Do you agree with this statement ? Advance your arguments in support of your answer.
10. Describe and evaluate the Government policies and their effects on entrepreneurial development in India. Offer your suggestion also.
11. What role is played by the small scale industries in the economic development of a country ? Discuss the policy followed by the Government of India for their promotion and growth, outlining its strengths and weaknesses.
12. Point out the main features of Small Sector Industrial Policy, 2002.
13. Explain the policies governing Small Industries in India. Do you agree with policy of dereservation for small scale units in the country.
14. Critically examine the provisions already made in Ninth Plan for the development of small scale sector in India.
15. "Planning Commission is not so sensitive to the development of SSI sector in the country." Do you agree ? Support your answer with reasons.

16. "Adhocism in policy and programmes for SSI sector is the main cause for its poor competitive image." Comment.
17. Examine the significant features of the Industrial policy of the government of India. How far has this policy been successful in creating an entrepreneurial climate in the country ?

Short Answer Questions

1. Examine the Government of India policies governing small scale industries.
2. Examine the impact of economic reforms on Small Scale Sector.
3. Examine the position of SSIs in Ninth Plan.
4. Critically examine the public sector outlays on Small Industries.

Objective Type Questions

1. Investment limit was raised to ₹20 lakh by :
   (a) IPR-1980 (b) IPR-1997
   (c) IPR-1956 (d) IPR-1991
2. Tiny Sector was launched by :
   (a) IPR-1956 (b) IPR-1970
   (c) IPR-1977 (d) IPR-1980
3. District Industries Centre was launched by
   (a) IPR-1948 (b) IPR-1956
   (c) IPR-1977 (d) IPR-1980
4. Investment ceiling was raised to ₹35 lakh for SSI by :
   (a) IPR-1977 (b) IPR-1980
   (c) IPR-1985 (d) IPR-1990
5. Public sector outlay for Small Industries in Ninth Plan was :
   (a) 4908 Crores (b) 4303 Crores
   (c) 4506 Crores (d) 4872 Crores

Answers

1. (a) 2 (c) 3 (c) 4 (c) 5 (b)

Reason Based Questions

State with reason whether the following statements are true or false :

1. Industrial Policy statement was declared on 6th August, 1999.
2. Tiny sector was brought in the Industrial Policy Statement of 1980.
3. Concept of limited liability partnership allowed foreign companies to invest in SSI sector upto a limit of 24 per cent of capital of the unit concerned.
4. Technology Development Cell is working in SIDO
5. Carry on Business (COB) licence is required for all SSI units.

30

INSTITUTIONAL SUPPORT FOR SMALL SCALE SECTOR

SSIs are generally promoted by first generation entrepreneurs. These entrepreneurs lack technical and managerial skills, strong financial background, knowledge about government sponsored infrastructural facilities and subsidies and tax incentives. They also lack information about existing support systems developed by the Central Government as well as State Governments. So, institutional support system is necessary to provide all needed help to the first generation entrepreneurs. Development of institutional support system is a must to accelerate the growth of entrepreneurship in the country.

The term 'institutional support system' generally refers to the economic environment of industry and business comprising authorities and institutions whose decisions and operational framework affect the level of business. These institutions include government owned agencies, statutory corporations and semi-autonomous and autonomous organisations. In our country, these authorities and agencies are government sponsored organisations and entrusted with sufficient powers to regulate and promote SSIs in specific areas of activities.

Basically, institutional support system is necessary at three stages of enterprise development. These are : (*i*) inception or promotion of a business or industrial unit; (*ii*) day to day management or routine management and (*iii*) expansion and diversification.

In the Indian context, institutional support systems include three dimensions : (*i*) support system developed by Central Government, (*ii*) support system developed by State Governments and (*iii*) Non-Government support system.

A. SUPPORT SYSTEM DEVELOPED BY THE CENTRAL GOVERNMENT

The Department of small scale industries was developed in 1991 under the Ministry of Industry. This department has been responsible for the development and monitoring of the following support system :

1. Small Scale Industries Board (SSI Board)

It was established in 1954 to provide effective coordination and inter-institutional linkages for the benefits of small scale sector. The Board being an apex body has been entrusted to play its advisory role in solving the problems of small scale sector.

The Board has been constituted with the following members:

(a)	Union Industry Minister	Chairman
(b)	State Industry Ministers	Members
(c)	Selected Members of Parliament	Members
(d)	Secretaries of Departments Concerned	Members
(e)	Financial Institutions	Members
(f)	Selected Public Enterprises	Members
(g)	Industry Associations	Members
(h)	Eminent Experts in the field	Members

2. National Board for Micro, Small and Medium Enterprises (NBMSME)

The Government established the National Board for Micro, Small and Medium Enterprises (NBMSME) under the Micro, Small and Medium Enterprises Development Act, 2006 and Rules made thereunder. The Board examines the factors affecting promotion and development of MSMEs and reviews policies and programmes from time to time relating to these enterprises and makes recommendations to the Government in formulating the policies for the growth of MSMEs.

The Government of India had constituted the National Commission for Enterprises in the Unorganised Sector (NCEUS) to examine the problems of the enterprises in the unorganised/informal sector. The Commission has made recommendations to provide technical, marketing and credit support to these enterprises and submitted 11 Reports to the Government.

3. Small Industries Development Organisation (SIDO)

It is another version of the office of Development Commissioner for small scale industries. It was constituted in 1954 to develop support services for the promotion of small scale sector. Additional Secretary to the Government of India is expected to work as Development Commissioner (SSI) in ex-officio capacity. It is responsible to work as a total organisation with regard to execution of government policies and programmes. The main ***objectives*** of the SIDO are given below :

(*i*) To formulate an all India policy and programme for the promotion of SSIs.

(*ii*) To provide coordination about policies and programmes of State Governments.

(*iii*) To maintain liaison with Central Government and different State Government departments. Planning Commission, Reserve Bank of India and All India Financial Institutions.

(iv) To collect and disseminate economic information concerned with SSIs.

(v) To provide wide range of extension services through allied institutions.

(vi) To promote facilities for technology upgradatlon, modernisation, quality improvement in SSI Sector.

(vii) To offer consultancy services in the area of technical and managerial field.

Services Rendered by SIDO : The SIDO is engaged in the provision of the following support services :

(i) Entrepreneurship Development and Management Training : The basic purpose of this programme is to identify entrepreneurial capabilities and motivate and train the entrepreneurs so that they can easily set up their industrial units with confidence. Under the guidance and administrative control of SIDO, the following organisations are responsible to provide such as :

(a) Small Industries Service Institutes (SISIs) and branch institutions are engaged in running a variety of Entrepreneurship Development Programmes and Management training programmes for potential entrepreneurs.

(b) The National Institute for Entrepreneurship and Small Business Development (NIESBUD) and the National Institute of Small Industry Extension and Training (NISIET) are required to organise Entrepreneurship Development Programmes and devise training materials for entrepreneurial trainers.

(ii) Provision of Extension and Training Services : The SIDO also ensures guidance and assistance on technical, economic, managerial and other matters to first generation entrepreneurs. The SISIs/Branch SISI's controlled workshops are engaged in initiating different types of job works from SSI units. Their services are quite cost-effective.

(iii) Efforts for Skill Development : The SIDO is trying its best to arrange training facilities for technical skill development to technicians and workers at SISI controlled workshops located in different parts of the country. Besides, testing centres, tool rooms and training centres, tool design institutes etc. are providing training facilities to workers engaged in SSI sector.

(iv) Preparation of Feasibility Reports for Different Products : The SIDO prepares project profiles related with different product groups. Assessment and preparation of industrial potentialities/feasibility reports for various product groups are also undertaken by the SIDO. In project profiles, detailed information on product manufacturing process, market potential, quality control and standards, investments requirement, availability of raw materials and machineries, viability are also evaluated and necessary advice to potential entrepreneurs are made available. The SIDO also tries to collect information on market and technologies and evaluate their suitability to SSI sector.

(v) *Provision of Testing Services* : SISI controlled testing centres are providing testing facilities to SSIs. These testing facilities are available at Regional Testing Centres at New Delhi, Mumbai, Kolkata and Chennai. Field testing stations are also doing the same job. Main functions of these testing centres and field stations are to provide certification facilities for quality assurance. It increases the marketability of products being produced by the SSI Sector.

(vi) *Establishment of Sub-Contract Exchanges* : Major SISIs have also promoted 16 sub-contract exchanges to develop ancillarisation programme in the country. Main functions of these exchanges are to (a) register spare capacities available in SSI and tiny units, (b) identify the items required by large units and match this need with spare capacity available in SSI sector, (c) ensure interaction between small and large units and, (d) organise vender development programmes, exhibitions and promotional programmes etc.

(vii) *Availability of Tool Room Facilities* : Generally, SSI units are unable to establish individual tool rooms facilities as huge investment is required in these tool rooms. However tool-room facility is the heart of engineering industry. Tool room facilities are available at Hyderabad, Ludhiana, Kolkata, Jalandhar, Nagaur, Aurangabad, Indore, Ahmedabad, Bhubaneshwar and Jamshedpur. The main functions of Tool Rooms are to (a) design/manufacture dies/tools, jigs and fixtures, gauges, tool components etc., (b) provide service facilities for manufacturing tools, heat treatment, testing etc., (c) arrange training to tools and die makers, (d) organise short term/part time courses for entrepreneurs, and (e) undertake product-cum-process development work in specific industry groups.

SIDO Administered Institutes/Centres : The SIDO has promoted the following Institutes and centres and is responsible for their management :

(i) *Small Industries Service Institutes* : At present SIDO has been administering 28 SISIs and 30 branch SISIs working in different parts of tie country. Actually, these institutes are responsible to undertake the following functions : (a) to interface between central and State governments, (b) to provide technical support services and consultancy services, (c) to undertake entrepreneurship development programmes, (d) to promote ancillarisation programme, and (e) to ensure efforts for export promotion and liaison activities.

(ii) *Product-cum-Process Development Centres* : These have been promoted to provide specific service to different types of small scale units concentrated in different locations. These centres are working at Ferozabad (glass industry), Kannauj (fragrance oils), Meerut (sport-goods), Ramnagar (electronic industry), Mumbai (electrical measuring instruments) and Agra (foundry and forging). These centres are responsible for the following functions : (a) to serve as research and development institutions in areas of dense industry clusters; (b) to encourage product design and innovation; (c) to develop new processes and upgrade the existing level of technology; (d) to act as centres of excellent in respective areas; and (e) to provide technical and managerial support services.

(iii) Regional Training Centres : These centres are located at Chennai. New Delhi. Mumbai and Kolkata. They are responsible for quality awareness programme among small units. For this purpose, they are engaged in systematic testing and technical consultancy services. These centres are also responsible to assist field testing stations which are expected to provide testing services to SSI units. These stations are available at Dehradun, Jaipur, Bhopal, Kolhapur, Hyderabad, Bangalore, Pondicherry and Changanacherry.

(iv) Establishment of Training Institutes : The SIDO is also controlling the affairs of NISIET (Hyderabad); NIESBUD (New Delhi) and integrated training centre (Industries) at Nilokheri. These institutes are responsible for arranging training facility to entrepreneurial trainers.

(v) Establishment of Central Footwear Training Institutes : These institutes are required to extend support services to SSI units in leather and footwear segments. These institutes are located in Agra, Chennai, Kolkata and Mumbai. The main functions of these institutes are to (a) provide training facility to manpower engaged in footwear industry, (b) develop designs and new types of footwear to promote export.

Thus, the SIDO has been playing very important role in promotion of different types of support services required for the development of SSI sector in India.

New Role of Development Commission of MSME

The O/o DC (MSME) was established as Small Industries Development Organisation (SIDO) {also referred to as Micro, Small and Medium Enterprises - Development Office (MSME-DO)} in 1954 on the basis of the recommendations of the Ford Foundation. The MSME-DO is playing a very constructive role by rendering comprehensive services including consultancy through institutional set-up of its field organisations spread over different parts of the country. The Office of the Development Commissioner (Micro, Small and Medium Enterprises) has been functioning as an apex/nodal organisation and provides link between the Ministry/Department and field organisations. It has been working as an attached office to the Ministry of Small Scale Industries (now Ministry of Micro, Small and Medium Enterprises) since September, 2001. Over the years, it has witnessed its role evolve into an agency for advocacy, handholding and facilitation of the small industries sector. It has over 60 offices and 21 autonomous bodies [including 2 Departmental Training Institutes (MSME-TIs) and one departmental Hand Tools Development Centre (MSME-TDCH and Tools)] under administrative control. These autonomous bodies include Tool Rooms; Training Institutions and Technology Development Centres. It provides a wide spectrum of services to the small industries sector, now enlarged to also include Micro, Small and Medium Enterprises. The Services, *inter-alia,* include facilities for testing, tool making, training for entrepreneurship development, preparation of project and product profiles, technical and managerial consultancy, assistance for exports, pollution and energy audits etc. The organisation provides economic information services and also advises Government in policy formulation for the promotion and development of MSME sector. Its field offices also work as effective links between the Central and the State Governments in the area of MSME development.

As a result of the globalisation and liberalisation of the economy, the units in the sector were increasingly called upon to face new and bigger challenges not only from MNCs etc. but also from bigger domestic players. Recognising the dynamics of the new environment in which these units were operating, the O/o DC (MSME) now focuses on providing support in the fields of credit, marketing, technology and infrastructure. The emerging global trends and national developments have transformed the role of the organisation into that of catalyst of growth of small enterprises in the country.

Major Functions

The major functions of the Organisation are :

(i) Advising the Government in policy formulation for the promotion and development of MSME Sector;

(ii) Providing techno-economic and managerial consultancy, common facilities and extension services to the MSME Sector;

(iii) Making Available facilities for technology upgradation, modernisation, quality improvement and infrastructure;

(iv) Developing Human Resources through training and skill upgradation;

(v) Providing economic information services;

(vi) Maintaining a close liaison with the Central Ministries, Planning Commission, State Governments, Financial Institutions and other organisations concerned with development of MSME Sector; and

(vii) Evolving and coordinating Policies and Programmes for development of the Sector as ancillaries to large industries.

4. National Small Industries Corporation (NSIC)

The NSIC was promoted by Government of India as a public undertaking in 1955. It is responsible for promoting and developing small scale industries in the country. Its main objectives are to promote, aid and foster the development of SSI in India. Main functions of the NSIC are as follows :

(i) Supply of Machinery and Equipments : The NSIC is ensuring supply of machinery and equipments from different sources to SSIs. In this context it has two schemes : Hire-purchase scheme and Lease scheme. Under hire-purchase scheme, it arranges indigenous and imported machinery on easy instalments. In case of lease scheme, 100% financial facilities are available to small entrepreneurs which enable them to diversify and ensure technology upgradation. Besides, they can also claim tax rebate on lease rentals paid to NSIC.

(ii) Provision of Financial Assistance : The NSIC has established five financial centres to extend financial support to SSIs. These centres are located at New Delhi, Mumbai, Ahmedabad, Bangalore and Goa. The purposes for which these financial facilities are available include (i) marketing, (ii) bills discounting, (iii) purchase of raw materials, (iv) export activities.

(iii) Assistance for the Arrangement of Raw Materials : The NSIC assists SSIs in arranging raw materials. These assistance are generally available in the form of (a) supply of raw materials under the off the shelf basis scheme; (b) import of raw materials; (c) supply of scarce raw materials on priority basis and (d) supply of raw materials from deposits, godowns created by the NSIC for the purpose.

(iv) Establishment of Technology Transfer Centres : At the enterprise level, SSIs are interested to avail facilities for technology acquisition, adoption and upgradation. The NSIC assists SSIs in these areas through its technology information and promotion services. For this purpose a separate technology transfer centre has been promoted at Okhla (Delhi). Besides, NSIC also provides different types of services to SSI sector which include (a) information dissemination on technology, business and investment opportunities, (b) arranging business partners and latest technology world wide, (c) ensuring technology transfer programmes through missions, delegations and expositions, (d) provisioning training consultancy and technology evaluation facilities and providing library facilities and development of network to access database.

Technical Service Centres (TSC). established by NSIC In different parts of the country, provide diverse technical support to small scale sector. The centres have done significant work in meeting the manpower and technology needs of the small units.

(v) Arrangement of Marketing Assistance : The NSIC has been authorised by the government to ensure marketing assistance to SSI sector. In this context, NSIC is responsible to (a) ensure adequate margin or return to small entrepreneurs, (b) encourage standardisation and quality control for the products of SSI sector, (c) assist in the development of brand/command brand making the products more marketable, (d) try to upgrade technology by supplying sophisticated machinery and equipment, and (e) ensure effective advertising and publicity for SSI products.

(vi) Priority in Government Purchase Programme : Under this programme only registered SSI units are allowed to avail the benefits of single point registration scheme. These benefits include (a) supply of tender form free of cost; (b) prior information with regard to tenders issued by JDG S & D; (c) freedom from security deposit upto the monetary limit for the unit is registered; (d) exemption from payment of earnest money; (e) issue of competency certificate in case the value of an order exceeds the monetary limit after due verification; (f) and price preference upto 15 percent on merit over the price quoted by large units and the procurement as per the reserve list.

5. Small Industries Development Bank of India (SIDBI)

The SIDBI, over the years has striven to fulfil the role enshrined in its charter by formulating and reorienting its policies, gearing up operations and enlarging the profile of its promotional and developmental activities aimed at facilitating entrepreneurial entry and strengthening the small scale sector to enable them to meet the emerging challenges. From mere traditional refinancing institution, it has emerged stronger in meeting the varied requirements of the SSI sector by exploring new areas and seeding option for future growth, like launching new financial products and instruments and support service programmes.

Small Industries Development Bank of India (SIDBI), a wholly-owned subsidiary of Industrial Development Bank of India (IDBI), set up by an Act of Parliament, is the principal financial institution for the promotion, financing and development of industry in the small, tiny and cottage sectors and for co-ordinating the functions of the institutions engaged in similar activities. It commenced its operations on April 2, 1990 by taking over the outstanding portfolio and activities of IDBI pertaining to the small scale sector and has emerged, over the years as the main purveyor of credit to small, tiny and cottage sectors.

Given the apex role, the approach of SIDBI has been to supplement the efforts of existing institutions, strengthening their capabilities through financial and support services and instituting suitable co-ordination mechanism while providing assistance for the small scale sector. While continuing with the schemes operated by IDBI under Small Industries Development Fund (SIDF), the Bank took initiatives by identifying the gaps in existing credit delivery system and devised tailor-made schemes for direct lending to small scale sector so as to supplement the efforts of Primary Lending Institutions (PLIs), which include State Financial Corporations (SFCs), State Industrial Development Corporations (SIDCs) (including twin-function IDCs), Scheduled Commercial Banks (SCBs) both in public and private sector, State Co-operative Banks, scheduled Urban Co-operative Banks and Regional Rural Banks (RRBs).

Under indirect assistance, assistance to small scale sector is channelised through the large network of PLIs across the country by way of refinance, bills rediscounting and resource support in the form of lines of credit in lieu of refinance etc.

New Initiatives of SIDBI for MSMEs : In the recent years SIDBI has provided various supports to the MSMEs in the country. These supports are as follows :

(i) Promoting Energy Efficiency *:* The MSMEs in India have good potential for improving productivity and competitiveness through Energy Efficiency (EE) measures in production process. In order to upscale EE financing for the MSME sector, SIDBI contracted bilateral Lines of Credit from Japan International Cooperation Agency (JICA), Japan; KfW, Germany and French Development Agency (AFD), France. During the year under review, the Bank introduced a Scheme for "Promoting Investment in Energy Efficiency projects in MSME sector" to provide loan assistance at concessional terms to MSMEs to invest in energy saving technologies. To have wider coverage, the Bank has provided resource support to banks, SFCs and NBFCs for onlending to MSMEs for energy saving projects. Simultaneously, the Bank has launched awareness campaigns on EE measures in the energy intensive MSME clusters and has also provided technical support services to MSMEs for identifying EE technology/equipments.

(ii) Promoting Clean Production Measures : To promote investment in clean technologies, CETPs, waste recycling and management in MSME units/clusters, the Bank availed a World Bank Line of Credit based on Environmental and Social (E&S) standards. The utilisation of the World Bank loan has been satisfactory. Further, the Bank introduced a scheme to provide "Assistance for Clean Production Options" from April 2010, under which, apart from financial assistance at concessional terms, technical support is also provided to MSMEs for investing in environmentally friendly technologies.

(iii) World Bank Global Environment Facility Project (WB-GEF) : SIDBI, along with BEE, is implementing a new initiative on financing EE measures under WB-GEF in 5 MSME clusters, *viz.* Kolhapur, Pune, Tirunelveli, Ankaleshwar and Faridabad to improve EE and reduce Green House Gas (GHG) emissions from MSMEs utilising increased commercial financing for EE.

(iv) Assistance to Mumbai Taximen : The Hon'ble High Court of Maharashtra had passed an order for phasing out taxis plying in Mumbai which are more than 25 years old. SIDBI devised a special scheme for providing assistance to these taxi owners for replacing the old taxis with latest energy efficient versions, using a simplified credit delivery arrangement with active involvement of the two local taxi associations. Under the arrangement, assistance at concessional rate is offered with credit guarantee coverage by Credit Guarantee fund Trust for Micro and Small Enterprises (CGTMSE). So far, over 800 taxi owners have been provided collateral free loans for buying new CNG taxis in place of older polluting ones.

(v) Auto Rickshaw Financing : 600 LPG fitted Auto Rickshaws were provided assistance in Chandigarh by Delhi Finance Corporation (DFC). SIDBI provided refi nance to DFC for this clean energy initiative.

(vi) Solar Lanterns : Friends of Women's World Banking (FWWB), a Micro Finance Institution (MFI), was sanctioned assistance of ₹10 crore for providing assistance to micro entrepreneurs in Manipur and other North Eastern States for purchasing Solar Lanterns of 2 watts each. 50,000 micro entrepreneurs are proposed to be covered under the assistance.

(vii) Rickshaw Sangh Programme : SIDBI signed an MoU with American India Foundation (AIF) to provide livelihood support to the low-income groups through a joint initiative called the "Rickshaw Sangh Programme", under which the Bank sanctioned financial assistance of ₹50 lakh to Bhartiya Micro Credit (BMC) under its Micro Credit Scheme for microfinance as well as for financing livelihood programmes. BMC, under the Programme, has provided 500 Rickshaws to disadvantaged persons residing in and around Lucknow with the credit support from the Bank and technical support from AIF. As a part of the Bank's Corporate Social Responsibility, these clients are also being provided various non-credit support, such as, getting the licence and Municipal permits, uniforms, life insurance covers for client and spouse, accident insurance for the rickshaw clients, opening of savings bank account etc. The initiative is proposed to be scaled up in other backward states through more MFIs.

(viii) Green Rating : As part of its commitment to sustainable development, the Bank supported SME Rating Agency of India Ltd. (SMERA) to develop Green Rating model for MSMEs. Green rating assesses the compatibility of an industrial unit to adhere to manufacturing processes, along with efficient use of resources with minimum environmental damage. It also takes into account compliance of environmental regulatory norms by MSMEs. To encourage MSMEs to go for green rating, SIDBI gives concession in interest rate upto 50 bps in its loan assistance to MSMEs obtaining green rating of 'SMERA Green 3' and above.

(ix) MSME Receivable Finance Scheme : SIDBI operates the MSME Receivable Finance Scheme (RFS) for MSME sellers/ eligible service providers in respect of sales & services rendered to purchaser companies. Under the Scheme, SIDBI fixes limits to well performing purchaser companies and discounts usance bills of MSMEs/ eligible services, etc. So that the MSME/ services sector units realise their sale proceeds quickly. SIDBI also offers invoice discounting facilities to the MSME suppliers of purchaser companies.

(x) NTREES: SIDBI, along with National Stock Exchange (NSE), took an initiative for setting up an electronic platform for discounting of MSME receivables. The e-platform is named as NTRESS (NSE Trade Receivables Engine for E-discounting in association with SIDBI). Operations on the platform are on RTGS basis and all the participants are beging provided with system generated passwords for accessing the site. At present, trade receivables under MSME Receivable Finance Scheme limits sanctioned by SIDBI have been shifted on NTRESS.

(xi) CART : SIDBI had been using Credit Appraisal and Rating Tool (CART), an IT-based mechanism for appraising and rating loan exposure uptro ₹100 lakhs for existing profit making MSMEs. With the experience gained, it is now being used for loan exposure upto ₹200 lakhs. So far, more than 4,000 loan applications have been processed in CART, snstioning more than ₹800 crore. The Tool has been used as an effective mechanism for quantification of credit risk of small loans, there by enabling faster credit delivery processes, protfolio analysis, migration studies etc. With user-friendly features and auto-workflow, it has helped in reduction of Turn-around-Time (TAT) resulting in faster credit appraisal and sanctions. SIDBI has shared the tool with banks and MoU SFCs free of cost and has also been giving training to the officials of banks/FIs to facilitate its smooth implementation.

(xii) Customised Financing : SIDBI's business initiatives are strategised to develop tailor-made, customised financial products to meet the diverse credit needs of the MSMEs. The financial support is based on project vaibility and entrepreneurs' capabilities. To enable the MSMEs to weather economic crisis, the bank had, *inter-alia* taken certain specific measures, the important ones being:

(a) The Bank alloed need-based restructuring of repayment schedules to affected MSMEs as a support during the difficult times.

(b) In order to augment greater credit flow to MSE sector, the Bank decided to provide all loans upto ₹100 lakhs without collateral and/or third party guarantee under the Credit Guarantee Scheme of CGTMSE. More and more loans upto ₹100 lakhs are being provided to MSEs without collateral.

(xiii) Risk Capital Fund : Pursuant to the announcement made in the Union Budget 2008-09, the Risk Capital Fund was created by SIDBI to provide Risk Capital assistance to MSMEs in the form of Equity, Preference capital, Optionally Convertible Debenture, Optionally Convertible Debt etc. The Bank has also started operations under its Start-up Assistance initiative on pilot basis, where early stage ventures operating in innovative/technology space, including those being incubated at technology incubators are offered financial assistance on flexible terms. Further, assistance to Venture Capital Funds was extended under Risk capital. An aggregate sum of ₹310 crore has been committed out of the Fund to VC funds during the financial year under review. The Bank proposes to further expand its risk capital operations by reaching out to a larger group of MSMEs through banks and other institutions.

MSME Financing and Development Project (MSMEFDP)

SIDBI is implementing a multi-agency/multi-activity MSME Financing and Development Project (MSMEFDP). The Department of Financial Services Ministry of Finance, Government of India is the Nodal Agency for the Project The World Bank, Department for International Development (DFID) UK, KfW and GTZ, Germany are the international partners in the Project. The primary objective of the Project is to meet both the demand and supply side concerns of MSMEs through a judicious blend of financial and non-financial services.

The progress of the Project has been quite noticeable as it has so far reached out to about 28,000 beneficiaries comprising 26,000 MSMEs and 2,000 banker and other stakeholders. The Project has received Merit Award from Association of Development Financing Institutions in Asia and the Pacific (ADFIAP) in 2010 The Project has two major components : Credit Facility by World Bank and KfW and Technical Assistance by DFID, UK; KfW and GTZ, Germany.

1. Credit Facility (CF)

Long term financing is a critical input for supporting capital formation and technological upgradation. Looking beyond traditional approaches, the Project helps facilitate MSME growth for survival and sustainability by providing Credit Facility.

2. Technical Assistance (TA)

(i) Business Development Services (BDS) : The BDS programme under MSMEFDP is being implemented in 26 clusters. The BDS activities have benefitted 17,500 MSMEs in these clusters mainly to strengthen MSMEs' acce to marketing, skill upgradation, technological changes and various other services in these clusters. Under one such initiative, the Project supported activities which have helped more than 3,500 rural youth to get trained in various skills and then becoming gainfully employed. Most of these people belonged to disadvantaged sections of our society.

(ii) Credit Information and Credit Rating : The Project has supported capacity building of Credit Information Bureau of India Ltd. (CIBIL) for strengthening credit information on MSMEs.

(iii) Technical Assistance to Banks/FIs : This component of the Project aims at capacity building of banks in innovating the delivery mechanisms, modifying processes, launching new products, training of officials in MSME lending etc.

(iv) Policy Advocacy : In order to strengthen the policy/legal/regulatory framework, the Project provides technical assistance in promoting informed and evidence based dialogue in the public domain on key policy measures that are critical to establishing a more effi cient policy framework for MSME development.

3. Other Promotional Initiatives

(i) Micro Enterprises Business Information Counsellors (MEBIC) : In order to foster entrepreneurship and remove information asymmetry within micro enterprises of underserved regions, the Project took an initiative for developing a cadre of BDS providers for counselling, initial handholding and development of micro enterprises in North-Eastern region as Micro Enterprise Business Information Counsellors (MEBIC).

(ii) National Level Mentoring to MSMEs : Capacity building assistance has been sanctioned to PRIME Database for development of a portal *www.msmementor.in* This web-based platform would host the database of different categories of service providers and s earch tool for the MSMEs to avail such services. Through this e-platform, MSMEs are expected to get various benefits from the concerned BDS professionals.

(iii) Support to Faridabad Small Industries Associations (FSIA) : A grant has been sanctioned to build the capacity of FSIA to channelise larger credit flow to its MSME members for meeting their unplanned credit needs.

(iv) Modified Rural Industries Programme : The project has started the modified version of Rural Industries Programme (RIP) in 2 pilot locations with a focus on sustainability of the activities.

(v) Support to METALAB, a Common Testing Facility Centre at Jamnagar : The support from the Project has helped the Jamnagar Factory Owners Association to set up a common facility centre in a record time. The centre has provided its services to about 900 MSMEs. The Centre has also leveraged additional Government funds and already started generating cash surplus.

(vi) Scheme on Energy Efficiency in MSME Clusters : S1DB1 has launched a programme on Energy Efficiency, initially in 19 MSME clusters with focus to train about 5,000 MSME units and complete energy audit of 500 enterprises. Besides capacity building, the MSMEs will also be linked to credit assistance by banks/FIs.

Initiatives Relating to SFCs

(i) Memorandum of Understanding (MoU) with SFCs : In order to improve the operational and financial performance of SFCs, the Bank has MoU with 12 SFCs. The financial position of 10 MoU SFCs registered improvement in the post-MoU period. Looking at the need for continued mentoring and hand-holding support and with a view to further consolidating the gains made so far and also to address the emerging challenges, it was decided to renew the MoU with SFCs concerned for a further period of five years.

(ii) Regulatory Directives : SIDBI has taken various initiatives as part of compliance to RBI regulatory requirements. Up-to-date Income Recognition and Asset Classifications (IRAC) norms have been issued to SFCs and their compliance thereto is being monitored. The MoU SFCs have switched over to accrual system of accounting. SIDBI has circulated draft valuation policy for SFCs for their loans and advances and also other assets for implementation. The Bank is also in the process of preparing a draft "Loan Policy" and "Risk Management Policy" for adoption and use by SFCs.

(iii) Refinance Scheme under JICA-LoC : In view of the growing need for energy saving and importance of energy conservation for sustainable development and improvement in profitability as an outcome of implementing energy saving measures, a new Refinance Scheme for Energy Saving Projects (RSES) for MSMEs was launched under Japan International Co-operation Agency — Line of Credit (JICALoC). The overall objective of the RSES is to promote energy saving in the MSME sector, thereby contributing to environmental improvement and economic development in the country.

(iv) Joint Financing with SFCs : In order to provide adequate and timely assistance to MSMEs on a risk sharing basis and also help SFCs to retain existing good MSME clients and broaden their operating canvass, the Bank on a pilot basis, had launched joint financing with Andhra Pradesh State Financial Corporation (APSFC) and Rajasthan Financial Corporation (RFC). The arrangement was subsequently extended to Kerala Financial Corporation (KFC) and Tamilnadu Industrial Investment Corporation (TIIC). With a view to bringing about further flexibility in the arrangement, refinance was also extended to SFCs for the term ioan sanctioned by them under such joint financing arrangement.

(v) Enhancement in Limit of Accommodation and ceiling on refinance for SFCs : In order to encourage MSMEs to corporatise their establishments and to ensure faster credit delivery to MSMEs from SFCs, the Bank has, in terms of proviso to Section 26 of the SFCs Act, decided to permit SFCs to provide assistance to individual units upto ₹10 crore in case of a corporation or a company or a cooperative society under Section 26(i) of the Act. Consequently, refinance ceiling per unit at 100% of the loan amount was enhanced from ₹5 crore to ₹10 crore in case of a corporation/company/cooperative society in the sector. However, refinance to medium enterprises stood reduced to 80% of the term loan amount subject to a ceiling of Rs 10 crore. The refinance ceiling in case of proprietorship concerns/partnership/trusts, etc. has, however, been retained at ₹2 crore per enterprise.

Bank Credit of SSI Sector

The outstanding bank credit to SSIs by public, private sector and foreign banks in India as at end-March, 2004 was ₹71,613 crore. as compared to ₹63,654 crore as at end-March, 2003. This outstanding balance formed 9.4 per cent and 10.3 per cent share of the net bank credit at the end of respective years. In order to boost the flow of credit of SSIs, public sector banks have thus far opened more than 500 specialised SSI branches.

B. STATE GOVERNMENT SUPPORT SYSTEM

Director of Industries is the highest authority at state level to execute the policies and programmes with regard to SSIs, medium and large scale enterprises. Director/commissioner is responsible for the overall supervision of support system developed for the SSIs in the state. These support systems are as follows :

1. District Industries Centres (DICs)

The concept of DIC was developed by the Industrial Policy 1977. However DIC Programme was initiated on 1st May 1978 as a centrally sponsored scheme but this sponsorship was withdrawn in 1993-94. These centres are responsible for effective promotion of cottage and small scale industries at district level. These centres are also to provide support facilities/concessions/ services to develop tiny, cottage and small scale units. The basic purpose of these DICs is to generate more employment opportunities for rural people. The DICs are responsible to provide the following services to SSI sector (i) identification of local resources, (ii) arrangement of machinery and equipments, (iii) supply of raw materials from different suppliers, (iv) provision of credit facilities, (v) extension of quality control facilities, (vii) undertaking marketing, consultancy and extension services.

(i) Structural Framework : The DIC is headed by a General Manager. He is assisted by 4 Functional Managers and 3 Project Managers having technical background and specialisation equipped in certain areas of SSIs in the respective districts.

(ii) Operational Framework : The DICs being the focal point of promotion at the state level have a General Manager who supervises extension services for technology, raw materials, credit, economic investigating, training, marketing and village industries. Actually, DICs were originally set up as promotional agencies currently function mainly as regulators and are used extensively as registration centres for SSIs. While most areas have been delicensed SSI registration is necessary to avail of the various incentives available. The DICs administer the incentive programmes of State Governments such as capital subsidies, fiscal incentives, raw material allocations, power subsidies and the like. They are also supposed to provide single window clearance.

The studies suggest that the services at the DICs are rudimentary and more complex problems are referred to SSIs. However, "evaluation suggests that they have not succeeded in achieving even this limited objectives. Entrepreneurs still have to shuttle between a variety of departments for clearance of projects. The extension work of DICs is far from satisfactory and they do not have updated their information. A fair arrangement would be that the DICs are unable to cope with administrative overload."[1]

Thus, a completely new look be taken on the functioning of the District Industry Centres in order to make them more promotional rather than regulatory. DICs would acquire additional significance if they can weave a web of linkages with other institutions. They should function as key conduits for information flowing from a variety of channels for dissemination to local business firms. DICs can function with greater efficiency if they can draw on other resources from business. They can work in association with local councils constituted of members from industry, banks, training institutions etc. The function of the Councils should be to solve day to day problems.

2. State Financial Corporations

The State Financial Corporations were set up under the separate State Financial Corporation Act, 1951 on the lines of Industrial Finance Corporation. State Financial Corporations (SFCs), the state-level institutions, play an important role in the development of small and medium enterprises in their respective states with the main objectives of financing and promoting these enterprises for achieving balanced regional growth, catalyse investment, generate employment and widen the ownership base of industry. In tandem with the changing business environment, SFCs have also expanded the scope of their activities and coverage of their assistance. The State Financial Corporations (SFCs) are operating as regional development banks for development of small and medium enterprises in their respective states in tandem with national priorities. There are 18 SFCs in the country, of which 17 were set up under the SFCs Act, 1951. Tamil Nadu Industrial Investment Corporation Ltd. established in 1949 under the Companies Act as Madras Industrial Investment Corporation, also functions as SFC.

In tandem with changing business environment, the SFCs are expanding the scope of their activities and coverage of their assistance. The financial assistance include term loans, direct subscription to equity/debentures, guarantees, discounting of bills of exchange and seed/special capital. The SFCs operate a number of schemes of refinance and equity type assistance on behalf of IDBI/SIDBI in addition to special schemes for artisans and special target groups such as SC/ST, women, ex-servicemen, physically handicapped, etc. The refinance scheme was modified in view of changes in financial sector, so as to make it more cost-efficient and market-friendly. The major features were abolition of upfront fee, raising of loan ceilings for PLIs, extension of line of credit (LOC) facility to all SFCs/SIDCs and increase in the extent of refinance to 100% by SIDBI and to 80% by IDBI.

(i) Financing Arrangement : With the increasing diversification/expansion in the Indian industry especially since the outset of economic reforms, SFCs have started providing assistance to newer types of business activities including floriculture, tissue culture, poultry farming, commercial complexes and services related to engineering, marketing etc. With a view to enable SFCs to finance/undertake new industrial/business activities, definition of industrial concern under Section2(c) of SFCs Act has been reviewed to include activities like construction of commercial complexes, show-rooms and sales outlets independent of hotel business, establishment of departmental stores,shopping malls and tourism homes, setting-up of vocational training centres for imparting technical knowledge to the entrepreneurs for setting up and running the units efficiently and produce quality goods. SFCs have also started offering facilities such as equipment leasing and have entered the field of consultancy, merchant banking, debenture trusteeship and capital related services. With the changing pattern of financing of industrial enterprises, SFCs are giving a thrust to their investment activities and capital market related operations.

(ii) Operational Arrangement : SFCs provide financial assistance to small and medium enterprises in the forms of term loans, direct subscription to equity/debentures, guarantees, discounting of bills of exchange and seed capital assistance.

Critical Evaluation : Today's liberalised environment calls for a new approach by SFCs which have borne the brunt of term lending in the last four decades, credit sanctions and disbursements by SFCs have grown but average recovery rate has been very low.

The scope of activities of the SFIs needs to be widened, their resource base enlarged and their organisation transformed to ensure operational autonomy. In this context recommendations of Mr. S.H. Khan committee are quite noteworthy which suggested certain changes. These changes are as follows :

(i) Widening the definition of industrial concern and addition of certain business activities.

(ii) Increasing the share capital and changes in shareholding pattern.

(iii) Borrowings from other sources and deployment of funds in other securities.

(iv) Restructuring the Board of Directors to ensure functional autonomy.

(v) Exposure limit in the borrowing companies and

(vi) Recovery of SFC dues.

Thus, they have to be restructured to meet the growing expectations of small and medium enterprises in globalised era.

3. State Small Industries Development Corporations (SSIDCs)

State Small Industries Development Corporations (SSIDCs) were established under the Companies Act, 1956 as State Government undertakings with specific objectives of promoting and developing small, tiny and village industries in the State/Union Territories under their jurisdiction.

Some of the important functions performed by SSIDCs include: (*i*) procurement and distribution of raw materials; (*ii*) supply of machinery on hire-purchase basis; (*iii*) providing assistance for marketing of the products of small scale units; (*iv*) construction of industrial estates/sheds, providing allied infrastructure facilities and their maintenance; (*v*) extending seed capital assistance on behalf of the respective State Governments: (*vi*) providing management assistance to production units; and (*vii*) management of State Emporia for providing sale window for handlooms, handicrafts and SSI items.

To keep pace with the changing environment, SSIDCs have initiated various measures to expand the scope of their activities. Though their prime operation continues to be distribution of raw materials, SSIDCs also pay attention to various aspects of small industry development, especially marketing; and thus, helping the tiny and small industries increase their market share. Some of the SSIDCs are setting up centres for display of/and information dissemination on SSI products to needy SSI units on export marketing in addition to development of web pages for them and acting as common export manager.

Information on the operations of SSIDCs during 1998-99 was available in respect of eight SSIDCs located in Chandigarh, Goa, Gujarat, Kerala, Madhya Pradesh. Maharashtra, Rajasthan and Tamil Nadu. The discussion that follows pertains to these eight SSIDCs.

(i) Distribution of Raw Materials : Distribution of raw materials to small scale units continues to be one of the main activities of SSIDCs. The aim is to reduce the exploitation faced by small entrepreneurs in an oligopolistic market by supplying them the right amount of quality raw materials at right time.

(ii) Marketing Assistance : Apart from distribution and supply of raw materials, SSIDCs also assist small scale industries by marketing their products in domestic and international markets. They procure bulk orders for and on behalf of SSI units through participation in national/international trade fairs and from government departments/undertakings. SSIDCs also provide credit facility to SSI units for purchase of raw materials required for execution of orders, discounting of bills and arranging for advance/prompt payments.

(iii) Promotional and Developmental Activities : SSIDCs provide infrastructure facilities such as industrial sheds/estates, godowns and common production facilities to small scale units. They also run production-cum-training centres, provide guidance/consultancy to entrepreneurs' and organise buyer-seller meets. With the help of SIDBI they provide assistance for rehabilitation of sick small units.

4. State Industrial Development Corporations

The State Industrial Development Corporations (SIDCs) act as catalyst for promotion and development of medium and large enterprises in their respective states. In tandem with changing business environment, SIDCs are making efforts to diversify their activities to cover a range of services and schemes and have entered into the areas of equipment leasing, merchant banking, venture capital and mutual funds.

The State Industrial Development Corporations (SIDCs) incorporated under the Companies Act as wholly-owned undertakings of State Governments for promotion and development of medium and large industries in respective states, provide financial assistance in the form of rupee loans, underwriting/direct subscriptions to shares/debentures, guarantees, inter-corporate deposits and also opens letters of credit on behalf of its borrowers. They are also involved in setting up of medium and large industrial projects in the joint sector/assisted sector in collaboration with private entrepreneurs or wholly-owned subsidiaries. They undertake a range of promotional activities which include preparation of feasibility reports, conducting industrial potential surveys, entrepreneurship training & development programmes and developing industrial areas/estates. Some SIDCs also offer a package of developmental services which include technical guidance, assistance in plant location and co-ordination with other agencies. In tandem with the changing business environment, many SIDCs are making efforts to diversify their activities and enter into areas of equipment leasing, merchant banking, venture capital and mutual funds. Refinance scheme run by SIDBI/IDBI has been modified by extending loan ceilings for PLIs, extension of line of credit LoC to all SIDCs, enhancement in the ceiling of the cost of infrastructure projects to ₹20 crore, increase in the extent of refinance to 100% by SIDBI and to 80% by IDBI. Some of the SIDCs provide an option of fixed/floating rate of interest.

Of the 28 SIDCs in the country, those in Andaman & Nicobar, Arunachal Pradesh, Daman & Diu and Dadra & Nagar Haveli, Goa, Manipur, Meghalaya, Mizoram, Nagaland, Tripura, Pondicherry and Sikkim function also as SFCs to provide assistance to small and medium enterprises and act as promotional agencies.

5. Technical Consultancy Organisations

Indian financial institutions alongwith commercial banks and state-level financial/development institutions established a network of Technical Consultancy Organisations (TCOs) during the seventies and eighties to cater to the consultancy needs of the small and medium industries and new entrepreneurs with a view to making available the technical expertise and filling up the gaps in the process of industrialisation. At present there are 17 TCOs operating in various states; some of them covering more than one state. Besides, Karnataka has a state sponsored TCO, viz. Technical Consultancy Services Organisation of Karnataka (TECSOK).

TCOs provide a complete package of consultancy services at reasonable rates to small and medium enterprises, individual entrepreneurs, government departments and agencies, various state level institutions, commercial banks and other institutions in their task relating to industrial development and financing. Though initially, TCOs focussed on preinvestment studies, over the years they have diversified their services to include :

(i) preparation of project profiles and feasibility studies,

(ii) undertaking industrial potential surveys,

(iii) identification of potential entrepreneurs and providing them technical and management assistance,

(iv) undertaking market research and surveys for specific products,

(v) undertaking energy audit and energy conservation assignments.

(vi) project supervision and where necessary rendering technical and administrative assistance,

(vii) taking up assignments on turn-key basis,

(viii) undertaking export consultancy for export-oriented projects based on modern technology,

(ix) offering management consultancy services, especially for diagnostic study of sick units or for improvement in the existing units and their rehabilitation programmes,

(x) conducting entrepreneurship development programmes (EDPs) and skill upgradation programmes, and

(xi) offering merchant banking services.

The performance of TCOs is somewhat mixed. While some TCOs are performing well and are self-sustaining, there are others which are facing operational and financial problems. In order to identify strengths and weaknesses of TCOs in the changed environment and envisage future role of these entities, IDBI has commissioned a study on TCOs by a reputed consultant with the following terms of reference :

(a) To review the performance since inception, of all TCOs in general and IDBI-led TCOs in particular and one strong/weak TCO-each led by IFCI/ICICI and also analysing reasons for good/poor performance and evolving strategy for growth in future.

(b) Study of the existing management structure including constitution of the Boards and suggest measures to make them more effective.

(c) Existing shareholding pattern & changes therein, if any. with a view to providing better flexibility in managing the affairs of TCOs.

(d) To evaluate the performance of TCOs in the light of changes, post-liberalisation phase.

(e) Any other measures to streamline the functioning of TCOs.

Some Highlights of Latest Support Systems

1. Credit Rating Agency for SME Sector

With a view to providing comfort to the bank officials in their credit decisions and helping SME sector gain expeditious access to credit SIDBI, in association with select public sector banks has taken initiatives to set up a specialised rating agency for the SME sector. The proposed agency would have partnership with leading rating and information dissemination agencies of the country. The agency aims at providing affordable, creditable and independent ratings to the SMEs which would help enhancing their credibility and standing. It is felt that with the setting up of the agency, banks would be provided with an independent external assessment for quicker decisions in extension of credit to the SME sector.

2. Small and Medium Enterprises Fund

Pursuant to the announcement made by the Government of India on January 09, 2004 regarding creation of SME Fund for making available adequate and timely credit to SMEs and appointing SIDBI as the Nodal Agency, the Bank made the Fund operational with effect from April 01, 2004.

3. SME Growth Fund

The Working Group set up by the Reserve Bank of India on Flow of Credit to SSI Sector, headed by Dr. A.S. Ganguly had recommended setting up of a national level SME Fund promoted by SIDBI/banks to fund export oriented, high technology SMEs to play catalytic role in the advancement of the SME sector. To meet the need of risk capital for SME units, SIDBI set up a ₹500 crore national level venture capital fund for SMEs, named "SME Growth Fund", on October 25, 2004. The Fund is intended to be utilised by investing in equity and equity-linked instruments in the growth sectors including life sciences, retailing, light engineering, food processing, information technology, infrastructure related to services like health care, logistics and distributions, etc. SME Growth Fund is an 8-year close-ended venture capital fund. The Fund has received commitments for the entire amount of ₹500 crore from various banks that include State Bank of India, Punjab National Bank, Bank of Baroda, Oriental Bank of Commerce, Bank of India, Union Bank of India, Corporation Bank and Central Bank of India, including SIDBfs commitment of ₹100 crores.

4. World Bank-led Project on Financing and Development of SMEs

With a view to upscaling credit flow to the sector and raising resources for the SME Fund, SIDBI has negotiated a Project with the World Bank for financing and development of SMEs in India. The Project has three components :

(i) Line of Credit,

(ii) Risk Sharing Facility, and

(iii) Technical Assistance.

5. Risk Management in the Bank

In line with the Credit Risk Management (CRM) policy, comprehensive Credit Risk Management Systems and Operational Risk Management Systems developed by CRISIL Ltd., have been set up in the Bank. The CRM Policy, *inter alia,* lays down the Bank's Risk Philosophy and covers the credit risk organisation, risk measurement exposure limit framework, pricing etc. Risk Assessment Models, in the form of software tools, have been developed and implemented for credit risk rating of various borrower segments. A Risk Management Committee, comprising senior executives of the Bank, has been constituted which guides the risk management functions of the Bank and also oversees and monitors the effective implementation of the CRM Policy.

6. Rationalisation of the Existing Schemes

(i) Technology Upgradation Fund Scheme : For expeditious disbursal of the interest reimbursement under TUFS for textiles and jute industry to the medium scale units assisted by SIDBI, Government of India authorisation was obtained to release the interest reimbursement to directly assisted medium sector units.

(ii) Credit Linked Capital Subsidy Scheme : Pursuant to the announcement by the Ministry of SSI, GoI, units assisted under National Equity Fund Scheme have also been made eligible for availing subsidy under the Credit Linked Capital Subsidy Scheme, provided other terms and conditions of the same were satisfied.

(iii) *Credit Linked Capital Subsidy Scheme — Technology Upgradation Fund Scheme :* Consequent upon the announcement "by "Ministry di "Textiles, GoI. THe operations of the CLCS-TUF scheme were extended upto March 31, 2007.

7. Increase in the limit of accommodation to SFCs under Refinance

In terms of proviso to section 26 of the SFCs (Amendment) Act, 2000, the SFCs are allowed to provide assistance to units beyond ₹5 crores and upto ₹20 crores in case of a corporation or a company or a cooperative society and beyond ₹2 crores and up to ₹8 crores in case of others on case to case basis, subject to the SFCs raising additional resources for meeting additional fund requirement. The ceiling on the extent of refinance, based on the categorisation of SFCs and the ceiling on cost of project, which was fixed at ₹12 crore in respect of SSI units and ₹20 crore in respect of service sector units, was done away with. Accordingly, the extent of refinance would be 100 per cent subject to an enhanced ceiling of ₹500 lakh. However, SFCs were permitted to finance all projects in SME sector irrespective of project cost.

8. International Cooperation

During the year under review, discussions were held with various visiting missions from abroad and embassies of different countries in India to explore opportunities for collaborative arrangement relating to areas where SIDBI has developed expertise. A number of high level delegations from Algeria, Egypt,

Mauritius, Namibia, Senegal, South Africa and Sri Lanka visited the Bank and held discussions with senior officials. The Bank also represented in Joint Working Groups set up by the GoI under mutual cooperation programmes with the Government of Mauritius, Government of Egypt and the Republic of Algeria. Some of these nations have evinced interest in seeking SIDBI's expertise in the institution building and financing of SMEs in their respective countries. Dialogue continued with multilateral/bilateral agencies, *viz.*, the World Bank, DFID, KfW, GTZ, SECO and IFAD in respect of the ongoing projects.

9. WTO Impact Assessment Studies

SIDBI had identified 16 industries in the SME sector for assessing the impact of WTO provisions in view of significant contribution of SME Sector to the Indian economy. The Bank has, so far, completed such studies in respect of 9 industrial sectors in two phases. While the studies in the six sectors were completed in the first phase by FY 2003, in the second phase, 3 sectors, *viz.*, Food Processing, Biotechnology and Bicycle and Bicycle Parts were taken up and completed during FY 2005. Summary reports of the studies were disseminated to various Government departments, banks/State-level institutions, Industry Associations and other stakeholders.

10. Initiatives to Support State Financial Corporations

(i) Memorandum of Understanding with SFCs : In the series of entering into MoUs with State Financial Corporations, three more SFCs, viz., Delhi Financial Corporation, Himachal Pradesh Financial Corporation and Tamil Nadu Industrial and Investment Corporation signed tripartite MoU with SIDBI and respective State Governments during the year, taking the total number of MoU with SFCs to ten. These SFCs have expressed that the concessions given by SIDBI under the arrangement have helped them in reducing their cost of borrowing and making them competitive in SME credit dispensation. Most of the SFCs that have entered into MoU seemed to be moving towards achieving various milestones stipulated under the arrangement. These SFCs have honoured their commitments to SIDBI in terms of payment of dues on time. Greater emphasis is being lain to cut down the cost of borrowing through debt swap arrangement, negotiation with banks, taking up with the respective State Governments for funding support and obtaining guarantees, etc. In order to improve the outcome of the package, SIDBI brought in modification/relaxations in the existing package/scheme of restructuring, wherever required.

(ii) Development Loan Scheme for SFCs : Considering the need for SFCs to upgrade their infrastructure and technology for installation of sufficient and effective operating systems, Mis, etc., a Development Loan Scheme for SFCs has been introduced by the Bank.

(*iii*) Training for Officers of SFCs : As a part of the capacity building initiatives for strengthening the SFCs and to enable them to adopt better systems and processes so as to improve functional efficiencies, SIDBI has tied up with

Bankers Training College, RBI wherein four residential training programmes on different topics of interest to the SFCs were organised. Around 75 officials from various SFCs had benefited from these programmes. The cost of the training programmes was entirely borne by SIDBI.

11. Technical Group for Refinancing Institutions

Pursuant to the announcement made in the Credit Policy 2004-05, the RBI constituted a Technical Group for Refinancing Institutions to evaluate the efficiency of regulatory and supervisory systems of the refinancing institutions and make recommendations for strengthening the framework. SIDBI was represented in the Group by the Chairman and Management Director. The recommendations of the Group address the issues relating to supervision and regulation of SFCs as well.

12. Other Initiatives

(*i*) *Computerisation of Borrowers' Accounts* : As part of the measures for strengthening credit monitoring and follow-up mechanism, units are encouraged to consider inclusion of need based hardware/software in the schemes and cost thereof is included in the cost of the project. This not only helps the entrepreneur to ensure day-to-day/periodical monitoring of the operations of the unit, but also assists them in submitting the required data to SIDBI/banks, without much difficulty.

(*ii*) *Simplification of Direct Credit Process* : As part of the ongoing simplification/automation of Direct Credit Process, an electronic workflow system has been developed and launched. The system integrates and automates the main credit functions of sanction, documentation and disbursement. The system is aimed at standardising the processes and reducing the transaction time.

(*iii*) Interest Rate Structure : During the year under review, the Bank's Prime Lending Rate reduced from 11.50 per cent per annum in 2010-11 to 9 percent 2014-15.

C. SUPPORT SYSTEM PROVIDED BY OTHER AGENCIES

Besides, Central Government and State Government agencies, there are some Non-Governmental agencies who are also supporting the cause of small scale industries in the country. These agencies include Non-Government organisations and industry associations. They provide a common platform to voice SSI needs and initiate cooperative efforts. Government policies have stressed the increasing role of these associations and NGOs in setting up common facilities and other cooperative ventures in technology, marketing and other support systems. Some of these major associations are as follows :

1. Indian Council of Small Industries.
2. Laghudyog Bharti.
3. Federation of Associations of Small Industries of India.

4. World Association for Small and Medium Enterprises.
5. Federation of Indian Chambers of Commerce and Industry.
6. PHD Chambers of Commerce and Industry.
7. Confederation of Indian Industry.
8. Federation of Indian Exporters Organisations.

1. Indian Council of Small Industries (ICSI)

It was established in 1979 to help tiny, cottage & small industries and artisans of rural areas. Membership of ICSI constitutes about 1500 associations of the decentralised sector. Its main functions are as follows :

(i) Information dissemination.
(ii) Entrepreneurship development.
(iii) Consultancy and managerial support.
(iv) Training & Research.

In its operational behaviour, council follows consortium approach to extend marketing services, testing facilities and quality control backups. The ICSI is expected to protect the interest of its members by giving suggestions for appropriate policy making.

2. Laghudyog Bharti (LUB)

It was founded in 1995 to promote and safeguard the interest of tiny and small scale industries. It has been given representation on the national and state level government bodies responsible for the development of SSIs. It is responsible to undertake

(i) entrepreneurial training,
(ii) support for technology upgradation and
(*iii*) marketing services. However, it would be better for LUB to necessary steps in channelising resources from its members. Sufficient fund is necessary to meet out growing needs of the above functions.

3. Federation of Associations of Small Industries of India (FASII)

It was promoted in 1959 to represent the problems of SSIs with the **government and lcaisoning** with other agencies involved in promotion of SSI sector. Its objectives are as follows :

(i) to promote the development of small scale tiny and cottage
(ii) to cooperate with industrial business, educational institutions in collecting and exchanging information pertaining to the small scale sector,
(iii) to undertake professional, technical and management consultation services;
(iv) to undertake studies, surveys and research assignments,

(v) to further the cause of small industries by interacting with Union and State Governments and other bodies.

(vi) to establish and operate trade centres display centra, sub-contract exchanges and other promotional institutions for the benefit of the small scale sector and

(vii) to establish test centres, laboratories and common facility centres for the SSI sector.

In operational behaviour, it represents associations of small industries and indvidual SSI units. It also evolved in monitoring the performance of SSI sector. organising seminar/conferences, and coordinating the SSI issues with the Government.

4. World Association for Small and Medium Enterprises (WASME)

It was established in 1981 to ensure business cooperation among its members. Its membership represents chamber of commerce, small countries.

It facilitates technology transfer, manpower training, maintaining a register of experts/consultants, organising seminars and conferences and acting as fdearing house of information and marketing services etc.

5 Federation of Indian Chambers of Commerce and Industry (FICCI)

The FICCI was established in 1927 as the national agency through which the chambers of commerce and trade association in India could crystallise their views on current economic Problems, It serves as the coordinating agency for the commercial and industrial interests as represented by various chambers of commerce and trade associations.

The representative functions occupy the foremost place in the activities of the federation. The administrative decisions and the decisions taken by the legislative bodies vastly concern the businessmen in their individual business judgements and actions. The Federation maintains very close relations with the Union Government. The Federation is also represented on over sixty-five advisory committees appointed by government and other leading organisations. The business community's viewpoint is put forward at the meetings of these committees.

6. Associated Chambers of Commerce & Industry of India (Assocham)

Assocham is another apex organisation like Ficci to which some of the older chambers of commerce are affiliated. It was founded in December, 1920. It seeks to make the businessmen's voice heard and to ensure that their views are taken into account in the moulding of the nation's economic life. It also undertakes persuasive activities directed to the administrative departments and to the law makers with a view to acquaint them with the viewpoint of the members. It has also been given representation on some 65 consultative and advisory bodies that have been set up to assist government in dealing with specialised aspects of economic affairs.

7. PHD Chambers of Commerce & Industry

It was promoted in 1905 to represent the interest of trade and industry in northern India. It provides a meeting ground for representatives of commerce and industry with the government. It also constitutes various expert committees and task forces through which members representing various interest, pool knowledge and experience are required to work in the interest of business community. The association has also launched a new system in 1995—small industries and business (SIB) Help Line to assist and support the SSIs. It is responsible for the coordination between SSI units and commercial banks and financial institutions.

8. Confederation of Indian Industry (CII)

It was created in 1992 by changing the name of Confederation of Engineering Industry (ECI). The CEI itself was a creation of two merging associations like Indian Engineering Association (1912) and Engineering Association of India (1942) in 1974.

It is responsible for advisory, consultative and representative services to industry and the government. It has been given representation on major policy formulating bodies, related with the industry. It is also expected to work as a nodal agency for international industrial cooperation.

The CII has submitted an eight points plan[2] *to* the Union Government for stimulating the small scale industries (SSI) sector to make it more competitive in the global market. These points are as follows :

(i) The Indian small and medium industries have to keep pace with the quick changes to penetrate in the global market in the free market economy.

(ii) There is urgent need for expansion and the development of SSIs, enhancement in excise duty exemption from the present threshold of ₹50 lakhs to ₹1 crore for new business opportunities to cater to the export markets.

(iii) Income tax reduction on R&D (Research and Development) expenditure may be raised from the present ceiling and amendments in Income-tax Act for full depreciation benefits for the company to purchase the fixeo assets of a sick unit.

(iv) Recommendations of Nayak Committee on banking sector to be accepted and implemented to meet out the working capital requirements of SSI.

(v) Tiny sector units be exempt from the provisions of Factories Act and priority should be given to such sector for new power connections as well as for marketing outlets to promote their products.

(vi) Respite should be ensured for the SSIs from the "Inspector Raj" by formulating a comprehensive law and a waiver from labour laws for employing 50 to 100 workers.

(vii) Workmen's Compensation Act may be an alternative to the ESI scheme for SSI units.

(viii) Government should provide more opportunities to SSIs the vital sector of Indian economy for ensuring the country's overall economic development.

9. Federation of Indian Exporters Organisation (FIEO)

This is an appex organisation set up in October, 1965 by the Ministry of Commerce. It represents the Indian entrepreneurs' spirit of enterprise in the global market. The Federation performs activities of common nature such as sending trade delegations abroad and inviting trade delegations from foreign countries, sponsoring commodity and market surveys collection and dissemination of commercial intelligence. It provides facilities for settlement of trade disputes arising in the course of foreign trade and advises government on all matters relating to export trade.

Its membership comprises mainly Export Houses. Trading Houses, Star Trading Houses, Super Star Trading Houses and Consultancy exporting firms. Members generally belong to manufacturing, international trading investment and joint ventures abroad etc.

EXAMINATION QUESTIONS

Long Answer Questions

1. What are the institutional sources of financing small business enterprises in India?
2. Describe the role of National Small Industries Corporation in the development of small scale industries in India. To what extent has it been successful in its objectives ?
3. Describe the role of Small Industries Development Organisation" in the development of small scale industries in India. To what extent has it been successful in its objectives ?
4. Discuss the assistance provided by National Small Industries Corporation to small scale units in India.
5. What do you mean by Institutional Support System? Examine the present position of Institutional Support System available to SSIs in India.
6. Discuss the different components of support system. Critically examine their present position in Indian context.
7. Evaluate the role of All India Financial Institutions in entrepreneurial development.
8. Critically examine the contributions of institutional finance with reference to entrepreneurship development.
9. Write an essay on Institutional Finance and entrepreneurship.

10. Critically examine the role of technical consultancy organisations for entrepreneurial development in India.
11. Critically examine the role of state agencies involved in promotion of SSIs in India.
12. What do you mean by Non-Government agencies involved in promotion of SSIs in India ? Do you think that industry associations are more forceful to NGOs in promoting the interest of SSIs ? Explain.
13. Critically examine the role of District Industries Centre in the development of Small Scale Industries.
14. Critically examine the role of National Small Industries Corporation in the development of Small Scale industries.
15. What are the main sources of short and long term finance for a small entrepreneur ? Discuss the role of SIDBI in the context of financing of small enterprises.
16. Describe the role of Small Industries Development Organisation in the development of small scale industries in India. To what extent it has been successful in its objectives ?
17. What role has been played in this regard by he special financial institutions set-up by the Government of India during the plan period ?

Short Answer Questions

1. Describe the functions of District Industries Centre.
2. Explain the composition of Small Scale Industries Board.
3. Describe the services rendered by the SIDO.
4. Discuss the functions of NSIC.
5. Examine the different forms of State Government Support systems.

Objective Type Questions

1. SSI Board was established in :

   (a) 1947 (b) 1954

   (c) 1964 (d) 1957

2. Small Industries Service Institutes are run by :

   (a) SSI Board (b) SIDBI

   (c) SIDO (d) NSIC

3. NSIC was promoted in :

   (a) 1955 (b) 1960

   (c) 1965 (d) 1970

4. DIC was developed by the Industrial policy of :

   (a) 1956 (b) 1970

   (c) 1977 (d) 1991

5. FASII is a :

   (a) Government Organisation (b) Liaisonlng organisation

   (c) Small Scale unit (d) None of the above.

Answers

1 (b) 2 (c) 3 (a) 4 (c) 5 (b)

Reason Based Questions

State with reason whether the following statements are true or false :

1. The Small Scale Industries Board (SSI Board) was established in 1954.
2. The District Industries Centres are responsible for industrial development of the district concerned.
3. Most of the state financial corporations in states are working as joint stock companies.
4. District Industry Centre (DIC) is the nodal agency for institutional support of SMEs.
5. State Small Industries Development Corporations are responsible for supply of raw materials to SSI units.
6. Indian Council of Small Industries was established in 1979.

REFERENCES

1. Abid Hussain *Committee Report,* p. 71.
2. SIDBI *Report on SSI sector,* 1999, p. 81.
3. *Business Line,* August 7, 2000, p. 1.

31

VENTURE CAPITAL

Basically, venture capital is a source of finance for new or relatively new, high risk, high profit potential projects undertaken by a firm. These projects are usually promoted by first generation entrepreneurs attempting to break new ground for commercial activity or industrial product. In this situation, venture capital comes to their help for arranging resources.

In practice, venture capital helps budding entrepreneurs, having skills and business acumen to realise their dreams. In most of the cases, first generation entrepreneur comes forward with a new idea or attractive product and approaches a venture capitalist for financial assistance in implementing his projects. Being a new concept, traditional public of financial institutions are unable to extend financial support to them. In such cases, venture capitalists provide the needed resources—financial as well as managerial, to implement the project. As soon as the project reaches the stage of profitability, venture capitalist sell their equity holdings at the market price. Venture capitalists are rewarded for their risk taking behaviour as these enterprises earn high rate of profit. The object of the investment is to provide capital appreciation.

The venture capitalists are generally professionals drawn from various fields. They provide funds to these firms after carefully scrutinising the projects. Their main aim is to earn huge returns on their investments. " They know very well that if they may suffer losses in some project, the others will compensate the same due to high returns. They take active participation in the management of the company as well as provide the expertise and qualities of a good banker, technologist, planner and managers." Thus, the venture capitalist and the entrepreneur literally act as partners in an innovative project.

Venture capital is meant for investment, in an enterprise that offers profitability along with the possibility of loss. It is the money provided by the professionals who invest alongside the management in young, rapidly growing companies that have the potential to develop into significant economic contributors. Thus, the venture capital has privately raised external equity capital and has been used to fund early-stage firms with attractive growth prospects. Earlier, it was known as "risk capital". But, now, the term venture capital is used for the purpose.

Nature of Venture Capital

Venture capital is long term risk capital to finance high technology project which involves risk but having strong potential for growth. Venture capitalists pool their resources including managerial abilities to assist new entrepreneurs in the early stage of the project. Once the project reaches the stage of profitability, they sell their equity holdings at high premium and ensure their exit from the firm at appropriate time.

A venture capital company is defined as "a financing institution which joins an entrepreneur as a co-promoter in a project and shares the risks and rewards of the enterprise."

In a broad-sense, venture capital refers to the commitment of capital as shar holding, for the formulation and setting up of small firms specialising in new ideas or new technologies. It ensures an injection of funds into a new firm as well as facilitates a simultaneous input of skill needed to set up the firm, design its marketing strategy and organise and manage it. It is an association with successive stages of firm's development with distinctive types of financing appropriate to each state of development.

Characteristics of Venture Capital

(i) Investment in equity capital appreciates in course of time and investors can sell their shares at high premium.

(ii) Only new projects of high technology, having high risk as well as scope for windfall profits, are taken up.

(iii) It not only provides finance but also assist in the management of the enterprise to ensure smooth implementation.

(iv) The investment in new ventures lacks marketability/liquidity until the project is implemented and profits are generated.

(v) The venture capitalists take speedy decisions in appraising projects and releasing funds.

Emergence of Venture Capital in India

In India, the growth of venture capital is at its infancy stage. It makes the rise of the new class of technocrat entrepreneurs, coming out with new technologies, new processes and new products; requiring financial assistance, which cannot be provided by the financial institutions in accordance with the appraisal criteria. At present, venture capital is emerging as a thrust area for finance companies. Flexibility in financing encourages new ventures. An agreement is entered into between the venture capital fund and the assisted company that the venture will go public at a convenient time to offload shares without any compulsion.

Indian venture capital Funds/companies have different objectives. Some companies are engaged in providing finance in the early stage of the project in the form of seed capital. Medium companies like credit capital venture fund cannot wait for three year lock-in period and look for ways to offload their equity in a company as soon as possible. Other small funds are risk-averse and really do not provide assistance to new entrepreneurs.

In India, the venture capital funds (VCFs) can be categorised into the following groups :

(i) Those promoted by the Central Government controlled development finance institutions, for example :
  (a) ICICI Venture Funds Ltd.
  (b) IFCI Venture Capital Funds Limited (IVCF)
  (c) SIDBI Venture Capital Limited (SVCL)

(ii) Those promoted by State Government controlled development finance institutions, for example :
  (a) Gujarat Venture Finance Limited (GVFL)
  (b) Kerala Venture Capital Fund Pvt. Ltd.
  (c) Punjab Infotech Venture Fund
  (d) Hyderabad Information Technology Venture Enterprises Limited (HITVEL)

(iii) Those promoted by public banks, for example :
  (a) Canbank Venture Capital Fund
  (b) SBI Capital Markets Limited

(iv) Those promoted by private sector companies, for example :
  (a) IL&FS Trust Company Limited
  (b) Infinity Venture India Fund

(v) Those established as an overseas venture capital fund, for example :
  (a) Walden International Investment Group
  (b) SEAF India Investment and Growth Fund
  (c) BTS India Private Equity Fund Limited

All these venture capital funds are governed by the Securities and Exchange Board of India (SEBI). The SEBI is the nodal agency for registration and regulation of both domestic and overseas venture capital funds. Accordingly, it has made the following regulations, namely, Securities and Exchange Board of India (Venture Capital Funds) Regulations, 1996, and Securities and Exchange Board of India (Foreign Venture Capital Investors) Regulations, 2000. These regulations provide broad guidelines and procedures for establishment of venture capital funds both within India and outside it; their management structure and setup as well as size and investment criteria of the funds.

SEBI GUIDELINES FOR VENTURE CAPITAL

Registration of Venture Capital Fund

The applicant for grant of registration as a Venture Capital Fund under SEBI (Venture Capital Funds) Regulations, 1996 should make an application to SEBI in Form A along with all the necessary documents.

Generally, on receipt of application, the applicant will receive a reply from SEBI within 21 working days. The time taken for registration, however, depends on how fast the requirements are complied with by the applicant.

The applicant is advised to go through the SEBI (Venture Capital Funds) Regulations, 1996 for checking the eligibility criteria and such other details which may help expedite the registration process. As an integral part of the registration process, the applicant will submit :

1. Form A along with the application fees of ₹1,00,000 and documents as under:

   (a) Copy of Memorandum and Articles of Association in case the applicant is set up in the form of a Company.

   or

   Copy of Registered Trust Deed in case the applicant is set up in the form of a trust

   or

   Copy of main objective of constitution in case the applicant is set up in the form of a body corporate.

   (b) Copy of Investment Management Agreement.

Apart from the above documents/declarations as required under Form A, the applicant will also be required to submit the details/information as under :

2. Details of the Sponsor/Settler :

   (i) Write up on the activities of the sponsor/settler, its shareholding pattern/profile of the directors. In case of an individual, please state whether the individual is a director/employee of any entity registered with SEBI.

   (ii) State whether, the sponsor/settler has floated venture capital funds previously, which are registered with SEBI. If so give details. Also state whether they (Sponsor or their directors) were refused a certificate by the Board or its certificate has been suspended under regulation 30 or cancelled under regulation 31.

   (iii) State whether the sponsor/settler is registered with SEBI, RBI or any other regulatory authority in any capacity along with the details of its registration.

   (iv) State whether any of its group companies is registered with SEBI, RBI or any regulatory authority along with the details of its registration.

   (v) State whether sponsor/settler or its holding company, is listed on any of the recognised stock exchanges in India. If so details thereof.

   (vi) State whether the sponsor/settler or its directors are involved in any litigation connected with the securities market and any order passed against them for violation of securities laws. If so give details.

3. Details of the Trustees/Trustee Company :

   (i) Write-up on the activities of the Trustee Company/Profile of Trustees.

   (ii) Shareholding pattern and the write-up on profile of the Directors.

(iii) State whether the Trustee Company is registered with SEBI, RBI or any other regulatory authority in any capacity along with the details of its registration.

4. Details of the Investment Manager/Investment Advisor/Asset Management Company (AMC).

   (i) Write up on the activities of the Investment Manager/Investment Advisor/AMC.

   (ii) Shareholding pattern along with the profile of the Directors.

   (iii) State whether the Investment Manager/Advisor/AMC is registered with SEBI, RBI or any' other regulatory authority in any capacity, along with the details.

   (iv) Details of Key Personnel/Management Team. Also state whether they are also the employees of any SEBI registered entity. If so give details;

5. Investment Strategy :

   Disclose in detail the investment strategy of the fund Investment strategy should disclose the investment style or pattern, preferred sectors/industries for investment, proposed corpus, the class of investors, life cycle of the fund and any other information.

6. Declarations to be submitted by the applicant:

   (i) An undertaking under Regulation 11(3) of SEBI (Venture Capital Funds) Regulations, 1996.

   (ii) Undertaking under Third Schedule to SEBI (Venture Capital Funds) Regulations, 1996.

   (iii) Declaration in respect of "Fit and Proper Person" criteria as per regulation 4-A of the SEBI (Venture Capital Funds) Regulation, 1996 and as specified under Schedule II of the Securities and Exchange Board of India (Intermediaries) Regulation, 2008.

7. Grant of Certificate of Registration.

Once all requirements including the 'Fit and Proper Person' criteria have been complied with and on intimation from SEBI for payment of registration fees of ₹5,00,000 as per Second Schedule to Regulations, SEBI will grant the applicant, certification of registration as a SEBI Registered Venture Capital Fund.

Types of Venture Capitalists

(1) Generalists : Venture capitalists are quite wide. They invest in various industry sectors or various geographic locations, or various stages of company's life. Since, they are ready to finance any area of the industry, they are called generalist venture capitalists. These venture capitalists are interested in investing in any business idea with high prospects of success. Actually, they are inclined to invest in emerging areas. These areas are IT industry, financial services, medical and health care, manufacturing and others. They do not have any reservation about the level of financing. They also invest in early start up (seed investing), or may provide funds to start up a company . in its first or second stage of development known as "early stage investing", or may provide funds for expansion of the company,

"Expansion state financing". Actually, venture capitalists invest in a company throughout the company's life cycle.

(2) Specialists : They are interested to invest in one or two industries or sectors or may seek to invest in only a localised geographic area. Specialists help companies in the acquisition, turnaround or recapitalisation of public and private companies that represent favourable investment opportunities. These venture capitalists are expert in specific areas and they exploit the emerging opportunities available in the existing businesses. Identification of profitable business opportunities is a complex process and specialist venture capitalists easily identify these opportunities.

Process of Venture Capital Investment

(1) Deal Origination : Deals may originate in various ways. Parent organisations, trade partners, industry associates are playing very important role in generating and referring deals to the venture capital funds. Networks, trade fairs, conferences, seminars, workshops etc, and intermediaries also help the venture capital funds in generating these business deals. Generally, some professions and trade associates mediate and match VCFs and potential entrepreneurs.

(2) Screening : This is a step in which the venture capitalists reach an initial decision to investigate liability of further investment. The Venture capitalists screen proposals with an initial glance at the business place, and determine whether the proposals are related with the area of its areas of expertise. In case of need, the venture capitalists assess the business plan more thoroughly to identify the potential of the product or idea to obtain first impression of the management.

(3) Evaluation (Due Diligence) : It deals with detailed analysis of the venture. The Entrepreneur is required to provide detailed information of the business plan to the venture capitalists. Assessment of concepts, assessment of principles and assessment of returns are the broad criteria on which venture capitalists evaluate proposals for investment. What (what is the problem that promoter is trying to solve), where (where are the consumers who are having problems), and how (how do you reach the consumer?) are the three broad criteria generally considered by venture capitalists at the time of evaluation" of the proposal.

(4) Deal Structuring : It deals with the decisions regarding terms and conditions of agreement to be signed by the venture capitalists and entrepreneur. It is concerned with the instruments through which funds provided, percentage share of profit or share in management, liquidity of investment, board membership and right to replace management if there is need to do so.

(5) Post-investment Activities. (It is also called Monitoring) : It deals with continuous evaluation of performance of portfolio of venture capital investment. Appreciation in the investment value is the most important objective of the venture capital fund. Monitoring enables the VCFs to get an idea about the fulfilment of this objective.

(6) Exit : Higher appreciation in the investment value, and expiry of investment horizon, if any, motivate the VCFs to opt for exit from the business. In the exit stage, the important aspect is the form or ways or alternatives for exit. Generally, there are three alternatives available to exit from the business. They are going public (IPO); selling to another company; sale of the enterprise or selling the management to a new investor.

Venture Funding for Effective Business Plan

Venture capitalists are the investors with high risk-bearing capacity. If they are ready to assume high risk, naturally they can expect high returns, and *vice-versa*. Venture capitalists balance the risk-return ratio by selecting the investing in a venture which fit in their investment criteria at the time of "Due Diligence".

Venture capitalists generally take into account different criteria for funding. These are location of the business; size of the market; industry structure; option of involvement of venture capitalists; complementary team; etc. However, venture capitalists assess the following aspects before deciding to fund a particular business plan :

1. **Superior Performance :** Sound businesses plans with superior (ideas) products or services, which are targeted at huge, fast growing untapped market, with intellectual property or patents motivate the venture capitalists to extend funding facility. Actually, venture capitalists provide finance for a product or service which cannot easily be imitable.
2. **Quality and Depth of Management:** Quality and depth of the management team decide the liability of the business plan. Management team should professionally be qualified, have a multidisciplinary background, and quality [value added] experience in the business. Besides, integrity and reputation of the team members also carry weight in the assessment process. Great team always help the enterprise to achieve its goal in right direction.
3. **Appropriate Investment Structure :** Venture capitalists are interested in funding projects which has the potential to generate high returns on investment. Financial feasibility report, funds requirement, utilisation of funds, expected returns, expenditure to generate revenues, net profit and internal rate of return etc. are the bases for evaluation of investment structure. Venture capitalists are always interested to have management control as it help them to

improve the performance of the firm. They prefer equity funding to get management control of the firm.

4. **Exit Opportunity** : Venture capitalists provide medium term funds about 3 to 7 years. At the time of evaluating a proposal they clearly look for exit opportunity for their investments. The exit option may be through listing in the stock markets [IPO], or through buyback by the promoters or a third party acquisition or strategic sale to another. In the Indian context, IPO is the most preferred route.

Modes of Financing

1. Equity

Venture capital funds generally provide financial support to entrepreneurs in the form of equity. It is also generally restricted to 49% of the total equity. This is to ensure that the ownership and overall control remains with the entrepreneur. Equity financing is the safest mode of financing as it carries no periodical servicing cost. Moreover, in the initial years of working companies face lower cash in-flows in their income streams. Even these cash inflows are quite uncertain in the initial years. But, in case of debt investments, they require periodical servicing of department.

2. Conditional Loan

Equity is an unsecured instrument, hence, a less preferable option than a secured debt instrument. A conditional loan usually involves either no interest at all or a coupon payment at nominal rate. But, entrepreneur is required to agree pay a royalty in addition to interest. Payment of royalty is generally based on sales turnover. As the units pick up in sales levels, the interest rates are increased and royalty amounts are decreased.

3. Convertible Loans

The convertible loan is subordinate, to all other loans. In case of default in payment of interest in time, there is generally a provision in the agreement that loan is to be converted into equity. It gives ownership rights to the venture capitalists.

Stages of Venture Capital/Financing

1. Early Stage Financing

It includes the following types of financing :

(i) **Seed Capital** : Venture capitalists are generally interested in providing seed finance to turn the business plans into a business. Venture capital funds are also interested to undertake risks and make investment in such R & D projects promising higher returns in future.

(ii) **Start Ups** : Start ups may include new industries/businesses set up by the experienced persons in the area in which they have knowledge. Research bodies or large corporations, having patent or other rights want to go for mutual collaboration with venture capitalists once, provided they are industrially experienced partners. Similarly, new companies having new technology are also interested to commercialise it with the support of venture capital funds.

(iii) Second Round Financing : It deals with the financing when product has already been launched in the market but has not earned enough profit to attract new investors. Additional funds are needed at ' this stage to meet the growing needs of business. Venture capital funds provide large funds at this stage to finance its requirement in the form of debt capital for upto 7 years.

2. Later Stage Financing

It includes the following types of financing :

(i) Development Capital : It refers to the financing of an enterprise which has overcome the highly risky stage and have stal ted earning profits but cannot go public, thus, needs financial support. Funds are needed lor the purchases of new equipment/plant, expansion of marketing and distributing facilities etc. The time scale of investment generally range from one year to three years. It is also called medium risk category.

(ii) Expansion Financing : It deals with the finance required for expansion purpose either by growth implying bigger factory, large warehouses, new factories, new products or new markets or through purchases of exiting business. The timeframe of this type of investment ranges from one year to three years. It represents the last round of financing before a planned exit.

(iii) Buyouts : It is concerned with the transfer of management control by creating a separate business by separating it from their existing owners. It may be of two types :

(a) ***In Management Buyouts (MBOs)*** **:** Venture capital provide financial support to enable the current operating management/ investors to acquire an existing product line/business. They represent an important part of the activity undertaken by the specialists type of venture capitalists.

(b) ***Management Buying (MBIs)*** **:** Venture capitalists provide funds to enable an outside group of professional managers or entrepreneur to buy an existing company. Thus, in this process, there are three parties which comprise a management team, a target company and an investor (i.e., Venture capital funds). MBIs are more risky than MBOs and, hence, are less popular because it is difficult for new management to assess the actual potential of target company. Usually, MBIs are able to target the weaker or underperforming companies.

(iv) **Replacement Capital** : It deals with the arrangement of funds for the purchases of existing share of owners. Basic reasons behind this type of sale of share are the personal need of finance, conflict in the family, or need for association of a well-known name. The time scale of investment is one year to three year and involve low risk.

(v) **Turnarounds Financing** : It involves medium to high risk and a time scale of three years to five years. It also involves buying the control of a sick company which required very specialised skills. Rescheduling company's borrowings, change in management or a change in ownership are the different options before the venture capital funds. Venture capitalists are required to adopt a very active "hands on" approach in the initial crisis period to make the turnaround process a viable process.

Importance of Venture Capital

1. **Advantages to investing public** : Venture capital provides a viable investment platform to the investing public. Direct investment in capital issues may be risky and venture capital fund is promoted by experienced, competent and professionally trained venture capitalists. With their expertise in the field and continuous involvement in the business, they would be able to stop malpractices by management.
2. **Advantage of promoters** : The entrepreneur for the success of public issues is required to convince underwriters, brokers and thousands of investors. Even then, these parties are ready to support and cooperate with first generation entrepreneurs.

General

However, in case of venture capital, the state entrepreneur is expected to convince only venture capitalists about his business ideas. Technological innovation needs its commercial exploitation in time. Venture capital reduces the time lag between the two. This process accelerates the pace of industrial development under this category.

Disinvest Mechanism

The objective of venture capitalists is to invest at appropriate time and sell the investment at substantial capital gains. Venture capitalists generally use the following exit options :

(i) Buyback of equity by promoters

(ii) Public offerings

(iii) Strategic Sale

(iv) Management buyouts.

Thus, venture capitalists are always interested to invest their fund in high risky but most profitable businesses. Their investment horizon ranges from 3 years to 7 years. Ultimately, they have to disinvest their stake in the financed firms through the above mechanism.

EXAMINATION QUESTIONS

Long Answer Questions

1. Define Venture Capital ? Examine its role and limitations.
2. Distinguish between venture capital and private equity. Examine their relevance in Indian context.
3. Examine the process of venture capital investment.
4. Explain the importance and stages of venture capital financing.
5. Critically examine the emergence of venture capital in India.

Short Answer Questions

1. What is venture capital ?
2. What do you mean by generalist venture capitalists ?
3. What are the functions of specialist venture capitalists ?
4. What is management buyouts ?
5. What is deal structuring ?

Objective Type Questions

1. Venture capital is concerned with
   (a) new project having potential for higher profit
   (b) New project of high technology
   (c) New project having high risk
   (d) All of the above
2. Venture capital fund is specially meant for
   (a) Existing entrepreneurs
   (b) First generation entrepreneurs
   (c) Potential entrepreneurs
   (d) None of the above.
3. Deal structuring is concerned with
   (a) Instruments through which funds are provided
   (b) Instrument through which risk is shared
   (c) Instrument through which profit is shared
   (d) Instrument through which exit option is carried out.

4. Venture capitalists are interested in
   (a) Average profit
   (b) Superior profit
   (c) Net profit
   (d) Minds fall gains
5. Seed capital is meant for converting
   (a) The business idea into plan.
   (b) The business plan into business
   (c) The business into viable enterprise
   (c) The business into a multinational enterprise.

Answer Required

1. (a) 2. (b) 3.(c) 4, (b). 5 , (b)

True/False Questions

Whether the following statements are true or false :

1. Venture capital is a risky capital
2. Generalise Venture Capitalists have a wide scope.
3. Venture Capitalists invest their funds for a long period.
4. Due diligence is concerned with detailed analysis of the venture.
5. Management buyout means transfer of management control to outside entrepreneurs.

32

NEW VENTURE FINANCING (START-UPS FINANCING)

One is supposed to have money to make money. Finance is the lifeline of business. A business firm requires finance to commence its operations, to continue its operations and for its expansion and growth. There must be continuous flow of funds in and out of business. Sound plans, efficient production and marketing are all dependent on smooth flow of finance. Hence, a financial plan needs to be prepared, which indicates the requirements of finance, sources for raising the finance and the application of funds. Financial planning for starting a business begins with estimating the total amount of capital required by the firm for the various needs of the business. There are different source of financing for business enterprises. Traditional source of financing for an existing business enterprise includes short-term, medium-term and long-term of financing. For a new enterprise, specially small enterprise, environment of financing business plan is quite different are quite innovative in modern era. New entrepreneurs specially first generation entrepreneurs are facing problems in moblisation of resources. These entrepreneurs at the first instance depend on their own resources.

Thus, sources of financing most new businesses are built without raising substantial amounts of outside capital. They are founded with small infusions of cash from the founders, perhaps augmented by support from relatives or wealthy individuals. In doing so, the founders avoid the effort and dilution of raising capital from institutional investors. The vast majority of small businesses remain small and their founders are happy maintaining family control and pursuing modest growth. In technology, however, two factors confound this common pattern: (i) Founders tend to be very ambitious about growth and liquidity, and (ii) The rapid pace of technological progress makes slow growth unsustainable. Because some technology companies use capital as a competitive weapon to progress more rapidly, all their competitors are compelled to do so as well.

Recognising the necessity to develop and grow rapidly, and the resulting need to raise large amounts of outside capital, first generation entrepreneurs are faced with a range of options, each appropriate to a different stage of growth. Early in the company's development angels and founders can provide the relatively modest amounts of capital (less than ₹50 Lakhs) to get the business plan written, the core management team assembled and a prototype developed. At that point, the promoter or founder turns to professional venture investors for larger amounts of capital, and for the expertise essential to building a larger business firm. Finally, the successful new venture (start-up) turns to major corporations or the public markets for access to even larger blocks of capital and for liquidity for the founders, employees and investors. In recent years, start-up's or new venture financing is getting importance as it is at the initial stage, small business promoters channelise their private resources to finance their new ventures.

EVOLUTION OF NEW VENTURE FINANCING

After the Great depression, which was blamed in part on a rise in speculative investments in unregulated small companies, New venture (start-up) investing was primarily a word of mouth activity reserved for the friends and family of a start-up's co-founders. In the United States, this has been the case ever since the implementation of the Securities Act of 1933. Many nations implemented similar legislations to prohibit general solicitation and general advertising of unregistered securities, including shares offered by start-up companies. Title II of the Jumpstart Our Business Startups Act, first implemented on September 23, 2013, granted start-ups and start-up co-founders or promoters the right to generally solicit and advertise publicly using any method of communication on the condition that only accredited investors are allowed to purchase the securities.

Nature of New Venture Financing

New venture investing is the action of making an investment in an early stage company (the start-up company). The solicitation of funds became easier for start-ups as result of the creative work. Prior to the advent of crowdfunding for equity or debt securities offerings, a form of online investing which has been legalised in several nations, start-ups did not advertise themselves to the general public as investment opportunities until and unless they first obtained approval from regulators for an Initial Public Offering (IPO) which typically involved a listing of the start-up's securities on a stock exchange. Today, there are many alternative forms of IPO commonly employed by start-ups and start-up promoters that do not include an exchange listing, thus enabling start-ups to avoid certain regulatory compliance obligations including mandatory periodic disclosures of financial information and factual discussion of business conditions by management that investors and potential investors routinely receive from registered public companies.

New Venture Financing Cycle

New venture companies can come in all forms and sizes. A critical task in setting up a business is to conduct research in order to validate, assess and develop the ideas or business concepts in addition to opportunities to establish further and deeper understanding on the ideas or business concepts as well as their commercial potential. Business models for start-ups are generally found via a bottom-up or top-down approach. A company may cease to be a start-up as it passes various milestones, such as becoming publicly traded in an IPO, or ceasing to exist as an independent entity via a merger or acquisition. Companies may also fail and cease to operate altogether. Investors are generally most attracted to those new companies distinguished by their risk/reward profile and scalability. That is, they have lower bootstrapping costs, higher risk and higher potential return on investment. Successful start-ups are typically more scalable than an established business, in the sense that they can potentially grow rapidly with limited investment of capital, labor or land.

Startup Financing Cycle

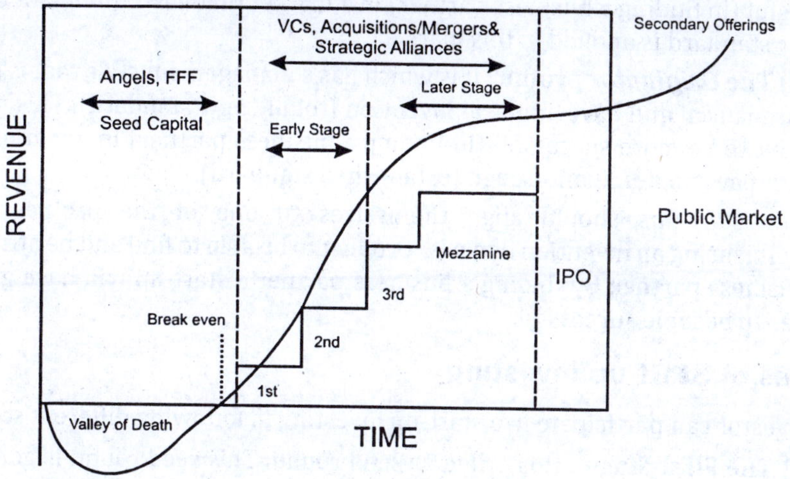

New Venture Cycle

Start-ups encounter several unique options for funding. Venture capital firms and angel investors may help start-up companies begin operations, exchanging seed money for an equity stake. In practice though, many start-ups are initially funded by the founders themselves. Factoring is another option, though not unique to start-ups. Some new funding opportunities are also developing in crowd funding.

New Venture Financial Plan

Financial Plan of a new venture is to be formulated keeping in mind the following factors :

(*i*) The financial objectives of the company.

(*ii*) Nature and size of the business.

(*iii*) The image and credit-worthiness of the enterprise.

(*iv*) Growth and expansion plans.

(*v*) Capital market trends.

(*vi*) Government regulations.

Business Profile of New Venture

Start-ups usually need to form partnerships with other firms to enable their business model. To become attractive to other businesses new venture need to align their internal features, such as management style and products with the market situation. Popular form of a business profile of a new venture is as follows:

(i) The *Inheritor* profile : It calls for management style that is not too entrepreneurial (more conservative) and the startup should have an incremental invention (building on a previous standard). This profile is set out to be more successful (in finding a business partner) in a market that has a dominant design (a clear standard is applied in this market).

(*ii*) The *Originator* profile : It is which has a management style that is highly entrepreneurial and have a radical invention (totally new standard). This profile is set out to be more successful (in finding a business partner) in a market that does not have an dominant design (established standard).

New start-ups should align themselves to one of the profiles when commercialising an invention or a new product to be able to find and be attractive to a business partner. By finding a business partner a start-up will have greater chances to become successful.

Stages of Start-up investing

Investor can participate in a start-up investing in following different stages :

(i) The First Stage : It is called as seed round. This seed round is generally when the start-up is still at the very early days of execution and when their product is still at a prototype phase. At this level, angel investors will be the ones participating.

(ii) The Series—A Stage : At this point the company already has traction and may be making revenue.

(iii)The Series—A Round: Venture capital firms will be participating alongside angels or super angel investors.

(iv)The Series—B, C, and D Rounds : These three stages are the ones leading to the IPO. Venture Capital firms and Private Equity firms will be participating.

Journey of New Venture (Business Start-ups)

(i) Completion of a prototype.

(ii) Completion of the management team.

(iii) Conclusion of beta testing for a product.

(iv) Selling to initial active customers.

(v) Getting customers to place repeat orders.

(vi) Reaching cash flow break-even and profitability.

(vii) Filling out a fuller product line and

(viii) Completing a series of profitable and, growing quarters on plan.

Requisites of Ideal Financing for New Venture

Financing start-ups is a craft, not a science. The company's performance, macroeconomic fluctuations, capital market fads and serendipity each play a role in determining what the best course of action is at any time in a young company's growth. There are many right answers and there is never a time to rest. The best CEOs are always selling their companies, always raising money. Financing a company, like starting a company, is an exercise in predicting the future. Consultation process with management team, board, attorney, and finally consult family team. But do not run out of cash. Requisites of ideal financing for new ventures are as follows :

(*a*) Designing a complete solution to help entrepreneurs to achieve their goals.

(*b*) Working capital to supplement an existing line of credit.

(*c*) Fixed assets.

(*d*) Fund marketing and start-up fees.

(*e*) A franchise purchase.

(*f*) Consulting services.

Sources of New Venture Financing

For decades, entrepreneurs have followed a traditional stair-step of financing methods to vault their companies through successive stages of growth. Starting with personal savings, they would often then raise seed money from personal contacts, move on to banks, angel investors and/or venture capitalists. Eventually, a successful start up would offer shares to investors and become a publicly traded company.

But openings on to that well-trodden paths are narrowing. Banks and venture firms are less liberal with funds since the financial crisis of 2008. Initial public offerings of shares are also harder to float.

However, new fund raising mechanisms have been springing up. The new culture of social media has produced hybrid online platforms with elements of contributing, investing and marketing. Through Kickstarter and Indiegogo, business innovators rely on the kindness of web strangers to back their projects. While supporters celebrate the new opportunities, some experts see dangers of investor fraud, as well as possible pitfalls for unwary start ups. However, major sources of new venture or startups are as follows :

1. Sweat Equity: Entrepreneurs can "fund" the first stage of their business by using their own unpaid labour and resources to create value. Rather than contributing cash, they might write code for a new system or build a workshop in their garage. By investing own resources without outside funding, entrepreneurs are required to develop an idea on his own time. He should control the decisions and any intellectual property he creates. If entrepreneurs have partners efforts are made to provide full credit for their contributions. There is need to have a "deal memo" on the ownership percentage for each partner. A truly original idea conceived in an instant can be worth hours of computer programming. It is better to maintain accounting books. Unequal financial contributions or sweat equity among the partners may change their views on the ownership shares they deserve. There must be a clear agreement and it will avoid lawsuits years later if the enterprise takes off.

2. Personal Financing : Personal saving of an entrepreneur is generally a seed money for the small business. The initial funding for a fledgling private business has often come from its founders. A budding entrepreneur might draw on a personal savings account to finance an indie film. It may not be very creative, but it amazed at the number of "wannabe" entrepreneurs who haven't thought about saving any money before they start, or wouldn't think of using their own savings to start a business. No investor will put money into a deal if they see that potential entrepreneur have no "skin in the game." The entrepreneur can retain control of their project. They are also proving to future funders that they're willing to put their own money at risk to launch their business.

3. Personal Credit Lines: Entrepreneur may qualify for a secured personal credit line based on his personal credit efforts. A credit card can be used to pay for the machine tools needed to build a sample product or prototype. Credit cards can usually be acquired with even less history. It is well known fact that start-ups have been built on one or both of these. The advantage is that entrepreneur retain total ownership and control, as long as he make minimum payments.

4. Friends and Family: These are people who should believe in the entrepreneur, without waiting to see if his idea works, or waiting until he have real customers, revenue, and hard assets. These commitments should always be positioned in writing as promissory notes, or so-called bridge-loans, which convert to equity at a rate determined by later investors. When a young enterprise produces promising early results, the founders' friends and family have often been the first outsiders who chip in money to help it grow. The entrepreneurs' parents may give them a loan, or their college friends may buy small ownership stakes. Friends and family often help because they want to support the entrepreneurs, not for an expected profit.

5. Bank Loans: Banks and credit unions make loans to small businesses that need cash to fund their next growth spurt. If the small company is already profitable, lenders may advance the cash for business expansions, such as new store locations, that will increase profits.

Entrepreneurs may qualify for loan guarantees or lower interest rates through programs of the small business chamber of commerce or local economic development agencies. The bank takes no ownership share of the company promoted by the entrepreneurs. Banks see small business loans as risky investments. To get a loan on favorable terms, entrepreneurs need a solid business plan, extensive documentation of entrepreneurs creditworthiness and possibly assets to post as collateral. To help entrepreneurs navigate the loan process, web-based outfits such as Multifunding.com is now offering to connect entrepreneurs with lenders, guide entrepreneurs, choice among banks or facilitate loan applications of the entrepreneurs.

6. Peer-to-Peer Lending: This is a process whereby a group of people comes together to lend money to each other. It's been around many years, in examples like small business groups or ethnic groups supporting similar efforts. In the start-up context, look for a successful entrepreneur peer willing to fund similar new ideas.

7. Microloans: There are many private companies and non-profits organisations that offer small loans, up to 2 crores, to promote entrepreneurship, to individuals who would not normally quality for bank financing. For example, SKS Finance Ltd.

8. Vendor Financing: If entrepreneurs need tangible products for inventory, many manufacturers and distributors can be convinced to defer their payment until the goods are sold by them. This really means an extension of the normal 30-day payment terms to a period of months or longer, depending on their credit worthiness and extra fees.

9. Purchase Order Financing: The most common scaling problem faced by startups is the inability to accept a large new order, since they don't have the cash to build and deliver the product. (Purchase Order) financing companies will often advance the required funds directly to the supplier, allowing the transaction to complete and profit to flow to the start-up.

10. Factoring Accounts Receivables: This is similar in concept to PO financing, but applies the advance to unpaid amounts not yet due or collected from customers. In high volume start-ups starting to scale up, this will provide cash on entrepreneurs sales immediately, rather than waiting for 30 to 60 days or longer for payment.

11. Investment Retirement Accounts (IRA) Financing: Investment Retirement Account funds are arguably the single most accessible alternative funding source available today for start-ups. It is the amount that has already withdrawn from a viable venture to be used again for some other start-ups destination. Entrepreneur cannot use his own self-directed funds for his start-up, but many others are willing and able to loan you money from theirs, for the right terms, if they believe in the entrepreneur and his cause.

12. Angel Investors: An Angel investor or angel (also known as a business angel or informal investor or angel funder) is an affluent individual who provides capital for a business start-up, usually in exchange for convertible debt or ownership equity. A small but increasing number of angel investors organise themselves into angel groups or angel networks to share research and pool their investment capital, as well as to provide advice to their portfolio companies. Angel investors are often experienced entrepreneurs, who can become valuable advisers to a young company. Wealthy individuals called angel investors like to make financial bets on early stage private companies that are capable of rapid growth, but that are still too small to seek millions from venture capital firms. Angels, often take an ownership stake in exchange for their private investment of personal funds. Such sales of company shares are called "private placements."

13. Crowdfunding: Entrepreneurs generally use the power of the internet to find a crowd of like-minded people, with small amounts each, to back their efforts. This approach is now spreading beyond non-profits, pre-sales and memento rewards, to soon include the ability to make small equity investments. Innovative businesses can now use social media sites such as Kickstarter and Indiegogo to appeal for financial support through "crowdfunding" campaigns. Entrepreneurs attract backers by posting their imaginative plans and often, by promising perks to those who pitch in some money. Those perks range from product samples to an invitation to join a company-sponsored activity. This new form of crowdfunding authorised by the government will allow private sales of company shares through social media sites and other intermediaries. Companies could raise as much as 10 crore a year through small private investments from an unlimited number of people. Crowdfunding websites are expected to crop up the fund raised programmes for the companies. These fundraising platforms are expected to emerge after the government formulates necessary regulations for small companies. The regulatory requirements, such as financial disclosures, would be less stringent than general SEBI rules for registering securities or for making an initial public offering of shares. But the most important limiting factor in this funding arrangement is that many new shareholders have rights under the regulatory laws. Complying with those rights could soak up company's time and money. A start-up's crowdfunding investors may also look like a cumbersome burden to some venture capital firms you'd counted on for the next round of financing of the company.

14. Revenues: The least dilutive way to finance a company is with profits. It is the most popular source of financing a new venture though it is quite slow and time taking. Before raising capital, entrepreneurs are also required to control costs and increase revenues. If income statement of the companies cannot provide any more help, then it would be better to take a look at the balance sheet. There is hidden cash in old receivables—and if they're old because of unhappy customers, the company will need to resolve those problems before prospective investors begin their calls.

15. Venture Capital: This is a popular vehicle for leveraging an initial venture investment. Many of these firms can provide a flexible array of services also that allow the small entrepreneurs to devote their more expensive capital to people rather than computers and cubicles. Venture capitalists also like this vehicle because it helps improve their return on investment as well. Price is by no means the most important factor in choosing a venture debt firm. Ask for reference CEOs of difficult accounts to learn how the lender reacts in tough times. Venture capital firms, can devote several crores to the growth of a young company that has established its potential to market valuable new technology, goods or services. Venture firms invest pools of money, raised from wealthy individuals, in enterprises with potentially high rates of return. Venture firms bring management expertise and guidance in realising the full financial payoff for investments in fast growing companies. In exchange for risking their capital, venture firms seek a substantial ownership stake and often, seats on the funded company's board of directors.

16. Corporate Partners: Corporate investors represent a double-edged sword to small companies. They can bring great resources to bear. They can also impose ponderous decision-making processes on fragile start-up companies. Venture capitalists only have one agenda in their investing, the maximisation of stock value. That happens to be the same agenda as the company's founders. Corporate investors usually have a more complex and less compatible agenda in mind such as a pipeline of technology or products, or access to key people. The people making the initial investment frequently change jobs and the relationship with the company can fall hostage to corporate politics.

17. Mergers and Acquisitions: An entrepreneur's tiny private company may reach its next stage of growth by becoming part of a large corporation that offers to buy it. Big companies often acquire creative enterprises whose new product or service dovetails with their own business activities. Original promoter partners and investors can get a cash payout for betting on a winning idea and bringing it to life. After this "exit" from their investment, they can use their financial gains to start another company, or to rest from your labours. Companies may forfeit even greater financial rewards that might have been reaped from retaining control of your company and offering ownership shares to the investing public in an IPO. And if the acquiring corporation doesn't ask promoter of merging company by the merging company to stay on, other people will explore the full potential of the business you nurtured.

18. Initial Public Offering: A privately owned company can raise a substantial amount of fresh capital for further growth by offering shares to the general public in an initial public offering. The private enterprise becomes a publicly traded company whose shares can be bought and sold on the NSE and BSE. After the IPO, the pre-existing ownership stakes of the company founders and early investors have a specific value determined by the stock's daily trading price.

Small company can fund new growth opportunities through IPO. The company and other shareholders may benefit if share prices rise with profits. But also, founders and early investors, such as venture firms, have opportunities to cash out, or "exit" from the investment by selling their shares on a stock exchange.

The value of company shares may fall well below their initial offering price, depending on the ongoing performance of the business and economic conditions. Registration as a publicly traded company brings new requirements for frequent public disclosures of financial reports, and compliance with other SEBI rules. However, there may be certain relations from the regulatory requirements for up to five years for "emerging growth companies" that conduct IPOs. These companies can delay compliance with certain SEBI rules, including some auditing requirements. But they must comply fully once they complete the relation time set for them.

ANGEL INVESTOR

Angel investors are high net-worth individuals who represent an essential source of funding for early stage, high-risk ventures. They are estimated to provide 90% of all seed and start-up capital, while the venture capital community provides less than 2% of start-up financing.

An investor who provides financial backing for small start-ups or entrepreneurs. Angel investors are usually found among an entrepreneur's family and friends. The capital they provide can be a one-time injection of seed money or ongoing support to carry the company through difficult times.

Angel investors are often retired entrepreneurs or executives, who may be interested in angel investing for reasons that go beyond pure monetary return. These include wanting to keep abreast of current developments in a particular business arena, mentoring another generation of entrepreneurs and making use of their experience and networks on a less than full-time basis. Thus, in addition to funds, angel investors can often provide valuable management advice and important contacts. Because there are no public exchanges listing their securities, private companies meet angel investors in several ways, including referrals from the investors' trusted sources and other business contacts; at investor conferences and symposia; and at meetings organised by groups of angels where companies pitch directly to investor in face-to-face meetings.

Angel investors are generally secretative in nature. Their desire for privacy makes them difficult to identify and contact. A number of formal sources have developed, including directories, conventions, incubators, and electronic networks. In addition, professional advisors, such as attorneys, accountants and bankers, can provide assistance in the search for private investors. Placement agents can be hired, but this is a more expensive route. The most valuable source is the entrepreneur's own network of friends and family who can provide personal endorsement to the investor.

Historical Perspective

The term "angel" originally comes from Broadway, where it was used to describe wealthy individuals who provided money for theatrical productions. In 1978, William Wetzel, then a professor at the University of New Hampshire and founder of its Center for Venture Research, completed a pioneering study on how entrepreneurs raised seed capital in the USA and he began using the term "angel" to describe the investors that supported them.

Beginning in the late 1980s, angels started to coalesce into informal groups with the goal of sharing deal flow and due diligence work and pooling their funds to make larger investments. Angel groups are generally local organisations made up of 10 to 150 accredited investors interested in early-stage investing. In 1996, there were about 10 angel groups in the United States. It used to be that angel investors were wealthy people the business owner knew. Or they might be veteran entrepreneurs who were discovered through old-fashioned networking at the local Chamber of Commerce. These days, though, angel groups are proliferating, offering plenty of mentoring and coaching on top of the money provided.

In India, the Finance Act, 2012, introduced a provision through amendment of section 56 which was called 'Startup Tax' or 'Angel Tax'. Under this, share premium above the fair value of investment by Indian angel investors is taxed SEBI regulation in 2013 provided relief to angels investing through a fund, but not for individuals. Angels need to stay invested for 36 months to benefit from long terms capital gains tax.

On an average, active angel investors who back startups invest ₹60-70 lakhs per year. Angel investors cut cheques starting from ₹ 5 lakhs personal allocation among entrepreneurs can range from 5% to 50%, but majority of their personal wealth is locked up in their own business and real estate.

Indian Angel Network, which backed data security company Druva Software in 2008, has seen some angels exit the company with 22 times returns. Mobile advertisement firm In Mobi also saw certain investors from Mumbai Angels exit at over 20-30x in early 2010. Ratan Tata bought stake from angel investor Kenneth Glass in e-tailer Snapdeal, after it was valued at $1 billion. Sequoia Capital giving partial exit to angels in OYO Rooms at ₹140-150 crore valuation, as compared to entry valuation of ₹ 3-5 crore.

Features of Angel Investments

(*i*) Angel investments bear extremely high risks and are usually subject to dilution from future investment rounds. As such, they require a very high return on investment. Because a large percentage of angel investments are lost completely when early stage companies fail.

(*ii*) Professional angel investors seek investments that have the potential to return at least ten or more times their original investment within 5 years, through a defined exit strategy, such as plans for an initial public offering or an acquisition.

(*iii*) They use Current 'best practices' : It suggets that angels might do better setting their sights even higher, looking for companies that will have at least the potential to provide a 20x-30x return over a five- to seven-year holding period.

(*iv*) Angle investors need to cover failed investments and the multi-year holding time for even the successful ones, the actual effective internal rate of return for a typical successful portfolio of angel investments is, in reality, typically as 'low' as 20–30%.

(*v*) Angle investor's need for high rates of return on any given investment can thus make angel financing an expensive source of funds, cheaper sources of capital, such as bank financing, are usually not available for most early stage ventures

(*vi*) They offer expertise, experience, and contacts that can be invaluable to the new venture. Angel investors often work in groups to improve the efficiency of their due diligence and to allow them to complete larger deals.

(*vii*) They raise small funds to invest more broadly in seed stage companies — earning the name "Super Angels" and blurring the line between angels and venture capitalists.

Sources of Angel Funding

(*i*) They invest their own funds.

(*ii*) They manage the pooled money of others in a professionally-managed fund.

(*iii*) They use business, limited liability company, investment fund, or other vehicle.

(*iv*) They fill the gap in start-up financing between "friends and family", who provide seed funding, and formal venture capital.

Thus, angel investment is a common second round of financing for high-growth start-ups, and accounts in total for almost as much money invested annually as all venture capital funds. There is no "set amount" for angel investors, and the range can go anywhere from a few thousand, to a few million rupees.

Working Process of Angel Investing

(*i*) Angel investments — which in India range from ₹50 lakh to ₹3 crore — are typically done in groups of at least 5-6 investors.

(*ii*) Some members of the angel consortium also take a board seat.

(*iii*) Angels invest their personal money in a start-up, mostly in their area of expertise, often marking it the first outside capital for a start-up.

(*iv*) It is followed by venture capital funding, which is institutional capital

(*v*) Angels typically exit after series B or C round of funding, while some continue to hold shares even after the IPO.

Merits of Angel Investments

(*i*) They give more favorable terms than other lenders, as they are usually investing in the person rather than the viability of the business.

(*ii*) They are focused on helping the business succeed, rather than reaping a huge profit from their investment. Angel investors are essentially the exact opposite of a venture capitalist.

(*iii*) They take much less time, on average, to meet with and receive funds from a private investor than a venture capital firm.

(*iv*) The due diligence is less involved with an angel investor and angels typically expect a lower rate of return.

(*v*) Angel investors take a board position or an important advising role (*vi*) Angel investments has become a status symbol in the start-up ecosystem, entrepreneurs should cover their basic financial needs like a house and financial liquidity before venturing into it.

Limitations of Angles Investments

(*i*) Angel-funded entrepreneurs can be dissatisfied with the level of involvement. Venture capitalists often provide considerably more support in the management of the business, setting of targets and staffing.

(*ii*) An entrepreneur in search of capital must identify the start-up's non-financial needs and determine the required skills for investors. Before accepting angel financing, the entrepreneur should understand the investor's motivations and goals and establish guidelines for their respective roles.

(*iii*) Any financing round that involves selling shares to new investors can reduce the entrepreneur's freedom to make business decisions unilaterally. The new ownership structure may also limit valuations and options for the next round of financing. Privately held shares have traditionally been hard to sell to others.

(*iv*) Angel investments are also highly illiquid, so funds are not accessible in case of urgency.

(*v*) Investors who have a fixed return expectation and requirement should avoid angel investments as it is a high-risk and return assets class.

CROWDFUNDING

It is the practice of funding a project or venture by raising monetary contributions from a large number of people, typically via the internet. It is generally described as "the practice of raising funds from two or more people over the internet towards a common service, project, product, investment, cause, and experience or otherwise."

The crowdfunding model is popular among three types of actors: the project initiator who proposes the idea and/or project to be funded; individuals or groups who support the idea; and a moderating organisation (the "platform") that brings the parties together to launch the idea.

The inputs of the individuals in the crowd trigger the crowdfunding process and influence the ultimate value of the offerings or outcomes of the process. Each individual acts as an agent of the offering, selecting and promoting the projects in which they believe. They will sometimes play a donor role oriented towards providing help on social projects. In some cases, they will become shareholders and contribute to the development and growth of the offering. Each individual disseminates information about projects they support in their online communities, generating further support (promoters).

Motivation for consumer participation stems from the feeling of being at least partly responsible for the success of others' initiatives (desire for patronage), striving to be a part of a communal social initiative (desire for social participation), and seeking a payoff from monetary contributions (desire for investment). An individual who takes part in crowdfunding initiatives tends to reveal several distinct traits: innovative orientation, which stimulates the desire to try new modes of interacting with firms and other consumers; social identification with the content, cause or project selected for funding, which sparks the desire to be a part of the initiative; (monetary) exploitation, which motivates the individual to participate by expecting a payoff.

Types of Crowdfunding

Main types of croudfunding are as follows:

(i) Reward-based Crowdfunding: Under reward-based crowdfunding, entrepreneurs pre-sell a product or service to launch a business concept without incurring debt or sacrificing equity/shares. Reward-based crowdfunding has been used for a wide range of purposes, including motion picture promotion, free software development, inventions development, scientific research and civic projects. Generally, there are, two types of reward-based crowdfunding :

(*a*) ***'Keep-it-All' (KIA):*** Where the entrepreneurial firm sets a fundraising goal and keeps the entire amount raised regardless of whether or not they meet their goal.

(*b*) ***'All-or-Nothing' (AON):*** Where the entrepreneurial firm sets a fundraising goal and keeps nothing unless the goal is achieved."

"Overall, [all-or-nothing] fundraising campaigns involved substantially larger capital goals, and were much more likely to be successful at achieving their goals." The study suggests that potential investors are more inclined to support "all-or-nothing strategy" initiatives, whereby a substandard product will not be released if the funding goal is not achieved. The study further suggests that "AON" campaign typically provide more detailed information on the campaign.

(ii) Equity-based Crowdfunding: Equity crowdfunding (also known as "hyperfunding") is a mechanism that enables broad groups of investors to fund start-up companies and small businesses in return for equity. Investors give money to a business and receive ownership of a small piece of that business. If the business succeeds, then its value goes up, as well as the value of a share in that business—the converse is also true. Coverage of equity crowdfunding indicates that its potential is greatest with start-up businesses that are seeking smaller investments to achieve establishment, while follow-on funding (required for rapid growth) may come from other sources.

Selling investments via crowdfunding has been called crowdfund investing, crowdinvesting, or even simply crowdfunding, as in "legalise crowdfunding". Some have called for standardisation of the terminology in a way that distinguishes the practice from other forms of crowdfunding. Investment crowdfunding can be debt-based or equity-based, or can follow other models, including profit-sharing and hybrid models. It is notable that under equity-based crowdfunding, the backer receives unlisted shares of a company, usually in its early stages, in exchange for the money pledged. The company's success is determined by how successfully it can demonstrate its viability. Actually, equity-based crowdfunding is the collective effort of individuals to support efforts initiated by other people or organisations through the provision of finance in the form of equity.

Investment crowdfunding can breach various securities laws, because soliciting investments from the general public is often illegal, unless the opportunity has been filed with an appropriate securities regulatory authority, such as the SEBI. The Howey test says that a transaction constitutes an investment contract (therefore a security) if there is (i) an exchange of money (ii) with an expectation of profits arising (iii) from a common enterprise (iv) which depends solely on the efforts of a promoter or third party. Any crowdfunding arrangement in which investors are asked to contribute money in exchange for potential profits based on the work of others would be considered a security. As such, the applicable investment contract would have to be registered with a regulatory agency, unless it qualified for one of several exemptions.

(iii) Credit-based Crowdfunding : Debt crowdfunding allows a group of lenders to lend funds to individuals or businesses in return for interest payment on top of capital repayments. Also known as Peer to peer lending or Peer to business lending. Borrowers must demonstrate creditworthiness and the capability to repay the debt, making it unsuitable for NINA or start-ups.

In recent years in foreign countries, credit-based crowdfunding from non-banks became more prominent as a form of crowdfunding. Prospective borrowers of the Lending Club first submit their requirements, and are then matched with pools of investors who are willing to accept the credit terms. Platforms such as the Lending Club gained popularity, as banks increased interest rates or reduced their level of lending activity.

Crowdfunding Platforms

Internationally, there is big growth of crowdfunding platforms. Project creators need to do their own due diligence in order to understand which platform is the best to use depending on the type of project that they want to launch. There are fundamental differences in the services provided by many crowdfunding platforms.

For instance, CrowdCube and Seedrs are both Internet platforms which enable small companies to issue shares over the Internet and receive small investments from registered users in return. While CrowdCube is meant for users to invest small amounts and acquire shares directly in start-up companies, Seedrs on the other hand pools the funds to invest in new businesses, as a nominated agent. Curated crowdfunding platforms such as SeedInvest and FundersClub serve as a "network orchestrators" by curating the offering that are allowed on the platform.

They create the necessary organisational systems and conditions for resource integration among other players to take place.

Relational mediators act as an intermediary between supply and demand (e.g., SellaBand, Kickstarter). They replace traditional intermediaries (such as traditional record companies, venture capitalists). These platforms link new artists, designers, project initiators with committed supporters who believe in the persons behind the projects strongly enough to provide monetary support. Growth engines focus on the strong inclusion of investors. They dis-intermediate by eliminating the activity of a service provider previously involved in the network. The platforms that use crowdfunding to seek stakes from a community of high net worth, private investors and match them directly with project initiators.

Merits of Crowdfunding

(i) **Profile:** It helps in raising a producer's profile and provide a boost to their reputation.

(ii) **Marketing:** Project initiators can show there is an audience and market for their project. In the case of an unsuccessful campaign, it provides good market feedback.

(iii) **Audience Engagement:** Crowd funding creates a forum where project initiators can engage with their audiences. Audience can engage in the production process by following progress through updates from the creators and sharing feedback via comment features on the project's crowdfunding page.

(iv) **Feedback:** It offers pre-release access to content or the opportunity to beta-test content to project backers as a part of the funding incentives provides the project initiators with instant access to good market testing feedback.

Limitations of Crowdfunding

(i) Reputation: If new venture fails to meet campaign goals or to generate interest result in a public failure. Reaching financial goals and successfully gathering substantial public support but being unable to deliver on a project for some reason can severely negatively impact the reputation of the new venture.

(ii) IP Protection : Many Interactive Digital Media developers and content producers are reluctant to publicly announce the details of a project before production due to concerns about idea theft and protecting their IP from plagiarism.

(iii) Donor Exhaustion : There is a risk that if the same network of supporters is reached out to multiple times, that network will eventually cease to supply necessary support.

(iv) Public Fear of Abuse : Concern among supporters that without a regulatory framework, the likelihood of a scam of abuse of funds is high. The concern may become a barrier to public engagement.

(v) Lack of Due Diligence : Investors don't always do their due diligence to determine if it's a sound investment before investing, which leads to making investment decisions based on emotion rather than financial logic.

INITIATIVE IN INDIA FOR START-UPS FINANCING

In a move that will help start-ups struggling to raise funds, SEBI is warming to the idea of allowing crowdfunding, a popular concept in developed countries. Crowdfunding is seeking funds (in small amounts) from multiple investors through a web-based platform or a social networking for a specific project, business venture or social cause. SEBI came out with a consultation paper on crowdfunding on Tuesday to provide alternative financing sources to start-ups. It wants the issue fund-raising capped at ₹10 crore a year for each start-up. However, companies which want to raise more than ₹10 crore may do so by listing shares on an SME platform or main board of a recognised stock exchange.

To ensure that retail investors do not end up bearing all the risks of start-up ventures, the market regulator proposes to permit only certain retail and accredited investors to participate in crowdfunding. Retail investors who can participate in crowdfunding should be getting advice from an investment consultant or a portfolio manager or should have passed an appropriateness test (may be conducted by an institution accredited by the National Institute of Securities Markets or the crowdfunding platform). Also, only investors with a minimum annual gross income of ₹10 lakh and those who have filed income-tax returns for at least three financial years will be eligible to participate.

Investors "have to issue a certificate that will not invest more than ₹60,000 in an issue through the crowdfunding platform and not invest more than 10 per cent of their net worth, which excludes the value of the primary residence or any loan secured on such property." Accredited investors, the other set that can invest in start-ups, include qualified institutional buyers, companies with a minimum net worth of ₹20 crore and high networth individuals (HNIs) with a minimum net worth of ₹2 crore. Though there is no cap on QIBs, a maximum of 200 HNIs and retail investors can participate in an issue.

Restrictions

There are curbs on fund raisers too. According to the SEBI proposal, a company promoted, sponsored or related to an industrial group with a turnover in excess of ₹25 crore or which has an established business is not eligible for crowdfunding.

Also barred are realty companies, listed corporates and firms which have been in existence for more than two years. The crowdfunding route is not open to a company that proposes to use the funds raised to provide loans or make investments in other entities.

Start-ups shall not use multiple crowdfunding platforms nor advertise their offering or solicit investments from the public. The issuer should compulsorily route all crowdfunding issues through a SEBI—recognised platform. Only national stock exchanges and SEBI-registered depositories are eligible to set up a crowdfunding platform. SEBI is also open to allowing technology business incubators promoted by the Centre or a State government to set up a crowdfunding platform. Now, the market regulator will wait for comments and suggestions on the consultation paper from industry and market participants.

Steps To Ease Start-ups

Who can raise funds?

A company intending to raise capital not exceeding ₹10 crore in a period of 12 months.

A company which is not promoted, sponsored or related to an industrial group that has a turnover of over ₹25 crore.

Investment Eligibility are as follows :

(*i*) *Accredited investors*

- Qualified institutional buyers
- Companies with a minimum net worth of ₹20 crore
- HNIs with a minimum net worth of ₹2 crore

(*ii*) *Retail investors*

- Who receive advice from an investment consultant or portfolio manager
- With a minimum annual income of ₹10 lakh

Who have filed Income-Tax return for at least 3 financial years.

SMALL AND MEDIUM ENTERPRISES EXCHANGES (SME EXCHANGE)

Small and Medium Enterprises (SMEs) are small-sized companies often at the beginning of their growth cycle. When an organisation is starting out, either promoters use their own funds or get the help of financing investors such as private equity funds and venture capitalists. Of course, there is an option of adding debt, which also helps improve the overall return on equity, but the cost of raising debt for SMEs is relatively higher. High interest expense does not look very good on the profit and loss statement of a growing company. Thus, in order to fund the next stage of growth without excessive interest cost burden, companies look to access equity funds via capital market. This is where listing in an exchange comes into the picture.

A large group of investors could be interested in SME exchanges. Private equity (PEs) to venture capital (VCs)/ angel investors, High networth individuals (HNIs) to strategic investors, VC-assisted companies looking for next round of funding, subsidiaries of large firms looking to unlock value, are some who would be interested to invest on SMEs listed on these platforms. Unlike regular companies, the SME's IPO paper's are vetted by bourses rather than SEBI. Any company with an issue capital smaller than ₹10 crore at the IPO time, will be allowed to list on SME platform. Any firm can list on the main bourse if its issue capital crosses ₹25 crore subsequently as per SEBI guidelines.

The SME platform is a completely different regime, where it is a classic development role for the stock exchanges. That would mean setting higher benchmarks and not playing the numbers game to be one up a rival bourse and being choosy in the kind of companies it wants to list and the intermediaries who stay the course with them. More so this time because another botched attempt could lead to regulatory overkill and any potential loss of credibility will hurt the smallest of firms hoping to attract risk capital in a difficult environment.

Historical Perspective

During 2013-14, a land mark development was initiated in country's financial sector with the launch of an exchange dedicated to small and medium enterprises (SMEs.). While the concept of SME exchange is not new to India, focused efforts from the regulator and exchanges would be required to make a successful beginning in this niche field. According to the Securities and Exchange Board of India (SEBI), the new platform has been formulated after a detailed study of best practices from across the world and feedback from market participants. It has also taken into learning from past attempts. One was Over-the-counter Exchange of India (OTCEI), launched in 1990 with aim of becoming the Nasdaq of India. It introduced many concepts that were new to the Indian capital markets then such as screen-based nationwide trading, sponsorship of companies, market making and scripless trading. However, the 1992 scam and the bear market that followed killed the initiative. India has, in the past, experimented unsuccessfully with Over-The-Counter Exchange of India (OTCEI) in 1989, and the Indo-Next Platform for SME on BSE in 2005.

For the third time in the Indian stock market history, small and medium enterprises (SMEs) now have a new platform to access funds from people other than friends and family in the Bombay Stock Exchange (BSE) SME exchange that completed its first initial public offer (IPO) in February, 2014.

So., where India's Big Two – the National Stock Exchange and BSE – stipulate a minimum paid-up capital of ₹10 crore, companies with lower paid-up capital can raise as little as ₹50 lakh on this new SME platform.

BSE Indonext, launched in 2007, was specially created to cater to SMEs listed on region exchanges were unable to attract trader attention for lack of advanced technology, BSE tried give them a lease of life under the new platform. The companies listed on BSE IndoNext, however, did not attract much market participation either.

Both BSE Ltd. and National Stock Exchange of India Ltd have launched their versions of an SME exchange this year. The BSE SME Exchange took off with the listing of BCB Finance Ltd. in March 2014 and the NSE equivalent. Emerge, took off with the listing of Thejo Engineering Ltd. April, 2014.

The only exception is retail investors who have nothing to benefit from these SME platforms as they are virtually barred since the minimum lot size for an IPO as well as trading is ₹ 1 lakh.

Rationale of SME Exchanges

(*i*) An SME exchange helps small companies with a good track record to raise capital through equity shares.

(*ii*) Generally, many good enterprises are denied a listing, since they do not meet the minimum paid-up capital requirement of the main exchanges.

(*iii*). An SME-focused stock exchange would correct the situation and boost the confidence of small enterprises.

(*iv*) Availability of easy and low-cost capital through dedicated exchanges gives a fillip to the SME sector and boost domestic employment.

(*v*) The governance process and practices of SMEs will become more transparent as Sebi acting as the regulator for SME exchanges.

(*vi*) Strict listing norms impart discipline in their overall functioning, especially in accounting standards.

(*vii*) Listing enhances the status of small companies, and give them spin-off gains in brand building, visibility and recognition.

(*viii*) SME exchanges, facilitate the future growth of the MSME sector.

(*ix*) Issuers and exchanges will have to face straightaway in terms of identifying the kind of merchant bankers that can provide enough capital to act as market-makers and also ensure good quality issuance.

(*x*) It spawn a new category of bankers capable of both fund and feebased activities and for whom the levels of due diligence are far higher in handling public share sales.

(xi) They need to be guided on governance provisions as they prepare to list with the rules making it mandatory for them to have more independent directors on board. That is not easy when top-rung listed firms are struggling to attract good quality professionals to serve as independent directors.

(xii) The intermediaries who are working with the platform, are not too keen because they feel the money is too little. Even if a banker charges five per cent of the money raised, which is usually the upper end of the fee for big public offers, he will get a princely ₹50 lakh for managing an issue of ₹10 crore. They would rather spend their resources running free services for government share sales and boost league.

Exchanges as an Alternative Source of Financing

Accounting to various estimates, India has nearly three millions SMEs. Collectively, they account for almost 50 per cent of industrial output and 42 per cent of total exports. The sector has been clamouring for higher fund flows for a long time. There are about 26 million small firms employing more than twice that number of big enterprises. SME exchanges are now an important alternative source of finance for SMEs globally. A dedicated SME exchange gives SMEs an opportunity to boost their capital and presents private and corporate investors with a wide array of investment options. Across the world, such exchanges have been playing a key role in financing small enterprises, thereby facilitating the evolution and growth of well-managed, quality enterprises.

Internationally also, countries have provided for a separate exchange/trading platform to facilitate listing of securities of growth companies/new economy companies/small and medium companies. Some of the cases in point are the Alternative investment Market (AIM), London, the Growth Enterprises Market (GEM), Hong Kong and Mothers, Japan. Out of these, the GEM is a separate dedicated stock exchange whereas, the AIM and the MOTHERS are trading platforms of their respective man stock exchanges.

The BSE SME is different from other Stock exchanges in its operational behaviour. The concept is similar to the OTCEI, but additional safeguards such as 100 per cent underwriting of offerings, easier compliance norms such as half-yearly reporting instead of quarterly for bigger firms and the provision to migrate to the main board have been put in place. SEBI has also waived listing conditions such as profitability for three years, approval of prospectus by SEBI and so on.

The SME exchange is off the blocks with BCB Finance, a Mumbai-based firm, launching its IPO. A good start is important in a race but in the case of the SME exchange, there are no podium finishes; the prize is for breasting the tape. And the exchange needs a lot of running to do before it can get anywhere near the finish line.

Estimates put the contribution of SMEs to the country's gross domestic product at eight per cent. The big exchanges, which are considered barometers of India's trillion-dollar economy, heave a market capitalisation of around a trillion dollars. Therefore, a SME exchange, which represents eight per cent of the company, should have a market capitalisation of $80 billion or ₹4 lakh crore. Assuming SME promoters will sell stocks worth 30 per cent of their companies in the exchange, we should see initial share sales of ₹1.5 lakh crore.

Mechanism of SME Exchange

The minimum depth of the quote shall be ₹1,00,000. However, the investors with holdings of value less than ₹1,00,000 shall be allowed to offer their holding to the market in that scrip provided that he sells his entire holding in that scrip in one lot along with a declaration to the effect to the selling broker. The market maker's role, thus, is crucial because it gives investor an exit option.

To start with, the regulator has ensured that the onus of issuance, due diligence and post-listing is on the merchant banker; much like in other markets. Market-making and underwriting of the full issue is mandatory which is sure to fob off some of the big boys in the business — who are anyway more keen on the pecking order in the league tables.

The rules on market-making for merchant bankers may well be restrictive considering that not even institutions or non-banking finance companies with deeper pockets are allowed to offer such two-way quotes. The regulator has mandated that the market-maker should provide two-way quote for 75% of the time during a day. The NSE is working on an auction mechinsm so that at a pre-determined time during the day, there will be and attempt to match the interest of buyers and sellers.

While these are second-level issues post-listing, what is critical to the success of the venture this time is identification of the kind of companies that the stock exchanges want to showcase on the new exchange platforms. Unlike on the main board or the main stock exchange, SMEs will need to recast their financial statements to comply to migrate to more rigorous accounting standards.

The Bombay Stock Exchange has been quick off the draw, with the listing of a finance, company, while the National Stock Exchange is expected to list a few SMEs that are into manufacturing. The timing may not be bad, coming as it does at a time when companies are squeezed for capital and with lenders wary of exposure to a sector that they regard as far more riskier and vulnerable to an economic downturn. And the policy design this time appears to have taken into account some of the mistakes of the past and building on practices elsewhere.

Challenges before SME Exchanges

SME Exchanges are generally facing following challenges -

(*i*) The biggest challenge is in ensuring gate-keeping and nudging only good quality issuers. It would also mean stepping in to prevent a race to the bottom and being patient to stay on course.

(*ii*) Design flaws can always be corrected in the process of handling transactions. So, the promised land is beckoning. The faithful are eager to get there. Right now, there is no road. It has to be paved with the intentions of the intermediaries. The regulators relies more on market makers and merchant bankers but less on the platform itself.

(*iii*) For the merchant banker to play his role is much harder than for a bigger company. He has to ensure that issue is underwritten fully and 15 per cent of the issue has to be underwritten by his own balance sheet.

(*iv*) The minimum ticket size is set at ₹1 lakh. Merchant bankers have to sell it to savvier and wealthier investors. Convincing these investors about a relatively little-known company is a difficult and time-consuming task.

(*v*) It is the responsibility of the merchant banker to appoint a stock broker as the market maker for the issue and under the rules such market making should be done for a period of three years. And the market's engagement has to be deep: he will be required to provide a two-way quote for 75 per cent of the trading time in a day.

(*vi*) For the exchanges that are trying to promote the cause of SMEs, there is much more to do. Investors, even if it means with a high net worth or institutions, need information on some of the companies that are in line to list on the SME platform.

(*vii*) Ratings agency crisil, which provides a lot of research reports on listed firms on the main board, will hopefully subsidies the cost of bringing out similar reports on SME listings. However, it is a difficult task in practice.

(*viii*) India's stock exchanges will have to do a great deal of hand-holding to ensure a smooth transition for firms promoted by young first-generation entrepreneurs in many cases to making the cut as public listed firms. That is not unusual. Alternative, which offers an electronic trading platform for small firms in Europe, offers the carrot of low listing fees and other services related to public listing.

(*ix*) The SME Exchanges in their developmental role, would also need to woo some of India's biggest institutional investors and get them to buy into some of these companies.

(*x*) The smaller merchant bankers are either scared to make the three-year commitment or have to charge exorbitantly to be viable. The market for the first IPO is charging ₹75,000 a month. At one per cent of the money raised every year, it makes the equity expensive for the SME.

(*xi*) There is a lack of clarity on operational issues such as what will happen if the entire floating stock ends up with the market maker or the opposite position, where he is left with no stock at all to deliver. Exchanges have made representations to the regulator on these issues.

EXAMINATION QUESTIONS

Long Answer Questions :

1. What is new venture financing? What are its stages?
2. What do you mean by new venture financing cycle? How does it work?
3. What do you mean by start-ups firms? What are the different sources of their financing?
4. What is angels investing? Explain its merits and limitations.
5. What do you mean by crowdfunding? What are its merits and limitations?

Short Answer Questions:

1. What do you mean by start-ups?
2. What is angel investing?

3. What is crowdfunding?
4. What is venture capital?
5. What is private equity financing?

Objective Type questions :

1. A business firm requires finance to except :
   (a) Commence its operations (b) Finance promoters family
   (c) Continue its operations (d) Ensure expansion and growth
2. New venture financing is concerned to :
   (a) An early stage company (b) Running company
   (c) Diversified company (d) Expanded company
3. Inheritor profile is concerned with :
   (a) More dynamic approach
   (b) More modern in approach
   (c) More conservative in approach
   (d) None of the above
4. Angel investors are :
   (a) Low net worth individuals (b) High net worth individuals
   (c) High growth individuals (d) Low growth individuals
5. Keep it All is concerned with :
   (a) Angel investors (b) Crowdfunding
   (c) Venture capitalists (d) Private equity investors

Answers

1. (b), 2. (a), 3. (c), 4. (b), 5. (b)

33

INCENTIVES AND SUBSIDIES

The SSI sector plays a vital role in industrial production, employment generation and exports. In the context of growing domestic and international competition, the strategy of the government is to support this sector through promotional policies of financial assistance, incentives, subsidies and technology. Actually, these incentives are the major support facilities for the promotion of small industries in India. Entrepreneurs need these incentives for setting up industries of their own. Further, these incentives are also necessary for existing small industries to initiate expansion and modernisation programme. Assistance and incentives are necessary to create market imperfections and to accelerate the process of industrialisation so as to drive the forces of supply and demand reach the equilibrium point. New ventures involve high risk and first generation entrepreneurs are generally not inclined to assume high risk of entrepreneurial activities. However, risks of new ventures and ventures in new areas can be minimised with the support of incentives and subsidies.

Meaning of Incentives and Subsidy

Incentives are motivational forces which improve productivity of entrepreneurs. They enable the entrepreneurs to take appropriate decisions and give capacity to implement them. In practice, incentives are concerned with actions to encourage productive activities.

Generally, incentives include three variables : concessions, subsidies and bounties. Incentives are financial as well as non-financial. These incentives are necessary to encourage entrepreneurs for undertaking entrepreneurial activities and achieving their goals.

Concessions are relaxations in policies and guidelines which motivate the entrepreneurs to undertake a particular entrepreneurial activity in a given environment. They may be monetary reliefs and right to enjoy certain freedoms from restrictions imposed by the Government from time to time.

Subsidy relates with a single lumpsum payment given by the government to an entrepreneur compensating him for the excess cost over administered price for a particular product or service.

Bounty means a bonus or financial assistance given by the government to a particular industry or product improving its capacity to compete with other units or products in the country or in a foreign market.

Thus, the basic purpose of incentives is to encourage an entrepreneur to undertake new entrepreneurial activities for increasing the supply of goods and services in the country.

Need for Assistance and Incentives

1. Balanced Regional Development : Entrepreneurs are generally not inclined to set up industries in underdeveloped and far flung areas of the country. These areas also lack the experience of industrial administration, departmental support system, and environmental growth potentialities. Infrastructural facilities are also not availabe in these areas. So, the government provides incentives and other assistance to lure entrepreneurs to develop their units removing all these deficiencies. Basically, policy of incentives and assistance forces the entrepreneurs to locate their industrial units in areas as identified by the government rather than that of their own choice.

2. Removal of Economic Constraints : The first generation entrepreneurs face many impediments and constraints. These are inadequate infrastructural facilities, distance between administrative organs and project sites, lack of supporting services like marketing intelligence, entrepreneurial guidance and training, technical consultancies and merchant banking facilities, lack of effective institutional mechanism and ineffective orientation of promotional institutions developed by the government. These constraints generally discourage entrepreneurs to undertake entrepreneurial activity. However, assistance, incentives and support system tend to mitigate some or all of the constraints. Industrial estates, industrial parks and growth centres, concessional finance, fiscal incentives and different types of subsides are quite effective in removing all these constraints.

3. To Provide Competitive Strength and Growth : Some incentives are made available by the government at the time of promotion of business enterprises and some other incentives are available for a comparatively long period. During this period, they are expected to improve their competitive strength with existing units. For example, reservation of items for small scale sector is meant for improving the competitive strength of SSI units working in the sector. Price preference, concessional finance etc. also help SSI units in improving their competitive strength and growth.

Advantages of Incentives and Subsidies

1. They motivates entrepreneurs to undertake new entrepreneurial activities.
2. They stimulate the new and existing entrepreneurs to develop their units in backward area districts and zero industries districts.
3. They ensure uniformity in the development process of all regions.
4. They encourage first generation entrepreneurs to work for industrial development of the country.

5. They improve the competitive capacity of entrepreneurs to face the competitive environment of the industry.
6. They solve the problems of impediments and constraints generally available before the entrepreneurs.

Problems of Incentives and Subsidies

1. Entrepreneurs generally develop bogus units to avail incentives and subsidies.
2. Incentives encourage incompetencies in business units. They cover their inefficiency under the cover of incentives and subsidies.
3. Incentives and subsidies encourage unviable use of resources employed in business units and they are just a drain on public exchequer.
4. Incentives and subsidies develop favouritism and rampant corruption.
5. Incentives and subsidies have a demoralising effect on other industrial units or efficient units.

Classification of Assistance and Incentives

Government assistance and incentives are classified under the following categories :

A. Government Assistance :

1. Technical assistance.
2. Assistance for obtaining raw materials.
3. Cash assistance.
4. Supply of plant and machinery on hire-purchase basis.
5. Marketing assistance.
6. Assistance to small entrepreneurs.
7. Rural industrial project assistance.

B. Government Incentives :

1. Subsidy relating to investment.
2. Export/Import subsidies and bounties.
3. Subsidy relating to research and development.
4. Subsidy relating to taxes.
5. Subsidy relating to resources.
6. Capital subsidy scheme for technology upgradation.
7. Excise duty exemption.

A. Government Assistance

Following government assistances are available to entrepreneurs.

***(i)* Technical Assistance** : The SIDO through Small Industries Service Institutes and Extension Centres provides technical assistance and guidance to the existing small industrialists and the intending entrepreneurs. These institutes are manned by experts in different fields/trades/industries like mechanical, electrical, chemical engineering, electronics, foundry and forging, blacksmith, leather technology, glass and ceramics, wood working and joinery, sports goods, industrial designing, industrial management and industrial economics. These experts are required to visit various small industries, study their problems on the spot and give technical assistance and guidance. The NSIC has established a Technology Transfer Centre (TTC) at Okhla (Delhi) to upgrade technology in the changed economic scenario under economic reforms. At the enterprise level, the primary concern is to assist small scale enterprises in technology acquisition, adoption and upgradation through its technology information and promotion services. Government has introduced the techno-economic and managerial consultancy service scheme under which Small Industry Service Institute solves the technical problems of entrepreneurs. Industrial Extension Service Scheme has also been introduced by the government to help small entrepreneurs. There are 16 Service Institutes, 5 Branch Institutes and 64 Extension Centres which are extending technical assistance to the entrepreneurs.

***(ii)* Raw Material Assistance** : Earlier small units were offered assistance in the procurement of scarce and controlled raw materials by the Small Industries Development Organisation at the central level and the Directorate of Industries at the state level. Now, District Industries Centre is authorised to sponsor the SSI units for procuring scarce and controlled raw materials. Now it is obligatory for the small scale units to obtain registration certificate from the concerned Directorate of Industries for proouring essential raw materials. National Small Industries Corporation (NSIC) is also helping SSI units in (a) supply under the off-the-shelf basis; (b) import of raw materials; (c) providing scarce raw materials on priority basis; (d) supplies through NSIC depots/godowns.

***(iii)* Cash Scheme** : Government provides cash assistance under self-employment scheme to rural youths. Similarly, cash assistance is also made available to scheduled castes/scheduled tribes and women entrepreneurs.

***(iv)* Supply of Machinery and Equipment on Hire-Purchase Basis** : An entrepreneur is required to purchase machinery etc. for launching new industrial unit or for expansion of the existing plant. If his financial position permits, he purchases machinery on his own, otherwise he can procure it from the National Small Industries Corporation or State level Small Industries Corporations. These corporations ensure supply of indigenous and imported machinery (the value of which would not exceed ₹3 crore inclusive of the value of machinery and equipment already installed) on easy financial terms, mainly targeted at first generation entrepreneurs, women entrepreneurs, weaker sections, the handicapped and ex-servicemen. Besides, they also arrange machinery and equipment on lease basis. They provide 100% finance to facilitate SSIs in diversification and technology upgradation. Entrepreneurs can also avail tax rebate on full year rentals.

***(v)* Marketing Assistance** : The success of small entrepreneurs is generally governed by the ability and efficiency of these units in marketing their products.

For the purpose of marketing assistance, small units are required to get registered themselves with the NSIC. The objectives of the marketing programme of NSIC are as under : (a) ensure fair margin to producers of goods; (b) standardisation and quality control with testing facilities; (c) market products under common brand name; (d) provide publicity to SSI products; (e) upgrade technology by supplying sophisticated machinery and equipment. Besides, for the supply of goods to government and public enterprises, SSIs registered under the single point registration scheme with NSIC are given the following facilities : (a) issue of tender forms/sets free of cost; (b) advance intimation of tenders issued by DGS & D; (c) exemption from payment of earnest money; (d) waiver of security deposit upto the monetary limit for which the unit is registered; (e) issue of competency certificate in case the value of an order exceeds the monetary limit after due verification.

***(vi)* Assistance to Small Entrepreneurs** : The NSIC has developed five financial centres at New Delhi, Mumbai, Ahmedabad, Bangaluru and Goa to provide finance to small entrepreneurs for activities relating to marketing, bills discounting, raw materials purchases and exports. To train and equip the first generation entrepreneurs, government has developed various training institutes in the field of entrepreneurial activities/entrepreneurship development programmes. The NISIET (Hyderabad), NIESBUD (New Delhi); and Integrated Training Centre (Industries) (Nilokheri) are the main training institutes which function under the administrative control of SIDO.

***(vii)* Rural Industrial Project Assistance** : The SIDBI has been assigned a very crucial role in the identification of viable and self-sustaining SSIs in rural and semi-rural areas. These units are expected to provide an intensive thrust to address the problems of rural unemployment, urban migration, under-utllisation of physical resources and skills of the rural areas. The Rural Industries Programme (RIP) of SIDBI provides a cohesive and integrated package of basic inputs like information, motivation, training and credit, backed by appropriate technology and market linkages.

For the purpose, SIDBI has identified implementing agencies such as NGOs, development professionals, technical consultancy organisations (TCO), and these are assigned the task of developing RIP at a fee given by the bank. The implementing agency either by itself or by networking with appropriate agencies provides the following professional services : (a) identification and motivation of potential entrepreneurs in the rural areas; (b) identifying potential investment opportunities for these entrepreneurs; (c) facilitating skill upgradation; (d) assisting in securing finance from banks and other lending institutions; (e) helping entrepreneurs in selection, sourcing, installation and operation of machinery; (f) arranging market support wherever necessary and (g) guiding entrepreneurs till their units commence commercial production.

SIDBI meets part of the manpower costs of the implementing agency, mainly in the form of performance fee which is linked to units actually grounded by identified rural entrepreneurs. In deserving cases, the Bank even provides startup expenses. Further, the Bank extends credit support by way of refinance through PLIs.

B. Government Incentives

(*i*) Subsidy Relating to Investment : Government has initiated different scheme of investment subsidy for the benefits of entrepreneurs so that they may be encouraged to establish more and more SSI units. These schemes are capital investment subsidy, transport subsidy, power generators subsidy, special investment scheme for women entrepreneurs, provision for seed capital, subsidy for technical/feasibility study etc. Besides, being an apex bank for SSI sector, the SIDBI is also arranging equity type assistance schmes e.g. seed capital scheme, National Equity Fund scheme, single window scheme to provide both term loan and working capital, venture capital fund with a corpus of ₹80 crores etc. to accelerate the pace of investment in small scale sector.

(*ii*) Export/Import Subsidies and Bounties : 100 percent export-oriented units (EOUs) and units in the export processing zones (EPZs) enjoy a package of incentives and facilities, which include duty free imports of all types of capital goods, raw material, and consumables in addition to tax holidays against export.

(*iii*) Subsidy Relating to Research and Development : To encourage continuous research and development activities in the small scale sector, government provides subsidy. A provision of ₹50 crores had been made in the budget 2000-2001, for Technology Information Forecasting and Assessment Council. Besides, another provision of ₹50 crores had also been made in the budget for launching New Millehnium Indian Technology Leadership Initiative. The Government has already approved a modernisation project of ₹75 crores for the patent office and strive to remove all impediments related with the project.

(*iv*) Subsidy Relating to Taxes : Central Government as well as State Governments are trying to encourage entrepreneurs through tax subsidy schemes enabling them to accelerate the pace of establishment of industrial units. These are exemption from estate duty, tax relief to NRIs, rebate in income-tax, interest-free sales tax loan, sales tax subidy, exemption from sales tax etc.

(*v*) Subsidy Relating to Resources : Small Industries need infrastructural facilities and government is trying to provide these facilities at subsidised rates. Subsidy for purchase of testing tools, subsidy for industrial estates and parks, allotment of land and buildings at concessional rates, supply of water at concessional rates, arrangement of developed or constructed production sheds, arrangement of raw materials at concessional rates or controlled rates are some of the important subsidies which are available to the small scale units.

(*vi*) Capital Subsidy, Scheme for Technology Upgradation : In November 2000, the Central Government had introduced a capital subsidy scheme for small scale industries (SSIs) in select sectors for technology upgradation. Under the scheme styled "credit linked capital subsidy scheme for technology upgradation of the small scale industries" a 12 percent back ended capital subsidy will be admissible on loans and advanced to SSI units by the scheduled commercial banks/designated state financial corporations.

***(vii)* Credit Linked Capital Subsidy Scheme (CLCSS)** : The M/o MSME is implementing a Scheme, namely, Credit Linked Capital Subsidy Scheme (CLCSS) for technology upgradation of micro and small enterprises (MSEs) by providing 15% capital subsidy on institutional finance availed by them for induction of identified technology in selected sub-sectors/products. The maximum limit of eligible loan for calculation of capital subsidy under the revised scheme has also been raised from ₹40 lakhs to ₹100 Lakhs w.e.f. 29.9.2005. The ceiling of capital subsidy under the scheme is ₹15 lakhs. The admissible capital subsidy is calculated with reference to purchase price of the plant and machinery, instead of the term loan availed by the beneficiary.

Entrepreneurs availing of this scheme should not avail of any other benefit including interest subsidy under any other scheme of the Central Government and should have competent management to carry out the upgradation programme and manage the unit subsequently. For calculation of subsidy, a maximum loan amount of ₹8 lakh should be considered for tiny units with investment in plant and machinery of less than ₹10 lakhs. Similarly, a maximum loan ceiling of ₹20 lakhs is allowed for subsidy calculation for tiny units with investment in plant and machinery between ₹10 lakhs and ₹25 lakhs. For SSI units, the maximum ceiling for calculation of subsidy would be ₹40 lakhs, for investment in plant and machinery above ₹25 lakhs.

However, the maximum amount for calculation of subsidy would be limited to the actual investment if it is less than the ceiling specified for calculation of subsidy. Some of the sectors covered by the scheme are leather and leather products, including footwear and garments, food processing. IT (hardware), drugs and pharmaceuticals, auto-parts and components, toys, dyes and intermediaries, handtools and foundries, ferrous and cast-iron.

***(viii)* Credit Guarantee Fund Scheme For Micro And Small Enterprises** : The Government of India launched the Credit Guarantee Fund Scheme for Micro and Small Enterprises in August, 2000, with the objective of making available credit to micro and small enterprises (MSEs), particularly micro enterprises, without collateral/third party guarantees. The Scheme is being operated through the Credit Guarantee Fund Trust for Micro and Small Enterprises (CGTMSE) set up jointly by the Government of India and Small Industries Development Bank of India (SIDBI).

The Scheme covers collateral free credit facility (term loan and/or working capital) extended by eligible member lending institutions (MLIs) to new and existing micro and small enterprises upto ₹100 lakhs per borrowing unit. The guarantee cover provided is upto 75% of the credit facility upto ₹50 lakh with an incremental guarantee of 50% of the credit facility above ₹50 lakhs and upto ₹100 lakhs (85% for loans upto ₹5 lakhs provided to micro enterprises, 80% for MSEs owned/operated by women and all loans to domicile of NER). One time guarantee fee of 1.5% of the credit facility sanctioned (0.75% for NER) and Annual Service Fee of 0.75% is collected from the MLIs.

(ix) Micro Finance Programme : The Ministry has been operating the Scheme of Micro Finance Programme, since 2003-04, which has been tied up with the existing Micro Credit Scheme of SIDBI. Under the scheme, the Government of India provides funds to SIDBI under a 'Portfolio Risk Fund' (PRF), which is utilised for security deposit requirement of the loan amount from the MFIs/ NGOs. At present, SIDBI takes fixed deposit equal to 10% of the loan amount. Under the PRF, the share of MFIS/NGOs is 2.5% of the loan amount (i.e., 25% of security deposit) and balance 7.5% (i.e., 75% of security deposit) is adjusted from the Funds provided by the Government under the scheme. The Funds under PRF are to be utilised for extending loans in the underserved States like North Eastern States, Sikkim, Bihar, Jharkhand, West Bengal, Orissa, Madhya Pradesh, Chhattisgarh, Uttar Pradesh, Jammu & Kashmir, Rajasthan and Uttarakhand and the under-served pockets/districts of other States.

(x) Excise Duty Exemption : The most important incentive for Small Scale units is the excise duty concessions. However, it was watered down by MODVAT (modified value added tax) and the reduction in excise duty rates. In the era of protection, large companies had to pay very high levels of duty and excise waivers and concessions afforded small firms an automatic price advantages over large firms. As a result of the fall in excise duty rates and MODVAT the relative difference in the tax burden for large and small companies has declined. Large companies can claim MODVAT benefits on inputs and capital goods so that the cascading effect of excise duty taxation is factored out. For many commodities, especially consumer goods, the rates of excise duty have also fallen. In this liberalisation process, small firms were the losers on this account.

Now, the Government has increased the excise duty exemption limit from ₹50 lakhs to ₹1 crore. This is the second increase in excise exemption limit since 1998. In practice, the government will incur some losses due to increased exemption limit but it is worth it.

However, due to this modification, any small scale unit where the inputs do not attract excise duty would find itself priced out of the market once its sales exceed ₹1 crore. Consequently, if a small scale unit wishes to utilise its idle plant capacity beyond the turnover, of ₹1 crore, it would have no option but to undertake clandestine sales for which the inputs would also have to be procured from the parallel economy. The policy effectively prohibits any incentive for the growth of the unit.

Indigeneous manufacturers of raw materials (especially in the small scale sector) would find themselves at a disadvantage since the reduction of duty on imports would render them non-competitive. A small scale unit which sells its products to a large scale unit and therefore has a derived demand for its products, does not enjoy any price advantage on account of excise exemption since large scale units are also covered under the MODVAT-Scheme. Similarly, the practice of multiple sourcing by the parent unit may make it impossible for the ancillary unit to achieve sales of ₹1 crore if the parent unit Is the lone buyer and in case the ancillary unit does not have a multiple product mix. If it does, then the product meant for the market may not be saleable on account of incidence of excise duty which is linked to the total sales.

***(xi)* National Manufacturing Competitiveness Programme (NMCP):** The Government had announced formulation of National Competitiveness Programme in 2005 with an objective to support the Small and Medium Enterprises (SMEs) in their endeavour to become competitive and adjust the competitive pressure caused by liberalisation and moderation of tariff rates. The National Manufacturing Competitiveness Council (NMCC) has conceptualised and finalised the components of the programme incorporating suitable inputs from the stakeholders. The National Manufacturing Competitiveness Programme (NMCP), as conceptualised by the NMCC, was accepted by the Government and announced for implementation in the Budget, 2006-07.

***(xii)* Marketing Assistance/Support to MSEs (Bar Code)** : The objective of the 'Marketing Assistance/Support to MSEs' scheme of NMCP is to popularise the Bar Code registration and motivate the Small and Micro Manufacturing Enterprises to adopt the Bar Code Certification on large scale and to sell their value added products worldwide and enable higher export price realisation. It also helps in domestic marketing (wholesale and retail). 75% of annual fee (recurring) of Bar Code certification for the first three years are reimbursed to Micro and Small Entrepreneurs, under the Scheme.

***(xiii)* Support for Entrepreneurial and Managerial Development of MSMEs (INCUBATOR)** : The concept of Business Incubation is a relatively new concept for MSMEs. The "Support for Entrepreneurial and Managerial Development of Small and Medium Enterprises (INCUBATOR)" Scheme of the NMCP makes available a new window for supporting and nourishing businesses based on new ideas. Under the Scheme, Knowledge Institutions like Engineering Colleges, Research Labs etc. are provided financial assistance for incubating each of the new ideas. The Incubator provides technology guidance, workshop and lab support and linkages with other agencies for successful launching of the business and guides the entrepreneurs in running the business for the next 2-3 years.

***(xiv)* Setting up Mini Tool Room and Training Centres under PPP Mode** : The Tool Room facilities are the backbone of manufacturing sector as these create dies, tools, moulds, jigs, fixtures, gauges and precision components in the absence of which production units cannot operate at all. The M/o MSME started implementing the scheme called "Setting up Mini Tool Room and Training Centres under the PPP Mode", by providing financial assistance to Private Partners/ States/State Agencies. The objective of the Scheme is to establish more tool room facilities in private sector and well within the reach of all industries in the country. The scheme will be implemented through the following three models in order of preference :

(*xv*) Building Awareness on Intellectual Property Rights (IPRs) : The objective of "Building Awareness on Intellectual Property Rights (IPRs)" for the MSMEs is to create and enhance awareness about IPRs among the MSMEs so as to enable them to take appropriate measure for protecting their ideas and business strategies and also avoiding infringement of the intellectual property belonging to others. The scheme provides financial assistance for taking up the following identified initiatives :

(1) Awareness/Sensitisation Programmes on IPRs;
(2) Pilot Studies for Selected Clusters/Groups of Industries;
(3) Interactive Seminars/Workshops;
(4) Specialised Training;
(5) Assistance for Grant of Patent/GI Registration;
(6) Setting up of IP Facilitation Centre and
(7) Interaction with International Agencies.

These initiatives are being developed through PPP mode for encouraging economically sustainable models for overall development of MSMEs. The eligible applicants/beneficiaries contribute a minimum of 10% of the Central financial assistance. The Project Implementation Committee (PIC) responsible for the day-to-day implementation of the programmes has approved organising of 23 Awareness/Sensitisation Programmes on IPRs throughout the country; setting up of an IP Facilitation Centre specially for Bio-tech Units; organising of four Workshops on IPRs for Leather Cluster/IT Cluster and a Pilot Study for the Bamboo Cluster.

(*xvi*) Lean Manufacturing Competitiveness Programme for MSMEs: Under the Lean Manufacturing Programme (LMP), MSMEs will be assisted in reducing their manufacturing costs, through proper personnel management, better space utilisation, scientific inventory management, improved process flows, reduced engineering time and so on. LMP also brings improvement in the quality of products and lowers costs which are essential for competing in national and international markets. The broad activities planned under the scheme include Total Productive Maintenance (TPM), 5S, Visual Control, Standard Operation Procedures, Just in Time, Kanban System, Cellular Layout, Poka Yoke, TPM etc. The scheme has been approved as a pilot project for lean technique intervention in 100 Mini Clusters.

(*xvii*) Enabling Manufacturing Sector to be Competitive through Quality Management Standards (QMS) and Quality Technology Tools (QTT) : This scheme was launched in the year 2008-09. The scheme aims at improving the quality of the products in the MSME sector and inculcating quality consciousness among MSMEs. The major activities to be undertaken under this scheme are :

(a) Introduction of Appropriate Modules for Technical Institutions with target coverage of 2000 technical institutions;
(b) Organising 100 Awareness Campaigns every year for MSEs;

(c) Organising Competition-Watch (C-Watch) every year in two Sectors; Implementation of Quality Management Standards and Quality;

(d) Technology Tools in 100 selected MSEs every year; and

(e) Monitoring at least 2 International Study Missions per year.

***(xviii)* Technology and Quality Upgradation Support** : The objective of the Scheme is to sensitise the manufacturing (MSME) sector in India to upgrade their technologies, usage of energy efficient technologies to reduce emissions of Greenhouse gases, adoption of other technologies mandated as per the global standards, improve their quality and reduce cost of production etc, towards becoming globally competitive. The major activities planned under the scheme include capacity building of MSMEs clusters for energy efficiency/clean development interventions, implementation of energy efficient technologies in MSME sector, setting up of carbon credit aggregation centres and encouraging MSMEs to acquire product certification licences from National/International bodies.

***(xix)* Marketing Assistance and Technology Upgradation Scheme** : The objective of this scheme is to identify and encourage those clusters of MSMEs which have quality production and export potential and assist them to achieve competitiveness in the national and international markets. The scheme aims at improving the marketing competitiveness of MSME sector by improving their techniques and technology for promotion of exports. The broad activities planned under the scheme include technology upgradation in packaging, development of modern marketing techniques, competition studies etc.

***(xx)* Design Clinics Scheme** : The main objective of the scheme is to bring the MSME sector and design expertise into a common platform and to provide expert advice and solutions on real time design problems, resulting in continuous improvement and value-addition for existing products. It also aims at value-added cost effective solutions. The broad activities planned under the scheme include creation of Design Clinics Secretariat along with regional centres for intervention on the design needs of the MSME sector.

***(xxi)* Promotion of Information and Communication Technology (ICT)** : The objectives of this programme envisages that some of those clusters of SMEs, which have quality production and export potential, shall be identified and encouraged and assisted in adopting ICT applications to achieve competitiveness in the national and international markets. The broad activities planned under the scheme include identifying target clusters for ICT intervention, setting up of e-readiness infrastructure, developing web portals for clusters, skill development of MSME staff in ICT applications, preparation of local software solution for MSMEs to enhance their competitiveness, construction of e-catalogue, e-commerce etc. and networking MSME cluster portals on the National Level Portals in order to outreach MSMEs in global markets.

***(xxii)* ISO-9000/ISO-14001/HACCP Certification Reimbursement Scheme :** The scheme envisages one time reimbursement of charges for acquiring

ISO 9000/14001/HACCP (or its equivalent) certification to the extent of 75% of the cost subject to a maximum of ₹75,000 in total.

New Incentives and Subsidies for Small Scale Sector

The primary responsibility to develop village and small industries in the States/UTs rests with the respective State/UT Governments. However, the Government of India announces, from time to time, various incentive schemes/concessions and support services for promotion of industries, particularly in industrially backward areas and other special regions with the intention of reducing regional imbalances. The package of incentives and facilities currently available from the Central Government are discussed hereunder.

Fiscal incentives are provided in the form of exemptions, rebate, refund or postponement of direct or indirect taxes leviable on production or profits, besides special tax concessions. Such measures include : (i) Income Tax concessions, (ii) Customs duty drawbacks, (iii) Exemption and preferential treatment in respect of Excise duty, (iv) Exemption from Sales Tax, (v) Tax holiday for new industrial units, etc.

1. Tax Incentives/Concessions/Deduction from profits and gains

(i) IT Section 80-HH—20 per cent for 10 years for industries to be set up under the Factories Act in backward areas.

(ii) IT Section 80-HHA—20 per cent for 10 years for SSI units to be set up in rural areas.

(iii) IT Section 80-I—20 per cent for 7 to 9 years for SSI units to be set up under Factories Act, 25 cent for 11 years in case of cooperative societies, 35 per cent for companies.

(iv) IT Section 80-IA—25 per cent for 10 years for industries to be set up under Factories Act, 100 per cent for 5 years and 25 per cent for next 5 years for backward areas only.

(v) IT Section 80-IB—the small scale units commencing production between April 01, 1995 and March 31, 2000 are allowed a deduction of 25 per cent of their profits (30 per cent for Companies) for a period of 10 years.

2. Incentives for exports including duty drawbacks

(i) Deduction in respect of profits and gains from projects outside India (Section 80-HHB)

(ii) Deduction in respect of Export Turnover (Section 80-HHC)

(iii) Deduction in respect of earnings in convertible foreign exchange (80-HHD).

(iv) Deduction for consultancy exports (80-O).

(v) Ten Year Tax Holiday for newly established industrial undertaking in the Free Trade Zones, or Electronic Hardware Technology Parks and Software Technology Parks (Sec. 10-A)

(vi) Ten Year Tax Holiday for newly established 100 per cent Export Oriented Undertaking (Section 10-B)

(vii) Duty drawaback facilities are provided in two ways :

(a) Drawback of the whole of import duty on imported articles, components and raw materials, and excise duty paid on excisable components used in the manufacture of the product when it is exported. (b) Drawback of 90 per cent of duty paid on imported article when it is exported.

3. Exemptions and preferential treatment from excise duties

For SSIs having clearances in the preceding financial year not exceeding ₹30 million, the present rates of excise duty are as under:

Clearances	Rate of Duty for SSIs Avail Modvat Credit	Rate of Duty for SSIs Avail Modvat Credit
Not exceeding ₹1 0 Million Nil 60% of normal rate ₹10 to 30 million Normal Normal Goods for capital consumption	Nil	Nil

Note : Commodity specific exemption for small scale units, namely, articles of plastics/cosmetics and toilet preparation, tread rubber, air conditioning and refrigeration machinery and parts have been merged with the General SSI Exemption Scheme with effect from April 01, 2000

4. Modvat Credit

Modvat credit is allowed at the rate of 100 per cent of duty paid on inputs, be it excise duty or special duty or additional duty of customs. It also covers capital goods purchased and used by the manufacturers.

5. Exemptions from Sales Tax

(i) No liability under State Sales Tax, Law for import of the goods into or export of goods out of the territory of India.

(ii) Export sales have been exempted from levy of sales tax under Central Sales Tax Act, 1957.

6. Other Incentives

(a) Capital Inverstment Subsidy : Capital Investment Subsidy Scheme 1997 had been notifed on June 01, 1998 under the Prime Minister's new initiatives for the North Eastern Region. Under the Capital Investment Subsidy Scheme, subsidy at the rate of 15 per cent of the investment in plant and machinery subject to a maximum ceiling of ₹3 million is payable to industry located in the growth centres and to new industrial units and/or their substantial expansion in other identified areas in the North Eastern Region. The Scheme is operated through the respective State Governments.

(b) Transport Subsidy : The Transport Subsidy Scheme was introduced in July 1971 to promote industries in hilly, remote and inaccessible areas. The scheme is applicable to the States of Himachal Pradesh J&K, the North Eastern States, Sikkim, Union Territories of Andaman & Nicobar Islands and Lakshadweep, Darjeeling District of West Bengal and eight hill districts of Uttaranchal. Under the scheme, a susbsidy ranging from 50 per cent to 90 per cent is admissible on transport costs incurred on the movement of raw materials and finished goods from designated rail heads/parts upto the location of the industrial units and vice-versa.

(c) Incentives for Electronics and Information Technology

(i) The electronics industry, except aerospace and defence electronics, has been fully delicensed.

(ii) Export earnings from Information Technology (IT) products not to be taxed.

(iii) Depreciation of IT products to be allowed at 60 per cent.

(iv) Units located in Electronics Hardware Technology Parks . (EHTP) and Software Technology Parks (STP) have been exempted from payment of corporate income tax for 10 years.

(v) Income derived by foreign companies as dividend and interest would be taxed at the rate of 20 per cent.

(vi) The payments in the form of royalty and technical service fee to be taxed at 30 per cent.

(vii) Under section 80-HHE of the Income Tax Act. definition of Computer Software has been widened to include transmission of data.

(viii) Exemption of withholding tax on interest on external commercial borrowings has been extended to the IT sector.

(ix) The tariff levels are being brought in line with the average international levels in a phased manner.

Measures taken for development of North Eastern Region

In order to accelerate the setting up of SSI units in North Eastern Region, several steps have been taken by the government.

Incentives And Subsidies Policies At State Level

The State Governments formulate their respective policies for development of industries in general and small scale industries in particular and also implement the incentive schemes through the District Industries Centres and other

Departments and Coporations set up for this purpose. They provide technical and other support services to SSIs. The main areas of support and facilities are listed below :

(i) Respective Industrial Development and Investment Cororations to develop and manage industrial areas.

(ii) Financial support services by State Financial Corporations.

(iii) Technical guidance by Technical Consultancy Organisations.

(iv) Human resources development through Training Institutions.

(v) Infrastructure development by the concerned corporation.

(vi) Export promotion by Small Industries and Export Corporations.

(vii) Single window assistance by District Industries Centres. Apart from these, the State governments also offer a range of incentives for providing an impetus to industrialisation. Incentives to SSIs are provided mainly by way of provision of land and developed plots/sheds in industrial estates on easy terms, capital subsidy on investment (in selected areas), subsidy on power generating sets, exemptions/deferment on sales tax and stamp duty, water supply at reduced rates, seed capital assistance, relief on electricity duty, interest subsidy, financial assistance for preparation of project reports, subsidy for obtaining technical know-how, subsidy for testing the products in approved test houses, etc. All these concessions are not uniform in all the States/UTs; their nature, contents, quantum and periodicity vary from State to State.

Development Schemes for Industrially Backward Areas

The Department of Industrial Policy and Promotion. Ministry of Commerce and. Industry is implementing the following important schemes for the development of industrially backward areas in the country.

1. Growth Centre Scheme : Under this scheme growth centres are to be developed throughout the country which would be provided with basic infrastructure facilities like power, water, tele-communication, sewage, effluent disposal etc. enabling them to attract industries. The growth centres approved by the Government of India are to be developed by the State Governments with a central assistance component of ₹10 crore per acre (Rs. 15 crore in the case of North Eastern region).

2. Transport Subsidy Scheme : This scheme was introduced in July 1971 to promote industries in hilly, remote and inaccessible areas. Under the scheme, subsidy ranging from 50%-90% is admissible on transport costs incurred on movement of raw materials and finished goods from designated rail heads/ ports upto the location of the industrial units and *vice-versa* for a period of five years from the date of commencement of commercial production. The scheme is applicable to all industrial units (except plantations, refineries and power generation units) irrespective of their size, located in the North Eastern region.

3. Capital Investment Subsidy Scheme : Under this scheme, a subsidy @ 15% of the investment in plant and machinery subject to maximum of ₹30 lakh would be admissible to industries located in the growth centres and to new industrial units and/or their substantial expansion in other identified areas in the North-Eastern Region. The scheme is operated through the agency of the State Government. The North Eastern Development Financial Corporation (NEDFC) has been designated as the nodal agency to release subsidy to the eligible units on the basis of recommendations of the state level committee/State Governments. The scheme was notified in 1998.

4. Central Interest Subsidy Scheme.: Under this scheme, notified on 19.2.99, interest subsidy @ 3% on the working capital loan would be payable to the new industrial units in the North Eastern Region for a period of 10 years after the unit goes into production.

5. Comprehensive Insurance Scheme : This scheme notified on 14.7.99 envisages reimbursement of insurance premium to all industrial units set up in the North-Eastern regions after 24th December 1997 and included in fire policy (as per All India Fire Tariff). The insured party shall pay initial premium which shall be reimbursed by the nodal insurance company out of a revolving fund maintained by the company. Funds for this revolving fund shall be contributed by the Department of Industrial Policy & Promotion. Now, this scheme has been extended to 31.3. 2017.

6. Integrated Infrastructure Development Scheme : The office of the Development Commissioner (Small Scale Industries), Ministry of Small Scale Industries & Agro and Rural Industries is also implementing the Integrated Infrastructure Development scheme (IID). The scheme introduced in 1994 envisages development of infrastructural facilities for location of industries in rural/backward areas. Under the scheme 52 IID centres have been sanctioned in various states.

7. State Policies for Assistance and Incentives: The very size and dispersed nature of the small sector implies that the onus of promotion and development rests mainly on State Governments and institutions. The central policy framework acts as a guiding principle in this regard. Small units are encouraged to register with the District Industries Centre which helps them avail of the various incentives and direct support programmes of the central and State Governments. The important aspects of state policies are:

(*i*) Development and management of industrial areas by the industrial development and investment corporations.

(*ii*) Capital investment subsidy ranging from 15 to 25 per cent on fixed investment (subject to an outer ceiling) to new units.

(*iii*) Sales tax exemptions/deferment to units for 5 to 10 years, limited by fixed capital investment as well as tax liabilities.

(*iv*) Incentives/subsidies for using power derived from alternative energy sources.

(*v*) Special assistance programme for women and weaker sections.

(*iv*) Seed capital/margin money assistance scheme on soft terms.

(*vii*) Underwriting costs on feasibility studies/consultancy for modernisation, technology upgradatio

(*viii*) Empowered committees at the district/state level to accord clearances and settle disputes.

(*ix*) Higher incentives to set up pioneer units in backward/zero industry districts.

(*x*) Equity participation by state corporations in joint/assisted sector projects.

EXAMINATION QUESTIONS

Long Answer Questions

1. What facilities and concessions have been given to small scale industries in India by the central and state government for their promotion.
2. How do the incentives and subsidies, motivate the entrepenurs in undertaking new entrepreneurial projects ? Give a brief account of the various assistance and incentives that are available to the small scale industries in India.
3. Describe in brief the different types of state assistance available for technological upgradation.
4. What do you understand by Incentives ? Discuss the government incentives which are made available to small entrepreneurs.
5. Explain 'the various incentives given by the governmen t for the development of small business.
6. "Concessions for small units are deterrents in the long run." Comment.
7. What do you know by incentives and subsidies ? Discuss their role In entrepreneurship development.
8. What are the various incentives offered by the central and state governments for the promotion and growth of small business in India ?
9. Discuss the concessions and facilities made available to small scale industries in India.
10. Critically examine the government policy with regard to assistance and incentives for the development of small units.

Short Answer Questions

1. Distinguish between Incentives and subsidy.
2. Explain the rationale of assistance and incentives.
3. Explain the technical assistance extended by the SIDO.
4. What is market assistance ?

5. Discuss the various excise duty exemption available to SSIs.
6. Discuss the main incentives available to Small Scale Industries.

Objective Type Questions

1. Incentives are :
   (a) Motivational forces (b) Financial forces
   (c) Non financial forces (d) None of the above.
2. Subsidy is a :
   (a) Cash payment (b) Incentives
   (c) Cash payment to cover cost of production.
   (d) Cash payment to compensate loss to the manufactures.
3. Technical assistance to be given by :
   (a) SIDO (b) SIDBI
   (c) IDBI (d) None of the above.
4. Rural Industries Programme is initiated by :
   (a) MSIC (b) SIDBI
   (c) SIDO (d) UPSIC
5. Growth Centre scheme has covered :
   (a) 70 growth centres (b) 68 growth centres
   (c) 71 growth centres (d) None of the above.

Answers

1 (a) 2 (b) 3 (a) 4 (b) 5 (b)

Reason Based Questions

State with reason whether the following statements are true or false :

1. Subsidy is a single lumpsum payment given by the government to an entrepreneur.
2. Bounty is a bonus or financial assistance.
3. Concession and bounties are the same.
4. Growth centre scheme was introduced in 1988.
5. IID is concerned with infrastructural facilities for industries in rural/backward areas.

34

Entrepreneurial Monitoring Techniques

Entrepreneur invests their valuable fund and energy for the establishment of an enterprise. The basic expectation of the entrepreneur is to make the enterprise competitive and viable. For this purpose, he needs continuous and regular support mechanisms to ensure its successful operations. For failure, he should try for introspection and for success, he should visualise for immediate challenges. Both these problems can be solved with the help of entrepreneurial consultancy and monitoring. These mechanisms provide continuous basis for entrepreneurship development. Generally, an entrepreneur faces large number of problems during the course of production or business process and to solve these problems he needs effective and useful consultancy services. There are technical consultancy organisations who extend their services to entrepreneurs, specially first generation entrepreneurs. However, it is their duty to provide consultancy services from time to time for making them more motivated in fulfilment of entrepreneurial mission. These consultancy organisations are required to set the real effect of their consultancy services in solving the problems of entrepreneurs. They should try to assess to what extent these entrepreneurs are successful in operating their enterprises a successful venture. At the same time, these consultancy organisations should also develop monitoring activities effectively so that they can get effective feed back and thereafter suggest necessary modification in their consultancy support system. Moreover, there is a relationship of professional consultant and customer between the entrepreneurs and consultancy organisations. Effectiveness of these organisations are also judged on the basis of entrepreneurial success of an enterprise generally seen as a basic point for the success of these consultancy organisations.

In practice, consultancy is a process of starting the function of planned progress of customer and motivating him with ancillary relationships." In practical terms, consultancy and assistance are used as complementary to each other. But in technical sense, both are different concepts. Consultancy develops base for any activity or operation. However, assistance improves the utility of that particular activity or operation. In this way we can say that assisting process ensures value addition in the effectiveness or usefulness of consultancy made available by the consultant to his customer. Ultimately, it helps the customer to achieve his objectives early and effectively. In practice, it may also be a tool in the development process of the customer. But assisting the customer is an important part of the activities being undertaken by the institution concerned.

Managerial Consultancy : An entrepreneur is an owner of the business as well as its manager. He coordinates the productive resources. To get his venture a success, he needs managerial consultancy. The institution engaged in the entrepreneurship development process provides consultancy services with regard to entrepreneurship development function. In this process, consultancy organisation or organisation involved in entrepreneurship development programme, provide managerial consultancy services at various stages and activities of entrepreneurship development. However, managerial consultancy system depends on the nature and level of entrepreneurship. Actually, entrepreneur is just a customer for the organisations engaged in entrepreneurship development or consultancy organisations. The success of these organisations is directly linked with the level of success of the entrepreneur.

Main **objectives** of entrepreneurial consultancy are as follows:

(i) To study the entrepreneurial behaviour by evaluating the background, personality, knowledge and skill of an entrepreneur.

(ii) To know the entrepreneurial environment under which entrepreneurs are working.

(iii) To identify the problems of entrepreneurs under pre planning and post planning situations of entrepreneurship.

(iv) To know the entrepreneurial feasibility for starting and running an entrepreneurial unit.

(v) To enable the entrepreneur for making his plan of action as a real life workable business unit.

Consultancy Process : An entrepreneur is required to take different types of decisions under entrepreneurial process. He feels the need for consultancy in ensuring effective formulation and implementation of entrepreneurial objectives. In this way, under consultancy process, a consultant provides consultancy to the entrepreneur for evaluating the socio–economic conditions of the society as such and motivate him to adjust with the existing environment. Consultancy is a short but useful process for fulfilling the entrepreneurial objectives. However, consultation process is relatively a broader framework under which support systems and helps are extended to the prospective entrepreneur. Consultancy helps in seeking professional aids, involving in entrepreneurial discussions and solving the problems of entrepreneurship.

In practice, entrepreneur identify the problems and thereafter consultants are supposed to analyse the approaches of entrepreneur in solving these problems. Thus, the consultants extend their consultancy services to the entrepreneurs as per the nature of problems and again try to activate the entrepreneurs. Consultancy can be helpful to the entrepreneurs at any level of their decision making process. However, it totally depends upon the forms of consultancy required by the entrepreneurs and how this consultancy is useful for a particular level of entrepreneurial behaviour. Moreover, need for consultancy arises at pre-planning level of the potential entrepreneurial behaviour and it also needs a broader framework of information at this stage. In this way, it is clear that the functionality of consultants is generally governed by the need and nature of entrepreneurial decision making process.

Merits: Important merits of the method are as follows:

(i) It facilitates detailed study of the proposed or existing business.

(ii) It encourages effective interaction between the consultant and the entrepreneur.

(iii) It enables the entrepreneur to get specialised expertise in his business field.

(iv) It ensures higher level of satisfaction to entrepreneur.

(v) It helps in guiding the entrepreneur on continuous basis.

Methods of Consultancy

1. Direct Method: Under this method, consultant extends advisories to entrepreneurs by seeking information about his proposed or existing business. He argues his case before the entrepreneur and also gives his lecture before him. At the end of it, he tries to solve the problem or queries asked by the entrepreneur. Thereafter it may be converted into question answer. Now a days, it has been replaced by presentation form before the entrepreneur and his managerial team. This method enables the consultant to extend his consultancy as per his standing or goodwill in the industry and provides sufficient time to the entrepreneur to take his own decisions with regard to the business proposed or operated. But this method is not so practical as it fails to motivate the entrepreneur to think on his own intensively about his business problem. Actually, entrepreneur becomes totally dependent upon the consultant for every problem of his business and fails to solve these problems on his own thinkings and initiatives. This method also mars the creativity of the entrepreneur which is the essence of the entrepreneurship.

2. Indirect Method: Under this method, entrepreneur gets sufficient opportunities to grasp the problems and solve them without taking any advice or directions from the consultant. The consultant is supposed to act as patient listener in place of discussion. Under this method, consultant tries to motivate the entrepreneur for identifying the problem and think and take initiative to solve them. The consultant only develops the base for solving the problem before the entrepreneur, and motivates the entrepreneur to take his own decisions. In other words, consultancy is not supposed to solve the problem directly but drives the entrepreneur towards solution of the problem.

Merits: Important merits of the method are as follows:

(i) It provides an opportunity of entrepreneurial awareness among the entrepreneurs.

(ii) It enables the entrepreneurs to undertake intensive study of environment.

(iii) It ensures implementation of self formulated directives by the entrepreneur for his own development.

(iv) It facilitates the formulation and implementation of work/business plan by the entrepreneur.

(v) It encourages the entrepreneur to seek the expertise of consultants for reviewing his work performance.

(vi) It facilitates the entrepreneur to identify the merits and limitations of his own judgments/decisions by reviewing his own work performance.

(vii) It encourages the entrepreneur to use previous successful decisions as a base for future decisions. In this way, he can minimise his dependence on consultancy organisations.

Necessary Elements for Consultancy Process

(i) Development of open environment is necessary for both the parties —consultant and entrepreneur, to bring effectiveness in consultancy process. It will enable the entrepreneur to undertake intensive study of the problem.

(ii) Exchange of information should be undertaken on regular basis between an entrepreneur and government officials.

(iii) Consultants are required to give assistance through their consultancy skill by attending the meeting organised for the entrepreneur and government official.

(iv) Government officials should be trained in providing information and assisting formally or informally to the entrepreneur.

(v) Consultant should be fully prepared for effective consultancy and use his previous experiences and information for effective consultancy.

(vi) Organisations engaged in entrepreneurship development functions should develop effective consultancy structure on regular basis because they are generally related with every stage of entrepreneurship development.

Entrepreneurial Monitoring

Success of any business depends upon the monitoring and consequently implementation of remedial actions. Thus, effectiveness of an entrepreneurial development programme is directly related with continuous and regular monitoring process. Entrepreneurship development programme should be result oriented. There is a need to evaluate each and every stage or phase of the entrepreneurship development in terms of performance achieved. If entrepreneur fails to take timely evaluation there may be a possibility of negative physical and financial performance. There is also possibility of huge accumulated losses if remedial actions also fail to generate anything. It would be seen to what extent entrepreneur is able to monitor his enterprise and in which direction he has implemented remedial action effectively and adequately. So, there is need to evaluate and monitor the whole process of entrepreneurship development programme to implement remedial action on time.

Definition of Monitoring: "Monitoring may be defined as a process through which it guides the entrepreneur and develops awareness to know where he is in the process of developing his enterprise".

Thus, it is clear that monitoring process is highly essential to get an idea about the different stages of enterprises' development.

Features: Important features of monitoring are given below:

(i) It is a continuous process.

(ii) It develops entrepreneurial awareness.

(iii) It guides the entrepreneur where he is in his economic mission.

(iv) It integrates the different phases/stages of enterprise development.

(v) It ensures effective coordination in entrepreneurial activities.

In this context it is important to note that institutions engaged in entrepreneurship development should try to give more importance on monitoring mechanism for desired success. These institutions should also involve themselves in having effective mutual relations and trust with the entrepreneurs. Monitoring process facilitates the enterprise development in proper perspective. In practice, sponsoring agency is responsible for monitoring of the entrepreneurship development activities. Sometimes, specialised financial institutions, training institutes, companies engaged in development of infrastructural facilities also undertake monitoring activities with regard to entrepreneurship development. So there must be an effective coordination among these institutions on monitoring activities to avoid duplication. In these situations these institutions can really help the entrepreneurs for success.

Monitoring Techniques: Following techniques are being used in monitoring process of entrepreneurial development.

1. Log Book Technique: Log book is generally used as an important mechanism for effective monitoring. Log books are filled up by the regular worker or officials of the sponsoring agency. This book contains separate page for each and every entrepreneur. All information related with entrepreneurial activities is feeded in this book. Moreover, this book is also used as a reference book by the institutions engaged in entrepreneurial training. In most of the cases, other assisting institutions also prepare separable log book for each and every entrepreneurship development programmes.

2. History Cards Technique: History cards are an arrangement which keep continuous watch on the process of the entrepreneurship development. All information, like different stages which have been completed by the entrepreneur at different points of time, problems already being faced by the entrepreneur at various levels, how he solved these problems, what are the levels of performance at various levels of entrepreneurial activities etc. are detailed in the history card. Institutions engaged in entrepreneurship development monitors the activities of entrepreneur on the basis of these cards.

At this stage, it would be better to say that whatever experience we have received with regard to monitoring of entrepreneurship development process, we can say that this process is still at infancy stage. However, institutions engaged in the monitoring process, are playing crucial role. Institutions are relying more and more on their Cooperating institutions for monitoring activities. So it needs further coordination. Actually, it is for the sponsoring agency to monitor the progress of enterprise development directly and get a direct feedback about the operational performance. It will reduce the time lag between getting the feed back and implementing the remedial actions. Then, we can ensure a better consultancy and monitoring process with regard to entrepreneurship development.

EXAMINATION QUESTIONS

Long Answer Questions:

1. What do you mean by entrepreneurial consultancy? Discuss its objects.
2. Critically examine the consultancy process.
3. What are the different methods of consultancy? Examine their suitability.
4. Discuss the necessary elements for consultancy process.
5. What do you understand by entrepreneurial monitoring? Discuss its techniques.

Short Answer Questions:

1. What is consultancy?
2. What are objectives of entrepreneurial consultancy?
3. What is consultanc process?
4. What is entrepreneurial monitoring?
5. What do you mean by Log Book Technique?

Objective Type Questions:

1. Consultancy relates with the following except,
   (a) Planned process of customer
   (b) Rewarding the customer
   (c) Motivation of customer
   (d) Ancillary relationships

2. Direct method of consultancy covers the following except,
   (a) Collection of information
   (b) Providing direct consultancy
   (c) Giving arrangements in support of his position
   (d) Motivating entrepreneurs think intensively
3. History Cards Technique relates with the following:
   (a) Monitoring of procurements process of the enterprises
   (b) Monitoring of entrepreneurs' public relations
   (c) Monitoring of entrepreneurial activities
   (d) Monitoring of financial performance of the enterprise
4. Log Book Technique deals with
   (a) Consultancy
   (b) Monitoring
   (c) Performance appraisal
   (d) Profitability evaluation
5. Indirect methods of consultancy facilitates the entrepreneurs
   (a) To be more aware about himself
   (b) To study the immediate environment more intensively
   (c) To seek expertise for the review of his own performance appraisal
   (d) All of the above

Answers

1-(d) 2-(b) 3-(c) 4-(b) 5-(d)

35

ETHICS AND SOCIAL RESPONSIBILITY OF ENTREPRENEUR

Entrepreneurs generally develop their business into three popular forms of organisations. These are sole tradership or proprietory form, partnership form and corporate form of business organisations. However, corporate form is the most popular form of business organisation in the country. Most of the entrepreneurs prefer floating their businesses in corporate form as it is more convenient, legally suitable and flexible. Corporates are legal entity and they are free to formulate their own vision and mission. They are also supposed to set the tone of their operational behaviour. Operational behaviour integrates the practices that are the base for relationships management with different parties. Companies have their own separate identity with their shareholders. Traditional thinking advocates that managers have to maximise the value of the firm and consequently maximising the wealth of their shareholders as they are the risk bearers of the business. But at practical parlance, it is not fair. Contemporary theory suggests that there are many contributors in the well being of the company. These contributors are called as stakeholders. These stakeholders include managers, employers, customers, suppliers, creditors, government employees, shareholders and the community. These stakeholders need care and consideration at the hands of companies.

Managers take the risk and transfer the risk to the shareholders and employees are also working hard to achieve the goal of the company. Similarly, suppliers ensure timely and steady supply of materials and related services to the company. The society bears the cost of growing pollution and other hazards created by the industries. The customers being a part of the society also create demand for the products and services being produced by the company. Bankers are providing funding facilities to the company. The government facilitates the transition from project idea to selling the products and services. These contributors do not expect any reward or pie from the profits of the company. These stakeholders just want to know the answer for their contributions—What they should expect from the company? They expect from the company only implementation of principles of honesty, quality rationality, justifiability, sincerity and societal orientation in its working behaviour. They want integration of morality in their corporate behaviour.

Business has to promote its growth with fairness and trust. Stakeholders are always concerned with the level of ethical behaviour of the company as it enable the company to develop a long-term brand equity. The business is also expected to share a part of its prosperity with the community in the midst of which it is located by offering amenities and services not otherwise available to the needy in that community. Business decisions and activities affect the expectations of stakeholders. Each enterprise faces unique political, economic, social and technological pressures. Each and every enterprise has its own organisational culture that influences its stakeholders. However, behaviour model of the company can demonstrate a process through which owners and managers can identify enterprise stakeholders. They are required to foster reasonable stakeholder expectations; and inspire, encourage and support for remedial actions in the interest of these stakeholders.

(I) ENTREPRENEURIAL ETHICS

The terms—ethos, values, ethics and morals can be used interchangeably to explain similar set of ideas. Human concern for values has been a subject matter of deliberation among intellectuals and practioners in India. The concept of values is called as 'dharma'. The word "dharma" is derived from "dhri" which means to sustain. It also means duties and obligations. Dharma is not the same thing as religion. Dharma is seen as performance of one's duties towards ourselves, family, organisation, society and the entire world. Dharma is the prerogative of humans, without which they are not worthy of being called humans.

Nature of Entrepreneurial Ethics

Ethics are defined by the concise Oxford Dictionary as "moral principles" or as "rules of conduct". It is a combination of moral principles or manner of actions, which are acceptable or unacceptable in any field of human activity. Corporate ethics is a specialised study of morality in the area of business. It concentrates on moral standards as they apply to business policies, institutions and behaviour. The ethical issues involve judgement about the rightness or wrongness of behaviour. These issues are also guiding force for the behaviour and decision-making process in the company. Various laws strive to advocate ethical standards at the minimum floor level, in actual practice corporate should strive to practice ethical conduct in their various activities at a higher level. Dharma is also equivalent to ethics. The concept of "Dharma" refers to what we ought to hold and to which we ought to fasten ourselves. A code of conduct is not merely a set of regulations of do's and don'ts. It is an endeavour to define the norms of behaviour of corporates which uses the wealth of the society.

Management of Entrepreneurial Ethics

Concept of corporate ethics generally applied to the business having separate entity from its owners. However, these separate entities are not involved in the decision-making process. Managers at different levels are required to take decision within the business entity. Top level managers take decisions that affect the organisation's policies and that determine how lower level managers confront decisions that involve applying organisational policies to their day to day circumstances. Since managers are taking decisions it is their sense of right and wrong that ultimately determines the extent of corporate ethical environment. Corporate ethics is a form of applied ethics or professional ethics that examines ethical principles and moral or ethical problems that arise in a business environment. It applies to all aspects of business conduct and is relevant to the conduct of individuals and business organisations as a whole.

The study of ethics in management addresses individual decisions in the context of certain rules of conduct or moral standards. Ethical behaviour, then refers to individual conduct that is considered "right" or "good" in the context of a governing moral code. "It confirms not only to the law, but also to a broader set of moral principles expected by all or by a segment of society. In contrast, unethical behaviour covers any individual conduct that is "wrong" or "bad" within this moral code. It may or may not be illegal, but it falls short of the broader set of moral principles expected by society." [3]

Human beings are the active segments of the corporate business. The companies cannot and shall not be immune to ethics. The goal of corporate business is to provide goods and services to customers and earn profits. The company has to ensure the supply of goods and services at reasonable price and of a reasonable quality. A society consists of people who have common ends and whose activities are organised by a system of institutions designed to achieve these ends. Family, community, society, schools, religions, temples, government etc. are the basic institutions which are the base for formulation of values and moral standards. These institutions helps in designing the sub-systems : (*a*) Production of the goods and services the members of society want and need, and (*b*) Distribution of these goods and services to the various members of society. Thus, economic institutions determine who will carry out the work of production, how that work will be organised, what resources that work will consume and how its products and benefits will be distributed among society's members. Corporate enterprises are the economic institutions through which people in modern societies carry on the tasks of producing and distributing the goods and services. They provide the fundamental structures within which the members of society combine their scarce resources—land, labour, capital, and technology—into usable goods and they provide the channels through which these goods are distributed in the form of consumer products, employee salaries, investors' return and government taxes.

Thus, corporate ethics is a study of moral standards and how these apply to the systems and organisations through which modern societies produce and distribute goods and services and to the people who work within these organisations. It includes not only the analysis of moral norms and moral values, but also attempts to apply the conclusions of this analysis to that assortment of institutions, technologies, transactions, activities and pursuits that we call business enterprises.

Corporate Values and Image

Corporate value reflect the values of entrepreneurs at the top level. The esteem of a company generally governed by the values that the entrepreneurs/promoters of any organisation cherish. Some organisations emphasise on integrity, independence etc., while other values hard work, interdependence and cooperation. Consistent values help in formulation of organisational norms. Some values like tolerance, empathy, risk-taking etc., get embedded in the fabric of an organisation culture.

The values and attitude of people are important for any company as social factors affect its strategic management decisions. This is more important for a growing company as it has to form an image in society. There is growing trend that the real success of an entrepreneur depends on the adherence of social norms valued by the society. It is the public image of the company that carries for a long period amongst its stakeholders. Public interest is to be taken care of by the company as it is the most important value dimension of the public image. Toothpaste is very personal to people and hence it enjoys a brand loyalty. In a society where herbal ingredients are valued by the users, the presence of turmeric or meswak is advertised by the manufacturer to woo his customers. The soft drink similarly enjoys a brand loyalty and a news item in the paper about traces of lizards eggs in the water used for soft drinks would definitely mar its image and the product may never to take off. A courier service company may built a public image for fast delivery of goods, and any action by the company contrary to this public image may be extremely harmful to the company."

Factors Governing Entrepreneurial Ethics

1. Legislative Framework: Ethics is a voluntary phenomenon. It cannot be forced but it should be persuaded. However, if corporates are not giving due weightage to ethics in their behaviour it is for the laws to intervene in the process. Laws are generally passed as result of low ethical standards or the failure to recognise social issues. Legal action or government directives are the result of social pressure. A practice can be made illegal if society views it as being unethical. For example, if contributions to political parties by corporates are being viewed as excessive and unethical then the practice can be banned.

2. Regulatory Framework of the Government: From time to time, government regulates the working conditions, product safety, statutory warnings (on cigarettes and other harmful products) etc. These are all supported by laws or guidelines. These guidelines help the entrepreneurs in determining the working behaviour as per the acceptable standards and practices. Similarly, Jago Grahak Jago is another persuading strategy among the potential consumers about the corporate business practices. This has also been launched by the Ministry of Consumer Affairs to improve awareness about corporate defaults in their marketing practices.

3. Corporates Ethical Codes: Many times company provides specific guidelines to their managers and employees about the ethical codes of behaviour.

One important question in such instances is whether individuals within organisations are really governed by the code of ethics or give lip services to the guidelines.

4. Societal Obligations: Social forces and pressure have considerable influence on ethics in business. Job reservation to the handicapped in corporates is an important example of societal obligations being fulfilled by them. Society in fact, forces the entrepreneurs to alter their decisions by taking a broader view of the environment and the needs of society.

5. Entrepreneurial Vision and Mission: Everyday ethical decisions are usually made between the lesser of the two evils rather than obvious right and wrong dimension of the judgement. These judgements generally include different types of values being persued by the industrial house in the vision and mission of the group companies. In this context, we can include the norms of ethical standards formulated by the Tata and Birla group of companies.

Scope of Entrepreneurial Ethics

Entrepreneurial ethics include three dimensions. These are systemic, corporate and individual environment.

1. Systemic Issues: These are ethical questions raised about the economic, political, legal, and other social systems within which corporate enterprises are expected to operate. These are set by the society, government and other agencies involved in ethical movements. These include questions about the morality of economic system, laws, regulations, industrial structures and social practices within which Indian corporate enterprises are required to achieve their vision and mission.

2. Corporate Issues: These are ethical questions raised about a particular company. These include questions about the morality of the activities, policies, practices or organisational structure of an individual company taken as a whole. Individual behaviour of the company set the agenda for other companies working in the industry concern and managers and employees are expected to comply with these standards. Generally, individual companies try to formulate their own ethical standards.

3. Individual Issues: These are ethical questions raised about a particular individual or particular individuals within a company. These include questions about the morality of the decisions, actions or character of an individual manager.

Sources of the Ethical Behaviour

1. Values and Goals: There is an important relationship between goals and values of an organisation. The goals of the organisation are influenced by leadership, knowledge and skills, amity, influence and power, and survival. All these factors change the goals of the organisation and consequently corporates expect values based behaviour from their individual managers.

2. Values Forming Institution: The life and development of society produce values. There are so many organisations like family, school, state and religion which are the basic sources of values for individuals. The basic purpose of values formation by these institutions is that they prescribe what is good or bad for an individual. And at a later stage, inculcation of these values enable the managers to work for values in their companies.

3. Work and Career: Work consists of the tasks or responsibilities associated with the job or position in an organsiation. In organisation, the work is organised and directed for the achievement of desired end. An individual's experience over a period of time constitutes his career work and career creates special values that give unity, cohesion and meaning to persons and groups.

4. Professional's Codes: In recent days, more and more professionals are being appointed by the corporates. These professionals are required to go by the values and code of conduct prescribed by the relevant professional institutes and associations. Professional's codes are the sources of ethical norms for managers in business organisations. These codes are consistent with customs, beliefs, social values, public laws and generally desirable behaviour. The Institute of Chartered Accountant of India, Institution of Engineers, Institute of Company Secretaries of India and All India Management Association etc., have prescribed a set of code of conduct for their members.

Rationale of Entrepreneurial Ethics

1. Survival of Business: Any individual business will collapse if all of its managers, employees and customers come to think that it is morally permissible to steal from, lie to, or break their agreements with the company.

2. Need of a Stable Society: All businesses require a stable society in which they are supposed to carry on their business dealings. Stability of any society requires that its members adhere to some minimal standards of ethics. It will create a conducive environment for the development of economic and social institutions.

3. Consistent with Business Objectives: Ethics should be brought into business by showing that ethical considerations are consistent with business pursuits, in particular with the pursuit of profit. That ethics is consistent with the pursuit of profit can be shown by simply finding examples of companies where a history of good ethics has existed side by side with a history of profitable operations.

4. Growing Clout of Business: The power and influence of business in society is greater than ever before. Evidence suggests that many members of the public are uneasy with such developments. Ethics helps us to understand why this is happening, what will be its implications and how we will address this situation.

5. Safeguarding Public from Business Malpractices: Business malpractices have the potential to inflict enormous harm on individuals, communities and the environment. Ethics seeks, to improve the human condition' by focusing on the causes and consequences of these malpractices being done by the corporates.

6. Effective Decision Making: Ethics help to improve the corporate ethical decision-making with the appropriate knowledge and tools that allow them to correctly identify, diagnose, analyse and provide solutions to the ethical problem and dilemmas they are confronted with day to day decision making having implications for the stakeholders.

7. Entrepreneurial Effectiveness: Ethics develops the ability to assess the benefits and problems associated with different ways of managing ethics in organisations. It also improves the knowledge that transcends the traditional framework of business studies which have focused on the relevance of ethics in business.

Importance of Entrepreneurial Ethics

1. Basic Human Needs: Ethics corresponds to basic human needs. It is human trait that man desires to be ethical: not only in his private life but also in his business affairs where, being a manager, he knows his decisions may affect the lives of thousand of employees or customers.

2. Improve Creditability: Values create credibility with the public. A company perceived by the public to be ethically and socially responsive would be honoured and respected even by those who have no intimate knowledge of its actual working. There will be an instinctive prejudice in favour of its product, since people believes that the company offers value for their money. Public issues attract an immediate response from the company as it affects its credibility.

3. Improves Coordination: Values gives credibility to the management by coordinating the language of value from the top to the lower level in the organisations. Organisational ethics, when perceived by the employees as genuine and create common goals, improves ethical environment. The entrepreneur has credibility with its employees precisely because it has credibility with the public. Neither sound business strategy, nor a generous compensation policy and fringe benefits can win the employee credibility. Perceived moral and social uprightness about the company by its employees can be the basis for credibility among the employees.

4. Better Decision Making: Values help better decision making. An ethical attitude helps the management to make better decisions, *i.e.*, decisions which are in the interest of the public, their employees and the company's own long good, even through the decision making is slower. Ethics force a management to take various aspects of economic, social decisions keeping in mind their ethical implications.

5. Trade-off between Ethics and Profits: Ethics and profit can go together. A company, which is inspired by ethical conducts, can also be a profitable one. Value driven companies are sure to be successful in long-run, though in the short-run they can loose money. Ethics help the company to develop a long-term brand equity in the society which ultimately improves sales and profit.

6. Humanitarian Approach: An ethical oriented management takes measures to prevent pollution and protects workers health. Leading business houses had already initiated social responsibility initiatives to protect the environment, provides social welfare amenities to the workers etc. These business houses are incurring huge expenditures without any mandatory initiative of the government. It is a sharing of wealth by the company in favour of society at large.

Morality

Moral norms can usually be expressed as general rules or statements. These norms describe the objects or features of objects that have worth, such as "Honesty is good" and "Injustice is bad." These norms or standards differ from country to country and from culture to culture.

Typically, a person's moral standards are first absorbed as child from family, friends, and various societal influences such as church, school, television, magazines, music and associations. Person grows up, experience, learning, and intellectual development may lead the maturing person to revise these standards Some are discarded and new ones may be adopted to replace them. Moral standards can be contrasted with standards we hold about things that are not moral.

Features of Moral Standards

(*i*) Moral standards deal with matters that can seriously injure or seriously benefit human beings. Human being constitutes the society. Society is supposed to formulate moral standards for its members and they are required to follow them in their actual life. If individual members of the society are not following it, then members' reputation will be affected in the society itself.

(*ii*) Moral standards are not established or changed by the decisions of particular authoritative bodies. Laws and legal standards are established by the authority of a legislature or the decisions of voters. However, moral standards, however, are not established by authority nor does their validity rest on voting procedures. The validity of moral standards rests on the adequacy of the reasons that are taken to support and justify them; so long as these reasons are adequate, the standards remain valid.

(*iii*) Moral standards are more important to other values including self-interest. If a person has a moral obligation to do something, then he is supposed to do it even if he has conflicts with other non-moral values or self-interest.

(*iv*) Moral standards are based on impartial considerations. Basically, the moral point of view goes beyond personal interests. It is concerned with "universal" standpoint in which everyone's interests are impartially counted as equal. Moral standards are associated with special emotions and have a special vocabulary.

(*v*) Moral standards deal with matters of serious consequences. They are based on good reasons and not on authority, overriding self-interest and ego. These are based on impartial considerations and whose transgression is associated with feelings of guilt and shame.

(*vi*) Ethics is the discipline that examines the moral standards of a society. It asks how these standards apply to our lives and whether these standards are reasonable or unreasonable *e.g,* whether they are supported by good reasons or poor ones. Therefore, a person starts to do ethics when he takes the moral standards absorbed from family, church, and friends. The person himself is a part of the society.

(*vii*) Ethics is the study of moral standards. The ultimate aim of ethics is to develop a body of moral standards that are reasonable to hold. The standards should be justifiable and must have societal acceptance.

(*viii*) Ethics is a normative study of ethics. A normative study is an investigation that attempts to reach normative conclusions *i.e.,* conclusions about what things are good or bad or about what actions are right or wrong. It aims to discover what should be? Ethics is the study of moral standards whose explicit purpose is to determine as far as possible which standards are correct or supported by the best reasons and so it attempts to reach conclusions about morally right and wrong and morally good and bad.

(*ix*) The social sciences are engaged in a descriptive study of ethics. A descriptive study is one that does not try to reach any conclusions about what things are truly good or bad or right or wrong. It attempts to explain the world without reaching any conclusions about whether the world is as it should be.

Moral Reasoning

Moral reasoning refers to the reasoning process by which human behaviour, institutions, or policies are judged to be in accordance with or in violation of moral standards. Moral reasoning always involves two essential components: (*a*) An understanding of what reasonable moral standards require, prohibit, value, or condemn; and (*b*) Evidence or information that shows that a particular person, policy, institution, or behaviour has the kinds of features that these moral standards require, prohibit, value, or condemn. However, moral reasoning should fulfill the following conditions:

(*i*) Logical Moral Reasoning: The analysis of moral reasoning requires that the logic of the arguments used to establish a moral judgement by rigorously examining, all the unspoken moral and factual assumptions. However, both assumptions and premises be displayed and subjected to criticism.

(*ii*) Factual Evidence Required: Factual evidence cited in support of a person's judgment must be accurate, relevant and complete. Factual evidence lays the foundation for moral reasoning. It provides practice orientation for moral reasoning.

(*iii*) **Consistent Moral Standards:** They must be consistent with other standards and beliefs the person holds. Inconsistency between a person's moral standards can be uncovered and corrected by examining situations in which these moral standards require incompatible things.

Morality vs. Ethics

In common usage, the terms 'ethics' and 'morality' are often used interchangeably. However, sometime a technical difference makes differences between the two terms. Morality is concerned with the norms, values, and beliefs embedded in social processes which define right and wrong for an individual or a community. Ethics is concerned with the study of morality and the application of reason to elucidate specific rules and principles that determine right and wrong for any given situation. These rules and principles are called ethical theories.

Trusteeship

A trust is normally created when a fund or asset is earmarked for a specific purpose. A wealthy person may set apart some funds for a specific purpose and request a trusted individual or a corporate like a bank, to manage it and make sure that the benefits are made available to the specified beneficiaries. Gandhian concept is also relevant to corporate enterprises. In his trusteeship concept Gandhiji had made the following observations.

(*i*) Ownership is a costly and illusory concept to ensure permanency and succession.

(*ii*) It gives birth to attachment, exploitation, possessiveness and greed, exploitation and revenge.

(*iii*) All assets must be held in trust and used for the good of all.

(*iv*) Distribution of assets and the benefits of the operations be equitable, not equal.

(*v*) The owner of wealth has the right to a honourable livelihood and the rest is that of the community.

The Gandhian concept of Trusteeship also said that "Trusteeship provides a means of transforming the present capitalist order of society into an egalitarian one. It gives no quarter to capitalism but gives the present owning class, a chance of reforming itself. It is based on the faith that human nature is never beyond redemption. It does not recognise any right of private ownership of property, except so far as it may be permitted by society for its own welfare. It does not exclude legislative regulation of the ownership and use of wealth."[4] "Thus, under state regulated ownership, an individual will not be free to hold or use his wealth for selfish satisfaction or in disregard of the interests of society."[5]

Gandhiji's concept of trusteeship was founded on non-violence. He thought that the very idea of ownership was at the root of violence. People really are together only when they rise above conflicts of interests, envy and competition. Trusteeship was seen as a means of bringing people together. He had said, "If one has come by a fair amount of wealth, either by way of legacy or by mean of trade and industry, he must know that all that wealth does not belong to him. What belongs to him is the right to an honourable livelihood." Trusteeship followed the vedic dictum or renounce (rights and pleasures of self) and enjoy (in the pleasures of others). This is also the basis of the commandment in all religions: to share one's strengths and assets with others.

Ethical Code

An ethical code is adopted by an organisation is to assist the persons working in its own system. They are generally persuaded to understand the difference between 'right' and 'wrong' and to apply this understanding their decision making process. The ethical code therefore generally implies documents at three levels:

(*i*) Code of Ethics (Corporate ethics): A code of ethics often focuses on social issues. It may set out general principles about an organisation's beliefs on matters such as mission, quality, privacy or the environment. It may delineate proper procedures to determine whether a violation of the code of ethics has occurred and if so, what remedies are available to correct it. The effectiveness of such codes of ethics depends on the extent to which management supports these corrective measures. These codes of ethics are voluntary in nature.

(*ii*) Code of Conduct (Employee ethics): A code of conduct is a document designed to influence the behaviour of employees. They set out the procedures to be used in specific ethical situations, such as conflicts of interest or the acceptance of gifts and delineate the procedures to determine whether a violation of the code of ethics occurred and if so, what remedial actions are in place to make the behaviour of employees more acceptable to the ethical environment. The effectiveness of such codes of ethics depends on the extent to which management supports them with sanctions and rewards. Violations of a code of conduct may subject the violator to the organisation's remedies which can under particular circumstances result in the termination of employment.

(*iii*) Code of Practice (Professional ethics): A code of practice is adopted by a profession or by a governmental or non-governmental organisation to regulate that profession. A code of practice may be styled as a code of professional responsibility, which discusses difficult issues, difficult decisions that will often need to be made and provide a clear account of what behaviour is considered "ethical" or "correct" or "right" in the relevant circumstances. In a membership context, failure to comply with a code of practice can result in expulsion from the professional organisation. Professional ethics concerns the moral issues that arise because of the specialist knowledge that professionals attain, and how the use of this knowledge should be governed when providing a service to the public at large.

Social Charter for Indian Corporates[6]

Ex-Prime Minister Dr. Manmohan Singh outlined a 10 point social charter for Indian Industry to make our country's growth process both efficient and inclusive. Dr. Singh invited corporate India to be a partner in making ours a more humane and just society.

The 10 point social charter spelt out by the prime minister are :

(*i*) Healthy respect for workers and their investment in welfare.

(*ii*) Corporate social responsibility.

(*iii*) Employment to the less privileged.

(*iv*) Resist excessive remuneration and discourage conspicuous consumption.

(*v*) Investment in people and in their skills.

(*vi*) Desist from non-competitive behaviour.

(*vii*) Invest in environment-friendly technologies.

(*viii*) Promote enterprise and innovation.

(*ix*) Fight corruption at all levels.

(*x*) Promote socially responsible media and finance socially responsible advertising.

(II) ENTREPRENEURIAL SOCIAL RESPONSIBILITY

Business enterprises are the basic cells of modern economic life and their phenomenal success in converting natural resources into economic wealth is quite important. These business enterprises are playing active role in transformational process of social and physical environment in the interest of society at large. Basically, they are the institutional members of society. If individual members have an obligation to improve the level and standard of society, then corporates also have responsibility to enrich the society as per its requirements. They are also the citizens who have civic duties and responsibilities. The corporate performance affects the economy and creates social problems. An equal amount of social responsibility is needed to match their social power. Business enterprises are expected to perform its role in an orderly manner so that they can have a claim for the well being of the society. Thus, the measurement and reporting of social performance of profit-oriented firms form the core of Corporate Social Responsibility (CSR).

Nature of Social Responsibility of Business

The term 'Social Responsibility of Busines's reflects the impact of a corporation's activities on society. This embodies the performance of its economic function and other actions taken to contribute to the quality of life. These activities may extend beyond meeting the letter of law due to the pressures of competition or the requirements of contracts.

'Corporate social responsibility is operating a business in a manner which meets or excels the ethical, legal, commercial and public expectations that a society has from the business.'

The term corporate social responsibility refers to the concept of business being accountable for how it managers the impact of its processes on stakeholders on a voluntary basis.

The NAA Committee has identified four major areas of social performance: community development, human resources, physical resources and environmental contribution and product or service contributions. The responsibility of business itself indicates the desire to ensure the optimum use of resources, development and expansion, operation and management, promotion of research environment and environmental management etc. Since corporates have to draw on the community in which they operate for all resources, they also have obligations to their multiple stakeholders. Stakeholders are defined as those who get affected by corporate policies and practices. It is acknowledged fact that business has not just financial accountability but also has the social and environmental responsibility. It is generally known as the triple bottom-line of good governance. The license to operate in the societies trust that an organisation will work in the best interest of the society. Society itself is increasingly being critical about the operating norms in the industry. Business cannot be seen as aggravating the problems of the merger, poverty, depletion of natural resources or inequities. Entry barriers, adverse judgment from judiciaries or earlier, business was expected to serve the purpose of its stockholders as a creator of financial wealth. But now business is assigned to fulfill the expectations of different stakeholders like consumers, employees, shareholders, society, community, environment and government etc.

Need for Social Responsibility of Business

The Indian corporate sector has seen the current decade as a period of high growth and the emergence of a strong India Inc. having a significant global footprint. The decade also saw the financial crisis that shook the global markets. While the corporate sector is recovering from the jolt of the global financial crisis, the future is looking bright. However, the corporate sector is also standing in the midst of a sustainability crisis that poses a threat to the very existence of business. What we have before us is a cross-road where one path leads us to inclusive growth and the other may lead to unsustainable future. However, the first path will require careful nurturing for which all stakeholders need to assume and discharge their respective responsibilities. Business sector generating wealth and value for the shareholders in the last sixty years, but simultaneously we also have the problems of poverty, unemployment, illiteracy, malnutrition etc. facing the nation. The corporate growth is sometimes seen as widening the gap between India and Bharat through its income-skewing capability. This gap needs to be bridged. While the Government undertakes extensive developmental initiatives through a series of sectoral programmes, the business sector also needs to take the responsibility of exhibiting socially responsible business practices that ensures the distribution of wealth and well being of the communities in which the business operates. The Indian business has traditionally been socially responsible. From inactive philanthropy to the incorporation of the stakeholders' interest in the business model, the Indian business sector practices various methods of discharging its social responsibility. While a lot of human and economic energy is available for utilisation in this area, a suitable mechanism is required to channelise this energy for which the Government, corporate sector and the communities need to partner together.

The subject of entrepreneurial social responsibility has evolved during last few decades from simple philanthropic activities to integrating the interest of the business with that of the communities in which it operates. By exhibiting socially, environmentally and ethically responsible behaviour in governance of its operations, the business can generate value and long-term sustainability for itself while making positive contribution in the betterment of the society. Although, we have seen a period of sustained economic growth in the current decade, we still continue to face major challenges on the human side in India. The problems like poverty, illiteracy, malnutrition etc. have resulted in a large section of the population remaining as "un-included" from the mainstream. We need to address these challenges through suitable efforts and interventions in which all the state and non-state actors need to partner together to find and implement innovative solutions. Indian business has traditionally been socially responsible and some of the business houses have demonstrated their efforts on this front in a laudable manner. However, the culture of social responsibility needs to go deeper in the governance of the businesses.

Approaches towards Entrepreneurial Social Responsibility (ESR)

1. Profit Maximisation Approach: The first approach originates in classical economic theory as expressed in the hypothesis that the firm has one and only one objective, which is to maximise profit. By extension, the objective of a company should be to maximise shareholders' wealth. In striving to attain this objective within the constraints of existing legal and ethical. framework, business corporations are acting in the best interests of society at large. This classical interpretation of the concept of corporate social responsibility has been advocated as—there is one and only one social responsibility of business—to use its resources and engage in activities designed to increase its profit, as long as it stays within the rules of the game. Participation of corporates in open and free competition, without deception or fraud may be considered as an important aspect of the social responsibility. "Few trends could so thoroughly undermine the very foundations of our free society as the acceptance by corporate officials of a social responsible firm other than to make as much money for their shareholders as possible."[1]

2. Social Objective Approach: It was developed in the 1970s, recognising the significance of social objectives in relation to the maximisation of profit. According to this approach, corporate managers should make decisions which maintain an equitable balance between the claims of stakeholders *viz.*, shareholders, employees, customers, suppliers and the general public. The corporation represents, therefore, a coalition of interests and the proper consideration of the various interests of this coalition is the only way to ensure that the corporation will attain its long-term profit maximisation objective.

3. Balancing Approach: It regards profit as a means to an end and not as an end in itself. The promoters/executives of a company have the problem of reconciling the demands of employees for more wages and improved benefit plans, customers for lower prices and greater values, shareholders for higher dividend and greater capital appreciation & all within a framework that will be constructive and acceptable to society. Balancing stakeholders needs understanding their concern, priporitising them and making them a part of the business process is essential. It is generally believed that industry cannot be an island of prospering in a sea of prosperity. Accordingly, "organisational decisions should be concerned with the selection of socially responsible alternatives. Instead of seeking to maximise profit generally, the end result should be a satisfactory level of profit which is compatible with the attainment of a range of social goals."[2]

Trusteeship model of Mahatma Gandhi also advocates that whereby the wealth you create has to be ploughed back for the benefit of society. In fact, today the debate is not about whether corporates need to take on social responsibility, because that is taken as given, but how this responsibility is to be discharged and how it is to be measured, audited and continuously improved upon. It is a fact that, the success of companies is measured by their turnover, size, market capitalisation, profit after tax or shareholder value created. But the real purpose of business corporations is to improve the quality of life in society. How and to what extent corporates have improved the life of society at large is to be analysed, interpreted and reported in proper manner is one of the main theme of modern business.

Scope of Entrepreneurial Social Responsibility

Ernst and *Ernst* have identified six areas in which corporate social responsibility is expected: [3]

(*i*) Environment: This area involves the environmental aspects of production, covering pollution control in the conduct of business operations, prevention or repair of damage to the environment resulting from processing of natural resources and the conservation of natural resources. Corporate social objectives are to be found in the abatement of the negative external social effects of industrial production and in adopting more efficient technologies to minimise the use of irreplaceable resources and the reduction of waste.

(*ii*) Energy: This area covers conservation of energy in the conduct of business operations and increasing the energy efficiency of the company's products.

***(iii)* Fair business practices:** This area concerns the relationship of the company to special interest groups. In particular it deals with:

(*a*) Employment of minorities (*b*) advancement of minorities (*c*) employment of women (*d*) advancement of women (*e*)employment of other special interest groups (*f*) support for minority business (*g*) socially responsible practices abroad.

(iv) Human resources: This area concerns the impact of organisational activities on the people who constitute the human resources of the organisation. These activities include:

(*a*) Recruiting practices (*b*) training programmes (*c*) experience building-job rotation (*d*) job enrichment (*e*) wage and salary levels (*f*) fringe benefit plans (*g*) congruence of employee and organisational goals, (*h*) mutual trust and confidence, (*i*) job security, stability of workforce, layoff and recall practices (*j*) transfer and promotion policies (*k*) occupational health.

(v) Community involvement: This area involves community activities, health-related activities, education and the arts and other community activity disclosures.

(vi)Products: This area concerns the qualitative aspects of the products, for example their utility, life-durability, safety and serviceability, as well as their effect on pollution. Moreover, it includes customer satisfaction, truthfulness in advertising, completeness and clarity of labelling and packaging. Many of these considerations are already important from a marketing point of view. It is clear, however, that the social responsibility aspect of the product contribution extends beyond what is advantageous from a marketing angle.

Objectives of Entrepreneurial Social Responsibility

1. To identify and measure the periodic net social contribution of an individual firm, which includes not only the social costs and benefits internalised to the firm, but also those arising from externalities affecting different social segments;

2. To help in determining an individual firm's strategy and practices, which directly affect the relative resource and power status of individuals, communities, social segments and generations are consistent with widely shared social priorities, on the one hand and individuals' legitimate aspirations on the other.

3. To make available in an optimal manner to all social constituents relevant information on a firm's goals, policies, programmes, performance and contribution to social goals.

There has been a long-standing debate over scope of the corporate social responsibility but it is a fact that its scope is affected by the change available in the business environment. Social responsibility of business is a continuous process as the business is a regular and on-going activity and it is composed of two-way traffic. The business as well as the different sections of the society have mutual interests.

Conceptual Framework of Corporate Citizenship

The growing domination of global economic forces is pushing business to acquire greater responsibility for social well-being. As a result, a new concept is emerging in the new millennium: 'Corporate Citizenship' resembling the 'Corporate Social Responsibility.' A company's reputation in terms of corporate citizenship can be a key asset in attracting and retaining customers, opening up new markets and attracting and retaining a loyal and productive workforce. Corporates which fail to undertake this social responsibility face the prospects of shrinking consumer base and consequently profits. Some of the world's most successful companies, including Shell, Nike, Union Carbide and Exxon, operating entirely within the law have experienced devastating public relations and disasters due to negative public perceptions of their social responsibility. These perceptions have hurt the reputation and credibility of these companies and correspondingly shareholders' value.

"CSR encourages increased understanding and active participation of corporates in equitable social development as an integral part of good business practice. It focuses on finding ways for corporates to behave in a manner that maximises their society's wealth and consequently stake holders' value."[4] Corporate social responsibility is a continuing commitment by business to behave ethically and contribute to economic development while improving the quality of life of the workforce and their families as well as of the local community and society at large. Corporate social responsibility is considered a must for any company under the public gaze.

CSR is not a concept Indian corporates are unfamiliar with, though their activities may not always have borne the CSR tag. For instance, as long back as the 1920s, Tata Steel was engaged in philanthropic activities like maternity benefits, payment of provident fund, working hours etc. on which legislation was later enacted by government. Today, in post-liberalisation era, more companies have begun thinking on similar lines. With MNCs (multi-national corporations) focusing on CSR, many Indian corporates now keep aside sums ranging from 0-15 per cent of their profits after tax for CSR. Understanding of corporate social responsibility is a fledgling area of serious economic activity.

"Corporate responsibility norms seem to rise as wealth increases. Growing demand for more responsible corporate behaviour creates business opportunities. Firms that meet the demand at an early stage stand to win; laggards are put at risk."[5] A company that puts the interests of its stakeholders first through good corporate governance finds its stock more attractive to investors.

The manner in which the business community is contributing to the developmental issues is also undergoing a change. The old style paternalistic philanthropy of 'doing for the community'& building schools and hospitals in the name of the company's founder—is giving way to the idea of 'working with the community'. These ideas include: sharing marketing, technical and managerial skills; using communities as channel members to distribute the company's products; setting up ancillary units managed by communities and supplying products and using employees as volunteers, trainers and mentors. In simple terms, being socially responsible makes good business sense and firms could be rewarded by increased patronage. Corporates are expected to continuously improve their social, environmental and financial performance. The criteria of CSR as considered by companies includes environment, health and safety, sustainable development, human rights, ethics, gender equity, customer relations etc. The World Business Council for Sustainable Development in its publication "Making Good Business Sense" clearly stated how companies behaviour affects many people, including the flora and fauna and not just the shareholders. A company should be a responsible member of the society in which it operates. That means contributing to sustainable development by working to improve the quality of life of employees, their families, the local community and stakeholders up and down the supply chain. It can mean a day care facility for working mothers, a new clinic, health insurance, playgrounds; it can also mean bio-degradable packaging, cleaner fuel for buses and trucks, community tree plantation drives, reduced water and energy consumption.

Regulatory Base of Entrepreneurial Social Responsibility (ESR)

1. Legislation: It outlaws undesirable social activities. Many examples exist of public concern with undesirable features of business activity and of legislation to suppress such activities. For example, legislation relating to child labour in India has made employment of a child less than 14 years as illegal.

2. Licensing systems: They may be employed to limit the extent of activities which are useful to society, but present a potential social problem. The licensing of lorries, for example, has been made the subject of certificates of road-worthiness, and attention is now being paid to the control of exhaust emission. Thus, licensing may be qualitative as well as quantitative.

3. Taxation: Taxation is a convenient manner of internalising external social costs of activities having negative effects on society. The objective is to impose taxes on the firm equal in magnitude to the damage sustained by society from the firm's activities. The obvious purpose of such taxes would be to encourage firms to abate the effects of such activities or, alternatively, to finance public programmes for controlling these effects. There should be a tariff of taxes designed to encourage firms to locate an area where their methods of production would do least harm to the environment. Environment Protection Control Act, 1988 has made necessary provisions with regard to pollution control process in India.

Entrepreneurial Social Communication Process

Social Performance Reports are the latest trend in corporate communication indicating the level of compliance of social responsibility. The growing popularity of corporate social reporting and organisations' desire to know their stakeholders' view on corporate social performance suggests two possibilities.

(i) that stakeholders are interested in corporate behaviour, and business attitudes are changing from a predominantly managerial emphasis to collaborative one.

(ii) that there is an infrastructure of management information systems underpinning the whole process of reporting and providing the information behind organisationl decision-making. Social accounting systems identify and measure social performance. If an organisation then chooses to disclose this information in the interests of transparency and openness, its stakeholders must be confident that the information is true.

Reliable information systems reduce the risk that reporting of inaccurate information could damage the firm's reputation. Many organisations collect information that is pertinent to stakeholder groups, but all of them do not disclose it. Corporate attitudes towards stakeholders are changing; rather than holding stakeholders at arm's length, many organisations are now seeking to engage with them. It is a definite change from the hostile encounters that gave rise to early forms of social auditing and reporting. Stakeholders are becoming more articulate about their interests and concerns and organisations are getting better at communicating about social performance issues. "Corporate social reporting is increasingly popular for communicating data about social performance of corporates to multiple constituents. The wave of corporate communication is under-pinned by existing management information system. But while popular management accounting tools are being used for social responsibility decision-making, they require skillful adaptation if they are to demonstrate transparency and accountability. They have to perceive the value of business as holistic and not additive."[6] The organisations take advantage of their good social reputation in their marketing campaigns.

Social image of organisations is extremely important for several stakeholder groups. The groups they identified are similar in all forms of organisations: communities, customers, employees, environment, shareholders and suppliers. But the priority given to different stakeholder groups varies. The organisations are planning to develop links between the externally-reported measures and their internal reporting. But, despite lacking such a system, the firms are concerned about their social performance. *Barry H. Spicer* suggests that following measures are required to ensure effective compliance of social responsibility. "[7]

Action Plan for ESR : Following components of the action plan for entrepreneurial social responsibility are:

(*i*) To establish an implementation team that includes a management accountant and managers. (*ii*) Consult managers about the social information and performance measures they need (*iii*) Develop links between the organisation's mission statement/objectives and its internally reported social performance measures (*iv*) Develop internal social performance measures for each of organisation's stakeholder groups (*v*) Check that the internally reported social performance measures include both input and output measures (*vi*) Set up a system for the internal monitoring and management of social performance, (*vii*) Develop explicit links between managers' evaluation and their contribution to the organisation's social performance.

"The social values and culture of an organisation are critical factors affecting its social performance—often through informal group control and self-control."[8] External social reporting is important, but so is management information on social performance. Ultimately, it is the strategic and operating decisions of managers and other employees that determine the social performance of an organisation.

VOLUNTARY GUIDELINES FOR ENTREPRENEURIAL SOCIAL RESPONSIBILITY

The Ministry of Corporate Affairs has issued voluntary guidelines for the corporate social responsibility in 2009. These guidelines are as follows: [9]

Preamble

The 21st century is characterised by unprecedented challenges and opportunities, arising from globalisation, the desire for inclusive development and the imperatives of climate change. Indian business, which is today viewed globally as a responsible component of the ascendancy of India, is poised now to take on a leadership role in the challenges of our times. It is recognised the world over that integrating social, environmental and ethical responsibilities into the governance of businesses ensures their long-term success, competitiveness and sustainability. This approach also reaffirms the view that businesses are an integral part of society, and have a critical and active role to play in the sustenance and improvement of healthy ecosystems, in fostering social inclusiveness and equity and in upholding the essentials of ethical practices and good governance. This also makes business sense as companies with effective CSR, have image of socially responsible companies, achieve sustainable growth in their operations in the long run and their products and services are preferred by the customers. Indian entrepreneurs and business enterprises have a long tradition of working within the values that have defined our nation's character for millennia. India's ancient wisdom, which is still relevant today, inspires people to work for the larger objective of the well being of all stakeholders. These sound and all-encompassing values are even more relevant in current times, as organisations grapple with the challenges of modern-day enterprise, the aspirations of stakeholders and of citizens eager to be active participants in economic growth and development.

CSR is not philanthropy and CSR activities are purely voluntary—what companies will like to do beyond any statutory requirement of obligation. To provide companies with guidance in dealing with the above-mentioned expectations, while working closely within the framework of national aspirations and policies, following voluntary guidelines for corporate social responsibility have been developed. While the guidelines have been prepared for the Indian context, enterprises that have a transnational presence would benefit from using these guidelines for their overseas operations as well. Since the guidelines are voluntary and not prepared in the nature of a prescriptive road-map, they are not intended for regulatory or contractual use. While it is expected that more and more companies would make sincere efforts to consider compliance with these Guidelines, there may be genuine reasons for some companies in not being able to adopt them completely. In such a case, it is expected that such companies may inform their stakeholders about the guidelines which the companies have not been able to follow either fully or partially. It is hoped that "India Inc." would respond to these guidelines with keen interest.

After considering the experience of adoption of these guidelines by Indian Corporate Sector and consideration of relevant feedback and other related issues, the Government may initiate the exercise for review of these guidelines for further improvement after one year.

Fundamental Principle of Entrepreneurial Social Responsibility

1. Core Elements: Each business entity should formulate a CSR policy to guide its strategic planning and provide a roadmap for its CSR initiatives, which should be an integral part of overall business policy and aligned with its business goals. The policy should be framed with the participation of various level executives and should be approved by the Board. The CSR Policy should normally cover following core elements:

(i) Care for all Stakeholders: The companies should respect the interests of and be responsive towards all stakeholders, including shareholders, employees, customers, suppliers, project affected people, society at large etc. and create value for all of them. They should develop mechanism to actively engage with all stakeholders, inform them of inherent risks and mitigate them where they occur.

(ii) Ethical Functioning: Their governance systems should be under-pinned by ethics, transparency and accountability. They should not engage in business practices that are abusive, unfair, corrupt or anti-competitive.

(iii) Respect for Workers' Rights and Welfare: Companies should provide a workplace environment that is safe, hygienic and humane and which upholds the dignity of employees. They should provide all employees with access to training and development of necessary skills for career advancement, on an equal and non-discriminatory basis. They should uphold the freedom of association and the effective recognition of the right to collective bargaining of labour, have an effective grievance redressal system, should not employ child or forced labour and provide and maintain equality of opportunities without any discrimination on any grounds in recruitment and during employment.

(iv) Respect for Human Rights: Companies should respect human rights for all and avoid complicity with human rights abuses by them or by third party.

(v) ***Respect for Environment:*** Companies should take measures to check and prevent pollution; recycle, manage and reduce waste, should manage natural resources in a sustainable manner and ensure optimal use of resources like land and water, should proactively respond to the challenges of climate change by adopting cleaner production methods, promoting efficient use of energy and environment friendly technologies.

(vi) ***Activities for Social and Inclusive Development:*** Depending upon their core competency and business interest, companies should undertake activities for economic and social development of communities and geographical areas, particularly in the vicinity of their operations. These could include: education, skill building for livelihood of people, health, cultural and social welfare etc., particularly targeting at disadvantaged sections of society.

2. Implementation Guidance

1. The CSR policy of the business entity should provide for an implementation strategy which should include identification of projects/activities, setting measurable physical targets with timeframe, organisational mechanism and responsibilities, time schedules and monitoring. Companies may partner with local authorities, business associations and civil society/non-government organisations. They may influence the supply chain for CSR initiative and motivate employees for voluntary effort for social development. They may evolve a system of need assessment and impact assessment while undertaking CSR activities in a particular area. Independent evaluation may also be undertaken for selected projects/activities from time to time.

2. Companies should allocate specific amount in their budgets for CSR activities. This amount may be related to profits after tax, cost of planned CSR activities or any other suitable parameter.

3. To share experiences and network with other organisations the company should engage with well established and recognised programmes/platforms which encourage responsible business practices and CSR activities. This would help companies to improve on their CSR strategies and effectively project the image of being socially responsible.

4. The companies should disseminate information on CSR policy, activities and progress in a structured manner to all their stakeholders and the public at large through their website, annual reports and other communication media.

Recommendations of Standing Committee of Parliament on Finance (SCF)

The Standing Committee of Parliament on Finance which has thoroughly examined the Companies Bill, 2009 on the extent which of Corporate Social Responsibility (CSR) being undertaken by corporates and the need for a comprehensive CSR policy, the Ministry of Corporate Affairs have agreed that the Bill may now include provisions to mandate that every company having [(net worth of ₹500 crore or more, or turnover of ₹1000 crore or more)] or [a net profit of ₹5 crore or more during a year] shall be required to formulate a CSR Policy to ensure that every year at least 2% of its average net profits during the three immediately preceding financial years shall be spent on CSR activities as may be approved and specified by the company. The directors shall be required to make suitable disclosures in this regard in their report to members. In case any such company does not have adequate profits or is not in a position to spend prescribed amount on CSR activities, the directors would be required to give suitable disclosure/reasons in their report to the members.

While welcoming the Ministry's acceptance of the Committee's suggestion to bring Corporate Social Responsibility (CSR) in the statue itself, the Committee feels that separate disclosures required to be made by companies in their Annual Report by way of CSR statement indicating the company policy as well as the specific steps taken there under will be a sufficient check on non-compliance.

EXAMINATION QUESTIONS

Long Answer Questions

1. "Corporate should be socially accountable." Comment on this statement.
2. What do you mean by corporate social responsibility? Examine its different approaches.
3. What is corporate social responsibility? Evaluate its scope.
4. Explain the nature of corporate social responsibility. Also examine its objectives.
5. What do you mean by corporate citizenship? Examine the regulatory base of corporate social responsibility.
6. Examine the process of corporate social communication. Also evaluate the issues involved in corporate social responsibility.
7. Critically examine the different aspects of corporate social responsibility in Indian scenario.
8. What is business ethics? Examine its relevance.
9. Examine the concept of trusteeship. How does it affect the working the Indian corporate sector.

Short Answer Questions

1. What is culture?
2. What do you mean by ethics?
3. What is trusteeship?
4. What do you mean by business ethics?
5. What do you mean by ethical code?

6. What is morality?
7. What is entrepreneurial social responsibility?
8. What is corporate citizenship?
9. What do you mean by entrepreneurial social communication process?
10. What do you mean by fair business practices?

Objective Type Questions:

1. A teleological approach to business ethics proposes that the guiding principle should be:
   (*a*) People (*b*) Purpose
   (*c*) Power (*d*) Practice
2. Ethical behaviour is a matter of:
   (*a*) Obeying the rule
   (*b*) Juggling standards and business needs
   (*c*) Action on a considered judgement
   (*d*) None of these
3. Morality is not concerned with:
   (*a*) Norms (*b*) Believes
   (*c*) Values (d) Principles
4. Business ethics helps in solving except:
   (*a*) Ethical expectations (*b*) Ethical problems
   (*c*) Ethical code (*d*) Ethical dilemmas
5. The term 'culture' has its root in:
   (*a*) Sociology (*b*) Social anthropology
   (*c*) Vedic studies (*d*) Ethnography
6. Stake holders does not include the following :
   (*a*) Shareholders (*b*) Bankers
   (*c*) Employees (*d*) Debtors
7. Profit Maximisation Approach originals from :
   (*a*) Classical economic theory (*b*) Neo classical economic theory
   (*c*) Modern Economic theory (*d*) None of the above

Answers

1. (*b*) 2. (*c*) 3. (*d*) 4. (*c*) 5. (*b*) 6. (*c*) 7 (*a*)

REFERENCES

1. Friedman, M, *"Capitalism and Freedom"*, Chicago: University of Chicago Press, (1962), p.123
2. Ramnathan, K.V., *"Towards a Theory of Corporate Social Accounting,"* The Accounting Review, July, 1996

3. Ernst, & Ernst , *Social Responsibility Disclosure& Survey.* Cleve land, Ohio, (1978), p.70
4. Dewhurst, J., "*The Green Resource Audit,*" The Accountant, October, (1989), p.89
5. Accounting Standards Committee, *"The Corporate Report,"* Institute of Chartered Accounts in England and Wales, (1975), p.102
6. Ditzler, Patricia *"Corporate Social Performance,"* Management Accountant, February, (1983), p.119
7. Spicer, Barry H. *"Investors' Corporate Social Performance and Information Disclosure,"* The Accounting Review, January, (1978), p.145
8. Rearce, D.W.A. Markandaya and E.B. Barlier, *"Blueprint for a Green Economy,"* Earth Scan, (1989)
9. *"Voluntary Guidelines on Corporate Social Responsibility"*, Ministry of Corporate Affairs, 2009, p.7
10. Satpathy. Biswajit, *"Indian Ethos and Values"*, Elite Publications, 2002, p1
11. Raj Rituparna, *"A Study in Business Ethics,"* Himalaya Publishing House, Mumbai, 2003, p77
12. Courtland. L. Bovee, John V.Thill, Marian Burk Wood, George P. Dovel, "*Management*", McGraw-Hill. Inc. 1993, p.118
13. "*Mahatma Gandhi- Harijan*". 14.5.1939
14. Pyarelal. *"Harijan"*. 25.10.1952
15. *Kaleido Scope*, Vol, 27, No.1, June 2007

36

STRATEGIES FOR GROWTH

Environmental analysis helps the management in the process of identifying the organisational strengths, opportunities, weaknesses and threats. The SWOT analysis enables the management to evolve different alternative strategies in meeting emerging situations. These strategies are to be carefully examined by the business enterprises in terms of prevailing business environment.

In this context, entrepreneur is supposed to implement strategies like : (*i*) Stability strategy (*ii*) Growth strategy. An enterprise is free to select any one or the combination of these strategies as its basic strategy for operational behaviour.

Enterprise management has to be keenly aware not only of what is happening in society but also what is going to happen so that they may formulate growth strategies and prepare to meet the opportunities of the year ahead. "A future oriented management strategy could lead to decisions which prove profitable in the long-run and to the discounting of short sighted though immediately profitable measures." So, entrepreneurs must live with the problems of the present in the future and should, therefore, develope a strategy of meeting them on that basis and design policies which assume their continued experience.

1. STABILITY STRATEGY

A stability strategy deals with the assumption that the firm should concentrate on better utilisation of its resources to develop its competitive strength in the market. In this strategy, management is expected to maintain the *status quo* in the prevailing situations. However, this strategy makes possible only a limited growth or improvement in the present level of performance.

Features of Stability Strategy

(i) It implies no major change in the product or service line, market or functions.

(ii) It continues to pursue the same objectives and mission of the firm by ensuring current annual growth rate.

(iii) It concentrates on resources to maintain the same level of competitive advantage.

(iv) It lays down importance on incremental improvement in functional operations.

Retionale of Stability Strategy

(i) The firm is able to achieve its objective which is generally treated as satisfactory. So, management may be more inclined to continue with the same activities.

(ii) The firm does not expect a major change in environment in terms of opportunities and threats.

(iii) The firm evaluates that neither opportunities are attractive nor threats are serious. So, there is no major risk involved in changing the product market posture.

(iv) Key personnel of the firm are not inclined to welcome innovative processes like new products, new market or new organisational functions. Personnel are habitual of resisting change available in the environment.

Criteria for Stability Strategy

(i) **Return on Capital:** This principle is generally implemented to maintain the *status quo*. However, rate of return should be sufficient to meet the operating expenses including provisions for renewal and replacements. Similarly, retention of profit should also be initiated to meet future unforeseen problems.

(ii) **Expected Cash Flow:** A firm should expect a positive cash flow to avoid any shortage of funds in near future. Success of stability is generally governed by financial factors so a proper assessment of future expected cash flow from existing operation is desirable.

(iii) **Manpower:** Manpower is the active factor in the process of production. In a fast changing technological scenario, availability of suitable and competent manpower is a challenge before the management. Provisions for attractive compensation packages, conducive working conditions, opportunities for internal growth and promotion and harmonious inter-personal relations are major considerations for stability strategy.

2. GROWTH STRATEGY

Under growth strategy, an enterprise is expected to increase its level of business operations than its immediate past. Actually, in this strategy, a firm increases its expected performance in terms of market share, sales revenue, earnings etc. "A growth strategy is one that an enterprise pursues when it increases its level of objectives upward in a significant increment much higher than an extrapolation of its past achievement level."[1] The basic purpose of this strategy is to achieve higher growth by initiating growth mechanism. These mechanisms are entering new market, capturing large share of the markets by improved product, developing new products, acquiring latest technology, acquiring better resources and inculcating professionalism in management.

Features of Growth Strategy

(*i*) Strategy which involves holding the relative position of the firm in a high-growth product market areas.

(*ii*) Increase market share in high growth market.

(*iii*) Increase market share in slow growth (matured markets).

(*iv*) Hold strong relative position in slow growth market : use excess cash flow, funds capacity and other resurces to support penetration of multi-national markets with existing product line.

(v) Hold strong relative position in a maturing market ; use excess cash flow, external funds capability and other resources to support penetration of new product market areas domestically.

(*vi*) Hold strong relative position in multinational markets with present product line, use excess cash flow, funds capability and other resources to diversify products.

(*vii*) Hold strong position in diversified product line domestically, use excess cash flow, funds capability and other resources to diversify markets.

Rationale of Growth Strategies

(*i*) Growth company holds better public image and ables to attract professional managers.

(*ii*) Growth firm easily adjusts itself with the changing scenario specially in terms of opportunities available, technological changes etc.

(*iii*) Growth firm motivates management for high performance by initiating higher compensation packages and satisfying power and recognition needs.

Approaches to Growth Strategy

1. Intensive Expansion : It deals with protection and development of product market line of the firm. It helps the firm to expand its share of market, sales volume and profit volume. Intensive expansion is possible in three ways : (*i*) Market penetration (*ii*) Market development and (*iii*) Product development.

(*i*) *Market Penetration :* In this process, company assesses the scope of its present product in the market. If it is possible for the company to increase its volumes of sales and profits by initiating aggressive marketing efforts then it will try to improve the product quality and design. Because, these steps enable the company to increase its market share permanently. Market penetration is achieved through the following steps : (*a*) Inducing customers through mass media to buy its products more frequently and in larger quantities (*b*) Attracting existing customers by providing better service and improving brand image of the products, (*c*) Initiating price reduction and offensive advertising programmes to convert potential customers into real customers.

(ii) Market Development : It deals with launching of existing products in new market. Generally, it is possible through the appointment of sales agents and dealers, development of new channels of distribution, franchising etc. Thus, in market development process, the firm tries to move into new geographical areas with its existing products. However, the firm should try to incorporate some minor modifications, if any, in existing products the local conditions of that particular geographical area.

(iii) Product Development : It incorporates improvements in the quality and standard of the existing product as well as launching of new product in the market. Product developmpent is made prossible through (*a*) Launching of new product through research and development (*b*) Product innovation, (*c*) Increase in product brand range.

2. Integration : A company tries to expand externally. It is a growth strategy wherein new products or services are added which are complementary to the existing product or service line. It is characterised by the extension of the firm's business definition in two possible directions from the present backward and forward.[2] It is generally motivated by taking into account the growth and survival possibilities. It is of two types :

(i) Backward Integration : It is the creation of facilities for the production of raw materials and components to ensure smooth current production behaviour. It is setting up of facilities for the production of raw materials and components required for the current operation of the firm.

(ii) Forward Integration : It is the creation of facilities for manufacturing products for which current products serve as inputs. It is the use of company's current products as inputs for manufacture of another product of the same organisation.

3. Merger : A merger is a combination of two or more business in which one acquires the assets and liabilities of the other in exchange for cash, stock or both are companies dissolved and assets and liabilities are combined and new equity shares are issued. According to *Prof. L.H. Haney*, it is 'a form of business organisation which is established by the outright purchase of the properties of constituents, organisations and the merging or amalgamating of such properties into a single business unit." Thus, merger is the result of forming new company by amalgamating two or mora existing companies or by absorbing one business enterprise by another unit.

Types of Mergers

(*i*) ***Horizontal Merger :*** It involves merger of two firms operating and competing in the same kind of business activity. Its main intension is to avail benefit of economies of scale.

(*ii*) ***Vertical Merger :*** It occurs between firms who are in different stages of production operation. This type of merger takes place when two or more firms are engaged in complementary production bases. The rationale rests primarily on the costliness of market exchange and contracting.

(iii) ***Conglomerate Merger :*** It involves firms engaged in unrelated type of business activities. Conglomerate mergers are possible mainly on three lines[3] : (*a*) Product-extension mergers broaden the product lines of firms ; these are mergers between firms in related business activities and may also be called concentric mergers. (*b*) A geographic market extension merger involves two firms whose operations have been conducted in non-overlapping geographic areas. (*c*) The other conglomerate mergers which are often referred to as pure conglomerate mergers involve unrelated business activities.

(iv) ***Concentric Merger :*** It involves combination of two or more firms which are related to each other in terms of customer functions, customer groups or technology. For example, combination of shoe company with a hosiery firm engaged in production of socks.

4. Diversification : It is a mode of business expansion. It involves addition of units that produce different products that can be distributed through the same channel. Under this process, a firm switches over to new products and markets rather than continuing with the existing ones only. Diversification can be achieved in three different ways :[4]

(*i*) A firm can diversify internally by using standard organisation or new venture organisation.

(*ii*) It can diversify through ventures or by forming mergers or amalgamation with other business enterprises.

(*iii*) It can be achieved by forming a conglomeration.

(i) Mergers and Acquisition Process : It involves external diversification when a firm is interested to take over another firm working in other new field or allied areas. Actually, these are the areas where production units are adopting strategies to enter the field. These fields are generally treated as sunrise industries. Mergers and acquisitions are the best methods to achieve this target. Actually, it is possible for the firm to use securities in obtaining other companies whereas it might not be able to finance the acquisition of equivalent assets and capabilities internally.

(ii) Joint Venture : It involves mutual cooperation of two independent firms who are interested to participate in a business venture. "Joint ventures are a special case of consolidation where two or more companies form a temporary partnership for a specified purpose."[5] In practice, joint venture allows to implement changes in strategic posture and also allows to defend the strategic posture jointly against forces which could be difficult to defend individually.

Basically, in joint venture, participants continue to exist as separate firms with a joint venture representing a newly created business enterprise. The joint ventures are usually described as having the following characteristics[6] : (*i*) Contribution by partners of money, property, effort, knowledge, skill or other asset, to a common undertaking (*ii*) Joint property interest in the subject-matter of the ventures (*iii*) Right of mutual control or management of the enterprise (*iv*) Expectation of profit or presence of adventure (*v*) Right to share in profit (*vi*) Usual limitation of the objective to a single undertaking or *ad-hoc* enterprise.

Rationale for Joint Ventures

(i) To augment insufficient financial or technical ability to enter a particular line of business.

(ii) To share technology and/or generic management services in organisation planning and control.

(iii) To diversify risk.

(iv) To obtain distribution channel or raw material supply.

(v) To achieve economies of scale.

(vi) To extend activities with similar investment that is done independently.

(vii) To take advantage of favourable tax treatment or political incentives (particularly in foreign ventures).

(iii) Conglomeration : It is another technique to diversify in other areas. Diversification activities related with product extention and market extension are included in conglomerate diversification process. The motivation on the part of the diversifying or acquiring firm is in expectation that it has or will have excess capacity of general managerial capabilities in relation to its existing product, market activities or technological capabilities. It may also enable the firm to develop industry specific managerial experience and firm specific organisation capital over time.

NEW FRONTIERS OF ENTREPRENEURSHIP

There are some key findings from a study on entrepreneurship conducted by the Monitor Group in collaboration with Business Standard.[7] However, any discussion on entrepreneurship in India quickly leads to the question : "Why do Indians do so well abroad but do not achieve the same degree of success at home?"

The survey in India sought to answer three key questions :

- What are the characteristics of India's entrepreneurship policy environment—as perceived by people operating in that environment?
- What are the relative strengths and what are the areas that need to be bolstered for improving entrepreneurship in India ?
- What lessons can we learn from policies implemented in top performing countries ?

Key Highlights

The survey was administered to entrepreneurs and other participants in their ecosystem like venture capitalists, private equity firms, banks and industry associations across seven regions in India.

The sample has a large proportion of executives working for small and medium companies. For instance, less than a fifth of respondents were from companies with more than 500 employees or hand revenues of greater than ₹150 crores. Majority of respondents were the entrepreneur/founder in a lead management role and most of the companies had shown commendable revenue growth over the last three years.

The good news is that India had the highest aggregate score for policy drivers (see chart : Policy drivers—Aggregate country scores). These overwhelmingly positive responses may be due, in part, to India's recent economic success. The Indian economy is currently one of the world's fastest growing with even the most conservative forecasts estimating the GDP to average 6 per cent in the coming years. These recent successes, in conjunction with comparison to what it was earlier, have bred overly positive expectations.

The bad news is that the ranking was driven by superior performance in a few areas of entrepreneurship assets and business assistance, instead of being more broad-based. The other areas of policy accelerators and motivations showed significant under-performance in some instances; especially, in relation to interactions with the government, physical infrastructure and technology. These areas require more fundamental changes.

The focus will be on findings that have a direct implication policy formulation. As such, recommendations outlined here elaborate more on what needs to be improved rather than where we are already doing well.

(i) Entrepreneurship assets refers to supply and access to financial, human and infrastructure resources. Supply of equity, debt, venture or seed capital were not an issue in that respondents placed the country first in all of these areas, possibly a function of the large amount of funds currently available to entrepreneurs. Also, cost of capital was not considered a hindrance in company formation and growth; a reflection of the interest rate regime of the past couple of years.

What is insightful from a policy formulation perspective is that while 60-70 per cent of respondents felt that the supply of equity and debt capital for new firms was adequate, only 40 50 per cent of respondents agreed in terms of venture and seed capital.

This is especially relevant as our previous work had shown that "easy of entry" and specifically access to angle investors for early stage seed funding had a disproportionate impact in stimulating entrepreneurship.

(ii) Business assistance is a composite indicator for entrepreneurship support services, both government and from other professional services firms.

While India has relatively high rating from a policy formulation perspective, the critical finding is that as compared to other countries, there are not a sufficient number of government programmes to support new and growing firms.

There is a high level of dissatisfaction on this issue. Seventy-seven per cent of respondents indicated that government programmes do not provide high quality services to new firms; 75 per cent believe these programmes are not easy to access and 78 per cent believe these are not available through a single agency.

This is a significant area of underperformance for India with only Russia having a lower composite score.

(iii) ***Policy accelerators*** refers to various aspects of the regulatory environment, and is a composite indicator measuring enacted legislation and the administrative burden imposed in adhering to the legislation. India's underperformance in policy accelerators is a function not so much of the legislation, but of the administrative burden. For instance, only 28 per cent of the respondents agreed that the government makes it easy for new and growing firms to get required permits and licences.

Of particular urgency is the fact that only one-third of the respondents indicate that the time taken to start a business is acceptable and approximately two thirds agree that the number of permits and licences required is excessive—both areas where India is among the bottom two countries.

While our research from other countries shows that administrative burdens matter relatively less in stimulating performance; India's current position at the bottom of the table is far from satisfactory. These low rankings point to the need for significant structural and governance issues.

(iv) ***Individual motivations*** composed on various cultural and attitudinal factors had a disproportionate impact on performance. As illustrated in the chart composite indicators score—India vs "Best in class," indicators relating to motivations are among the weakest policy drivers for India.

Half the respondents felt that fear of bankruptcy prevents people from starting firms, as opposed to 30 per cent in the survey leader, China. In addition, two-thirds of Indian respondents agree that starting a business and failing is a disgrace, versus about a quarter in the US and China. The problem is aggravated when one considers the financial impact of declaring bankruptcy with three-fourth or respondents declaring that bankruptcy has excessively negative financial consequences, as opposed to 40 per cent in the US and 48 per cent in China.

These policy changes have the most impact in explaining why some countries do better than others in creating a positive entrepreneurship environment. These same policy drivers are also among the hardest to implement in that changing a society's attitudes about many of these topics are especially difficult to make progress on.

Relative Strengths	Policy Implications
Supply of equity and debt capital.	Establish more formal, organised angle investor and VC networks in order to institutionalise and streamline seed and VC capital mechanisms.
Financing and exit strategies.	Facilitating ease of buy-outs, closure and restructuring and enact labour reform to iron out to issues preventing scale-up.
Competency/experience.	Create and institutionalise mechanisms for education and training of entrepreneurship, including mentoring and hand-holding by networks. Facilitate mechanisms for exchange of people and expertise between academia and industry.
Affordable and accessible technology.	Facilitate commercialisation of R&D through increased private-public partnerships, incentives for sub-contracted research and so on. Improve technology transfers among universities, government and entrepreneurs.
Legitimacy/career choice.	Draw attention to and promote entrepreneurs that emphasis social responsibility and philanthropic aspects of their success, not just absolute wealth creation.
Areas for Improvement	**Policy Implications**
Attitudes towards bankruptcy.	Significantly bring about structural changes to simplify and streamline bankruptcy proceedings. Create mechanisms to change perceptions about bankrupt impact on social status.
Administrative burdens and transaction costs.	Improve quality of governance and leverage technology to reduce effort, cost and time to set up new enterprises.
Preparation of entrepreneurs through training and education.	Establish more high-quality vocational training and management development programmes that allow current managers to become more effective as their firms become more global, well-established enterprises.
Quality of an access to government assistance programmes.	Regional governments to provide adequate, high-quality assistance to local industry clusters through more organised efforts.
Availability and cost of adequate infrastructure.	Improve physical infrastructure that directly impacts : ability of small firms to access more national and international markets and do so across a wide range of regions.

Prospects

SMEs play a dominant role in most of the economies—development and developing—in shapping their industrial destiny and path of economic growth. So, vital is the small business that a few, if any, parts of the global economy could go on without its product and services. Innovation has been the unique and biggest strength of SMEs the world over. In the Indian context, the small-scale industries symbolise the rich heritage and economic strength of the nation. With their continued innovations and resilience, they have shown excellent growth trends surpassing both the industry sector and overall rate of growth of the economy. However, in view of the post-WTO dynamics and the need to align Indian SME segment with the global trends, the Hon'ble Union Finance Minister in the Budget Speech 2004-05, while appreciating the contribution of Small Scale Sector as the engine of growth, acknowledged that small units must be given space to grow into medium enterprises and all over the world, policies are devised to meet such growth objectives. In diference to the announcement, a SME development bill has been placed before the Parliament. Once approved, the new legislation would further strengthen the power of the sector to accelerate the process of overall growth in output and employment.

Another important structural change in the Indian financial sector that is currently on is that large enterprises are not any more dependent on financial intermediaries. It is the small and medium business, which is offering abundant opportunities of financing. Hence, fulfilment of credit and credit related needs of SMEs has emerged as a critical issue. The conventional instruments of financing the sector served in reasonable well over the long haul. But, the cataclysmic changes unleashed by the current environment have brought into focus severe limitations of the conventional approach. There has been a very strong felt need for a paradigm shift in SME financing to meet the challenges of the present and expectations of the future. Depending on the requirements of each niche market and the sector, the credit delivery would vary from pure debt finance to providing risk capital or hybrid of both. These innovations have been instrumental "in developing different kinds of institutional structures, credit delivery mechanisms and financing channels for small and medium entrepreneurs.

With the new developments like the introduction of SME Development Bill, as stated above, increasing interest of multi-nationals and multi-lateral agencies in the development of small and medium sector and the inherent strength of these enterprises, the landscape of SME sector in India is projected to change from a protection seeking segment to a dynamic force.

In order to improve the flow of credit to small and medium enterprise sector, strategic business initiatives were taken by the bank during Financial Year 2005 by broad basing certain schemes in line with the changing requirements of the sector. Steps were taken to enhance the scale of operations under direct finance schemes, in addition to refinance activities. Greater emphasis was laid